UNDERSTANDING
SOCIAL PROBLEMS

Second Canadian Edition

UNDERSTANDING
SOCIAL PROBLEMS

Second Canadian Edition

Linda A. Mooney
East Carolina University

David Knox
East Carolina University

Caroline Schacht
East Carolina University

Adie Nelson
University of Waterloo

THOMSON
✳
NELSON

Australia   Canada   Mexico   Singapore   Spain   United Kingdom   United States

THOMSON

NELSON

Understanding Social Problems
Second Canadian Edition

Linda A. Mooney, David Knox,
Caroline Schacht, and Adie Nelson

Editorial Director and Publisher:
Evelyn Veitch

Executive Editor:
Joanna Cotton

Acquisitions Editor:
Cara Yarzab

Marketing Manager:
Lenore Taylor

Developmental Editor:
Glen Herbert

Production Editor:
Wendy Yano

Copy Editor:
Alex Moore

Proofreader:
Gilda Mekler

Indexer:
Elizabeth Bell

Production Coordinator:
Helen Locsin

Interior Design:
Ellen Pettengell

Interior Design Modifications:
Peter Papayanakis

Creative Director:
Angela Cluer

Cover Design:
Peter Papayanakis

Cover Photos:
Top left: Andrew Ward/Lifefile/
PhotoDisc. Top right: PhotoDisc Collection.
Bottom left: Plush Studios/PhotoDisc.
Bottom right: Mel Curtis/PhotoDisc.

Compositors:
Andrew Adams/Carol Magee

Printer:
Transcontinental

**National Library of Canada
Cataloguing in Publication Data**

Understanding social problems /
Linda A. Mooney ... [et al.].—2nd
Canadian ed.

Includes bibliographical references
and indexes.

ISBN 0-17-622483-1

1. Social problems—Canada.
2. Canada—Social conditions—
1991-. 3 Social problems. 4. Social
history. I. Mooney, Linda A.

H103.5.U65 2003   361.1'0971
C2003-9003033-4

Brief Contents

Detailed Contents

SECTION 1 — Problems of Well-Being 28

SECTION 2   Problems of Human Diversity   174

SECTION 3 Problems of Inequality and Power   304

Preface

Violence in the home, school, and street; impoverished living conditions among millions of people throughout the world; increasing levels of environmental pollution and depletion of the earth's natural resources; persistent conflict between and within nations; ongoing oppression of minorities; and the widening gap between the "haves" and the "have-nots" paint a disturbing picture of our modern world. In *A Guide for the Perplexed*, B.F. Schumacher questions whether a "turning around will be accomplished by enough people quickly enough to save the modern world" (quoted in Safransky 1990: 115). Schumacher notes, "this question is often asked, but whatever the answer given to it will mislead. The answer 'yes' would lead to complacency; the answer 'no' to despair. It is desirable to leave these perplexities behind us and get down to work."

In *Understanding Social Problems*, we "get down to work" by examining how the social structure and culture of society contribute to social problems and their consequences. Understanding the social forces that contribute to social problems is necessary for designing strategies for action—programs, policies, and other interventions intended to ameliorate the social problem.

Academic Features of the New Edition

In response to feedback from teachers, reviewers, and students who have read the first Canadian edition of *Understanding Social Problems* (2001), we have retained several features and added several others.

Strong Integrative Theoretical Foundations

The three major sociological approaches—structural functionalism, symbolic interactionism, and conflict theory—are introduced in the first chapter and discussed and applied, where appropriate, to various social problems throughout the text. Other theories of social problems, as well as feminist approaches, are also presented where appropriate.

Emphasis on the Structure and Culture of Society

As noted above, the text emphasizes how the social structure and culture of society contribute to and maintain social problems, as well as provide the basis for alternative solutions.

Review of Basic Sociological Terms

An overview of basic sociological terms and concepts is presented in the first chapter. This overview is essential for students who have not taken an introductory course and is helpful, as a review, for those who have.

Unique Organization

The order of the 14 chapters reflects a progression from micro to macro levels of analysis, focusing first on problems of health care, drug use, and crime, and then broadening to the widening concerns of science and technology and population growth and environmental problems.

Two chapters merit special mention: "Sexual Orientation" (Chapter 9) and "Science and Technology" (Chapter 13). Whereas traditional texts discuss sexual orientation under the rubric of "deviance," this topic is examined in the section on problems of human diversity along with the related issues of age, gender, and racial and ethnic inequality. The chapter on science and technology includes such topics as biotechnology, the computer revolution, and the Internet. This chapter emphasizes the transformation of society through scientific and technological innovations, the societal costs of such innovations, and issues of social responsibility. This chapter is particularly relevant to students, many of whom have never known a world without computers.

Expanded Coverage of Global Issues

In the second edition, we place an even greater emphasis on examining social problems from a global perspective. Each chapter contains a heading entitled "The Global Context," and the number and scope of references to international issues have been expanded.

Consistent Chapter Format

Each chapter follows a similar format: the social problem is defined, the theoretical explanations are discussed, the consequences of the social problem are explored, and the alternative solutions and policies are examined. A concluding section assesses the current state of knowledge for each social problem.

Increased Media Content

New to the second edition is an emphasis on the media and the role it plays in defining, exacerbating, and ameliorating social problems. Examples include portrayals of alcohol and drug use in children's animated films (Chapter 3) and minority representations on prime-time television shows (Chapter 8 and Chapter 9).

Standard and Cutting-Edge Topics

In addition to problems that are typically addressed in social problems courses and texts, new and emerging topics are examined. Topics new to the second edition include racial profiling after 9/11 (Chapter 4), gender tourism (Chapter 8), genetically modified crops (Chapter 10) and eco-terrorism and environmental refugees (Chapter 14).

Pedagogical Features of the New Edition

Opening Vignettes

New to the second edition, each chapter begins with a vignette designed to engage the student by illustrating the current relevance of the topic under discussion. Topics of opening vignettes include the heinous and lethal "gay bashing" of Vancouver resident Aaron Webster (Chapter 9) and life as Mr. Dot-ComGuy (Chapter 13).

Student-Friendly Presentation

To enhance the book's appeal to students, the second edition includes expanded information relevant to this population. In Chapter 1, for example, we present data on the beliefs of Canadian teens about various social problems, and Chapter 3 contains a section on binge drinking and other student alcohol-related problems. Further, Chapter 8 contains expanded coverage on race and ethnic diversity on campus, and in Chapter 12, "Problems in Education," students may complete a "Student Alienation Scale."

Self and Society

Each chapter includes a social survey designed to help students assess their own attitudes, beliefs, knowledge, or behaviour regarding some aspect of a social problem. Examples include a Criminal Activities Survey (Chapter 4), a Beliefs About Women Scale (Chapter 7), and an Attitudes towards Economic Opportunity in Canada Inventory (Chapter 10).

The Human Side

To personalize the information being discussed, each chapter includes a feature entitled "The Human Side." These features describe personal experiences of individuals who have been affected by the social problem under discussion. Examples include the powerful statements of Elijah Harper (Chapter 2) and Celia Haig-Brown (Chapter 12), the tragic experience of Kimberly Rogers (Chapter 10), and the pioneering efforts of Craig Kielburger, the founder of Free the Children (Chapter 6).

Social Problems Research Up Close

Now in every chapter, boxes called "Social Problems Research Up Close" present examples of social science research. These boxes demonstrate for students the sociological enterprise from theory and data collection, to findings and conclusions. Examples of topics covered include "Perceptions of Marriage among Low-Income Single Mothers" (Chapter 5), "Family, Gender Ideology, and Social

Change" (Chapter 7) and "The Social Construction of the Hacking Community" (Chapter 13).

Focus on Technology

Boxes called "Focus on Technology" also now appear in every chapter. These boxes present information on how technology may contribute to social problems and their solutions. For example, in Chapter 4, "Crime and Violence," the Focus on Technology feature highlights the use of DNA testing in criminal investigations. In Chapter 14, "Population and Environmental Problems," environmental and health hazards associated with computers are discussed.

Is It True?

Each chapter begins with five true–false items to stimulate student interest and thinking.

Critical Thinking

Each chapter ends with a brief section called "Critical Thinking" that raises several questions related to the chapter topic. These questions invite the student to use critical thinking skills in applying the information discussed in the chapters.

World Wide Web Home Page

As an additional pedagogical tool, *Understanding Social Problems* has its own home page on the World Wide Web: www.socialproblems2e.nelson.com.

New to this Edition—A Chapter-by-Chapter Look

In addition to the academic and pedagogical features noted above, *Understanding Social Problems'* content areas have been significantly revised. Over 30 new citations have been added to every chapter. Further, in addition to expanded and updated coverage of important topics from the first edition, we have added new areas of research and theorizing. A partial list of new or expanded topics follows:

Chapter 1: Thinking about Social Problems The "sociological enterprise," journal article content, reading tables, and triangulation.

Chapter 2: Illness and Health Care New sections on mental illness, models of mental health care, health practices of young Canadians, and expanded coverage of HIV/AIDS worldwide.

Chapter 3: Alcohol and Other Drugs Club drugs, mandatory drug testing, images of alcohol and tobacco in children's animated films, and drug policies in other countries.

Chapter 4: Crime and Violence Transnational crime, racial profiling, restorative justice, Canada's Terrorist Act, and legislative measures to curtail child sexual exploitation.

Chapter 5: Family Problems Parental alienation syndrome, interactive computer parenting, expanded global information on abuse of women, and expanded coverage of single-parent families.

Chapter 6: The Young and the Old Dependency ratio, beliefs about the elderly, children and grandchildren as caregivers for the elderly, the "greying" of the Canadian workforce, and an expanded section on children, violence, and the media.

Chapter 7: Gender Inequality Beliefs about gender equality, expanded section on media, language and cultural sexism, the "war on boys," and a new section on international efforts towards gender equality.

Chapter 8: Race and Ethnic Relations Hate on campus, expanded discussion of aversive and modern racism, and new Census data on Canada's increasing diversity.

Chapter 9: Sexual Orientation Updated terminology (lesbigay, transgender, LGBT), expanded coverage, both national and global, of laws concerning sexual orientation, and new sections on the impact of Internet filtering and monitoring on sexual orientation minorities, and how homophobia affects heterosexuals.

Chapter 10: The Haves and the Have-Nots New global qualitative research findings on poverty, new section on the advantages/disadvantages of agricultural biotechnology as a solution to global hunger, and updated information on national and international responses to poverty.

Chapter 11: Work and Unemployment Expanded and updated coverage on the changing Canadian workforce, work–family concerns, and labour unions.

Chapter 12: Problems in Education Results of international testing, expanded discussion on bullying and violence within schools, and the effects of budget cuts in education.

Chapter 13: Science and Technology Completion of the Human Genome Project, the 2000 Discovery Innovation Awards, and cyberstalking.

Chapter 14: Population and Environmental Problems Environmental education, intergovernmental report on global warming and its effects, online environmental activism, and corporate involvement in the environmental movement.

Online Resources

For a variety of resources that support this text, visit our Web site at www.socialproblems2e.nelson.com.

Instructor's Test Bank

There are multiple-choice and true–false questions available for each chapter, all with page references. The test bank also includes short-answer questions and essay questions for each chapter. Available upon adoption.

Acknowledgments

This text reflects the contributions of many people. At Nelson, we are especially grateful to Brad Lambertus and Glen Herbert for their consummate professionalism, constant good humour, and patient readiness to indulge requests for Luddite-friendly file formats and last-minute changes to incorporate just-released census data. We also gratefully acknowledge the assistance provided by Wendy Yano, Gilda Mekler, and Alex Moore. Additionally, we are indebted to those who reviewed this work in draft form and provided valuable insights and suggestions:

Anne Charles, Conestoga College
Brian Finnigan, Brandon University
Lindsay Harris, Algonquin College
Beverly Matthews, Mount Royal College
Victor Ujimoto, University of Guelph

Finally, we are always interested in ways to improve the text and invite your feedback and suggestions for new ideas and material to be included in subsequent editions.

Adie Nelson
Department of Sociology
University of Waterloo
Waterloo, ON N2L 3G1
E-mail address: <eds@watarts.uwaterloo.ca>

Thinking about Social Problems

Is It True?

1. For at least three decades, Canadians have identified the economy, unemployment, and crime as their foremost social concerns.

2. Before the nineteenth century, it was considered a husband's legal right and marital obligation to discipline and control his wife using physical force.

3. Currently, 1.2 billion people live on less than a dollar a day.

4. Questions involving values, religion, and morality can be answered only through scientific research.

5. In a national survey of Canadians 18 and older, about half agreed with the statement, "Anyone who works hard will rise to the top."

Answers: 1 = T, 2 = T, 3 = T, 4 = F, 5 = T

U nless someone like you cares a whole awful lot, nothing is going to get better. It's not.

DR. SEUSS
The Lorax

We enter the new millennium with our optimism for the future necessarily tempered by recognition of the persistence of such social problems as crime, unemployment, drug abuse, suicide, racism, sexism, and family violence. Consider, for example, that for the past three decades Canadians have consistently identified the economy, unemployment, and crime as primary areas of social concern (Bibby 1995: 94–5; Bibby 2001: 43). In addition, the September 11, 2001 attacks on the Pentagon and the World Trade Center "forced us to look beyond the comforts of our borders and drove home the fact that the world is, and for some time will continue to be, a dangerous place" (Gregg 2001/2002: 22) (see Figure 1.1).

A global perspective on social problems is even more troubling. In 1990, the United Nations Development Programme published its first annual Human Development Report, which measured the well-being of populations around the world according to a "human development index" (HDI). This index measures three basic dimensions of human development—longevity, knowledge (i.e., educational attainment), and standard of living. The most recent report reveals that "globalization is increasing human insecurity by accelerating the spread of crime, disease, and financial volatility" (May 2000: 219). The results—100 million children live and work on the streets, 1.2 billion people live on less than a dollar a day, and 18 million people die every day from communicable diseases.

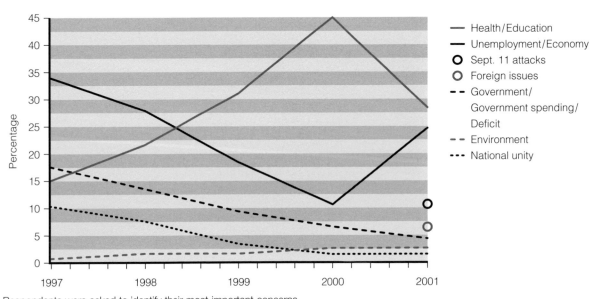

Respondents were asked to identify their most important concerns.

■ **Figure 1.1** *Terrorism Matters, But So Do Older Concerns*

SOURCE: Gregg, Allan R. (2001/2002). "Scary New World." *Maclean's*, December 31, 2001–January 7, 2002: 25.

Problems related to poverty and malnutrition, inadequate education, acquired immunodeficiency syndrome (AIDS) and other sexually transmitted diseases (STDs), inadequate health care, crime, conflict, oppression of minorities, environmental destruction, and other social issues are both national and international concerns. Such problems present both a threat and a challenge to our national and global society.

The primary goal of this text is to facilitate increased awareness and understanding of problematic social conditions in Canadian society and throughout the world. Although the topics covered in this text vary widely, all chapters share common objectives: to explain how social problems are created and maintained; to indicate how they affect individuals, social groups, and societies as a whole; and to examine programs and policies for change. We begin by looking at the nature of social problems.

What Is a Social Problem?

There is no universal, constant, or absolute definition of what constitutes a social problem. Rather, social problems are defined by a combination of objective and subjective criteria that vary across societies, among individuals and groups within a society, and across historical periods.

Objective and Subjective Elements of Social Problems

Although social problems take many forms, they all share two important elements: an objective social condition and a subjective interpretation of that social condition. The **objective element** of a social problem refers to the existence of a social condition. We become aware of social conditions through our own life experience, through the media, and through education. We see the homeless in the streets and battered children in hospital emergency rooms. We read about employees losing their jobs as businesses downsize and factories close. In television news reports, we see the anguished faces of parents whose children have been killed by drunk drivers.

The **subjective element** of a social problem refers to the belief that a particular social condition is harmful to society, or to a segment of society, and that it should and can be changed. We know that crime, drug addiction, poverty, racism, violence, and pollution exist. These social conditions are not considered social problems, however, unless at least a segment of society believes that these conditions diminish the quality of human life.

By combining these objective and subjective elements, we arrive at the following definition: A **social problem** is a social condition that a segment of society views as harmful to members of society and in need of remedy.

Variability in Definitions of Social Problems

Individuals and groups frequently disagree about what constitutes a social problem. For example, some Canadians view the availability of abortion as a social problem, while others view restrictions on abortion as a social problem. Similarly, some Canadians view homosexuality as a social problem, while others view prejudice and discrimination against homosexuals as a social problem.

> Social problems are fundamentally products of collective definition. ... A social problem does not exist for society unless it is recognized by that society to exist.
>
> **HERBERT BLUMER**
> *Sociologist*

> We rarely find that people have good sense unless they agree with us.
>
> **FRANÇOIS, DUC DE LA ROCHEFOUCAULD**

Such variations in what is considered a social problem are due to differences in values, beliefs, and life experiences.

Definitions of social problems vary not only within societies, but across societies and historical periods as well. For example, prior to the nineteenth century, it was a husband's legal right and marital obligation to discipline and control his wife through the use of physical force. Today, the use of physical force is regarded as a social problem and a criminal offence rather than a marital right.

Because social problems can be highly complex, it is helpful to have a framework within which to view them. Sociology provides such a framework. Using a sociological perspective to examine social problems requires knowledge of the basic concepts and tools of sociology. In the remainder of this chapter, we discuss some of these concepts and tools: social structure, culture, the "sociological imagination," major theoretical perspectives, and types of research methods.

Elements of Social Structure and Culture

Although society surrounds us and permeates our lives, it is difficult to "see" society. By thinking of society in terms of a picture or image, however, we can visualize society and therefore better understand it. Imagine that society is a coin with two sides: on one side is the structure of society, and on the other is the culture of society. Although each "side" is distinct, both are inseparable from the whole. By looking at the various elements of social structure and culture, we can better understand the root causes of social problems.

Elements of Social Structure

Sometimes a cigar is just a cigar.

SIGMUND FREUD
Founder of psychoanalysis

The *structure* of a society refers to the way society is organized. Society is organized into different parts: institutions, social groups, statuses, and roles.

Institutions An **institution** is an established and enduring pattern of social relationships. The five traditional institutions are family, religion, politics, economics, and education, but some sociologists argue that other social institutions, such as science and technology, mass media, medicine, sport, and the military, also play important roles in modern society.

Many social problems are generated by inadequacies in various institutions. For example, unemployment may be influenced by the educational institution's failure to prepare individuals for the job market and by alterations in the structure of the economic institution.

Social Groups Institutions are made up of social groups. A **social group** is defined as two or more people who have a common identity, interact, and form a social relationship. For example, the family in which you were reared is a social group that is part of the family institution. The religious association to which you may belong is a social group that is part of the religious institution.

A social group may be categorized as primary or secondary. A **primary group**, which tends to involve a small number of individuals, is characterized by intimate and informal interaction. Families and friends are examples of primary groups. A **secondary group**, which may involve a small or large number of individuals, is task-oriented and characterized by impersonal and formal interaction. Examples of secondary groups include employers and their employees, and clerks and their customers.

Statuses Just as an institution consists of social groups, a social group consists of statuses. A **status** is a position a person occupies within a social group. The statuses we occupy largely define our social identity. The statuses in a family may consist of mother, father, stepmother, stepfather, wife, husband, child, and so on. Statuses may be either ascribed or achieved. An **ascribed status** is one that society assigns to an individual on the basis of factors over which the individual has no control. For example, we have no control over the sex, race, ethnic background, and socioeconomic status into which we are born. Similarly, we are assigned the status of "child," "teenager," "adult," or "senior citizen" on the basis of our age—something we do not choose or control.

An **achieved status** is assigned on the basis of some characteristic or behaviour over which an individual has some control. Whether or not you achieve the status of university graduate, spouse, parent, bank president, or prison inmate depends largely on your own efforts, behaviour, and choices. One's ascribed statuses may affect the likelihood of achieving other statuses, however. For example, if you are born into a poor socioeconomic status, you may find it more difficult to achieve the status of "university graduate" because of the high cost of a university education.

Every individual has numerous statuses simultaneously. You may be a student, parent, tutor, volunteer fundraiser, female, and have a physical disability. A person's **master status** is the status that is considered the most significant in a person's social identity. Typically, a person's occupational status is regarded as his or her master status. If you are a full-time student, your master status is likely to be "student."

Roles Every status is associated with many **roles**, or the set of rights, obligations, and expectations associated with a status. Roles guide our behaviour and allow us to predict the behaviour of others. As a student, you are expected to attend class, listen and take notes, study for tests, and complete assignments. Because you know what the role of teacher involves, you can predict that your teacher will lecture, give exams, and assign grades based on your performance on tests.

A single status involves more than one role. For example, the status of prison inmate includes one role for interacting with prison guards and another role for interacting with other prison inmates. Similarly, the status of nurse involves different roles for interacting with physicians and with patients.

Elements of Culture

Whereas social structure refers to the organization of society, culture refers to the meanings and ways of life that characterize a society. The elements of culture include beliefs, values, norms, sanctions, and symbols.

Beliefs **Beliefs** refer to definitions and explanations about what is assumed to be true. The beliefs of an individual or group influence whether that individual or group views a particular social condition as a social problem. Does second-hand smoke harm nonsmokers? Are nuclear power plants safe? Does violence in movies and on television lead to increased aggression in children? Our beliefs regarding these issues influence whether we view the issues as social problems. Beliefs not only influence how a social condition is interpreted, they also influence the existence of the condition itself. For example, young women who believed that forced interactions with former boyfriends were romantic (i.e., he

When I fulfil my obligations as a brother, husband, or citizen, when I execute contracts, I perform duties that are defined externally to myself....Even if I conform in my own sentiments and feel their reality subjectively, such reality is still objective, for I did not create them; I merely inherited them.

Émile Durkheim
Sociologist

Man is made by his belief. As he believes, so he is.

Bhagavad Gita

brought flowers, a card, or a gift) were less likely to define the relationship as frightening and, thus, less likely to terminate it (Dunn 2000). The *Self and Society* feature in this chapter allows you to assess your own beliefs about various social issues and compare your beliefs with national samples of Canadian adults 18 years of age and older, surveyed in 1975, 1985, 1995, and 2000.

> When people cherish some set of values and do not feel any threat to them, they experience well-being. When they cherish values but do feel them to be threatened, they experience a crisis—either as a personal trouble or as a public issue.
>
> C. WRIGHT MILLS
> *Sociologist*

Values Values are social agreements about what is considered good and bad, right and wrong, desirable and undesirable. Frequently, social conditions are viewed as social problems when the conditions are incompatible with or contradict closely held values. For example, poverty and homelessness violate the value of human welfare; some types of crime contradict the values of honesty, private property, and nonviolence; racism, sexism, and heterosexism violate the values of equality and fairness.

Values play an important role not only in the interpretation of a condition as a social problem but also in the development of the social condition itself. Sylvia Ann Hewlett (1992) explains how the values of freedom and individualism are at the root of many of our social problems:

> There are two sides to the coin of freedom. On the one hand, there is enormous potential for prosperity and personal fulfilment; on the other are all the hazards of untrammelled opportunity and unfettered choice. Free markets can produce grinding poverty as well as spectacular wealth; unregulated industry can create dangerous levels of pollution as well as rapid rates of growth; and an unfettered drive for personal fulfilment can have disastrous effects on families and children. Rampant individualism does not bring with it sweet freedom; rather, it explodes in our faces and limits life's potential. (pp. 350–51)

Absent or weak values may contribute to some social problems. For example, many industries do not value protection of the environment and thus contribute to environmental pollution.

Norms and Sanctions Norms are socially defined rules of behaviour. Norms serve as guidelines for our behaviour and for our expectations of the behaviour of others.

There are three types of norms: folkways, laws, and mores. **Folkways** refer to the customs and manners of society. In many segments of our society, it is customary to shake hands when being introduced to a new acquaintance, to say "excuse me" after sneezing, and to give presents to family and friends on their birthdays. Although no laws require us to do these things, we are expected to do them because they are part of the cultural traditions, or folkways, of the society in which we live.

Laws are norms that are formalized and backed by political authority. A person who eats food out of a public garbage container is violating a folkway; no law prohibits this behaviour. However, throwing trash onto a public street is considered littering and is against the law.

Some norms, called **mores**, have a moral basis. Violations of mores may produce shock, horror, and moral indignation. Both littering and child sexual abuse are violations of law, but child sexual abuse is also a violation of our mores because we view such behaviour as immoral.

All norms are associated with **sanctions**, or social consequences for conforming to or violating norms. When we conform to a social norm, we may be rewarded by a positive sanction. These may range from an approving smile to a

Personal Beliefs about Various Social Problems

Indicate whether you agree or disagree with each of the following statements:

Statement	Agree	Disagree
1. There are some circumstances in which a doctor would be justified in ending a patient's life.	_____	_____
2. It should be possible for a pregnant woman to obtain a *legal* abortion if she wants it for any reason.	_____	_____
3. It should be possible for a pregnant woman to get a *legal* abortion if there is a strong chance of a serious defect in the baby.	_____	_____
4. The death penalty should be exercised in some instances.	_____	_____
5. Immigrants to Canada have an obligation to learn Canadian ways.	_____	_____
6. Marijuana should be legalized.	_____	_____
7. Homosexuality is "always wrong" or "almost always wrong."	_____	_____
8. Homosexuals are entitled to the same rights as other Canadians.	_____	_____
9. Birth control information should be available to teenagers who want it.	_____	_____
10. Natives have too much power in our nation's affairs.	_____	_____
11. There are racial and cultural groups that are discriminated against in my community.	_____	_____
12. Law enforcement is applied evenly to all those who break the law.	_____	_____
13. Anyone who works hard will rise to the top.	_____	_____
14. Corporations have far too much power in national life.	_____	_____
15. Bilingualism is a policy worth supporting.	_____	_____
16. In general, values in Canada have been changing for the worse.	_____	_____

Percentage* of Canadians Agreeing with Belief Statements

Statement Number	Percentage Agreeing			
	1975	1985	1995	2000
1. Doctor-assisted euthanasia	–	–	75	75
2. Abortion "on demand"	–	37	39	43
3. Abortion if "serious defect" in child	85	86	88	–
4. Use of death penalty	79	84	82	74
5. Assimilation expectations	85	–	88	–
6. Legalization of marijuana	27	–	31	47
7. Disapproval of homosexuality	72	71	52	–
8. Extending rights to homosexuals	–	76	67	71
9. Birth control information to teens	94	91	94	–
10. Natives have too much power	7	13	33	–
11. Racial and cultural discrimination	–	54	67	–
12. Law enforcement equitable	37	27	25	–
13. Self-efficacy	45	50	53	49
14. Corporations have too much power	83	73	69	–
15. Endorsement of bilingualism	49	53	55	60
16. Values changing for the worse	–	54	74	56

* Each Project Canada sample consists of a highly representative sample of approximately 1500 Canadian adults 18 years of age and older.
SOURCES: Adapted from Bibby, Reginald W. 1995. *The Bibby Report: Social Trends Canadian Style.* Toronto: Stoddart; and Bibby, Reginald W. 2001. *Canada's Teens: Today, Yesterday, and Tomorrow.* Toronto: Stoddart.

■ **Table 1.1** *Types and Examples of Sanctions*

	Positive	Negative
Informal	Being praised by one's neighbours for organizing a neighbourhood recycling program.	Being criticized by one's neighbours for refusing to participate in the neighbourhood recycling program.
Formal	Being granted a citizen's award for organizing a neighbourhood recycling program.	Being fined by the city for failing to dispose of garbage properly.

public ceremony in our honour. When we violate a social norm, we may be punished by a negative sanction, which may range from a disapproving look to life in prison. Most sanctions are spontaneous expressions of approval or disapproval by groups or individuals—these are referred to as informal sanctions. Sanctions that are carried out according to some recognized or formal procedure are referred to as formal sanctions. Types of sanctions, then, include positive informal sanctions, positive formal sanctions, negative informal sanctions, and negative formal sanctions (see Table 1.1).

Symbols A **symbol** is something that represents something else. Without symbols, we could not communicate with each other or live as social beings.

The symbols of a culture include language, gestures, and objects whose meaning is commonly understood by the members of a society. In our society, a red ribbon tied around a car antenna symbolizes Mothers Against Drunk Driving, a peace sign symbolizes the value of nonviolence, and a police badge symbolizes the authority of law. Sometimes people attach different meanings to the same symbol. The swastika is an ancient symbol that was supposed to bring good luck. However, its adoption as the official emblem of the Nazi Party and Nazi Germany has encouraged many to view it as a symbol of anti-Semitism, White supremacy, and bigotry.

The elements of the social structure and culture just discussed play a central role in the creation, maintenance, and social response to various social problems. One of the goals of taking a course in social problems is to develop an awareness of how the elements of social structure and culture contribute to social problems. Sociologists refer to this awareness as the "sociological imagination."

The Sociological Imagination

Freedom is what you do with what's been done to you.

JEAN-PAUL SARTRE
Philosopher

The **sociological imagination**, a term developed by C. Wright Mills (1959), refers to the ability to see the connections between our personal lives and the social world in which we live. When we use our sociological imagination, we are able to distinguish between "private troubles" and "public issues" and to see connections between the events and conditions of our lives and the social and historical context in which we live.

For example, that one man is unemployed constitutes a private trouble. That thousands of people are unemployed in Canada constitutes a public issue. Once we understand that personal troubles such as HIV infection, criminal victimization, and poverty are shared by other segments of society, we can look for the elements of social structure and culture that contribute to these public issues and private troubles. If the various elements of social structure and culture contribute to private troubles and public issues, then society's social structure and culture must be changed if these concerns are to be resolved.

Rather than viewing the private trouble of being unemployed as being due to an individual's faulty character or lack of job skills, we may understand unemployment as a public issue that results from the failure of the economic and political institutions of society to provide job opportunities to all citizens. Technological innovations emerging from the Industrial Revolution led to individual workers being replaced by machines. During the economic recession of the 1980s, employers fired employees so the firms could stay in business or could maximize profits, or both. Thus, in both these cases, social forces rather than individual skills largely determined whether a person was employed or not.

Theoretical Perspectives

Theories in sociology provide us with different perspectives from which to view our social world. A perspective is simply a way of looking at the world. A theory is a set of interrelated propositions or principles designed to answer a question or explain a particular phenomenon; it provides us with a perspective. Sociological theories help us to explain and predict the social world in which we live.

Sociology includes three major theoretical perspectives: the structural-functionalist perspective, the conflict perspective, and the symbolic interactionist perspective. Each perspective offers a variety of explanations about the causes of and possible solutions for social problems.

> The most incomprehensible thing about the world is the fact that it is comprehensible.
>
> **ALBERT EINSTEIN**
> *Scientist*

Structural-Functionalist Perspective

The structural-functionalist perspective is largely based on the works of Herbert Spencer, Émile Durkheim, Talcott Parsons, and Robert Merton. According to **structural-functionalism**, society is a system of interconnected parts that work together in harmony to maintain a state of balance and social equilibrium for the whole. For example, each of the social institutions contributes important functions for society: family provides a context for reproducing, nurturing, and socializing children; education offers a way to transmit a society's skills, knowledge, and culture to its youth; politics provides a means of governing members of society; economics provides for the production, distribution, and consumption of goods and services; and religion provides moral guidance and an outlet for worship of a higher power.

The structural-functionalist perspective emphasizes the interconnectedness of society by focusing on how each part influences and is influenced by other parts. For example, the increase in lone-parent and dual-earner families has contributed to the number of children who are failing in school because parents have become less available to supervise their children's homework. As a result of changes in technology, colleges and universities are offering more technical programs, and many adults are returning to school to learn new skills that are required in the workplace. The increasing number of women in the workforce has contributed to the formulation of policies against sexual harassment and job discrimination.

> Some see the glass half-empty, some see the glass half-full. I see the glass as too big.
>
> **GEORGE CARLIN**
> *Comedian*

Education has for its object
the formation of character.

HERBERT SPENCER
Sociologist

Structural-functionalists use the terms "functional" and "dysfunctional" to describe the effects of social elements on society. Elements of society are functional if they contribute to social stability and dysfunctional if they disrupt social stability. Some aspects of society may be both functional and dysfunctional for society. For example, crime is dysfunctional in that it is associated with physical violence, loss of property, and fear. But, according to Durkheim and other functionalists, crime is also functional for society because it leads to heightened awareness of shared moral bonds and increased social cohesion.

Sociologists have identified two types of functions: manifest and latent (Merton 1968). A **manifest function** is a consequence that is intended and commonly recognized. A **latent function** is a consequence that is unintended and often hidden. For example, the manifest function of education is to transmit knowledge and skills to society's youth. But public elementary schools also serve as babysitters for employed parents, and colleges and universities offer a place for young adults to meet potential mates. The babysitting and mate selection functions are not the intended or commonly recognized functions of education—hence, they are latent functions.

Structural-Functionalist Theories of Social Problems

Two dominant theories of social problems grew out of the structural-functionalist perspective: social pathology and social disorganization.

Social Pathology According to the social pathology model, social problems result from some "sickness" in society. Just as the human body becomes ill when our systems, organs, and cells do not function normally, society becomes "ill" when its parts (i.e., elements of the structure and culture) no longer perform properly. For example, problems such as crime, violence, and poverty are often attributed to the breakdown of the family institution, the decline of the religious institution, and inadequacies in our economic, educational, and political institutions.

Social "illness" also results when members of a society are not adequately socialized to adopt its norms and values. Persons who do not value honesty, for example, are prone to dishonesties of all sorts. Early theorists attributed the failure in socialization to "sick" people who could not be socialized. Later theorists recognized that failure in the socialization process stemmed from "sick" social conditions, not "sick" people. To prevent or solve social problems, members of society must receive proper socialization and moral education, which may be accomplished in the family, schools, churches, workplace, and/or through the media.

Social Disorganization According to the social disorganization view of social problems, rapid social change disrupts the norms in a society. When norms become weak or are in conflict with each other, society is in a state of **anomie** or normlessness. Hence, people may steal, physically abuse their partner or children, abuse drugs, commit sexual assault, or engage in other deviant behaviour because the norms regarding these behaviours are weak or conflicting. According to this view, the solution to social problems lies in slowing the pace of social change and strengthening social norms. For example, although the use of alcohol by teenagers is considered a violation of a social norm in our society, this norm is weak. The media portray young people drinking alcohol, teenagers teach each other to drink alcohol and buy fake identification cards to purchase alcohol, and parents model drinking behaviour by having a few drinks after work or at a social event. Solutions to teenage drinking may involve strengthening norms against it through public education, restricting media depictions of youth and alcohol, imposing stronger sanctions against the use of fake IDs to purchase alcohol, and educating parents to model moderate and responsible drinking behaviour.

Conflict Perspective

Whereas the structural-functionalist perspective views society as comprising different parts working together, the **conflict perspective** views society as comprising different groups and interests competing for power and resources. The conflict perspective explains various aspects of our social world by looking at which groups have power and benefit from a particular social arrangement.

The origins of the conflict perspective can be traced to the classic works of Karl Marx. Marx suggested that all societies go through stages of economic development. As societies evolve from agricultural to industrial, concern over meeting survival needs is replaced by concern over making a profit, the hallmark of a capitalist system. Industrialization leads to the development of two classes of people: the bourgeoisie, or the owners of the means of production (e.g., factories, farms, businesses), and the proletariat, or the workers who earn wages.

The division of society into two broad classes of people—the "haves" and the "have-nots"—is beneficial to the owners of the means of production. The workers, who may earn only subsistence wages, are denied access to the many resources available to the wealthy owners. According to Marx, the bourgeoisie use their power to control the institutions of society to their advantage. For example, Marx suggested that religion serves as an "opiate of the masses" in that it soothes the distress and suffering associated with the working-class lifestyle and focuses the workers' attention on spirituality, God, and the afterlife rather than on such worldly concerns as living conditions. In essence, religion diverts the workers so that they concentrate on being rewarded in heaven for living a moral life rather than on questioning their exploitation.

Conflict Theories of Social Problems

There are two general types of conflict theories of social problems: Marxist and non-Marxist. Marxist theories focus on social conflict that results from economic inequalities; non-Marxist theories focus on social conflict that results from competing values and interests among social groups.

Marxist Conflict Theories According to contemporary Marxist theorists, social problems result from the class inequality inherent in a capitalistic system. A system of "haves" and "have-nots" may be beneficial to the "haves" but often translates into poverty for the "have-nots." As we shall explore later in this text, many social problems, including physical and mental illness, low educational achievement, and crime, are linked to poverty.

> Promises of better things to come, repeated for years and years, are a cruel hoax on those who are hoping and waiting.
>
> DAVID LEWIS
> *Politician, lawyer, academic*

In addition to creating an impoverished class of people, capitalism also encourages "corporate violence." Corporate violence may be defined as actual harm and/or risk of harm inflicted on consumers, workers, and the general public as a result of decisions by corporate executives or managers. Corporate violence may also result from corporate negligence, the quest for profits at any cost, and wilful violations of health, safety, and environmental laws (Hills 1987). Our profit-motivated economy may provide encouragement for those who are otherwise good, kind, and law-abiding to participate knowingly in the manufacturing and marketing of defective brakes on jets, fuel tanks on automobiles, and unsafe contraceptive devices such as some intrauterine devices (IUDs). The profit motive has also caused individuals to sell defective medical devices, toxic pesticides, and contaminated foods to developing countries. As Eitzen and Baca Zinn note, the "goal of profit is so central to capitalistic enterprises that many corporate decisions are made without consideration for the consequences" (Eitzen and Baca Zinn 2000: 483).

Marxist conflict theories also focus on the problem of **alienation**, or powerlessness and meaninglessness in people's lives. In industrialized societies, workers often have little power or control over their jobs, which fosters a sense of powerlessness in their lives. The specialized nature of work requires workers to perform limited and repetitive tasks; as a result, the workers may come to feel that their lives are meaningless.

Alienation is bred not only in the workplace, but also in the classroom. Students have little power over their education and often find the curriculum is not meaningful to their lives. Like poverty, alienation is linked to other social problems, such as low educational achievement, violence, and suicide.

Marxist explanations of social problems imply that the solution lies in eliminating inequality among classes of people by creating a classless society. The nature of work must also change to avoid alienation. Finally, stronger controls must be applied to corporations to ensure that corporate decisions and practices are based on safety rather than on profit considerations.

Non-Marxist Conflict Theories Neo-Marxist conflict theorists such as Ralf Dahrendorf are concerned with conflict that arises when groups have opposing values and interests. For example, anti-abortion activists value the life of unborn embryos and fetuses; pro-choice activists value the right of women to control their own bodies and reproductive decisions. These different value positions reflect different subjective interpretations of what constitutes a social problem. For anti-abortionists, the availability of abortion is the social problem; for prochoice advocates, restrictions on abortion are the social problem. Sometimes the social problem is not the conflict itself, but rather the way that conflict is expressed. Even most pro-life advocates agree that shooting doctors who perform abortions and blowing up abortion clinics constitute unnecessary violence and lack of respect for life. Value conflicts may occur between diverse categories of people, including non-Whites versus Whites, heterosexuals versus homosexuals, young versus old, liberals versus conservatives, and environmentalists versus industrialists.

Solutions to the problems that are generated by competing values may involve ensuring that conflicting groups understand each other's views, resolving differences through negotiation or mediation, or agreeing to disagree. Ideally, solutions should be win–win; both conflicting groups should be satisfied with the solution. However, outcomes of value conflicts are often influenced by power; the group with the most power may use its position to influence the outcome of value conflicts.

Symbolic Interactionist Perspective

Both the structural-functionalist and the conflict perspectives are concerned with how broad aspects of society, such as institutions and large social groups, influence the social world. This level of sociological analysis is called **macro sociology**: it looks at the "big picture" of society and suggests how social problems are affected at the institutional level.

Micro sociology, another level of sociological analysis, is concerned with the social psychological dynamics of individuals interacting in small groups. **Symbolic interactionism** reflects the micro-sociological perspective and was largely influenced by the work of early sociologists and philosophers such as Max Weber, George Simmel, Charles Horton Cooley, G. H. Mead, W. I. Thomas, Erving Goffman, and Howard Becker. Symbolic interactionism emphasizes that human behaviour is influenced by definitions and meanings that are created and maintained through symbolic interaction with others.

Sociologist W. I. Thomas ([1931] 1966) emphasized the importance of definitions and meanings in social behaviour and in its consequences. He suggested that humans respond to their definition of a situation rather than to the objective situation itself. Hence, Thomas noted that situations we define as real become real in their consequences.

Symbolic interactionism also suggests that our identity or sense of self is shaped by social interaction. We develop our self-concept by observing how others interact with us and label us. By observing how others view us, we see a reflection of ourselves that Charles Horton Cooley calls the "looking-glass self."

Lastly, the symbolic interaction perspective has important implications for how social scientists conduct research. Max Weber (1864–1920) argued that in order to understand individual and group behaviour, social scientists must see the world from the eyes of that individual or group. Weber called this approach *Verstehen*, which in German means "empathy." Verstehen implies that in conducting research, social scientists must try to understand others' view of reality and the subjective aspects of their experiences, including their symbols, values, attitudes, and beliefs.

> Each to each a looking glass, reflects the other that doth pass.
>
> CHARLES HORTON COOLEY
> *Sociologist*

Symbolic Interactionist Theories of Social Problems

A basic premise of symbolic interactionist theories of social problems is that a condition must be defined or recognized as a social problem in order for it to be a social problem. Based on this premise, Herbert Blumer (1971) suggested that social problems develop in stages. First, social problems pass through the stage of "societal recognition"—the process by which a social problem, for example, drunk driving, is "born." Second, "social legitimation" takes place when the social problem achieves recognition by the larger community, including the media, schools, and churches. As the visibility of traffic fatalities associated with alcohol increased, so did the legitimation of drunk driving as a social problem. The next stage in the development of a social problem involves "mobilization for action," which occurs when individuals and groups, such as Mothers Against Drunk Driving, become concerned about how to respond to the social condition. This mobilization leads to the "development and implementation of an official plan" for dealing with the problem, involving, for example, highway checkpoints, lower legal blood-alcohol levels, and tougher penalties for drunk driving.

Blumer's stage development view of social problems is helpful in tracing the development of social problems. For example, although sexual harassment and date rape have occurred throughout the past century, these issues did not begin to receive recognition as social problems until the 1970s. Social legitimation of these problems was achieved when high schools, colleges and universities, churches, employers, and the media recognized their existence. Organized social groups mobilized to develop and implement plans to deal with these problems. For example, groups successfully lobbied for the enactment of laws against sexual harassment and the enforcement of sanctions against violators of these laws. Groups also mobilized to provide educational seminars on date rape for students and to offer support services to victims of date rape.

Some disagree with the symbolic interactionist view that social problems exist only if they are recognized. According to this view, individuals who were victims of date rape in the 1960s may be considered victims of a problem, even though date rape was not recognized at that time as a social problem.

Labelling theory, a major symbolic interactionist theory of social problems, suggests that a social condition or group is viewed as problematic if it is labelled as such. According to labelling theory, resolving social problems sometimes involves changing the meanings and definitions that are attributed to people and situations. For example, as long as teenagers define drinking alcohol as "cool" and "fun," they will continue to abuse alcohol. As long as our society defines providing sex education and contraceptives to teenagers as inappropriate or immoral, the teenage pregnancy rate in our country will continue to grow.

Table 1.2 summarizes and compares the major theoretical perspectives, their criticisms, and social policy recommendations as they relate to social problems. The study of social problems is based on research as well as theory, however. Indeed, research and theory are intricately related. As Wilson (1983) states,

> Most of us think of theorizing as quite divorced from the business of gathering facts. It seems to require an abstractness of thought remote from the practical activity of empirical research. But theory building is not a separate activity within sociology. Without theory, the empirical researcher would find it impossible to decide what to observe, how to observe it, or what to make of the observations....(p. 1)

Social Problems Research

Most students taking a course in social problems will not become researchers or conduct research on social problems. Nevertheless, we are all consumers of research that is reported in the media. Politicians, social activist groups, and organizations attempt to justify their decisions, actions, and positions by citing research results. As consumers of research, it is important to understand that our personal experiences and casual observations are less reliable than generalizations based on systematic research. One strength of scientific research is

■ **Table 1.2** *Comparison of Theoretical Perspectives*

	Structural-Functionalism	Conflict Theory	Symbolic Interactionism
Representative Theorists	Émile Durkheim Talcott Parsons Robert Merton	Karl Marx Ralf Dahrendorf	George H. Mead Charles Cooley Erving Goffman
Society	Society is a set of inter-related parts; cultural consensus exists and leads to social order; natural state of society—balance and harmony.	Society is marked by power struggles over scarce resources; inequities result in conflict; social change is inevitable; natural state of society—imbalance.	Society is a network of interlocking roles; social order is constructed through interaction as individuals, through shared meaning, make sense out of their social world.
Individuals	Society's institutions socialize individuals; socialization is the process by which social control is exerted; people need society and its institutions.	People are inherently good but are corrupted by society and its economic structure; groups with power control institutions; "order" is part of the illusion.	Humans are interpretative and interactive; they are constantly changing as their "social beings" emerge and are moulded by changing circumstances.
Cause of Social Problems?	Rapid social change: social disorganization that disrupts the harmony and balance; inadequate socialization and/or weak institutions.	Inequality; the dominance of groups of people over other groups of people; oppression and exploitation; competition between groups.	Different interpretations of roles; labelling of individuals, groups, or behaviours as deviant; definition of an objective condition as a social problem.
Social Policy/ Solutions	Repair weak institutions; assure proper socialization; cultivate a strong collective sense of right and wrong.	Minimize competition; create an equitable system for the distribution of resources.	Reduce impact of labelling and associated stigmatization; alter definitions of what is defined as a social problem.
Criticisms	Called "sunshine sociology"; supports the maintenance of the status quo; needs to ask "functional for whom?" Does not deal with issues of power and conflict; incorrectly assumes a consensus.	Utopian model; Marxist states have failed; denies existence of cooperation and equitable exchange. Can't explain cohesion and harmony.	Concentrates on micro issues only; fails to link micro issues to macro-level concerns; too psychological in its approach; assumes label amplifies problem.

that it is subjected to critical examination by other researchers (see this chapter's *Social Problems Research Up Close* feature). The more you understand how research is done, the better able you will be to critically examine and question research, rather than to passively consume research findings. The remainder of this section discusses the stages of conducting a research study and the various methods of research used by sociologists.

The Sociological Enterprise

Each chapter in this book contains a *Social Problems Research Up Close* box that describes a research report or journal article examining some sociologically significant topic. Some examples of the many journals in sociology are the *Canadian Journal of Sociology, Canadian Review of Sociology and Anthropology, Recherches Sociographiques, Sociologie et Sociétés* and *Cahiers de Sociologie*. Journal articles are the primary means by which sociologists, as well as other scientists, exchange ideas and information. Most journal articles begin with an *introduction* and *review of the literature*. It is here that the author examines previous research on the topic, identifies specific research areas, and otherwise "sets the stage" for the reader. It is often in this section that research hypotheses, if applicable, are set forth. A researcher, for example, might hypothesize that the primary social concerns of Canadian teenagers adolescents vary on the basis of sex.

The next major section of a journal article is entitled *sample and methods*. In this section the author describes the characteristics of the sample, if any, and the details of the type of research conducted. The type of data analysis used is also pre-sented in this section. Using the above research question, a sociologist might obtain data from the Project Teen Canada 2000 Survey. This national survey, based on a highly representative sample of more than 3500 Canadian high school students, aged 15 to 19, was carried out from the University of Lethbridge.

The final section of a journal article includes the *findings and conclusions*. The findings of a study describe the results, that is, what the researcher found as a result of the investigation. Findings are then discussed within the context of the hypotheses and the conclusions that can be drawn. Other research results are presented in tabular form. Reading tables carefully is an important part of drawing accurate conclusions about the research hypotheses. In reading a table you should follow the steps below (see the table on the next page):

1. *Read the title of the table and make sure that you understand what the table contains.* The title of the table indicates the unit of analysis (high school students), the dependent variable (social concerns), the independent variable (sex), and what the numbers represent (percentages).

2. *Read the information contained at the bottom of the table, including the source and any other explanatory information.* For example, the information at the bottom of this table indicates that the data are from the Project Teen Canada 2000 survey and that the sample was restricted to Canadians 15 to 19 years old in grades 10 to 12 across Canada, including CEGEP I's in Quebec.

3. *Examine the row and column headings.* This table looks at the social concerns that were identified as "very serious" by male and female teenagers in Canada.

4. *Thoroughly examine the data contained within the table, carefully looking for patterns.* As indicated in the table, there is a general tendency for far more female than male teenagers to see any "person-related" issue as serious. For example, child abuse is seen as "very serious" by 66 percent of females but just 44 percent of males. Similar large differences can be noted in relation to AIDS, violence in schools, teenage suicide, drugs, discrimination, violence against women, poverty, crime, and youth gangs. However, the differences between male and female teenagers are minor in relation to "institutional-related issues" such as the environment, American influence, the economy, the threat of

---

Stages of Conducting a Research Study

Sociologists progress through various stages in conducting research on a social problem. This section describes the first four stages: formulating a research question, reviewing the literature, defining variables, and formulating a hypothesis.

Formulating a Research Question A research study usually begins with a research question. Where do research questions originate? How does a particular researcher come to ask a particular research question?

nuclear war, lack of Canadian unity, and Native–White and French–English relations.

5. *Use the information you have gathered in step 4 to address the hypotheses.* Clearly, young women are much more likely than young men to express concern about social issues that have a strong person-centred emphasis. However, when more abstract, structurally related social concerns are raised, male teenagers match or exceed female teenagers in their identification of the issue as "very serious."

6. *Draw conclusions consistent with the information presented.* From the table can we conclude that a "compassion gap" exists between male and female teenagers in Canada? Can we conclude, as some have, that "[y]oung females are far more caring, sympathetic, and responsive towards people in general and the disprivileged in particular" (Bibby and Posterski 1992: 141)? Although the data may imply it, it would be premature to come to such a conclusion. More information, from a variety of sources, is needed. The use of multiple methods and approaches to study a social phenomenon is called **triangulation**.

Primary Social Concerns of Canadian High School Students*, by Sex			
	% Viewing as "Very Serious"		
	Nationally	**Males**	**Females**
Child abuse	56%	44%	66%
AIDS	55	46	62
Violence in schools	50	40	59
Teenage suicide	49	36	60
Drugs	48	41	55
Racial discrimination	47	40	53
The environment	42	41	44
Violence against women	42	33	51
Poverty	41	34	47
Crime	40	29	49
Youth gangs	32	28	34
Unequal treatment of women	32	23	39
American influence	25	27	22
Economy	25	27	23
The threat of nuclear war	24	22	24
Lack of Canadian unity	21	22	21
Native–White relations	21	20	21
French–English Relations	20	20	20

*The Project Teen Canada 2000 sample was restricted to Canadians, 15 to 19 years old, in grades 10 to 12 across Canada, including CEGEP I's in Quebec.
SOURCE: Bibby, Reginald W., and Donald C. Posterski. 1992. *Teen Trends: A Nation in Motion*. Toronto: Stoddart. Table source: Bibby, Reginald W. 2001. *Canada's Teens: Today, Yesterday, and Tomorrow*. Toronto: Stoddart. p. 43.

In some cases, researchers have a personal interest in a specific topic because of their own life experience. For example, a researcher who has experienced spousal abuse may wish to do research on such questions as "What factors are associated with domestic violence?" and "How helpful are battered women's shelters in helping abused women break the cycle of abuse in their lives?" Other researchers may ask a particular research question because of their personal values—their concern for humanity and the desire to improve human life. Researchers who are concerned about the spread of human immunodeficiency virus (HIV) infection and AIDS may conduct research on such questions as "How does the use of alcohol influence condom use?" and "What educational strategies are effective for increasing safer sex behaviour?" Researchers may also want to test a particular sociological theory, or some aspect of it, in order to establish its validity or conduct studies to evaluate the effect of a social policy or program. Research questions may also be formulated by the concerns of community groups and social activist organizations in collaboration with academic researchers. Government and industry also hire researchers to answer questions such as "How many children are victimized by episodes of violence at school?" and "What types of computer technologies can protect children against being exposed to pornography on the Internet?"

Reviewing the Literature After a research question is formulated, the researcher reviews the published material on the topic to find out what is already known about it. Reviewing the literature also provides researchers with ideas about how to conduct their research and helps them formulate new research questions. A literature review also serves as an evaluation tool, allowing a comparison of research findings and other sources of information, such as expert opinions, political claims, and journalistic reports.

Defining Variables A **variable** is any measurable event, characteristic, or property that varies or is subject to change. Researchers must operationally define the variables they study. An **operational definition** specifies how a variable is to be measured. For example, an operational definition of the variable "religiosity" might be the number of times the respondent reports going to church or synagogue. Another operational definition of "religiosity" might be the respondent's answer to the question, "How important is religion in your life? (1 = not important, 2 = somewhat important, 3 = very important)."

Operational definitions are particularly important for defining variables that cannot be directly observed. For example, researchers cannot directly observe concepts such as "mental illness," "sexual harassment," "child neglect," "job satisfaction," and "drug abuse." Nor can researchers directly observe perceptions, values, and attitudes.

Formulating a Hypothesis After defining the research variables, researchers may formulate a **hypothesis**, which is a prediction or educated guess about how one variable is related to another variable. The dependent variable is the variable that the researcher wants to explain; that is, it is the variable of interest. The independent variable is the variable that is expected to explain change in the **dependent variable**. In formulating a hypothesis, the researcher predicts how the **independent variable** affects the dependent variable. For example, Mouw and Xie (1999) hypothesized that fluent bilingual children have higher levels of academic achievement than children who are English-only fluent. However, their analysis found "no evidence that fluent bilinguals do better than students who are fluent only in English" (p. 250). In this example, the independent variable is bilingualism and the dependent variable is school achievement.

In studying social problems, researchers often assess the effects of several independent variables on one or more dependent variables. For example, Jekielek (1998) examined the impact of parental conflict and marital disruption (two independent variables) on the emotional well-being of children (the dependent variable). Her research found that both parental conflict and marital

> Science is meaningless because it gives no answer to the question, the only question of importance for us: "What shall we do and how shall we live?"
>
> COUNT LEO NIKOLAYEVITCH TOLSTOY
> *Novelist*

disruption (separation or divorce) negatively affect children's emotional well-being. However, children in high-conflict intact families exhibit lower levels of well-being than children who have experienced high levels of parental conflict but whose parents divorce or separate.

Methods of Data Collection

After identifying a research topic, reviewing the literature, and developing hypotheses, researchers decide which method of data collection to use. Alternatives include experiments, surveys, field research, and secondary data.

Experiments An **experiment** involves manipulating the independent variable in order to determine how it affects the dependent variable. It requires one or more experimental groups that are exposed to the experimental treatment(s) and a control group that is not exposed. After the researcher randomly assigns participants to either an experimental or a control group, she or he measures the dependent variable. After the experimental groups are exposed to the treatment, the researcher measures the dependent variable again. If participants have been randomly assigned to the different groups, the researcher may conclude that any difference in the dependent variable among the groups is due to the effect of the independent variable.

An example of a "social problems" experiment on poverty would be to provide welfare payments to one group of unemployed single mothers (experimental group) and no such payments to another group of unemployed single mothers (control group). The independent variable would be welfare payments; the dependent variable would be employment. The researcher's hypothesis would be that mothers in the experimental group would be less likely to have a job after 12 months than mothers in the control group.

The major strength of the experimental method is that it provides evidence for causal relationships; that is, how one variable affects another. A primary weakness is that experiments are often conducted on small samples, usually in artificial laboratory settings; thus, the findings may not be generalizable to other people in natural settings.

Surveys **Survey research** involves eliciting information from respondents through questions. An important part of survey research is selecting a sample of those to be questioned. A **sample** is a portion of the population, selected to be representative so that the information from the sample can be generalized to a larger population. For example, instead of asking all abused spouses about their experience, you could ask a representative sample of them and assume that those you did not question would give similar responses. After selecting a representative sample, survey researchers either interview people, ask them to complete written questionnaires, or elicit responses to research questions through computers.

> My latest survey shows that people don't believe in surveys.
>
> LAURENCE PETER
> *Humorist*

1. *Interviews.* In interview survey research, trained interviewers ask respondents a series of questions and make written notes about or tape-record the respondents' answers. Interviews may be conducted over the telephone or face to face. One advantage of interview research is that researchers are able to clarify questions for the respondent and follow up on answers to particular questions. Researchers often conduct face-to-face interviews with

groups of individuals who might otherwise be inaccessible. For example, some AIDS-related research attempts to assess the degree to which individuals engage in behaviour that places them at high risk for transmitting or contracting HIV. Street youth and intravenous drug users, both high-risk groups for HIV infection, may not have a telephone or address because of their transient lifestyle (Catania et al. 1990). These groups may be accessible, however, if the researcher locates their hangouts and conducts face-to-face interviews. Research on homeless individuals may also require a face-to-face interview survey design.

> When I was younger I could remember anything—whether it happened or not.
>
> **MARK TWAIN**
> *Humorist and writer*

The most serious disadvantages of interview research are cost and the lack of privacy and anonymity. Respondents may feel embarrassed or threatened when asked questions that relate to personal issues such as drug use, domestic violence, and sexual behaviour. As a result, some respondents may choose not to participate in interview research on sensitive topics. Those who do participate may conceal or alter information or give socially desirable answers to the interviewer's questions (e.g., "No, I do not use drugs").

2. *Questionnaires.* Instead of conducting personal or phone interviews, researchers may develop questionnaires that they either mail or give to a sample of respondents. Questionnaire research offers the advantages of being less expensive and time-consuming than face-to-face or telephone surveys. In addition, questionnaire research provides privacy and anonymity to the research participants. This reduces the likelihood that they will feel threatened or embarrassed when asked personal questions and increases the likelihood that they will provide answers that are not intentionally inaccurate or distorted.

The major disadvantage of mail questionnaires is that it is difficult to obtain an adequate response rate. Many people do not want to take the time or make the effort to complete and mail a questionnaire. Others may be unable to read and understand the questionnaire.

3. *"Talking" Computers.* A new method of conducting survey research is asking respondents to provide answers to a computer that "talks." Romer et al. (1997) found that respondents rated computer interviews about sexual issues more favourably than face-to-face interviews and that the former were more reliable. Such increased reliability may be particularly valuable when conducting research on drug use, deviant sexual behaviour, and sexual orientation as respondents reported the privacy of computers as a major advantage.

Field Research **Field research** involves observing and studying social behaviour in settings in which it occurs naturally. Two types of field research are participant observation and nonparticipant observation.

In participant observation research, the researcher participates in the phenomenon being studied to obtain an insider's perspective of the people and/or behaviour being observed. Coleman (1990), a middle-class White male, changed clothes to live on the streets as a homeless person for 10 days. In nonparticipant observation research, the researcher observes the phenomenon being studied without actively participating in the group or the activity. For example, Dordick (1997) studied homelessness by observing and talking with homeless individuals in a variety of settings, but she did not live as a homeless person as part of her research.

> Feminists in all disciplines have demonstrated that objectivity has about as much substance as the emperor's new clothes.
>
> **CONNIE MILLER**
> *Feminist scholar*

Sometimes sociologists conduct in-depth detailed analyses or case studies of an individual, group, or event. For example, Skeen (1991) conducted case studies of a prostitute and her adjustment to leaving the profession, an incest survivor, and a person with AIDS.

The main advantage of field research on social problems is that it provides detailed information about the values, rituals, norms, behaviours, symbols, beliefs, and emotions of those being studied. A potential problem with field research is that the researcher's observations may be biased (e.g., the researcher becomes too involved in the group to be objective). In addition, because field research is usually based on small samples, the findings may not be generalizable.

Secondary Data Research Sometimes researchers analyze secondary data, which are data that have already been collected by other researchers or government agencies or that exist in forms such as historical documents, police reports, school records, and official records of marriages, births, and deaths. A major advantage of using secondary data in studying social problems is that the data are readily accessible, so researchers avoid the time and expense of collecting their own data. Secondary data are also often based on large representative samples. The disadvantage of secondary data is that the researcher is limited to the data already collected.

> The gulf between knowledge and truth is infinite.
>
> HENRY MILLER
> *Novelist*

Goals of the Text

This text approaches the study of social problems with several goals in mind.

1. *Provide an integrated theoretical background.* This text reflects an integrative theoretical approach to the study of social problems. More than one theoretical perspective can be used to explain a social problem because social problems usually have multiple causes. For example, youth crime is linked to (1) little or no parental supervision (social disorganization), (2) young people having no legitimate means of acquiring material wealth (anomie theory), (3) youth being angry and frustrated at the inequality and racism in our society (conflict theory), and (4) teachers regarding youth as "no good" and treating them accordingly (labelling theory).

2. *Encourage the development of a sociological imagination.* The most recent Project Canada (2000) national surveys found that about one in two Canadian adults and no less than 7 in 10 Canadian teenagers believe that "anyone who works hard will rise to the top" (Bibby 2001: 243). In general, the expectations of Canadian teenagers are extremely high. Approximately 8 in 10 expect to obtain the job they want upon graduation (86 percent), marry and stay with the same partner for life (88 percent), and be more financially comfortable than their parents (79 percent); almost all expect to own their own home (96 percent) (Bibby 2001: 136). However, a major insight of the sociological perspective is that various structural and cultural elements of society have far-reaching effects on individual lives and societal well-being. This insight, known as the sociological imagination, enables us to understand how social forces underlie personal misfortunes and failures as well as contribute to personal successes and achievements. Each chapter in this text emphasizes how structural and cultural factors contribute to social problems. This emphasis encourages you to develop your sociological imagination by recognizing how structural and cultural factors influence private troubles and public issues.

> For the first time in history, the 21st century should give each person the right to choose their government and enjoy the freedom to participate in decisions that affect their lives.
>
> UNITED NATIONS DEVELOPMENT PROGRAMME
> **Human Development Report 2000**

In a certain sense, every single human soul has more meaning and value than the whole of history.

NICHOLAS BERDYAEV
Philosopher

3. *Provide global coverage of social problems.* The modern world is often referred to as a "global village." The Internet and fax machines connect individuals around the world, economies are interconnected, environmental destruction in one region of the world affects other regions of the world, and diseases cross national boundaries. Understanding social problems requires an awareness of how global trends and policies affect social problems. Many social problems call for collective action involving countries around the world; efforts to end poverty, protect the environment, control population growth, and reduce the spread of HIV are some of the social problems that have been addressed at the global level. Each chapter in this text includes coverage of global aspects of social problems. We hope that attention to the global aspects of social problems broadens students' awareness of pressing world issues.

4. *Provide an opportunity to assess personal beliefs and attitudes.* Each chapter in this text contains a section called *Self and Society*, which offers you an opportunity to assess your attitudes and beliefs regarding some aspect of the social problem discussed. Earlier in this chapter, the *Self and Society* feature allowed you to assess your beliefs about a number of social problems and compare your beliefs with a national sample of Canadians.

Activism pays the rent on being alive and being here on the planet....If I weren't alive politically, I would feel as if I were sitting back eating at the banquet without washing the dishes or preparing the food. It wouldn't feel right.

ALICE WALKER
Novelist

5. *Emphasize the human side of social problems.* Each chapter in this text contains a feature called *The Human Side*, which illustrates how social problems have affected individual lives. By conveying the private pain and personal triumphs associated with social problems, we hope to elicit a level of understanding and compassion that may not be attained through the academic study of social problems alone. This chapter's *The Human Side* presents stories about how students, disturbed by various social conditions, have participated in social activism.

6. *Encourage students to take prosocial action.* Individuals who understand the factors that contribute to social problems may be better able to formulate interventions to remedy those problems. Recognizing the personal pain and public costs associated with social problems encourages some to initiate social intervention.

I am not very patriotic, in the usual meaning of that word. I cannot say, "My country right or wrong" in any political, social, or literary context.

MARGARET LAURENCE
Novelist

Individuals can make a difference in society by the choices they make. Individuals may choose to vote for one candidate over another, demand the right to reproductive choice or protest government policies that permit it, drive drunk or stop a friend from driving drunk, repeat a racist or sexist joke or chastise the person who tells it, and practise safe sex or risk the transmission of sexually transmitted diseases. Individuals can also "make a difference" by addressing social concerns in their occupational role, as well as through volunteer work.

Although individual choices have an important impact, collective social action often has a more pervasive effect. For example, in 1971, engineer Jim Bohlen, lawyer Irving Stone, and law student Paul Cote formed the Greenpeace Foundation in Vancouver to protest U.S. nuclear tests at Amchitka. In their first direct action, the 11 members of the Greenpeace Foundation set sail in a chartered trawler boat into the bomb testing range. In doing so, they attracted the interest of Canadians living downwind of the test site. The issue was subsequently brought before the U.S. Supreme Court; four additional tests that had been planned at Amchitka were cancelled. Since that time Greenpeace has continued in its pursuit of "a moratorium on all those things poisoning us" and

Student Activism

Some people believe that in order to promote social change one must be in a position of political power and/or have large financial resources. However, the most important prerequisite for becoming actively involved in improving levels of social well-being may be genuine concern and dedication to a social "cause." The following vignettes provide a sampler of student activism—students making a difference in the world.

- In May 1989, hundreds of Chinese university students protested in Tiananmen Square in Beijing, China, because Chinese government officials would not meet with them to hear their pleas for a democratic government. These students boycotted classes and started a hunger strike. On June 4, 1989, thousands of students and other protesters were massacred or arrested in Tiananmen Square.
- In October 1969, less than four months after the "Stonewall Riots" in New York (an event that marked the symbolic beginning of the gay liberation movement) (Goldie 2001), the first meeting of the first gay liberation organization in Canada, the University of Toronto Homophile Association (UTHA), was convened. In 1970, a group of eight gay students who perceived the need for an organization that would assist gays living in a heterosexual-dominated world formed Waterloo Universities Gay Liberation Movement (WUGLUM), a group encompassing both the University of Waterloo and Wilfrid Laurier University. In the autumn of 1971 in Saskatoon, the Gay Students Alliance became the first gay group in Saskatchewan. The following year, Gay McGill (originally GAY) became the first anglophone gay organization in Quebec. The costs of student activism at this time and on this issue were often steep. However, organizations for lesbian, bisexual, gay, and transgendered peoples are now common on most campuses and provide such support services as "coming out" discussion groups and help lines, furnish educational materials, and organize a wide variety of social events.
- On December 6, 1989, the largest mass shooting in Canada occurred when 25-year-old Marc Lepine, armed with a Sturm Ruger Mini-14 semiautomatic rifle, knives, and bandoliers of ammunition, entered the École Polytechnique in Montreal and killed 14 female students and wounded 13 other students (9 women and 4 men). His rampage, which had deliberately targeted women, ended with his suicide. In the suicide note he left, Lepine wrote, "I have decided to send the feminists, who have always ruined my life, to their maker....I have decided to put an end to these viragos." This tragedy, which occurred in the University of Montreal's School of Engineering building, prompted the Canadian government to proclaim December 6 the National Day of Remembrance and Action on Violence Against Women. Since 1989, student activists across Canadian have held annual commemorative events to remember the women killed and to promote an end to violence in all its forms. For example, on the anniversary of the Montreal Massacre, the Engineering Undergraduate Society and the Association of Engineering at the University of British Columbia share a minute of silence and light candles in memory of the Montreal victims. In Nova Scotia, a Purple Ribbon campaign pays tribute to the murdered women, attempts to raise public awareness of violence against women, and collects donations to benefit transition houses for abused women and their children. The group Men for Change also formed in response to the tragedy, with the purpose of working toward an end to violence.

(continued)

- In the early 1970s, U.S. citizen activist Ralph Nader launched PIRGs (Public Interest Research Groups) as a means of harnessing the energy and talent of students in solving social problems. Today, there are over 200 PIRG chapters in the United States and 19 in Canada (3 in B.C., 1 in Nova Scotia, 4 in Quebec, and 11 in Ontario) funded through voluntary student fees. The goals of PIRGs are to motivate civic participation and responsibility by encouraging individuals to become informed, concerned, and active in their communities; to recognize and pursue integrative analyses of societal and environmental issues; to respect and encourage local and global ecosystem integrity; to encourage diversity and social equality for all people by opposing all forms of oppression; to work in a cooperative way, employing a consensual decision-making process; and to work in solidarity with other like-minded environmental and social justice movements. PIRGs in Canada have produced a variety of issue-oriented publications and audio-visual materials on such topics as the food industry, acid rain, nuclear power, tenant rights, Ontario Hydro, freedom of information, and the management of toxic waste. Students Against Sweatshops—Canada (SAS-C), formed after a student networking conference held at the University of Toronto in 1999, often works through PIRGs (Campuslife 2002).

- In Canada, Britain, and the United States, students have increasingly challenged campus–corporate parternship. "Whether it's bankers on the board of governors, corporate-endowed professorships or the naming of campus buildings after benefactors, all are facing scrutiny from a more economically politicized student body" (Klein 2000: 405).

- The Canadian Federation of Students, founded in 1981, a cooperative alliance of over 60 students' unions that unites over 450 000 Canadian college and university students, has declared February 6th a "day of action" to protest the soaring costs of post-secondary education in Canada. On that date in 2002, events were held in more than 70 communities across Canada, including St. John's, Halifax, Charlottetown, Toronto, Windor, Thunder Bay, Winnipeg, Regina, Vancouver, and Victoria (Canadian Federation of Students Newswire 2002).

Students who are interested in becoming involved in student activism, or who are already involved, might explore the Web site for the Center for Campus Organizing (2000)—an organization that supports social justice activism and investigative journalism on campuses—or the Student Activism Clearinghouse (2002). These organization recognize that students and faculty, as part of an "affluent conscience constituency" (Carroll 1997: 11) have long played a critical role in larger social movements for social justice in our society, including the Civil Rights movement, the anti–Vietnam War movement, the anti-Apartheid movement, the women's rights movement, and the environmental movement (Axelrod 1990, 1995; Eyerman and Jamison 1991).

SOURCES: Axelrod, Paul. 1990. *Making a Middle Class: Student Life in English Canada During the Thirties*. Montreal and Kingston: McGill-Queen's University Press. Axelrod, Paul. 1995. "Spying on the Young in Depression and War: Students, Youth Groups and the RCMP, 1935–1942," *Labour/Le Travail* 35, Spring: 43–63. Campuslife. 2002. "Students Against Sweatshops-Canada." http://www.campuslife.utoronto.ca/groups/opirg/groups/sweatshops/sas-c.html. Canadian Federation of Students Newswire. 2002. "Students Declare February 6 Day of Action." (4 February). http://action.web.ca. Carroll, William K. 1997. "Social Movements and Counterhegemony: Canadian Contexts and Social Theories." In *Organizing Dissent: Contemporary Social Movements in Theory and Practice*, edited by William K. Carroll, pp. 3–38. Toronto: Garamond Press. Center for Campus Organizing. 2000. http://www.cco.org/about.html. Eyerman, R., and A. Jamison. 1991. *Social Movements: A Cognitive Approach*. Cambridge: Polity Press. Goldie, Terry. 2001. "Queer Nation?" In *In a Queer Country: Gay & Lesbian Studies in the Canadian Context*, edited by Terry Goldie, pp. 7–26. Vancouver: Arsenal Pulp Press. Klein, Naomi. 2000. *No Logo: Taking Aim at the Brand Bullies*. Toronto: Vintage Canada. Student Activism Clearinghouse. 2002. http://e-activism.sourceforge.net/main3.php.

become one of the largest environmental groups in the world, with offices in Argentina, Australia, Austria, Belgium, Canada, Costa Rica, Denmark, Ireland, West Germany, Finland, France, Italy, Japan, Luxembourg, the Netherlands, New Zealand, Norway, Spain, Sweden, Switzerland, the United Kingdom, and the United States. However, as Bohlen has himself remarked, "As individuals we are weak. Our strength is created by putting ourselves at risk" (in Nader et al. 1993: 100).

Schwalbe (1998) reminds us that we do not have to join a group or organize a protest to make changes in the world.

> We *can* change a small part of the social world single-handedly. If we treat others with more respect and compassion, if we refuse to participate in re-creating inequalities even in little ways, if we raise questions about official representation of reality, if we refuse to work in destructive industries, then we are making change. (p. 206)

Understanding Social Problems

At the end of each chapter to follow, we offer a section entitled *Understanding* in which we re-emphasize the social origin of the problem being discussed, the consequences, and the alternative social solutions. It is our hope that the reader will end each chapter with a "sociological imagination" view of the problem and how, as a society, we might approach a solution.

Sociologists have been studying social problems since the Industrial Revolution in the nineteenth century. Industrialization brought about massive social changes: the influence of religion declined; families became smaller and moved from traditional, rural communities to urban settings. These and other changes have been associated with increases in crime, pollution, divorce, and juvenile delinquency. As these social problems became more widespread, the need to understand their origins and possible solutions became more urgent. The field of sociology developed in response to this urgency. Social problems provided the initial impetus for the development of the field of sociology and continue to be a major focus of sociology.

There is no single agreed-upon definition of what constitutes a social problem. Most sociologists agree, however, that all social problems share two important elements: an objective social condition and a subjective interpretation of that condition. Each of the three major theoretical perspectives in sociology—structural-functionalist, conflict, and symbolic interactionist—has its own notion of the causes, consequences, and solutions of social problems.

> Although the world is very full of suffering, it is also full of the overcoming of it.
>
> HELEN KELLER
> *Social activist*

Critical Thinking

1 People are increasingly using information technologies as a means of getting their daily news. Research indicates that news on the Internet is beginning to replace television news as the primary source of information among computer users (see Chapter 13). What role do the media play in our awareness of social problems, and will definitions of social problems change as sources of information change?

2 Each of you occupies several social statuses, each one carrying an expectation of role performance, that is, what you should and should not do given your position. List five statuses you occupy, the expectations of their accompanying roles, and any role conflict that may result. What types of social problems are affected by role conflict?

3 Definitions of social problems change over time. Identify a social condition that is now widely accepted that might be viewed as a social problem in the future.

Key Terms

achieved status	latent function	secondary group
alienation	laws	social group
anomie	macro sociology	social problem
ascribed status	manifest function	sociological imagination
beliefs	master status	status
conflict perspective	micro sociology	structural-functionalism
dependent variable	mores	subjective element
experiment	norms	survey research
field research	objective element	symbol
folkways	operational definition	symbolic interactionism
hypothesis	primary group	triangulation
independent variable	roles	values
institution	sample	variable
labelling theory	sanctions	

Section 1

Problems of Well-Being

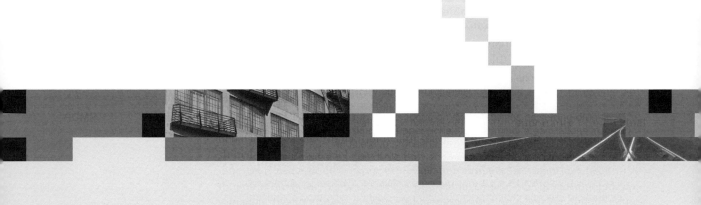

Section 1 deals with problems that are often regarded as private rather than public issues; that is, they are viewed as internally caused or as a function of individual free will. People often respond to these problems by assuming that the problem is the victims' fault—that in some way they have freely chosen their plight. In this set of problems, blame is most often attached to the individuals themselves. Thus, the physically and mentally ill (Chapter 2), the alcoholic and the drug addict (Chapter 3), the criminal and the delinquent (Chapter 4), and the divorced person and the child abuser (Chapter 5) are thought to be bad, weak, immoral, or somehow different from the average person. Consider the following scenarios.

A woman with a limited income decides not to fill an expensive prescription to be able to afford nutritious food for her children. When her condition worsens, she is blamed for failing to follow her doctor's orders to fill the prescription. As sociologists, we would say that the woman did not want to be sick, but rather chose what she perceived as the least of several unfortunate alternatives. In this case, factors that underlie her illness include poverty, the costs of

medication not covered by government plans, and the value system that stresses parental responsibility and sacrifice.

A teenager from an urban lower-class neighbourhood decides to sell drugs rather than stay in school or get a regular job. Such a teenager is generally viewed as being "weak" or having "low" morals. Sociologists view such a person as a lower-class, poorly educated individual with few alternatives in a society that values success. Raised in an environment where the most successful role models are often criminals, legitimate opportunities are few, traditional norms and values are weak, and peer pressure to use and sell drugs is strong, what are his choices? He can pump gas or serve fast food for minimum wage, or he can sell drugs for as much as $5000 a week.

A mother comes home from work and finds her children playing and the house in disorder. She had told the children to clean the house while she was gone. She decides they need to be whipped with a belt because of their disobedience. The physical abuse she engages in is viewed as a reflection of her mental instability and her inability to control her temper. Research indicates, however, that fewer than

10 percent of identified child abusers are severely psychologically impaired.

If being mentally unstable does not explain the majority of child abuse cases, what does explain them? A history of being abused as a child is the strongest independent predictor of who will be a child abuser as an adult. Additionally, the culture of society includes myriad beliefs that contribute to child abuse: acceptance of corporal punishment of children and the ambiguity surrounding what constitutes appropriate discipline, the belief that parental control is an inalienable right, and the historical and lingering belief that children are property.

A student drinks alcohol daily and often cuts classes. Although the public views such behaviour as a personal weakness, sociologists emphasize the role of the individual's socialization and society. For example, a disproportionate number of individuals with drinking problems were reared in homes where one or both parents drank heavily. In the general culture, media portrayals of drinking as desirable, fun, glamourous, and a source of status further promote drinking. Student culture itself often emphasizes bars and drinking parties as primary sources of recreation and affiliation.

These examples illustrate that many behaviours result more from social factors than from individual choice. To the degree that individuals do make choices these choices are socially determined, in that the structure and culture of society limit and influence individual choices. For example, customers in a restaurant cannot choose anything they want to eat; they are limited to what is on the menu. Sociologically, one's social status—male, female, young, old, rich, poor, able-bodied, differently abled—determines one's menu of life choices.

In each of the above examples, the alternatives were limited by the individual's position in the social structure of society and by the cultural and subcultural definitions of appropriate behaviour. While conflict theorists, structural-functionalists, and symbolic interactionists may disagree about the relative importance and mechanisms of the shared structure and culture of society in determining the problems identified, all would agree that society, not the individual, is the primary source of the solutions. In this and the following sections, we emphasize the importance of the social structure and culture of society as the sources of and the solutions to social problems.

2

Illness and Health Care

Outline

The Global Context: Patterns of
Health and Disease

HIV/AIDS: A Global Health
Concern

Mental Illness:
The Invisible Epidemic

Sociological Theories of Illness
and Health Care

Social Factors Associated with
Health and Illness

Problems in Canadian
Health Care

Strategies for Action: Improving
Health and Health Care

Understanding Illness
and Health Care

Is It True?

1. In 2002, the life expectancy of
Canadian males exceeded that of
females.

2. Worldwide, the predominant
mode of HIV transmission is
through heterosexual contact.

3. One in five Canadians will be
affected by a mental illness at some
time in their lives.

4. Lower education levels are associated with higher rates of health
problems and mortality.

5. Although men are more likely to
attempt suicide, women are more
likely to succeed at it.

Answers: 1 = F, 2 = T, 3 = T, 4 = T, 5 = F

It is ironic that in some parts of the world hundreds of millions of people suffer daily from a lack of basic health care while in other parts millions of people spend money on things that are not healthy. Think what a billion dollars could do to help immunize people against deadly diseases in developing countries. A billion dollars is not much money—it is what Americans spend on beer every twelve days and what Europeans spend on cigarettes every five days.

DAVID WRIGHT
Telemedicine and Developing Countries

In August 1997, Jeanne Calment, then the oldest woman in the world, died in France at the age of 122. When she was born in 1875, Thomas Edison had not yet discovered electricity; before she died, photographs from the planet Mars had been transmitted to Earth. During Jeanne Calment's lifetime, the world changed in unimaginable ways. One of the most profound changes over the last century has been the increase in the average length of life. Since the end of World War II, longevity of life in most developed and developing countries has increased by almost 25 years—the greatest increase seen in the history of humankind (LaPorte 1997).

Despite overall improvements in living conditions and medical care, health problems and health care delivery are major concerns of individuals, families, communities, and nations. In this chapter, we review health concerns in Canada and throughout the world. The World Health Organization (1946) defines **health** as "a state of complete physical, mental, and social well-being" (p. 3). Sociologists are concerned with how social forces affect and are affected by health and illness, why some social groups suffer more illness than others, and how illness affects individuals' sense of identity and relationships with others. Sociologists also examine health care systems and explore how these systems can be improved.

The Global Context: Patterns of Health and Disease

The study of patterns of health and disease is called **epidemiology**. The field of epidemiology incorporates several disciplines, including public health, medicine, biology, and sociology. An **epidemiologist** is concerned with the social origins and distribution of health problems in a population and how patterns of health and disease vary between and within societies. Next, we look at global patterns of morbidity, longevity, mortality, and disease burden.

Patterns of Morbidity

Morbidity refers to acute and chronic illnesses and diseases and the symptoms and impairments they produce. An **acute condition** is short term; by definition, it can last no more than three months. A **chronic condition** is a long-term health problem. The rate of serious morbidity in a population provides one measure of the health of that population. Morbidity may be measured according to the incidence and prevalence of specific illnesses and diseases. **Incidence** refers to the number of new cases of a specific health problem within a given population during a specified period. **Prevalence** refers to the total number of cases of a specific health problem within a population that exist at a given time. For example, the incidence of HIV infection worldwide was 5.3 million in 2000, meaning that there were 5.3 million people newly infected with HIV in 2000. In the same year, the worldwide prevalence of HIV was 36.1 million, meaning that a total of 36.1 million people worldwide were living with HIV infection in 2000 ("Global Summary of the HIV/AIDS Epidemic" 2001).

As we discuss later in this chapter, patterns of morbidity vary according to social factors such as social class, education, sex, and race. Morbidity patterns also vary according to the level of development of a society and the age structure of the population. In the less developed countries, malnutrition, pneumonia, and infectious and parasitic diseases such as HIV disease, malaria (transmitted by mosquitoes), and measles are major health concerns. In the industrialized world, advances in sanitation, immunizations, and antibiotics have largely controlled infectious and parasitic diseases. Noninfectious diseases such as heart disease, cancer, mental disorders, and respiratory diseases pose the greatest health threat to the industrialized world. However, the widespread use of antibiotics in industrialized countries has contributed to a rise in infectious disease, as antibiotics kill the weaker disease-causing germs while allowing variants resistant to the drugs to flourish. Worldwide, the most alarming consequence of the development of drug-resistant germs is the resurgence of tuberculosis, which kills more people yearly than any other infectious disease. Tuberculosis is caused by bacilli that attack and destroy lung tissue and is spread when infected individuals cough or sneeze. The World Health Organization estimates that one-third of the world's population is infected, although only about 10 percent of infected persons ever develop symptoms (Weitz 2001).

The shift from a society characterized by low life expectancy and parasitic and infectious diseases to one characterized by high life expectancy and chronic and degenerative diseases is called the **epidemiological transition**. Declining birthrates and increased longevity have resulted in the aging of the world's population, which means that the major sources of morbidity are becoming those of adults rather than those of children. As societies make the epidemiological transition, diseases that need time to develop, such as cancer, heart disease, Alzheimer's disease, arthritis, and osteoporosis become more common, and childhood illnesses, typically caused by infectious and parasitic diseases, become less common.

Patterns of Longevity

One indicator of the health of a population is the average number of years individuals born in a given year can expect to live, referred to as **life expectancy.** Worldwide, life expectancy has increased dramatically over the last 50 years.

However, wide disparities exist in life expectancy for different populations between and within societies. "Japan was the first country to attain an average lifespan of over 80 years—more than double that of many less-developed countries" (Ash 2001: 57). In 2000, Japan had the longest life expectancy: 81 years. In the same year, life expectancy was less than 50 in several countries (see Table 2.1). In Canada, a female born in 2002 could expect to live 83.2 years, a man, 76.3 years (Ash 2001: 53).

Patterns of Mortality

Rates of **mortality** or death—especially those of infants, children, and women—provide sensitive indicators of the health of a population. Worldwide, the leading cause of death is infectious and parasitic diseases (World Health Organization 1998). In Canada, the leading causes of death for both women and men are cardiovascular diseases and cancer. In 1999, over a third of deaths (36 percent) were due to diseases of the circulatory system (e.g., ischaemic heart disease and cerebrovascular diseases) while malignant neoplasms (cancers) accounted for 28 percent of all deaths (Statistics Canada 2002). Later, we discuss how patterns of mortality are related to social factors, such as social class, sex, and education. Mortality rates also vary by age. For example, it is only among 15- to 19-year olds that rates for external causes of death (e.g., suicide, motor vehicle and other types of accidents) are higher than rates for non-external causes of death (deaths arising from natural physiological processes). Among this age group, external causes account for almost eight in ten deaths among boys and seven in ten among girls. Motor-vehicle accidents are the leading cause of death for both males and females in this age group (responsible for about four in ten deaths). Suicide is the second leading cause of death among teenagers 15 to 19 (Statistics Canada 1998c: 110; Nelson and Robinson 2002: 389).

Table 2.1 *Countries with the Longest and Shortest Life Expectancies at Birth (Years 2000–05)*

Lowest Life Expectancies		Highest Life Expectancy	
Country	Life Expectancy	Country	Life Expectancy
Botswana	36.1	Japan	81.5
Mozambique	38.0	Sweden	80.1
Swaziland	38.1	Iceland	79.4
Malawi	39.3	Australia	79.2
Lesotho	40.2	Israel	79.2
Sierra Leone	40.5	Martinique	79.1
Burundi	40.6	Switzerland	79.1
Djibouti	40.6	Canada	79.0
Rwanda	40.9	France	79.0
Zambia	42.2	Norway	78.9

SOURCE: Adapted from United Nations Population Division. 2000. *World Population Prospects: The 2000 Revision*, Annex Table 4, available at www.un.org/esa/population/publications/publications.htm.

Infant and Childhood Mortality Rates The **infant mortality rate**, the number of deaths of live-born infants under one year of age per 1000 live births (in any given year), provides an important measure of the health of a population. In 1999, 25 countries had infant mortality rates over 100 (UNICEF 2001). That means that in 25 countries, one in every ten live-born babies died before they reached age one. The African nation of Sierra Leone had the highest infant mortality rate in the world—an alarming 182 infants out of every 1000 live births died before they reached their first birthday. The lowest rates of infant mortality in 1999 were in Sweden and Switzerland, where only 3 of every 1000 live-born babies died in their first year of life. In 1999, the Canadian infant mortality rate was 5.3. The mortality rate of infant boys in that year (5.7) was slightly higher than the mortality rate for infant girls (4.8) (Statistics Canada 2002).

The **under-five mortality rate**, another useful measure of child health, refers to the rate of deaths of children under age five. Approximately 12 million children younger than five years of age die every year; most of these children live in developing countries. More than half of these deaths are attributed to diarrhea, acute respiratory illness, malaria, or measles, conditions that are either preventable or treatable with low-cost interventions (Rice et al. 2000). Malnutrition is associated with about half of all deaths among children (Rice et al. 2000). Mortality among infants and children has been declining in most developing countries from the mid-1980s through the 1990s. However, this decline has recently slowed, stopped, or reversed itself in some countries of sub-Saharan Africa, largely as a result of the rate of HIV infection among infants and children (Rustein 2000).

Maternal Mortality Rates The **maternal mortality rate**, a measure of deaths that result from complications associated with pregnancy, childbirth, and unsafe abortion, also provides a sensitive indicator of the health status of a population. Maternal deaths are the leading cause of death and disability for women ages 15 to 49 in developing countries (Family Care International 1999).

Of all the health statistics monitored by the World Health Organization, maternal mortality has the largest discrepancy between developed and developing countries. Women's lifetime risk of dying from pregnancy or childbirth is 1 in 48 in all developing countries compared to 1 in 1800 in all developed countries (Family Care International 1999). In Africa, 1 in 16 women dies from pregnancy or childbirth. The highest rate of maternal death is in Niger, where one woman in nine dies in pregnancy or childbirth. The lowest maternal mortality rate is in Norway, where only one in 7300 die in pregnancy or childbirth (Lay 2000). In Canada, the maternal mortality rate is 3.7 deaths per 100 000 live births (Turner et al. 2002) (see Figure 2.1).

Several factors contribute to high maternal mortality rates in less developed countries. Poor quality and inaccessible health care, malnutrition, and poor sanitation contribute to adverse health effects of pregnancy and childbirth. In developing countries, only 53 percent of all births are attended to by professionals and nearly 30 percent of women who give birth in developing countries receive no care after the birth (United Nations Population Fund 2000). Also, women in less developed countries experience higher rates of pregnancy and childbearing and begin childbearing at earlier ages. Thus, they face the risk of maternal death more often and before their bodies are fully developed (see also

> For a woman to die from pregnancy and childbirth is a social injustice. Such deaths are rooted in women's powerlessness and unequal access to employment, finances, education, basic health care, and other resources.
>
> Safe Motherhood Initiative

> It is not uncommon for women in Africa, when about to give birth, to bid their older children farewell.
>
> United Nations Population Fund
> The State of the World Population Report 2000

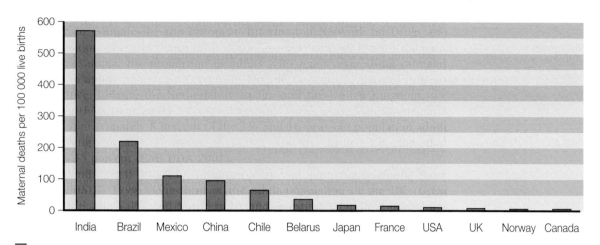

■ Figure 2.1 *Maternal Mortality Rates in Selected Countries (1999 Estimates)*

SOURCE: Turner, Linda A., Margaret Cyr, Robert A. Kinch, Robert Liston, Michael S. Kramer, Martha Fair, and Maureen Heaman. 2002. "Under-reporting of Maternal Mortality in Canada: A Question of Definition." *Chronic Diseases in Canada*, 23(1). Health Canada, © 2002. Reproduced with the permission of the Minister of Public Works and Government Services Canada, 2003.

Chapter 14). Women in many countries also lack access to family planning services and/or do not have the support of their male partners to use contraceptive methods such as condoms. Consequently, many women resort to abortion to limit their childbearing, even in countries where abortion is illegal.

Illegal abortions in less developed countries have an estimated mortality risk of 100 to 1000 per 100 000 procedures (Miller and Rosenfield 1996). In contrast, the Canadian mortality risk for therapeutic abortions is very low (Health Canada 1999b). Each year, women worldwide undergo an estimated 50 million abortions, 20 million of which are unsafe, resulting in the deaths of 78 000 women (United Nations Population Fund 2000).

Patterns of Burden of Disease

Although infant and maternal mortality rates are sensitive indicators of the health of populations, researchers have developed a new approach to measuring the health status of a population that combines mortality and disability. This new approach provides an indicator of the overall **burden of disease** on a population through a single unit of measurement that combines not only the number of deaths but also the impact of premature death and disability on a population (Murray and Lopez 1996). This comprehensive unit of measurement, called the **disability-adjusted life year (DALY)**, reflects years of life lost to premature death and years lived with a disability. More simply, one DALY is equal to one lost year of healthy life. For example, The Global Burden of Disease Study (Murray and Lopez 1996) calculated the burden of disease for various diseases and injuries. The study concluded that worldwide, tobacco is a more serious threat to human health than any single disease, including HIV (see also Chapter 3). Table 2.2 lists the top 10 risks globally in terms of the burden of disease they cause. Together, these account for more than one-third of all deaths worldwide (World Health Organization 2000).

■ Table 2.2 *Ten Leading Risk Factors Globally**

1. Underweight
2. Unsafe sex
3. High blood pressure
4. Tobacco consumption
5. Alcohol consumption
6. Unsafe water, sanitation, and hygiene
7. Iron deficiency
8. Indoor smoke from solid fuels
9. High cholesterol
10. Obesity

*Among all member states of the World Health Organization.

SOURCE: World Health Organization. 2002. *The World Health Report 2002*. http://www.who.int.

HIV/AIDS: A Global Health Concern

HIV/AIDS Epi Update 2002

An estimated 10.3 million people age 15–24 are living with HIV/AIDS, and half of all the new infections that are occurring worldwide are occurring among young people.

HEALTH CANADA

One of the most urgent public health concerns around the globe is the spread of the human immunodeficiency virus (HIV), which causes acquired immuno-deficiency syndrome (AIDS). HIV is transmitted through sexual intercourse; through sharing unclean intravenous needles; perinatally (from infected mother to fetus or newborn); through blood transfusions or blood products; and, rarely, through breast-milk. Worldwide, the predominant mode of HIV transmission is through heterosexual contact (Inciardi and Harrison 1997). The second most common mode of transmission worldwide is **perinatal transmission**—the transmission of HIV from an infected mother to a fetus or newborn. An esti-mated 15 percent to 30 percent of babies born to HIV-infected mothers are HIV positive (Ward 1999). Although homosexual activity accounts for less than 10 percent of new cases worldwide (Stine 1998), men who have sex with other men are the group most at risk for developing HIV/AIDS in Canada. The pro-portion of new infections attributed to this group declined steadily from over 80 percent in 1981–83 to 30 percent in 1996 but, in 1999, increased to 38 percent (see Figure 2.2) (Statistics Canada 1998b, Health Canada 2002c) .

Since the beginning of the epidemic, AIDS has claimed more than 18 million lives (Joint United Nations Programme on HIV/AIDS 2000e). HIV/AIDS is the fourth most common cause of death worldwide, and the leading cause of death in Africa (United Nations Population Fund 2000). In 16 countries in sub-Saharan Africa, more than one in ten persons ages 15 to 49 are HIV-infected. In seven countries in southern Africa, at least 20 percent of the adult population is living with HIV. In Botswana, where about one in three adults are HIV-infected—the highest prevalence in the world—at least two-thirds of today's 15-year-old boys will die prematurely of AIDS (Joint United Nations Programme on

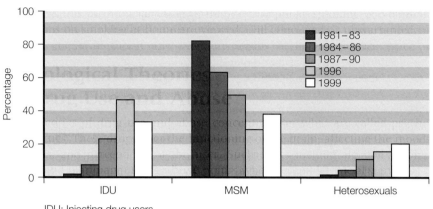

■ **Figure 2.2** *Estimated Exposure Category Distribution (%) among New HIV Infections in Canada by Time Period*

SOURCE: HIV/AIDS Epi Update, p. 3, Figure 1, © Health Canada, April 2002. Reproduced with the permission of the Minister of Public Works and Government Services Canada, 2003.

IDU: Injecting drug users
MSM: Men who have sex with men
Heterosexual: Heterosexual exposure

HIV/AIDS 2000b). Since the epidemic began, over 13 million children—95 percent of them in Africa—have lost their mother or both parents to AIDS (Joint United Nations Programme on HIV/AIDS 2000c). Although HIV/AIDS originally emerged as adult health problems, they have become a major killer of under-five-year-old children, especially in developing countries (Adetunji 2000).

The high rates of HIV in developing countries, particularly sub-Saharan Africa, are having alarming and devastating effects on societies. The HIV/AIDS epidemic creates an enormous burden on the limited health care resources of poor countries. Gains in life expectancy achieved in recent decades have been reversed in some countries. In Botswana, Zambia, and Zimbabwe—countries with high HIV prevalence—life expectancy at birth was lower in 2000 than it was in 1975 (Adetunji 2000). Economic development is threatened by the HIV epidemic, which diverts national funds to health-related needs and reduces the size of a nation's workforce.

HIV/AIDS in Canada

In 1999 in Canada, there were 431 deaths (365 male, 66 female) due to the human immunodeficiency virus (HIV) (Statistics Canada 2002). In that year, there were an estimated 49 800 individuals in Canada living with HIV infection (including AIDS), including an estimated 4190 who became infected in that year (Health Canada 2002c). Between 1982, when the disease was first diagnosed in Canada, and December 31, 2001, 17 810 cumulative AIDS cases in adults had been reported to the Centre for Infectious Disease Prevention and Control. The overwhelming majority of these cases involved men (92.2 percent). Although before 1993 there was one woman with AIDS for every 15 men, women account for a growing proportion of positive HIV test reports. Women accounted for less than one in ten positive HIV test reports between 1985 and 1995, but almost one in four between January 1999 and December 31, 2001 (Health Canada: 2002a). Heterosexual contact with a high-risk partner and injection drug use are the two major risk factors for HIV infection in women (Health Canada 2002a).

Currently, young Canadians compose only a small proportion of the total reported cases. Of the cumulative reported AIDS cases in Canadian youth aged 10 to 19 years of age, approximately two out of three cases were attributed to the receipt of infected blood and blood products. Among youths aged 20 to 24, half were attributed to men who have sex with men, and 21 percent to heterosexual contact with a person at risk (Health Canada 2002b). While HIV prevalence is currently low among Canadian youth, risk behaviour data on young Canadians suggests cause for concern. Although a national survey of Canadian teens found that over one in two (55 percent) saw AIDS as a "very serious" issue (Bibby 2001: 43), many Canadian youths are engaging in unsafe sexual practices (see "The Student Sexual Risks Scale" in this chapter's *Self and Society* feature). For example, according to the National Population Health Survey, among sexually active youth age 15 to 19, 51 percent of females and 29 percent of males reported never or only sometimes using a condom in the past year. Among those 20 to 24 years old, the corresponding figures were 53 percent and 44 percent (Health Canada 2002b; Statistics Canada 1998a).

Mental Illness: The Invisible Epidemic

The concepts of mental illness and mental health are not easy to define. What it means to be mentally healthy varies across and within cultures. Furthermore, mental health and mental illness may be thought of as points on a continuum. **Mental health** has nevertheless been defined as "the successful performance of mental function, resulting in productive activities, fulfilling relationships with other people, and the ability to adapt to change and to cope with adversity" (U.S. Department of Health and Human Services 1999: ix). **Mental illness** refers collectively to all mental disorders. A **mental disorder** is a health condition that is characterized by alterations in thinking, mood, and/or behaviour associated with distress and/or impaired functioning. Although we all experience problems in living, functioning, and emotional distress, such problems are not necessarily considered as mental illness, unless they meet specific criteria (such as level of intensity and duration) specified in the classification manual used to diagnose mental disorders: The Diagnostic and Statistical Manual of Mental Disorders (American Psychiatric Association 2000).

Some examples of mental disorders are presented in Table 2.3 (see page 41).

Extent and Impact of Mental Illness

Although cross-national estimates of the prevalence of mental disorders vary, one study found a 12 percent lifetime prevalence of any mental disorder in Turkey, a 20 percent lifetime prevalence in Mexico, a 37.5 percent lifetime prevalence in Canada and a 40 percent lifetime prevalence in the Netherlands and the United States (WHO International Consortium in Psychiatric Epidemiology 2000). At any given time, three million Canadians are living with some kind of mental illness (Simmie and Nunes 2001). According to the Canadian Mental Health Association (2002), one in five Canadians will be affected by a mental illness at some time in their lives. The most common mental disorder, depression, is estimated to affect one in four Canadian women and one in ten Canadian men at some point in their lives (Canadian Psychiatric Association

The Student Sexual Risks Scale

The following self-assessment allows you to evaluate the degree to which you may be at risk for engaging in behaviour that exposes you to HIV. Safer sex means sexual activity that reduces the risk of transmitting the AIDS virus. Using condoms is an example of safer sex. Unsafe, risky, or unprotected sex refers to sex without a condom, or to other sexual activity that might increase the risk of AIDS virus transmission. For each of the following items, check the response that best characterizes your opinion.

A = Agree

U = Undecided

D = Disagree

	A	U	D
1. If my partner wanted me to have unprotected sex, I would probably give in.	___	___	___
2. The proper use of a condom could enhance sexual pleasure.	___	___	___
3. I may have had sex with someone who was at risk for HIV/AIDS.	___	___	___
4. If I were going to have sex, I would take precautions to reduce my risk of HIV/AIDS.	___	___	___
5. Condoms ruin the natural sex act.	___	___	___
6. When I think that one of my friends might have sex on a date, I ask him/her if he/she has a condom.	___	___	___
7. I am at risk for HIV/AIDS.	___	___	___
8. I would try to use a condom when I had sex.	___	___	___
9. Condoms interfere with romance.	___	___	___
10. My friends talk a lot about safer sex.	___	___	___
11. If my partner wanted me to participate in risky sex and I said we needed to be safer, we would still probably end up having unsafe sex.	___	___	___
12. Generally, I am in favour of using condoms.	___	___	___
13. I would avoid using condoms if at all possible.	___	___	___
14. If a friend knew that I might have sex on a date, he/she would ask me whether I was carrying a condom.	___	___	___
15. There is a possibility that I have HIV/AIDS.	___	___	___
16. If I had a date, I would probably not drink alcohol or use drugs.	___	___	___
17. Safer sex reduces the mental pleasure of sex.	___	___	___
18. If I thought that one of my friends had sex on a date, I would ask him/her if he/she used a condom.	___	___	___
19. The idea of using a condom doesn't appeal to me.	___	___	___
20. Safer sex is a habit for me.	___	___	___
21. If a friend knew that I had sex on a date, he/she wouldn't care whether I had used a condom or not.	___	___	___
22. If my partner wanted me to participate in risky sex and I suggested a lower-risk alternative, we would have the safer sex instead.	___	___	___
23. The sensory aspects (smell, touch, etc.) of condoms make them unpleasant.	___	___	___
24. I intend to follow "safer sex" guidelines within the next year.	___	___	___

(continued)

25. With condoms, you can't really give yourself over to your partner.　　——　——　——

26. I am determined to practise safer sex.　　——　——　——

27. If my partner wanted me to have unprotected sex and I made some excuse to

use a condom, we would still end up having unprotected sex.　　——　——　——

28. If I had sex and I told my friends that I did not use a condom, they would be angry

or disappointed.　　——　——　——

29. I think safer sex would get boring fast.　　——　——　——

30. My sexual experiences do not put me at risk for HIV/AIDS.　　——　——　——

31. Condoms are irritating.　　——　——　——

32. My friends and I encourage each other before dates to practise safer sex.　　——　——　——

33. When I socialize, I usually drink alcohol or use drugs.　　——　——　——

34. If I were going to have sex in the next year, I would use condoms.　　——　——　——

35. If a sexual partner didn't want to use condoms, we would have sex without

using condoms.　　——　——　——

36. People can get the same pleasure from safer sex as from unprotected sex.　　——　——　——

37. Using condoms interrupts sex play.　　——　——　——

38. It is a hassle to use condoms.　　——　——　——

(To be read after completing the scale.)

SCORING: Begin by giving yourself 80 points. Subtract one point for every undecided response. Subtract two points every time that you disagreed with odd-numbered items or with item number 38. Subtract two points every time you agreed with even-numbered items 2 through 36.

INTERPRETING YOUR SCORE: Research shows that students who make higher scores on the SSRS are more likely to engage in risky sexual activities, such as having multiple sex partners and failing to consistently use condoms during sex. In contrast, students who practise safer sex tend to endorse more positive attitudes toward safer sex, and tend to have peer networks that encourage safer sexual practices. These students usually plan on making sexual activity safer, and they feel confident in their ability to negotiate safer sex even when a dating partner may press for riskier sex. Students who practise safer sex often refrain from using alcohol or drugs, which may impede negotiation of safer sex, and often report having engaged in lower-risk activities in the past. How do you measure up?

(BELOW 15) LOWER RISK: (Of 200 students surveyed by DeHart and Birkimer, 16 percent were in this category.) Congratulations! Your score in the SSRS indicates that relative to other students your thoughts and behaviours are more supportive of safer sex. Is there any room for improvement in your score? If so, you may want to examine items for which you lost points and try to build safer sexual strengths in those areas. You can help protect others from HIV by educating your peers about making sexual activity safer.

(15 TO 37) AVERAGE RISK: (Of 200 students surveyed by DeHart and Birkimer, 68 percent were in this category.) Your score on the SSRS is about average in comparison with those of other university students. Although it is good that you don't fall into the higher-risk category, be aware that "average" people can get HIV, too. In fact, a recent survey indicated that the rate of HIV among university students is 10 times that in the general heterosexual population. Thus, you may want to enhance your sexual safety by figuring out where you lost points and work toward safer sexual strengths in those areas.

(38 AND ABOVE) HIGHER RISK: (Of 200 students surveyed by DeHart and Birkimer, 16 percent were in this category.) Relative to other students, your score on the SSRS indicates that your thoughts and behaviours are less supportive of safer sex. Such high scores tend to be associated with greater HIV-risk behaviour. Rather than simply giving in to riskier attitudes and behaviours, you may want to empower yourself and reduce your risk by critically examining areas for improvement. On which items did you lose points? Think about how you can strengthen your sexual safety in these areas. Reading more about safer sex can help, and sometimes student health clinics offer courses or workshops on safer sex.

SOURCE: Reprinted by permission of Dana D. DeHart, Ph.D., Center for Child and Family Studies, University of South Carolina, College of Social Work, Columbia, SC, 29208.

Table 2.3 *Mental Disorders Classified by the American Psychiatric Association*

Classification	Description
Anxiety Disorders	Disorders characterized by anxiety that is manifest in phobias, panic attacks, or obsessive–compulsive disorder
Dissociative Disorders	Problems involving a splitting or dissociation of normal consciousness such as amnesia and multiple personality
Disorders First Evident in Infancy, Childhood, or Adolescence	Including mental retardation, attention-deficit hyper-activity, and stuttering
Eating or Sleeping Disorders	Including such problems as anorexia and bulimia or insomnia and other problems associated with sleep
Impulse Control Disorders	Including the inability to control undesirable impulses such as kleptomania, pyromania, and pathological gambling
Mood Disorders	Emotional disorders such as major depression and bipolar (manic-depressive) disorder
Organic Mental Disorders	Psychological or behavioural disorders associated with dysfunctions of the brain caused by aging, disease, or brain damage (such as Alzheimer's disease)
Personality Disorders	Maladaptive personality traits that are generally resistant to treatment, such as paranoid and antisocial personality types
Schizophrenia and Other Psychotic Disorders	Disorders with symptoms such as delusions or hallucinations
Somatoform Disorders	Psychological problems that present themselves as symptoms of physical disease, such as hypochondria
Substance-Related Disorders	Disorders resulting from abuse of alcohol and/or drugs such as barbiturates, cocaine, or amphetamines

Mental illness is the most pervasive health problem in Canada.

JOHN T. GOODMAN
Director, Dept. of Psychology, Children's Hospital of Eastern Ontario

2002). In 2001, major depression was the leading cause of disability in developed nations, including Canada (World Health Organization 2001). Worldwide, mental disorders accounted for approximately 12 percent of all disability-adjusted life years lost in 2001 (Brundtland 2000; World Health Organization 2001). Five of the leading causes of disability worldwide are mental disorders: major depression, schizophrenia, bipolar disorders, alcohol use, and obsessive-compulsive disorders (Brundtland 2000). Mental disorders also contribute to mortality, with suicide representing one of the leading preventable causes of death in Canada and worldwide.

Causes of Mental Disorders

Mental illnesses are the result of a number of biological and social factors. A broad scope of research has linked many mental disorders with genetic or neurological causes involving some pathology of the brain. However, social and environmental influences, such as poverty, history of abuse, or other severe emotional trauma, also affect individuals' vulnerability to mental illness and mental health problems. The global increase in life expectancy has contributed to mental illnesses that affect the elderly, such as Alzheimer's disease and other

Low scores for psychological well-being, high scores for probable depression and high rates of suicide are warning signs that many of Canada's young people are greatly troubled....[E]nhanced employment opportunities, incentives for higher education and nurturing communities are all prerequisites for improving the well-being of Canada's young people.

HEALTH CANADA
Toward a Healthy Future 1999

forms of dementia. War within and between countries may also contribute to mental illness in such forms as combat-related post-traumatic stress disorder. In addition, "many societies and communities that customarily offered support to their needier members through family and social bonds now find it much harder to do so" (Brundtland 2000: 411). Garfinkel and Goldbloom (2000) explain, "the radical shifts in society towards technology, changes in family and societal supports and networks and the commercialization of existence...may account for the current epidemic of depression and other psychiatric disorders" (p. 503). It may be safe to conclude that "the causes of most mental disorders lie in some combination of genetic and environmental factors, which may be biological or psychosocial" (U.S. Department of Health and Human Services 1999: xiv).

Sociological Theories of Illness and Health Care

The sociological approach to the study of illness, health, and health care differs from medical, biological, and psychological approaches to these topics. Next, we discuss how three major sociological theories—structural-functionalism, conflict theory, and symbolic interactionism—contribute to our understanding of illness and health care.

Structural-Functionalist Perspective

Diseases respect no national borders. With rising globalization, diseases are spreading rapidly from developing to industrialized nations.

ROSE WEITZ
Sociologist

The structural-functionalist perspective is concerned with how illness, health, and health care affect and are affected by changes in other aspects of social life. For example, the women's movement and changes in societal gender roles have led to more women smoking, drinking, and experiencing the negative health effects of these behaviours. Increased modernization and industrialization throughout the world have resulted in environmental pollution—a major health concern. Increasingly, patterns of health and disease are affected by globalization—the economic, political, and social interconnectedness among societies throughout the world. For example, increased business travel and tourism has encouraged the globalization of disease, such as the potentially fatal West Nile encephalitis. The virus first appeared in North America in 1999 (Weitz 2001) and the first confirmed case in Canada came in August 2001 when it was discovered in a bird in Windsor, Ontario (Higgins 2002). In 2003, Severe Acute Respiratory Syndrome (SARS) surfaced in 13 countries with a cumulative total of 1550 cases and 54 death as of March 29, 2003. As of that date, Canada had reported 8 cases of SARS (WHO 2003).

Just as social change affects health, health concerns may lead to social change. The emergence of HIV and AIDS in the gay male population was a force that helped unite and mobilize gay rights activists in both Canada and the United States. Concerns over the hazards of using cellular phones while driving led to a 2001 editorial in the Canadian Medical Association Journal, which called for laws restricting the use of cellular phones while operating a vehicle (Drivers.com 2001) (see this chapter's *Focus on Technology* feature).

According to the structural-functionalist perspective, health care is a social institution that functions to maintain the well-being of societal members and, consequently, of the social system as a whole. Illness is dysfunctional in that it interferes with people performing needed social roles. To cope with nonfunctioning individuals and to control the negative effects of illness, society assigns a temporary and unique role to those who are ill—the sick role (Parsons 1951). This role assures that societal members receive needed care and compassion, yet at the same time, the social role carries with it an expectation that the person who is ill will seek competent medical advice, adhere to the prescribed regimen, and return as soon as possible to normal role obligations.

Structural-functionalists additionally explain the high salaries of physicians by arguing that society must entice people into the medical profession by offering high salaries. Without such an incentive, individuals would not be motivated to endure the rigours of medical training or the stress of being a physician.

Conflict Perspective

The conflict perspective focuses on how wealth, status, and power, or the lack thereof, influence illness and health care. Worldwide, the have-nots not only experience the adverse health effects of poverty, but they also have less access to quality medical care. In societies where women have little status and power, women's life expectancy is lower than in industrialized countries because of several social factors: eating last and eating less, complications from frequent childbearing and sexually transmitted diseases (because they have no power to demand abstinence or condom use), infections and hemorrhages following genital mutilation (which is practised in 29 countries), and restricted access to modern health care (World Health Organization 1997). Consider, as well, that while public health measures, improved sanitation systems, proper housing, immunization, and antibiotics have virtually eliminated many of the infectious diseases (such as smallpox, tuberculosis, and cholera) that ravaged Canada's cities and towns in the nineteenth century, not all Canadians have equally benefited. Currently, one-fifth of all tuberculosis cases in Canada occur among First Nations people, largely due to crowded living conditions (with housing densities twice the national average) and poor nutrition. First Nations and Inuit people have a rate of tuberculosis that is almost seven times the Canada-wide average (Health Canada 1999b).

Medical research agendas are also shaped by wealth, status, and power. Although malaria kills twice as many people annually as does AIDS, malaria research receives less than one-tenth as much public funding as AIDS research (Morse 1998). Similarly, pneumonia and diarrheal diseases constitute 15.4 percent of the total global disease burden, but only 0.2 percent of the total global spending on research (Visschedijk and Simeant 1998). This is because northern developed countries, which provide most of the funding for world health-related research, do not feel threatened by malaria, pneumonia, and diarrheal diseases, which primarily affect less developed countries in Africa and Asia.

Worldwide, public health systems have been slower to address and more likely to neglect women's health issues than men's. For example, a year after the male impotence drug Viagra made its debut in 1998, the Constitutional Court in Colombia decreed that state-run health services must reimburse men needing the pill for impotence due to chronic or terminal diseases. In a country where the public health system is so overburdened that patients often have to

Health Hazards and Cellular Phones

Since they were introduced in 1983, cellular phones have become widespread, with more than 400 million cell phones in use worldwide (Greenwald 2000). In 1999, five million Canadians used cell phones. It is anticipated that by 2006, the number of cell-phone users in Canada will grow to 13 million (Bronskill 1999). Cell phones have been under scrutiny for possible contributions to two health problems: traffic accidents and cancer.

Do Cell Phones Contribute to Traffic Accidents?

Surveys have found that 80 to 90 percent of cellular phone owners use these devices while driving (Lissy et al. 2000). Some research suggests that cellular phone use is associated with a significantly increased rate of traffic accidents (Redelmeier and Tibshirani 1997; Violanti 1997). The Harvard Centre for Risk Analysis concluded that "cellular phone use while driving poses a risk to the driver, to other motorists, and to pedestrians" (Lissy et al. 2000: 1). This report adds, however, "the risks appear to be small...but are uncertain because existing research is limited" (p. 2). Researchers at the Transportation Safety Laboratory of the Université de Montréal who recently conducted a major study on the risks of road accidents and the use of cellular phones concluded that while "[h]eavy users of the cell phone have twice the accident risk of drivers who use the phone infrequently or not at all," this association "does not constitute a direct demonstration of cause and effect, since there is no direct observation of wireless telephone use and other factors at the time of the accident" (Drivers.com 2001a).

Public perceptions of the dangers of driving while using cell phones are also mixed. A bumper sticker that reads "Hang Up and Drive" reflects the growing concern that driving while using a cell phone distracts drivers (Kelley 2000). At least 22 nations have cell phone restrictions on drivers, ranging from a mandate against hand-held cell phones in Britain to an outright ban on the use of all types of cell phones by drivers in Japan (Clines 2001).

Critics of such bans argue that cellular phones improve safety on the road by enabling people to contact emergency services in the event of accidents and alerting police to drunk drivers. Unfortunately, this benefit of cell phone use is a mixed blessing: multiple calls for the same incident produces a significant burden on emergency response resources in some jurisdictions. Some localities have reported more than one hundred "911" calls for a single incident (National Highway Traffic Safety Administration 1998). Critics also argue that if cell phone use while driving is banned, so should be other distracting activities such as eating and drinking, putting on makeup, and smoking.

In response to research that finds even hands-free cell phone use to be distracting to drivers (Redelmeier and Tibshirani 1997), critics ask if listening to radio talk shows or even having conversations with passengers is just as distracting. According to Émilie Thérien, president of the Canada Safety Council, "What about other distractions? How many collisions are caused by kids' misbehaving, adults' quarreling, eating, drinking coffee, putting on a CD, talking to passengers, or even listening to the radio? Where and how do you draw the line? Any ban would be counter-productive, irresponsible, and unenforceable. There are far more effective ways to spend money to save lives and enhance traffic safety" (quoted in Drivers.com 2001b).

Can Using Cell Phones Cause Cancer?

Another public health issue concerning cell phones is the debate about whether they can cause cancer (Schultz and Terrell 2000; Senior 2000). Cell phones emit low levels of radiation, measured in "specific absorption rates," or SARs. An SAR measures the energy in watts per kilogram that one gram of body tissue absorbs from a cell phone. In both Canada and the United States, the SAR limit for mobile phones used by the public is 1.6 watts/kg (W/k) averaged over one gram of tissue (Cellular Telecommunications and Internet Association 2002). Although researchers have not been able to demonstrate a clear link between cell phone use and cancer, they have not been able to rule out the possibility either. An expert panel of scientists and physicians in Britain concluded, "it is not possible at present to say that exposure to [cell phone] radiation, even at levels below national guidelines, is totally without potential adverse health effects" (Raloff 2000: 326). This panel concludes that the available research findings on the cancer risks of cell phones justify a "precautionary approach." The British panel and other researchers and public health officials who are concerned about cancer risks and cell phone use

recommend that consumers take the following precautions:

1. Use hands-free cell phones. Some research suggests that hands-free cell phones offer substantially reduced exposure to radiation (Dobson 2000).
2. Choose cell phones with lower SAR levels. In fall 2000, cell phone makers began including data on SAR levels in the packaging of the newest cell phone models (Greenwald 2000). Teral Communications Commission declares all phones that emit radiation below the SAR ceiling of 1.6 as being safe. Although there is no evidence that a cell phone with an SAR level of 0.24 is any safer than one with an SAR level of 1.49, concerned consumers may choose a phone with a lower SAR level.
3. Limit the time one talks on cell phones. One study reports that cell phone users spend an average of 150 minutes a month using their cell phones (Greenwald 2000).
4. Discourage children's use of cell phones. Because children's developing brains absorb more radiation than adult brains, children should be discouraged from using cell phones. "Parents should permit children to use cell phones only for calls essential to safety" (Raloff 2000: 326).

SOURCES: Bronskill, Jim. 1999. "Health Canada Probes Cellphone Dangers—Suspicion of Ill Effects Refuses to Go Away." *The Ottawa Citizen,* February 1. www.safecellularphones.com/pages/articles/ottawa_citizen_020199.htm. Cellular Telecommunications and Internet Association (CTIA). 2002. http://phonefacts.net. Clines, Francis X. 2001. "Deaths Spur Laws Against Drivers on Cell Phone." *New York Times.* http://www.nytimes.com/2001/02/18/technology/18CELL.html?ex=983524085dei=1. Dobson, Roger. 2000. "'Hands-free' Mobile Phones May Be Safer than the Rest." *British Medical Journal* 321(7259), August 19: 468. Drivers.com. 2001a. "Cell Phones May Increase Crash Risk 38%." August 16. www.drivers.com/cgi-bin/go.cgi?type=ARTand8d=000000449 andstatic=1. Drivers.com. 2001b. "Bad Drivers Cause Accidents, Not Cell Phones." May 31. www.drivers.com/cgi-bin/go.cgi?type=ARTandid=000000393andstatic=1. Greenwald, John. 2000. "Do Cell Phones Need Warnings?" *Time,* October 9: 66–67. Kelley, Tina. 2000. "Phoning While Driving Is Now Illegal in Suffolk." *New York Times,* October 4. www.nytimes.com/2000/10/04/nyregion/04CELL. Lissy, Karen, Joshua Cohen, Mary Park, and John D. Graham. 2000. "Cellular Phones and Driving: Weighing the Risks and Benefits." *Risk in Perspective* 8(6), July: 1–6. Harvard Center for Risk Analysis. National Highway Traffic Safety Administration. 1998. "Cellular Telephone Use in America and Perceptions of Safety." www.nhtsa.dot.gov/. Raloff, J. 2000. "Two Studies Offer Some Cell-Phone Cautions." *Science News* 157(21), May 20: 326. Redelmeier, Donald A., and Robert J. Tibshirani. 1997. "Association Between Cellular Telephone Calls and Motor Vehicle Collisions." *New England Journal of Medicine* 336(17): 453–58. Schultz, Stacey, and Kenneth Terrell. 2000. "Could Your Phone Cause Cancer? Don't Get Hung Up On It." *U.S. News and World Report* 129(8), August 28: 54. Senior, Kathryn. 2000. "Mobile Phones: Are They Safe?" *The Lancet* 355(9217), May 20: 1793. Violanti, J.M. 1997. "Cellular Phones and Traffic Accidents." *Public Health* 111(6): 423–28.

provide their own syringes and people die of gangrene after amputation, it is disconcerting to note a high-court ruling that requires the government to pay for some men's use of a very expensive drug (*KW Record* 1999: A16). Women have also been excluded from participating in major health research studies that have looked at the relationship between aspirin use and heart disease or how cholesterol levels, blood pressure, and smoking affect heart disease (Johnson and Fee 1997).

The conflict perspective also focuses on how the profit motive influences health, illness, and health care. The profit motive underlies much of the illness, injury, and death that occur from hazardous working conditions and dangerous consumer products.

Symbolic Interactionist Perspective

Symbolic interactionists focus on (1) how meanings, definitions, and labels influence health, illness, and health care and (2) how such meanings are learned through interaction with others and through media messages and portrayals. According to the symbolic interactionist perspective of illness, "there are no illnesses or diseases in nature. There are only conditions that society, or groups within it, have come to define as illness or disease" (Goldstein 1999: 31). Psychiatrist Thomas Szasz ([1961] 1970) argues that what we call "mental illness" is no more than a label conferred on those individuals who are "different," that is, who don't conform to society's definitions of appropriate behaviour.

Definitions of health and illness vary over time and from society to society. In some countries, being fat is a sign of health and wellness; in others, it is an indication of mental illness or a lack of self-control. Before medical research documented the health hazards of tobacco, our society defined cigarette smoking as fashionable. Cigarette advertisements still attempt to associate positive meanings (such as youth, sex, and romance) with smoking to entice people to smoke. A study of top-grossing American films from 1985 to 1995 revealed that 98 percent had references that supported tobacco use and 96 percent had references that supported alcohol use (Everett et al. 1998).

A growing number of behaviours and conditions are being defined as medical problems—a trend known as **medicalization**. Hyperactivity, insomnia, anxiety, and learning disabilities are examples of phenomena that some view as medical conditions in need of medical intervention. Increasingly, "normal" aspects of life, such as birth, aging, sexual development, menopause, and death, have come to be seen as medical events (Goldstein 1999).

Symbolic interactionists also focus on the stigmatizing effects of being labelled "ill." A **stigma** refers to any personal characteristic associated with social disgrace, rejection, or discrediting. (Originally, the word stigma referred to a mark burned into the skin of a criminal or slave.) Individuals with mental illnesses, drug addictions, physical deformities and impairments, and HIV and AIDS are particularly prone to being stigmatized. Stigmatization may lead to prejudice and discrimination and even violence against individuals with illnesses or impairments.

Having a stigmatized illness or condition often becomes a master status, obscuring other aspects of a person's social identity. One individual who uses a wheelchair commented: "When I am in my chair I am invisible to some people; they see only the chair" (Ostrof 1998: 36).

Social Factors Associated with Health and Illness

Public health education campaigns, articles in popular magazines, post-secondary-level health courses, and health professionals emphasize that to be healthy, we must adopt a healthy lifestyle. In response, many people have at least attempted to quit smoking, eat a healthier diet, and include exercise in their daily or weekly routine. However, health and illness are affected by more than personal lifestyle choices. In the following section, we examine how social factors such as social class and poverty, education, race, and gender affect health and illness. Health problems related to environmental problems are discussed in Chapter 14.

Social Class and Poverty

Poverty has been identified as the world's leading health problem by an international group of physicians ("Poverty Threatens Crisis" 1998). Poverty is associated with unsanitary living conditions, hazardous working conditions, lack of access to medical care, and inadequate nutrition (see also Chapter 10).

In Canada, socioeconomic status is related to numerous aspects of health and illness (Health Canada 1999b). For example, self-rated health is strongly linked to income. According to the 1996–97 National Population Health Survey, Canadians who lived in the lowest income households were four to seven times more likely (depending on race, ethnicity, and sex) to report fair or poor health than those who lived in the highest income households (Figure 2.3). In addition, at each rung up the income ladder, Canadians have less sickness, longer life expectancies, and improved health. "It is estimated that if the death rates of the highest income earners applied to all Canadians, more than one-fifth of all years of life lost before age 65 could be prevented" (Health

> Recent years have seen a tendency to blame individuals for their own health problems....Yet patterns of disease reflect social conditions as much as, if not more than individual behaviors or biological characteristics.
>
> **ROSE WEITZ**
> *Sociologist*

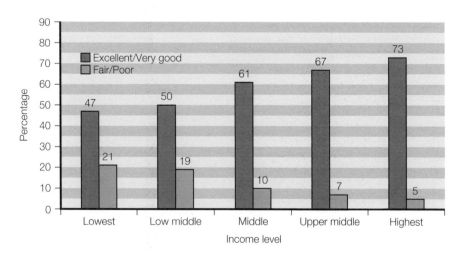

Figure 2.3 *Self-Rated Health, by Income Level,* Canadians Aged 12+, 1996–1997*

SOURCE: Statistics Canada. *National Population Health Survey, 1996–97.*

* Income levels in this figure represent total household incomes before taxes and are adjusted for family size and age-standardized.

Canada 1999a: 14). As Figure 2.4 indicates, there is a strong inverse relationship between career earnings and death rates for Canadian men. Compared with those in the lowest quartile of the income distribution, Canadian men in the highest quartile can expect to live 6.3 years longer and have 14.3 more years free of disability. For women, the differences are 3 and 7.6 years respectively (Health Canada 1999a: 26).

Poor persons are also more likely to report an unmet need for health care. Although in Canada access to universally insured health care remains largely unrelated to income, many low- and moderate-income Canadians have limited or no access to such health services as eye care, dentistry, mental health counselling, and prescription drugs (Health Canada 1999a).

Low socioeconomic status is also associated with increased risk of a broad range of psychiatric conditions (Williams and Collins 1999). Rates of depression and substance abuse, for example, are higher in the lower socioeconomic classes (Kessler et al. 1994). Why do poor people have higher rates of mental illness? One explanation suggests that lower-class individuals experience greater stress as a result of their deprived and difficult living conditions. Others argue that members of the lower class are simply more likely to have their behaviours identified and treated as mental illness.

Lower socioeconomic groups have higher rates of mortality, in part, because they have higher rates of health risk behaviours such as smoking, alcohol drinking, being overweight, and being physically inactive. Other factors that explain the relationship between socioeconomic status and mortality include exposure to environmental health hazards and inequalities in access to and use of preventive and therapeutic medical care (Lantz et al. 1998). In addition, the lower class tends to experience high levels of stress, while having few resources to cope with it (Cockerham 1998). Stress has been linked to a variety of physical and mental health problems, including high blood pressure, cancer, chronic fatigue, and substance abuse.

Education

In general, low levels of education are associated with higher rates of health problems and mortality (Health Canada 1999a; National Center for Health Statistics 2000). According to the 1996–97 National Population Health Survey,

■ **Figure 2.4** *Career Earnings and Death for 500 000 Canadian Men*

SOURCE: Wolfson, M.C. et al. 1993. "Career Earnings and Death: A Longitudinal Analysis of Older Men." *Journal of Gerontology: Social Sciences*, 47(4): S167–S179.

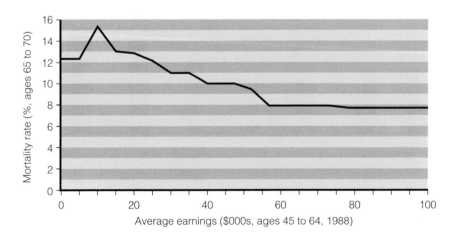

30 percent of respondents who were university graduates rated their health as "excellent" compared with 19 percent of respondents with less than a high school education (Health Canada 1999a: 42). In addition, less educated women and men have higher rates of suicide. Low birthweight and high infant mortality are also more common among the children of less educated mothers than among children of more educated mothers. Low-birthweight babies (weighing 2500 grams or less) are more likely to die in infancy, and those who survive are more likely to suffer illness, stunted growth, and other health problems into adult life. About 6 percent of babies in Canada are born with low birthweight (Statistics Canada 1998c: 107).

One reason that lower education levels are associated with higher rates of health problems and mortality is that individuals with low levels of education are more likely to engage in health-risk behaviours such as smoking and heavy drinking. The well educated, in contrast, are less likely to smoke and drink heavily and are more likely to exercise. Women with less education are less likely to seek prenatal care and are more likely to smoke during pregnancy. However, research findings suggest that the strong association between education and income best explains educational differences in health and mortality (Lantz et al. 1998).

Gender

Gender issues affect the health of both women and men. Gender discrimination and violence against women produce adverse health effects in girls and women worldwide. Violence against women is a major public health concern: at least one in three women has been beaten, coerced into sex, or abused in some way—most often by someone she knows (United Nations Population Fund 2000). "Although neither health care workers nor the general public typically thinks of battering as a health problem, woman battering is a major cause of injury, disability and death among...women worldwide" (Weitz 2001: 56). In Africa, where the leading cause of death is HIV/AIDS, HIV positive women outnumber men by two million, in part because African women do not have the social power to refuse sexual intercourse and/or to demand that their male partners use condoms (United Nations Population Fund 2000). As noted earlier, women in developing countries suffer high rates of mortality and morbidity due to the high rates of complications associated with pregnancy and childbirth. The low status of women in many less developed countries results in their being nutritionally deprived and having less access to medical care than do men. For example, in some countries in Asia and Africa, boys receive more medicine and medical treatment than girls. In Latin America and India, girls are often immunized later than boys or not at all (United Nations Population Fund 2000).

Before the twentieth century, the life expectancy of Canadian women was shorter than that of men because of the high rate of maternal mortality that resulted from complications of pregnancy and childbirth. Currently, however, Canadian women have a higher life expectancy than Canadian men (Statistics Canada 2002).

Although women tend to live longer than men do, they have higher rates of illness and disability than do men (Health Canada 1999a; Verbrugge 1999). Prevalence rates for nonfatal chronic conditions (such as arthritis, thyroid disease, and migraine headache) are typically higher for women. However, men tend to have higher rates of fatal chronic conditions (such as high blood pressure, heart disease, and diabetes). Women also tend to experience a higher incidence of acute conditions, such as colds and influenza, infections, and digestive conditions. "In sum, women live longer than men but experience more illness, whereas men experience relatively little illness but die quickly when illness strikes" (Weitz 2001: 55). Regarding mental health, men are more likely to abuse drugs and have higher rates of personality disorders, whereas women are more likely to suffer from mood disorders such as depression and anxiety (Cockerham 1998).

Men are more prone to chronic and life-threatening diseases, such as coronary disease, because they are more likely than women to smoke, use alcohol and illegal drugs, and work under hazardous conditions. Our culture socializes men to be aggressive and competitive and to engage in risky behaviours (such as dangerous sports, driving fast, and violence), which contributes to their higher risk of death from injuries and accidents (see the *Social Problems Research Up Close* feature in this chapter). Although women are more likely to attempt suicide, men are more likely to succeed at it because they use deadlier methods. In Canada in 1999, there were 3.8 suicides among men for every suicide among women (Statistics Canada 2002). HIV infections and AIDS deaths in men outnumber those in women on every continent except sub-Saharan Africa (Joint United Nations Programme on HIV/AIDS 2000b), in part because of socialization men receive which permits and even encourages them to engage in sexually promiscuous behaviour. Men are also less likely than women to seek medical care. Boys who are brought up to believe that "real men don't get sick" often see themselves as invulnerable to illness or risk. The under-use of health services by men reflects this (Joint United Nations Programme on HIV/AIDS 2000b).

Racial and Ethnic Minority Status

In Canada, the risks to health posed by inadequate income, welfare dependency, substandard living conditions, and stresses on mental health and well-being are manifestly apparent in the lives of First Nations peoples (Royal Commission on Aboriginal Peoples 1996). The life expectancy of Status Indians (i.e., those who names appear on the Indian Register maintained by the Department of Indian and Northern Affairs pursuant to the *Indian Act*) is seven to eight years shorter than for non-Aboriginal Canadians, and the infant mortality rate double that of the non-Aboriginal population. The rate of accidental death and injury among Aboriginal children is four times that of the non-Aboriginal population; death rates from causes such as birth defects, low birthweight, fetal alcohol syndrome, and respiratory illnesses are consistently and significantly higher among Aboriginal infants and children (Health Canada 1999a; National Council of Welfare 2001). Indigenous Canadians also experience a heightened risk of violent death and elevated rates of injuries, poisonings, and suicide (National Council of Welfare 2001). Among First Nation and Inuit males, the rates of violent death are especially high (Canadian Centre for Substance Abuse 1999).

Indigenous peoples also experience high rates of illicit drug use with First Nation and Métis youth more likely than non-Indigenous youth to use all types of drugs (*Canadian Aboriginal News* 2001). The use of solvents is significantly higher among Aboriginal youths and the risk of developing an alcohol problem

Young Canadians: A Summary of Personal Health Practices

The 1996–97 National Population Health Survey (NPHS) collected data on a broad range of health-risk behaviours including behaviours that contribute to unintentional and intentional injury; tobacco, alcohol, and other drug use; sexual behaviours that contribute to sexually transmitted infections, unhealthy dietary behaviours; and physical inactivity.

Adolescence and early adulthood are times when young people make important decisions related to sexuality, physical activity, nutrition and the use of alcohol, tobacco and other drugs. As we take a closer look at these years, we find significant differences in behaviours among young and older teens and those in their early 20s, and between males and females.

Physical activity. Rates of leisure-time physical activity dropped quickly as age increased, and there were large differences between males and females.

Smoking. Rates of smoking are higher among young women aged 12 to 17 than young men in the same age group. In the age group 18 to 24, men are more likely to smoke than women.

Healthy weights. Young women were more likely than young men to be concerned about their weight. In 1994, 28 percent of girls aged 12 to 14, 38 percent of those aged 15 to 19, and 43 percent of those aged 20 to 24 were trying to lose weight. Over half of the women in the age group 20 to 24 who were trying to lose weight were already within the healthy weight range.

Healthy eating. Among 15-year-olds, only 39 percent of girls and 40 percent of boys ate whole wheat bread once a day or more; 25 percent of girls and 32 percent of boys ate candy or chocolate bars once a day or more. Forty-eight percent of young women but only 19 percent of young men aged 15 to 19 reported that they were taking action to reduce dietary fat.

Drinking. The amount of alcohol consumed at one time increased with age for both genders. After age 18, young men drank significantly more than young women. At ages 18 and 19, young women were slightly more likely than young men to drive after drinking; after age 20 this pattern was dramatically reversed.

Bicycle helmet use. While 12- to 14-year-olds were the most likely of all age groups to wear a bicycle helmet (40 percent), young people aged 15 to 19 were the least likely to wear one (15 percent).

Sexual practices. Among sexually active young people (aged 20 to 24), 48 percent reported that they never or sometimes used condoms in the past year. In the age group 15 to 19, 40 percent reported inconsistent or non-use of condoms.

Multiple risk behaviours. Young men were more likely than young women to report multiple risk-taking behaviours. While smoking and binge drinking was the most common combination for both sexes, almost as many young men reported binge drinking combined with unsafe sex.

SOURCE: Health Canada. 1999. *Toward a Healthy Future: Second Report on the Health of Canadians.* Prepared by the Federal, Provincial and Territorial Advisory Committee on Population Health for the Meeting of Ministers of Health, Charlottetown, PEI, September 1999, pp. 128–29.

Percentage who were classified as "active" in their leisure time		
Age	Males	Females
12 to 14	54%	33%
15 to 17	53%	31%
18 and 19	39%	26%
20 to 24	32%	22%

	Percentage of drinkers who drank five or more drinks on at least one occassion		Percentage who drove after drinking five or more drinks on at least one occasion	
Age	Male	Female	Male	Female
12 to 14	16%	15%	—	—
15 to 17	53%	46%	—	—
18 and 19	71%	59%	17%	19%
20 to 24	71%	60%	23%	9%

two to six times greater than that of other Canadians (Scott 1997). The prevalence of daily smoking among adult Indigenous Canadians occurs at about twice the rate found among the general Canadian population (Canadian Centre for Substance Abuse 1999).

Racial and ethnic prejudice and discrimination may induce psychological distress that adversely affects both physical and mental health status and increases the likelihood of violence and substance abuse. Moreover, **environmental racism** or the tendency for hazardous waste sites and polluting industries to be located near areas inhabited by those who are poor and socially marginalized, may also contribute to lower levels of health. For example, in the 1980s, the mercury poisoning of the English-Wabigoon river system by local pulp and paper industries led to the virtual destruction of the Grassy Narrow Indians' lifestyle and means of livelihood (Shkilynk 1985). More recently,

> patterns of atmospheric cycling have made the North a dumping ground for industrial chemicals that...[are] never used there. The chemicals bioaccumulate, delivering a higher level of toxic concentration to each level up the food chain. As a result, the breast milk of Inuit mothers is 10 times as contaminated as that of southern Canadian women. In both the North and the South, mother's milk is so laden with toxic substances such as PCBs, DDT (and its breakdown product DDE) and lindane, that if it were offered for sale, it would be too contaminated to be approved as human food. (Barlow and May 2000: 184)

This chapter's *The Human Side* focuses attention on the health status of Canada's Indigenous peoples.

Problems in Canadian Health Care

In 2000, the World Health Organization released its report on the first ever analysis of the world's health systems (World Health Organization 2000). The report concluded that France provides the best overall health care among major countries, followed by Italy, Spain, Oman, Austria, and Japan. After presenting a brief overview of Canadian health care, we address some of the major health care issues in Canada.

Canadian Health Care: An Overview

Canada, like countries such as Great Britain, Sweden, Germany, and Italy, has a national health insurance system that is sometimes referred to as socialized medicine. Despite differences in how socialized medicine works in various countries, what is common to all systems of socialized medicine is that the government (1) directly controls the financing and organization of health services, (2) directly pays providers, (3) guarantees equal access to health care, and (4) allows some private care for individuals who are willing to pay for their medical expenses (Cockerham 1998). However, Canada does not truly have a system of "socialized medicine" in that the government does not employ Canadian physicians. Rather, the majority of Canada's physicians are independent practitioners in independent or group practices. They are generally paid on a fee-for-service basis and submit their claims directly to the provincial health insurance plan for payment.

An Excerpt from Elijah: No Ordinary Hero

Elijah Harper is a Canadian Ojibway-Cree leader, was chief of the Red Sucker Lake Band in Manitoba from 1978 to 1981, served in the Manitoba Legislature and as a provincial cabinet minister from 1981 to 1992, and was elected to the House of Commons in 1993. "To some Canadians, especially those of the First Nations, Elijah Harper is a hero...[and] known as the man who, almost singlehandedly, prevented the ratification of the Meech Lake Accord in 1990" (Morton and Weinfeld 1998: 32) in the belief that it did not adequately address the concerns of First Nations peoples. In this extract, taken from the introduction to Elijah: No Ordinary Hero, Harper eloquently reminds us why health care is not simply the "private problem" of individuals. Individuals can only do so much; the larger responsibility is society's.

As a Canadian and an aboriginal person, I could not support an amendment to the supreme law of the country that failed to recognize the place of all the founding cultures of the federation. The suffering of native people is too great.

Aboriginal people in Canada die on average 10 years younger than other Canadians do. Three out of 10 aboriginal families have no furnaces or heat in their homes, yet Canada has one of the highest standards of living in the world. Thirty-four percent have no indoor plumbing; our homes are overcrowded and in poor condition. About 45 percent of aboriginal people are on social assistance. Few of our people are in secondary schools. Only five percent graduate from secondary school. In my province, Manitoba, aboriginal people comprise seven percent of the population, yet they make up 45 percent of the jail population. Family income on reserves is about $10000, less than half the national average. Alcoholism, drunkenness and solvent abuse are epidemic on some reserves, and we suffer the negative stereotyping that naturally follows from that. Unemployment is about 66 percent; on some reserves, it is as high as 90 percent. Even our languages are in danger. Many have

already become extinct. Our religions were forbidden for long enough that much has been forgotten.

But these are only statistics. I cannot bring to you the despair. I bring to you the 15-year-old boy in Winnipeg who will never share a bright future because that child was so depressed by what he saw every day that he took his own belt and hanged himself....We must attack our problems on two levels. We must attack them as individual problems and we must work to eradicate their origins. We must change personal circumstances and the system. We must build houses for the homeless, but we must also build better communities around them. We must cure the sick, but we must also eliminate the poor water, inadequate sanitation, poor nutrition and poverty that make our people sick. If we don't solve all our problems on those two levels, we will be eternally fighting against a current over which we have no control.

The origins of a universal health care system in Canada can be traced back to 1919 when William Lyon Mackenzie King first raised the idea of national, publicly funded health insurance as part of the Liberal Party platform. However, it took approximately half a century of intense debate and the persistent efforts of then–Saskatchewan Premier Tommy Douglas, leader of the Co-Operative Commonwealth Federation (the precursor of the New Democratic Party), before the Canadian government would implement a universal health care system. In 1947 Douglas's government pioneered Canada's first universal hospital plan after testing prepaid medical insurance in the Swift Current health district and introducing a public insurance plan for hospital services. Public health care insurance also began in Saskatchewan with coverage provided for visits to and the services of physicians outside hospitals.

To me it seems to be sheer
nonsense to suggest that
medical care is something
which ought to be mea-
sured in dollars. When
we're talking about med-
ical care we're talking
about our sense of values.
Do we think human life is
important?

TOMMY DOUGLAS
Politician

Canada's health care system, known to Canadians as **Medicare**, provides access to universal comprehensive coverage for medically necessary in-patient and outpatient physician services. The role of the federal government in relation to health care is in the setting and administration of national principles for the health care system, assisting in the financing of provincial health services through fiscal transfers, and fulfilling certain functions for which it is constitutionally responsible. For example, the federal government is responsible for health service delivery to specific groups including veterans, Indigenous people living on reserves, members of the military, inmates of federal penitentiaries, and the Royal Canadian Mounted Police. However, the management and delivery of health services is the responsibility of each individual province or territory, which plans, finances, and evaluates the provision of hospital care, physician and allied health services, public health, and some aspects of prescription care. As such, our system of health care is perhaps best described as "12 interlocking provincial and territorial plans" (Statistics Canada 1998a).

In 1964, the Hall Royal Commission on Services recommended that the provincial and federal governments introduce a medical program that would eradicate the disparities in Canada's health care system. The costs of the program were to be borne through taxation. The federal government agreed to share the costs equally with the provinces if each provincial plan satisfied five requirements:

1. Accessibility: reasonable access should be guaranteed to all Canadians.
2. Comprehensiveness: all necessary medical services should be guaranteed, without dollar limit, and should be available solely on the basis of medical need.
3. Universality: all Canadians should be eligible for coverage on uniform terms and conditions.
4. Portability: benefits should be transferable from province to province.
5. Administration by a public, nonprofit agency or commission. (Grant 1993: 401)

In 1972, these recommendations became law.

Evidence suggests that our health care system is, in fact, accomplishing what it originally set out to do: eliminate inequality among Canadians in relation to health care services. For example, poor women in Toronto have a survival rate for breast cancer that is 30 percent higher than the rate for poor women in Detroit. For ovarian cancer, the survival rate is 38 percent higher, for cervical cancer it is 48 percent higher (Armstrong et al. 1998). However, while two-thirds of Canadians in one poll agreed with the statement "Canada's health care system is one of the best in the world," the last decade has seen massive cuts made to that system. As deficit-strapped governments in the 1990s ratcheted back health expenditures, the percentage of Canadians citing health care as a top concern has grown from five percent in 1993 to 64 percent in 2000. Between 1991 and 2000, the number of Canadians rating our health care system as very good or excellent has shrunk from 61 percent to 25 percent; the number of those rating the system as poor or very poor increased threefold over the same time period. Moreover, when forecasting 10 years into the future, 58 percent of Canadians believe that the state of health care in our country will get worse; only 24 percent believe it will get better (Bricker and Greenspon 2001: 189–90). It is evident that the question of how to sustain—if not improve—

public health care in Canada will continue to be the subject of intense concern, controversy, and debate.

Unmet Needs

In 2001, of the 30 countries in the OECD, only three—the United States, Germany, and Switzerland—spent more than Canada on health care as a proportion of GDP (Milne 2002). However, despite a total health care bill that surpassed $100 billion in 2001 (Kennedy 2001), Canadians increasingly confront the closing of emergency room departments and long waits in those that remain, continuing shortages of nurses, physicians, specialists and costly diagnostic equipment, persistent geographic differences in access to services, a decrease in the number of available hospital beds, and growing waiting lists for scheduled surgeries (Marshall 2001).

Although Canada's universal health insurance system is based on the premise that "all citizens will have access to the care they need within a reasonable time period" (Health Canada 1999b), there are no precise definitions of what constitutes "needed care" or a "reasonable time." One national survey conducted by the Canadian Medical Association (CMA 1999) suggests Canadians perceived a decline in access to health care services between 1996 and 1998. More recently, their 2001 national survey found that "[w]hen asked to assign a letter grade to the current health care system, Canadians gave it, on average, a B for overall quality." While Canadians assigned a grade of A to "access to family physicians," they awarded a grade of B to "access to community services for youth and seniors" and a C grade to "access to modern diagnostic equipment, emergency room services, mental health services and medical specialists" (Canadian Medical Association 2001).

In general, Canadians were far more critical of the government's performance in the delivery of health care. While health care providers, particularly physicians, were given a grade of B, the federal government was given a grade of C. They gave a failing grade (F) to their provincial government's performance on health care issues. When asked how our current system could be improved, over eight in ten identified the provision of long term, sustainable funding. A second option, advanced by almost six in ten Canadians, stressed more efficient management and the proper allocation of existing funds.

Patients are not the only Canadians complaining of inadequate services. At the 1999 annual meeting of the CMA, physicians asserted that Canada was heading towards a critical shortage of doctors that would threaten patient safety and emphasized that there already existed a serious shortage of physicians in rural areas and within certain specialties such as anesthesia, radiology, and obstetrics. It was noted that even in major Canadian cities such as Toronto, patients were being forced to wait for needed surgery because of the shortage (Bricker and Greenspon 2001: 217). It is estimated that by 2021, there will be only one doctor for every 718 patients (compared to one doctor for every 548 patients in 1998) (Kennedy 1999). In addition, physicians have acknowledged that their ability to assist their patients is being jeopardized by the unavailability of the costly equipment they need. For example, while PET (positron emission tomography) scanners are the best way to diagnose and evaluate tumours, there are no publicly funded PET scanners anywhere in B.C. In consequence, B.C. physicians must tell their patients who require a scan that "they can either pay

$2500 for one at a private PET facility in Vancouver, or go out of province or out of country to get it" (Milne 2002: 41). It is also evident that the aging of the Canadian population (see Chapter 6) will challenge the sustainability of our publicly funded health care system. Consider here that when economist James Frank superimposed the population profile of British Columbia in 2020 on that province's 2000–01 provincial budget, the effect was immense. "The impact of a more aged population immediately added $1.7 billion to health care spending, driving the province's deficit from its projected $1.2 billion that year upwards to nearly $3 billion" (Bricker and Greenspon 2001: 198).

In recent years, the premiers of Ontario and Alberta have both issued challenges to the federal government over health care. In the spring of 2000, for example, the Alberta government passed Bill 11, the Health Protection Act, which allowed private, for-profit clinics to perform minor surgical procedures and to keep patients overnight. More recently, the provincial government in Alberta seems poised to introduce changes that would allow for greater privatization. In like fashion, in Ontario, the provincial government has threatened that, if Ottawa does not increase transfer payments, it will withdraw pharmacare and home care services to senior citizens. Some applaud these developments and argue for privatization, that is, allowing private clinics to play an expanded role in the public system or for the creation of a parallel private system, as in Britain. They argue that privatization will facilitate timely access to quality care and allow provinces to cope with rising health costs. Others, however, suggest that privatization might result in the development of a two-tier system of a health care: one for those who can pay for quality care and a second for those who cannot. Among their concerns:

- ability to pay will become more important than need in determining access to quality health care;
- the facilities and doctors available to those with private money will be of a much higher quality than the ones available in the public system;
- the problems in the current system will not necessarily be solved by bringing in private money; and
- private money will only put more cash into the pockets of those in the system who want to increase their incomes; it won't deal with the problems being experienced in facilities or services (Bricker and Greenspon 2001: 196).

User fees are not about making the rich pay. They are about making the sick pay. And poor people tend to be in worse health than rich people.

ROBERT G. EVANS
Economist

The fifth annual Health Care in Canada survey, a nationwide investigation of the attitudes of 800 health professionals and 1200 members of the public, found that when asked what they thought of allowing Canadians to pay to receive speedier services from private clinics, opinion was almost evenly split: while approximately half (47 percent) of the general public rejected the notion, 49 percent favoured that two-tier approach (Milne 2002: 40). However, there is evidence that many Canadians cherish the ideal of a single-payee, public health system as an important component of our national identity. One study, for example, reported that 25 percent of Canadians identified our health care system as what makes us unique from other countries (receiving over three times as many mentions as other characteristics such as multiculturalism, freedom, and tolerance [all at seven percent]). Among those who cited health care as a major symbol of our national identity, almost three-quarters identified public funding and universality as "especially defining features" (Bricker and

Greenspon 2001: 196). A 2000 survey reported that while fully three-quarters of Canadians nationwide believe that finding a solution to the health care crisis will cost Canadians more money, 56 percent of Canadians say they are willing to pay more—either out-of-pocket or through a dedicated health tax—to sustain our system of public health care (Milne 2002: 40).

Access to Dental Care

According to the 1996–97 National Population Health Survey, only slightly more than half of all Canadians (55 percent) have dental insurance. Having dental insurance is much more common among children, youths, and working-age adults than among Canadian seniors. Among those 75 years of age and older in Canada, only 25 percent of men and 17 percent of women report having dental insurance. Income differences in relation to dental care are particularly notable: those in the highest income group are about three times as likely to have dental insurance as those in the lowest category. There is also interprovincial variation in insurance coverage, with slightly more than 60 percent of those in Ontario and Alberta having dental insurance versus lows of 40 and 43 percent in Quebec and Newfoundland, respectively. In Canada, dentists work independently of the health care system except where in-hospital dental surgery is required.

The High Cost of Medications

Except for medication received while in institutional care, the *Canada Health Act* does not cover prescription drugs, nonprescription drugs, and over-the-counter products (e.g., cough and cold remedies, oral hygiene products, and home diagnostic kits). Instead, payers include governments through pharmacare programs, private insurance (including insurance companies, employees, and unions), and patients paying out-of-pocket. According to the 1996–97 National Population Health Survey, the prescription drug costs of almost two-thirds (61 percent) of Canadians were covered to some extent by government plans or insurance, with the greatest percentage covered under private plans. However, although 75 percent of high-income Canadians had prescription drug plan subsidies in 1996–97, this benefit was available to only 54 percent of middle-income Canadians and 39 percent of low-income Canadians (Health Canada 1999a). For those Canadians who lack insurance, the costs of medically necessary drug products may he prohibitively high. A 2001 report by the Canadian Institute for Health Information noted that costs for Canadians paying out-of-pocket for prescription drugs, over-the-counter remedies and other non-prescribed products has jumped dramatically—by 125 percent—over the past 12 years. In 2000, the average Canadian spent approximately $478 on drugs. As health economist Jeremiah Hurley has observed, "[I]f drugs are going to continue to become an important part of medically necessary services, then what does it mean if we have a significant component of financing coming from direct payments by individuals and in what ways might that compromise public access to necessary treatment?" (in Arnold 2001).

At present, only four Canadian provinces provide universal drug plans; British Columbia is the only province that uses a reference-based pricing scheme (which pays for only the lowest cost drug in each of three designated

[T]he debate about expanding the use of private money to a mixed health system, taken from a British model, quickly transmutes into accusations about the "Americanization" of our health care system. The prevailing view in Canada is that anyone suggesting that pay-as-you-go should be an option is at best unpatriotic, and at worst, a Yankee in sheep's clothing.

DARRELL BRICKER
Political scientist/pollster
EDWARD GREENSPON
Journalist

"therapeutic categories" to help reduce costs). In provinces without universal plans, Armstrong et al. (1998) note that "not only are many individuals left out, especially among the 'working poor,' but it is very difficult for any particular plan to control costs. At the same time, each of them faces unnecessarily high administrative costs." In consequence, the National Forum on Health has called our current drug plan situation "incompatible with Canada's vision for the health care system," and has recommended the establishment of a single-payer, publicly funded system for pharmaceuticals.

Organ Replacement

In 1996, surgeons in Canada performed 1578 transplants of kidneys, hearts, lungs, and other organs. Nevertheless, between 1992 and 1996, more than 1000 individuals died while waiting for transplants. At the end of December 1997, there were 3072 Canadians waiting for an organ transplant. Between 1991 and 1997, the number of patients waiting for an organ transplant increased by 68 percent, with the largest number of those on waiting lists for transplants living in Ontario (48 percent), followed by Quebec (21 percent), and British Columbia (12 percent). Canada has one of the lowest organ donor rates of all developed countries. In 1996, Canada's donation rate was 14.1 donors per million population or almost half that of Spain (26.8 per million). Currently, men constitute the majority of transplant recipients (65 percent) in general and, in particular, among those who are recipients of heart transplants (84 percent) (Health Canada 1999b; Statistics Canada 1998a).

Strategies for Action: Improving Health and Health Care

In poor countries today there are 170 million underweight children, over 3 million of who will die this year as a result.

WORLD HEALTH ORGANIZATION
The World Health Report
2002

Because poverty underlies many of the world's health problems, improving the world's health requires strategies that reduce poverty (see Chapter 10). Other chapters in this text discuss strategies to alleviate problems associated with tobacco and illegal drugs (Chapter 3), health hazards in the workplace (Chapter 11), and environmental health problems (Chapter 14). Here, we discuss other strategies for improving health including global strategies to improve maternal and infant health, HIV/AIDS prevention and alleviation strategies, the use of computer technology in health care, and Canada's health care reform.

Improving Maternal and Infant Health

As discussed earlier, maternal deaths are a major cause of death among women of reproductive age in the developing world. In 1987, the Safe Motherhood Initiative was launched. This global initiative is a partnership of governments, non-governmental organizations, agencies, donors, and women's health advocates working to protect women's health and lives, especially during pregnancy and childbirth. Improving women's health also improves the health of infants: 30 to 40 percent of infant deaths are the result of poor care during labour and delivery (Safe Motherhood Initiative 1998). The cost of ensuring that women in low-income countries get health care during pregnancy, delivery, and after birth; family planning services and newborn care is estimated at only $3 (U.S.) per person per year (Family Care International 1999).

The Safe Motherhood Initiative advocates improving maternal and infant health by first identifying the powerlessness that women face as an injustice that countries must remedy through political, health, and legal systems. In many developing countries, men make the decisions about whether or when their wives (or partners) will have sexual relations, use contraception, or bear children. Improving the status and power of women involves ensuring that they have the right to make decisions about their health and reproductive lives.

A report published by the Save the Children Organization entitled "State of the World's Mothers 2000" found that access to family planning and female education are the two most important determinants of the well-being of mothers and their children (Lay 2000). Women must have access to family planning services, affordable methods of contraception, and safe abortion services where legal. The Safe Motherhood Initiative recommends reforming laws and policies to support women's reproductive health and improve access to family planning services. This implies removing legal barriers to abortion—a highly controversial issue in many countries. Promoting women's education increases the status and power of women to control their reproductive lives, exposes women to information about health issues, and also delays marriage and childbearing.

HIV/AIDS Prevention and Alleviation Strategies

One suggested strategy to curb the spread of HIV involves encouraging individuals to get tested for HIV so they can modify their behaviour (to avoid transmitting the virus to others) and so they can receive early medical intervention that can slow or prevent the onset of AIDS. Millions of HIV-infected people throughout the world are not aware they are infected. Many are hesitant to find out if they have HIV because of the shame and blame that can be associated with HIV/AIDS. Facilities for HIV testing are also inadequate in many developing countries. However, testing is not enough. Research suggests that individuals who have been diagnosed with HIV often continue to engage in risky behaviours such as unprotected anal, genital, or oral sex and needle sharing without bleach. One study compared risky behaviours in HIV-infected youth (younger than 25 years) and HIV-infected adults (25 years of older) and found that 66 percent of young women and 46 percent of adult women engaged in risky behaviours after HIV infection. Twenty-eight percent of young men with HIV infection and 16 percent of infected adult men engaged in risky behaviour (Diamond and Buskin 2000).

Alleviating HIV/AIDS also requires educating populations about how to protect against HIV and providing access to condoms. However, there continues to be widespread concern that providing sex education and access to condoms will encourage young people to become prematurely sexually active. Consequently, many sex education programs have focused solely upon abstinence. Several studies have concluded, however, that sex education programs that combine messages about abstinence and safer sex practices (e.g., condom use) may delay the initiation of sexual behaviour as well as increase preventive behaviours among young people who are already sexually active (Joint United Nations Programme on HIV/AIDS 2000d).

Alleviating HIV/AIDS requires making medical interventions accessible and affordable, especially to the poor populations in developing countries. In an effort to combat AIDS in Africa, five of the world's leading pharmaceutical companies have agreed to decrease the price of drugs used to treat HIV. But even at discounted prices, the drugs will be beyond what many Africans can afford.

There is currently no "cure" for HIV or AIDS. Although various prevention and alleviation strategies may help reduce the spread of HIV and AIDS deaths, the HIV pandemic "will ultimately be controlled only by immunization against HIV using a protective, cheap, simple, and widely available vaccine" (Ward 1999: 199). As of this writing, no such effective vaccine exists, although at least 29 AIDS vaccines have been clinically tested around the world without success (Gottlieb 2000).

Health Promotion

For at least 25 years, federal policy has recognized the importance of individual behaviour as a determinant of health status. While in recent years the focus has shifted from individual behaviour to the socioeconomic determinants of behaviour, there is no doubt that health education remains an important health promotion strategy at the levels of the individual and of the broader population. Canadian health education stresses that good nutrition, exercise, and abstaining from smoking are important to good health, and it seems that many Canadians are heeding the message. For example, the National Population Health Survey reported that in the 12 months prior to the survey, just less than half (47 percent) of their respondents had changed some facet of their behaviour to improve their health, while slightly more than half (54 percent) recognized that some change was needed. Among the latter group, more than two-thirds (69 percent) indicated their intent to change their behaviour in the next year. Among those who recognized a need for change, the need most commonly identified was for greater amounts of exercise followed by reductions in smoking, improved nutrition, and weight loss. An absence of time and personal willpower were identified as the main barriers to making the desired lifestyle changes.

Within this survey, women were more likely than men to report having made changes in their personal behaviours in the year before the survey; women were also more likely to voice their intention to make such changes in the forthcoming year. However, differences based on gender were less notable than differences based on age. With increasing age, "[t]here was a general decline in behaviour change—whether actual, needed, or intended" (Health Canada 1999b). Individuals in Ontario were more likely to report behaviour changes in the previous year and the least likely to report any intended changes in future years. Residents of Quebec (79 percent), British Columbia (73 percent), and Alberta (61 percent) were the most likely to report intentions to change in the next year.

People with Disabilities

It would be a grave mistake to forget the necessity of ensuring the physical and social health of those who have physical or mental disabilities. People with disabilities in Canada continue to face disadvantage in areas such as work, housing, support services, transportation, and income support. Moreover, depending on the specific nature of their disability, they may or may not have access to adequate health care and education services.

For example, when 17-year-old Calgarian Terry Urquhart was placed on a waiting list to receive a lung transplant, it marked the first time that anyone with Down's syndrome in Canada, and perhaps in the world, had been given serious consideration for a lung transplant. Although individuals with Down's syndrome commonly experience severe lung problems as part of their genetic disorder, Terry's parents were originally told that their son did not qualify for a transplant in that he failed to meet the program's written criterion of "satisfactory intelligence." It was not until his parents went to the media that Terry was placed on the waiting list. However, public reaction was not unequivocally in favour of Urquhart. Reportedly, "hundreds" of phone calls poured in to the University of Alberta Hospital in Edmonton to protest, with some threatening to destroy their donor cards if Terry received a lung transplant. Consider as well that only two decades ago, newborns with Down's syndrome often died in Canada because of physicians' recommendations that parents not correct a simple stomach blockage (Mitchell 1995: A10).

Graham (1999) has noted that "support programs and services available to persons with disabilities, which are so essential to viability within the wider community, vary enormously from one part of the country to another." He points out that in Lloydminster, which straddles the Saskatchewan–Alberta border, a person with a visual disability can obtain certain high-tech equipment on the Alberta side but not on the Saskatchewan side; "in other words, if you live in Saskatchewan you can get a white cane—but sorry, nothing high tech."

It has been suggested that a Canadian disability act is necessary to ensure that the rights and needs of people with disabilities in Canada are protected (Kerzner and Baker 1999). However, in the absence of such an act, organizations such as the Council of Canadians with Disabilities, the Canadian Association for Independent Living Centres, DAWN (the Disabled Actions Women's Network), the Coalition of Provincial Organizations of the Handicapped, and institutes such as the Roeher Institute, the Canadian Council on Rehabilitation and Work, the Canadian Centre on Disability Studies, and the National Aboriginal Clearing/Connecting House on Disability Issues attempt to ensure that both the health and social needs of peoples with disabilities are not ignored in Canada.

Telemedicine: Computer Technology in Health Care

Computer technology offers numerous ways to reduce costs associated with health care delivery and to improve patient care. **Telemedicine** involves using information and communication technologies to deliver a wide range of health care services, including diagnosis, treatment, prevention, health support and information, and education of health care workers. Telemedicine can involve the transmission of three main types of information: data, audio, and images. A patient's medical records or vital signs (such as heart rate and blood pressure) can be transmitted from one location to another. Many hospitals and clinics store their medical records electronically, allowing doctors to access information about their patients very quickly and to update patient data from a distance. Specialized medical databases, such as MEDLINE, can be accessed via the Internet and offer a valuable resource for health care practitioners and researchers. The public may also use the Internet to gain health information and support. The transmission of radiological images (such as X-ray and ultrasound images) from one location to another, for the purpose of interpretation or consultation, has become one of the most commonly used telemedicine services. Images of tissue samples may also be transmitted to a pathologist in another location, who can look at the image on a monitor and offer an interpretation.

Benefits of Telemedicine Telemedicine has the potential to improve public health by making health care available in rural and remote areas and by providing health information to health care workers and to the general population. In addition, "telemedicine allows the scarce resources of specialists and expensive equipment to be shared by a much greater number of patients. Doctors are no longer restricted by geographical boundaries; international specialists are able to spread their skills across continents, without leaving their own hospitals" (LaPorte 1997: 38).

Telemedicine can be used in training and educating health care professionals and providing health care workers with up-to-date health information. Telemedicine can also reduce health care costs by reducing the cost of travel to major health centres or to specialists and by reducing the length of hospitalization, since patients can be monitored at a distance.

Another benefit of telemedicine is the provision of health information and support services on the Internet, which helps empower individuals in managing their health concerns. According to one recent survey, over half of Canadians with Internet access visited a health site; three in 10 said they had done so at least once in the past week and another 45 percent at least once during the past month. Of those who visited a health site, half judged themselves to be more knowledgeable as a result of their efforts (Bricker and Greenspon 2001: 225). Through e-mail, bulletin boards, and chat rooms, individuals with specific health problems can network with other similarly affected individuals. This social support assists in patient recovery, reduces the number of visits to physicians and clinics, and "provides...individuals [with disabilities] with an opportunity to achieve levels of social integration that were simply not possible before" (LaPorte 1997: 33).

In the twentieth century, advances in public health were largely due to improvements in sanitation and immunization. Advocates of telemedicine have forecast that in the twenty-first century, improvements in public health will result from the increased uses of information technology (LaPorte 1997). Telemedicine holds the promise of improving the health of individuals, families, communities, and nations. But whether or not telemedicine achieves its promise depends, in part, on whether resources are allocated to provide the technology and the training to use it.

Understanding Illness and Health Care

Human health has probably improved more over the past half century than over the previous three millennia (Feachem 2000). Yet the gap in health between rich and poor remains very wide and the very poor suffer appallingly. Health problems are affected not only by economic resources, but also by other social factors such as aging of the population, gender, education, and race/ethnicity.

Our cultural values and beliefs emphasize the ability of individuals to control their lives through the choices they make. Thus, westerners view health and illness as resulting from individual behaviour and lifestyle choices, rather than resulting from social, economic, and political forces. We agree that an individual's health is affected by the choices that person makes—choices such as whether or not to smoke, exercise, engage in sexual activity, use condoms, wear a seatbelt, and so on. However, the choices individuals make are influenced by social, economic, and political forces that must be taken into account if the goal is to improve the health not only of individuals but also of entire populations. Further, by focusing on individual behaviours that affect health and illness, we often overlook not only social causes of health problems but social solutions as well. For example, at an individual level, the public has been advised to rinse and cook meat, poultry, and eggs thoroughly and to carefully wash hands, knives, cutting boards, and so on to avoid illness caused by *Escherichia coli* and salmonella bacteria. However, whether or not one becomes ill from contaminated meat, eggs, or poultry is affected by more than individual behaviours in the kitchen. Governmental actions can also offer solutions by providing for more food inspectors and stricter regulations on food industries.

Although certain changes in medical practices and policies may help to improve world health, "the health sector should be seen as an important, but not the sole, force in the movement toward global health" (Lerer et al. 1998: 18). Improving the health of a society requires addressing diverse issues, including poverty and economic inequality, gender inequality, population growth, environmental issues, education, housing, energy, water and sanitation, agriculture, and workplace safety. Health promotion is important not only in the hospital, clinic, or doctor's office—it must also occur in the various settings where people live, work, play, and learn (Antezana et al. 1998).

Perhaps the most critical public health agenda today is reducing the gap between the health of advantaged and disadvantaged populations. Feachem (2000) suggests that "addressing this problem, both between and within countries, constitutes one of the greatest challenges of the new century. Failure to do so properly will have dire consequences for the global economy, for social order and justice, and for civilization as a whole" (p. 1).

> The health of each person affects the health of our families, our workplaces, our communities, our economy, and our society.
>
> LINDA PEENO
> *M.D.*

Critical Thinking

1 An analysis of 161 countries found that, in general, countries with high levels of literacy have low levels of HIV (World Health Organization and United Nations Joint Programme on HIV/AIDS 1998). However, in the region of the world affected the worst by HIV, sub-Saharan Africa, there is also a relationship between literacy rates and HIV, but the direction of the relationship is reversed. In this region, the countries with the highest levels of HIV infection are also those whose men and women are most literate. What are some possible explanations for this?

2 The Centre for Disease Control and Prevention (CDC) recommends that people aged six and older engage regularly, preferably daily, in light to moderate physical activity for at least 30 minutes per day. Experts agree that if those "who lead sedentary lives would adopt a more active lifestyle, there would be enormous benefit to the public's health and to individual well-being" (Pate et al. 1995: 406). Yet, in a telephone survey of more than 87 000 adults, only about 22 percent reported being active at the recommended level; 24 percent reported that they led a completely sedentary lifestyle (that is, they reported no leisure-time physical activity in the past month). What social and cultural factors contribute to the sedentary lifestyle of many North Americans?

3 Why do you think The American Psychiatric Association (2000) avoids the use of such expressions as "a schizophrenic" or "an alcoholic" and instead uses the expressions "an individual with schizophrenia" or "an individual with alcohol dependence"?

Key Terms

acute condition	globalization	mental health
burden of disease	health	mental illness
chronic condition	incidence	morbidity
disability-adjusted life year (DALY)	infant mortality rate	mortality
	life expectancy	perinatal transmission
environmental racism	maternal mortality rate	prevalence
epidemiological transition	medicalization	stigma
epidemiologist	Medicare	telemedicine
epidemiology	mental disorder	under-five mortality rate

Alcohol and Other Drugs

3

Outline

The Global Context: Drug Use
and Abuse

Sociological Theories of Drug
Use and Abuse

Frequently Used Legal and
Illegal Drugs

Societal Consequences of Drug
Use and Abuse

Treatment Alternatives

Strategies for Action: Canada
Responds

Understanding Alcohol and
Other Drugs

Is It True?

1. Alcoholics are seven times more
likely to separate or divorce than
non-alcoholics.

2. Impaired driving is one of the
most common crimes committed by
Canadians and a major cause of
death in Canada.

3. Of all psychoactive drugs,
alcohol is the only one whose
consumption has been shown
to increase aggression.

4. The most commonly used illicit
drug in Canada is marijuana.

5. The Dutch have decriminalized
small quantities of heroin and have
one of the lowest addiction rates in
Europe.

Answers: 1 = T, 2 = T, 3 = T, 4 = T, 5 = T

3

At the age of 20, Justin Lambert-Belanger was considered a likely future Olympic athlete. In 1999, he had won the Ontario high school championship in the 3000-metre steeple-chase. The following year, he became the Canadian junior champion of this gruelling event. Despite his many accomplishments, Justin was humble and introspective. A high school essay recorded his aspirations for himself and his generation. "I do not measure success by what one has accomplished," he wrote. "I hope I find a job I like. I hope I find a woman I love. I hope to sit back as an old man and be satisfied with the choices I made." But most of all, he wrote, "I want to make a difference. I want to help" (in Remington 2001). After winning an academic and athletic scholarship to Campbell University in North Carolina, he transferred to the University of Wyoming and became the best runner on their cross-country team. On September 16, 2001, Justin, along with seven other University of Wyoming runners, was killed in a head-on crash with a drunk driver.

The abuse of alcohol and other drugs is a social problem when it interferes with the well-being of individuals and/or the societies in which they live—when it jeopardizes health, safety, work and academic success, family, and friends. But managing the drug problem is a difficult undertaking. In dealing with drugs, a society must balance individual rights and civil liberties against the personal and social harm that drugs promote—crack-addicted babies, suicide, drunk driving, industrial accidents, mental illness, unemployment, and teenage addiction. When to regulate, what to regulate, and who should regulate are complex social issues. Our discussion begins by looking at how drugs are used and regulated in other societies.

The Global Context: Drug Use and Abuse

Pharmacologically, a **drug** is any substance other than food that alters the structure or functioning of a living organism when it enters the bloodstream. Using this definition, everything from vitamins to aspirin constitutes a drug. Sociologically, the term drug refers to any chemical substance that (1) has a direct effect on the user's physical, psychological, and/or intellectual functioning, (2) has the potential to be abused, and (3) has adverse consequences for the individual and/or society. Societies vary in how they define and respond to drug use. Thus, drug use is influenced by the social context of the particular society in which it occurs.

Drug Use and Abuse around the World

According to estimates by the European Information Network on Drugs and Drug Addiction, the prevalence of drug use around the world varies dramatically. For example, the proportion of adults who report ever using cannabis ranges from approximately 10 percent in Finland to about 25 percent in Denmark, France, Ireland, the Netherlands, Spain, and the United Kingdom (see Figure 3.1) (EMCDDA 2001). Use by adolescents varies as well. In Sweden and Portugal, approximately 8 percent of the 15- and 16-year-old population admit to ever using cannabis. However, in France and the United Kingdom that number is 35 percent (EMCDDA 2001).

In England, illegal drug use continues to spread, particularly among those under 25 (ISDD 1999). One-third of the adult population of the UK (Great Britain, Scotland, Wales, and Northern Ireland) is estimated to have used drugs at some time in their life—49 percent of those under 30. Statistics also indicate that drug users in the UK are more likely to be male, unemployed, and living in or around London when compared with non-users.

Some of the differences in international drug use may be attributed to variations in drug policies. The Netherlands, for example, has had an official government policy of treating the use of such drugs as marijuana, hashish, and heroin as a health issue rather than a crime issue since the mid-1970s. In the first decade of the policy, drug use did not appear to increase. However, increases in marijuana use were reported in the early 1990s with the advent of "cannabis

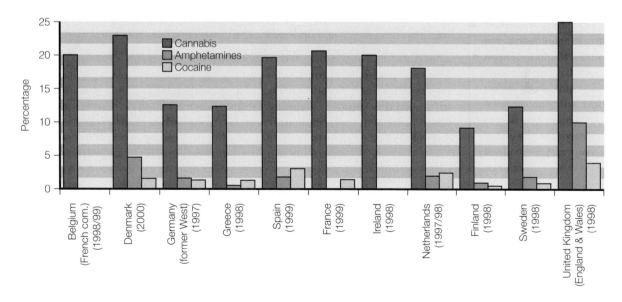

NB Data are from the most recent national surveys available in each country. The age range is from 15–18 years old to 59–69 years old. Variation in age ranges may partially influence disparities between countries. In Belgium the range is 18–49.

■ **Figure 3.1** *Lifetime Experience of Cannabis, Amphetamines, and Cocaine among Adults in Some EU Countries, Measured by National Population Surveys*

SOURCE: © European Monitoring Centre for Drugs and Drug Addiction.

cafés." These coffee shops sell small amounts of marijuana for personal use and, presumably, prevent casual marijuana users from coming into contact with drug dealers (MacCoun and Reuter 2001). More recent evidence suggests that marijuana use among Dutch youth is decreasing (Sheldon 2000).

Great Britain has also adopted a "medical model," particularly in regard to heroin and cocaine. As early as the 1960s, English doctors prescribed opiates and cocaine for their patients who were unlikely to quit using drugs on their own and for the treatment of withdrawal symptoms. By the 1970s, however, British laws had become more restrictive, making it difficult for either physicians or users to obtain drugs legally. Today, British government policy provides for limited distribution of drugs by licensed drug treatment specialists to addicts who might otherwise resort to crime to support their habits. Recent increased drug use, however, has led to discussions of a British "zero-tolerance" policy (Francis 2000).

In stark contrast to such health-based policies, other countries execute drug users and/or dealers, or subject them to corporal punishment. The latter may include whipping, stoning, beating, and torture. Such policies are found primarily in less developed nations such as Malaysia, where religious and cultural prohibitions condemn any type of drug use, including alcohol and tobacco.

Drug Use and Abuse in Canada

According to government officials and the media, there is a drug crisis in Canada—a crisis so serious that it demands that we engage in a "war on drugs." Canadians' concern with drugs, however, has varied over the years. Although in 1975 almost one in two Canadians (46 percent) identified drugs as a "very serious" problem in our country, by 1995, this figure had declined to about one in three (34 percent). Similarly, while 64 percent of Canadian teens viewed drugs as a "very serious" social concern in 1992, in 2000, only 48 percent did so (Bibby 2001: 181).

In Canada, the use of alcohol is much more widespread than the use of illicit drugs such as marijuana and cocaine, but our response to drug use is contradictory—condemning it on the one hand (e.g., heroin), yet encouraging and tolerating it on the other (e.g., alcohol). At various times in our history, many drugs that are illegal today were legal and readily available. In the 1800s and the early 1900s, opium was routinely used in medicines as a pain reliever, and morphine was taken as a treatment for dysentery and fatigue. Amphetamine-based inhalers were legally available until 1949, and cocaine was an active ingredient in Coca-Cola until 1906, when it was replaced with another drug—caffeine (Witters et al. 1992). In the 1950s, anabolic steroids were viewed as "wonder drugs" that could enhance the well-being of sick and malnourished people, promote quick weight gain in cattle, and potentially provide a cure to cancer. It was arguably not until 1988, when Canadian athlete Ben Johnson lost his gold medal at the Seoul Olympics for taking a performance-enhancing drug, that many Canadians became aware that the use of anabolic steroids could be problematic. Even now, while the majority of Canadians (86 percent) indicate that they are aware of the health risks of environmental tobacco smoke (ETS), more than three million Canadians aged 12 and older (or 14 percent of the Canadian population) believe that there are no health risks for nonsmokers or have no opinion on the subject (Health Canada 1999: 155). It would seem likely that among these Canadians,

There are but three ways for the populace to escape its wretched lot. The first two are by route of the wine-shop or the church; the third is by that of the social revolution.

MIKHAIL A. BAKUNIN
Anarchist and revolutionary

such measures as municipal bylaws that restrict public smoking or voluntary restrictions on smoking at home are viewed as ill conceived or unwarranted.

Sociological Theories of Drug Use and Abuse

Most theories of drug use and abuse concentrate on what are called psychoactive drugs. These drugs alter the functioning of the brain, affecting the moods, emotions, and perceptions of the user. Such drugs include alcohol, cocaine, heroin, and marijuana. **Drug abuse** occurs when acceptable social standards of drug use are violated, resulting in adverse physiological, psychological, and/or social consequences. For example, when an individual's drug use leads to hospitalization, arrest, or divorce, such use is usually considered abusive. Drug abuse, however, does not always entail drug addiction. **Drug addiction**, or **chemical dependency**, refers to a condition in which drug use is compulsive—users are unable to stop because of their dependency. The dependency may be psychological, in that the individual needs the drug to achieve a feeling of well-being, and/or physical, in that withdrawal symptoms occur when the individual stops taking the drug.

Various theories provide explanations for why some people use and abuse drugs. Drug use is not simply a matter of individual choice. Theories of drug use explain how structural and cultural forces, as well as biological factors, influence drug use and society's responses to it.

Structural-Functionalist Perspective

Functionalists argue that drug abuse is a response to the weakening of norms in society. As society becomes more complex and rapid social change occurs, norms and values become unclear and ambiguous, resulting in anomie—a state of normlessness. **Anomie** may exist at the societal level, resulting in social strains and inconsistencies that lead to drug use. For example, research indicates that increased alcohol consumption in the 1830s and the 1960s was a response to rapid social change and the resulting stress (Rorabaugh 1979). Anomie produces inconsistencies in cultural norms regarding drug use. For example, while public health officials and health care professionals warn of the dangers of alcohol and tobacco use, advertisers glorify the use of alcohol and tobacco, and the government subsidizes alcohol and tobacco industries. Further, cultural traditions, such as giving away cigars to celebrate the birth of a child and toasting a bride and groom with champagne, persist.

Anomie may also exist at the individual level as when a person suffers feelings of estrangement, isolation, and turmoil over appropriate and inappropriate behaviour. An adolescent whose parents are experiencing a divorce, who is separated from friends and family as a consequence of moving, or who lacks parental supervision and discipline may be more vulnerable to drug use because of such conditions. Thus, from a structural-functionalist perspective, drug use is a response to the absence of a perceived bond between the individual and society, and to the weakening of a consensus regarding what is considered acceptable. Consistent with this perspective, Nylander et al. (1996) found that adolescents who reported that religion was important in their lives were less likely to use drugs than those who didn't.

Conflict Perspective

Conflict perspectives emphasize the importance of power differentials in influencing drug use behaviour and societal values concerning drug use. From a conflict perspective, drug use occurs as a response to the inequality perpetuated by a capitalist system. Societal members, alienated from work, friends, and family, as well as from society and its institutions, turn to drugs as a means of escaping the oppression and frustration caused by the inequality they experience. Further, conflict theorists emphasize that the most powerful members of society influence the definitions of which drugs are illegal and the penalties associated with illegal drug production, sales, and use.

For example, alcohol is legal because it is produced and often consumed by those who enjoy power, privilege and influence. In 2000–01, for example, the alcohol industry enjoyed sales of more than $13.6 billion and generated $3.8 billion in revenue for provincial governments as well as considerable federal revenue (Statistics Canada 2002a). Consider the irony: Of the $18.5 billion cost of substance abuse to the Canadian economy, the costs of legal drugs were the most significant, with tobacco accounting for $9.6 billion, alcohol $7.5 billion, and illicit drugs $1.4 billion (CCSA 1999).

Conversely, the consumption of "street drugs" such as cocaine and heroin is associated with the powerless and disenfranchised: the poor, minority group members, and, in particular, visible minorities. As Hackler (2000: 213) observes, "the societal demand to punish, stigmatize, and exclude users of certain substances *is not based on pharmacological evidence*" and evidence of such damage "plays a secondary role in drug policy." The use of opium by Chinese immigrants in the 1800s provides an historical example. The Chinese, who had been brought to Canada to work on the railroads, regularly smoked opium as part of their cultural tradition. However, hostility to the use of opium emerged in part because of a labour surplus that followed the completion of railway construction and the diminished intensity of the Gold Rush. Green (1986) notes that before this time, in the midst of a labour shortage, "the Chinese were regarded as industrious, sober, economical and law-abiding individuals" (p. 25). As jobs became scarce and the Chinese were viewed as competitors for the positions that existed, "the earlier friendly feelings toward the Chinese changed to hostility....There was a great demand that Chinese immigration be restricted or discontinued" (p. 24). Simultaneously, opium use, which had been previously viewed as, at worst, "an individual medical misfortune or personal vice, free of severe moral opprobrium" (p. 25), became defined as a significant social "evil." Morgan (1978) observes:

> The first opium laws...were not the result of a moral crusade against the drug itself. Instead, it represented a coercive action directed against a vice that was merely an appendage of the real menace—the Chinese—and not the Chinese per se, but the labouring "Chinamen" who threatened the economic security of the white working class. (p. 59)

The criminalization of other drugs, including cocaine, heroin, and marijuana, follows similar patterns of social control of the powerless, political opponents, and/or minorities. In the 1940s, marijuana was used primarily by minority group members and carried with it severe criminal penalties. However, after White middle-class students began to use marijuana in the 1970s, various lobby groups sought to reduce the penalties associated with its use. Though the nature and pharmacological properties of the drug had not changed, the population of

[I]llegal drugs are all over the place. For whatever reasons, only a minority of teens bother to use them. Maybe that's the *real* drug story. The big things they are into are alcohol and cigarettes.

REGINALD W. BIBBY
Sociologist

users was now connected to power and influence. Thus, conflict theorists regard the regulation of certain drugs and drug use itself as a reflection of differences in the political, economic, and social power of various interest groups.

Symbolic Interactionist Perspective

Symbolic interactionism, emphasizing the importance of definitions and labelling, concentrates on the social meanings associated with drug use. If the initial drug use experience is defined as pleasurable, it is likely to recur, and over time, the individual may earn the label of "drug user." If this definition is internalized so that the individual assumes an identity as a drug user, the behaviour will likely continue and may even escalate.

Drug use is also learned through symbolic interaction in small groups. Friends, for example, are the most common source of drugs for teenagers (Leinwand 2000). First-time users learn not only the motivations for drug use and its techniques, but also what to experience. Becker (1966) explains how marijuana users learn to ingest the drug. A novice being coached by a regular user reports this experience:

> I was smoking like I did an ordinary cigarette. He said, "No, don't do it like that." He said, "Suck it, you know, draw in and hold it in your lungs...for a period of time." I said, "Is there any limit of time to hold it?" He said, "No, just till you feel that you want to let it out, let it out." So I did that three or four times. (p. 47)

Marijuana users not only learn how to ingest the smoke, but also learn to label the experience positively. When peers define certain drugs, behaviours, and experiences as not only acceptable but pleasurable, drug use is likely to continue.

> Because they [first-time users] think they're going to keep going up, up, up till they lose their minds or begin doing weird things or something. You have to like reassure them, explain to them that they're not really flipping or anything, that they're gonna be all right. You have to just talk them out of being afraid. (Becker 1966: 55)

Interactionists also emphasize that symbols may be manipulated and used for political and economic agendas. "[A]meliorative programs which are imbued with...potent symbolic qualities...are virtually assured wide-spread public acceptance (regardless of actual effectiveness) which in turn advances the interests of political leaders who benefit from being associated with highly visible, popular symbolic programs" (Wysong et al. 1994: 461).

Biological and Psychological Theories

Drug use and addiction are likely the result of a complex interplay of social, psychological, and biological forces. Biological research has primarily concentrated on the role of genetics in predisposing an individual to drug use. According to a recent report by the National Institute on Alcohol Abuse and Alcoholism (NIAAA 2000: xiii), "50 to 60 percent of the risk for developing alcoholism is genetic." Research also indicates that by examining inherited traits science "can predict [in] childhood with 80 percent accuracy who is going to develop alcoholism later in life" (AAP 1998). At the same time, many alcoholics do not have parents who abuse alcohol, and many alcoholic parents have offspring who do not abuse alcohol.

Biological theories of drug use hypothesize that some individuals are physiologically predisposed to experience more pleasure from drugs than others and, consequently, are more likely to be drug users. According to these theories, the central nervous system, which is composed primarily of the brain and spinal cord, processes drugs through neurotransmitters in a way that produces an unusually euphoric experience. Individuals not so physiologically inclined report less pleasant experiences and are less likely to continue use (Jarvik 1990; Alcoholic Alert 2000).

Psychological explanations focus on the tendency of certain personality types to be more susceptible to drug use. Individuals who are particularly prone to anxiety may be more likely to use drugs as a way to relax, gain self-confidence, or ease tension. For example, research indicates that female adolescents who have been sexually abused or who have poor relationships with their parents are more likely to have severe drug problems (NIDA 2000a). Psychological theories of drug abuse also emphasize that drug use may be maintained by positive and negative reinforcement.

Frequently Used Legal and Illegal Drugs

Social definitions regarding which drugs are legal or illegal have varied over time, circumstance, and societal forces. In Canada, two of the most dangerous and widely abused drugs, alcohol and tobacco, are legal (Table 3.1).

Table 3.1 *Illicit and Legal Substances that Can Be Abused*

Substance	Examples	Illegal Acts
Tobacco	Cigarettes, cigars	Use in some public places, sale to minors
Alcohol	Wine, beer, spirits	Driving while intoxicated, sale to minors, use in prison
Substances covered by the *Controlled Drugs and Substances Act**	Heroin, LSD, cocaine, marijuana, ecstasy, medications such as antidepressants and tranquilizers, and sport-enhancing substances such as anabolic steroids	Possession and trafficking of cocaine and heroin, medications obtained without a proper prescription from a physician, possession of a banned substance by an athlete, smuggling cocaine into the country aboard an aircraft, possession of proceeds from selling drugs illegally
Other substances	Inhalants such as model airplane glue and gasoline	Not illegal but very harmful when abused

* Use of many substances under the *Controlled Drugs and Substances Act* is legal under restricted circumstances, such as drugs prescribed by a physician, including most recently "medicinal" marijuana. Many can also be used legally, without a medical prescription, such as mild pain relief pills that are available over the counter and contain low dosages of codeine, a controlled substance.

SOURCE: *Report of the Auditor General of Canada—2001*, Office of the Auditor General of Canada, 2001. Reproduced with the permission of the Minister of Public Works and Government Services, 2003.

Alcohol

Canadians' attitudes toward alcohol have had a long and varied history (this chapter's *Self and Society* box deals with attitudes toward alcohol). Although alcohol was a common beverage in early Canada, "the moral climate in Canada after the turn of the century was one in which middle class persons with strong religious convictions were willing to believe the worst of alcohol, tobacco and other drugs....The typical reaction to these perceived threats was to press for total prohibition" (Giffen et al. 1991: 150). Many have argued that the push for Prohibition was, in fact, a "moral crusade" (Gusfield 1963) against immigrant groups who were perceived as more likely to use alcohol. Today, Canada is experiencing a resurgence of concern about alcohol. What has been called a "new temperance" has manifested itself in increased concern about fetal alcohol syndrome, teenage drinking, and calls for strict enforcement of drinking and driving regulations.

Alcohol is the most widely used and abused drug in Canada among both adults and youths (Table 3.2). Although most people who drink alcohol do so moderately and experience few negative effects, alcoholics are psychologically and physically addicted to alcohol and suffer various degrees of physical, economic, psychological, and personal harm.

According to the 1996–97 National Population Health Survey (NPHS), more than half (53 percent) of Canadians 12 years of age and older (12.7 million Canadians) reported drinking at least one alcoholic drink per month in the previous year. The largest proportion of regular drinkers (43 percent) consumed, on average, one to six drinks each week. Men were significantly more likely than women were to be regular drinkers (63 percent versus 43 percent), especially

> Drunkenness is the ruin of reason. It is premature old age. It is temporary death.
>
> ST. BASIL
> *Bishop of Caesarea*

Table 3.2 *Drug Use among Teenagers, Canada, 2000*

"How often do you..."	Weekly or More	Once or Twice a Month	Less than Once a Month	Never
Smoke cigarettes	23%	5%	9%	63%
Males	22	5	9	64
Females	24	6	9	61
Drink beer, wine, other alcohol	22	30	26	22
Males	29	29	22	20
Females	16	31	28	25
Under 18 total	18	29	26	27
Males	26	31	22	21
Females	14	31	29	26
Smoke marijuana or hashish	14	10	13	63
Males	19	11	13	57
Females	9	8	14	69
Use other illegal drugs	3	4	7	86
Males	4	4	8	84
Females	2	4	7	87

SOURCE: Bibby, Reginald W. 2001. *Canada's Teens: Today, Yesterday, and Tomorrow.* Toronto: Stoddart, p. 98.

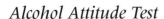
Alcohol Attitude Test

If you strongly agree with the following statements, write in 1. If you agree, but not strongly, write in 2. If you neither agree nor disagree, write in 3. If you disagree, but not strongly, write in 4. If you strongly disagree, write in 5.

Set 1

_____ 1. If I tried to stop someone from driving after drinking, the person would probably think I was butting in where I shouldn't.

_____ 2. Even if I wanted to, I would probably not be able to stop someone from driving after drinking.

_____ 3. If people want to kill themselves, that's their business.

_____ 4. I wouldn't like someone to try to stop me from driving after drinking.

_____ 5. Usually, if you try to help someone else out of a dangerous situation, you risk getting yourself into one.

_____ Total score for questions 1 through 5

Set 2

_____ 6. My friends would not disapprove of me for driving after drinking.

_____ 7. Getting into trouble with my parents would not keep me from driving after drinking.

_____ 8. The thought that I might get into trouble with the police would not keep me from driving after drinking.

_____ 9. I am not scared by the thought that I might seriously injure myself or someone else by driving after drinking.

_____ 10. The fear of damaging the car would not keep me from driving after drinking.

_____ Total score for questions 6 through 10

Set 3

_____ 11. The speed limit on the open roads spoils the pleasure of driving for most teenagers.

_____ 12. Many teenagers use driving to let off steam.

_____ 13. Being able to drive a car makes teenagers feel more confident in their relations with others their age.

_____ 14. An evening with friends is not much fun unless one of them has a car.

_____ 15. There is something about being behind the wheel of a car that makes one feel more adult.

_____ Total score for questions 11 through 15

Scoring

Set 1. 15–25 points: takes responsibility to keep others from driving when drunk; 5–9 points: wouldn't take steps to stop a drunk friend from driving.

Set 2. 12–25 points: hesitates to drive after drinking; 5–7 points: is not deterred by the consequences of drinking and driving.

Set 3. 19–25 points: perceives auto as means of transportation; 5–14 points: uses car to satisfy psychological needs, not just transportation.

SOURCE: Courtesy of National Highway Traffic Safety Administration. National Center for Statistics and Analysis, from _Drunk Driving Facts_. Washington, D.C.: NHTSA, 1988.

among those aged 15 to 44, where almost three-quarters of men (74 percent) and half of women (49 to 50 percent) were regular drinkers. Men who were regular drinkers were also more likely to drink more frequently and to report a higher average weekly consumption than women were (Health Canada 1999: 171–72). The 2000 Project Canada youth survey also finds that while one in five Canadian teens drank beer, wine, or other forms of alcohol at least once a week, the weekly level for males was almost twice that of females (Bibby 2001: 97).

Binge drinking, defined as the consumption of five or more alcoholic beverages on at least one occasion, is most common among youth. According to the 1996–97 NPHS, more than one-third (36 percent) of Canadians aged 20 to 24 who were current drinkers drank five or more drinks at least 12 times in the previous year and more than one in 10 (13 percent) did so 52 or more times in the previous year. Binge drinking is more prevalent among young Canadian men aged 15 to 19 (52 percent) than among young Canadian women (35 percent). However, the majority of both sexes in the 20- to 24-year-old age group (73 percent of men and 51 percent of women) reported at least one episode of binge drinking (Health Canada 1999: 171).

A study (Wechsler et al. 1998) of more than 17 000 students at 140 U.S. four-year colleges and universities indicates that:

- In the two weeks before the survey, 44 percent of students had engaged in binge drinking.
- Seventy-three percent of men and 68 percent of women reported that getting drunk was an important reason for drinking.
- Students who were White, members of a fraternity or sorority, or athletes were the most likely to binge.
- Sixty-one percent of men and 39 percent of women drank alcohol on 10 or more occasions in the past 30 days.
- More than 80 percent of women and men reported having a hangover, more than 50 percent doing something they regretted later, more than 40 percent missing class due to drinking, and more than 30 percent getting behind in schoolwork because of drinking.

> ■ Most Canadians still think drinking is the stuff of comedy.
>
> **EDWARD PHILLIPS**
> **Sunday Best**

Not only were binge drinkers more likely to report using other controlled substances, but also the more frequently a student binged, the higher the probability of reporting other drug use. The most commonly reported other drugs used by frequent binge drinkers were, in order, cigarettes, marijuana, hallucinogens, and chewing tobacco (HHS 1998).

According to the NPHS, there is a *positive* relationship between education and drinking. That is, as education increases, so too does the likelihood that Canadians are regular drinkers. "University graduates were most likely (61 percent) to drink at least once a month, while those with less than high school were least likely (44 percent) to do so." It additionally notes that the relationship between amount consumed and educational attainment "is similar, though less pronounced: with each successive level of education, the likelihood of having had one or more drinks weekly increased. However, university graduates were least likely to have had 14 or more drinks weekly" (Health Canada 1999: 172). This survey also found that the proportion of Canadian men and women who drank at least once per month rose steadily with increases in income and men and women with higher incomes tended to be heavier drinkers. Among men in the two lower-income levels who were drinkers, 24 percent reported at least one episode of heavy or "binge" drinking, compared with 43 percent of men in the highest income bracket. The rate of heavy drinking among women drinkers in the lowest income level was 13 percent. This rate dropped to 10 percent at the next income level, then slowly climbed to 19 percent at the highest income level.

Tobacco

Tobacco is probably our most dangerous drug. It kills more of us than all the others combined and doubled.

NEIL BOYD
Criminologist

Although nicotine is an addictive psychoactive drug and the dangers of second-hand smoke form the basis for Canada's Non-Smoker's Health Act, tobacco continues to be one of the most widely used drugs in Canada. According to the Canadian Tobacco Use Monitoring Survey (CTUMS), in 2001, 5.4 million Canadians (22 percent of the population aged 15 years and older) were smokers. In that year, about one in four men (24 percent) and one in five women (20 percent) smoked tobacco. However, compared to two decades ago, there are fewer Canadians that smoke and those that smoke on a daily basis are smoking less (down from 20.6 cigarettes in 1985 to 16.2 in 2001). In 2001, more Canadians identified themselves as "former smokers" than "current smokers" (Health Canada 2001).

Much of the concern about smoking surrounds the use of tobacco by young people (see Figure 3.2). In this chapter's *Social Problems Research Up Close* feature, images of tobacco and alcohol use in children's animated films are examined. In 2001, 22.5 of Canadian teens aged 15–19 reported themselves as current smokers (24 percent of girls and 21 percent of boys). However, at 32 percent, young Canadians aged 20–24 have the highest smoking rate of any age group (29 percent of females and 35 percent of males) (Health Canada 2001).

Under Canada's *Tobacco Act (1997)*, it is a summary conviction offence for any person to furnish (i.e., sell, give, or send) a tobacco product to a person under 18 in any public place (Solomon 1999: 11). The Tobacco Act also prohibits retailers from selling cigarettes in packages of fewer than 20, restricts the placement of tobacco machines, requires retailers to post signs indicating that giving or selling tobacco products to those under 18 is prohibited, and specifies that those who violate these provisions may be fined up to $3000 for a first offence

■ **Figure 3.2** *Trends in Youth Smoking since 1981*

SOURCE: *The Scoop on Smoking.* Health Canada for Youth Web site, © 2002. Reproduced with the permission of the Minister of Public Works and Government Services Canada, 2003.

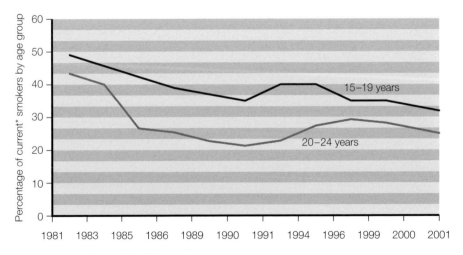

* Current/Daily/Non-daily smokers

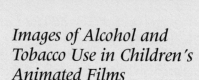

Images of Alcohol and Tobacco Use in Children's Animated Films

The impact of media on drug and alcohol use is likely to be recursive—media images affect drug use while, alternatively, societal drug use helps define media presentations. Previous research has documented the rate of tobacco and alcohol use in print media, advertising, and Hollywood movies. In the present research, Goldstein, Sobel, and Newman (1999) use content analysis to investigate the prevalence of tobacco and alcohol use is children's animated films as one step in assessing the growing concern with media influence on children's smoking and drinking behaviour.

Sample and Methods

The researcher's examined all G-rated animated films released between 1937 (*Snow White and the Seven Dwarfs*) and 1997 (*Hercules*, *Anastasia*, *Pippi Longstocking*, and *Cats Don't Dance*). Criteria for sample inclusion included that the film be at least 60 minutes in length and, before video distribution, have been released to theatres. The resulting sample included all of Disney's animated children's films produced during the target years with the exception of three that were unavailable on videocassette. The remaining films included all children's animated films produced by MGM/United Artists, Universal, 20th Century Fox, and Warner Brothers since 1982. Variables coded included the: (1) presence of alcohol or tobacco use, (2) length of time of use on screen, (3) number of characters using alcohol or tobacco, (4) value of the character using tobacco or alcohol (i.e., good, neutral, or bad), (5) any implied messages about the drug use, and (6) the type of tobacco or alcohol being used.

Findings and Conclusions

Of the 50 films analyzed, at least one episode of alcohol and/or tobacco use was portrayed in 34 (68 percent) with tobacco use (N=528) slightly exceeding portrayals of alcohol use (N=25). Tobacco was used by 76 different characters with an onscreen time of 45 minutes—an average of 1.62 minutes per movie. Characters were most likely to use cigars followed by cigarettes, and pipes. Of the 76 characters using tobacco, 28 (37 percent) were classified as good. Surprisingly, the use of tobacco products by "good" characters has increased rather than decreased over time.

Sixty-two characters, averaging 2.5 per film, were shown using alcohol, with a total duration of 27 minutes across all films. Characters were most likely to consume wine, followed by beer, spirits, and champagne. The number of good characters using alcohol was similar to the number of characters classified as bad. In 19 of the 25 films in which alcohol use was portrayed, tobacco use was also pictured. Although several films portrayed the physical consequences of smoking (N=10) (e.g., coughing) or drinking (N=7) (e.g., passing out), no film verbally referred to the health hazards of either drug.

One particularly interesting finding of the research concerned the use of alcohol and tobacco as a visual prop in character development. For example, although cigar smokers were portrayed as tough and powerful (e.g., Sykes in Oliver and Company), pipe smokers were most often older, kindly, and wise (e.g., Geppetto in Pinocchio), and cigarette smokers independent, witty, and intelligent (e.g., the Genie in Aladdin). There was also a tendency for alcohol and tobacco use to be portrayed together. When one, the other, or both are associated with positively defined characters the impact may be detrimental to the lifestyle choices of viewers.

Although this study cannot assess the "impact question," advertising campaigns have been linked to detrimental results. Although in each of these cases the motivation for the use of such appealing characters is clear, the presentation of "good" characters using alcohol and tobacco products in children's animated films remains unexplained. Interpretation of the results is further complicated by the lack of change over time, that is, as our knowledge of the harmful effects of these products increased, their presence in children's films did not, as expected, decrease. In light of these results, the researchers call for an end to the portrayal of alcohol and tobacco use in all children's animated films and associated products (e.g., posters, books, games).

SOURCE: Goldstein, Adam, Rachel Sobel, and Glen Newman. 1999. "Tobacco and Alcohol Use in G-rated Children's Animated Films." *Journal of the American Medical Association* 281: 1121–36.

and $50 000 for a subsequent offence. In addition, the Act governs the marketing activities of tobacco manufacturers and retailers, requires tobacco packaging to list certain information and to carry health warnings (the size, location, and colouring of which are governed by the regulation), and "severely limits all sponsorship, advertising and promotion of tobacco products" (p. 308).

Tobacco was first cultivated by Indigenous people and used as part of their religious rituals. European settlers believed that tobacco had medicinal properties and its use spread throughout Europe, assuring the economic success of the colonies in the New World. Tobacco was initially used primarily through chewing and snuffing, but in time, smoking became more popular even though scientific evidence that linked tobacco smoking to lung cancer existed as early as 1859 (Feagin and Feagin 1994). Today, the health hazards of tobacco use are well documented. Smoking is associated with lung cancer, cardiovascular disease, strokes, emphysema, spontaneous abortion, premature birth, and neonatal death. In Canada, it is estimated that one person dies every 12 minutes of a tobacco-related disease (Health Canada 2001). Tobacco smoke kills more than 45 000 Canadians yearly—more than the combined total of all murders, alcohol-related deaths, car accidents and suicides (see Figure 3.3). Smoking also reduces the number of years that a person may hope to live without any disability. "Among both men and women, two-thirds of non-smokers will survive without any disability to the age of 65, compared with less than half of smokers. In addition, 25 percent of male non-smokers and 30 percent of female non-smokers who live to the age of 80 will have no disability, compared with less than 10 percent for both men and women who smoke" (Statistics Canada 2001).

By the year 2030, tobacco-related diseases will be the number-one cause of death worldwide, killing one of every six people. Eighty percent of the deaths will take place in poor nations where many smokers are unaware of the health hazards associated with their behaviour (Mayell 1999). In an attempt to discourage the use of tobacco by Canadians, various control measures, by all levels of government, have been introduced including media campaigns and public education programs; and increased restrictions on access by minors to cigarettes, public smoking and sponsorship promotion by the tobacco industry (Health Canada 2002b). Most recently, in June 2002, the federal government announced

> For thy sake, tobacco, I would do anything but die.
>
> CHARLES LAMB
> *Novelist*

■ **Figure 3.3** *Estimated Deaths in Canada, 1996*

SOURCE: Health Canada for Youth Web site, © 2002. Reproduced with the permission of the Minister of Public Works and Government Services Canada, 2003.

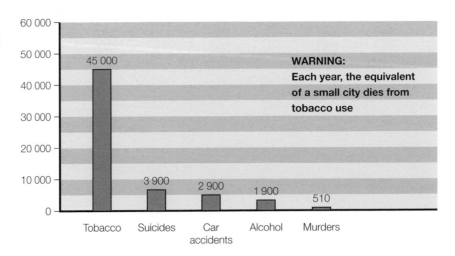

a $3.50-per-carton increase in federal taxes on cigarettes. This increase, which restored federal tobacco tax rates to their pre-1994 levels, was to take effect in conjunction with a number of provincial tobacco tax increases. In announcing the increase, Minister of Health Anne McLellan observed: "We know that increasing taxes on tobacco directly reduces the incidence of smoking, which contributes to the overall health of Canadians" (Department of Finance Canada 2002).

Marijuana

Although drug abuse ranks among the top concerns of many Canadians, surveys indicate that illegal drug use of all kinds is far less common than alcohol and tobacco abuse. Marijuana remains the most commonly used and most heavily trafficked illicit drug in the world. It is estimated that over 40 million Europeans have tried cannabis at least once in their lifetime and that there are 200 to 250 million marijuana users worldwide, predominantly in Africa and Asia. According to the Canadian Centre on Substance Abuse (CCSA 1999), cannabis is also the most commonly used "illicit drug" in Canada.

Marijuana's active ingredient is (THC) (delta-9-tetrahydrocannabinol) which, in varying amounts, may act as a sedative or as a hallucinogen. Marijuana use dates back to 2737 B.C. in China and has a long tradition of use in India, the Middle East, and Europe. In North America, hemp, as it was then called, was used for making rope and as a treatment for various ailments. Nevertheless, in the 1920s, Judge Emily Murphy was the first to draw the attention of Canadians to "Marihuana—A New Menace" in her book, *The Black Candle*. Although the drug was virtually unknown in Canada at the time, Murphy's book suggested that marijuana had an insidious effect on its users and drove them "completely insane. The addict loses all sense of moral responsibility. Addicts to this drug, while under its influence, lose all sense of moral responsibility…are immune to pain…become raving maniacs and are liable to kill or indulge in any forms of violence to other persons, using the most savage methods of cruelty…without any sense of moral responsibility." To Murphy, all drugs, including marijuana, produced one predictable pattern: "moral degeneration, crime, physical and mental deterioration and disease, intellectual and spiritual wastage, and material loss through drug-induced negligence." However, as Green (1986: 31) has noted, racism appears to have been a "critical component" in Murphy's analysis of the drug problem. According to Murphy, narcotics were part of an international conspiracy "to injure the bright-browed races of the world" and a tactic used by "aliens of colour to bring about the degeneration of the white race." However, "[a]s a result of the considerable media attention devoted to *The Black Candle* and the paucity of challenge or contradictory statements, Murphy's conception of the scourge-like effects of drug use came to dominate Canadian narcotics ideology" (Green 1986: 33).

In general, Canadian men are twice as likely as women to be current users of cannabis with the highest rate of current use reported by young men aged 15 to 24 (26 to 28 percent) (CCSA 1999; Health Canada 1999). Over the past decade, the number of young people who believe marijuana is dangerous has steadily declined and marijuana use among young people has steadily increased. The 2000 Project Canada national survey of youth reports that 50 percent of Canadian teens (58 percent of males and 42 percent of females) favour the legalization of marijuana use—up from 27 percent in 1992 (Bibby 2001: 188). Similarly, while in 1992, 18 percent of Canada's teens reported regular or occasional use of marijuana (19 percent of males and 17 percent of females), in 2000, 37 percent of Canada' teens (43 percent of males and 31 percent of females) indicated that they regularly or occasionally smoked marijuana or hashish (Bibby 2001: 186). Among certain groups of young Canadians, cannabis use is even higher. For example, compared with others in the same age cohort, street youth in Canada report elevated rates of both illicit drug use and heavy drinking. In various studies, the percentage of street youth reporting cannabis use ranges from 66 percent to 88 percent, while between one-quarter and one-half report heavy drinking (Health Canada 1999). This chapter's *The Human Side* feature notes the role played by alcohol and other drugs in both the backgrounds and daily lives of Canada's street youths.

Although the effects of alcohol and tobacco are, in large part, indisputable, there is less agreement about the effects of marijuana. Although the carcinogenic effects of marijuana are as lethal as nicotine's, other long-term physiological effects are unknown. An important concern is that marijuana may be a **gateway drug** that causes progression to other drugs such as cocaine and heroin. More likely, however, is that persons who experiment with one drug are more likely to experiment with another. Indeed, most drug users are polydrug users with the most common combination being alcohol, tobacco, and marijuana (Health Canada 1999).

Cocaine

Cocaine is classified as a stimulant and, as such, produces feelings of excitation, alertness, and euphoria. Although such prescription stimulants as methamphetamine and dextroamphetamine are commonly abused, over the past 10 to 20 years societal concern over drug abuse has focused on cocaine. Its increased use, addictive qualities, physiological effects, and worldwide distribution have fuelled such concerns. More than any other single substance, cocaine has led to the present "war on drugs."

Cocaine, which is made from the coca plant, has been used for thousands of years, and anti-cocaine sentiment did not emerge until the early twentieth century in either the United States or Canada. In the United States, where cocaine was heavily used by urban Blacks, "stereotypes about the effects of cocaine—particularly in producing 'superhuman strength, cunning and efficiency'" coincided "with a wave of repressive measured defined to ensure the subordination of blacks" (Giffen et al. 1991: 14). In Canada, it has been suggested that efforts to suppress the nonmedical use of cocaine stemmed from a highly publicized cocaine scare in Montreal and, in particular, the pioneering efforts of a probation officer of the Montreal Children's Aid Society (pp. 37, 85). In 1911, the *Opium and Drug Act* confined the legal use of cocaine and morphine to medical prescriptions and made any other possession a criminal offence. Cocaine remains an illicit drug under the 1997 *Controlled Drug and Substances Act* (CDSA), but its use and effects continue to be misunderstood. For example, a 1982 *Scientific American* article suggested that cocaine was no more habit forming than potato chips (Van Dyck and Byck 1982). The percentage of Canadians reporting cocaine use is low—below 1 percent. Its use is higher among Canadian men than among Canadian women, highest among 25- to 34-year-olds (followed by 35- to 44-year-olds and 20- to 25-year-olds), and varies regionally, with British Columbia having the highest rates of use and Newfoundland the lowest (CCSA 1999).

Crack is a crystallized product made by boiling a mixture of baking soda, water, and cocaine. The result, also called rock, base, and gravel, is relatively inexpensive and was not popular until the mid-1980s. Crack is one of the most dangerous drugs to surface in recent years. Crack dealers often give drug users their first few "hits" free, knowing the drug's intense high and addictive qualities are likely to lead to returning customers. Recent data, however, suggest that the number of new users may be decreasing as young people begin to associate crack use with "burnouts" and "junkies" (ONDCP 1998).

Other Drugs

Other drugs abused in Canada include "club drugs" (e.g., LSD, ecstasy), heroin, prescription drugs (e.g. tranquilizers, amphetamines), and inhalants (e.g., glue).

Club Drugs Club drugs is a general term used to refer to illicit, often synthetic drugs commonly used at nightclubs or all-night dances called raves. Club drugs include ecstasy (MDMA), ketamine ("Special K"), LSD ("acid"), GHB ("liquid ecstasy"), and Rohypnol ("roofies"). Ecstasy, manufactured and trafficked from Europe, is the most popular of the club drugs, ranging in price from $20 to $30 a dose (DEA 2000). Use of ecstasy is small compared with other drug use—less than one percent of the population—but is growing in numbers. Ecstasy is associated with feelings of euphoria and inner peace, yet critics argue that as the "new cocaine," both long-term (e.g., permanent brain damage) and short-term (e.g., hypothermia) negative effects are possible (Cloud 2000; DEA 2000).

Ketamine and LSD (lysergic acid diethylamide) both produce visual effects when ingested. Ketamine, an anaesthetic for human and animal use, costs veterinarians $7 a vial, drug dealers $30 to $40 a vial, and drug users $100 to $200 a vial. Use of ketamine can also cause loss of long-term memory, respiratory problems, and cognitive difficulties. LSD is a synthetic hallucinogen, although many other hallucinogens are produced naturally (e.g., peyote). Although the rate of hallucinogen use is low in Canada, one Ontario survey reported increased use of such hallucinogens as mescaline, psilocybin (magic mushrooms), and LSD in the late 1990s (CCSA 1999).

GHB (gamma hydroxybutyrate) and Rohypnol (flunitrazepam) are often called **date-rape drugs** because of their use in rendering victims incapable of resisting sexual assaults. Rohypnol, presently illegal in both Canada and the United States, is lawfully sold in Europe and Latin America. It belongs to a class of drugs known as benzodiazepines, which also includes such common prescription drugs as Valium, Halcion, and Xanax. Rohypnol is tasteless and odourless; 1 mg of the drug can incapacitate a victim for up to 12 hours (NIDA 2000b; DEA 2000). The first major seizure of Rohypnol occurred in Canada in January 1999, when 3500 doses were seized in a raid at a home in North Vancouver, B.C. Following the raid, a RCMP spokesperson remarked, "[T]he RCMP had been under the impression, up till now, that there wasn't any Rohypnol [problem] in Canada....Guess what—it's here, so we need to be concerned" (*Vancouver Sun*, January 26, 1999: A1).

Heroin In Canada, the most commonly injected drug is heroin. Although the precise number of illicit drug users who inject drugs is not known, it is estimated that in 1998 their numbers were between 50 000 and 100 000. Injected drug use is most common in Montreal, Toronto, and Vancouver. In 1999, an estimated

> ■ Crack is a drug peddler's dream: it is cheap, easily concealed and provides a short-duration high that invariably leaves the user craving more.
>
> TOM MARGANTHAU
> *Journalist*

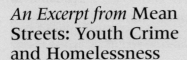
An Excerpt from Mean Streets: Youth Crime and Homelessness

In *Mean Streets: Youth Crime and Homelessness* (1997) Canadian sociologists John Hagan and Bill McCarthy describe the backgrounds and current experiences of homeless youths on the streets of two Canadian cities, Toronto and Vancouver. They report that substance abuse by parents and siblings is common in the backgrounds of these young people and that it is often coupled with poverty, neglect, and physical or sexual abuse.

Sebastian: "My parents threw me out....They're drug addicts. Hash, weed, coke, crack—everything....I didn't want to leave but they just threw me out. I had a huge fight with my dad. We'd fight 'cause I'd go, 'quit drugs,' and he would go 'no.'...I'd go, 'quit drinking.' He'd say 'no.' So we just argued about that most of the time. And one day he goes, 'I think it's about time you

leave, get on your own.' So I just left." (p. 25)

Robert: "Both my parents were alcoholics, and I had a younger sister and older brother, and, uh, it just got to a point...I mean, we used to get beat up at least four or five times a week. It got to a point where we'd hide and just wait for them to find us...and, um, finally I just couldn't take it anymore." (pp. 25–6)

Jeremy: "When I was 12, I was sent home from school, and my mom said, 'You're out of here' and I said, 'What do you mean?' and she goes, 'You're going to live with your father again.' I said, 'Oh shit.' So I went down to my father's. My dad was an alcoholic, and he always abused me—physically. He'd punch me and stuff like that—throw me up against the walls. And like one night we were going at it, and I turned around, like he punched me a couple of times. I turned around and got a baseball bat out of the bedroom, and I hit him in the head, and then he got back up, and he started pounding on me big time.

Well, the cops came and they took him, and they said 'You can go live with your mother, right?' My mother had already said, 'We don't want you,' so I said, 'Okay, I'm going to my mother's' and [instead] I went out in the streets." (p. 26)

Gord: "I started smoking dope when I was, like, 8, 9 years old, like literally when I was 8 or 9 years old....Just, sittin' around the pool halls, you know, people giving you joints and stuff....My family was always poor. Like my mom was always poor. She was, you know, she was always on welfare. So, my older brother sold dope, did whatever he could to make money to help out and to take care of himself. I used to hang out in a pool hall.... And all my brother's friends would get me to hold their dope and stuff, 'cause the cops would come in and I'd be playing video games, you know....After that it just, you know, I got to know when I was like 10, 10 years old I knew, you know, how to weigh out grams and knew there was sixteen ounces in a pound and

> The only livin' thing that counts is the fix....Like I would steal off anybody— anybody, at all, my own mother gladly included.
>
> *Heroin addict*

34 percent of all new HIV infections stemmed from injection drug use (Auditor General 2001). Among Indigenous people, the percentage of AIDS cases attributable to injection drug use is especially high and has risen dramatically over time (from 29.5 percent in 1992–1996 to 52.9 percent during 1997–2001). Among Aboriginals with a reported AIDS diagnosis up to December 31, 2001, 26.9 percent of males and 64.9 percent of women were injection drug users (Health Canada 2002). In Canada, as in other countries, injection drug use is a major cause of the heterosexual transmission of HIV infection, hepatitis, and other infectious diseases (Health Canada 1999).

Prescription Drugs Tranquilizers and antidepressants are often used in the treatment of psychiatric disorders. For example, Prozac, Valium, and Halcion are often prescribed for the treatment of insomnia, anxiety, and depression. In Canada, women are more likely than men are to use these types of drugs:

twenty-eight grams in an ounce. So when I needed to make my own money, it just seemed totally natural because I knew so many people that would, just, give me dope and say, 'Okay, pay me when you can, right?' It was pretty easy actually. It seemed like the only logical thing to do." (p. 111)

Hagan and McCarthy's research additionally notes that drug use is a common part of the daily lives of homeless youths themselves; more than 80 percent of their respondents acknowledged smoking marijuana, 55 percent used crack or other chemicals, and 43 percent used cocaine. However, they note that drug use is simply one part of the "downward spiral of deviance, danger, and despair" that marks the lives of street youths.

Eva: "Oh, it was fun for a while—we met some really nice people, lots of partying—but down here [Vancouver's East Side] it was different. I found like, people were more violent, and everybody was into using hard drugs, and every-

thing was just really different, and I ran into things, like I started prostituting and doing illegal stuff [using and selling heroin and armed robbery] and all kinds of crazy stuff down here." (pp. 113–14)

Jordy: "I was selling a bit of drugs here and there, stealing still, doing some shoplifting—videos and records from stores, clothing, everything basically. Just being a hustler, man, just going out and hustling money wherever which way I could. If I could con some old man on the street for five bucks, I'd do it." (p. 115)

Alan: "Like when I walk down the street and I see people panhandling for money, like, I turn around and I look at them, and I go, 'Why are you sittin' here panhandling for money? Why don't you sell some drugs, or go rob someone or something', right? Why do you have to, like, sit there and ask everyone walkin' by for some money?'" (p. 53)

Kathy: "I beat this girl, really, really bad. I was on acid. I was just mad at the whole world. I just wanted anybody to beat up, and she was

pouring, bleeding, and I was just hitting her with a steel bar and everything, and everybody's saying, 'What?' and I'm saying to everybody, 'Am I hurting her yet?' (p. 118)

Simon: "Fifty dollars that you make out there lasts about as long as five dollars does that you make from a paycheck....With myself I am so ashamed or so mad, and I have really bad feelings about pulling tricks, you know, like I was being used enough sexually in my life, and then I subject myself to it again. So then I need to sedate how I'm feeling, so I usually go and get really drunk. So then 80 percent of that money ends up being drinking money. And, like, you know, you have nothing to do all day and then having fifty bucks, you know, you're looking for a place to spend your money. You're looking for anything to entertain yourself." (p. 222)

SOURCE: Hagan, J., and Bill McCarthy. 1997. *Mean Streets: Youth Crime and Homelessness*. Cambridge, MA: Cambridge University Press. Reprinted with the permission of Cambridge University Press.

3.4 percent versus 2.0 for tranquilizers, 4.7 percent versus 2.5 percent for anti-depressants, and 4.0 percent versus 2.9 percent for sleeping pills. Their use is also more common among the elderly than among the young. For example, Canadians over the age of 75 have the highest level of use of sleeping pills (10.6 percent) and anti-depressants (5.3 percent), while those between the ages of 65 and 74 are most likely to use tranquilizers. The divorced, separated, or widowed in Canada are also more likely to use these drugs than those who are single or married, and the use of these drugs decreases as income increases (CCSA 1999). Despite the fact that these drugs are most often obtained through prescription, these drugs continue to be abused, and an illegal market for them persists.

Amphetamines are stimulants rather than "downers," and are legal when prescribed by a physician. Illegal use of amphetamines, made in clandestine laboratories, has increased in recent years. Worldwide, the production of amphetamines has increased dramatically in recent decades (*World Drug Report* 1997).

Inhalants Common inhalants include lighter fluid, air fresheners, hair spray, glue, paint, and correction fluid, although over 1000 other household products are currently abused. Canadian surveys suggest Canadians between the ages of 15 and 17 are the most likely to abuse inhalants (CCSA 1999). Regionally, solvents were used most by people in Quebec (0.2 percent), Ontario (0.1 percent), and Alberta (0.1 percent) (CCSA 1999). Solvent use is also considerably higher among Indian and Métis youth than among non-Indigenous populations (Gfellner and Hundelby 1995). Young people often use inhalants believing they are harmless, or that any harm caused requires prolonged use. In fact, inhalants are very dangerous because of their toxicity and may result in what is called Sudden Sniff Death Syndrome (Join Together 1998).

Societal Consequences of Drug Use and Abuse

Drugs are a social problem not only because of their adverse effects on individuals, but also as a result of the negative consequences their use has for society as a whole. Everyone is a victim of drug abuse. Drugs contribute to problems within the family and to crime rates, and the economic costs of drug abuse are enormous. Drug abuse also has serious consequences for health at both the individual and societal level.

Family Costs

The cost to families of drug use is incalculable. When one or both parents use or abuse drugs, needed family funds may be diverted to purchasing drugs rather than necessities. Children raised in such homes have a higher probability of neglect, behavioural disorders, and absenteeism from school, as well as lower self-concepts and increased risk of drug abuse (Easley and Epstein 1991; Tubman 1993; AP 1999; ONDCP 2000). Drug abuse is also associated with family disintegration. For example, alcoholics are seven times more likely to separate or divorce than nonalcoholics, and as many as 40 percent of family court problems are alcohol related (Sullivan and Thompson 1994: 347).

Abuse between intimates is also linked to drug use. Research indicates that between 25 to 50 percent of men who are involved in domestic violence have substance abuse problems, and drug use contributes to seven out of ten cases of child maltreatment (ONDCP 2000). In a study of 320 men who were married or living with someone, twice as many reported hitting their partner only after they had been drinking, compared with those who reported the same behaviour while sober (Leonard and Blane 1992). According to Statistics Canada's Violence Against Women Survey (VAWS), "women who are married or living with heavy drinkers are five times more likely to be assaulted by their partners than are women who live with nondrinkers" (Johnson 1996: 11). Half of all wife batterers in this survey were reported to have been drinking at the time they assaulted their wives. Women who suffered very serious abuse were approximately twice as likely to report that their spouse had been drinking at the time. The results of the VAWS indicate that "the more a man drinks the greater the likelihood that drinking will be involved in incidents of assault against his wife" (p. 1).

Crime Costs

One way of measuring the extent of the crime-drug problem, both nationally and internationally, is to consider the sales of illicit drugs. "While estimates vary, the United Nations believes that the annual global sales of illicit drugs are between $450 billion and $750 billion. In Canada, the government's estimates of sales range from $7 billion to $18 billion" (Auditor General 2001).

The drug behaviour of persons arrested, those incarcerated, and those in drug treatment programs provides evidence of the link between drugs and crime. Drug users commit a disproportionate number of crimes. In Vancouver, for example, it is estimated that 70 percent of criminal activity is associated with illicit drugs (Auditor General 2001). In 45 to 75 percent of date rape cases either the victim, the offender, or both had used alcohol (ONDCP 2000). Consider as well that, among those serving criminal sentences of over two years in length, almost two-thirds (63 percent) have drug abuse problems (Auditor General 2001). However, as Roth (1994) has observed, "Of all psychoactive substances, alcohol is the only one whose consumption has been shown to commonly increase aggression." In 1998, a Canadian survey reporting on the use of drugs and alcohol within solved firearm homicides from 1991 to 1996 found that the accused was reported to have used alcohol in 20.6 percent of these homicides, to have used both alcohol and drugs in 12.3 percent, and to have used drugs alone in 4.5 percent (Department of Justice 1998).

The relationship between crime and drug use, however, is a complex one. Sociologists disagree as to whether drugs actually "cause" crime or whether, instead, criminal activity leads to drug involvement. Further, because both crime and drug use are associated with low socioeconomic status, poverty may actually be the more powerful explanatory variable. After extensive study of the assumed drug-crime link, Gentry (1995) concludes that "the assumption that drugs and crime are causally related weakens when more representative or affluent subjects are considered" (p. 491).

In addition to the hypothesized crime–drug use link, some criminal offences are drug defined. For example, driving while intoxicated is one of the most common drug-related crimes. In 2001, Canadian police agencies reported over 90 000 incidents of impaired driving (Statistics Canada 2002b). Other criminal offences include possession, cultivation, production, and sale of controlled substances, public intoxication, and drunk and disorderly conduct. One may consider that in 1999, approximately 50 000 people in Canada were charged with offences under the Controlled Drugs and Substances Act in cases where the most serious offence was drug-related. As Table 3.3 indicates, 90 percent of the charges related to cannabis and cocaine. In 1999, cannabis accounted for more than two-thirds of these charges and approximately half of the charges laid were for possession. In that year, an estimated 19 percent of offenders in the federal correctional system were serving sentences for drug offences (Auditor General 2001). In 2001, there were almost 92 000 drug offences recorded by Canadian police agencies. Once again, cannabis offences were the most common and, in 2001, accounted for three out of four drug offences (Statistics Canada 2002b).

The relationship between drugs, organized crime and violence has become a major concern in Canada in recent years. In 1998, a federal government report on organized crime concluded that

I've never had the slightest problem defending clients whom other people have regarded as "professional" or "organized" criminals. I've defended such clients (among many other things) on drug-related charges of various kinds. I might have had a big problem, though, had I ever been called upon to defend the *idea* of say, trafficking in illicit drugs.

EDWARD L. GREENSPAN
Lawyer

■ **Table 3.3** *Number of Persons Charged* for Offences under the Controlled Drugs and Substances Act in Canada during 1999*

Substance	Possession	Trafficking	Importation	Cultivation	Total	Percentage
Heroin	351	800	23	–	1 174	21
Cocaine	3 375	6 990	184	–	10 549	21
Other drugs	1 797	1 561	157	–	3 515	7
Cannabis	21 381	8 112	157	4 697	34 347	70
Total	26 904	17 463	521	4 697	49 585	100
Percentage	54	35	1	10	100	

Note: Data report number of persons charged by most serious offence in a given incident. For example, if a person were charged with armed robbery and possession of a small quantity of drugs at the same time, the drug charge would not show up in the above figures. This prevents double counting of the number of persons charged.

*"Number of persons charged" means persons charged by police or persons whom the police recommended that charges should be laid against.

SOURCE: *Report of the Auditor General of Canada—2001*, Office of the Auditor General of Canada, 2001. Reproduced with the permission of the Minister of Public Works and Government Services, 2003.

the drug trade has a significant impact on Canadians and entails substantial violence....[W]ith drugs as its primary source of revenue, organized crime has intimidated police officers, judges, juries, and correctional officers. Such intimidation is a direct threat to Canada's philosophy of peace, order, and good government. Of note is that more than 150 deaths since 1994 have been attributed to "biker" wars in Quebec over control of organized crime, including the illicit drug trade. (Auditor General 2001)

The federal Integrated Proceeds of Crime initiative, whose mandate involves investigating organized crime groups and seizing assets gained through criminal activities is acknowledged as largely a drug-related initiative with an estimated 90 percent of seizures related to drugs. According to the RCMP's Performance Report, the value of assets seized in 1999–2000 was $32 million (Auditor General 2001). In addition, the 2001 Report of the Auditor General of Canada emphasizes that illicit drugs represent a continuing source of income for terrorist groups—a concern that has been echoed by the United Nations.

Economic Costs

The economic costs of drug use are high. As Health Canada (1999: 184) has noted, "The 'war on drugs' currently being waged by governments around the world consumes significant government resources in an attempt to deal with drug problems." In 1996, the Canadian Centre on Substance Abuse released a study that estimated that substance abuse cost more than $18.4 billion in Canada a year or $649 per capita. The largest economic costs for alcohol, which accounted for $7.5 billion, were for lost productivity due to sickness and premature death ($4.14 billion), followed by law enforcement ($1.36 billion), and direct health care costs ($1.30 billion). The economic costs of tobacco amounted to more than $9.6 billion—including $6.8 billion for lost productivity and $2.68 billion for direct health care costs. The costs of illicit drug use were estimated to be $1.4 billion, including $823 million for lost productivity due to sickness and disease and $400 million spent on the costs of law enforcement. Since then, the estimated costs have only gone up. For example, the 2001 Report of the Auditor General of Canada estimates that the economic costs of illicit drugs alone now exceed $5 billion a year in Canada (Auditor General 2001).

Health Costs

The physical health consequences of drug use for the individual are tremendous: shortened life expectancy; higher morbidity (e.g., cirrhosis of the liver, lung cancer); exposure to HIV infection, hepatitis, and other diseases through shared needles; a weakened immune system; birth defects such as fetal alcohol syndrome; drug addiction in children; and higher death rates. Death rates from drug-induced and alcohol-induced causes are significantly higher for males and First Nations peoples than for females and Whites (CCSA 1999; Health Canada 1999). However, the incidence of lung cancer in women has increased dramatically as their smoking rates have increased. In 1998, more Canadian women died from lung cancer (6500) than from breast cancer (5300); lung cancer accounts for almost one in three (32 percent) male cancer deaths and more than one in five female cancer deaths (22 percent) (Health Canada 1999).

Concern that on-the-job drug use may impair performance or cause fatal accidents has led to drug testing. For some employees, such tests are routine, both as a condition for employment and as a requirement for keeping their job. This chapter's *Focus on Technology* reviews some of the issues related to drug testing in Canada.

Heavy alcohol and drug use are also associated with negative consequences for an individual's mental health. Longitudinal data on both male and female adults have shown that drug users are more likely to suffer from anxiety disorders (e.g., phobias), depression, and antisocial personalities (White and Labouvie 1994). Other data confirm that drug users, particularly in adolescence, have a higher incidence of suicide (Bureau of Justice Statistics 1992; Cooper et al. 1992). Marijuana is also linked to short-term memory loss, learning disabilities, motivational deficits, and retarded emotional development.

The *societal* costs of drug-induced health concerns are also extraordinary. Health costs include the cost of disability insurance, the effects of second-hand smoke, the spread of AIDS, and the medical costs of accident and crime victims, as well as unhealthy infants and children. For example, cocaine use by pregnant women may lead to low birth weight babies, increased risk of spontaneous abortions, and abnormal placental functioning (Klutt 2000).

Treatment Alternatives

Drug treatment reduces drug use by approximately 40 to 60 percent and is as effective as treating many other chronic diseases (e.g., diabetes, asthma) (NIDA 1999: 15). Helping others to overcome chemical dependency is, however, expensive. For example, Health Canada's National Native Alcohol and Drug Abuse Programs spends about $80 million annually on substance abuse treatment and prevention for on-reserve Aboriginal people, with the majority of these funds used in relation to alcohol abuse (Auditor General 2001). Persons who are interested in overcoming chemical dependency have a number of treatment alternatives from which to choose. Some options include hospitalization, family therapy, counselling, private and public treatment facilities, behaviour

The Question of Drug Testing

The technology available to detect whether a person has taken drugs was used during the 1970s by crime laboratories, drug treatment centres, and the military. Today, employers in private industry have turned to chemical laboratories for help in making decisions on employment and retention, and parents and school officials use commercial testing devices to detect the presence of drugs. An individual's drug use can be assessed through the analysis of hair, blood, or urine. New technologies include portable breath (or saliva) alcohol testers, THC detection strips, passive alcohol sensors, interlock vehicle ignition systems, and fingerprint screening devices. Counter technologies have even been developed, for example, shampoos that rid hair of toxins and "Urine Luck," a urine additive that is advertised to speed the breakdown of unwanted chemicals.

Canadians are, perhaps, most familiar with drug testing in the context of international sporting events. For example, in August 1999, officials at the 1999 Pan American Games stripped the Canadian roller-hockey team of its gold medal when drug tests showed high levels of an anabolic steroid (Nadrolone) and two stimulants (ephedrine and pseudoephedrine) in the urine samples of the Canadian goaltender, Steve Vézina (Clark 1999: B14). Some argue that testing for drugs should not be limited to athletes but extended to those in a variety of jobs, including, for example, air traffic controllers, police officers, technicians at nuclear power plants, doctors, nurses, and school bus drivers (McMillan 1991: 30).

While workplace drug and alcohol testing is common in the United States, it is less so in Canada. In 1990, for example, the Toronto-Dominion Bank introduced a mandatory drug-testing policy for both newly hired and returning employees. According to the policy, screening employees for drug-use represented an attempt to "maintain a safe, healthy and productive workforce, to safeguard bank and customer funds and information and to protect the bank's policy" (Schmidt 2001). A complaint was filed with the Canadian Human Rights Tribunal that alleged that the policy constituted discrimination on the basis of disability ("any previous or existing mental or physical disability and includes disfigurement and previous or existing dependence on alcohol or a drug"). Although a Canadian Human Rights tribunal initially issued a finding of non-discrimination, a federal Court of Appeal ruled in 1998 that the policy *did* constitute "adverse-effect discrimination." As defined by then Supreme Court of Canada justice Bertha Wilson, adverse-effect discrimination refers to "a rule that is neutral on its face but has an adverse discriminatory effect on certain members of the group to whom it applies" (in Dranoff 2001: 38). In consequence, the policy was found to be in violation of the Canadian Human Rights Act because it could discriminate against certain employees and because it was not sufficiently related to job performance.

A similar decision was reached in relation to Imperial Oil's drug and alcohol testing policy for "safety-sensitive" positions within that company. In 1992, four employees of Imperial Oil filed complaints of discrimination with the Ontario Human Rights Commission. One of the complainants maintained that, despite giving up alcohol eight years earlier and participating in a company-sponsored substance-abuse program, he had been demoted as a result of the policy. The Ontario Human Rights Commission later ruled that, under the Ontario Human Rights Code, alcoholism is a handicap protected from discrimination and that the employer has the duty to accommodate the employee. The Commission ordered Imperial Oil to reinstate the employee in his "safety sensitive" position and awarded the complainant $21 241 in damages. When Imperial Oil appealed this decision, the Ontario Court of Appeal ruled in July 2000 that Imperial Oil's use of both a pre-employment drug screening test and random drug testing for employees was discriminatory and in violation of the province's human rights code. The court held that a Breathalyzer is permissible for people in high-risk jobs such as oil refinery workers, pilots, and train engineers because it determines whether someone is impaired at the moment the test is administered. However, because drug testing only measures past use, not present impairment, future impairment or likely impairment on the job, the court ruled that Imperial Oil could not justify pre-employment testing or random drug testing for employees.

Under the *Canadian Human Rights Act*, which applies to federal government employees, Crown corporations, and companies in the federal jurisdiction (e.g., banks and air-lines), discrimination based on alcohol or drug dependency is prohibited. In 1999, the Canadian Human Rights Commission instituted a policy on drug testing which specified that, unless safety is an issue, drug testing cannot be justified as a bona fide occupational requirement. However, while drug test requirements by employers in the federal jurisdiction are normally considered to be discriminatory, "[n]o law in Canada states that it is illegal for an employer to insist, before or after hiring, that an employee take a test to confirm the absence of drug use....There is also no constitutional protection against drug testing" (Dranoff 2001: 37). In consequence, a prospective employee who is asked to take a drug test and refuses cannot later complain if he or she is not hired. Similarly, if the job applicant consents to take the test and it reveals drug use, the applicant may have no legal remedy if he or she is not hired. "It all depends on whether freedom from drug use is a reasonable requirement of the job, and therefore whether human rights protections are infringed" (Dranoff 2001: 37).

Some maintain that if employees in any industry are using drugs, human lives may be in jeopardy because of impaired job perfor-mance. An alternative perspective is that drug testing may be harmful. One concern is accuracy of the tests. Faulty tests may result in either "false positives" (the person who does not use drugs is identified as doing so) or "false negatives" (the person who uses drugs is identified as not doing so). The false-positives problem is serious: an innocent person could lose his or her job because of faulty technology (Brannigan 2000). A second concern is that drug testing may also reveal that a person is pregnant, is being treated for heart disease, or has epilepsy. The person may want these aspects of his or her private life to remain private (Kahn 2000). Third, as we have seen, drug testing may violate basic human rights. The question in a complex and increasingly technologically dependent society is how to balance the rights of an individual with the needs of society as a whole.

SOURCES: Brannigan, Mariha. 2002. "Labs that Test Transportation Workers for Drugs Face Inquiry Over Samples." *Wall Street Journal*, October 2: A4. Dranoff, Linda Silver. 2001. *Everyone's Guide to the Law*, 2nd ed. Toronto: HarperCollins Publishers Ltd. Kahn, Jeffery. 2000. "Criminally Pregnant." CNN.com. October 30. Schmidt, Steve. 2001. "Canadian Courts Restrict Drug Tests." *National Post*, December 19: A1, A8. Clark, Campbell. 1999. "Vézina Says Sorry, but Not for Taking Banned Substances." *National Post*, August 3: B14. McMillan, D. 1991. *Winning the Battle against Drugs*. New York: Franklin Watts.

modification, pharmacotherapy (use of treatment medications), community care programs, drug maintenance programs, and employee assistance programs. Two commonly used techniques are inpatient/outpatient programs and supportive communities.

Inpatient/Outpatient Treatment

Inpatient treatment refers "to the treatment of drug dependence in a hospital and includes medical supervision of detoxification" (McCaffrey 1998: 2). Most inpatient programs last between 30 and 90 days and target individuals whose withdrawal symptoms require close monitoring (e.g., alcoholics, cocaine addicts). Some drug-dependent patients, however, can be safety treated as outpatients. Outpatient treatment allows individuals to remain in their home and work environments and is often less expensive. In outpatient treatment the patient is under the care of a physician who evaluates the patient's progress regularly, prescribes needed medication, and watches for signs of a relapse.

The longer a patient stays in treatment, the greater the likelihood of a successful recovery. Variables that predict success include the user's motivation to change, support of family and friends, criminal justice or employer intervention, a positive relationship with therapeutic staff, and a program of recovery that addresses many of the needs of the patient.

Peer Support Groups

Twelve-Step Programs Both Alcoholics Anonymous (AA) and Narcotics Anonymous (NA) are voluntary associations whose only membership requirement is the desire to stop drinking or taking drugs. AA and NA are self-help groups in that they are operated by nonprofessionals, offer "sponsors" to each new member, and proceed along a continuum of 12 steps to recovery. Members are immediately immersed in a fellowship of caring individuals with whom they meet daily or weekly to affirm their commitment. Some have argued that AA and NA members trade their addiction to drugs for feelings of interpersonal connectedness by bonding with other group members.

> AA members essentially trade addiction to the bottle to a network of friends who share a common bond.
>
> **BARRY LUBETKIN**
> *Psychologist*

Symbolic interactionists emphasize that AA and NA provide social contexts in which people develop new meanings. Abusers are surrounded by others who convey positive labels, encouragement, and social support for sobriety. Sponsors tell the new members that they can be successful in controlling alcohol and drugs "one day at a time" and provide regular interpersonal reinforcement for doing so. Although thought of as a "crutch" by some, AA members may also take medications to help prevent relapses. In a study of 222 AA members, Rychtarik and colleagues (2000) found that although over half of those surveyed thought the use of relapse-preventing medication was or might be a good idea, 29 percent reported pressures from others to stop taking the medication.

Therapeutic Communities In **therapeutic communities**, which house between 35 and 500 people for up to 15 months, participants abstain from drugs, develop marketable skills, and receive counselling. Synanon, which was established in 1958, was the first therapeutic community for alcoholics and was later expanded to include other drug users. The longer a person stays at such a facility, the greater the chance of overcoming the dependency. Symbolic inter-actionists argue that behavioural changes appear to be a consequence of revised self-definition and the positive expectations of others.

In the United States, Stay'N Out, a therapeutic community for the treatment of incarcerated drug offenders, has demonstrated its success in reducing recidi-vism. When participating in the program for at least nine months, only 23 per-cent of the inmates reoffended, compared with 50 percent of those not receiving treatment. The Cornerstone Program has also been successful with drug abusers in prison. Both programs include a holistic treatment approach that focuses on the social and psychological difficulties of returning to acceptable social roles (Lipton 1994: 336). However, in Canada, there are no therapeutic communities for the treatment of incarcerated drug users outside Quebec, which runs both the ECHO and STOP programs. Elsewhere, the two core substance abuse pro-grams offered by Corrections Canada are the Offender Substance Pre-release Program (which involves approximately 32 three-hour counselling sessions offered over several months), and Choices (a cognitive-behavioural modifica-tion program that involves approximately 60 hours of counselling over three to four months).

Strategies for Action: Canada Responds

Drug use is a complex social issue exacerbated by the structural and cultural forces of society that contribute to its existence. While the structure of society perpetuates a system of inequality creating in some the need to escape, the cul-ture of society, through the media and normative contradictions, sends mixed messages about the acceptability of drug use. Thus, developing programs, laws, or initiatives that are likely to end drug use may be unrealistic. Nevertheless, since 1987 Canada's Drug Strategy has emphasized the need for a "balanced" approach that combines prevention and education with law enforcement. Among its stated objectives: "reducing the demand for drugs; reducing drug-related mortality and morbidity by reducing high-risk behaviours, such as spreading HIV/AIDS through needle sharing; improving the effectiveness of and accessibility to substance abuse information and interventions; restricting the supply of illicit drugs; reducing the profitability of illicit trafficking; and reducing the costs of substance abuse to Canadian society" (Auditor General 2001).

In recent years, the majority of the federal government's changes to legisla-tion in relation to illicit drugs have targeted the issue of supply rather than demand. These efforts have included the amendment of the Canadian Criminal Code to include organized crime offences and the creation of the Financial Transactions and Reports Analysis Centre of Canada. The latter attempts to detect money laundering by monitoring financial transactions (see Table 3.4).

> ▪ Managing the illicit drug problem in Canada is inherently difficult. It requires the efforts of three levels of government—federal, provincial/ territorial, and municipal—and many non-government organizations....Although integrating the efforts of three levels of government is difficult, it is essential.
>
> **Report of the Auditor General of Canada—2001**

Government Regulations

Drawing upon Solomon (1999), we will review some of the major federal and provincial alcohol and drug laws. In Canada, the federal government regulates the importation and exportation of alcohol products, alcohol-related excise taxes, and broadcast advertising. At present, the federal regulations prohibit

■ **Table 3.4** *Addressing Illegal Drugs: The Federal Infrastructure*

Federally, 11 departments and agencies are involved in addressing illicit drug use in Canada. The major ones are:	
Health Canada	provides the leadership and coordination for Canada's Drug Strategy. It is involved directly in activities to reduce the demand for and the supply of illicit drugs. Its Office of Controlled Substances is responsible for the legislative control framework to control illicit drugs. The office administers the regulations of the *Controlled Drugs and Substances Act*, which includes processing the licensing and permit requirement for the use of controlled substances for legitimate purposes. The Office of Cannabis Medical Access deals with controls on the medical use of marijuana.
Solicitor General Canada	plays a leadership and coordinating role in policing, security and corrections under Canada's Drug Strategy. The Department is also engaged in related activities both domestically and internationally.
RCMP	The RCMP's federal drug efforts focus on such activities as seizing drugs, investigating and arresting the upper echelon of criminal organizations involved in the drug trade, and seizing proceeds of crime. The RCMP also undertakes drug enforcement as part of the provincial and municipal policing responsibilities it performs on contract. In addition to participation in many "joint force operations" aimed at combating organized crime, the RCMP also delivers drug prevention programs. It makes some 8000 presentations annually to students, parents, employees, and community groups.
Department of Justice	prosecutes drug cases and provides expertise to the development of legislation addressing organized crime. It has a pilot initiative, the Toronto Drug Treatment Court Program, that offers alternatives to traditional prosecution.
Canada Customs and Revenue Agency	contributes to reducing the supply of illicit drugs in two ways. Customs intercepts illegal drugs entering Canada at our borders. For instance, it estimates that in 1999 it seized illicit drugs with a street value estimated at $351 million. Taxation audits individuals suspected of selling illicit drugs or engaging in other illegal activities and raises assessments and levies penalties where it finds unreported income. Taxation also investigates suspected tax evasion and recommends prosecution of individuals.
Correctional Services Canada	is responsible for offenders serving criminal sentences over two years. These include individuals convicted of serious drug offences. CSC provides substance abuse and treatment programs to offenders with drug problems. It also uses security measures, including the use of sniffer dogs and urinalysis testing, to control the supply of illicit drugs in prisons.
Department of Foreign Affairs and International Trade	collaborates with other federal departments and represents Canada in the international aspects of Canada's Drug Strategy.

SOURCE: *Report of the Auditor General of Canada—2001*, Office of the Auditor General of Canada, 2001. Reproduced with the permission of the Minister of Public Works and Government Services, 2003.

broadcasting a range of messages, including those that encourage non-drinkers to consume alcohol; that direct their appeal to minors; that suggest that alcohol use is positively associated with social acceptance, personal accomplishment, or success in athletic or business endeavours; or that link the consumption of alcohol with high-risk activities. In addition, the provinces have some degree of control over the marketing and advertising of alcohol including such market practices as price discounting, drinking contests, the use of alcohol as prizes, or the dispensing of free drinks. The majority of provincial advertising regulations target lifestyle advertising that might otherwise encourage youths to drink, drink large amounts of alcohol, or drink and drive. Each province in Canada also regulates the control and sale of alcohol in its province. Currently, the legal drinking age in all Canadian provinces and territories is 19 with the exception of Quebec, Manitoba, and Alberta, where the minimum age is 18.

Under the Canadian *Criminal Code*, there are four specific types of drinking-and-driving offences. The first is "operating or having care or control of a motor vehicle while one's ability to drive is impaired by alcohol or a drug." The term "drug" is broadly defined here to include any substance, legal or illegal, which can cause impairment. The second type of offence is "[e]ngaging in impaired driving causing death or bodily harm." The 1985 introduction of this offence was intended to make the penalties for causing serious accidents while impaired harsher than those for "simply" driving while impaired. The maximum penalty for impaired driving causing bodily harm is 10 years' imprisonment and 10 years' driving prohibition; the maximum penalty for impaired driving causing death is 14 years' imprisonment and 10 years' driving prohibition. The third type is "[o]perating or having care or control of a motor vehicle with a blood alcohol concentration (BAC) over 0.08 percent." Even if you drive safely, driving with a BAC over this level is a criminal offence in Canada. The specific amount of alcohol that must be consumed to have a BAC over the specified level can vary depending on such factors as, for example, when the individual last ate, that person's weight and percentage of body fat, and how quickly the alcohol was consumed. Nevertheless, BAC can be determined through an analysis of a person's blood or urine. The final type of offence is "[f]ailing to provide breath or blood samples for analysis without a reasonable excuse." The term "reasonable excuse" refers to, for example, an inability to comprehend the demand or to physically comply with it. The minimum penalty for both the third and fourth types of offence is a $300 fine and a three-month driving prohibition for a first offence, 14 days' imprisonment and a six-month driving prohibition for a second offence, and 90 days' imprisonment and a one-year driving prohibition for a subsequent offence. The maximum penalty when charged as a summary conviction offence is a $2000 fine, six months' imprisonment, and a three-year driving prohibition. As an indictable offence, the maximum penalty is five years' imprisonment, a three-year driving prohibition, and a fine of any amount that may be imposed by the court.

In addition, provincial highway traffic legislation gives police the authority to stop vehicles in a random manner to determine whether the driver has been drinking; the provinces also have the authority to issue, suspend, revoke, and reinstate driving licences. The majority of Canadian provinces have created provisions for automatic provincial licence suspensions such that a person convicted of any federal drinking and driving offence is subject to an automatic mandatory provincial licence suspension. The length of the suspension for a first, second, or subsequent conviction varies in the different provinces and territories. For example, in Manitoba, a 12-month suspension is given for a first offence and a five-year suspension for a second; in Alberta and Saskatchewan, the respective time periods are one and two years, and, in the Yukon, three months and a year. Moreover, with the exception of Nova Scotia and Quebec, provincial legislation authorizes police to temporarily suspend a driver's licence at roadside if, for example, a driver refuses an officer's demand to provide a breath sample or registers a BAC of 0.05 or higher. In the majority of provinces, the duration of the suspension is 24 hours. Six provinces have enacted additional legislation that authorizes police to impose 90-day administrative licence suspensions (ALS) on those who register a BAC over 0.08 percent or refuse to provide a breath or blood sample. The provinces have also created several drinking-and-driving countermeasures, such as graduated licence programs for new drivers, which require that they abstain from drinking any alcohol prior to driving; vehicle impoundment programs to deter offenders from driving while prohibited or suspended; alcohol interlock programs, which involve the connection of a small breath-testing instrument to a vehicle that prevents it from being started or driven if the driver's BAC is over a preset limit; and mandatory remedial measures that require offenders to attend, for example, an alcohol awareness program for a first offence or, for a second or subsequent offence, undergo alcohol assessment or participate in a treatment program. The cost of participating in such programs is generally borne by the offender.

In Canada, the *Controlled Drugs and Substances Act* outlines the six federal criminal offences of possession, trafficking, possession for the purpose of trafficking, production, importing or exporting, and "prescription shopping." While the penalties for possession vary depending on the type of drug, the maximum penalties under this act for the majority of offences are severe. For example, for "Schedule 1 Drugs" (i.e., cocaine, heroin, opium, phencyclidine, and those drugs that, prior to May 1997, were dealt with under the Narcotics Control Act), the maximum penalty for trafficking, possession for the purpose of trafficking, producing, and importing and exporting is life imprisonment. Life imprisonment is also the maximum penalty for importing or exporting any amount of any form of cannabis.

We earlier noted federal and provincial legislation that regulates tobacco in Canada. In addition to those previously noted, British Columbia has enacted legislation "to assist the provincial government and smokers in suing tobacco manufacturers to recover for tobacco-related costs, illness and disabilities. Moreover, the province has sued the manufacturers for the smoking-related costs that the government has incurred" (Solomon 1999: 309). Although similar legislation is being contemplated in other Canadian provinces, the tobacco companies have, not unexpectedly, challenged the constitutionality of this measure.

Despite all the attempts to regulate the use of alcohol and drugs, some would argue that the war on drugs has done more harm than good. Duke and Gross (1994) argue that the war on drugs, much like Prohibition, has only intensified other social problems: drug-related gang violence and turf wars, the creation of syndicate-controlled black markets, unemployment, the spread of AIDS, overcrowded prisons, corrupt law enforcement officials, and the diversion of police from other serious crimes. Consistent with conflict theory, still others argue that the "war on drugs" is a war on the poor, while the drug use of the affluent goes largely ignored (Duster 1995).

Further, national drug policies have implications that extend beyond domestic concerns. They can affect international relations and the economies of foreign countries. Many of the countries in which drug trafficking occurs are characterized by government corruption and crime, military coups, and political instability. Some argue that trade sanctions should be imposed in addition to crop eradication programs and interdiction efforts. Others, however, noting the relative failure of such programs in reducing the supply of illegal drugs entering the country, argue that the "war on drugs" should be abandoned and that legalization is preferable to the side effects of regulation.

Deregulation or Legalization: The Debate

Deregulation is the reduction of government control over certain drugs. For example, Ontario has opened up the sale of wine to private stores. Since 1999, Canadians who require marijuana for medical purposes have been able to apply for an exemption under Section 56 of the Controlled Drugs and Substances Act. In 2002, over 800 Canadians were permitted by Health Canada to possess marijuana for medical purposes. Moreover, the Marijuana Medical Access Regulations (MMAR) allow people with authorizations to possess and cultivate marijuana for medical purposes (McLellan 2002). Extending this approach, in April 1999, the board of directors of the Association of Canadian Police Chiefs made a recommendation to the federal government that simple possession of marijuana and hashish be **decriminalized**—that is, that it no longer be an offence under the Criminal Code. They suggested that this strategy would clear a backlog of drug cases in the courts and allow Canadian police services to focus their resources on more serious crimes like drug trafficking (Fife 1999). Currently, about 2000 Canadians go to jail every year for cannabis possession at a cost of approximately $150 per day per offender (CCSA 1999). Decriminalization would promote a medical rather than criminal approach to drug use that would encourage users to seek treatment and adopt preventive practices. For example, making it a criminal offence to sell or possess hypodermic needles without a prescription encourages the use of nonsterile needles that spread infections such as HIV and hepatitis.

Proponents for the **legalization** of drugs affirm the right of adults to make an informed choice. They also argue that the tremendous revenues realized from drug taxes could be used to benefit all citizens, that purity and safety controls could be implemented, and that legalization would expand the number of distributors, thereby increasing competition and reducing prices. Drugs would thus be safer, drug-related crimes would be reduced, and production and distribution of previously controlled substances would be taken out of the hands of the underworld.

Those in favour of legalization also suggest that the greater availability of drugs would not increase demand, pointing to countries where some drugs have already been legalized or decriminalized.

Opponents of legalization argue that it would be construed as government approval of drug use and, consequently, drug experimentation and abuse would increase. Further, although the legalization of drugs would result in substantial revenues for the government, because some drugs (e.g., crack) some would remain illegal, drug trafficking and black markets would still flourish. Legalization would also require an extensive and costly bureaucracy to regulate the manufacture, sale, and distribution of drugs. Finally, the position that drug use is an individual's right cannot guarantee that others will not be harmed. It is illogical to assume that a greater availability of drugs will translate into a safer society.

Collective Action

If some drunk gets out and kills your kid, you'd probably be a little crazy about it, too.

KATHY PRESCOTT
Former MADD President

Social action groups such as Mothers Against Drunk Driving **(MADD)** have successfully lobbied legislators to lower maximum blood alcohol levels for drivers and to introduce zero allowable blood alcohol for young drivers. MADD, with 3.5 million members and 600 chapters in North America, has also put pressure on alcohol establishments to stop "two-for-one" offers and has pushed for laws that hold the bartenders personally liable if a served person is later involved in an alcohol-related accident. Even hosts in private homes can now be held liable if they allow a guest to drive who became impaired while drinking at their house. Most importantly perhaps, MADD seeks to change the meaning of alcohol use by, for example, redefining drunk driving "accidents" as violent crimes.

Sensitized to the danger of driving while impaired, some high-school principals and school boards have encouraged students to become members of Students Against Drunk Driving (SADD). Members often sign a formal pledge and put an emblem on their car to signify a commitment against alcohol. "Dry grads" also encourage students to refrain from drinking alcohol. To reduce the number of teenagers driving while drinking, local groups of parents have also organized parties at bowling alleys or school gyms as alternatives to high-school graduation parties.

Understanding Alcohol and Other Drugs

In summarizing what we know about substance abuse, drugs and their use are socially defined. As the structure of society changes, the acceptability of one drug or another changes as well. As conflict theorists assert, the status of a drug as legal or illegal is intricately linked to those who have the power to define acceptable and unacceptable drug use. There is also little doubt that rapid social change, anomie, alienation, and inequality further drug use and abuse. Symbolic interactionism also plays a significant role in the process—if people are labelled as "drug users" and expected to behave accordingly, drug use is likely to continue. If there is positive reinforcement of and/or a biological predisposition to use drugs, the probability of drug involvement is even higher. Thus, the theories of drug use complement rather than contradict one another.

Drug use must also be conceptualized within the social context in which it occurs. In a study of high-risk youths who had become involved with drugs, Dembo et al. (1994) suggest that many youths in their study had been "failed by society":

> Many of them were born into economically-strained circumstances, often raised by families who neglected or abused them, or in other ways did not provide for their nurturance and wholesome development...Few youths in our sample received the mental health and substance abuse treatment services they needed. (p. 25)

However, many treatment alternatives, emanating from a clinical model of drug use, assume that the origin of the problem lies within the individual rather than in the structure and culture of society. Although admittedly the problem may lie within the individual at the time treatment occurs, policies that address the social causes of drug abuse provide a better means of dealing with the drug problem in Canada.

Prevention is preferable to intervention, and given the social portrait of hard drug users—young, male, minority—prevention must entail dealing with the social conditions that foster drug use. Some data suggest that marginal youth are particularly vulnerable to drug involvement because of their lack of legitimate alternatives (Van Kammen and Loeber 1994):

> Illegal drug use may be a way to escape the strains of the severe urban conditions and dealing illegal drugs may be one of the few, if not the only, ways to provide for material needs. Intervention and treatment programs, therefore, should include efforts to find alternate ways to deal with the limiting circumstances of inner-city life, as well as create opportunities for youngsters to find more conventional ways of earning a living. (p. 22)

However, social policies dealing with drug use have been predominantly punitive rather than preventive.

In Canada and throughout the world, millions of people depend on legal drugs for the treatment of a variety of conditions, including pain, anxiety and nervousness, insomnia, depression, and fatigue. Although drugs used for these purposes are relatively harmless, the cultural message "better living through chemistry" contributes to alcohol and drug use and their consequences. But these and other drugs are embedded in a political and economic context that determines who defines what drugs, in what amounts, are licit or illicit and what programs are developed in reference to them.

Critical Thinking

1 Are alcoholism and other drug addictions a consequence of nature or nurture? If nurture, what environmental factors contribute to such problems? Which of the three sociological theories best explains drug addiction?

2 Measuring alcohol and drug use is often very difficult. This is particularly true given the tendency for respondents to acquiesce, that is, respond in a way they believe is socially desirable. Consider this and other problems in doing research on alcohol and other drugs, and how such problems could be remedied.

3 If, as symbolic interactionists argue, social problems are those conditions so defined, how might the manipulation of social definitions virtually eliminate many "drug" problems?

Key Terms

anomie	decriminalization	gateway drug
chemical dependency	deregulation	legalization
club drugs	drug	MADD
crack	drug abuse	therapeutic communities
date-rape drugs	drug addiction	

4

Crime and Violence

Outline

The Global Context:
International Crime and Violence

Sources of Crime Statistics

Sociological Theories of Crime
and Violence

Types of Crime

Demographic Patterns of Crime

Costs of Crime and Violence

Strategies for Action: Responding
to Crime and Violence

Understanding Crime
and Violence

Is It True?

1. In 2001, about half of the 2.4 million *Criminal Code* incidents (excluding traffic offences) reported to Canadian police services involved violent crimes.

2. Although sociologists have different theories about the causes of crime, they agree that crime is always harmful to society.

3. The majority of Canadians believe that capital punishment should be exercised in some circumstances.

4. Less than 1 percent of Canadians regard prostitution as a "very serious" social issue.

5. The majority of Canadian homicide victims had some type of relationship with their murderers.

Answers: 1 = F, 2 = F, 3 = T, 4 = T, 5 = T

U

njust social arrangements are themselves a kind of extortion, even violence.

JOHN RAWLS
A Theory of Justice

On November 22, 1999, the cover story of Time *magazine directed attention to the Pokémon craze among children 12 years of age and under and pointedly drew attention to two incidents, one in Laval, Quebec, and the other in Long Island, New York, in which one preteen had stabbed another in a dispute over the collectible cards (Chua-Eoan and Larimer 1999). While the Pokémon craze is new, the suggestion that certain recreational activities lead to crime or are criminogenic is not. Olmsted (1988) has noted that, in the past, such diverse pastimes as billiards, parachuting, surfing, pinball, attending the theatre, amateur archaeology, horse racing, butterfly collecting, motorcycling, target shooting, and ballroom dancing have all been identified as morally disreputable and socially problematic activities. In the 1950s, a book entitled* Seduction of the Innocent *blamed the increase in crime in general, and juvenile delinquency in particular, on the reading of comic books (Gorelick 1992). Since that time, various social commentators have suggested that crime is best explained with reference to such activities as listening to rap music, watching certain television programs or cartoons, playing certain video games, or surfing the Internet. All attest to our continuing attempts to understand and prevent crime in our society.*

The social problems of crime and violence rank among Canadians' foremost social concerns (Bibby 2001). This chapter examines the criminal justice system as well as theories, types, and demographic patterns of criminal behaviour. The economic, social, and psychological costs of crime and violence are also examined. The chapter concludes with a discussion of social policies and prevention programs designed to reduce crime and violence in Canada.

The Global Context: International Crime and Violence

According to the *United Nations Global Report on Crime and Justice*, several facts about crime are true throughout the world. First, crime is ubiquitous; that is, there is no country where crime does not exist. Second, most countries have the same components in their criminal justice system—police, courts, and prisons. Third, worldwide, adult males comprise the largest category of crime suspects, and, fourth, there is no general trend toward increased use of incarceration. Finally, in all countries, theft is the most common crime committed, with violent crime being a relatively rare event—about 10 to 15 percent of all reported crime (Global Report 1999).

Dramatic differences do exist, however, in international crime and violence rates. While tiny Gibraltar, with a total area of 6.5 square kilometres, has the

With ready-made opinions one cannot judge of crime. Its philosophy is a little more complicated than people think. It is acknowledged that neither convict prisons, nor the hulks, nor any system of hard labour ever cured a criminal.

FYODOR DOSTOYEVSKY
Writer

Crime is no longer bound by the constraints of borders. Such offences as terrorism, nuclear smuggling, computer crime, and drug trafficking can spill over from other countries.

LOUIS FREEH
Director, FBI

That the violent crime rate of the Canadian metropolis is only 10 to 20 percent of that of the American (murders average 70 a year in Toronto but 700 in Detroit) is more than a matter of strict gun control in Canada and the lack of it in the United States. It is a matter of the two societies differing in their attitudes toward authority.

WILLIAM KILBOURN
Historian

highest reported crime rate of any country in the world (at 18 316 per 100 000 population) (Ash 2001: 66), in general, industrialized countries have higher rates of reported crime than nonindustrialized countries. There are also variations within industrialized countries. The U.S. homicide rate is three times higher than Canada's, four times higher than Western Europe's, six times higher than Great Britain's, and seven times higher than Japan's (Doyle 2000; Gannon 2001) (see Figure 4.1).

Recent concerns have focused on **transnational crime**, defined by the United Nations as "offences whose inception, prevention, and/or direct or indirect effects involve more than one country" (Finckenauer 2000: 3). For example, Russian arms and precious metals are smuggled out of that country daily. Chinese triads operate in large cities worldwide, netting billions of dollars a year from prostitution, drugs, and other organized crime activities; children are trafficked throughout Canada, the United States, and Mexico for use in pornography rings; and Colombian cocaine cartels flourish and spread to sub-Saharan countries with needy economies (United Nations 1997; INTERPOL, 1998; Finckenauer 2000). Transnational crime is facilitated by recent trends in globalization, including enhanced transportation and communication technologies. For example, recent estimates suggest that, worldwide, there are over 100000 Web sites involved in child pornography (ABCNews 2001).

Figure 4.1 *Rates of Homicide, Canada and the United States, 1961–2000*

SOURCE: Gannon, Marie. 2001. "Crime Comparisons Between Canada and the United States." Canadian Centre for Justice Statistics, Cat. No. 85-002-XPE, 21(11): 5.

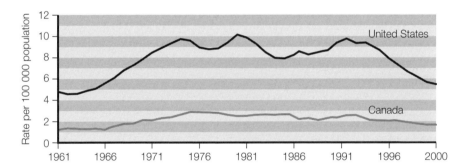

Sources of Crime Statistics

From the *National Symbol of Canada Act*, which identifies the beaver as symbolic of Canadian sovereignty, to the *Income Tax Act*, whose rules and regulations are bound in an almost 2000-page volume amended yearly, our social life is bound together by laws (Statistics Canada 1998). Although there are 40 000 federal and provincial statutes and a broad range of municipal bylaws that define behaviour in violation of some penal law, "[u]nder the terms of the *Constitution Act*, only those offences defined by federal law can technically be called crimes" (Brantingham et al. 1995). Most of the behaviours that we would commonly recognize as crimes (e.g., assault, kidnapping, sexual assault, murder) are contained within the federal *Criminal Code*. Unlike the United States, which has many state criminal codes, Canada has a single criminal code.

A simple definition of **crime** would be "any act that violates the criminal law." For a violation to be a crime, however, the offender must have acted voluntarily and with intent and have no legally acceptable excuse (such as insanity) or justification (such as self-defence) for the behaviour. Three major types of statistics are used to measure crime: official statistics, victimization surveys, and self-report offender surveys.

Official Statistics

Since the establishment of the first modern police force, the London Metropolitan Police Force (Scotland Yard) in 1829, police agencies have collected information about crime. Systematic national police statistics have been collected since 1857 in England and Wales, since 1920 in Canada, and since 1930 in the United States (Brantingham et al. 1995). Since 1962, Canada has used a system called the Canadian Uniform Crime Reports (UCR) that was developed by Statistics Canada and the Canadian Association of Chiefs of Police "to provide a measure of reliability for crime statistics through providing police agencies with a standardized set of procedures for collecting and reporting crime information" (Evans and Himelfarb 2000).

Under the UCR system, information is collected monthly from more than 400 municipal police departments, services, and agencies across Canada on 91 detailed categories of crime and offences. This information is compiled and published each year with counts and calculated rates per 100 000 population presented for each province and territory and for Canada as a whole. Within UCRs, crimes known to the police are grouped into major categories of crime. For example, "Crimes of Violence" group together such acts as homicide, attempted homicide, assault, abduction, sexual assault, and robbery. "Property Offences" include such offences as breaking and entering, theft of motor vehicles, possession of stolen goods, fraud, and so on. Uniform Crime Reports additionally provide information on the numbers of persons charged with different types of offences, with separate counts for adults and youths, males and females. The crimes known to police are compiled and published annually in Canada by the Canadian Centre for Justice Statistics (CCJS), the operational arm of the National Justice Statistics Initiative (NJSI). Since its establishment in 1985, the mandate of the NJSI has been (a) "[t]o provide information to the justice community and the public on the nature and extent of crime and the administration of criminal justice in Canada," and (b) to direct energies toward "the production of useful information to support the legislative, policy, management and research agenda of the Partners, and to inform the public" (CCJS 1999).

These statistics have several shortcomings (DiIulio 1999) (see this chapter's *Social Problems Research Up Close* feature). Not only do many incidents of crime go unreported, but also not all crimes reported to the police are recorded. Alternatively, some rates may be exaggerated. Motivation for such distortions may come from the public (e.g., demanding that something be done) or from political or organizational pressures (e.g., budget requests). For example, a police department may "crack down" on drug-related crimes in a given year. The result is an increase in the recorded number of these offences. Such an increase reflects a change in the behaviour of law enforcement personnel, not a change in the number of drug violations. Thus, official crime statistics may be a better indicator of what police are doing than what criminals are doing.

What's Wrong with These Numbers?

We tend to invest statistics with tremendous authority. But like any other information, how useful they are depends on how and why they are collected.

These numbers were complied from records collected and distributed every day to the media by the Metropolitan Toronto Police. *Globe and Mail* reporter Gay Abbate sifted through each day's records for 1992 and 1993 and picked out robberies and attempted robberies and the victim's description of each robber. She then sorted the suspected robbers into groups according to the race the police had recorded for each. (Toronto police are not allowed to compile such data themselves.)

The *Globe and Mail* attempted this exercise to show the difficulties in collecting statistics by race. While the chart conveys some information, the overwhelming number of caveats shows how unreliable such numbers can be.

Many people think any attempt to link crime with the skin colour of a suspect is spurious. Others believe that if the method of collecting them were improved, they could say a great deal about discrimination against a particular group.

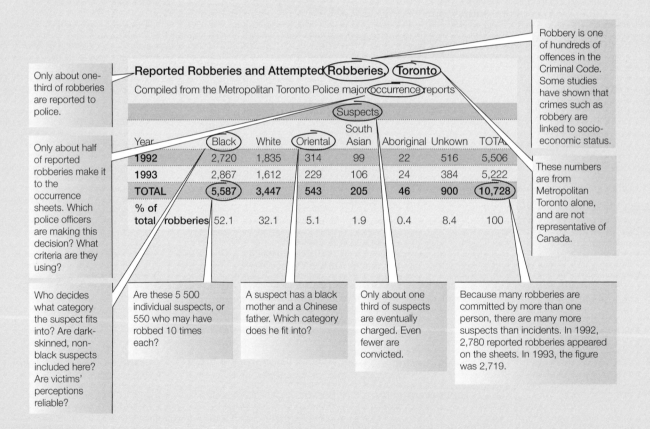

Reported Robberies and Attempted Robberies, Toronto

Compiled from the Metropolitan Toronto Police major occurrence reports

| | | | | Suspects | | | | |
Year	Black	White	Oriental	South Asian	Aboriginal	Unkown	TOTAL
1992	2,720	1,835	314	99	22	516	5,506
1993	2,867	1,612	229	106	24	384	5,222
TOTAL	5,587	3,447	543	205	46	900	10,728
% of total robberies	52.1	32.1	5.1	1.9	0.4	8.4	100

Only about one-third of robberies are reported to police.

Only about half of reported robberies make it to the occurrence sheets. Which police officers are making this decision? What criteria are they using?

Who decides what category the suspect fits into? Are dark-skinned, non-black suspects included here? Are victims' perceptions reliable?

Are these 5 500 individual suspects, or 550 who may have robbed 10 times each?

A suspect has a black mother and a Chinese father. Which category does he fit into?

Only about one third of suspects are eventually charged. Even fewer are convicted.

Robbery is one of hundreds of offences in the Criminal Code. Some studies have shown that crimes such as robbery are linked to socio-economic status.

These numbers are from Metropolitan Toronto alone, and are not representative of Canada.

Because many robberies are committed by more than one person, there are many more suspects than incidents. In 1992, 2,780 reported robberies appeared on the sheets. In 1993, the figure was 2,719.

SOURCE: Bennell, Bertrand. 1994. "What's Wrong With These Numbers?" *Globe and Mail*, June 11. Reprinted with permission from *The Globe and Mail*.

Victimization Surveys

Victimization surveys ask people if they have been victims of crime. Although the first victimization surveys were carried out in the United States in 1966 for the President's Commission on Law Enforcement and Administration of Justice, victimization surveys in Canada have a much shorter history. As Fattah (1991) observes, "[n]o truly national victimization survey was done in Canada until the General Social Survey was carried out by Statistics Canada in 1988." For Statistics Canada's 1999 General Social Survey (GSS), 26 000 people, aged 15 and older, were interviewed by telephone and asked if they had been victimized by crime and, if so, where and when the crime had occurred and whether or not it had been reported to the police. Respondents were also queried on their perceptions of the level of crime in their neighbourhood, their personal fear of crime, and their views on the criminal justice system (Tufts 2000).

In addition to national surveys, the International Crime Victim Survey (ICVS) collected victimization data using the same questionnaire in many countries, including Canada, in 1989, 1992, 1996–97, and 2000 (Besserer 2002). This survey examines householders' experience with crime, policing, crime prevention, and feelings of being unsafe. According to this survey, on average, only 55 percent of victimization incidents are reported to police, with property crimes more likely to be reported than crimes against persons. In part, this reflects the general requirement by insurance companies that individuals seeking compensation for property stolen or damaged as the result of a criminal act file a police report. Although victimization surveys provide detailed information about crime victims, they provide less reliable data about offenders.

Self-Report Offender Surveys

Self-report surveys ask offenders about their criminal behaviour. The sample may consist of a population with known police records, such as a prison population, or it may include respondents from the general population, such as university students. Self-report data compensate for many of the problems associated with official statistics but are still subject to exaggerations and concealment. The Criminal Activities Survey in this chapter's *Self and Society* feature asks you to indicate whether you have engaged in a variety of illegal activities.

Self-report surveys reveal that virtually every adult has engaged in some type of criminal activity. Why then is only a fraction of the population labelled as criminal? Like a funnel, which is large at one end and small at the other, only a small proportion of the total population of law violators is ever convicted of a crime. For example, for every 1000 burglaries that occur, only 495 are reported to the police, 72 lead to an arrest, 21 to a conviction, and 16 to an offender being incarcerated (Felson 1998: 7). If we review Figure 4.2 (see page 105), it becomes evident why research based on samples of incarcerated offenders may not have broad generalizability beyond inmate populations.

Sociological Theories of Crime and Violence

Some explanations of crime and violence focus on psychological aspects of the offender, such as psychopathic personalities, unhealthy relationships with parents, and mental illness. Other crime theories focus on the role of biological

Criminal Activities Survey

Read each of the following questions. If, since the age of 18, you have ever engaged in the behaviour described, place a "1" in the space provided. If you have not engaged in the behaviour, put a "0" in the space provided. After completing the survey, read the section on interpretation to see what your answers mean.

Questions	1 (Yes)	0 (No)
1. Have you ever shared a joint with a friend or offered to do so?	_____	_____
2. Have you ever given a cigarette to a person under 18 in any public place?	_____	_____
3. Have you ever advertised a reward, "no questions asked," for the return of anything lost or stolen?	_____	_____
4. Have you ever caused a disturbance in or near a public place by fighting, shouting, swearing, singing, or using insulting or obscene language?	_____	_____
5. Have you ever begun and/or participated in an office basketball or football pool?	_____	_____
6. Have you ever used "filthy, obscene, annoying, or offensive" language while on the telephone?	_____	_____
7. Have you ever punched out for a friend on a time clock so that it appeared that s/he left work later that s/he actually did?	_____	_____
8. Have you ever stolen anything from a dollar store?	_____	_____
9. Have you ever written a cheque when you knew it was bad?	_____	_____
10. Have you ever threatened to injure a pet bird or animal?	_____	_____
11. Have you, at a friend's request, used that friend's bank card to pay his/her bills or withdraw money for him/her?	_____	_____
12. Have you ever, while driving, damaged a parked car (e.g., in a parking lot) and failed to leave a note for the other driver with your name and address on it?	_____	_____
13. Have you ever driven your parents' car without their permission?	_____	_____

Interpretation

Each of the activities described in these questions represents criminal behaviour that was subject to fines, imprisonment, or both under the *Criminal Code* of Canada in 2002. For each activity, the following table lists the maximum prison sentence and/or fine for a first-time offender. To calculate your "prison time" and/or fines, sum the numbers corresponding to each activity you have engaged in.

Maximum Prison Sentence	Maximum Fine	Offence
1. Five years less a day	n.a.	Trafficking (Schedule II drug)
2. Six months	$2000	Furnishing a tobacco product to young person
3. Six months	$2000	Advertising a reward with immunity (e.g. "no questions asked")
4. Six months	$2000	Causing disturbance
5. Six months	$2000	Betting, pool-selling, book-making, etc.
6. Six months	$2000	Indecent telephone calls
7. Six month	$2000	Falsifying employment record
8. Two years	$2000	Theft
9. Ten years	$5000	False pretence or false statement
10. Two years	$2000	Uttering threats
11. Ten years		Unauthorized use of a computer system
12. Five years	$2000	Failing to stop vehicle at scene of accident
13. Six months	$2000	Taking motor vehicle without consent

SOURCES: Rodrigues, Gary P. (ed.). 1999. *The Police Officer's Manual of Criminal Offences and Criminal Law;* Toronto: Carswell. Solomon, Robert. 1999. "Alcohol and Drug Law." In *Canadian Profile 1999: Alcohol, Tobacco and Other Drugs*, p.p. 295–315. Ottawa: Centre on Substance Abuse and Centre for Addiction and Mental Health.

Total incidents reported to police = 2 832 800

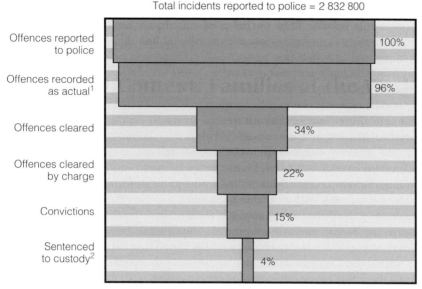

■ **Figure 4.2** *Caseload within the Canadian Criminal Justice System, 1996*

SOURCE: *Uniform Crime Reporting Survey, Adult Court Survey,* and *Youth Court Survey,* Canadian Centre for Justice Statistics, Statistics Canada. Adapted from *Juristat,* Catalogue. no. 85–002.

Offences reported to police — 100%

Offences recorded as actual[1] — 96%

Offences cleared — 34%

Offences cleared by charge — 22%

Convictions — 15%

Sentenced to custody[2] — 4%

Percentage of police-reported offences

[1] An offence is considered "actual" when, following an initial investigation, the police confirm that a criminal offence has occurred. An offence is "cleared" when police are satisfied that they have identified an offender. However, it may not be possible to lay a charge against an offender because he or she is dead, under age 12, has diplomatic immunity, is already in prison, and so on. If, in the view of the police, it is possible to lay a charge against an offender, the offence is cleared by charge.

[2] Includes secure custody only for young offenders and any custodial sentence for adults.

variables such as the central nervous system malfunctioning, stress, hormones, vitamin or mineral deficiencies, chromosomal abnormalities, and a genetic predisposition toward aggression. Sociological theories of crime and violence emphasize the role of social factors in criminal behaviour and societal responses to it.

Structural-Functionalist Perspective

According to Durkheim and other structural-functionalists, crime is functional for society. One of the functions of crime and other deviant behaviour is that it strengthens group cohesion:

> The deviant individual violates rules of conduct [that] the rest of the community holds in high respect; and when these people come together to express their outrage over the offense…they develop a tighter bond of solidarity than existed earlier. (Erikson 1966: 4)

Crime may also lead to social change. For example, an episode of local violence may "achieve broad improvements in city services…[and] be a catalyst for making public agencies more effective and responsive, for strengthening families and social institutions, and for creating public–private partnerships" (National Research Council 1994: 9–10).

While functionalism as a theoretical perspective deals directly with some aspects of crime and violence, it is not a theory of crime per se. Three major theories of crime and violence have developed from functionalism, however. The

No written law has ever been more binding than unwritten custom supported by popular opinion.

CARRIE CHAPMAN CATT
Suffragist and peace advocate

Every time you stop a
school, you will have to
build a jail. What you gain
at one end you lose at the
other. It's like feeding a
dog on its own tail. It
won't fatten the dog.

MARK TWAIN
Author

first, called **strain theory**, was developed by Robert Merton (1957), using
Durkheim's concept of anomie, or normlessness. Merton argues that when
legitimate means (for example, a job) of acquiring culturally defined goals (for
example, money) are limited by the structure of society, the resulting strain may
lead to crime.

Individuals, then, must adapt to the inconsistency between means and goals
in a society that socializes everyone into wanting the same thing but only provides opportunities for some (see Table 4.1). Conformity occurs when individuals accept the culturally defined goals and the socially legitimate means of
achieving them. Merton suggests that most individuals, even those who do not
have easy access to the means and the goals, remain conformists. Innovation
occurs when an individual accepts the goals of society, but rejects or lacks the
socially legitimate means of achieving them. Innovation, the mode of adaptation most associated with criminal behaviour, explains the high rate of crime
committed by uneducated and poor individuals who do not have access to legitimate means of achieving the social goals of wealth and power.

Another adaptation is ritualism, in which the individual accepts a lifestyle of
hard work, but rejects the cultural goal of monetary rewards. The ritualist goes
through the motions of getting an education and working hard, yet is not committed to the goal of accumulating wealth or power. Retreatism involves
rejecting both the cultural goal of success and the socially legitimate means of
achieving it. The retreatist withdraws or retreats from society and may become
an alcoholic, drug addict, or vagrant. Finally, rebellion occurs when an individual rejects both culturally defined goals and means and substitutes new goals
and means. For example, rebels may use social or political activism to replace
the goal of personal wealth with the goal of social justice and equality.

The greatest of evils and
the worst of crime is
poverty.

GEORGE BERNARD SHAW
Playwright

While strain theory explains criminal behaviour as a result of blocked opportunities, **subcultural theory** argues that certain groups or subcultures in
society have values and attitudes that are conducive to crime and violence.
Members of these groups and subcultures, as well as other individuals who
interact with them, may adopt the crime-promoting attitudes and values of the
group. For example, subcultural norms and values contribute to street crime.

■ **Table 4.1** *Merton's Five Types of Adaptation*

	Culturally Defined Goals	Structurally Defined Means
1. Conformity	+	+
2. Innovation	+	−
3. Ritualism	−	+
4. Retreatism	−	−
5. Rebellion	−/+	−/+

Key: (+) = acceptance of/access to; (−) = rejection of/lack of access to; (−/+) = rejection of culturally
defined goals and structurally defined means and replacement with new goals and means.

SOURCE: Reprinted with permission of The Free Press, a division of Simon & Schuster Adult Publishing Group, from *Social Theory and Social Structure* by Robert K. Merton. Copyright © 1957 by
The Free Press; copyright renewed 1985 by Robert K. Merton.

Sociologist Elijah Anderson (1994) explains that many inner-city youths live by a survival code on the streets that emphasizes gaining the respect of others through violence—the tougher you are and the more others fear you, the more respect you have in the community.

However, if blocked opportunities and subcultural values are responsible for crime, why don't all members of the affected groups become criminals? **Control theory** may answer that question. Hirschi (1969), consistent with Durkheim's emphasis on social solidarity, suggests that a strong social bond between individuals and the social order constrains some individuals from violating social norms. Hirschi identified four elements of the social bond: attachment to significant others, commitment to conventional goals, involvement in conventional activities, and belief in the moral standards of society. Several empirical tests of Hirschi's theory support the notion that the higher the attachment, commitment, involvement, and belief, the higher the social bond and the lower the probability of criminal behaviour. For example, Laub et al. (1998) found that a good marriage contributes to the cessation of a criminal career. Further, Warner and Rountree (1997) report that local community ties, although varying by neighbourhood and offence, decrease the probability of crimes occurring.

Conflict Perspective

Conflict theories of crime suggest that deviance is inevitable whenever two groups have differing degrees of power; in addition, the more inequality in a society, the greater the crime rate in that society. Social inequality may lead individuals to commit crimes such as armed robbery and burglary as a means of economic survival. Other individuals, who are angry and frustrated by their low position in the socioeconomic hierarchy, may express their rage and frustration through crimes such as drug use, assault, and homicide. In Argentina, for example, the soaring violent crime rate is hypothesized to be "a product of the enormous imbalance in income distribution...between the rich and the poor" (Pertossi 2000).

According to the conflict perspective, those in power define what is criminal and what is not, and these definitions reflect the interests of the ruling class. Laws against vagrancy, for example, penalize individuals who do not contribute to the capitalist system of work and consumerism. Rather than viewing law as a mechanism that protects all members of society, conflict theorists focus on how laws are created by those in power to protect the ruling class. For example, wealthy corporations contribute money to campaigns to influence politicians to enact tax laws that serve corporate interests (Jacobs 1988), and the "criminal justice system grows increasingly punitive as labour surplus increases," that is, as greater social control is felt to be needed (Hochstetler and Shover 1997).

Furthermore, conflict theorists argue that law enforcement is applied differentially, penalizing those without power and benefiting those with power. For example, female prostitutes are more likely to be arrested than are the men who seek their services. Unlike street criminals, corporate criminals are often punished by fines rather than by lengthy prison terms. Consider that in Canada in 2000–01, 61 percent of adult offenders convicted of break and enter but just 35 percent of convicted fraud cases resulted in a prison sentence (Thomas 2002: 9).

> Potentially today's expelled student in Toronto is next month's armed robber in Alberta.
>
> SCOTT NEWARK
> *General Counsel for the Canadian Police Association*

We are mad, not only individually, but nationally. We check manslaughter and isolated murders; but what of war and the much vaunted crimes of slaughtering whole peoples?

SENECA
Epistles

Societal beliefs also reflect power differentials. For example, "rape myths" are perpetuated by the male-dominated culture to foster the belief that women are to blame for their own victimization, thereby, in the minds of many, exonerating the offender. Such myths include the notion that when a woman says "no" she means "yes," that "good girls" don't get raped, that appearance indicates willingness, and that women secretly want to be raped. Not surprisingly, in societies where women and men have greater equality, there are fewer rapes (Sanday 1981).

Symbolic Interactionist Perspective

Two important theories of crime and violence emanate from the symbolic interactionist perspective. The first, **labelling theory**, focuses on two questions: How do crime and deviance come to be defined as such, and what are the effects of being labelled as criminal or deviant? According to Howard Becker (1963):

> Social groups create deviance by making rules whose infractions constitute deviance, and by applying those rules to particular people and labelling them as outsiders. From this point of view, deviance is not a quality of the act a person commits, but rather a consequence of the application by others of rules and sanctions to an "offender." The deviant is one to whom the label has successfully been applied; deviant behaviour is behaviour that people so label. (p. 238)

Labelling theorists make a distinction between **primary deviance**, which is deviant behaviour committed before a person is caught and labelled as an offender, and **secondary deviance**, which is deviance that results from being caught and labelled. After a person violates the law and is apprehended, that person is stigmatized as a criminal. This deviant label often dominates the social identity of the person to whom it is applied and becomes the person's "master status," that is, the primary basis on which the person is defined by others.

Thou call'dst me a dog before thou hadst a cause, But since I am a dog, beware my fangs.

WILLIAM SHAKESPEARE
The Merchant of Venice

Being labelled as deviant often leads to further deviant behaviour because (1) the person who is labelled as deviant is often denied opportunities for engaging in nondeviant behaviour, and (2) the labelled person internalizes the deviant label, adopts a deviant self-concept, and acts accordingly. For example, the teenager who is caught selling drugs at school may be expelled and thus denied opportunities to participate in nondeviant school activities (e.g., sports, clubs) and associate with nondeviant peer groups. The labelled and stigmatized teenager may also adopt the self-concept of a "druggie" or "pusher" and continue to pursue drug-related activities and membership in the drug culture.

The assignment of meaning and definitions learned from others is also central to the second symbolic interactionist theory of crime, **differential association**. Edwin Sutherland (1939) proposed that, through interaction with others, individuals learn the values and attitudes associated with crime as well as the techniques and motivations for criminal behaviour. Individuals who are exposed to more definitions favourable to law violation (e.g., "crime pays") than unfavourable (e.g., "do the crime, you'll do the time") are more likely to engage in criminal behaviour. Thus, children who see their parents benefit from crime, or who live in high-crime neighbourhoods where success is associated with illegal behaviour, are more likely to engage in criminal behaviour.

Types of Crime

Most Canadians would be understandably alarmed to hear that in 2001, 2.4 million *Criminal Code* incidents (excluding traffic incidents) were reported to Canadian police departments and agencies (Statistics Canada 2002) (Figure 4.3). However, while it might be assumed that all these incidents were interchangeable with the dramatic cases reported on the nightly news, this is not the case. In 2001, more than half (52 percent) of these *Criminal Code* incidents involved property crimes, 13 percent involved violent crimes, and just over one in three (35 percent) involved other *Criminal Code* incidents such as mischief, disturbing the peace, prostitution, or arson.

Criminologists use the terms **conventional crime** or **street crime** to refer to "those traditional illegal behaviours that most people think of as crime" (Koenig 2000). Included here would be offences such as murder, sexual assault, assault, armed robbery, break and enter, and theft. In contrast, the term *non-conventional crime* is employed with reference to such crimes as, for example, organized crime, white-collar crime, corporate crime, and computer crime.

Street Crime: Violent Offences

Violent crime includes homicide, attempted murder, assault, sexual assault, other sexual offences, abduction, and robbery. While Canada's violent crime is about 54 percent higher than it was two decades ago (Figure 4.4), "if common assaults (the least serious form of assault, which accounts for more than six in ten violent crimes) were excluded, the violent crime rate would actually be 15 percent lower than 10 years ago" (Logan 2001). Each year, minor assaults account for approximately two-thirds of all violent crimes in Canada (Statistics Canada 2002). During the fiscal year 2000/01, for example, common assault was the most frequently heard offence in adult criminal court (Thomas 2002) (Figure 4.5). Between 2000 and 2001, the rate of minor assaults increased by 1 percent—and "was the key factor" in the rise in the total violent crime rate in Canada (Statistics Canada 2002).

Homicide refers to the wilful killing of one human being by another individual or group of individuals. Although homicide is the most serious of the

> Figures often beguile me, particularly when I have the arranging of them myself; in which case the remark attributed to Disraeli would often apply with justice and force: "There are three kinds of lies: lies, damned lies, and statistics."
>
> **MARK TWAIN**
> *Writer*

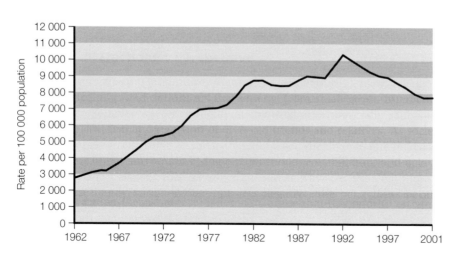

■ **Figure 4.3** *Crime, 1962–2001*

SOURCE: Statistics Canada. 2002. "Crime Statistics 2001." *The Daily*, July 17. http://www.statcan.ca/Daily/English/020717/d020717b.htm.

Figure 4.4 *Violent Crime Rate, Canada, 1962–2000*

SOURCE: Logan, Ron. 2001. "Crime Statistics in Canada, 2000." *Juristat* 21(8), July: 5. Catalogue no. 85-002-XPE.

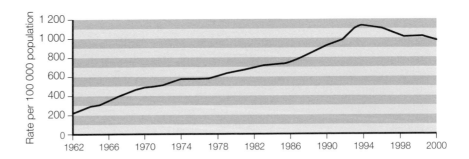

violent crimes, it is also the least common. In 2000, homicides and attempted murders, when tallied together, accounted for less than half of 1 percent of all violent incidents reported to police in Canada (Logan 2001: 6). In 2001, Canada's homicide rate, which has been declining since the mid-1970s, remained stable at 1.8 homicides for every 100 000 population (Statistics Canada 2002). The majority of homicides involve offenders who were known to their victims; in 2000, acquaintances committed 51 percent of homicides while 32 percent were family members (Logan 2001: 6).

Historically, and continuing into the present, about two-thirds of homicide victims have been men, as have almost 9 out of 10 (88 percent) of those accused of homicide (Fedorowycz 1999). For both homicide and other violent crimes, the highest risk group for offending is those 16 to 34 years old (Fedorowycz 1999).

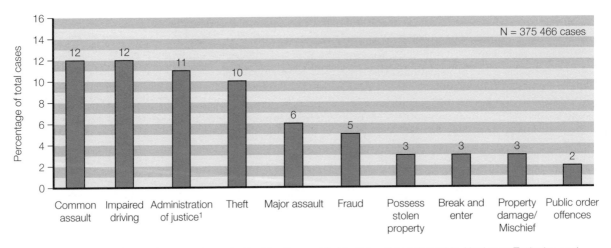

Note: Adult Criminal Court Survey data are not reported by New Brunswick, Manitoba, British Columbia, Northwest Territories, and Nunavut.

[1] Includes such offences as failure to appear in court and breach of probation.

Figure 4.5 *Ten Most Frequent Offences Heard in Adult Criminal Court, Eight Provinces and Territories in Canada, 2000/01*

SOURCE: Adult Criminal Court Survey, Canadian Centre for Justice Statistics, Statistics Canada.

The majority of homicides committed among marginal groups in North America (e.g., First Nations people, African-Americans) are intraracial (Hackler 2000).

Other forms of violent crime are sexual and nonsexual assaults. Both types of assault are distinguished by several categories. In relation to nonsexual assault, these categories are common assault (level 1), assault with a weapon or causing bodily harm (level 2), and aggravated assault (level 3) in which the victim is wounded, maimed, or disfigured. In addition, the *Criminal Code* outlines other types of assaults including those committed on a peace officer, an officiating member of the clergy, the Queen, an internationally protected person, and so on.

Sexual assaults are also classified into one of three levels that are distinguished by the degree of physical harm to the victim: level 1 sexual assault, level 2 sexual assault (sexual assault with a weapon, threats to a third party, or causing bodily harm), and level 3 aggravated sexual assault (in which an offender, in committing a sexual assault, wounds, maims, disfigures, or endangers the life of the victim). In relation to both types of assaults, sexual and nonsexual, the least serious are the most common. For example, while there was a slight increase in police-reported sexual assaults between 2000 and 2001 (of 0.7 percent), the rate of sexual assaults with a weapon and aggravated sexual assaults actually declined (by 17 percent and 9 percent, respectively). In 2001, the rate of sexual assaults in Canada was 78.6 per 100 000 population (Statistics Canada 2002).

Over the past decade, increasing attention has been directed to **acquaintance rape**—sexual assaults committed by someone the victim knows. The term is somewhat misleading as it does not appear within the *Criminal Code* of Canada, and the act so described is actually subsumed within the three levels of sexual assault already noted. Nevertheless, it has been reported that although sexual assaults committed by acquaintances are the most likely to occur, they are the least likely to be reported and the most difficult to prosecute. Unless the sexual assault is what Williams (1984) calls a **classic rape**—that is, the offender was a stranger who used a weapon and the attack resulted in serious bodily harm—victims hesitate to report the crime out of fear of not being believed. In addition, the use of "rape drugs," which render their victims unconscious (see Chapter 3), may lower reporting levels even further. It is estimated that only one in ten sexual assaults are reported each year.

Robbery, although involving theft, also involves force, the threat of force, or putting a victim in fear, and is thus considered a violent crime. The 2001 rate of robbery in Canada was 88.2 per 100 000 population (Statistics Canada 2002). Since 1991, robberies involving firearms have declined; in 2001, about one in every seven robberies was committed with the use of a firearm. Robberies involving other weapons (e.g., knives) or no weapon increased between 2000 and 2001 by 4 percent and 2 percent, respectively (Statistics Canada 2002). Robberies are generally committed by young people; in the late 1990s, for example, the median age of female robbers in Canada was 16, and of male offenders, 21 (Kong 1999).

Street Crime: Property Offences

Property crimes involve acts committed with the intent to gain property that do not involve the use or threatened use of violence. Examples of property crime include theft, breaking and entering, motor vehicle theft, fraud, and possession of stolen property. Property crimes have declined since the early 1990s, with the 2001 rate of property crime the lowest in nearly three decades (Statistics Canada 2002). Nevertheless, in 2000, property crimes accounted for almost one-half (46 percent) of youth crime and a third of adult crime (Logan 2001). Consistent with previous years, theft under $5000 was the most common type of property crime in 2000, occurring at a rate of 2155 per 100 000 population. In that year, there were 662 616 police-reported incidents of theft under $5000; 54 238 adults and 20 117 youths were charged with this offence (Statistics Canada 2001). Theft under $5000 was the most common type of case processed in youth courts in 2000/01 (deSouza 2002) (Figure 4.6).

Breaking and entering entails entering a structure, usually a house, with the intent to commit a crime while inside. Official statistics indicate that 282 512 incidents of breaking and entering were reported to the police in 2001—a rate of 908.9 per 100 000 population (Statistics Canada 2002). During the fiscal year 2000/01, breaking and entering accounted for one in ten of the cases heard in Canada's youth courts (deSouza 2002).

Vice Crimes

A vice crime is an illegal activity that has no complaining party and is therefore often called a **victimless crime**. Vice crimes include using illegal drugs, communicating for the purposes of prostitution, and illegal gambling. Compared with crimes such as murder or robbery, less consensus exists, nationally or internationally, that such crimes should be subject to the criminal law. In the Netherlands, for example, the Prostitution Information Centre in Amsterdam offers a six-day course on "prostitution as a career option," while the Australia Council of Trade Unions recently recognized women in prostitution as a labour sector (CATW 1997). In general, "prostitution is not an issue Canadians have been seeing as particularly pressing" (Bibby 1995). While one in five Canadians identified "prostitution" as a "very serious" social concern in 1985, a decade later, it

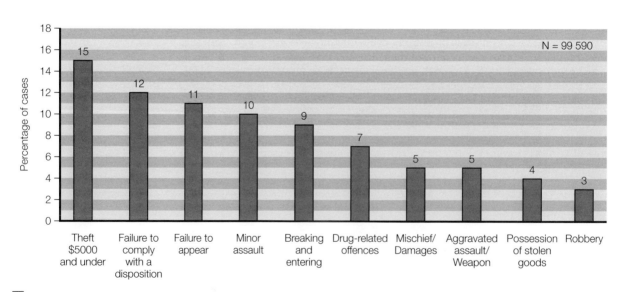

■ **Figure 4.6** *Principal Charge in Youth Courts, 2000/01*

SOURCE: Youth Court Survey, Canadian Centre for Justice Statistics.

was mentioned by less than 1 percent. While prostitution is not illegal in Canada, it is an offence to publicly communicate with another person for the purpose of buying or selling sexual services; since 1985, the law has clearly applied to both buyers and sellers.

Organized crime refers to criminal activity conducted by members of a hierarchically arranged structure devoted primarily to making money through illegal means. The *Criminal Code* defines a "criminal organization" as any group, association or other body consisting of five or more persons, whether formally or informally organized, having as one of its primary activities the commission of an indictable offence for which the maximum punishment is imprisonment for five years or more. Although often discussed under victimless crimes because of its association with prostitution, drugs, and gambling, organized crime often uses coercive techniques. For example, organized crime groups may force legitimate businesses to pay "protection money" by threatening vandalism or violence.

The traditional notion of organized crime is the Mafia—an international band of interlocked Italian families—but members of many ethnic groups engage in organized crime. Other organized crime groups in Canada include Chinese triads, the Colombian Mafia, outlaw motorcycle gangs, the Russian Mafia, and other ethnic-based drug trafficking groups. Their activities include drug trafficking, prostitution, terrorism, extortion, and such violent crimes as serious assaults and homicide (Stamler 2000). In addition, the Organized Crime Impact Study concluded that between $5 and $17 billion is laundered annually in Canada. "Money laundering is any act or attempted act to conceal or disguise the identity of illegally obtained proceeds so that they appear to have originated from legitimate sources" (Solicitor General 1999).

Organized crime also occurs at the international level, such as smuggling illegal drugs and arms. Since the fall of the Soviet Union, it is estimated that as much as 25 percent of the Russian gross national income is from organized crime activities generated by 5600 separate crime groups. Organized crime is now considered "one the most important political problems in Russia" whereby a "Russian citizen's personal safety" can no longer be guaranteed (Shabalin et al. 1995). In 1999, Canada's Extradition Act came into force, expanding Canada's ability to extradite those who are involved in organized crime. In recognition of the borderless nature of organized crime, "Canada is...working in the G-8, the United Nations and the Organization of American States to develop and promote international standards to combat transnational crime, and organized crime in particular" (Solicitor General 1999).

White-Collar Crime

White-collar crime includes both occupational crime, where individuals commit crimes in the course of their employment, and corporate crime, where corporations violate the law in the interest of maximizing profit. For example, Bre-X, reputedly one of the world's largest stock frauds, cost investors $6 billion. In this case, the Calgary-based company's geologist had sought to make a worthless mining property seem valuable by salting core samples with gold. After his actions became known, the market for Bre-X stock collapsed and the company's shares became worthless (Hagan 2000). Table 4.2 summarizes some of the major categories of white-collar crime.

A man may see how this world goes with no eyes. Look with thine ears: see how yond justice rails upon yond simple thief. Hark, in thine ear: change places; and, handy-dandy, which is the justice, which is the thief?

WILLIAM SHAKESPEARE
King Lear

Table 4.2 *Types of White-Collar Crime*

Crimes against Consumers	Crimes against Employees	Crimes against the Public	Crimes against Employers
Deceptive advertising	Health and safety violations	Toxic waste disposal	Embezzlement
Antitrust violations	Wage and hour violations	Pollution violations	Pilferage
Dangerous products	Discriminatory hiring practices	Tax fraud	Misappropriation of government funds
Manufacturer kickbacks	Illegal labour practices	Security violations	Counterfeit production of goods
Physician insurance fraud	Unlawful surveillance practices	Police brutality	Business credit fraud

Occupational crime is motivated by individual gain. Employee thefts of merchandise, or pilferage, is one of the most common types of occupational crime. Other examples include embezzlement, forgery and counterfeiting, and insurance fraud. "Churning" is one example of corporate crime, that is, crime that benefits the organization. As Sherrill notes, "churning" is:

> a racket in which as many as 10 million customers were sweet-talked into using the case value of their old insurance policies to pay the premiums of new, more expensive policies. They were not warned that the upgrading could be so costly that it would eat up their equity, leaving them with premiums they couldn't afford—and therefore no coverage. (2000: 304)

Price-fixing and anti-trust violations are other examples of corporate crime.

Corporate violence, another form of corporate crime, refers to the production of unsafe products and the failure of corporations to provide safe working environments for their employees. Corporate violence is the result of negligence, the pursuit of profit at any cost, and intentional violations of health, safety, and environmental regulations. For example, in 1999, GM was ordered to pay $4.9 billion (U.S.) to six people who were severely burned when their car exploded in flames after a rear-end collision. In court, lawyers for the plaintiffs produced a internal GM study that acknowledged that the gas tanks in the Chevrolet Malibu and El Camino, Pontiac Grand Am, and Oldsmobile Cutlass were mounted in unsafe positions—27 centimetres from the rear bumper. However, the GM study had also pointed out that it would be cheaper to settle lawsuits that might arise from accidents in which victims were fatally burned (calculated to be $2.40 per car produced) than to change where the tanks were placed (calculated to be $8.59 per car produced). Here, a profit-motivated decision was made and the placement of the gas tanks in these cars remained unaltered from 1979 to 1983. Even though the amount awarded was both the biggest product-liability award and the largest personal injury verdict in U.S. history, legal experts opined that the enormous punitive award was unlikely to stand on appeal. "Even with awards in the tens of millions, it is rare for a plaintiff to actually get anything close to the jury's verdict" (White 1999).

The first thing we do, let's kill all the lawyers.

WILLIAM SHAKESPEARE
King Henry VI

In Canada, some have argued that the term *corporate murder* (Swartz 1978) is an appropriate label for deaths resulting in such circumstances. Among the best-known cases are the failures of administrators within the Johns-Manville Corporation to alert workers to the serious health hazards posed by asbestos. Hagan (2000) notes that although these hazards have been recognized "since the turn of the century...people working with it were not informed, and the government bureaucracy and the medical community ignored the hazard." Similarly, he notes that the 1992 explosion at the Westray coal mine in Pictou County, Nova Scotia, which killed 26 miners, "was not an accident, but...the result of conscious decisions by those responsible for the safety of the miners." An official inquiry into the disaster resulted in a report tellingly entitled *The Westray Story: A Predictable Path to Disaster*. In it, Justice Richard concludes that the managers at Westray had "displayed a certain disdain for safety and appeared to regard safety-conscious workers as the wimps in the organization" (in Hagan 2000).

Computer Crime

Computer crime refers to any violation of the law in which a computer is the target or the means of criminal activity. Hacking, or unauthorized computer intrusion, is one type of computer crime. In just one month, hackers successfully attacked the computer systems of Walt Disney World, Yahoo, eBay, and Amazon.com through "denial of service" invasions (Kong and Swartz 2000). *Identity theft*—the use of someone else's identification (e.g., social insurance number, birth date) to obtain credit—is another (Miller 1999; Fields 2000). Although mail theft is one of the most common modes of obtaining the needed information, new technologies have contributed to the increased rate of this offence on an international basis. For example, in 2000, American government officials travelled to Russia to investigate the theft of 300 000 credit card numbers from CD Universe, an online music retailer (Fields 2000: 6a).

Conklin (1998) has identified other examples of computer crime:

- Two individuals were charged with theft of 80 000 cellular phone numbers. Using a device purchased from a catalogue, the thieves picked up radio waves from passing cars, determined private cellular codes, reprogrammed computer chips with the stolen codes, and then, by inserting the new chips into their own cellular phones, charged calls to the original owners.
- A programmer made $300 a week by programming a computer to round off each employee's paycheque down to the nearest 10¢ and then to deposit the extra few pennies in the offender's account.
- An oil company illegally tapped into another oil company's computer to get information that allowed the offending company to underbid the other company for leasing rights.

Demographic Patterns of Crime

Although virtually everyone violates a law at some time, persons with certain demographic characteristics are disproportionately represented in the crime statistics. Victims, for example, are disproportionately young, lower-class, minority males from urban areas. Similarly, the probability of being an offender varies by gender, age, race, social class, and region.

> ■ Think about it: How many victims of violent crime do you know? Now think: How many people do you know who are affected by something like the collapse of a major company? Millions of Canadians suffer when incompetence, misapplication or malfeasance strike a financial institution or professional body....It isn't the morons on the street who are a danger to most of us, it's the men in suits.
>
> **H.S. Bhabra**
> *Novelist*

Gender and Crime

Both official statistics and self-report data indicate that males commit more crimes than females (Table 4.3). Canadian adult criminal court statistics for the fiscal year 2000/01 indicate that 83 percent of cases involved a male accused. (Please note that data in this paragraph are drawn from an analysis of adult criminal courts in eight provinces and territories; at the time that the analysis was conducted, data was unavailable for New Brunswick, Manitoba, British

■ **Table 4.3** *Persons Charged by Age Group and Sex, Selected Incidents, Canada, 2000*

	Adults (18 and over)		Youth (12 to 17)	
	Male	Female	Male	Female
Homicide[1]	90	10	88	12
Attempted murder	89	11	89	11
Assaults	84	16	71	29
Sexual assaults	98	2	96	4
Other sexual offences	97	3	96	4
Abduction	55	45	25	75
Robbery	91	9	85	15
Violent crime—total	85	15	75	25
Break and enter	93	7	91	9
Motor vehicle theft	92	8	85	15
Fraud	70	30	63	37
Theft over $5000	77	23	85	15
Theft $5000 and under	71	29	66	34
Property crime—total	78	22	77	23
Mischief	88	12	88	12
Arson	81	19	86	14
Prostitution	49	51	14	86
Offensive weapons	93	7	93	7
Criminal code—total	82	18	77	23
Impaired driving[2]	88	12	87	13
Cannabis offences	87	13	87	13
Cocaine offences	82	18	79	21
Other drug offences	83	17	83	17

[1] These data are based on the Homicide Survey, CCJS.

[2] Includes impaired operation of a vehicle causing death, causing bodily harm, alcohol rate over 80 mg., failure/refusal to provide a breath/blood sample. Age of persons charged with impaired driving comes from the Incident-based survey (UCR2).

SOURCE: Uniform Crime Reporting Survey, CCJS.

Columbia, the Northwest Territories and Nunavut.) Males accounted for 85 percent of crimes against a person, 78 percent of crimes against property and 86 percent of Criminal Code traffic violations. Women accounted for a significant percentage of offenders in only a small number of crimes. Specifically, they accounted for 43 percent of those involved in morals-sexual offences (primarily soliciting), 44 percent of those charged with abduction (mainly child-related), 28 percent of those charged with fraud, and 27 percent of those charged with theft (including shoplifting) (Thomas 2002: 4). This pattern reappears for cases processed in the youth courts of Canada.

Although the increase in the rate of female youths charged with violent crime over the last decade was more than double that for male youths (+61 percent and +25 percent, respectively), "[t]he rate of male youths charged with violent crime (1342 per 100 000 population) is still almost three times that of female youth (481 per 100 000 population)" (Logan 2001: 18). In 2000/01, males accounted for eight in ten offenders in cases heard in Canada's youth courts (deSouza 2002: 5).

Why are males more likely to commit crime than females? One explanation is that society views female lawbreaking as less acceptable and thus places more constraints on female behaviour: "women may need a higher level of provocation before turning to crime—especially serious crime. Females who choose criminality must traverse a greater moral and psychological distance than males making the same choice" (Steffensmeier and Allan 1995: 88). Further, data suggest that males and females tend to commit different types of crimes. Men, partly because of more aggressive socialization experiences, are more likely than women are to commit violent crimes. Females are less likely than males to commit serious offences, and the monetary value of female involvement in theft, property damage, and illegal drugs is typically less than that for similar offences committed by males. Nevertheless, a growing number of women have become involved in characteristically male criminal activities such as gang-related crime and drug use.

The recent increases in crimes committed by females have led to the development of a feminist criminology. Feminist criminology focuses on how the subordinate position of women in the social structure affects the criminal behaviour of women. For example, Chesney-Lind and Shelden (1998) report that arrest rates for runaway juvenile females are higher than for males, not only because they are more likely to run away as a consequence of sexual abuse in the home, but also because police with paternalistic attitudes are more likely to arrest female runaways than male runaways. Feminist criminology thus adds insights into understanding crime and violence often neglected by traditional theories by concentrating on gender inequality in society.

Young Offenders

According to police-reported data, age 16 is the peak age of offending for both violent and property offences (Statistics Canada 2002). The rate of youths (aged 12 to 17) formally charged by police declined from 1991 to 1999 but increased slightly in both 2000 (by 1 percent) and in 2001 (by 1 percent) (Logan 2001; Statistics Canada 2002). While property crimes account for the majority of youth crime (Figure 4.7), the violent crime rate for youths

■ **Figure 4.7** *Youth*
Charged, by Type of
Offence, Canada,
1990–2000

SOURCE: Uniform Crime Reporting
Survey, CCJS.

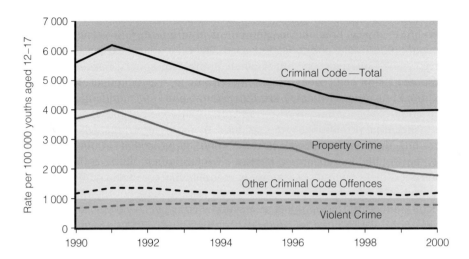

increased in both 2000 (by 7 percent) and in 2001 (by 2 percent) (Logan
2001; Statistics Canada 2002). The rate of rate of youths charged with robbery, for example, increased by 10 percent between 2000 and 2001. However,
while over the past decade an average of 48 youths a year have faced charges
of homicide only 30 youths were accused of homicide in 2001 (the lowest
level in more than three decades).

Age and Crime

People who have not reached middle age commit most crime. The 15- to 24-year-
old age cohort is the most crime prone. While this age cohort represented merely
14 percent of the total Canadian population in 2000, they accounted for 45 percent of those charged with a property crime and 31 percent of those charged with
a violent crime (Logan 2001: 3). Various commentators have linked Canada's
decreasing crime over the last decade to Canada's aging population structure (see
Figure 4.8). Specifically, while those between the ages 15 to 24 have a high risk

■ **Figure 4.8** *Crime Rate*
and Selected Demo-
graphics, Canada,
1962–2000

SOURCE: Logan, Ron. 2001. "Crime
Statistics in Canada 2000." Canadian Centre for Crime Statistics,
21 (8): 4. Catalogue no. 85-002-XPE

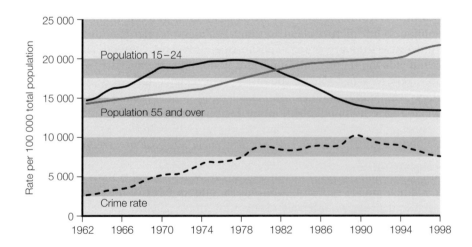

[1] Note that the population 15–24 and population 55 and over lines refer to changes
in the population for these age groups and not changes in crime rates.

of offending, this high-risk age group has decreased in size by 6 percent since 1991 (Logan 2001: 3). Unlike the 1960s, when the "baby boom" generation (i.e., those born between 1947 and 1966) came into their years of highest risk, the 1990s saw the products of the "baby bust" years (1967 to 1979). Simply put, "[t]here has been a smaller pool of people who are at the greatest risk with respect to criminal behaviour" (John Howard Society 1999a: 2).

Why is criminal activity more prevalent among individuals in their teens and early 20s? One reason is that juveniles are insulated from many of the social and legal penalties for criminal behaviour. Younger individuals are also more likely to be unemployed or employed in low-wage jobs. Thus, as strain theorists argue, they have less access to legitimate means for acquiring material goods.

Some research suggests, however, that high school students who have jobs become more, rather than less, involved in crime (Felson 1998: 120). In earlier generations, teenagers who worked did so to support themselves or their families. Today, teenagers who work typically spend their earnings on recreation and "extras," including car payments and gasoline. The increased mobility associated with having a vehicle also increases opportunities for criminal behaviour and reduces parental control.

Race, Social Class, and Crime

Race is a factor in who is arrested. The overrepresentation of Aboriginal peoples in the Canadian criminal justice system has been commented on for decades by various commissions and task forces. Although Aboriginal peoples represent 2 percent of the adult population in Canada, they have consistently accounted for 15–18 percent of admissions to both provincial/territorial and federal sentenced custody for the past two decades (Lonmo 2001: 8). The overrepresentation of Aboriginal persons in Canada's prisons is particularly marked in the Prairie provinces (Figure 4.9). One survey of all inmates in Canada's adult correctional facilities found that while Aboriginals represented 9 percent of Manitoba's population, they accounted for 61 percent of the adult inmate population. In Alberta, where Aboriginals make up 4 percent of the provincial population, they account for more than one-third (34 percent) of inmates (Lonmo 2001: 8).

> Poverty is the parent of revolution and crime.
> ARISTOTLE
> The Politics

Possible explanations for the overrepresentation of Aboriginal people in Canada's prisons include differential treatment by the criminal justice system (that is, Aboriginal people are being discriminated against by the police, the courts, etc.); differential commission of crime and differential offence patterns (that is, Aboriginal people commit crimes that are more detectable—more serious or more visible—than those committed by non-Aboriginal people); the sociostructural deprivation of Canada's Aboriginal peoples; the decline of informal mechanisms of social control within Aboriginal communities; and systemic racism (Hartnagel, 2000). Although some investigators have claimed that certain "races" are more or less law-abiding than others, such research typically fails to define "race," assumes racial purity as a given, treats crime as a unitary phenomenon, and simply presents correlational data on race and crime (Roberts and Gabor 1990). Demonstrating that a correlation exists does not, of course, prove causation.

There are a number of reasons why it would be inaccurate to conclude that race and crime are causally related. First, official statistics reflect the behaviours

Figure 4.9 *Aboriginal Persons—Proportion of Adult Population and Inmates by Jurisdiction*

SOURCE: Robinson, David, Frank J. Porporino, and William A. Millson. 1999. "A One-Day Snapshot of Inmates in Canada's Adult Correctional Facilities." In *Canadian Centre for Justice Statistics, The Juristat Reader: A Statistical Justice System*, pp. 53–66. Toronto: Thompson Educational Publishing, Inc. Reprinted with permission.

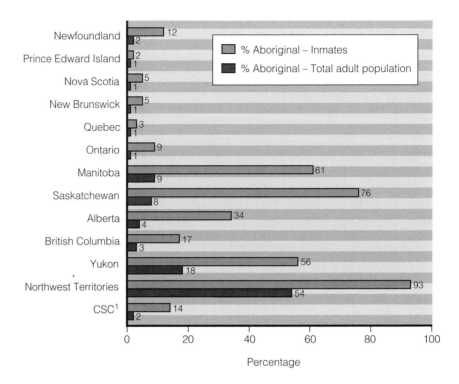

¹ National population and population within federal correctional Services Canada facilities.

and policies of criminal justice actors. Thus, the high rate of arrests, conviction, and incarceration of Aboriginal people may be a consequence of individual and institutional bias (e.g., police prejudice) not only against Aboriginal people, but also against the lower class in general. Second, race and social class are closely related in that Aboriginal people are overrepresented in the lower classes. Since lower-class members lack legitimate means to acquire material goods, they may turn to instrumental, or economically motivated, crimes. Further, while the "haves" typically earn social respect through their socioeconomic status, educational achievement, and occupational role, the "have-nots" more often live in communities where respect is based on physical strength and violence, as subcultural theorists argue. Thus, the apparent relationship between race and crime may be, in part, a consequence of the relationship between these variables and social class.

In recent years, changes made by Parliament to the sentencing provisions of the Canadian *Criminal Code* have attempted to do something about the overrepresentation of Aboriginal peoples in Canada's inmate population. For example, section 718.2 specifies that "all available sanctions other than imprisonment that are reasonable in the circumstances should be considered for all offenders, *with particular attention to the circumstances of aboriginal offenders*" (emphasis added). While being Aboriginal does not automatically result in a lesser sentence, the Supreme Court of Canada has urged judges, when sentencing an Aboriginal offender, to recognize the "broad systemic and background factors affecting Aboriginal people" (Lonmo 2001: 8). The Correctional Service of Canada has also attempted to assist Aboriginal people who are incarcerated by including culturally sensitive substance abuse programs, Native liaison services, and Elders' services. The Okimaw Ohci Healing Lodge for federally sentenced Aboriginal women in Maple Creek, Saskatchewan, was developed with and for the First Nations community. Sixty percent of the staff working at this facility, which places a strong emphasis on Aboriginal culture and spirituality, are of Aboriginal descent (Solicitor General 2002).

Region and Crime

In Canada, the distribution of crime varies by region. Historically, crime rates in Canada have generally increased from east to west, with Nova Scotia and Alberta providing exceptions to this general trend. That is, Nova Scotia's crime rate has generally been higher, and Alberta's crime rate lower, than those of their neighbouring provinces (Logan 2001). In 2001, as in previous years, the highest provincial crime rates occurred in Saskatchewan, followed by British Columbia and Manitoba. The lowest crime rates in that year were in Newfoundland and Labrador and Quebec, where the crime rate fell by 2 percent and 3 percent, respectively. In 2001, Saskatchewan and Manitoba reported the highest violent crime rates, while Quebec and Prince Edward Island reported the lowest. The highest property crime rate was reported in British Columbia, while Newfoundland and Labrador had the lowest property crime rates (Statistics Canada 2002).

Although folk wisdom might suggest that there is more crime in larger cities than in small cities or towns, this is not, in fact, the case. While greater numbers of crime do, indeed, occur in larger than in smaller cities, this must be set against the greater number of people living in such areas. For example, in 2001, the rate of violent crime in Toronto, Canada's largest metropolitan area, was 876 per 100 000—substantially below that of Regina (1614), Saskatoon (1663), Vancouver (1053), and Winnipeg (1309). The rate of property crime in Toronto (2932) was also lower than the property crime rate in these cities. In 2001, the property crime rate in Regina was 9661 per 100 000 population, while in Saskatoon it was 6616, in Vancouver 7347, and in Winnipeg 5967. Indeed, in 2001, Toronto, along with Chicoutimi-Jonquière, Québec, and Trois-Rivières, had the lowest crime rate among Canada's 25 census metropolitan areas (Statistics Canada 2002).

Costs of Crime and Violence

Crime does not result only or primarily in physical injury and loss of life or property; other, less tangible costs are incurred. Although the immediate victims of criminal acts bear the costs of crime most acutely, a far broader constituency may experience the economic, social, and psychological costs of crime.

Economic Costs of Crime and Violence

Conklin (1998: 71–72) suggests that the financial costs of crime can be classified into at least six categories. First are direct losses from crime, such as the destruction of buildings through arson, of private property through vandalism, and of the environment by polluters. Second are costs associated with the transferring of property. Bank robbers, car thieves, and embezzlers have all taken property from its rightful owner at tremendous expense to the victim and to society. For example, the Organized Crime Impact Study reported that such economic crimes as securities fraud and telemarketing scams cost Canadians a minimum of $5 billion each year (Solicitor General 1999).

A third major cost of crime is that associated with criminal violence, such as the loss of productivity of injured workers and the medical expenses of victims. Fourth are the costs associated with the production and sale of illegal goods and services, that is, illegal expenditures. The expenditure of money on drugs, gambling, and prostitution diverts funds away from the legitimate economy and enterprises and lowers property values in high-crime neighbourhoods. Fifth is the cost of prevention and protection, that is, the millions of dollars spent on house alarms, security devices, weapons for protection, bars for windows, timers for lights, automobile security systems, and the like.

Finally, there is the cost of the criminal justice system. According to the Business Network on Crime Prevention (2001), "governments spend almost $12 billion a year on Canada's police services, courts and corrections that make up our criminal justice system." They emphasize that this is a conservative figure, which "represents only a small portion of the total costs of crime." If the personal and physical costs, such as those associated with pain and suffering of victims or lost productivity are included, the annual costs of crime may exceed $58 billion (Figure 4.10). It should be noted that this estimate does *not* include the costs of white-collar crimes, tax evasion, or stock market manipulation.

Social and Psychological Costs of Crime and Violence

Crime and violence entail social and psychological, as well as economic, costs. According to the 2000 International Crime Victimization Survey, more than eight out of ten Canadians (83 percent) report feel very or fairly safe when

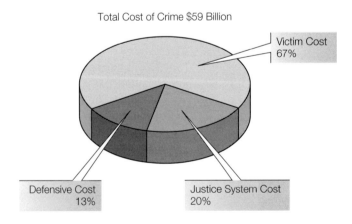

Total Cost of Crime $59 Billion

Victim Cost 67%

Defensive Cost 13%

Justice System Cost 20%

Defensive Costs $7.49 Billion (13%)
    Expenditure on Security
    Insurance Administration
Victim Costs $39.44 Billion (67%)
    Property Stolen and Damaged
    Emotional and Physical Impact on Victims
    Lost Output
    Health Services
    Victim Support Services
    Drug-Related Costs
Justice System Costs $11.97 Billion (20%)
    Police
    Prosecution
    Legal Aid
    Courts
    Adult correction
    Youth correction
TOTAL $58.91 Billion

■ **Figure 4.10** *Total Cost of Crime: $59 Billion*

SOURCE: Statistics Canada, *Juristat*, November 2002, www.canada.justice.gc.ca/en/ps/rs.

walking alone in their area after dark. However, Canadians were more pessimistic than those living in Finland, Sweden, the United States, or Scotland when asked about their perceived likelihood of experiencing a break-in. Only 66 percent of Canadians believed that the chance of a break-in was unlikely—compared with 84 percent in Finland, 79 percent in Sweden, 78 percent in the United States, and 71 percent in Scotland. In consequence, it is, perhaps, not surprising that no fewer than 80 percent of Canadians reported the use of at least one type of security measure (e.g., a burglar alarm, special door locks, special window/door grilles, a high fence, and so on) (Besserer 2002).

In various ways, it is evident that the fear of crime and violence affects community life:

> If frightened citizens remain locked in their homes instead of enjoying public spaces, there is a loss of public and community life, as well as a loss of "social capital"—the family and neighbourhood channels that transmit positive social values from one generation to the next. (National Research Council 1994: 5–6)

This is particularly true of women and the elderly who restrict their activities, living "limited lives," as a consequence of fear (Madriz 2000).

White-collar crimes also take a social and psychological toll at both the individual and the societal levels. Moore and Mills (1990) state that the effects of white-collar crime include "(a) diminished faith in a free economy and in business leaders, (b) loss of confidence in political institutions, processes and leaders, and (c) erosion of public morality" (p. 414). Crime also causes personal pain and suffering, the destruction of families, lowered self-esteem, shortened life expectancy, and disease.

Strategies for Action: Responding to Crime and Violence

In addition to economic policies designed to reduce unemployment and poverty, numerous social policies and programs have been initiated to alleviate the problem of crime and violence. These policies and programs are directed toward children at risk of being offenders, community crime prevention, criminal justice policies, and legislative action.

Youth Programs

Early intervention programs acknowledge that it is better to prevent crime than to "cure" it once it has occurred. Preschool enrichment programs, such as the Perry Preschool Project, have been successful in reducing rates of aggression in young children. After random assignment of children to either a control or experimental group, experimental group members received academically oriented interventions for one to two years, frequent home visits, and weekly parent–teacher conferences. When control and experimental groups were compared, the experimental group had better grades, higher rates of high-school graduation, lower rates of unemployment, and fewer arrests (Murray et al. 1997).

Recognizing the link between youthful offenders and adult criminality, many anticrime programs are directed toward at-risk youths. These prevention strategies include the federal government's Crime Prevention Initiative, with its focus

The eight blunders that lead to violence in society: wealth without work; pleasure without conscience; knowledge without character; commerce without morality; science without humanity; worship without sacrifice; politics without principle; rights without responsibilities.

MOHANDAS K. GANDHI
Indian nationalist leader and peace activist

on proactive programs for high-risk families. Others examples are youth programs such as Boys and Girls Clubs and the national Aboriginal Head Start program. These programs are designed to keep young people "off the streets," provide a safe and supportive environment, and offer activities that promote skill development and self-esteem. According to Gest and Friedman (1994), housing projects with such programs report 13 percent fewer juvenile crimes and a 25 percent decrease in the use of crack.

Finally, many youth programs are designed to engage juveniles in non-criminal activities. While sports are probably the most common example, other recreation-based programs entail music, theatre arts, dance, and the visual arts. One such program was developed in Chicago in 1991. Aimed at the city's thousands of inner-city, unemployed, low-income youths between the ages of 14 and 21, "Gallery 37" now provides more than 2000 paid apprenticeship positions with local artists. The program is so successful that similar programs now exist in 16 U.S. cities as well as in Adelaide, Australia, and London, England (OJP 1998).

Community Programs

Programs such as Neighbourhood Watch, Block Parents, Crime Stoppers, and Operation Identification involve local residents in crime-prevention strategies. The objective of such programs is to reduce crime by heightening community involvement in crime-prevention strategies. Neighbourhood Watch programs, which are developed with the help of local police departments or services, offer advice on how residents may best protect their homes and belongings and encourage participants to watch out for and report suspicious activities in their neighbourhoods to the police.

Law Enforcement Agencies

Police policies and practices can also affect crime rates. Seagrave (1997) noted that the mission statement of every Canadian police force in the 1990s contained evidence of formal commitment to the concept of **community policing**. Community-oriented policing involves collaborative efforts among the police, the citizens of a community, and local leaders. As part of community policing efforts, officers speak to citizens groups, consult with social agencies, and enlist the aid of corporate and political leaders in the fight against neighbourhood crime (COPS 1998; Lehrur 1999). Officers using community-policing techniques often employ "practical approaches" to crime intervention. Such solutions may include what Felson (1998) calls "situational crime prevention." Felson argues that simply minimizing the opportunity for its occurrence could prevent much crime. For example, cars could be outfitted with unbreakable glass, flush-sill lock buttons, an audible reminder to remove keys, and a high-security lock for steering columns (p. 168).

In addition, programs aimed at crime victims now exist in almost all police departments in Canada. Victim assistance programs are designed to provide crime victims with details on the progress of their case, facilitate the return of property to rightful owners, and act as a referral agency to other support groups in the local community. Often heavily dependent on volunteers, such services may signal the development of a partnership between the police and a local community agency or institution. In Ottawa, the Salvation Army works in collaboration with the Ottawa Police Department to supply victim services. In Montreal, the University of Montreal, in cooperation with the Montreal Urban Community Police, operates the Integrated Victim Assistance program (Seagrave 1997).

According to the 1999 General Social Survey, while the majority of Canadians feel that their local police are doing a good job, their perceptions of our criminal courts, prisons, and parole systems are less favourable (Tufts 2000).

Criminal Justice Policy

The criminal justice system is based on the principle of **deterrence**, that is, the use of harm or the threat of harm to prevent unwanted behaviours. It assumes that people rationally choose to commit crime, weighing the rewards and consequences of their actions. Thus, the recent emphasis on "get tough" measures holds that maximizing punishment will increase deterrence and cause crime rates to decrease. Research indicates, however, that the effectiveness of deterrence is a function of not only the severity of the punishment, but the certainty and swiftness of the punishment as well. Further, "get tough" policies create other criminal justice problems, including overcrowded prisons, and, consequently, the need for plea-bargaining and early release programs.

Capital Punishment With capital punishment, the state (the federal government in Canada) takes the life of a person as punishment for a crime. Although capital punishment has not been used in Canada since 1962 and was formally abolished in this country in 1976, the state, of course, retains the right to bring it back. Since the 1970s, Gallup polls have consistently noted that the majority of Canadians believe that the courts are too lenient with offenders: in the fall of 1943, Gallup reported that 80 percent of Canadians were in favour of capital punishment. In 1995, approximately 85 percent of a national random sample of Canadians maintained that the courts did not deal harshly enough with criminals, particularly young offenders, and about 82 percent believed that the death penalty should be exercised in some instances (Bibby 1995). Although support for the use of capital punishment has declined in recent years, data from the 2000 Project Canada survey indicates that 74 percent of Canadian adults and 59 percent of Canadian teenagers agree that "the death penalty should sometimes be used to punish criminals" (Bibby 2001: 244).

Proponents of capital punishment argue that executions of convicted murderers are necessary to convey public disapproval and intolerance for such heinous crimes. Those against capital punishment believe that no one, including the state, has the right to take another person's life and that putting convicted murderers behind bars for life is a "social death" that conveys the necessary societal disapproval.

Proponents of capital punishment also argue that it deters individuals from committing murder. Critics of capital punishment hold, however, that since most homicides are situational and are not planned, offenders do not consider the consequences of their actions before they commit the offence. Critics also point out that the United States has a much higher murder rate than Canada or Western European nations that do not practise capital punishment and that death sentences are racially discriminatory. For example, a recent study on federal capital cases in the United States found that Blacks were less likely than

We are creating the kind of society where the criminal is out of jail before his victim is out of hospital.

RICHARD NEEDHAM
Newspaper columnist

I do not believe that every vulture is a maladjusted nightingale.

T. GEORGE STREET
*Former chairman of the
National Parole Board of
Canada*

Whites to have their sentences reduced through plea bargaining (Worden 2000b).

Capital punishment advocates suggest that executing a convicted murderer relieves the taxpayer of the costs involved in housing, feeding, guarding, and providing medical care for inmates. Opponents of capital punishment argue that the principles that decide life and death issues should not be determined by financial considerations. In addition, taking care of convicted murderers for life may actually be less costly than sentencing them to death, due to the lengthy and costly appeal process for capital punishment cases (Garey 1985; "Myths" 1998).

Nevertheless, those in favour of capital punishment argue that it protects society by preventing convicted individuals from committing another crime, including the murder of another inmate or prison official. Opponents contend, however, that capital punishment may result in innocent people being sentenced to death. For example, since 1973, 76 death row inmates in the United States have been released when new evidence supported their innocence (*The Economist* 2000). Further, a recent report by the (U.S.) Justice Project entitled "A Broken System" found "serious, reversible error in nearly seven out of ten of the thousands of capital sentences" that were reviewed over the 23-year study period (Liebman et al. 2000). In Russia, it is reported that almost one in three (30 percent) of capital punishment cases may have had judicial errors that resulted in a wrongful execution (MacIntyre 1999). Even though 35 countries abolished the death penalty between 1985 and 1998, as of October 1, 2000, there were 3703 prisoners on death row in the United States (Ash 2001: 69; MacIntyre 1999).

The highly publicized cases of David Milgaard, Guy Paul Morin, and Donald Marshall should remind us that wrongful convictions do occur. David Milgaard served 23 years in various Canadian prisons, including the Oak Ridge institution for dangerous mentally ill offenders in Penetanguishene, Ontario, for the 1970 sex slaying of a Saskatoon nursing aide. He was finally exonerated in 1997 when DNA tests showed that he was not the killer (see this chapter's *Focus on Technology*). Donald Marshall, wrongfully convicted for the 1971 murder of a teenager who was stabbed to death in a Sydney, Nova Scotia park, spent 11 years in prison. Guy Paul Morin was wrongfully convicted in the sex slaying of a young Queensville, Ontario girl, faced two first-degree murder trials and spent 17 months in custody. In these cases, and a handful of others, the individuals have fought for their vindication on charges of murder and received, as partial redress, financial settlements from the federal and provincial governments. In the largest settlement to date for a wrongfully convicted person, Milgaard received $9.25 million in compensation for his legal fees (which alone totalled $1.5 million), pain and suffering, lost income, and out-of-pocket expenses; his mother received $750 000 for the legal and personal costs she had incurred during her long struggle to prove that her son was innocent (Bourrie 1999). There is, of course, no way of ever attempting to compensate those who have been wrongfully convicted and received, as a penalty, capital punishment.

Rehabilitation versus Incapacitation An important debate focuses on the primary purpose of the criminal justice system: Is it to rehabilitate offenders or to incapacitate them through incarceration? Both **rehabilitation** and **incapacitation** are concerned with recidivism rates, or the extent to which criminals

It is better to risk saving a guilty person than to condemn an innocent one.

VOLTAIRE (FRANÇOIS MARIE AROUET)
Zadig

My object all sublime,
I shall achieve in time—
to make the punishment fit the crime.

WILLIAM SCHWENCK GILBERT
Lyricist

DNA Evidence

Increasingly, law enforcement officers in Canada, the United States, and Europe are using what is called DNA fingerprinting in the identification of criminal suspects. DNA stands for deoxyribonucleic acid, which is found in the nucleus of every cell and contains an individual's complete and unique genetic makeup. Developed in the mid-1980s, DNA fingerprinting is a general term used to describe the process of analyzing and comparing DNA from different sources to the DNA of a suspect. Evidence that can be used includes evidence found at a crime scene, such as blood, semen, hair, saliva, fibres, and skin tissue.

In the fall of 1998, the FBI initiated the Combined DNA Index System. This database contains the DNA fingerprints of 250 000 convicted felons and more than 4600 DNA samples from unsolved crime scenes. Despite the database being in operation less than two years, the "FBI claims that 200 outstanding cases have already been solved" (Kluger 1999: 1). In 1995, Parliament enacted amendments to the *Criminal Code* of Canada to create the DNA warrant system. A DNA warrant could be issued during criminal investigations for a list of designated offences and DNA samples taken and stored. In that year alone, federal laboratories in Canada handled DNA evidence in the prosecution of 722 murders and 1289 assaults (Statistics Canada 1998: 510). DNA analysis is helpful not just to prosecutors—12 Canadian prisoners were released from custody on the strength of DNA evidence. DNA was used to vindicate Guy Paul Morin and David Milgaard, long after they were wrongfully convicted of murders they did not commit.

Despite these success stories, there is tremendous concern about the use of DNA evidence and, specifically, questions about how donors would be selected and what methods of data collection would be used. Libertarians fear possible violations of civil rights, particularly after a recent court decision by a French judge who ruled that all men in a village would be DNA tested to locate the killer of a 13-year-old girl. In England, police officials legally take samples of blood or skin tissue from every criminal suspect (Gleick 1997: 3). In two recent murder cases, Canadian police officers conducted mass DNA screenings and asked hundreds of potential suspects to consent to testing. In the first, the 1998 stabbing of a female employee at an adult-video store in Sudbury, Ontario, Sudbury Regional Police officers took DNA from more than 400 possible suspects. In the second, the Port Alberni (British Columbia) RCMP examined DNA from 350 suspects in relation to the 1996 sexual assault and murder of an 11-year-old girl. While asking possible suspects to consent to testing is legal, some have expressed fear that it may go too far. For example, Toronto lawyer James Lockyer rhetorically asks what will happen to those who refuse to provide samples and remarks, "That's where harassment might begin, if police don't take no for an answer." Toronto lawyer and forensic DNA authority Ricardo Federico queries, "Is this what we want, having the science police knocking on everybody's door?" (*Maclean's* 1999: 13). In addition, concerns have been expressed in relation to what methods of data collection will be used and potential abuses of analysis results. For example, DNA evidence might be used to simply *imply* guilt, as in the case of DNA information that indicates "proclivities for aggression" (McCullagh 1999:1). These concerns explain why, until relatively recently, England had the only nationwide DNA databank in the world (Gleick 1997; Goldberg 1998). Canada's national DNA data bank was established in 1998.

Nevertheless, the future of DNA fingerprinting is likely to be bright. It's less expensive than ever before, predicted to be as low as $10 a test within a few years, compared to earlier costs of $200 to $300. As technology has become increasingly sophisticated, the time it takes to conduct the analysis has decreased from weeks to days, and portable DNA analysis units are in the making (NIJ 2000a). Further, even if DNA fingerprinting doesn't survive the legal scrutiny it's likely to come under, it remains a valuable identification technique used in biology, archaeology, medical diagnosis, paleontology, and forensics.

SOURCES: Gleick, Elizabeth. 1997. "The Killer Left a Trace." *Time*, September 1: 150. Goldberg, Carey. 1998. "DNA Databanks Giving Police a Powerful Weapon, and Critics." *New York Times*, February 19: 1. Kluger, Jeffery. 1999. "DNA Detectives." *Time*, Canadian edition, January 11: 46–47. *Maclean's*. 1999. "Rounding up Suspects for Their DNA." December 13: 13. McCullagh, Declan. 1999. "The Debate of DNA Evidence." *Wired News*, July 12, 1. http://www.wirednews.com/news. National Institute of Justice. 2000. "National Commission on the Future of DNA Evidence." Washington, DC, U.S. Department of Justice. http://www.ojp.usdoj.gov/hij/dna. Statistics Canada. 1998. *Canada Yearbook 2000*. Ottawa: Ministry of Industry.

commit another crime. Advocates of rehabilitation believe changing the criminal can reduce recidivism, whereas proponents of incapacitation think it can best be reduced by placing the offender in prison so that he or she is unable to commit further crimes.

Societal fear of crime has led to a public emphasis on incapacitation, a demand for tougher mandatory sentences, and a reduction in the use of probation and parole (DiIulio 1999; Human Rights Watch 2000). Canada is, indeed, locking people up. In 2000, Canada had 31 467 people in prison for a rate of 118 per 100 000 population. In 1999–2000, Canada's prison population was composed of 12 816 inmates in federal institutions and 18 651 inmates in various forms of provincial/territorial custody. Although we imprison fewer members of our population that the United States (690 per 100 000 population) or Russia (675), our incarceration rate already exceeds those of many other Western democracies (Figure 4.11). In addition, under the Young Offenders Act, Canada had a record of youth custody that ranked "among the highest in the industrialized world, 10 to 15 times higher than in many European countries" (Campaign 2000 2001: 11).

According to the Solicitor General of Canada (2002), approximately $2 billion is spent on Canada's adult federal and provincial correctional systems each year. "The cost of keeping an offender in a federal penitentiary is about $50 000 per year. This compares to approximately $33 000 for a halfway house and $9000 to supervise an inmate on parole." It is emphasized that "[n]o matter how you add it up, locking offenders up and throwing away the key is an expensive proposition" (Solicitor General 2002).

While incapacitation is clearly enhanced by longer prison sentences, rehabilitation may not be. Rehabilitation assumes that criminal behaviour is caused by sociological, psychological, and/or biological forces rather than being solely a product of free will. If such forces can be identified, the necessary change can be instituted. Rehabilitation programs include education and job training, individual and group therapy, substance abuse counselling, and behaviour modification. While the evaluation of rehabilitation programs is difficult and results are mixed, incapacitation must of necessity be a temporary measure. Unless all criminals are sentenced to life, at some point about 98 percent will be returned to society.

If we closed every jail and prison tomorrow, data show that it would have zero effect—nothing would get worse, nothing would get better.

J.W. (Hans) Mohr
Specialist in criminal justice

Alternatives to Incarceration In addition to incarceration, there are other strategies that are being pursued. Offenders may be ordered by judges to provide restitution and financially compensate their victims for property loss and personal injury. Electronic monitoring involves offenders being required to wear an electronic bracelet that is generally placed around an ankle or wrist. "If they stray too far from a receiver unit attached to a telephone, when they are supposed to be home, an alarm sounds at the monitoring centre" (Solicitor General 2002). In cases where an offender does not pose a danger to the community and where the jail term that would normally be imposed would be less than two years, a conditional sentence may be used, requiring the offender to seek treatment, for example. Other community-based alternatives to incarceration include a community service order requiring an offender to perform a certain number of hours of work within the community.

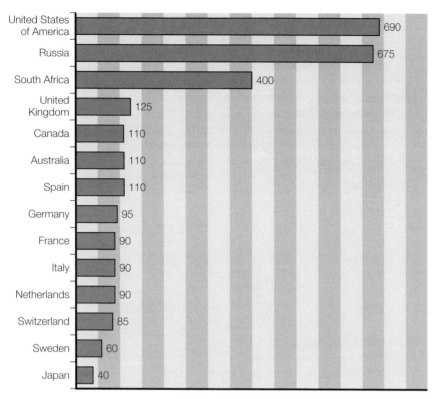

Figure 4.11 *Rate of Incarceration in Selected Nations, 1997–2000*

SOURCE: The Sentencing Project. 2001. http://www.sentencingproject. org. Reprinted by permission of The Sentencing Project.

Incarceration Rate (number of people in prison per 100 000 population)

Mediation services, which work in cooperation with the Crown Attorney's office, bring victimizers and their victims together in the belief that both will benefit. For example, if committing a crime requires, to varying degrees, that an offender discount the consequences of his or her act on the victim or blames the victim (e.g., "she's got insurance to cover the loss," "he was asking for it"), it is thought that face-to-face meetings will encourage a sense of personal culpability and compassion for the victim. Similarly, if the *hindsight effect* encourages victims to overestimate the extent to which they could have avoided victimization (Janoff-Bulman et al. 1985), confronting one's victimizer may result in a lessened amount of self-blame. Moreover, insofar as those who have experienced criminal victimization are likely to demonstrate a heightened fear of crime, it may prove personally empowering to see one's victimizer as simply another human being.

Victim and offender mediation represents one of many programs that may flow from a framework of **restorative justice**. Restorative justice "is an approach to justice that focuses on dealing with the harmful effects of crime by engaging victims, offenders and the community in a process of reparation and healing" (Solicitor General 2002). Many Aboriginal communities have traditionally emphasized this model of justice in which

- the focus is on problem solving and restoration of harmony;
- restitution and reconciliation are used as a means of restoration;
- the community acts as a facilitator in the restorative process;
- the offender is impressed with the impact of his action on the total community;
- the holistic context of an offence is taken into account including moral, social, economic, political, and religious and cosmic considerations;
- stigma of offences is removable through conformity;
- repentance and forgiveness are important factors;
- offenders take an active role in the restorative process (Bryant 1999: 21).

Unlike the traditional criminal justice process, restorative justice emphasizes individual and social healing, forgiveness, communication, and joint problem solving rather than punishment. Although the behaviour of the offender is condemned, the value of the offender as an individual is affirmed.

Legislative Action Throughout the last decade, the federal government has taken various steps to combat crime. In relation to organized crime, for example, these efforts include the 1994 Anti-Smuggling Initiative, which targets smuggling and distribution networks at the border, in Canada's ports, and across the country; and the 1996 establishment of the *Witness Protection Program Act*, which established a formal, national program to protect those who assist police investigations. Legislative amendments to the *Criminal Code* in 1997 included a package of anti-gang measures that made participation in a criminal organization an indictable offence, punishable by up to 14 years in prison. In 1998, amendments made to the Corrections and Conditional Release Act sought to ensure that those convicted of offences related to organized crime were ineligible for Accelerated Parole Review. In 2002, legislative changes included the introduction of three new offences that targeted those involved with criminal organizations; broader powers for law enforcement officers to seize the profits of crime and property used in a crime; and increased protection of law enforcement officers from criminal liability when they commit certain acts that would otherwise be considered illegal when investigating and infiltrating criminal organizations (Department of Justice 2002c).

Legislative efforts have also sought to curtail child sexual exploitation. For example, in 1997, amendments to the *Criminal Code* provided for the prosecution of persons who engage in child sex tourism in other countries and facilitated the apprehension and prosecution of persons who seek out the services of child victims of sexual exploitation in Canada. More recent legislation (Bill C-15A) that came into effect on July 23, 2002 makes it illegal to use the Internet to communicate with a child for the purpose of committing a sexual offence against that child, as well as to transmit, make available, export, or access child pornography. It also allows the courts to order the deletion of child pornography posted on Canadian computer systems, makes child pornography and the new Internet luring offence "triggering offences" for making an application to designate a person as a dangerous offender, allows for the seizure of materials or equipment used to commit a related offence, and simplifies the process of prosecuting Canadians who sexually exploit children in other countries (Department of Justice 2002a).

In 2001, in response to the September 11, 2001 terrorist attacks in New York City and Washington, D.C., Canada's highly controversial Anti-Terrorism Act

While there is a lower class I am in it, while there is a criminal element I am of it; while there is a soul in prison, I am not free.

EUGENE VICTOR DEBS
"Labor and Freedom"

(Bill C-36) passed through the Senate with a vote of 45 to 21 and became law. The Anti-Terrorism Act, like its counterpart in the United Kingdom, defines terrorist activity as encompassing acts of violence or destruction that are intended to influence government or intimidate the public. Both definitions require proof that an offence was committed out of religious, ideological, or political motivation. Among its provisions, Canada's Anti-Terrorism Act allows police to exercise "preventative arrest" powers and to detain, without judicial warrant, suspected terrorists for up to 48 hours. It also extends the valid period of a wiretap and lowers the standard required to obtain a wiretap. Unlike the United States, Canada does not seek to try suspected foreign terrorists in secret military tribunals. Unlike Britain, where the law provides for a 10-year maximum penalty for simply belonging to a terrorist organization, Canada has not banned membership.

Supporters of the Act have argued that, following the September 11 attack, it was necessary to bolster Canadian security in order to comply with Resolution 1373 of the United Nations Security Council that "called on all member countries to adopt the necessary measures to prevent any one country from becoming a haven for terrorists" (Chwialkowska 2001). Critics, however, maintain that the definition of terrorism used is too broad, that the Act contains measures that are open for abuse, and that there are only limited provisions for oversight. Moreover, some have expressed concern that **racial profiling**—the practice of targeting suspects based upon their race—will become a prominent feature of investigations conducted under this Act (see this chapter's *The Human Side* feature).

Canada's new Youth Criminal Justice Act (YCJA), which will replace the Young Offender's Act (1984), also represents an attempt to respond to the social problem of crime. The core principles of the YCJA are that:

- protection of society is the paramount objective of the youth justice system, which is best achieved through prevention, meaningful consequences for youth crime, and rehabilitation;
- young people should be treated separately from adults under criminal law and in a separate youth justice system that emphasizes fair and proportionate accountability, keeping in mind the dependency and level of development and maturity of youth;
- measures to address youth crime must hold the offender accountable; address the offending behaviour of the youth; reinforce respect for social values; encourage repair of the harm done to victims and the community; respect gender, ethnic, cultural, and linguistic differences; involve the family, community, and other agencies; and be responsive to the circumstances of youth with special requirements; and
- parents and victims have a constructive role to play in the youth justice system, and should be kept informed and encouraged to participate (Department of Justice 2002b).

Understanding Crime and Violence

What can we conclude from the information presented in this chapter? Research on crime and violence supports the contentions of both functionalists and conflict theorists. The inequality in society, along with the emphasis on

Racial Profiling after the Terrorist Attacks of 9/11

The following article, written by journalist Stephen Thorne, reminds us of the dangers of stereotyping certain groups within society as "criminals" in general and, in particular, of the human costs of racial profiling. The original, unabridged article can be found on the World Wide Web at http://www.1121_rights-cp.html.

He's lived in the same Toronto house for 32 years, and the thing about Canada that Ahmed Valiallah always loved most was that the people were friendly and helpful. But all that has changed since September 28, when the former schoolteacher was told insurance on his retirement investment, a building in downtown Toronto, was cancelled. The reason? Nabil Al-Marabh, a Kuwaiti with suspected links to the Sept. 11 hijackers, worked in his uncle's copy store in the building Valiallah owns.

It's the latest in a string of cases some say are changing the face of Canada as a fair and tolerant society following the hijackings and subsequent attacks by Islamic extremists. Incidents of ethnic or religious profiling are "quite prevalent and very under-reported," says Riad Saloojee, executive director of the Council on American-Islamic Relations Canada. Some contend that in the rush to fight terrorism, Canadians are losing the very values they're trying to defend. The council has documented 115 cases of threats, harassment, and profiling since the attacks on New York and Washington. Among them:

- The former head of the Canadian-Arab Foundation and once-esteemed member of the immigration review board is jailed for six days after she's caught up in a scam perpetrated by two men who came to her for immigration advice; her bail was set at $10 000.
- A nuclear engineer is questioned by RCMP and CCIS on everything from his religion to his friendships, then fired from his job at Chalk River. He's rehired after it apparently turns out to be a case of mistaken identity.
- A Muslim is asked at the border if he has a rocket launcher in his van.

There have been numerous incidents where Muslims, and Sikhs as well, have inexplicably been ordered off airplanes. It happened to Saloojee. Nobody told him why, except that it was "security-related." "There is this climate where Muslims have been collectively blamed for the actions of those terrorists," says Saloojee. "There is an increased wariness of people who look Arab or look Muslim. I think that's something that's come to light in a lot of these profiling incidents where terrorism is linked to ethnicity or religion."

Valiallah, whose grandfather immigrated to South Africa from India in the 1880s, thought he'd left that kind of persecution behind with South African apartheid in 1969. He has filed suit against the insurance company in Toronto

material well-being and corporate profit, produces societal strains and individual frustrations. Poverty, unemployment, urban decay, and substandard schools, the symptoms of social inequality, in turn lead to the development of criminal subcultures and definitions favourable to law violation. Further, the continued weakening of social bonds between members of society and society as a whole, the labelling of some acts and actors as "deviant," and the differential treatment of minority groups at the hands of the criminal justice system encourage criminal behaviour.

While crime and violence constitute major social problems in society, they are also symptoms of other social problems, such as poverty and economic inequality, racial discrimination, drug addiction, an overburdened educational system, and troubled families. The criminal justice system continues to struggle to find effective and just measures to deal with crime and criminal offenders. Many citizens and politicians have embraced the idea that society should "get small-claims court claiming that Al-Marabh's guilt or innocence should have no bearing on his property's risk assessment. The insurance company was "high-handed, wanton, abusive, and offensive," the suit says. "Such conduct was based on racial and religious profiling and stereotyping."

Profiling. Stereotyping. Racial discrimination. The words have come up time and time again since Sept. 11. Valiallah's counsel, Harry Kopyto, who successfully represented fired nuclear engineer Mohamed Attiah, says the incidents are driven by fear and mistrust. "As a general rule, persons who are in positions of power, including the police, are jumping the gun," says Kopyto. "They're assuming the worst based on perceived qualities. They see somebody's Arabic or Islamic, the assumption is almost that he must be guilty of something."...

But the RCMP and the Canadian Security Intelligence Service claim they've conducted business as usual. "The RCMP does not profile by race or religion," said Cpl. Benoit Desjardins, an Ottawa-based spokesman. "We do investigate, as in any other case apart from September 11, based on information or complaints we've received. We haven't changed policy about our investigations, except that we've concentrated efforts on that major file."

The Mounties' September 11 tip line had received 8500 calls by the first week of December. Some have been less justified than others, but that didn't necessarily stop the police. In one case, a neighbour's suspicions were aroused when visitors started showing up at the Muslim house next door. Police questioned the owners for several hours. It turned out there had been a death in the family. Retired general Lewis MacKenzie, new security adviser to the Ontario government, says authorities would be nuts not to exercise some degree of profiling based on country of origin—but not religion or ethnicity.

"People coming from states that sponsor terrorism have to be checked over a little more carefully when they arrive in the country," says MacKenzie. "It seems like common sense to me. It's not ethnic profiling." A bunch of "blond-haired, blue-eyed, six-foot-two Swedes" coming from Kabul, Afghanistan, would warrant just as much attention as anyone else on the plane, he said. MacKenzie says he doesn't believe there are many incidents like the Attiah and Valiallah cases because, if there were, Canadians would be hearing about them. "This type of offensive behaviour wouldn't be tolerated and it wouldn't be kept secret."...

For Valiallah, a proud Canadian, it has been a bitter disappointment. "From my experience, whenever I had difficulties or other people had difficulties and they went to different institutions, there was always a helping hand," he said. "And here, (the insurance company) was pushing me away. I wasn't a Canadian any more."

SOURCE: Thorne, Stephen. 2001. "Victims of Racial Profiling Say Canadians' Attitudes Changing for the Worse." December 21. http://www.canoe.ca/CNEWS2001Review/1221_rights-cp.html.

tough on crime." Get-tough measures include building more prisons and imposing lengthier mandatory prison sentences on criminal offenders. Advocates of harsher prison sentences argue that "getting tough on crime" makes society safer by keeping criminals off the streets and deterring potential criminals from committing crime. Yet, for example, an analysis of over 200 studies comparing institutionalized and non-institutionalized serious young offenders found that community-based treatment was superior to incarceration in lowering recidivism rates (Lipsey and Wilson 1998). Prison sentences may not only be ineffective in preventing crime, they may also promote it by creating an environment in which prisoners learn criminal behaviour, values, and attitudes from each other.

Rather than getting tough on crime after the fact, some advocate getting serious about prevention. Re-emphasizing the values of honesty, responsibility, and civic virtue is a basic line of prevention with which most agree. The recent move towards restorative justice, a philosophy primarily concerned with repairing the victim–offender–community relationship, is in direct response to concerns about an adversarial criminal justice system that encourages offenders to deny, justify, or otherwise avoid taking responsibility for their actions. As we have noted, restorative justice holds that the justice system should be a "healing process rather than a distributor of retribution and revenge" (Siegel 2000: 278). Key components of restorative justice include restitution to the victim, remedying the harm to the community, and mediation. At a recent meeting of the United Nations' Congress in Crime Prevention and Treatment of Offenders, a summary resolution called the *Vienna Declaration* was approved. The resolution calls for the worldwide use of restorative justice intervention (United Nations 2000).

Critical Thinking

1 Crime statistics are sensitive to demographic changes. Suggest how the aging of the Canadian population may affect Canadian crime rates as we move into the twenty-first century.

2 Some countries have high rates of gun ownership and low crime rates. Others have low rates of gun ownership and low crime rates. What do you think accounts for the differences between these countries?

3 One of the criticisms of crime theories is that they do not explain all crime, all of the time. Identify the theories of crime that are most useful in explaining categories of crime, for example, white-collar crimes, violent crimes, sex crimes, and so on. Explain your choices.

4 The use of technology in crime-related matters is likely to increase dramatically over the next several decades. DNA testing, and the use of heat sensors, blood-detecting chemicals, and computer surveillance are just some of the ways science will help fight crime. As with all technological innovations, however, there is the question, "Who benefits?" Are there gender, race, and class implications of these new technologies?

Key Terms

acquaintance rape	deterrence	restorative justice
classic rape	differential association	secondary deviance
computer crime	incapacitation	strain theory
control theory	labelling theory	street crime
conventional crime	organized crime	subcultural theory
corporate murder	primary deviance	transnational crime
corporate violence	racial profiling	victimless crime
crime	rehabilitation	white-collar crime

Family Problems

Is It True?

1. Since the 1970s, most Canadian women have been delaying their first childbirth until their late 20s and early 30s.

2. One in eight Canadians over the age of 15 provides some kind of care for others who are dealing with a long-term health care problem or a physical limitation.

3. If current rates are maintained, about 3700 out of every 10 000 marriages in Canada will end in divorce.

4. Only one in ten Canadians believes that an unfaithful partner or lack of love and respect are sufficient reasons to divorce.

5. In Canada, a husband who forces his wife to have sex is committing a criminal offence.

Answers: 1 = T, 2 = T, 3 = T, 4 = F, 5 = T

An unhealthy culture cannot have healthy families.

MARY PIPHER
The Shelter of Each Other: Rebuilding Our Families

Nafessa, a 20-year-old university student, usually sat in the front of her sociology class. She was one of those students who always had something to say about whatever the topic was for that day. One day mid-semester, Nafessa came to class 10 minutes late. Although it was a cloudy day, she wore sunglasses. Rather than sit in her usual seat, she took a seat at the back. On this day, Nafessa said nothing during the entire class—highly unusual for her. Concerned by Nafessa's atypical behaviour, her professor approached her after class. "Are you OK?" she asked. Nafessa's voice quivered as she replied, "I had a fight with my boyfriend last night and...well...things got out of hand. I'm sorry I was late." "Did he hurt you?" the professor asked. "He didn't mean to...he's real sorry." Underneath those sunglasses, Nafessa's eye was bruised and swollen.

Jennifer had maintained a 3.2 GPA and had a high B average in her sociology class. Her attendance had been perfect all semester, so when she missed three consecutive classes, her professor e-mailed her to inquire about her absences. In Jennifer's reply, she said she was having some personal problems. Her teacher asked Jennifer to meet with her during office hours. When Jennifer showed up, her face was pale and drawn and she looked exhausted. "What's going on?" the professor asked. Jennifer broke down and cried as she explained that she recently found out that her parents were planning to divorce. The professor encouraged Jennifer to make an appointment with a counsellor on campus. A week later, just three weeks before the end of the spring semester, the professor received an official notice that Jennifer was withdrawing from the course due to medical reasons. Jennifer's depression surrounding her parents' divorce required medication and ongoing counselling through the summer. By fall, she was well enough to return to school.

Eddie was excited about attending university even though it meant leaving his girlfriend Denise, a high-school student, behind. During his separation from Denise, Eddie kept in touch with her through letters, phone calls, and e-mails. About a month into the semester, Denise called Eddie to tell him she was pregnant. Although Eddie loved Denise, he was not sure he was ready to commit to one woman, and he knew he was not ready for the responsibilities of fatherhood. But for Denise, abortion was out of the question. "How could this have happened?" Eddie agonized. "What will happen to my future? My hopes and dreams?"

Each of the above scenarios depicts a real situation that is based on the authors' experiences with university students. These scenarios exemplify the major problems that are discussed in this chapter: violence and abuse in intimate and family relationships, problems of divorce, and problems associated with non-marital and teenage childbearing. Other problems facing families are discussed in other chapters in this text. For example, families are affected by health problems (Chapter 2), substance abuse (Chapter 3), problems of youth and the elderly (Chapter 6), problems with employment and poverty (Chapters 10 and 11), and so on. Before discussing these problems, we look briefly at diversity in families worldwide, and we provide an overview of the changing patterns and structures of households and families in Canada.

The Global Context: Families of the World

Family is a central aspect of every society throughout the world. But family forms are diverse. In Canada, the only legal form of marriage involves **heterosexual monogamy**—a marriage between two opposite-sex partners. However, this situation may soon change as a result of a July 2002 Ontario Superior Court ruling which found the federal law prohibiting same-sex couples from marrying to be unconstitutional. Although this judgment is under appeal at the time of writing, the issue of gay marriage has elicited varying responses in western countries. In 2001, the Netherlands became the first country in the world to legalize same-sex marriage. Cambodia (Kampuchea) has also extended full and equal marriage rights to homosexuals. Seven other countries, specifically Denmark (along with its dependency, Greenland), Hungary, Norway, Sweden, France, Iceland, Spain, and Germany, have enacted *registered partnership* legislation, which, to varying degrees, allows same-sex couples to receive some of the legal benefits of marriage. In contrast, the United States has shown significant opposition to same-sex marriages, with 32 states passing laws forbidding same-sex marriage (Reidmann et al. 2003).

While illegal in Canada since 1878, some societies practise **polygamy**—a form of marriage in which one person may have two or more spouses. The most common form of polygamy is **polygyny**—the concurrent marriage of one man with two or more women. Polygyny may be practised in some Islamic societies, including some regions of Africa. The second form of polygamy is **polyandry**—the concurrent marriage of one woman with two or more men. Polyandry is very rare, but does occur in some groups, including Tibetans and various African groups.

Family values, roles, and norms are also highly variable across societies. For example, unlike in Western societies, in Asian countries, some parents arrange marriages, selecting mates for their children. Another traditional Asian practice is for the eldest son and his wife to move in with the son's parents, where his wife takes care of her husband's parents. In some societies, it is normative for married couples to view each other as equal partners in the marriage, whereas in other societies social values dictate that wives be subservient to their husbands. The role of children also varies across societies. Some societies expect children as young as five years old to work full-time to help support the family. Social acceptance of unmarried couples having children also varies widely throughout the world. Acceptance of this lifestyle ranges from 90 percent or more in parts of Western Europe to fewer than 15 percent in Singapore and India (Global Study of Family Values 1998).

Finally, the ease of obtaining a divorce varies by country. Ireland did not allow divorce under any conditions until 1995, when voters narrowly approved a public referendum allowing divorce for the first time (Thompson and Wyatt 1999). In 2000, the Egyptian Parliament voted to allow women to file for

■ Change is not the same as crisis. We know family by what it does, not by any single "traditional" form.

ERIC W. SANGER
Director, Canadian Families Project

divorce on grounds of incompatibility (Eltahawy 2000). Prior to this new law, Egyptian women could file for divorce only in cases of proven physical or psychological abuse. By contrast, a man could simply say "I divorce you" three times or get a divorce by filing a paper with the marriage registrar without even notifying his wife. Under the new law, a woman who wants a divorce must return her husband's dowry and relinquish all financial claims, including alimony.

It is clear from the previous discussion that families are shaped by the social and cultural contexts in which they exist. As we discuss the family problems addressed in this chapter—violence and abuse, divorce, and nonmarital and teenage childbearing—we refer to social and cultural forces that contribute to these problematic events. Next we look at changing patterns and structures of Canadian families and households.

Changing Patterns and Structures in Canadian Families and Households

Changes in the Canadian census alert us to some of the changes that have occurred in relation to thinking about the family. For example, the 1981 Canadian Census was the first to report on common-law marriages. More recently, the 2001 Canadian Census included two questions that recognized same-sex partners (see Figure 5.1). You should note that Question #6 from the 2001 Census also explicitly recognizes children being raised in same-sex households, even in jurisdictions where provincial or territorial laws do not permit same-sex couples to formally adopt or share guardianship of their children. According to Statistics Canada, a **census family** is "a now married couple (with or without never-married sons and/or daughters of either or both spouses), a couple living common-law (again with or without never-married sons and/or daughters of either or both parents), or a lone parent of any marital status, with at least one never-married son or daughter living in the same dwelling."

As Figure 5.2 indicates, so-called "traditional families" are declining while common-law unions are increasing dramatically. Single-parent families are also on the rise and increasing numbers of couples are opting to live without children. The proportion of married families has declined from 83.1 percent in 1981 to 77.3 percent in 1991 and 70.5 percent in 2001. In contrast, common-law families have grown from 5.6 percent of families in 1981 to 9.8 percent in 1991 and 13.8 percent in 2001. The prevalence of common-law couples is about twice as high in Canada as it is in the United States. Although common-law unions are most popular in Quebec (where common-law families represented 30 percent of all couple families in 2001), Canada's other provinces and territories also have a higher proportion of common-law couples than the United States (11.7 percent versus 8.2 percent). Same-sex couples accounted for less than 1 percent of all Canadian couples and 3 percent of common-law couples in 2001. Moreover, the growth in lone-parent families has also changed the face of Canadian families and, in 2001, lone-parent families accounted for 15.7 percent of families, the vast majority of which were headed by women (Arnold 2002). While in the 1950s and 1960s, the death of a spouse was the major cause of lone parenthood in Canada (with over 60 percent of all lone-parent widows or widowers), currently, divorce, separation, and births outside of marriage have become the primary factors involved in the creation of lone-parent families.

5. **Is this person living with a common-law partner? Common law refers to two people of the opposite sex or of the same sex who live together as a couple but who are not legally married to each other.**

    ☐ Yes

    ☐ No

6. **Relationship to Person 1**

    For each person usually living here, describe his/her relationship to Person 1.

    Mark "X" or specify one response only.

    Stepchildren, adopted children and children of a common-law partner should be considered sons and daughters.

    If none of the choices apply, use the "Other" box to indicate this person's relationship to Person 1. Examples of "Other" relationships to Person 1:

    ☐ grandparent

    ☐ cousin

    ☐ niece or nephew

    ☐ lodger's husband or wife

    ☐ room-mate's daughter or son

    ☐ employee

    ☐ husband or wife of Person 1

    ☐ common-law partner (opposite-sex) of Person 1

    ☐ common-law partner (same-sex) of Person 1

    ☐ son or daughter of Person 1

    ☐ son-in-law or daughter-in-law of Person 1

    ☐ grandchild of Person 1

    ☐ father or mother of Person 1

    ☐ father-in-law or mother-in-law of Person 1

    ☐ brother or sister of Person 1

    ☐ brother-in-law or sister-in-law of Person 1

    ☐ lodger or boarder

    ☐ room-mate

    ☐ other—Specify

    _____

■ **Figure 5.1** *Questions #5 and #6 from the 2001 Canadian Census*

SOURCE: From the Statistics Canada publication, "2001 Canadian Census Questionnaire."

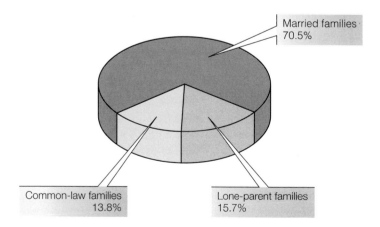

■ **Figure 5.2** *Canadian Families at a Glance: Distribution of Families by Structure*

SOURCE: Statistics Canada, General Social Survey, 1999.

Married families 70.5%

Common-law families 13.8%

Lone-parent families 15.7%

Divorce, remarriage, and stepfamilies have also become more common in the last several decades. Based on 1998 divorce rates, projections are that over a third of marriages (36 percent) will end in divorce within 30 years of marriage (Statistics Canada 2000a). Although remarriage remains the most common aftermath following divorce (with about 75 percent of divorced men and 65 percent of divorced women remarrying) remarriage is less common now than in previous years because of the increasing tendency to cohabit, particularly among younger divorced persons and among divorced men. Estimates suggest that divorced women in their 30s and 40s are now twice as likely to live common-law as to remarry (Le Bourdais et al. 2001).

Some view the trend towards diversification of family forms as signalling the disappearance of marriage and the breakdown of the family. But although traditionalists may view cohabitation (both heterosexual and homosexual), divorce, and single parenthood as threats to the institution of marriage, it is unlikely that marriage will disappear. Most people who cohabit eventually marry, although not necessarily to the person they cohabited with. Very few Canadians remain single: only 6.1 percent of men and 5.2 percent of women aged 60–64 were single (never married) in 1997 (Statistics Canada 1998c). Although the rising rate of marital dissolution seems to suggest a weakening of marriage, divorce may also be viewed as resulting from placing a high value on marriage, such that a less-than-satisfactory marriage is unacceptable. The rate of out-of-wedlock childbirth and single parenting is also not necessarily indicative of a decline in the value of marriage. Edin (2000) found that in a sample of low-income single women with children, most said they would like to be married, but just haven't found "Mr. Right." The persistent value placed on family is also evident in a national survey of Canadian teens that found that almost 9 out of 10 (88 percent) expected to get married and also to stay with the same partner for life (87 percent of males and 89 percent of females) (Bibby 2001: 136).

> [T]he essence of family is: who it is, how it feels, and what it does.
>
> LETTY COTTIN POGREBIN
> *Sociologist*

Sociological Theories of the Family

Three major sociological theories of the family—structural-functionalism, conflict theory, and symbolic interactionism—help to explain different aspects of the family problems we focus on in this chapter: violence and abuse, divorce, and teenage and nonmarital childbearing.

Structural-Functionalist Perspective

The structural-functionalist perspective views the family as a social institution that performs important functions for society, including reproducing new members, regulating sexual activity and procreation, socializing the young, and providing physical and emotional care for family members. According to the structural-functionalist perspective, traditional gender roles contribute to family functioning. Thus, heterosexual two-parent families in which women perform the "expressive" role of managing household tasks and providing emotional care and nurturing to family members and men perform the "instrumental" role of earning income and making major family decisions are viewed as "normal" or "functional." Other family forms (e.g., single-parent families, same-sex unions) are viewed as abnormal or dysfunctional.

> We grow up in families we do not choose, but when we have grown up, most of us choose to live in families. We need support and sympathy, connection and commitment.
>
> TRUDY GOVIER
> **Dilemmas of Trust**

According to the structural-functionalist perspective, increases in divorce and lone parent families signal a "breakdown" of the family. This breakdown is the result of rapid social change and social disorganization. The functionalist perspective views the breakdown of the family as one of the primary social problems in the world today—a problem of such magnitude that it leads to such secondary social problems as crime, poverty, and substance abuse.

Functionalist explanations of family problems examine how changes in other social institutions contribute to family problems. For example, a structural-functionalist view of divorce examines how changes in the economy (more dual-earner marriages) and in the legal system (such as the adoption of "no-fault" divorce) contribute to rising rates of divorce. Changes in the economic institution, specifically falling wages among unskilled and semi-skilled men, also contribute to both intimate partner abuse and the rise in female-headed lone parent households (Edin 2000).

Conflict Perspective

Conflict theory focuses on how social class and power influence marriages and families. Within families, the unequal distribution of power among women and men may contribute to domestic violence. The traditional male domination of families—a system known as **patriarchy**—includes the attitude that married women are essentially the property of husbands. When wives violate or challenge the male head-of-household's authority, the male may react by "disciplining" his wife or using anger and violence to reassert his position of power in the family. The unequal distribution of wealth between men and women, with men traditionally earning more money than women, contributes to inequities in power and fosters economic dependence of wives on husbands.

Conflict theorists also emphasize that social programs and policies that affect families are largely shaped by powerful and wealthy segments of society. The interests of corporations and businesses are often in conflict with the needs of families. Hewlett and West (1998) note that corporate interests undermine family life "by exerting enormous downward pressure on wage levels for young, child-raising adults" (p. 32). Government, which is largely influenced by corporate interests through lobbying and political financial contributions, enacts policies and laws that serve the interests of for-profit corporations, rather than families.

Symbolic Interactionist Perspective

Symbolic interactionism emphasizes that human behaviour is largely dependent upon the meanings and definitions that emerge from small group interaction. Divorce, for example, was once highly stigmatized and informally sanctioned through the criticism and rejection of divorced friends and relatives. As societal definitions of divorce became less negative, however, the divorce rate increased. The social meanings surrounding single parenthood, cohabitation, and delayed childbearing and marriage have changed in similar ways. As the definitions of each of these family variations became less negative, the behaviours became more common.

Symbolic interactionists also point to the effects of labelling on one's self-concept and the way the self-fulfilling prophecy can affect family members'

Some have cited facts such as the high rates of divorce, and changes in the older sexual morality...as evidence of a trend to disorganization in an absolute sense.

TALCOTT PARSONS
Sociologist

Stress occasioned by conflicts between work and family responsibilities extracts a cost—from families, employers, and their communities. Demands of the workplace often spill over into personal and family time to jeopardize not just the amount but also the quality of time spent with loved ones.

VANIER INSTITUTE OF THE FAMILY, 2000

behaviour toward one another. The **self-fulfilling prophecy** implies that we behave according to the expectations of others. For example, when a non-custodial divorced parent (usually a father) is awarded visitation rights, he may view himself as a visitor in his children's lives. The meaning attached to the visitor status can be an obstacle to the father's involvement, as the label "visitor" minimizes the importance of the non-custodial parent's role and results in conflict and emotional turmoil for fathers (Pasley and Minton 2001). Fathers' rights advocates suggest replacing the term "visitation" with such terms as "parenting plan" or "time-sharing arrangement," as these latter terms do not minimize either parent's role.

The symbolic interactionist perspective is useful in understanding the dynamics of domestic violence and abuse. For example, some abusers and their victims learn to define intimate partner violence as an expression of love (Lloyd 2000). **Emotional abuse** often involves using negative labels (e.g., "stupid," "whore," "bad") to define a partner or family member. Such labels negatively affect the self-concepts of abuse victims, often convincing them that they deserve the abuse. Next, we discuss violence and abuse in intimate and family relationships, noting the scope, causes, and consequences of this troubling social problem.

> The culture we have does not make people feel good about themselves. And you have to be strong enough to say if the culture doesn't work, don't buy it.
>
> MORRIE SCHWARTZ
> *Sociologist,* **Tuesdays with Morrie**

Violence and Abuse in Intimate and Family Relationships

Although intimate and family relationships provide many individuals with a sense of well-being, for others, these relationships involve physical violence, verbal and emotional abuse, sexual abuse, and/or neglect. Indeed, in Canadian society, people are more likely to be physically assaulted, abused and neglected, sexually assaulted and molested, and killed in their own homes and by other family members than anywhere else or by anyone else (Statistics Canada 2001). Before reading further, you may want to take the Abusive Behaviour Inventory in this chapter's *Self and Society* feature.

Intimate Partner Violence and Abuse

> All happy families resemble one another; every unhappy family is unhappy in its own fashion.
>
> COUNT LEO NIKOLAYEVITCH TOLSTOY
> *Novelist*

Globally, one woman in every three has been subjected to violence in an intimate relationship (United Nations Development Programme 2000). **Intimate partner violence** refers to actual or threatened violent crimes committed against persons by their current or former spouses, boyfriends, or girlfriends. The 1999 General Social Survey (GSS) found that, when asked, whether "in the past 5 years, your spouse/partner has (1) threatened to hit you with his/her fist or anything else that could have hurt you; (2) thrown anything at you that could have hurt you; (3) pushed, grabbed, or shoved you in a way that could have hurt you; (4) slapped you; (5) kicked, bit, or hit you with his/her fist; (6) hit you with something that could have hurt you; (7) beaten you; (8) choked you; (9) used or threatened to use a gun or knife on you; (10) forced you into any unwanted sexual activity by threatening you, holding you down, or hurting you in some way," the rates of violence reported by Canadian men and women were relatively similar (7 percent and 8 percent respectively). However, this survey found that women were more likely to experience severe forms of violence.

Abusive Behaviour Inventory

Circle the number that best represents your closest estimate of how often each of the behaviours happened in your relationship with your partner or former partner during the previous six months.

1. Never   2. Rarely   3. Occasionally   4. Frequently   5. Very frequently

1. Called you a name and/or criticized you.	1	2	3	4	5
2. Tried to keep you from doing something you wanted to do (e.g., going out with friends, going to meetings).	1	2	3	4	5
3. Gave you angry stares or looks.	1	2	3	4	5
4. Prevented you from having money for your own use.	1	2	3	4	5
5. Ended a discussion with you and made the decision himself/herself.	1	2	3	4	5
6. Threatened to hit or throw something at you.	1	2	3	4	5
7. Pushed, grabbed, or shoved you.	1	2	3	4	5
8. Put down your family and friends.	1	2	3	4	5
9. Accused you of paying too much attention to someone or something else.	1	2	3	4	5
10. Put you on an allowance.	1	2	3	4	5
11. Used your children to threaten you (e.g., told you that you would lose custody, said he/she would leave town with the children).	1	2	3	4	5
12. Became very upset with you because dinner, housework, or laundry was not done when he/she wanted it done or done the way he/she thought it should be.	1	2	3	4	5
13. Said things to scare you (e.g., told you something "bad" would happen, threatened to commit suicide).	1	2	3	4	5
14. Slapped, hit, or punched you.	1	2	3	4	5
15. Made you do something humiliating or degrading (e.g., begging for forgiveness, having to ask his/her permission to use the car or to do something).	1	2	3	4	5
16. Checked up on you (e.g., listened to your phone calls, checked the mileage on your car, called you repeatedly at work).	1	2	3	4	5
17. Drove recklessly when you were in the car.	1	2	3	4	5
18. Pressured you to have sex in a way you didn't like or want.	1	2	3	4	5
19. Refused to do housework or child care.	1	2	3	4	5
20. Threatened you with a knife, gun, or other weapon.	1	2	3	4	5
21. Spanked you.	1	2	3	4	5
22. Told you that you were a bad parent.	1	2	3	4	5
23. Stopped you or tried to stop you from going to work or school.	1	2	3	4	5
24. Threw, hit, kicked, or smashed something.	1	2	3	4	5
25. Kicked you.	1	2	3	4	5
26. Physically forced you to have sex.	1	2	3	4	5
27. Threw you around.	1	2	3	4	5
28. Physically attacked the sexual parts of your body.	1	2	3	4	5
29. Choked or strangled you.	1	2	3	4	5
30. Used a knife, gun, or other weapon against you.	1	2	3	4	5

Scoring: Add the numbers you circled and divide the total by 30 points to find your score. The higher your score, the more abusive your relationship.

The inventory was given to 100 men and 78 women equally divided into groups of abusers/abused and nonabusers/nonabused. The men were members of a chemical dependency treatment program in a hospital and the women were partners of these men. Abusing or abused men earned an average score of 1.8; abusing or abused women earned an average score of 2.3. Nonabusing/abused men and women earned scores of 1.3 and 1.6, respectively.

SOURCE: Shepard, Melanie F., and James A. Campbell. 1992. "The Abusive Behaviour Inventory: A Measure of Psychological and Physical Abuse." *Journal of Interpersonal Violence* 7(3), September: 291–305. Inventory is on pages 303–4. Used by permission of Sage Publications, 2455 Teller Road, Newbury Park, CA 91320.

Specifically, they were about twice as likely to report being beaten (25 percent versus 10 percent), or threatened by, or having had a knife or gun used against them (13 percent versus 7 percent). They were five times more likely to report being choked (20 percent versus 4 percent). Men were more likely than women to report that they had been slapped (57 percent versus 40 percent), kicked, bit, or hit (51 percent versus 33 percent), or had something thrown against them. Aboriginal peoples were more likely than other Canadians to report being assaulted by a spouse (about 20 percent of Aboriginal peoples compared with 7 percent of the non-Aboriginal population). "Aboriginal women in particular stand out as being at higher risk of spousal violence" (Johnson and Hotton 2001: 29) (see Figure 5.3).

Data from the 1999 GSS also indicates that women are three times more likely to be injured, five times more likely to receive medical attention, and also five times more likely than men to report that they feared for their lives as a result of the violence they had experienced. Women were also more likely than men to report multiple incidents of spousal violence. Sixty-five percent of women (versus 54 percent of men) who experienced spousal violence reported being assaulted on more than one occasion; 26 percent of women (versus 13 percent of men) said it happened more than 10 times (Bunge 2000: 14).

The GSS survey data reveals that women and men from all income and educational levels experience violence within common-law and marital relationships. Rates of violence ranged from a high of 3 percent for those who had a household income below $30 000 to a low of 1 percent for those with a household income of $60 000 or more. In addition, the survey found that, in general, younger people face the greatest risk of experiencing spousal violence, with the highest rates reported by young women under the age of 25 (5 percent). Younger men aged 25–34 also reported higher rates of violence (4 percent) than those who were older (1 percent). Consistent with earliest studies conducted in both Canada and the United States, the 1999 GSS reported that the risk of being a victim of spousal violence was higher for both men and women living in common-law unions (4 percent) than in legal marriages (1 percent).

Although research on intimate violence within gay and lesbian relationships is sparse, the few studies conducted to date on this issue suggest that it occurs at about the same rate as it does in heterosexual relationships (Lockhart et al. 1994). Many of the dynamics reported to characterize abusive heterosexual relationships, such as alcohol and/or drug abuse, are also found in same-sex abusive partnerships (Kurdek 1994; Renzetti and Milley 1996). Like hetero-

■ **Figure 5.3** *Aboriginal Women Report Higher Rates of Spousal Violence*

SOURCE: Statistics Canada, General Social Survey, 1999.

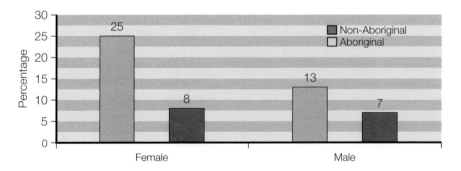

The difference in rates for Aboriginal and non-Aboriginal men is not statistically significant.

sexual abusers, the same-sex abuser is generally jealously possessive and uses violence or its threat to control his or her partner (Island and Letellier 1991).

Four patterns of partner violence have been identified: common couple violence, intimate terrorism, violent resistance, and mutual violent control (Johnson and Ferraro 2001). **Common couple violence** refers to occasional acts of violence arising from arguments that get "out of hand." Common couple violence usually does not escalate into serious or life-threatening violence. **Intimate terrorism** is violence that is motivated by a wish to control one's partner and involves the systematic use of not only violence but economic subordination, threats, isolation, verbal and emotional abuse, and other control tactics. Intimate terrorism is almost entirely perpetrated by men and is more likely to escalate over time and to involve serious injury. **Violent resistance** refers to acts of violence that are committed in self-defence. Violent resistance is almost exclusively perpetrated by women against a male partner. **Mutual violent control** is a rare pattern of abuse "that could be viewed as two intimate terrorists battling for control" (Johnson and Ferraro 2001: 169).

Intimate partner abuse also takes the form of sexual aggression, including forced sexual intercourse. **Sexual aggression** refers to sexual interaction that occurs against one's will through use of physical force, threat of force, pressure, use of alcohol/drugs, or use of position of authority. An estimated 7 to 14 percent of married women have been raped by their husbands (Monson et al. 1996). However, prior to 1983 and the introduction of Canada's sexual assault laws, it was legally impossible for a man in Canada to "rape" his wife because the rape law contained a *marital exemption*. A man could only be found guilty of rape on his own wife if he was party to someone else raping her (e.g., if he forcibly restrained his wife while another man raped her).

Violence in intimate relationships does not always end with the breakup of the relationship. Recognition that the most dangerous time for a victim of intimate violence was after leaving a violent relationship helped fuel the 1993 enactment of a law against "criminal harassment," an offence for which the maximum penalty is 10 years' imprisonment. This law is directed against "stalking" behaviours that may stem from a variety of motives including the adamant refusal of one relational partner "to believe that the relationship has ended" (Kong 1997). Stalking or criminal harassment includes repeatedly following, communication (via cards, letters, e-mails, and so on), or uttering direct or indirect threats or promises of violence or forcible intimacy. Women were the victims of over three-quarters (77 percent) of all incidents of criminal harassment reported to police in Canada in 1999. Although ex-husbands were the accused in more than a third (36 percent) of incidents reported by women, men were more likely to report being stalked by casual acquaintances than intimate partners. In that year, ex-wives accounted for 11 percent of the perpetrators of criminal harassment incidents reported by men (Johnson and Hotton 2001: 33). Although criminal harassment does not generally culminate in homicide, "between 1997 and 1999, it was identified as a precipitating factor in 12 percent of homicides committed by male ex-partners" (Johnson and Hotton 2001: 33).

Rates of spousal homicide have generally declined in recent years. Fedorowycz (1999) suggests this decline "may primarily be the result of reduced exposure to abusive or violent relationships as a consequence of the changing living arrangements of men and women, improvements in the economic status of women, and increases in the availability of domestic violence services (e.g., safe houses or shelters, counselling, financial aid)." However, women remained the most likely victims of lethal violence in spousal relationships from 1979 to 1999, with over three times as many wives as husbands killed by spouses (Figure 5.4). Aboriginal peoples in Canada suffer disproportionately from spousal homicide. From 1991 to 1999, spousal homicides claimed the lives of 62 Aboriginal women and 32 Aboriginal men—14 percent and 22 percent respectively of all spousal killings in Canada.

Between 1991 and 1999, women and men under the age of 25 years were at the greatest risk of being victims of spousal homicide. Following marital separation, Canadian women, but not men, also face a heightened risk of homicide victimization (Figure 5.5). Almost half (49 percent) of homicides committed by ex-spouses between 1991 and 1999 occurred within two months of the couple's separation, with another third (32 percent) occurring within 2 to 12 months. Among men who killed their ex-spouses, 39 percent killed themselves and 6 percent attempted suicide after the homicide. Among women who killed their ex-spouses, no murder-suicide occurred (Johnson and Hotton 2001: 34).

It is evident that intimate violence can have devastating consequences. In addition, many battered women are abused during pregnancy, resulting in a high rate of miscarriage and birth defects. Psychological consequences for victims of intimate partner violence can include depression, suicidal thoughts and attempts, lowered self-esteem, alcohol and other drug abuse, and post-traumatic stress disorder (National Center for Injury Prevention and Control 2000).

Battering also interferes with employment opportunities. Some abusers prohibit their partners from working. Other abusers will deliberately undermine the possibility of their partner's employment by "depriving them of transportation, harassing them at work, turning off alarm clocks, beating them before job interviews, and disappearing when they promise to provide child care" (Johnson and Ferraro 2001: 177). Battering also undermines employment by causing repeated absences, impairing ability to concentrate, and lowering self-esteem and aspirations.

Abuse, whether physical or emotional, is no doubt a factor in many divorces and is also a primary cause of homelessness. One study of homeless parents found that 22 percent were fleeing from abuse (National Coalition for the

■ **Figure 5.4** *Recent Decline in Rates of Spousal Homicide, 1978–1999*

SOURCE: Statistics Canada, Canadian Centre for Justice Statistics, Homicide Survey.

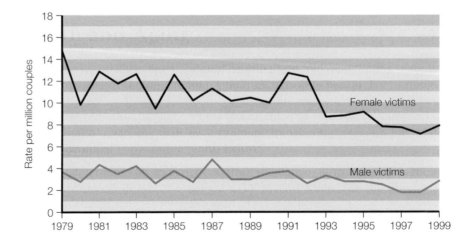

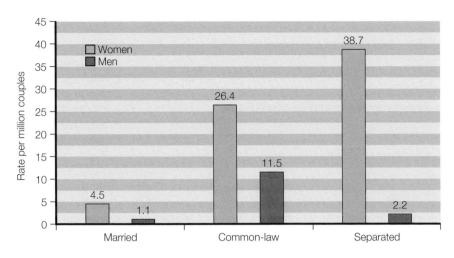

■ Figure 5.5 *Estranged Women at Greatest Risk of Spousal Homicide, 1991–1999*

SOURCE: Statistics Canada, Canadian Centre for Justice Statistics, Homicide Survey, 1991–1999.

The 1991 and 1996 Census was used to estimate the number of women and men aged 15 and older who were married, in a common-law union, and separated from legal marital partners during the reference period. Spousal homicide rates were not calculated for those separated from common-law partners, as there were no reliable estimates for this sub-population available from the Census. All known cases of homicide perpetrated by an ex-common law partner (as identified from police narratives) have been omitted from the separated rates. The denominators used for intercensal years were estimated by averaging the difference from the known population figures in 1991 and 1996.

Homeless 1999). A second reported that half of homeless women and children were fleeing from abuse ("Domestic Violence and Homelessness" 1998). According to Novac et al. (1996), homelessness and violence are inextricably linked for women. They observe that "homeless women with histories of family disruption and abuse distinguish being housed from being safe, so that homelessness is a problem for women, but is also a strategy for escaping violence. The relationship between violence and homelessness among women is complex, since there is also a great risk of violence when women are homeless."

According to the 1999 GSS, children are too frequently the observers of violence between spouses. In this survey, 46 percent of non-Aboriginal women and 57 percent of Aboriginal women reported that their child or children had witnessed the violence committed against them (Johnson and Hotton 2001: 29). Children who witness intimate violence may experience emotional, behavioural, and academic problems and may commit violence in their own relationships later (Parker et al. 2000). Children may also commit violent acts against a parent's abusing partner.

Why do abused adults stay in abusive relationships? Reasons include love, emotional dependency, commitment to the relationship, hope that things will get better, the view that violence is legitimate because they "deserve" it, guilt, fear, economic dependency, and feeling stuck. Abuse in relationships is usually not ongoing and constant, but rather occurs in cycles. The **cycle of abuse** involves a violent or abusive episode, followed by a makeup period where the abuser expresses sorrow and asks for forgiveness and "one more chance." This honeymoon period may last for days, weeks, or even months before the next outburst of violence occurs.

> ■ The great advantage of a hotel is that it's a refuge from home life.
>
> GEORGE BERNARD SHAW
> *Playwright*

Child Abuse

Child abuse refers to the "physical or mental injury, sexual abuse, negligent treatment, or maltreatment of a child under the age of 18 by a person who is responsible for the child's welfare..." (Willis et al. 1992: 2). According to the Canadian Incidence Study of Reported Child Abuse and Neglect (CIS), the first national study of child maltreatment investigations by child welfare services in Canada, the most common reason for investigations was suspected neglect (Figure 5.6). Investigations by child welfare substantiated 34 percent of cases involving suspected physical abuse, 38 percent of cases of suspected sexual abuse, 43 percent of suspected neglect cases, and 54 percent of cases involving suspected emotional maltreatment (Trocme and Wolfe 2001: 5). The majority (69 percent) of substantiated cases of child physical abuse involved inappropriate punishment (i.e., hitting a child with either a hand or object that led to physical harm or put the child at substantial risk of harm). The most common form of sexual abuse within substantiated cases involved touching and fondling of the genitals (68 percent); attempted and/or completed sexual intercourse accounted for about a third (35 percent) of all substantiated cases. The most common form of emotional maltreatment within substantiated cases was a child's exposure to family violence followed by emotional abuse (overtly hostile, punitive treatment, or habitual or extreme verbal abuse) (Trocme and Wolfe 2001).

According to the CIS, while biological mothers and, in particular, biological fathers largely committed physical abuse, sexual abuse was more likely to be perpetrated by other relatives or non-relatives (Figure 5.7). When alleged perpetrators were related to child sexual abuse victims, they were "equally likely to be a biological father or stepfather and less likely to be a child's biological mother or stepmother" (Trocme and Wolfe 2001: 8). Overall, however, the alleged perpetrator in substantiated child maltreatment investigations was most frequently the biological mothers (60 percent of cases) followed by biological fathers (41 percent), stepfathers/common-law partners (9 percent) and stepmothers/common-law partners (3 percent) (Trocme and Wolfe 2001: 8).

When compared to adults, children and youth are especially likely to be killed by family members (Locke et al. 2001: 15) (see Figure 5.8). Of the 1990 solved homicides of children and youths recorded by Canadian police agencies between 1974 and 1999, over six out of ten (63 percent) were committed by family members. During this time period, very young children, three years of age or less, were most likely to be killed in family homicides by their biological mothers.

> Children begin by loving their parents; as they grow older they judge them; sometimes they forgive them.
>
> OSCAR WILDE
> *Writer*

■ **Figure 5.6** *Child Neglect Most Common Reason For Child Maltreatment Investigation*

SOURCE: Health Canada. 1998. The Canadian Incidence Study of Reported Child Abuse and Neglect.

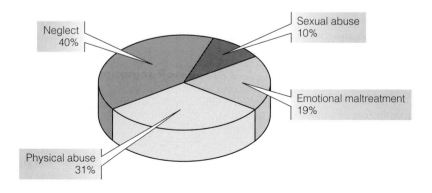

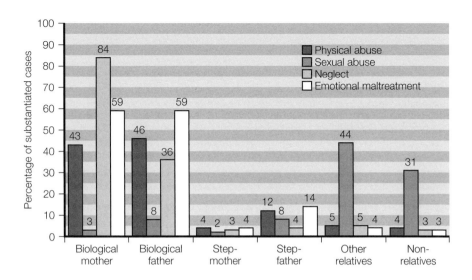

■ **Figure 5.7** *Physical Abuse Committed Largely by Biological Parents*

SOURCE: Health Canada. 1998. The Canadian Incidence Study of Reported Child Abuse and Neglect.

However, for all other age groups, children killed in family homicides were most likely to be killed by their fathers (Locke et al. 2001: 16).

The effects of child abuse and neglect vary according to the frequency and intensity of the abuse and neglect. Reviews of research on the effects of child abuse suggest that abused children are at higher risk for aggressive behaviour, low self-esteem, depression, and low academic achievement (Gelles and Conte 1991; Lloyd and Emery 1993). The CIS reports that in over one-half (56 percent) of cases of substantiated physical abuse, the child was described as having some type of difficulty, with behaviour problems, negative peer involvement, depression or anxiety, violence towards others, and developmental delay the most often indicated difficulties. Among child victims of substantiated sexual abuse, the five most frequently reported difficulties were depression or anxiety, age-inappropriate sexual behaviour, behaviour problems, negative peer involvement, and irregular school attendance (Trocme and Wolfe 2001). Adolescents and adults who were abused as children are more vulnerable to low self-esteem, depression, unhappiness, anxiety, increased risk of substance abuse, criminal activity, and suicide. Physical injuries sustained by child abuse cause pain, disfigurement, scarring, physical disability, and death.

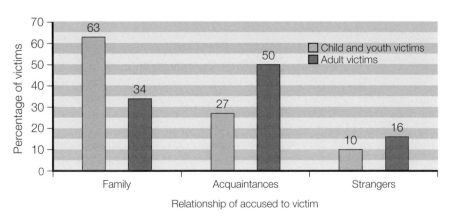

■ **Figure 5.8** *Children and Youth More Likely than Adults to be Killed by Family Members, 1974–1999*

SOURCE: Statistics Canada, Canadian Centre for Justice Statistics, Homicide Survey.

Percentages may not total 100% due to rounding.

Among females, early forced sex is associated with lower self-esteem, higher levels of depression, running away from home, alcohol and drug use, and more sexual partners (Jasinski et al. 2000; Lanz 1995; Whiffen et al. 2000). Sexually abused girls are also more likely to experience teenage pregnancy, have higher numbers of sexual partners in adulthood, and are more likely to acquire sexually transmitted infections and experience forced sex (Browning and Laumann 1997; Stock et al. 1997). Women who were sexually abused as children also report a higher frequency of post-traumatic stress disorder (Spiegel 2000) and suicide ideation (Thakkar et al. 2000). Spouses who were physically and sexually abused as children report lower marital satisfaction, higher stress, and lower family cohesion than spouses with no abuse history (Nelson and Wampler 2000).

Adult males who were sexually abused as children tend to exhibit depression, substance abuse, and difficulty establishing intimate relationships (Krug 1989). Sexually abused males also have a higher risk of anxiety disorders, sleep and eating disorders, and sexual dysfunctions (Elliott and Briere 1992).

Effects of child sexual abuse are likely to be severe when the sexual abuse is forceful, is prolonged, involves intercourse, and when the abuse was perpetrated by a father or stepfather (Beitchman et al. 1992). Not only has the child been violated physically, she or he has lost an important social support. One woman who had been sexually abused by her father described feeling that she had lost her father; he was no longer a person to love and protect her (Spiegel 2000).

Elder Abuse

Elder abuse includes physical abuse, psychological abuse, financial abuse (such as improper use of the elder's financial resources), and neglect. Elder neglect includes failure to provide basic health and hygiene needs such as clean clothes, doctor visits, medication, and adequate nutrition. Neglect also involves unreasonable confinement, isolation of elderly family members, lack of supervision, and abandonment.

The 1999 GSS asked Canadians 65 years of age or over a series of questions in relation to emotional and financial abuse by children, caregivers (individuals paid or unpaid who provide assistance or healthcare in the respondent's home), and spouses (including current and former spouses as well as common-law partners). In addition, it asked questions about possible physical or sexual abuse by children, caregivers, or spouses. This survey reports very little physical or sexual violence perpetrated against older Canadians residing in a private household. "[O]nly one percent of this population of seniors indicated that they had been physically or sexually assaulted by a spouse, adult child or caregiver in the five years prior to this survey" (Bunge 2000: 27). Seven percent reported experiencing some type of emotional or financial abuse, with spouses identified as the perpetrator in the vast majority of cases. The most common form of emotional abuse reported was being verbally put down or called names (3 percent), followed by limiting contact with family or friends (2 percent). Men were more likely than women (9 percent versus 6 percent) to report being victims of emotional or financial abuse by an adult child, caregiver, or spouse. The highest rates of emotional or financial abuse were reported by older adults whose household incomes were between

$30 000 and $39 000, who were divorced or separated, who lived in rural areas, and who had some postsecondary education. However, this survey did not include respondents living in institutions (e.g., retirement homes, hospitals) and, as such, cannot provide us with information on the experiences of older Canadians who live in such settings.

According to police-reported statistics, there were 802 cases of violence committed against older adults by family members in 1999, with the most frequent assailant an adult child (43 percent), followed by a spouse (28 percent) (Figure 5.9). The most common offence committed against an older adult, man or woman, by a family member was common assault (54 percent) followed by uttering threats (22 percent).

Factors Contributing to Intimate Partner and Family Violence and Abuse

Research suggests that cultural, community, and individual and family factors contribute to domestic violence and abuse (Willis et al. 1992).

Cultural Factors Violence in the family stems from our society's acceptance of violence as a legitimate means of enforcing compliance and solving conflicts at personal, national, and international levels (Viano 1992). Violence and abuse in the family may be linked to cultural factors such as violence in the media (see Chapter 4), acceptance of corporal punishment, gender inequality, and the view of women and children as property.

1. *Acceptance of corporal punishment.* **Corporal punishment** involves the use of physical force with the intention of causing a child to experience pain, but not injury, for the purpose of correction or control of a child's behaviour (Straus 2000). Many mental health professionals and child development specialists argue that it is ineffective and damaging to children. Children who experience corporal punishment display more antisocial

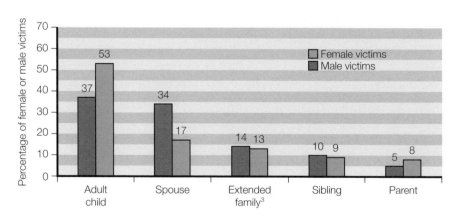

Figure 5.9 *Older Adults Most Frequently Victimized by Adult Children and Spouses, 1999*[1,2]

SOURCE: Statistics Canada. 2000. "Family Violence in Canada: A Statistical Profile," Cat. No. 85-224, July, p. 30.

[1] Data are not nationally representative. Data are based on a sample of 164 police departments, representing 46% of the national volume of crime in 1999.

[2] Includes all violent offences against victims 65 years and older.

[3] Extended family includes grandparents, aunts, uncles, cousins, sister/brother-in-laws, parents-in-laws, etc.

behaviour, are more violent, and have an increased incidence of depression as adults (Straus 2000). Yet, many parents accept the cultural tradition of spanking as an appropriate form of child discipline. Moreover, unlike such countries as Austria, Cyprus, Denmark, Finland, Italy, Norway, and Sweden where the use of corporal punishment in the home or school is against the law, Canadian law specifically allows for the corporal punishment of children. Section 43 of the *Criminal Code* of Canada specifies that "[e]very schoolteacher, parent, or person standing in the place of a parent is justified in using force by way of correction toward a pupil or child, as the case may be, who is under his care, if the force does not exceed what is reasonable under the circumstances." In effect, this section allows children to be assaulted by their parents and teachers, provided that the force used in the assault is "reasonable" and for the child's "correction."

2. *Gender role socialization.* Traditional male gender roles have taught men to be aggressive and to be dominant in male-female relationships. Male abusers are likely to hold traditional attitudes toward women and male–female roles (Lloyd and Emery 2000). Anderson (1997) found that men who earn less money than their partners are more likely to be violent toward them. "Disenfranchised men then must rely on other social practices to construct a masculine image. Because it is so clearly associated with masculinity in…[our] culture, violence is a social practice that enables men to express a masculine identity" (p. 667). Traditional female gender roles have also taught women to be submissive to their male partner's control.

3. *View of women and children as property.* Before the late nineteenth century, a married woman was considered to be the property of her husband. A husband had a legal right and marital obligation to discipline and control his wife through the use of physical force. This traditional view of women as property may contribute to men doing with their "property" as they wish.

4. The view of women and children as property also explains marital rape and father–daughter incest. Historically, the penalties for rape were based on property right laws designed to protect a man's property—his wife or daughter—from rape by other men; a husband or father "taking" his own property was not considered rape (Russell 1990).

Community Factors Community factors that contribute to violence and abuse in the family include social isolation and inaccessible or unaffordable health care, day care, elder care, and respite care facilities.

1. *Social isolation.* Living in social isolation from extended family and community members increases a family's risk for abuse. Isolated families are removed from material benefits, care-giving assistance, and emotional support from extended family and community members.

2. *Inaccessible or unaffordable community services.* Failure to provide medical care to children and elderly family members (a form of neglect) is sometimes due to the lack of accessible or affordable health care services in the community. Failure to provide supervision for children and adults may result from inaccessible day care and elder care services. Without elder care and respite care facilities, socially isolated families may not have any help with the stresses of caring for elderly family members and children with special needs.

Our culture promotes sexual victimization of women and children when it encourages males to believe that they have overpowering sexual needs that must be met by whatever means available.

EDWIN SCHUR
Sociologist

Individual and Family Factors Individual and family factors associated with intimate partner and family violence and abuse include a family history of violence, drug and alcohol abuse, poverty, and fatherless homes.

1. *Family history of abuse.* Mothers who have been sexually abused as children are more likely to physically abuse their own children (DiLillo et al. 2000). Although a history of abuse is associated with an *increased likelihood* of being abusive as an adult, *most* adults who were abused as children do not continue the pattern of abuse in their own relationships (Gelles 2000).
2. *Drug and alcohol abuse.* Alcohol use is reported as a factor in 50 to 70 percent of incidents of physical and sexual aggression in intimate relationships (Lloyd and Emery 2000). Alcohol and other drugs increase aggression in some individuals and enable the offender to avoid responsibility by blaming his or her violent behaviour on drugs/alcohol.
3. *Poverty.* Abuse in adult relationships occurs among all socioeconomic groups. However, Kaufman and Zigler (1992) point to a relationship between poverty and child abuse:

> Although most poor people do not maltreat their children, and poverty, per se, does not cause abuse and neglect, the correlates of poverty, including stress, drug abuse, and inadequate resources for food and medical care, increase the likelihood of maltreatment. (p. 284)

Strategies for Action: Preventing and Responding to Violence and Abuse in Intimate and Family Relationships

Strategies to prevent family violence and abuse include **primary prevention** strategies that target the general population, **secondary prevention** strategies that target groups at high risk for family violence and abuse, and **tertiary prevention** strategies that target families who have experienced abuse (Gelles 1993; Harrington and Dubowitz 1993).

Primary Prevention Strategies

Preventing violence and abuse may require broad, sweeping social changes such as eliminating the norms that legitimize and glorify violence in society and changing the sexist character of society (Gelles 2000). Specific abuse prevention strategies include public education and media campaigns that may help reduce domestic violence by conveying the criminal nature of domestic assault and offering ways to prevent abuse ("When you are angry at your child, count to 10 and call a friend..."). Other prevention efforts focus on parent education to teach parents realistic expectations about child behaviour and methods of child discipline that do not involve corporal punishment.

Another strategy involves reducing violence-provoking stress by reducing poverty and unemployment and providing adequate housing, child care programs and facilities, nutrition, medical care, and educational opportunities. This chapter's *The Human Side* also points to the need to broaden our understanding of what a family is and to challenge misleading stereotypes about people with disabilities—their intelligence, their credibility, and their sexuality—if we are to

> Family, it is said, is a "haven in a heartless world." However, violence among family members can turn the ideals of family upside down and violate the security, integrity and dignity of loved ones.
>
> VANIER INSTITUTE OF THE FAMILY

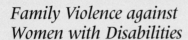

Family Violence against Women with Disabilities

Probably the single biggest factor affecting the incidence of family violence against women with disabilities is the extent of these women's "families." Women with disabilities must often depend on a variety of people to provide them with assistance in carrying out their everyday lives. For this reason, their "family" is understood to include not only parents, husbands, boyfriends, and other relatives, but also friends, neighbours, and caregivers. Caregivers can include attendants, interpreters, homemakers, drivers, doctors, nurses, teachers, social workers, psychiatrists, therapists, counsellors, and workers in hospitals and other institutions. This large number of people and the intimate physical and emotional contact involved in the care they provide greatly increase the risk of abuse to persons with disabilities.

Women who live in institutional settings, and women who are multiply or profoundly disabled, are most vulnerable to abuse because they are more dependent upon even larger numbers of people, and less able to get away. It is estimated that women with disabilities are 1.5 to 10 times as likely to be abused as women without disabilities are, depending on whether they live in the community or in institutions.

While a disability can make it more difficult for a woman to escape or report abuse, social attitudes toward persons with disabilities are probably a bigger factor in her increased vulnerability to violence. The way in which society views persons with disabilities handicaps these women in many ways:

- They tend to be viewed and treated as children, as lacking intelligence.
- They may be trained to be compliant and are sometimes punished for assertiveness or for challenging authority figures. This is in direct contrast to the streetproofing taught to many children in schools.
- Women with disabilities are considered to be non-sexual and are often not given sex education, which can result in an inability to distinguish between abusive behaviour and normal or necessary forms of touching.
- They may be considered incompetent witnesses by police and the courts, particularly if they have difficulty or require assistance in communicating.
- When they do report abuse, they may not be believed.

Prevalence of Abuse

- Research has only just begun in this area, but indications are that women and children with disabilities are one of the most highly victimized groups in our society.
- The degree of risk of sexual abuse of persons with disabilities appears to be at least 150 percent of that for individuals of the same sex and similar age without disabilities.
- It is estimated that only 20 percent of the cases of sexual abuse involving disabled people are ever reported to the police, community service agencies, or authorities.

Barriers to Obtaining Help

It is extremely difficult for any abused woman to leave a situation of abuse....Battering undermines self-esteem and can make a woman feel she is somehow responsible for her own abuse. For a woman with a disability, this situation is even more difficult. She may be dependent on her abuser for affection, communication, and financial, physical, and medical support. If she reports the abuse, she may risk poverty and loss of housing. She may fear she will not be heard or believed if she speaks out. She may face further violence, institutionalization, or loss of her children if she seeks help. She may not have access to information about existing support services for victims of violence. Even if she has this information, many sources of support may not be accessible. She may not be able to contact the police or women's shelters because they do not have communication devices such as Telecommunication Devices for the Deaf (TDDs). She may not be able to physically leave her situation because of a lack of accessible transportation. Her lack of options may leave her feeling so powerless and despairing that suicide seems the only viable choice. And if she seeks help in dealing with suicidal thoughts or attempts, she is unlikely to find counselling that takes account of her own reality....

be effective in both preventing violence within families and responding to it when it occurs.

Secondary Prevention Strategies

Families at risk of experiencing violence and abuse include low-income families, parents with a history of depression or psychiatric care, single parents, teenage mothers, parents with few social and family contacts, individuals who experienced abuse in their own childhood, and parents or spouses who abuse drugs or alcohol. Secondary prevention strategies, designed to prevent abuse from occurring in high-risk families, include parent education programs, parent support groups, individual counselling, substance abuse treatment, and home visiting programs.

In response to studies that noted that family violence is more prevalent in Aboriginal communities, the federal government allotted $7 million to the funding of short-term community-based projects related to family violence in Indian and Inuit communities as part of the Family Violence and Child Sexual Abuse Initiatives. More than 180 projects, focusing on public awareness, training, community workshops, and research and program development, were funded in Native communities across Canada in the 1990s, and care was taken to respect the strategies of intervention preferred within Aboriginal communities. Often, Aboriginal peoples view the problem of family violence as a sympton of community dysfunction. In consequence, solutions to the problem are viewed in terms of a holistic, community-wide healing process planned, developed, and implemented by Aboriginal peoples. For example, it is not uncommon to have workshops dealing with issues of abuse begin with a prayer and a sharing circle or a smudge ceremony using the local root. Communities may also use naming ceremonies and feasts to celebrate different points of healing or encourage survivors to take part in sweat lodges to ask for help for themselves and others. The Medicine Wheel, which explains that a healthy person must use all four parts of himself or herself—physical, mental, emotional, and spiritual—is also favoured as a healing tool with many versions of the Wheel used in counselling programs.

Tertiary Prevention Strategies

What social interventions are available to families that are experiencing abuse or neglect? Abused women and children may seek relief at one of Canada's 508 shelters for abused women and their children (Code 2001) or "safe houses." Although shelters differ (see Table 5.1), there are residential facilities in every Canadian province and territory that provide abused women and their children with housing, food, and counselling services. Safe houses are private homes of individuals who volunteer to provide temporary housing to abused women who decide to leave their violent homes. Battered men are not allowed to stay at women's shelters, but many shelters help abused men by providing money for a motel room, counselling, and support services. Some communities have abuse shelters for victims of elder abuse. In August 2002, www.Sheffernet.ca, a Web site providing point-and-click access to information about shelters across Canada, was launched in Toronto. A similar Web site, Hotpeachpages.org, also provides abused women with helpful information on shelters (Wherry 2002).

■ **Table 5.1** *Types of Shelters*

The term shelter is used broadly to refer to all residential facilities for abused women and their dependent children. The types of shelters are defined by the Transition Home Survey as:

Transition home—Short or moderate term (1 day to 11 weeks) first stage emergency housing.

Second Stage Housing—Long-term (3–12 months) secure housing with support and referral services designed to assist women while they search for permanent housing.

Safe Home Network—A network of private homes in rural or remote areas where there is no full-fledged operating shelter. It offers subsidiary very short-term (1–3 days) emergency housing.

Women's Emergency Centre/Shelter—Short-term (1–21 days) respite (temporary relief) for women and their dependent children.

Emergency Shelter—Short-term (1–3 days) respite for a wide population range, not exclusively abused women. Some facilities may provide accommodation for men as well as women. This type of facility may accommodate residents who are not associated with family abuse but are without a home due to an emergency situation (e.g., eviction for non-payment of rent). Other than residential (room and board) services, these shelters offer few additional client services.

Family Resource Centre—An Ontario government initiative that serves a wide range of clients and provides clients with an extensive array of information and referrals as well as residential services.

Other—All other facilities/shelters not otherwise classified. This category may include Rural Family Violence Prevention Centres in Alberta, Interim Housing in Manitoba, and other types of emergency shelters. These services may not be exclusive to abused women.

Source: Code, Ruth. 2001. "Children in Shelters for Abused Women." In Statistics Canada. 2001. *Family Violence in Canada: A Statistical Profile 2001*. July: 42 Catalogue no. 85-224-XIE.

Abused or neglected children may be removed from the home. Provincial child welfare laws permit abused or neglected children to be placed in out-of-home care, such as foster care. However, a preferred approach is to prevent family breakup when desirable and possible without jeopardizing the welfare of children in the home. **Family preservation programs** are in-home interventions for families who are at risk of having a child removed from the home due to abuse or neglect.

Alternatively, a court may order an abusing spouse or parent to leave the home. Abused spouses or cohabiting partners may obtain a restraining order prohibiting the perpetrator from going near the abused partner. However, legal action does not always protect victims of family violence. One Canadian study that tracked 133 cases of domestic violence through the courts for an eight-month period found that almost half of the men charged with assaulting their wives broke bail conditions by harassing, stalking, or moving back in with their wives. In addition, while 60 men had been convicted at the end of the eight-month period, "only 23 were jailed; the other 37 received the legal equivalent of a slap on the wrist, usually a probation sentence of one to three years, often with no criminal record" (Dranoff 2001: 173). Canadian courts have also been notably reluctant to curtail the access of abusive spouses to their children; the courts have held that a husband's commission of an assault upon his wife does not invalidate his application for child custody or the claim that he is a "good father." In situations in which a restraining order prohibits the abusive partner from establishing contact with a current or former spouse, the order itself may be unknowingly breached when the abused spouse voluntarily allows the abusive partner into the home to pick up or deliver their children.

Treatment for abusers—which may be voluntary or mandated by the court—typically involves group and/or individual counselling, substance abuse counselling and/or training in communication, conflict resolution, and anger management. Those who stop abusing their partners learn to take responsibility for their abusive behaviour, develop empathy for their partner's victimization, reduce their dependency on their partners, and improve their communication skills (Scott and Wolfe 2000).

Divorce

Between 1968 and 1987, Canada experienced a seven-fold increase in divorce (Ambert 1998: 4). However, divorce rates in Canada peaked in 1987 and have generally declined since then (see Figure 5.10). In 1987, the crude divorce rate (the number of divorces per 100 000 population) was 362.3; in 2000, it was 231.2 (Statistics Canada 2002). Individual and relationship factors that contribute to divorce include incompatibility in values or goals, poor communication,

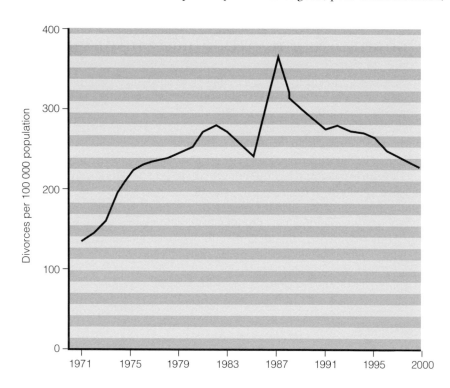

Figure 5.10 *Number of Divorces in Canada, 1986 to 1998*

SOURCE: Statistics Canada. 1997. "Divorces in the 1990s," *Health Reports*, 9(2): 53–8. Statistics Canada Cat. No. 82-003-XPB; Statistics Canada, Health Statistics Division, special tabulations.

lack of conflict resolution skills, sexual incompatibility, extramarital relationships, substance abuse, emotional or physical abuse, neglect, boredom, jealousy, and difficulty coping with change or stress related to parenting, employment, finances, in-laws, and illness. Other demographic and life course factors that are predictive of divorce include marriage order (second and subsequent marriages are more prone to divorce than first marriages), cohabitation (couples who live together before marriage are more prone to divorce), teenage marriage, premarital pregnancy, and low socioeconomic status.

Various social factors also contribute to the increased rate of divorce over the past three decades. These include the following structural and cultural forces.

1. *Changing family functions.* Before the Industrial Revolution, the family constituted a unit of economic production and consumption, provided care and protection to its members, and was responsible for socializing and educating children. During industrialization, other institutions took over these functions. For example, the educational institution has virtually taken over the systematic teaching and socialization of children. Today, the primary function of marriage and the family is the provision of emotional support, intimacy, affection, and love. When marital partners no longer derive these emotional benefits from their marriage, they may consider divorce with the hope of finding a new marriage partner to fulfill these affectional needs.

2. *Increased economic autonomy of women.* Before 1940, most wives were not employed outside the home and depended on their husband's income. However, by the end of the twentieth century, husbands were the sole earner in merely 14 percent of all husband–wife families (Vanier Institute of the Family 2000: 96). The last women to move into employment outside the home, mothers of young children, have also been entering the labour force in increasing numbers. By 1999, 61 percent of Canadian women with children less than three years of age were employed—more than double the figure in 1976 (Statistics Canada 2000c). Wives who are unhappy in their marriage are more likely to leave the marriage if they have the economic means to support themselves. Unhappy husbands may also be more likely to leave a marriage if their wives are self-sufficient and can contribute to the support of the children.

3. *Increased work demands and dissatisfaction with marital division of labour.* Another factor influencing divorce is increased work demands and the stresses of balancing work and family roles. Workers are putting in longer hours, often working overtime or taking second jobs. Many employed parents—particularly mothers—come home to work a **"second shift"**—the work involved in caring for children and household chores (Hochschild 1989). Wives are more likely than husbands to perceive the marital division of labour—household chores and child care—as unfair (Nock 1995). This perception of unfairness can lead to marital tension and resentment, as reflected in the following excerpt:

> My husband's a great help watching our baby. But as far as doing housework or even taking the baby when I'm at home, no. He figures he works five days a week; he's not going to come home and clean. But he doesn't stop to think that I work seven days a week. Why should I have to come home and do the housework without help from anybody else? My husband

Paid employment has greatly reduced the time available to wives for domestic work, and having paycheques has empowered them, giving them increased influence and independence. Conflict has resulted, over (1) husbands' reluctance to share the domestic work fairly, and (2) wives' refusal to be traditionally subservient.

CHARLES HOBART
Sociologist

and I have been through this over and over again. Even if he would just pick up things from the kitchen table and stack the dishes for me, that would make a big difference. He does nothing. On his weekends off, I have to provide a sitter for the baby so he can go fishing. When I have a day off, I have the baby all day long without a break. He'll help out if I'm not here, but the minute I am, all the work at home is mine. (quoted in Hochschild 1997: 37–8)

4 . *Liberalized divorce laws.* Before 1968, adultery was the only grounds for divorce in Canada, except in Nova Scotia, where cruelty was sufficient grounds even before Confederation (Morrison 1987). The 1968 *Divorce Act* expanded the "fault grounds" under which a divorce could be granted. In addition to adultery, proof that one's partner had engaged in prohibited activities, such as mental or physical cruelty, gross addiction to alcohol or other drugs, sodomy, bestiality, and homosexual acts, entitled the petitioner to an immediate divorce. The 1968 *Divorce Act* also introduced what are also termed **no-fault divorce** grounds that allowed couples to divorce without requiring them to stipulate their specific reason for doing so. In these cases of "marital breakdown," couples were required to live apart for a three-year period before applying for a divorce and jointly consent to being divorced. In the event that one party did not wish to be divorced, the court required that five years pass from the time of separation before applying for divorce. In addition, Morton (1990: 213) notes that "[a]s an added protection for the economically dependent spouse in cases of unilateral separation, courts were given the discretion to refuse a divorce if a 'granting of the decree would be unduly harsh or unjust or would affect the making of reasonable arrangements for the maintenance [financial support] of the spouse.'"

In 1985, a new divorce act became law. Under the current *Act,* there is only one ground available for divorce—marital breakdown—but this is defined in three ways: (1) the spouses have lived apart for one year; (2) one of the spouses has committed an act of adultery; (3) one spouse has treated the other with mental or physical cruelty. While proof of fault entitles couples to an immediate divorce, those opting for a one-year separation "may apply for a divorce any time after separation to ensure that their case is heard soon after the year is up" (Morton 1990: 214).

5 . *Changing cultural values.* Our society is increasingly characterized by **individualism**—the tendency to focus on one's individual self-interests rather than on the interests of one's family and community. The rising divorce rate has been linked to the continued rise of individualism. "For many, concerns with self-fulfillment and careerism diminished their commitment to family, rendering marriage and other intimate relationships vulnerable" (Demo et al. 2000: 281). **Familism**, in contrast, refers to the view that the family unit is more important than individual interests.

The value of marriage has also changed. The increased social acceptance of nonmarital sexuality, nonmarital childbearing, cohabitation, and singlehood reflect the view that marriage is an option, rather than an inevitability. The view of marriage as an option, rather than as an imperative, is mirrored by the view that divorce is also an acceptable option. Divorce today has less social stigma than in previous generations. "Marital

> ■ Housework, homework, classes, games, caregiving responsibilities, and meetings result in a new form of family work: the strategic organization of many schedules to keep pace with the accelerating culture.
>
> **KERRY J. DALY**
> *Sociologist*

> ■ It is now widely accepted that men and women have the right to expect a happy marriage, and that if a marriage does not work out, no one has to stay trapped.
>
> **SYLVIA ANN HEWLETT**
> *Family advocate*

dissolution, once considered to be a rare, unfortunate, and somewhat shameful deviation from normal family life" (Thompson and Amato 1999: xi) has become part of mainstream society.

6. *Increased life expectancy*. Finally, more marriages today end in divorce, in part, because people live longer than they did in previous generations. Because people live longer today than in previous generations, "till death do us part" involves a longer commitment than it once did. Indeed, one can argue that "marriage once was as unstable as it is today, but it was cut short by death not divorce" (Emery 1999: 7).

Consequences of Divorce

When parents have bitter and unresolvable conflict, and/or if one parent is abusing the child or the other parent, divorce may offer a solution to family problems. But divorce often has negative effects for ex-spouses and their children and contributes to problems that affect society as a whole.

Health Consequences A large number of studies have found that divorced individuals, compared to married individuals, experience lower levels of psychological well-being, including more unhappiness, depression, anxiety, and poorer self-concepts. Divorced individuals also have more health problems and a higher risk of mortality (Amato 2001; Waite and Gallagher 2000). Both divorced and never-married individuals are, on average, more distressed than married people because unmarried people are more likely than married people to have low social attachment, low emotional support, and increased economic hardship (Walker 2001).

Economic Consequences In families at the lowest income levels, divorce can improve women's income because men who earn little income can be a drain on the family's finances. However, "there is a clear pattern that the economic well-being of divorced women and their children plunges in comparison to predivorce levels" (Demo et al. 2000: 281). The economic costs of divorce are greater for women and children because women tend to earn less than men (see Chapter 8) and mothers devote substantially more time to household and child care tasks than fathers do. The time women invest in this unpaid labour restricts their educational and job opportunities as well as their income.

One or the ironies of marriage today is that it is about love and we have forgotten the economic union—until there's a divorce.

ALAN MIRABELLI
Representative, Vanier Institute of the Family

Men are less likely than women to be economically disadvantaged after divorce. Men often enjoy a better financial situation after divorce (Peterson 1996) as they continue to profit from earlier investments in education and career. However, men with low and unstable earnings often experience financial strain following divorce, which often underlies failure to pay child support. When custodial mothers who did not receive child support were asked the reasons why they did not receive it, 66 percent gave the reason as "father unable to pay" (Henry 1999).

Effects on Children Although divorce, following high conflict, may actually improve the emotional well-being of children relative to staying in a conflicted home environment (Jekielek 1998), for many children parental divorce has detrimental effects. With only one parent in the home, children of divorce, as well as children of never-married mothers, tend to have less adult supervision compared with children in two-parent homes. Lack of adult supervision is related to higher rates of criminality by youths, school failure, and teenage pregnancy (Popenoe 1993). A survey of 90 000 teenagers found that the mere physical presence of a parent in the home after school, at dinner, and at bedtime significantly reduces the risk of teenage suicide, violence, and drug use (Resnick et al. 1997). Many of the negative effects of divorce on children are related to the economic hardship associated with divorce. Economic hardship is associated with less effective and less supportive parenting, inconsistent and harsh discipline, and emotional distress in children (Demo et al. 2000).

In a review of the literature on the effects of parental divorce on university-age students, Nielson (1999) found that when their parents divorce and their mother remarries within a few years, most children do not suffer serious long-term consequences in terms of self-confidence, mental health, or academic achievements. However, in those cases where the mother does not remarry (about 15 percent), the consequences are more likely to be negative. Children of divorced women who do not remarry tend to experience a reduced standard of living and a lack of parental discipline. These children "fail to develop as much self-control, self-motivation, self-reliance, and self-direction as people their own age whose mothers have remarried" (Nielsen 1999: 547).

Children who live with their mothers may suffer from a damaged relationship with their nonresidential father, especially if he becomes disengaged from their lives. On the other hand, children may benefit from having more quality time with their fathers after parental divorce. Some fathers report that they became more active in the role of father after divorce. One father commented:

> In the last four and a half years, I have developed an incredibly strong and loving bond with my two sons. I am actively involved in all aspects of their lives. I have even coached their soccer and basketball teams....The time I spend with them is very quality time—if anything, the divorce has made me a better and more caring father...not to say this would not have happened if my marriage had worked out. (quoted in Pasley and Minton 2001: 248)

However, according to Canada's National Child Survey, following parental separation, about one-third of children have very little contact with their fathers (i.e., either irregular visits or no visits at all), with children born of common-law unions even less likely to see their fathers than are children born to married parents. "Since fathers who have low levels of contact with their children are least likely to pay child support, many Canadian children are at a high risk of losing both the personal and financial support of their fathers when their parents separate" (National Council of Welfare 1999: 51).

On occasion, custodial parents may actively attempt to alienate their children from their noncustodial parent. Some of these children may develop **parental alienation syndrome (PAS)**, which is defined as an emotional and psychological disturbance in which children engage in exaggerated and unjustified denigration and criticism of a parent (Gardner 1998). PAS has also been described as a form of child abuse in which one parent essentially encourages the child to hate the other parent (Schacht 2000). Long-term effects of PAS on children can include long-term depression, inability to function, guilt, hostility, alcoholism and other drug abuse, and other symptoms of internal distress (Family Court Reform Council of America 2000).

Some noncustodial divorced fathers discontinue contact with their children as a coping strategy for managing emotional pain (Pasley and Minton 2001). Many divorced fathers are overwhelmed with feelings of failure, guilt, anger, and sadness over the separation from their children (Knox 1998). Hewlett and West (1998) explain that "visiting their children only serves to remind these men of their painful loss, and they respond to this feeling by withdrawing completely" (p. 69).

In conclusion, we note that "while some children emerge from divorce with a strong sense of loss and feelings of anger or despair, others are capable of acknowledging that divorce has pain but also benefits for themselves and other family members" (Thompson and Amato 1999: xix). Factors that determine whether children are scathed or strengthened by parental divorce include the quality of the child's relationship with both parents, the extent of ongoing conflict versus cooperation between the parents, and the economic circumstances of the child's household. In most circumstances, children adapt to divorce, "showing resiliency, not dysfunction" (Thompson and Amato 1999: xix).

Strategies for Action: Responding to the Problems of Divorce

Two general strategies for responding to the problems of divorce are (1) strategies to prevent divorce and strengthen marriages and (2) strategies to strengthen post-divorce families.

Divorce Prevention Strategies

One strategy for preventing divorce is to require or encourage couples to participate in premarital education before getting married. Some have proposed legislation requiring or encouraging premarital education (Clark 1996; Peterson 1997). Proposed policies include mandating premarital education, lowering marriage licence fees for those who participate, and imposing delays on issuing marriage licences for those who refuse premarital education. Researchers have found that couples who participated in a widely used couples' education program called PREP (the Prevention and Relationship Enhancement Program) had a lower divorce and separation rate five years after completing the program compared with couples who did not participate (Stanley et al. 1995). Marriage enrichment programs for newlyweds have also been found to be effective in improving communication and conflict resolution and overall marital satisfaction (Cole et al. 2000).

Some family scholars and policymakers advocate strengthening marriage by reforming divorce laws to make divorce harder to obtain. In most cases, these measures are designed to make breaking up harder to do by requiring proof of fault (e.g., adultery, abuse) or extending the waiting period required before divorce is granted (Amato 2001). Opponents argue that **divorce law reform** measures would increase acrimony between divorcing spouses (which harms the children as well as the adults involved), increase the legal costs of getting a divorce (which leaves less money to support any children), and delay court decisions on child support and custody and distribution of assets.

I believe it would be a good thing to make marriage harder instead of easier, for there is too great a tendency on the part of people to rush into marriage without realizing either its hardships or its binding nature.

Agnes Macphail
Politician, pioneering Canadian feminist

In the United States, a novel idea arose when, in June 1997, the Louisiana legislature became the first in that nation to pass a law creating a new kind of marriage contract. Under the new law, couples can voluntarily choose between the standard marriage contract that allows a no-fault divorce (after a six-month separation) and a "**covenant marriage**" that permits divorce only under condition of fault or after a marital separation of more than two years. Couples who choose a covenant marriage must also get premarital counselling. The covenant marriage law was designed to strengthen marriages and discourage divorce. However, less than 1 percent of Louisiana couples have opted for a covenant marriage license (Flory 2000). As of this writing, several other states in the U.S. are considering marriage laws similar to the covenant marriage, but only one other state—Arizona—has passed a similar marriage law.

Strengthening marriages may be achieved through policies and services that provide greater resources to couples whose marriages are at risk. These supports include marriage counselling, flexible workplace policies that decrease work/family conflict, affordable child care, and economic support.

Strengthening Postdivorce Families

Negative consequences of divorce for children may be minimized if both parents continue to spend time with their children on a regular and consistent basis and communicate to their children that they love them and are interested in their lives. Parental conflict, in either intact families or divorced families, negatively influences the psychological well-being of children (Demo 1992). Ongoing conflict between divorced parents also tends to result in decreased involvement of nonresidential parents with their children (Leite and McKenry 2000). By maintaining a civil coparenting relationship during a separation and after divorce, parents can minimize the negative effects of divorce on their children.

> Although divorce ends a marriage, it does not end the family.
>
> Ross A. Thompson
> and Paul R. Amato
> The Postdivorce Family

What can society do to promote cooperative parenting by ex-spouses? One answer is to encourage, or even mandate, divorcing couples to participate in **divorce mediation**. In divorce mediation, divorcing couples meet with a neutral third party, a mediator, who helps them resolve issues of property division, child custody, child support, and spousal support in a way that minimizes conflict and encourages cooperation. Children of mediated divorces adjust better to the divorce than children of litigated divorces (Marlow and Sauber 1990). However, Canadian family lawyer Linda Silver Dranoff cautions that mediation is not always feasible and that "[s]pouses who have been bullied or dominated during the marriage may not be capable of holding their own in mediation, while rigid or abusive spouses may not be capable of the necessary flexibility and compromise" (2001: 254).

Another trend aimed at strengthening postdivorce families is the establishment of parenting programs for divorcing parents (Shapiro and Schrof 1995). For example, the B.C. Ministry of the Attorney-General is piloting a "Parenting after Separation" program for separated and divorced couples with children. Such programs emphasize the importance of cooperative co-parenting for the well-being of children. Parents are taught about children's reactions to divorce, nonconflictual co-parenting skills, and how to avoid negative behaviour toward their ex-spouse. In some programs, children participate and are taught that they are not the cause of the divorce, how to deal with grief reactions to divorce, and techniques for talking to parents about their concerns.

Nonmarital and Teenage Childbearing

In 1975, there were approximately 31 000 Canadian children born to not-married women (9 percent of all births). In 1996, there were about 103 500 births to not-married women and their babies accounted for just under a third (31 percent) of all births (Vanier Institute of the Family 2000: 55) (see Figure 5.11). To understand the rise in the number of children born to not-married women, we must consider several social factors. First, having a baby outside of marriage has become more socially acceptable and does not carry the stigma it once did. For example, over the past quarter century, all Canadian provinces and territories (with the exception of Alberta and Nova Scotia) have enacted legislation that dispenses with the distinction that used to exist in law between "legitimate" and "illegitimate" children. As a result, the distinction in legal terms between children born within and outside of marriage has been virtually eliminated in terms of financial support and inheritance rights (Dranoff 2001).

Singlehood has also become more acceptable and more common. The dictionary once defined a *spinster* as an unmarried woman above age 30. In previous generations, being a spinster meant the fear of isolation, living alone, and being somewhat of a social outcast. Today, women are "more confident, more self-sufficient, and...no longer see marriage as a matter of survival and acceptance" (Edwards 2000: 48). The women's movement created both new opportunities for women and expectations of egalitarian relationships with men. Increasingly, university-educated women in their 30s and 40s are making "the conscious decision to have a child on their own because they haven't found Mr. Adequate, let alone Mr. Right" (Drummond 2000: 54). This chapter's *Social Problems Research Up Close* feature examines attitudes of low-income single mothers toward marriage that help to explain why they are not married.

Increased acceptance of cohabitation and same-sex relationships has also contributed to the rising rate of nonmarital births. The term "nonmarital" includes births to the never-marrieds as well as the separated/divorced, widowed, and cohabiting. In 1996, three quarters of all Canadian children born to not-married women were born into common-law partnerships. In that year, the province with the highest number of births to women who were not married (50 percent) occurred in Quebec—the province with the highest proportion of couples living common law (24 percent) (Vanier Institute of the Family 2000:

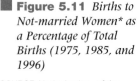 **Figure 5.11** *Births to Not-married Women* as a Percentage of Total Births (1975, 1985, and 1996)*

SOURCE: Vanier Institute of the Family. 2000. *Profiling Canada's Families II*. Nepean, ON: The Vanier Institute of the Family, p. 55.

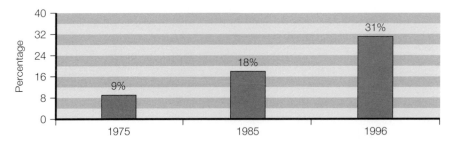

*Non-married women includes single women who may be part of a common-law relationship, and women who are divorced, separated, or widowed.

54). As such, "[t]he large majority of children born to mothers who are not married at the time of the child's birth nonetheless begin life in a family with both their biological parents present" (Vanier Institute of the Family 2000: 54).

A recent comparative study of teenage pregnancy in developed countries placed Canada in the "moderate" rate category (45.4 pregnancies/1000 females 15 to 19 years old) (Singh and Darroch 2000). Canada's teen pregnancy rate was about half of the "high" U.S. rate (83.6) but higher than the "low" or "very low" rates found in most developed European countries such as Belgium (14.1), Denmark (22.7), Sweden (24.9), and Norway (32.3) (Singh and Darroch 2000). Nevertheless, while the pregnancy rate among every other age group of fertile women is decreasing, the teenage pregnancy rate is increasing. Although well below their all-time highs, rates of teen pregnancies have increased from 41.1 per 1000 women aged 15 to 19 in 1987 to 47.1 per 1000 in 1995 to 59.2 in 1997 (Crawford 1997; Health Canada 1999). However, the number of live births is not as high as these figures suggest because approximately 40 percent of teenage pregnancies end in abortion (Figure 5.12).

Teenage pregnancy has been related to a variety of factors, including low self-esteem and hopelessness, low parental supervision, and perceived lack of future occupational opportunities (Jorgensen 2000; Luker 1996; McKay et al. 2000). Although lack of information about and access to contraceptives contributes to unintended teenage pregnancy, a U.S. study found that 30 to 40 percent of adolescent pregnancies are intended (Jorgensen 2000). Teenage females who do poorly in school may have little hope of success and achievement in pursuing educational and occupational goals. They may think that their only remaining option for a meaningful role in life is to become a parent. In addition, some teenagers feel lonely and unloved and have a baby to create a sense of feeling needed and wanted.

Social Problems Related to Nonmarital and Teenage Childbearing

Teenage and unmarried childbirth are considered social problems because of the adverse consequences for women and children that are associated with such births.

> ■ For many disadvantaged teenagers, childbearing reflects—rather than causes—the limitations of their lives.
>
> ELLEN W. FREEMAN
> AND KARL RICKELS

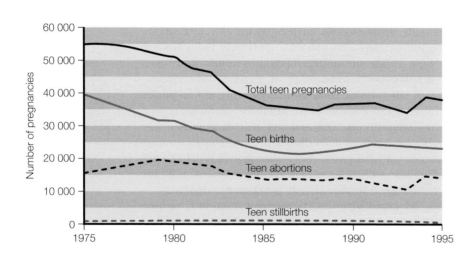

■ Figure 5.12 *Teenage Pregnancies, Births, and Abortions, Canada, 1975–1995*

SOURCES: Statistics Canada. 1999. Health Statistics Division *Health Indications*, Cat. No. 820221-XCB; and "Births and Deaths," Catalogue 84-210, May 1997.

Perceptions of Marriage among Low-Income Single Mothers

Single mothers with low incomes face both economic hardships and parenting challenges. These hardships and challenges could potentially be alleviated by marriage to a partner who contributes income to the family, and who shares the responsibilities of housework and child care and supervision. Yet, low-income single women have low rates of marriage and remarriage. U.S. Sociologist Kathryn Edin (2000) conducted research on the perceptions of marriage among low-income single mothers that helps explain why these mothers are not married. Here we summarize her research and its findings.

Sample and Methods

This study focused on transcripts and field notes collected from multiple qualitative interviews with 292 low-income single mothers. Initially, interviewers utilized the resources of community groups and local institutions to recruit eligible mothers. They then relied on references from the mothers themselves to gain access to others who might also participate in the interviews. Approximately half of the participants depended on welfare, and about half worked at low-wage jobs.

Researchers scheduled a minimum of two interviews with each mother to maximize rapport, and to encourage them to expand and clarify responses that may have been initially unclear. Interviewers asked respondents to describe the

circumstances surrounding the births of their children, their current family situations and relationship with each child's father, their views about how their family situations might change over time, and their views of marriage in general. Interviewers focused on two issues in their conversations with mothers: why women with few economic resources choose to have children and why these same women fail to marry or remarry.

Findings and Conclusions

Edin found four primary reasons why low-income single mothers do not marry. These include the low economic status of available men; the desire for parental, economic, and relationship control; mistrust; and domestic violence.

1. *Low economic status of men.* Edin found that men's income is a significant factor in poor single mothers' willingness to marry, as "they simply could not afford to keep an unproductive man around the house" (p. 118). Nearly every mother in Edin's sample said that it was important for any man they would marry to have a "good job." Although total earnings is the most important aspect for single mothers, also important are the regularity of those earnings, the effort men make to find and keep employment, and the source of the income. "Women whose male partners couldn't, or wouldn't find work, often lost respect for them and 'just couldn't stand' to keep them around" (p. 119). Mothers did not consider earn-

ings from crime (e.g., drug dealing) as legitimate earnings and reported that they wouldn't marry such a man no matter how much money he made from crime.

Respectability was also an issue for poor single mothers:

> Mothers said that they could not achieve respectability by marrying someone who was frequently out of work, otherwise underemployed, supplemented his income through criminal activity, and had little chance of improving his situation over time. Mothers believed that marriage to such a man would diminish their respectability, rather than enhance it. (p. 120)

Mothers also believed that marriage to a lower-class man would be unlikely to last because the economic pressures on the relationship would be too great. Mothers talked about the "sacred" nature of marriage, and believed that no "respectable" woman would marry a man whose economic situation would likely lead to a future divorce. Edin notes that:

> In interview after interview, mothers stressed the seriousness of the marriage commitment and their belief that "it should last forever." Thus, it is not that mothers held marriage in low esteem, but rather the fact that they held it in such high esteem that convinced them to forego marriage, at least until their prospective marriage partner could prove himself worthy economically or they could find

another partner who could. (pp. 120–121)

2. *Desire for parental, economic, and relationship control*. When asked what they liked best about being a single parent, the most common response was "I am in charge," or "I am in control."

Most mothers felt that the presence of fathers often interfered with their parental control. Single mothers in Edin's study felt that a husband might be "too demanding" of them and thus impede their efforts to spend time with their children. Mothers were also concerned about losing control of the family's economic situation. One mother said, "[I won't marry because] the men take over the money. I'm too afraid to lose control of my money again" (p. 121).

Regardless of whether or not the prospective wife worked, mothers feared that prospective husbands would expect to be the "head of the house," who, being "in charge," would want to make the "final" decisions about child rearing, finances, and other matters. Mothers also expressed the view that if they married, their husbands would expect them to do all of the household chores. Some women described their relationships with their ex-partners as "like having one more kid to take care of" (p. 122).

Most single mothers in Edin's sample wanted to marry eventually and thought that the best way to maximize their control in a marriage was by working and earning an income. One mother explained,

One thing my mom did teach me is that you must work some and bring some money into the household so you can have a say in what happens. If you completely live off a man, you are helpless. That is why I don't want to get married until I get my own [career] and get off of welfare. (p. 122)

Mothers also wanted to develop their labour market skills before marriage to ensure against destitution in the event of a divorce and to increase their bargaining power in their relationships. Mothers believed that women who were economically dependent on men had to "put up with all kinds of behaviour" because they could not legitimately threaten to leave.

> Mothers felt that if they became more economically independent...they could legitimately threaten to leave their husbands if certain conditions (i.e., sexual fidelity) weren't met. These threats would, in turn they believed, keep a husband on his best behaviour. (p. 122)

Many of the single mothers in Edin's study had held traditional gender role attitudes when they were younger and still in a relationship with their children's fathers. When the men for whom they sacrificed so much gave them nothing but pain and anguish, they felt they had been 'duped' and were no longer willing to be dependent or subservient to men.

3. *Mistrust*. Many of the single mothers in Edin's sample did not marry because they did not trust

their partners or men in general, and/or because their partners did not trust them. Some fathers claimed that the child was not theirs because the mother was "a whore." One partner of a pregnant woman in the sample told the interviewer, "how do I know the baby's mine? Who knows if she hasn't been stepping out on me with some other man and now she wants me to support another man's child!" (p. 124).

Mothers tended to mistrust men because their previous boyfriends and partners had been unfaithful. This experience was so common among respondents that many simply did not believe men could be faithful to only one woman. Most said they would rather never marry than to "let him make a fool out of me" (p. 124). "Nonetheless, many of these same women often held out hope of finding a man who was 'different', one who could be trusted" (p. 125).

4. *Domestic violence*. For some mothers in Edin's sample, domestic violence in either their childhood or adult lives played a role in their negative attitudes toward marriage. Many mothers reported physical abuse during pregnancy and several mothers had miscarriages because of such abuse. One woman who had been in the hospital three times because of abuse said, "I was terrified to leave because I knew it would mean going on welfare....But that is okay. I can handle that. The thing I couldn't deal with is being beat up" (p.126). Edin commented,

(continued)

The fact that women tended to experience repeated abuse from their children's fathers before they decided to leave attests to their strong desire to make things work with their children's fathers. Many women finally left when they saw the abuse beginning to affect their children's well-being. (p. 126)

In conclusion, low-income single mothers in Edin's study were reluctant to marry the father of their children because these men had low economic status, traditional notions of male domination in household and parental decisions, and patterns of untrustworthy and even violent behaviour. Given the low level of trust these mothers have of men and given their view that husbands want more control than the women are willing to give them, women realize that a marriage that is also economically strained is likely to be conflictual and short-lived. "Interestingly, mothers say they reject entering into economically risky marital unions out of respect for the institution of marriage, rather than because of a rejection of the marriage norm" (Edin 2000: 130). Low-income single mothers in Edin's study "say they are willing, even eager, to marry if the marriage represents an increase in their class standing and if...their prospective husbands' behaviour indicates he won't beat them, abuse their children, refuse to share household tasks, insist on making all decisions, be sexually unfaithful, or abuse alcohol or drugs" (p. 113):

In short, the mothers interviewed here believe that marriage will probably make their lives more difficult than they are currently.... If they are to marry, they want to get something out of it. If they cannot enjoy economic stability and gain upward mobility from marriage, they see little reason to risk the loss of control and other costs they fear marriage might exact from them. Unless low-skilled men's economic situations improve and they begin to change their behaviours toward women, it is quite likely that most low-income women will continue to resist marriage. (p. 130)

SOURCE: © 2000 by *The Society of Social Problems*. Reprinted from Edin, Katheryn. 2000. "What Do Low-Income Single Mothers Say about Marriage?" *Social Problems* 47(1), February 2000: 112–13, by permission.

1. *Poverty for single mothers and children.* Many unmarried mothers, especially teenagers, have no means of economic support or have limited earning capacity. Single mothers and their children often live in substandard housing and have inadequate nutrition and incomes. Even with public assistance, many unwed parents struggle to survive economically. The public bears some of the economic burden of supporting unmarried mothers and their children, but even with public assistance, many unwed and teenage parents often struggle to survive economically. While child poverty in Canada is not restricted to single-parent families, a far higher proportion of children of single parents and, in particular, lone-parent mothers, live in low-income circumstances (Riedmann et al. 2003).

2. *Poor health outcomes.* Compared with older pregnant women, pregnant teenagers are less likely to receive timely prenatal care and to gain adequate weight and are more likely to smoke and use alcohol and drugs during pregnancy (Jorgensen 2000; Ventura et al. 2000). As a consequence of these and other factors, infants born to teenagers are at higher risk of low birth weight, of premature birth, and of dying in the first year of life.

3. *Low academic achievement.* Low academic achievement is both a contributing factor and a potential outcome of teenage parenthood. Teens whose parents have not graduated from high school are at higher risk for becoming pregnant (Hogan et al. 2000). Three-fifths of teenage mothers drop out of school and, as a consequence, have a much higher probability of remaining poor throughout their lives. Because poverty is linked to unmarried parenthood, a cycle of successive generations of teenage pregnancy may develop.

    Some research has found that children of single mothers are more prone to academic problems. However, recent findings indicate that the mother's educational level and ability, rather than the absence of a father, have the most influence on a child's school readiness (Drummond 2000).

4. *Children without fathers.* Shapiro and Schrof (1995) report that children who grow up without fathers are more likely to drop out of school, be unemployed, abuse drugs, experience mental illness, and be a target of child sexual abuse. They also note that "a missing father is a better predictor of criminal activity than race or poverty" (p. 39). Popenoe (1996) believes that fatherlessness is a major cause of the degenerating conditions of our young.

    However, others argue that the absence of a father is not, in and of itself, damaging to children. Rather, other conditions associated with female-headed single-parent families, such as low educational attainment of the mother, poverty, and lack of child supervision contribute to negative outcomes for children.

Strategies for Action: Interventions in Teenage and Nonmarital Childbearing

Some interventions regarding teenage childbearing aim at prevention, while others attempt to minimize its negative effects. One preventive intervention is to provide sex education and family planning programs before unwanted or unintended pregnancy occurs. Schools, churches, family planning clinics, and public health departments may offer sex education programs. One obstacle to sex education in the schools is the fear that teaching youth about sex and contraception actually encourages sexual activity. However, the World Health Organization reviewed 35 controlled studies of sex education programs and found that students who participated in the programs did not initiate intercourse at an earlier age than students in the control group that were exposed to no programs (Berne and Huberman 1996).

Sex education programs that emphasize abstinence and do not provide students with access to contraception are unlikely to be highly successful in preventing teenage pregnancy (Jacobs and Wolf 1995). The European approach to teenage sexual activity is to provide widespread confidential and accessible contraceptive services to adolescents. The provision of contraceptive services to European teens is believed to be a central factor in explaining the rapid declines in teenage childbearing in northern and western European countries (Singh and Darroch 2000).

Other programs aim at both preventing teenage and unmarried childbearing and minimizing its negative effects by increasing the life options of teenagers and unmarried mothers. Such programs include educational programs, job training, and skill-building programs. Other programs designed to help teenage and unwed mothers and their children include public welfare prenatal programs to help ensure the health of the mother and baby, and parenting classes for both teenage fathers and unmarried mothers.

Strategies to increase and support fathers' involvement with their children are relevant to both children of unwed mothers and children of divorce. These include promoting responsible fatherhood by improving work opportunities for low-income fathers, increasing child support collections, providing parent education training for men, supporting access and visitation by noncustodial parents, and involving boys and young men in preventing teenage pregnancy and early parenting.

Because teenage parents are less likely than older parents to use positive and effective child-rearing techniques, parent education programs for teen mothers and fathers are an important component of improving the lives of young parents and their children. One such program that utilizes interactive computer technology is presented in this chapter's *Focus on Technology* feature.

Understanding **Family Problems**

Family problems can best be understood within the context of the society and culture in which they occur. Although domestic violence, divorce, teenage pregnancy and unmarried parenthood may appear to result from individual decisions, these decisions are influenced by a myriad of social and cultural forces.

The impact of family problems, including divorce, abuse, and nonmarital childbearing, is felt not only by family members, but by the larger society as well. Family members experience such life difficulties as poverty, school failure, low self-esteem, and mental and physical health problems. Each of these difficulties contributes to a cycle of family problems in the next generation. The impact on society includes public expenditures to assist single-parent families and victims of domestic violence and neglect, and combat youth crime and lower worker productivity.

> If we are to achieve a richer culture, rich in contrasting values, we must recognize the whole gamut of human potentialities, and so weave a less arbitrary social fabric, one in which each diverse human will find a fitting place.
>
> MARGARET MEAD
> *Anthropologist*

For some, the solution to family problems implies encouraging marriage and discouraging other family forms, such as single parenting, cohabitation, and same-sex unions. But many family scholars argue that the fundamental issue is making sure that children are well-cared for, whether or not their parents are married. Some even suggest that marriage is part of the problem, not part of the solution. According to Martha Fineman, "This obsession with marriage prevents us from looking at our social problems and addressing them....Marriage is nothing more than a piece of paper, and yet we rely on marriage to do a lot of work in this society: It becomes our family policy, our police in regard to welfare and children, the cure for poverty" (quoted in Lewin 2000: 2). Strengthening marriage is a worthy goal because strong marriages offer many benefits to individuals and their children. However, "strengthening marriage does not have to mean a return to the patriarchal family of an earlier era....Indeed, greater marital stability will only come about when men are willing to share power, as well as housework and childcare, equally with women" (Amato 2001: 184).

Parenting Wisely: An Interactive Computer Parenting Education Program

Parenting Wisely (FamilyWorks, Inc. 2000) is an interactive computer parenting education program that teaches communication skills (such as active listening), assertive discipline (such as using praise and setting consequences), and child supervision techniques (such as how to monitor homework and friends). The program contains nine case studies depicting nine problems common in families. After a video of a family problem is shown, three possible responses are presented. Some responses result in a worsening of the situation, whereas others improve the situation. Parents choose a response, see a video of how their choice would work, and get feedback on the pros and cons of their choice. Parents who have difficulty reading can choose to have the computer text read aloud. It usually takes two to three hours to work through the nine case studies.

The nine scenarios include two-parent, single-parent, and stepfamilies from diverse racial and ethnic backgrounds. Preteens and teenagers appear in the scenarios, but Parenting Wisely has been shown to be equally successful with parents of younger children.

Parents who are unfamiliar with computers, as well as those with computer experience, can use the program. It is designed to be entirely self-administered, eliminating the need for an instructor to guide parents through the program. Poorly educated parents with no computer experience have no difficulty using the program without assistance, and commonly report that the program is fun and highly engaging to use (FamilyWorks, Inc. 2000).

How effective is the Parenting Wisely program? A summary of research evaluating Parenting Wisely reveals that parents with pre-teens and teens showing significant behaviour problems demonstrated increased knowledge in parenting principles and skills, increased use of the parenting skills taught in the program, and reductions in problem behaviours of their children ("Parenting Wisely Evaluation Results" 2000). In one study (Lagges and Gordon 1999), 62 pregnant or parenting teens were randomly assigned to either the Parenting Wisely program or to a control group. Both groups attended a teen parenting class in their high schools. Compared with the control group, the intervention group scored significantly higher at two months follow-up in parenting knowledge, belief in the effectiveness of positive parenting practices over coercive practices (yelling and spanking), and application of positive parenting skills to hypothetical problem situations. In two studies, children's problem behaviour showed at least a 50 percent reduction one month after parents used the program ("Parenting Wisely Evaluation Results" 2000). A matched control group showed no improvement. In a study with teen mothers, use of the Parenting Wisely program resulted in improved knowledge of parenting principles and skills and problem-solving for toddler misbehaviour.

The effectiveness of Parenting Wisely may be attributed in part to the self-administered aspect of the computer program. "Parental resistance to change is minimal with this learning format. A person is not judging parents as in therapy. Parents also move through the program at their own pace, and can repeat a section when they wish" ("Parenting Wisely Evaluation Results" 2000: 1). Other benefits of using interactive computer technology in parenting education include that it can be disseminated fairly quickly and inexpensively. The convenience and lack of stigma can increase parent participation in computer-based parent education.

Evaluation results of the *Parenting Wisely* program suggest at least short-term improvements in children's behaviour after their parents complete the program. Ongoing evaluation is currently assessing longer-term effects.

SOURCES: FamilyWorks, Inc. 2000. "Parenting Wisely." 20 East Circle Drive, Suite 190. Athens, OH 45701-3751. "Parenting Wisely Evaluation Results." 2000. http://family-worksinc.com/index2.html. Lagges, A., and D. A. Gordon. 1999. "Interactive Videodisk Parent Training for Teen Mothers." *Child and Family Behavior Therapy* 21: 1937.

And strengthening marriage does not mean that other family forms should not also be supported. The reality is that the family comes in many forms, each with its strengths, needs, and challenges. Given the diversity of families today, social historian Stephanie Coontz (2000) suggests, "The only way forward at this point in history is to find better ways to make both marriage and its alternatives work" (p. 15).

> We recognize today that children can be effectively raised in many different family systems and that it is the emotional climate of the family, rather than its kinship structure, that primarily determines a child's emotional well-being and healthy development.
>
> DAVID ELKIND
> *Child development specialist*

Critical Thinking

1 Some scholars and politicians argue that "stable families are the bedrock of stable communities." Others argue that "stable communities and economies are the bedrock of stable families." Which of these two positions would you take and why?

2 Lloyd and Emery (2000) note that "one of the primary ways that power disguises itself in courtship and marriage is through the 'myth of equality between the sexes'....The widespread discourse on 'marriage between equals' serves as a cover for the presence of male domination in intimate relationships...and allows couples to create an illusion of equality that masks the inequities in their relationships" (pp. 25–26). Do you agree that the modern view of marriage between equal partners is an illusion? Why or why not?

3 Research has suggested that secondhand smoke from cigarettes represents a health hazard for those who are exposed to it. Consequently, smoking is now banned in many public places and workplaces. Do you think that parents should be banned from smoking in enclosed areas (home or car) to protect their children from secondhand smoke? Do you think that smoking in enclosed areas with one's children present should be considered a form of child abuse? Why or why not?

4 Some judges are imposing "shame sentences" on convicted abusers (e.g., sentencing an abusive husband to publicly apologize to his wife on the steps of City Hall, or to go to a local mall carrying a sign that reads, "I went to jail for assaulting my wife. This could be you" ["In the News" 1998]). What do you think about these types of "shame sentences" for batterers?

5 Is individualism necessarily incompatible with familism? Why or why not?

Key Terms

census family

child abuse

common couple violence

corporal punishment

covenant marriage

cycle of abuse

divorce law reform

divorce mediation

elder abuse

emotional abuse

familism

family preservation program

heterosexual monogamy

individualism

intimate partner violence

intimate terrorism

mutual violent control

no-fault divorce

parental alienation
    syndrome (PAS)

patriarchy

polyandry

polygamy

polygyny

primary prevention

second shift

secondary prevention

self-fulfilling prophecy

sexual aggression

tertiary prevention

violent resistance

Section 2

Problems of Human Diversity

People are diverse. They vary on many dimensions, including age, gender, sexual orientation, and race and ethnicity. In most societies, including Canada, these characteristics are imbued with social significance and are used to make judgments about an individual's worth, intelligence, skills, and personality. Such labelling creates categories of people who are perceived as "different" by others as well as by themselves and, as a result, are often treated differently.

A **minority** is defined as a category of people who have unequal access to positions of power, prestige, and wealth in a society. In effect, minorities have unequal opportunities and are disadvantaged in their attempt to gain societal resources. Even though they may be a majority in terms of numbers, they may still be a minority sociologically. Before Nelson Mandela was elected president of South Africa, South African Blacks suffered the disadvantages of a minority even though they were a numerical majority of the population.

Terms that may apply to minorities include *stereotyping*, *prejudice*, and *discrimination*. A stereotype is a set of assumptions or generalizations about the characteristics of a group of persons. Prejudice is an atti-

tude, often negative, that prejudges an individual. Discrimination is differential treatment by members of the majority group against members of the minority that has a harmful effect on members of the subordinate group. The groups we will discuss in this section are all victims of stereotyping, prejudice, and discrimination.

Minority groups usually have certain characteristics in common. In general, members of a minority group know that they are members of a minority, stay within their own group, have relatively low levels of self-esteem, are disproportionately represented in the lower socioeconomic strata, and are viewed as having negative traits. Other characteristics of specific minority groups are identified in the accompanying table.

In the following chapters, we discuss categories of minorities based on age (Chapter 6), gender (Chapter 7), race and ethnicity (Chapter 8), and sexual orientation (Chapter 9). Although other categories of minorities exist (e.g., people with disabilities, religious minorities), we have chosen to concentrate on these four groups because each is surrounded by issues and policies that have far-reaching social, political, and economic implications.

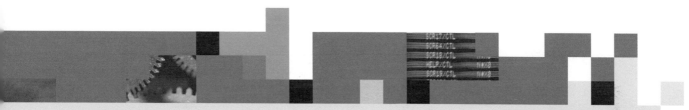

Nine Characteristics of Four Minorities

	Old/Young	Women	Racial and Ethnic Minorities	Homosexuals
1. Status ascribed based on	Age	Sex	Race/ethnicity	Sexual orientation
2. Visibility	High	High	High	Low
3. Attribution of minority status (correctly or incorrectly) based on	Hair Skin elasticity Size Posture	Anatomy Shape	Skin colour Facial features Hair	Mannerisms Style of dress
4. Summary image	Dependent	Weak	Inferior	Sick or immoral
5. Derogatory and offensive terms	Old codger Brat	Bitch Whore	Nigger Paki	Faggot Dyke
6. Control through feigning various characteristics*	Frailty Helplessness	Weakness	Ignorance	Heterosexuality
7. Discrimination	Yes	Yes	Yes	Yes
8. Victims of violence	Yes	Yes	Yes	Yes
9. Segregation	Yes	Yes	Yes	Yes

*Being aware of their lack of power, minority group members may try to exert control by feigning certain characteristics. For example, slaves could not tell their owners, "I'm not going to plough the fields—do it yourself!" However, by acting incompetent, slaves may have avoided the work. Gays may attempt to pass as straight by bragging about heterosexual conquests. The elderly in nursing homes whose family members might otherwise not visit may feign illness in the hope of eliciting a visit. The problem with these acts is that they contribute to and stabilize the summary images.

6

The Young and the Old

Outline

The Global Context: The Young and the Old around the World

Youth and Aging

Sociological Theories of Age Inequality

Problems of Youth in Canada

Demographics: The "Greying of Canada"

Problems of the Elderly

Strategies for Action: Growing Up and Growing Old

Understanding the Young and the Old

Is It True?

1. The concepts of "middle-age" and "adolescence" have always existed.

2. Every society assigns different social roles to different age groups.

3. It is estimated that three million children in Canada arrive at school hungry.

4. In Canada, there has been a steady increase in the percentage of seniors with low income.

5. By 2041, almost one-quarter of the Canadian population will be aged 65 or older, nearly double the proportion in 1995.

Answers: 1 = F, 2 = T, 3 = T, 4 = F, 5 = T

The quality of a nation is reflected in the way it recognizes that its strength lies in its ability to integrate the wisdom of elders with the spirit and vitality of its children and youth.

MARGARET MEAD
Anthropologist

In July 2002, World Youth Day 2002 drew hundreds of thousands of pilgrims from over 170 countries to Toronto for a 10-day festival of bible teachings, concerts, and discussions. World Youth Day was created in 1984 by Pope John Paul II with the goal of bringing together young people from around the world and is held every two or three years in cities across the globe. Although many had predicted that the pontiff would not address the crisis posed to the Catholic Church by increased reports of the sexual abuse of children by priests, he did so. Speaking before a congregation of approximately 800 000 who had gathered at an open-air service in Toronto, and beyond them, to a worldwide audience, he stated, "The harm done by some priests and religious to the young and vulnerable fills us with a deep sense of sadness and shame." He urged Catholics not to be discouraged and spoke of the resiliency of youth. "You are young, the Pope is old and a bit tired," he stated. "Although I have lived through much darkness, under harsh totalitarian regimes, I have seen enough violence to be unshakably convinced that no difficulty, no fear is so great that it can completely suffocate the hope that springs eternal in the hearts of the young" (in Vallis 2002).

The young and the old. Although age diversity is often celebrated (e.g., birthdays, high-school graduation, retirement), there are countless examples of how social life oppresses children and devalues the elderly. The young and the old represent major population segments of Canadian society. In this chapter, we examine the problems and potential solutions associated with youth and aging. We begin by looking at age in a cross-cultural context.

The Global Context: The Young and the Old around the World

The young and the old receive different treatment in different societies. Differences in the treatment of the dependent young and old have traditionally been associated with whether the country is developed or less developed. Although proportionately more elderly live in developed countries than in less developed ones, these societies have fewer statuses for the elderly to occupy. Their positions as caretakers, homeowners, employees, and producers are often usurped by those aged 18 to 65. Paradoxically, the more primitive the society the more likely that society is to practise **senilicide**—the killing of the elderly. In some societies, the elderly are considered a burden and left to die or, in some cases, actively killed.

Not all societies treat the elderly as a burden. Scandinavian countries provide government support for in-home care workers for elderly who can no longer perform such tasks as cooking and cleaning. Eastern cultures such as Japan

There were only two periods in the life of a Chinese male when he possessed maximum security and minimal responsibility—infancy and old age. Of the two, old age was the better because one was conscious of the pleasure to be derived from such an almost perfect period.

PAUL T. WELTY
Historian

Nobody knows anything, really, until he is fifty.

F.H. UNDERHILL
Political scientist

revere their elderly, in part because of their presumed proximity to honoured ancestors. By 2005, if present trends continue, Japan will have the highest proportion of elderly of any country in the world—19.6 percent of their population (Yamaguchi 2000).

Societies also differ in the way they treat children. In less developed societies, children work as adults, marry at a young age, and pass from childhood directly to adulthood with no recognized period of adolescence. In contrast, in industrialized nations, children are often expected to attend school for 12 to 16 years and, during this time, to remain financially and emotionally dependent on their families.

Because of this extended period of dependence, Canada treats "minors" differently from adults. Juveniles have a separate justice system and minimum ages for driving, drinking alcohol, joining the military, entering into a contract, marrying, dropping out of school, and voting. These limitations would not be tolerated if placed on individuals on the basis of sex or race. Hence, **ageism**, the belief that age is associated with certain psychological, behavioural, or intellectual traits, at least in reference to children, is significantly more tolerated than sexism or racism in Canada.

Despite this differential treatment, people in our country are fascinated with youth and being young. This was not always the case. The elderly were once highly valued—particularly older men who headed families and businesses. Younger men even powdered their hair, wore wigs, and dressed in a way that made them look older. It should be remembered, however, that in 1901, only 5.05 percent of the population was 65 or older and almost half the population (45 percent) was 19 years of age or under (Novak 1997). Being old was rare and respected; to some it was a sign that God looked favourably on that individual.

One theory argues that the shift from valuing the old to valuing the young took place during the transition from an agriculturally based society to an industrial one. Land, which was often owned by elders, became less important, as did their knowledge and skills about land-based economies. With industrialization, technological skills, training, and education became more important than land ownership. Called **modernization theory**, this position argues that as a society becomes more technologically advanced, the position of the elderly declines (Cowgill and Holmes 1972).

Youth and Aging

Age is largely socially defined. Cultural definitions of "old" and "young" vary from society to society, from time to time, and from person to person. For example, in ancient Greece or Rome, where the average life expectancy was 20 years, a person was old at 18; similarly, a person was old at 30 in medieval Europe.

Age is also a variable that has a dramatic impact on a person's life. Matras (1990) identified 1 to 4 of the points below:

1. Age determines life experiences, since the date of birth determines the historical period in which a person lives. Twenty years ago cell phones and palm-size computers were the stuff of science fiction.
2. Different ages are associated with different developmental stages (physiological, psychological, and social) and abilities. Ben Franklin observed, "at 20 years of age the will reigns; at 30 the wit; at 40 judgment."

3. Age defines roles and expectations of behaviour. The expression "act your age" implies that some behaviours are not considered appropriate for people of certain ages.
4. Age influences the social groups to which one belongs. Whether one is part of a sixth grade class, a labour union, or a seniors' bridge club depends on one's age.
5. Age defines legal status. It defines when you can get a driver's licence, vote, get married without your parents' permission, and become eligible for social security benefits.

> When I was young, I swore that when I was old enough I'd never forget what it was like to be young.
>
> SAM ORBAUM
> *Journalist*

Childhood, Adulthood, and Elderhood

Every society assigns different social roles to different age groups. **Age grading** is the assignment of social roles to given chronological ages (Matras 1990). Although the number of age grades varies by society, most societies make at least three distinctions: childhood, adulthood, and elderhood.

Childhood The period of childhood in our society is from birth through age 17 and is often subdivided into infancy, childhood, and adolescence. Infancy has always been recognized as a stage of life, but the social category of childhood only developed after industrialization, urbanization, and modernization took place. Before industrialization, infant mortality was high because of the lack of adequate health care and proper nutrition. Once infants could be expected to survive infancy, the concept of childhood emerged, and society began to develop norms in reference to children. In Canada, child labour laws prohibit children from being used as inexpensive labour, educational mandates require that children begin school by the age of six or seven, and the criminal law imposes severe penalties for the sexual exploitation of children.

> The adolescent or teenager is a twentieth-century invention, and a most ill-advised one.
>
> NORTHROP FRYE
> *Cultural critic*

Adulthood The period from age 18 through 64 is generally subdivided into young adulthood, adulthood, and middle age. Each status involves dramatic role changes related to entering the workforce, getting married, and having children. The concept of "middle age" is a relatively recent one that has developed as life expectancy has been extended. Some people in this phase are known as members of the "**sandwich generation**," since they are often emotionally and economically responsible for both their young children and their aging parents.

Elderhood At age 65, a person is likely to be considered elderly, a category that is often subdivided into the young-old, old, and old-old. Membership in one of these categories does not necessarily depend on chronological age. The growing number of healthy, active, independent elderly is often considered the young-old, whereas the old-old are less healthy, less active, and more dependent.

Sociological Theories of Age Inequality

Three sociological theories help explain age inequality and the continued existence of ageism in Canada. These theories—structural-functionalism, conflict theory, and symbolic interactionism—are discussed in the following sections.

Structural-Functionalist Perspective

Structural-functionalism emphasizes the interdependence of society—how one part of a social system interacts with other parts to benefit the whole. From a functionalist perspective, the elderly must gradually relinquish their roles to younger members of society. This transition is viewed as natural and necessary to maintain the integrity of the social system. The elderly gradually withdraw as they prepare for death, and society withdraws from the elderly by segregating them in housing such as retirement villages and nursing homes. In the interim, the young have learned through the educational institution how to function in the roles surrendered by the elderly. In essence, a balance in society is achieved whereby the various age groups perform their respective functions: the young go to school, adults fill occupational roles, and the elderly, with obsolete skills and knowledge, disengage. As this process continues, each new group moves up and replaces another, benefiting society and all of its members.

This theory is known as **disengagement theory** (Cummings and Henry 1961). Some researchers no longer accept this position as valid, however, given the increasing number of elderly who remain active throughout life (Riley 1987). In contrast to disengagement theory, **activity theory** emphasizes that the elderly disengage in part because they are structurally segregated and isolated, not because they have a natural tendency to do so. For those elderly who remain active, role loss may be minimal. In studying 1720 respondents who reported using a senior centre in the previous year, Miner et al. (1993) found that those who used the centre were less disengaged and more socially active than those who did not use it.

Conflict Perspective

The conflict perspective focuses on age grading as another form of inequality as both the young and the old occupy subordinate statuses. Some conflict theorists emphasize that individuals at both ends of the age continuum are superfluous to a capitalist economy. Children are untrained, inexperienced, and neither actively producing nor consuming in an economy that requires both. Similarly, the elderly, although once working, are no longer productive and often lack required skills and levels of education. Both young and old are considered part of what is called the dependent population; that is, they are an economic drain on society. Hence, children are required to go to school in preparation for entry into a capitalist economy, and the elderly are forced to retire.

Other conflict theorists focus on how different age strata represent different interest groups that compete with one another for scarce resources. Debates about funding for public schools, child health programs, and social security largely represent the conflicting interests of the young versus the old.

Symbolic Interactionist Perspective

The symbolic interactionist perspective emphasizes the importance of examining the social meaning and definitions associated with age. Teenagers are often portrayed as lazy, aimless, and awkward. The elderly are also defined in a number of stereotypical ways, contributing to a host of myths surrounding the inevitability of physical and mental decline. Table 6.1 identifies some of these myths.

I think that at the other end of life there is a chance and an unfolding and a new kind of splendour to life which should be siezed and enjoyed.

ROBERTSON DAVIES
Man-of-letters

Table 6.1 *Myths and Facts about the Elderly*

Health

Myth The elderly are always sick; most are in nursing homes.

Fact Almost three out of four seniors aged 65 and older and living at home rate their health as good to excellent. Among seniors aged 85 and older, more than three in four rated their health as good or very good. Although the likelihood that an individual will live in some type of special-care home for the aged (e.g., nursing homes, hospitals, etc.) increases with age, the 2001 census found that relatively few seniors live in such setting (9.2 percent of senior women and 4.9 percent of senior men); both of these proportions had declined from the time of the 1981 census (Dube 2002).

Automobile Accidents

Myth The elderly are dangerous drivers and the most likely age group to die in car accidents.

Fact Although older drivers are more likely to be seriously injured or to die in car crashes than are most of their younger counterparts, the worst record is actually held by the youngest drivers. According to Statistics Canada, the mortality rate for drivers aged 65 or older is 27.2 per 100 000. Although that rate falls to 14 deaths per 100 000 for drivers aged 25 to 64, the rate climbs to 40.6 per 100 000 for those aged 15 to 19 (Canadian Press 1999: B11). Up to age 75, older drivers tend to drive fewer kilometres than younger drivers and compensate for their reduced reaction time by driving more carefully. Nevertheless, the normal processes of aging, diminishing vision and hearing and decreasing attention spans, may interfere with the ability to drive a car (Canadian Press 1999).

Mental Status

Myth The elderly are senile.

Fact Although some of the elderly learn more slowly and forget more quickly, most remain oriented and mentally intact. Only 20 to 25 percent develop Alzheimer's disease or some other incurable form of brain disease. Senility is not inevitable as people age.

Crime

Myth The elderly are more likely to be victims of crime than the young are.

Fact Although older people express more fear of crime than younger people do, "studies in Britain, the United States, and Canada show that older people run less risk of victimization than any other group" (Novak 1997).

Sexuality

Myth Sexual satisfaction disappears with age.

Fact Many elderly persons report sexual satisfaction. For example, of couples 75 years of age and older, over 25 percent report having sexual intercourse once a week (Toner 1999).

Adaptability

Myth The elderly cannot adapt to new working conditions.

Fact A high proportion of the elderly are flexible in accepting change in their occupations and earnings. Adaptability depends on the individual: many young are set in their ways, and many older people adapt to change readily.

SOURCES: Binstock, Robert H. 1986. "Public Policy and the Elderly." *Journal of Geriatric Psychiatry* 19: 115–43. Canadian Press. 1999. "Older Drivers More at Risk." *KW Record*, November 17: B11. Dube, Francine. 2002. "25% of Households Have Only One Person." *National Post*, October 23: A9. Mulligan, T., and R. F. Pagluta Jr. 1991. "Sexual Interest, Activity and Satisfaction among Male Nursing Home Residents." *Archives of Sexual Behaviour* 20: 199–204. Novak, Mark. 1997. *Aging and Society: A Canadian Perspective*, 3rd ed. Scarborough, ON.: Nelson. Toner, Robin. 1999. "A Majority Over 45 Say Sex Lives Are Just Fine." *New York Times*, August 4: A10.

At 80, I'm in the prime of senility. All I worry about now is whether there will be anyone left to come to my funeral.

IRVING LAYTON
Poet

Media portrayals contribute to the negative image of the elderly. The young are typically portrayed in active, vital roles and are often overrepresented in commercials. In contrast, the elderly are portrayed as difficult, complaining, and burdensome and are often underrepresented in commercials. A study of the elderly in popular films from the 1940s through the 1980s concluded that "older individuals of both genders were portrayed as less friendly, having less romantic activity, and enjoying fewer positive outcomes than younger characters at a movie's conclusion" (Brazzini et al. 1997: 541).

The elderly are also portrayed as childlike in terms of clothes, facial expressions, temperament, and activities—a phenomenon known as **infantilizing elders** (Arluke and Levin 1990). For example, young and old are often paired together. When Grandpa Simpson babysits Bart and his siblings, he invariably falls asleep before Bart's baby sister, Maggie. Jack Lemmon and Walter Matthau in *Grumpy Old Men* get "cranky" when they get tired and, in the *Odd Couple II*, lose their luggage, direction, money, and car during a cross-country trip. Finally, the elderly are often depicted in role reversal, cared for by their adult children as in the situation comedies *Golden Girls* and *Frasier*.

Negative stereotypes and media images of the elderly engender **gerontophobia**—a shared fear or dread of the elderly, which may create a self-fulfilling prophecy. In a recent study, seniors received one of two types of subliminal messages—those negatively stereotyping the elderly (e.g., senile) and those positively stereotyping the elderly (e.g., wise). Compared with those who received negative messages, subjects who received the positive messages scored better on memory tests, and were more likely to respond that they would accept life-prolonging health interventions (Begley 2000).

Problems of Youth in Canada

In spite of the presumed benefits of being young, numerous problems are associated with childhood. Indeed, some of our most pressing social problems can be traced to early childhood experiences and adolescent behavioural problems (Weissberg and Kuster 1997). Not surprisingly, what happens to children is increasingly defined as a social problem.

Children and the Law

Since it is the Other within us who is old, it is natural that the revelation of our age should come to us from outside—from others.

SIMONE DE BEAUVOIR
Writer

Historically, children have had little control over their lives. They have been "double dependent" on both their parents and the state. Indeed, our ancestors regarded children as property. Beginning in the 1950s, however, the view that children should have more autonomy became popular and was codified in several legal decisions. In 1959, the United Nations General Assembly approved the *Declaration on the Rights of the Child*, which held that health care, housing, and education, as well as freedom from abuse, neglect, and exploitation, are fundamental children's rights. Canada is a signatory to the United Nations *Convention on the Rights of the Child*, a treaty that has been described as "the most comprehensive human rights document ever adopted by the international community," and ratified by all but two countries (the United States and Somalia) in the world.

As required under Article 44 of the Convention, in 1999 the Canadian Coalition for the Rights of Children issued its first five-year nongovernmental progress report to the United Nations. Entitled *The UN Convention on the Rights of the Child: How Does Canada Measure Up?*, the report concluded that Canada meets most of its obligations under the UN Convention on the Rights of the Child. It notes, for example, that children's right to education is assured in Canadian legislation, which provides for primary and secondary schooling and requires all children to attend school. It acknowledges that the *Canada Health Act* provides free universal health care for all Canadians; that refugee children are eligible for health care, education, and settlement services in Canada; and that our provincial and territorial governments have a duty to intervene to protect a child at risk from abuse or neglect. At the same time, however, the report concludes that Canada had some way to go before full compliance with the Convention is achieved. Among their findings:

- Canadian legislation rarely recognizes children specifically and there are few redress mechanisms available to them. As such, children's fundamental freedoms are very dependent on the goodwill of adults. Rights education is not part of our schools' core curricula and children's convention rights have not been widely promoted in Canada. In child welfare cases, the child's best interests are weighed against parental rights. In other areas, children's "best interests" are ignored or interpreted without considering the views of children at all. The general principle of maximum survival and development is not assured for our most vulnerable children, such as children with disabilities, Aboriginal children, and children in the care of the state.

- Where a child lives often determines the degree to which his or her rights are met. There can be significant differences in the programs and services children receive in different parts of the country. Home care services for families of children with disabilities vary widely and there is no effort to create standards or even to define basic services. Child welfare services are often fragmented and uncoordinated within jurisdictions, with resources unevenly allocated across regions. For Aboriginal children living on reserves, the delivery of services is further complicated by jurisdictional disputes.

- Resources for children's programs and services are often stretched or unstable. Cutbacks to education funding and the closing of schools have undermined access to and the quality of education, especially in special education, citizenship, social studies, and arts education. Child welfare services have taken a back seat to budget cuts in some provinces, despite growing caseloads, chronic waiting lists, and worker burnout. Even with the high number of Aboriginal children affected by disabilities, the delivery of services in Aboriginal communities is generally poor or nonexistent.

- Aboriginal children have a disability rate that is more than twice the national average. Aboriginal children are at greater risk of school failure than other Canadian children. A disproportionate number of Aboriginal children are victims of abuse and neglect compared to non-Aboriginal children. The suicide rate among Aboriginal youth is about five times the national average.

- An estimated 535 000 children and youth under age 20 have some form of disability. Children with disabilities have varying opportunities to live "full and decent lives" and the supports and services they need are not considered an entitlement but a privilege. Many families of children with disabilities do not receive adequate assistance. Early identification and intervention services are not universally available and the right to appropriate education in the most enabling environment is not guaranteed.

State Parties recognize the right of every child to a standard of living adequate for the child's physical, mental, spiritual, moral, and social development.

ARTICLE 27, UN CONVENTION ON THE RIGHTS OF THE CHILD

- Abused and neglected children continue to fall through the cracks in our child welfare systems. Inquests and inquiries into the deaths of children who were killed by their parents speak of inadequate risk assessments, insufficient training for social workers, a lack of service coordination and information sharing, a shortage of placement facilities, failed foster placements, a crisis orientation, and a lack of long-term planning for children who are in the care of the state.
- The refugee determination system is slow and the long wait unduly prolongs uncertainty in the lives of children and their families. Family reunification is rarely dealt with in a positive and expeditious manner. The interests of children are not taken into account in decisions to deport their parents. Children, even if born in Canada, do not have to be considered in the deportation hearings of their parents.
- Federal and provincial legislation prohibits discrimination against people with disabilities, but people with disabilities, and children in particular, still experience prejudice. Young people with disabilities experience more abuse and violence than those without disabilities. In addition, many disability issues are examined from the adult perspective and the special needs of children are overlooked. For example, provincial building codes include accessibility standards but they were not designed with children in mind.
- The few complaint mechanisms that are available to children and youth tend to be difficult to access.

These issues remain salient concerns within the Canadian Coalition for the Rights of Children 2001 Report (Covell 2001). The 2001 Report emphasizes that despite unanimous support in Parliament for an all-party resolution to eliminate child poverty by the year 2001, "a substantial gap remained between promise and reality" with increases in child poverty through the 1990s to the present (Covell 2001: 11) (Figure 6.1, Table 6.2).

Among other identified shortcomings, the 2001 Report notes Canada's failure to repeal Section 43 of the Criminal Code (which provides a defence in law for those who use corporal punishment as a form of discipline) and to ensure that quality child care is both affordable and available. Moreover, the Report expresses concern over the contents of the new Youth Criminal Justice Act, and the fear that "the government has attempted to appease public demands for punitiveness" (Covell 2001: 31).

That this House express its concern for the more than one million Canadian children currently living in poverty and seek to achieve the goal of eliminating poverty among Canadian children by the year 2000.

ALL-PARTY RESOLUTION PASSED WITH UNANIMOUS CONSENT BY THE HOUSE OF COMMONS ON NOVEMBER 24, 1989

■ **Figure 6.1** *Child Poverty Rate in Canada, 1989–1999*

SOURCES: 1989–1995 data prepared by the Canadian Council on Social Development using Statistics Canada's *Survey of Consumer Finances*, microdata files. 1996–1999 data prepared by the CCSD using Statistics Canada *Survey of Labour and Income Dynamics, 1999*.

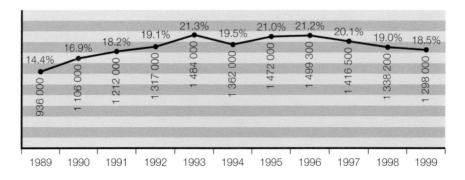

■ **Table 6.2** *What Has Happened to Child Poverty in Canada?*

Number of poor children* (1989–1999)	↑ 39%
Number of poor children in families with full-time, full-year employment (1989–1999)	↑ 15%
Number of poor children in two-parent families (1989–1999)	↑ 33%
Number of poor children in female lone-parent families (1989–1999)	↑ 44%
Number of children in unaffordable rental housing (1989–1996)	↑ 91%
Number of children in families with incomes less than $20,000 (constant $1999) (1989–1999)	↑ 32%
Average depth of poverty (1989–1999)	↑ 1.7%
Social assistance benefits (1990–2001)	↑ 19%
Average post-secondary tuition fees (1990–2000)	↑ 126%
Total number of visits to food banks (1989–2000)	↑ 90%

Notes

*Poor children are those living in families whose total income before taxes falls below the Low Income Cut-Off (LICO) as defined by Statistics Canada. Numbers in 1989–1991 use 1986-base LICO and numbers for 1992–1999 use 1992-base.

The Low Income Cut-Off (LICO) is the measure used by Statistics Canada to identify those families "who are substantially worse off than the average". A family at or below LICO is one that spends more than 55% of its income on food, shelter, and clothing.

Child is defined as a person under the age of 18 living with parent(s) or guardian(s), excluding those who are unattached individuals, those that are the major income earner, or those who are the spouse or common law partner of the major income earner.

Data for 1989 through 1995 prepared by Canadian Council on Social Development (CCSD) using Statistics Canada's *Survey of Consumer Finances*, 1997 microdata files; and data for 1996 through 1999 prepared by CCSD from Statistics Canada's *Survey of Labour and Income Dynamics*. Campaign 2000 follows Statistics Canada's example by seamlessly reporting the data from the two surveys.

Statistics Canada data excludes those on First Nations reserves; those in the Yukon, Northwest Territories, and Nunavut; and children living in institutions.

SOURCE: Campaign 2000. 2002. *Putting Promises Into Action: A Report on a Decade of Child and Family Poverty in Canada*. May, the UN Special Session on Children: 3. Reprinted by permission of Campaign 2000.

Poverty and Economic Discrimination

Canada has been less successful than many countries in preventing children from falling into poverty. According to the 2000 UNICEF report, "Child Poverty in Rich Nations," of the 23 rich nations belonging to the Organisation for Economic Co-operation and Development (OECD), Canada had the seventh highest rate of child poverty (Figure 6.2). Moreover, some children in Canada face a heightened risk of poverty. Specifically,

Among Aboriginal children, whether living on or off reserve, almost one or two lives in poverty....Rates of poverty are five times higher among families that have children with disabilities than among other families....Among racialized groups, the rate of poverty for children under six is 45 percent, compared to 26 percent for other children of the same age. (Campaign 2000 2002: 9–10) (See Figure 6.3.)

Childhood poverty is related to school failure (Fields and Smith 1998; NIH 2000), negative involvement with parents (Harris and Marmer 1996), stunted growth, reduced cognitive abilities, limited emotional development (Brooks-Gunn and Duncan 1997), and a higher likelihood of dropping out of school (Duncan et al. 1998). According to the National Longitudinal Survey of Children and Youth, one-quarter of children aged four and five from low-income households (less than $30 000 a year) scored poorly on verbal tests that indicate readiness to learn. In contrast, only 15.6 percent of those children from middle-income households and 9.2 percent of higher-income children scored poorly on these tests. In addition, this survey reported that 14.6 percent of low-income

■ **Figure 6.2** *Child Poverty in Selected OECD Nations*

SOURCE: UNICEF *Child Poverty in Rich Nations.* Innocenti Report Card, June 2000.

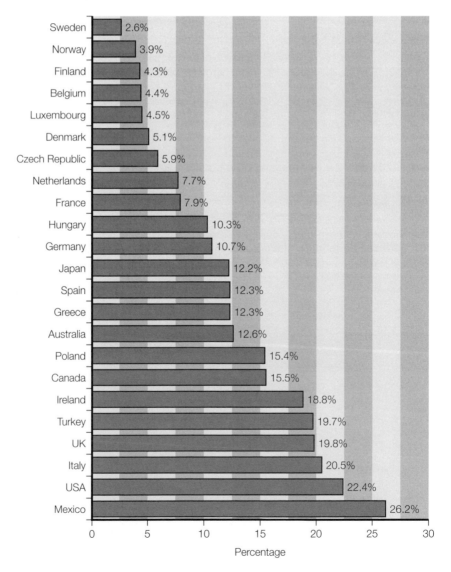

Country	Percentage
Sweden	2.6%
Norway	3.9%
Finland	4.3%
Belgium	4.4%
Luxembourg	4.5%
Denmark	5.1%
Czech Republic	5.9%
Netherlands	7.7%
France	7.9%
Hungary	10.3%
Germany	10.7%
Japan	12.2%
Spain	12.3%
Greece	12.3%
Australia	12.6%
Poland	15.4%
Canada	15.5%
Ireland	18.8%
Turkey	19.7%
UK	19.8%
Italy	20.5%
USA	22.4%
Mexico	26.2%

Percentage

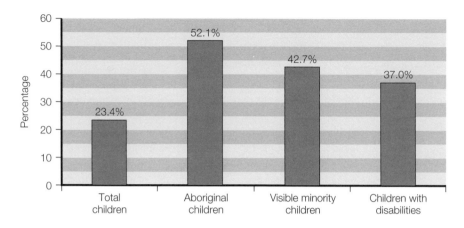

■ **Figure 6.3** *Aboriginal, Visible Minority Children, and Children with Disabilities (0–14 Years) More Likely To Be Poor*

SOURCE: Statistics Canada. 1996. Census 1996, custom tabulations by Canadian Council on Social Development.

Aboriginal refers to those persons who identified themselves with being North American Indian, Métis or Inuit. Visible minority persons are defined under the Employment Equity Act (1986) as those (other than Aboriginal persons) who are non-Caucasian in race or non-white in colour. Persons with disabilities are identified based on their responses to questions regarding their activity limitations or disabilities.

children were in households that were ranked as "dysfunctional" versus 7.5 percent of children in middle-income homes and 5 percent of children in high-income homes. About 15 percent of children in the lowest of four income groups had problems with aggression, depression, anxiety, or hyperactivity. Of those who were not in the poorest group, only 9 percent suffered behavioural problems. Finally, about 7 percent of those who were in the poorest groups had failed a grade. Among those who were not in the poorest group, only two percent had failed a grade (Fine 1999b).

Children are also discriminated against in terms of employment, age restrictions, wages, and training programs. Traditionally, children worked on farms and in factories but were displaced by the Industrial Revolution. In the 1880s, the *Factory Acts* "curbed the employment of both women and children on the grounds of protecting their health" (Krahn and Lowe 1993), and by 1929, children under age 14 were legally excluded from factory and mine employment in most provinces. Although the law was designed to protect children, it was also discriminatory in that it prohibited minors from having free access to jobs and economic independence. No such law exists for any other age group.

Young people in Canada often find it difficult to obtain any employment. In 1996, more than one out of every five Canadians between the ages of 15 and 24 had never held a job and the unemployment rate for this group was approximately 16 percent. A high rate of youth unemployment is not unique to Canada but part of an international trend, with young people in European countries finding it as difficult or more difficult to find work. Those who do manage to find work "are typically employed in low paid, tedious positions, often working long hours which interfere with school attendance and academic performance" (Covell 2001: 16).

Kids in Crisis

Childhood is a stage of life that is socially constructed by structural and cultural forces of the past and present. The old roles for children as labourers and farm helpers are disappearing, yet no new roles have emerged. While being bombarded

One of the really notable
achievements of twentieth
century Canada has been
to make the young old
before their time.

Robertson Davies
Tempest-Tost

by the media, children must face the challenges of an uncertain economic future, peer culture, music videos, divorce, incidents of abuse, poverty, and crime. Parents and public alike fear children are becoming increasingly involved with sex, drugs, alcohol, and violence. Some even argue that childhood as a stage of life is disappearing (Adler 1994).

Recent evidence, however, indicates that the lives of Canadian children *are* getting better: Infant, child and maternal mortality rates have significantly decreased in the last decade....[N]early all Canadian children have access to safe drinking water. High rates of basic education and completion of primary school by primary school–aged children have been maintained. In addition, progress has been made towards providing protections and services for particularly vulnerable populations of children such as Aboriginal children, children with disabilities, and sexually and economically exploited youth (Covell 2001: 5).

Moreover, although some describe children as pessimistic about their future and living in fear (Ingrassia 1993), this is not necessarily the case. Indeed, the 2000 Project Canada survey of Canadians teenagers found that the vast majority have very high expectations when it comes to their future lives (Table 6.3). While many of their expectations may be unfulfilled, "Canada's teens are dreaming and dreaming big" (Bibby 2001: 133). In addition, their aspirations are not always selfish. This chapter's *The Human Side* describes the growth of one organization for children, launched by a Canadian youth, that is run by children and devoted to improving the lives of children worldwide.

Table 6.3 *Expectations of Teenagers*

"Do you expect to..."	% indicating "Yes"		
	Nationally	Males	Females
Pursue a career	95%	93%	96%
Get the job you want when you graduate	86	86	86
Stay with the same career for life	62	61	62
Get married	88	87	89
Stay with the same partner for life	88	87	89
Eventually stay home and raise your children	45	47	43
Own your own home	96	97	96
Be more financially comfortable than your parents	79	81	77
Have to work overtime in order to get ahead	44	48	41
Travel extensively outside Canada	72	68	77
Be involved in your community	65	62	68
See the national debt paid off in your lifetime	43	51	47

SOURCE: Bibby, Reginald W. 2001. *Canada's Teens: Today, Yesterday, and Tomorrow*. Toronto: Stoddart, p. 136.

Free the Children: Children Helping Children

Free the Children, an international children's organization with over 100 000 members in more than 35 countries, was founded in 1995 by then 12-year-old Canadian Craig Kielburger. Kielburger first became an advocate for children's rights when he read about the murder of a child from Pakistan who had been sold into bondage as a carpet weaver. Free the Children is a registered nonprofit charitable organization whose mission statement identifies as its two main goals (1) to free children from poverty, exploitation, and abuse, and (2) to give children a voice, leadership training, and opportunities to take action on issues that affect them on a local or an international level.

Kielburger has received many awards for his work, including the Nuclear Age Peace Foundation Award for Leadership in Peace Building (2000), the Roosevelt Freedom Medal (1998), the Governor General's Medal of Meritorious Service (1998), and the State of the World Forum Award (1997). His organization has also flourished. Members have raised funds for the construction of over 300 primary schools in rural areas of developing nations, providing education every day to over 15 000 children. They have distributed approximately 100 000 school kits and over 2.5 million dollars worth of medical supplies to needy families. They also support potable water projects, health clinics, alternative income cooperatives, and primary schools in 21 developing nations. Their advocacy campaigns have also encouraged Canada, Mexico, and Italy to pass legislation that better protects sexually abused children. They have additionally lobbied corporations to adopt labels for child-labour-free products. In 2001, Craig's organization was selected by the United Nations and the Office of the Special Representative for Children in Armed Conflict to be the lead nongovernmental organization coordinating youth outreach for the decade of peace and non-violence towards children.

SOURCE: Adapted and abridged from freethechildren.org.

Demographics: The "Greying of Canada"

The population of Canada, as in many other countries around the world is "greying," that is, getting older (defined here as age 65 or beyond). In 2001, the median age (i.e., the point where precisely one-half of the population is older, and the other half younger) reached an all-time high of 37.6 years (Figure 6.4) (Statistics Canada 2002). The increase in median age is one indicator of Canada's changing population structure (Figure 6.5, see page 191).

The number of elderly is increasing for three reasons. First, the 10 million baby boomers born between 1947 and 1966 are getting older. Second, life expectancy has increased as a result of better medical care; sanitation, nutrition, and housing improvements; and a general trend toward modernization. Finally, lowered birthrates mean fewer children and a higher percentage of the elderly. For example, in Japan, low birth rates and rising life expectancies have contributed to the highest proportion of elderly in the world—19.6 percent of the population by 2005 (Yamaguchi 2000). While seniors aged 65 or over accounted for 13 percent of Canada's population in 2001, projections are that, if fertility rates remain low, their proportion will continue to increase in the years to come (Statistics Canada 2002).

■ **Figure 6.4** *Canada's Aging Population, 1901–2011*

SOURCE: Lewington, Jennifer. 2002. "Canada Facing Age Crunch." *The Globe and Mail*, July 17: A6.

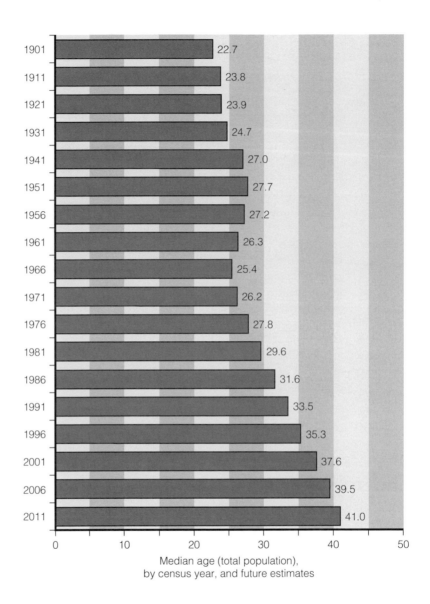

Median age (total population), by census year, and future estimates

Year	Median age
1901	22.7
1911	23.8
1921	23.9
1931	24.7
1941	27.0
1951	27.7
1956	27.2
1961	26.3
1966	25.4
1971	26.2
1976	27.8
1981	29.6
1986	31.6
1991	33.5
1996	35.3
2001	37.6
2006	39.5
2011	41.0

Age Pyramids

Age pyramids are a way of showing in graph form the percentage of a population in various age groups. In 1901 the Canadian age pyramid looked very much like a true pyramid: the base of the pyramid was large, indicating that most people were in their younger years, and the top of the pyramid was much smaller, showing that only a small percentage of the population was elderly (Figure 6.6, see page 192). However, Canada's age pyramid in 2001 (which scarcely resembles a "pyramid") reflects the aging of the Canadian population (Figure 6.7, see page 192).

The number of people at various ages in a society is important because the demand for housing, education, health care, and jobs varies as different age groups, particularly baby boomers, move through the pyramid. For example, as Canada "greys," colleges and universities will recruit older students, advertise-

The chart shows the actual population for 2001 by age group and the percentage change since 1991. The steepest decline can be seen among the younger workers age group. The highest rate of growth has occurred in seniors, aged 80 and over.

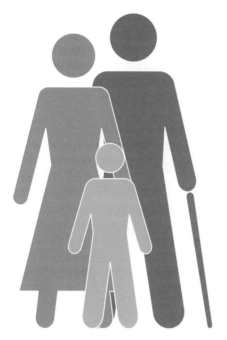

Preschool,
aged 0 to 4:
1.7 million   **−11%**

Kindergarten and elementary school,
aged 5 to 12:
3.2 million   **+6%**

High schools, colleges and universities,
aged 13 to 24:
4.8 million   **+4%**

Younger workers,
aged 25 to 34:
4 million   **−18%**

Mid-career,
aged 35 to 44:
5.1 million   **+17%**

Older workers,
aged 45 to 64:
7.3 million   **+36%**

Young retirees,
aged 65 to 69:
1.1 million   **+6%**

Seniors,
aged 70 to 79:
1.8 million   **+27%**

Older Seniors,
aged 80 and over:
932,000   **+41%**

■ **Figure 6.5** *Population Changes by Age Group*

SOURCE: Lewington, Jennifer. 2002. "Canada Facing Age Crunch." *The Globe and Mail*, July 17: A6.

ments will be directed toward older consumers, and elderly housing and medical care needs will increase.

Age and Region

Canada ages from west to east with one notable exception—British Columbia— a popular destination for many older Canadians. According to the 2001 Census, Canada's prairie provinces (i.e., Alberta, Saskatchewan, and Manitoba), Ontario, and the territories have relatively younger residents while Atlantic Canada and Quebec have populations that are older than the Canadian average. Nunavut and the Northwest Territories had the lowest median age in 2001 (22.1 years and 30.1 years, respectively) and the highest proportion of their population aged below 20. Reflecting the high fertility of both Nunavut and the Northwest Territories, approximately half (47 percent) of Nunavut's population, and over a third (35 percent) of those in the Northwest Territories, were aged 19 and under (compared to the national average of 26 percent). Because of birth rates that are higher than the Canadian average and lower life expectancies, Indigenous people as a group are younger than non-Indigenous peoples in Canada. The high fertility of the Aboriginal population also affects the age profile of both Manitoba and Saskatchewan. The older population of Canada's Atlantic region reflects two factors: low fertility in recent years and the exodus

Figure 6.6 *Canadian Population Pyramid, Age and Sex, 1901*

SOURCE: From *Canadian Population, Population: An Introduction*, 1st edition by McVey/Kalbach. © 1997. Reprinted with permission of Nelson, a division of Thomson Learning: www.thomsonrights.com. Fax 800-730-2215.

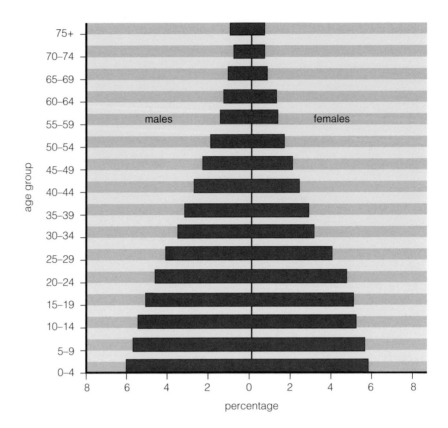

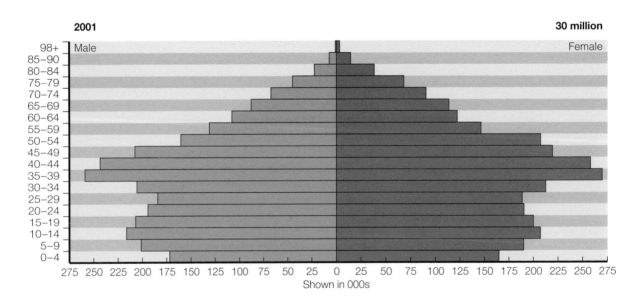

Figure 6.7 *Age Pyramid of Population of Canada, July 1, 2001*

SOURCE: Statistics Canada. 2002. 2001 Census: Canada. http://www.12.statcan.ca/english/census01/products/analytic/companion/age/ce.01pymd.cfm.

of the young to other areas of Canada. The aging of Quebec's population is largely the result of the low fertility rate in that province.

There are also differences in population age distributions that appear at the sub-provincial level. "In general, the population living in the nation's northern regions and in most census metropolitan areas had a lower median age than the Canadian average [while] [s]maller urban centres with core populations between 10 000 and 99 999, as well as small towns and rural areas, had older populations" (Statistics Canada 2002). Montreal and the adjacent region and British Columbia's Lower Mainland and southern Vancouver Island were two major urban regions that had somewhat older populations in 2001, with a median age in both of 38.1. In contrast, Ontario's extended Golden Horseshoe (with a median age of 36.4) and the Calgary–Edmonton corridor (with a median age of 35.2) were two large urban regions that had relatively young populations.

There is also an inverse relationship between population growth and aging. "In general, the 19 million people who lived in the 27 metropolitan areas were younger than the people who lived outside them" (Statistics Canada 2002). CMAs that experienced the largest growth in their population did so by attracting relatively young migrants (the majority aged between 20 and 39 with children). In 2001, Trois-Rivières, Quebec was the oldest of Canada's 27 census metropolitan regions, with a median age of 41.2 years, and Saskatoon, with a median age of 34.4 years, the youngest.

Age and Gender

In Canada, females make up 51 percent of the population (15.3 million). The **sex ratio**—the ratio of men to women in a given society or subgroup of society—is expressed in one number: the number of males to every 100 females. In 2001, the national average was 96.1 men for every 100 women (Statistics Canada 2002). In that year women outnumbered men in all provinces, especially in Atlantic Canada, where the sex ratio was 93.6 (i.e., 93.6 men for every 100 women). In all three territories, however, as well as the northern region of most provinces, men outnumbered women. This situation reflects the nature of employment opportunities in these areas as well as the relative youthfulness of their population.

The imbalance in the sex ratio is particularly notable at older ages. In 2001, there were 75 men per 100 women aged 65 and older. As an extreme example, there was one man for every four women aged 100 and older. Men die at an earlier age than women do for both biological and sociological reasons—heart disease, stress, and occupational risk (see Chapter 2). However, because of differences in death rates and a greater likelihood of previously widowed men remarrying, older women are more likely to be widowed and to retain this marital status. This can pose significant hardship in that the incidence of low income is higher among elderly persons who are living alone (Reidmann et al. 2003: 523).

Age and Social Class

Social class influences how long a person lives. In general, the higher the social class, the longer the person lives, the fewer the debilitating illnesses, the greater the number of social contacts and friends, the less likely the individual is to define him- or herself as "old," and the greater the likelihood of success in adapting to retirement. Higher social class is also related to fewer residential moves, higher life satisfaction, more leisure time, and more positively self-rated health. Functional limitations such as problems with walking, dressing, and bathing are also lower among higher income groups (Seeman and Adler 1998). In short, the higher one's socioeconomic status, the longer, happier, and healthier one's life.

Problems of the Elderly

The increase in the number of the elderly, worldwide, presents a number of institutional problems. The **dependency ratio**—the number of societal members that are under 18 or 65 and over compared with the number of people who are between 18 and 64—is increasing. By 2000, there were 62 "dependents" for every 100 persons between 18 and 64. By 2050, the estimated ratio will be 80 to 100 (AOA 2000). This dramatic increase, and the general movement toward global aging, may lead to a shortage of workers and military personnel, floundering pension plans, and declining consumer markets. It may also lead to increased taxes as governments struggle to finance elder care programs and services and heightening intergenerational tensions as societal members compete for scarce resources (Peterson 2000; Schieber 2000; Goldberg 2000). In addition to these macro level concerns, the elderly face a number of challenges of their own. This chapter's *Self and Society* feature tests your knowledge of the aged and some of these concerns.

> This is the century of old age, or, as it has been called, the "Age of Aging."
>
> ROBERT BUTLER
> *Gerontologist*

Work and Retirement

What one does (occupation), for how long (work history), and for how much (wages), are important determinants of retirement income. Indeed, employment is important because it provides the foundation for economic resources later in life. According to the 2000 Project Canada survey, only three of ten Canadian teens and adults agree that retirement should be mandatory at age 65 (Bibby 2001: 244). Moreover, depending upon where one lives in Canada, there are some legal protections against being forced to retire against one's will. For example, the Quebec Labour Standards Act prohibits compulsory retirement based on age or number of years of service, and in every other jurisdiction in Canada, human rights laws protect workers from discrimination based on age, including harassment because of age. Some exceptions do exist. For example, upper age limits are set at age 64 in the province of Saskatchewan and at age 65 in Ontario, British Columbia, and Newfoundland. Similarly, the Supreme Court of Canada ruled in 1995 that mandatory retirement at age 60 for police officers was not discriminatory but a "bona fide occupational requirement" (Dranoff 2001: 71).

For the elderly who want to work, entering and remaining in the labour force may be difficult because of negative stereotypes, lower levels of education, reduced geographical mobility, fewer employable skills, and discrimination. Moreover, Novak (1997: 197) notes that at least three economic forces may encourage Canadian workers to retire at age 65:

Facts on Aging Quiz

Answer the following questions about the elderly and assess your knowledge of the world's fastest-growing age group.

	True	False
1. Lung capacity tends to decline in old age.	_____	_____
2. The majority of old people say they are seldom bored.	_____	_____
3. Old people tend to become more religious as they age.	_____	_____
4. A person's height tends to decline in old age.	_____	_____
5. The aged are more fearful of crime than are younger persons.	_____	_____
6. The majority of old people live alone.	_____	_____
7. The five senses all tend to weaken in old age.	_____	_____
8. Older persons who reduce their activity tend to be happier than those who do not.	_____	_____
9. Older persons have more injuries in the home than younger persons.	_____	_____
10. Physical strength tends to decline with age.	_____	_____
11. The aged are the most law abiding of all adult age groups.	_____	_____
12. Older persons have more acute illnesses than do younger persons.	_____	_____

Answers: 1, 2, 4, 5, 7, 10, and 11 are true. The others are false.

SOURCE: Palmore, Erdman B. 1999. *Ageism: Negative and Positive.* © Springer Publishing Company, Inc.,

---

- First, some workers with good pension plans may earn more money in retirement than if they keep on working. Taxes, the cost of commuting, clothes, lunches, and other work-related expenses may make work an expensive option.
- Second, most private pension plans begin to pay full benefits at age 65...[and] many occupational pension plans penalize a person for staying on past retirement age....
- Third, OAS/GIS payments start at age 65, as do the Canada and Quebec Pension Plan payments. A person who works past age 65 will still get these benefits, but will lose a large portion of them through higher taxes.

Those who wish to enter the workforce at an older age or who, because of financial necessity, find it necessary to re-enter the labour force after retirement may be stymied in their attempts. The most common reason that workers over age 45 give for ending their job search is the perception that no work is available. Corroborating this perception to some degree is the fact that, from 1976 to 1994, the average time that unemployed 45- to 64-year-olds were out of work doubled from 17 weeks to 33 weeks. At present, older workers who look for work are likely to be unemployed for almost twice as long as those aged 15 to 24 (Statistics Canada 1998a). Although employers cannot advertise a position by age, they can state that the position is an "entry level" one or that "two to three years' experience" is required (Knoke and Kalleberg 1994).

Retirement is a relatively recent phenomenon. Before social security, individuals continued to work into old age. Today, the proportion of retirees under age 60 is double the rate it was in the late 1970s, and one-quarter of all new retirees are between the ages of 55 and 59. In 1984, the Quebec Pension Plan reduced its minimum age requirements for retirement benefits to age 60 and, in 1987, the Canadian Pension Plan followed suit. However, the desire to remain financially independent and a lack of confidence in the social security system may encourage many workers to remain in the labour force longer than the minimum age requirements allow (Simon-Rusinowitz et al. 1996).

Retirement can be difficult in that "work" is often equated with "worth." A job structures one's life and provides an identity; the end of a job culturally signifies the end of one's productivity. Retirement may also involve a dramatic decrease in personal income. While 60 percent of Canadian men retire between age 55 and 64, 27 percent are living in poverty on less than $10 000 a year and only 5 percent have an income of over $45 000 a year (Dranoff 2001: 70)

Retirement Income and Poverty

In 1996, the elderly and children were the groups most likely to be classified as low income. However, this was not true for elderly people living in families. Indeed, in that year, the elderly in families were the *least* likely to be low income (8 percent), while children under the age of 18 were the most likely. In the last four decades, seniors in Canada have benefited from rising incomes. While in 1951, the average senior earned slightly more than half the income of Canadians of working age, in 1995, the average senior earned $20 300 or almost $84 for every $100 earned by working-aged Canadians (Statistics Canada 1998a). However, one in five seniors (mostly unattached women) is still likely to be living in a low-income situation (National Council of Welfare 1998) (Figure 6.8). When compared to Canadian men, Canadian women are far less likely to have access to private-sector (i.e. non-governmental pensions) such as those provided by employers to employees. In 1997, among Canadians 65 to 68 years of age, for example, about one in two men—but only one in four women—received some income from a private pension (Lindsay 2000: 142). "Certain groups, such as First Nations women and women with disabilities, are particularly unlikely to be covered by private pension plans, and the likelihood of

■ **Figure 6.8** *People Aged 18 and Over Living in a Low-income Situation, by Family Status, 1997*

SOURCE: Statistics Canada, Income Statistics Division.

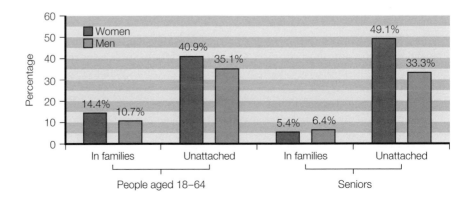

poverty is particularly pronounced among elderly women with disabilities" (Nelson and Robinson 2002: 483).

Even though the federal government has attempted to encourage Canadians to prepare for their own retirement by promising to increase the maximum annual tax-deductible RRSP contributions to $14 500 in 2004 and $15 500 in 2005 (and thereafter indexing them to inflation), it is evident that not all Canadians can afford to pursue such options. Although about two-thirds of Canadians report that they are putting away money for retirement, in general, the more individuals earn, the more likely they are to save. While the vast majority of those earning $40 000 or more invest in a RRSP (Registered Retirement Savings Plan) or RPP (Registered Pension Plan), four out of five who do not save have annual incomes less than $20 000 (Statistics Canada 1998). According to one 1999 survey, 11 percent of Canadians are hoping to use lottery winnings to support themselves during later life. However, "[s]ince the odds of winning the 6/49 lottery are about 14 million to one, this is not really a sound financial plan" (Kendall et al. 2000: 380).

At present, Canada's retirement income system is composed of three tiers: (1) governmental benefits such as Old Age Security (OAS) and the Guaranteed Income Supplement (GIS) designed to forestall the likelihood of poverty by furnishing all seniors with a taxable, flat-rate benefit (adjusted every three months as the Consumer Price Index increases) paid monthly regardless of their work histories or life circumstances; (2) the government-sponsored Canada Pension Plan (CPP) and the Quebec Pension Plan (QPP), which are designed to provide workers with a retirement income based on their pre-retirement earnings from ages 18 to 65; and (3) private savings, which include employer-sponsored private pensions plans, private investments, and RRSPs (Townson 1995: 27).

OAS pension benefits are based on age and residency. A person qualifies for a full OAS pension after having resided in Canada for 40 years after age 18. Those who are ineligible for a full pension may receive a prorated, partial pension after a minimum of 10 years residency in Canada. For the July–September 2002 period (amounts are adjusted quarterly), the maximum monthly OAS pension was $443.99. While OAS pension is payable at age 65, some exemptions do exist. For example, in 2002, those Canadian seniors whose net incomes exceeded $56 968 yearly were required to repay some or all of their OAS benefits. The full OAS pension was clawed back when an individual's net income exceeded $92 381.

The GIS was introduced in 1966 to assist those seniors with little or no income other than their OAS pension. The amount given depends on the pensioner's income, conjugal relationship status, and whether the recipient's partner also receives an OAS pension or Old Age Allowance income. For example, the July–September 2002 rate for the maximum monthly GIS payment to a single pensioner, or to a married person whose spouse or partner did not receive such benefits, was $527.66. In addition, married or common-law spouses of pensioners (opposite-sex or same-sex) as well as the conjugal survivors of deceased pensions may also qualify for an Old Age Allowance provided that they are between the ages of 60 and 64 and qualify under an income test.

Although GIS and OAS benefits are unrelated to an individual's prior income history, CPP/QPP benefits are directly based on a person's income earned between the ages of 18 and the time they claim retirement (between the ages of 60 and 70), and proportionately reflect their prior income patterns. Although full benefits do not begin until age 65, partial CPP/QPP payments can be received by retired persons, under certain circumstances, as early as age 60. In September 2002, the maximum pension payable at age 65 under the CPP was $788.75. Nevertheless, by the 1990s, "[t]he federal government was issuing dire warnings about the Canada Pension Plan's ability to meet its obligations" and forecasting that the CPP would be severely strained—if not depleted—by the retirements of Canada's baby boomers (Dranoff 2001: 314). One measure taken to avert this situation has been to significantly increase the contributions paid by workers and their employers.

Health Issues

The biology of aging is called **senescence**. It follows a universal pattern but does not have universal consequences. "Massive research evidence demonstrates that the aging process is neither fixed nor immutable. Biologists are now showing that many symptoms that were formerly attributed to aging—for example, certain disturbances in cardiac function or in glucose metabolism in the brain—are instead produced by disease" (Riley and Riley 1992: 221). Biological functioning is also intricately related to social variables. Altering lifestyles, activities, and social contacts affects mortality and morbidity. For example, a longitudinal study of men and women between 70 and 79 found that regular physical activity, higher numbers of ongoing positive social relationships, and a sense of self-efficacy enhanced physical and cognitive functioning (Seeman and Adler 1998).

Biological changes are consequences of either **primary aging**, caused by physiological variables such as cellular and molecular variation (e.g., grey hair), or secondary aging. **Secondary aging** entails changes attributable to poor diet, lack of exercise, increased stress, and the like. Secondary aging exacerbates and accelerates primary aging.

While three in four seniors 65 and over and living at home rate their health as good to excellent, health tends to decline as age increases (Statistics Canada 1998). For example, chronic ailments become more common with increased age. When hospitalized, the average length of stay also increases significantly with age (Health Canada 1999). While the average length of stay for hospitalized Canadians is 11 days, most age groups actually fall well below this. However, the 55 to 64 age group reaches this level and elderly Canadians surpass it (23 days for those 75 and over). Indeed, the Canadian average is actually skewed toward the older age groups (Health Canada 1999). Alzheimer's disease, named for German neurologist Alois Alzheimer, is a debilitating illness that is more common among the elderly. Over 300 000 Canadians have Alzheimer's disease or a related dementia: one in 13 people over the age of 65 and a third of Canadians over the age of 85. As Canada's population ages, the number of people with Alzheimer's is expected to grow considerably and reach 750 000 by 2031 (Picard 2002).

Some disturbing evidence suggests that health care may be rationed on the basis of age in Canada. For example, in what is believed to be the first large-scale Canadian study to examine treatment for heart attacks among the elderly, the researchers concluded that "[t]he older you are, the less likely you are to be treated." The research, conducted by Paula Rochon, of the Baycrest Centre for Geriatric Care in Toronto and the Institute for Clinical Evaluative Science, and published in the November 1999 issue of the *Canadian Medical Association Journal*, tracked more than 15 500 heart-attack patients aged 66 and older in

If exercise could be put in a pill it would be the number one anti-aging medicine.

ROBERT BUTLER
Gerontologist

Ontario between April 1993 and March 1995. The findings indicated that almost half (48 percent) of Canadian seniors were not getting life-saving drugs that greatly improve the chances of survival after a heart attack. Among the 5453 heart-attack patients deemed to be the best candidates for beta-blocker therapy, 30 percent were not provided with these drugs. Women were significantly less likely than men to receive drugs, and seniors who lived in long-term care facilities were twice as likely not be treated with them. The study also reported that older, frailer patients were three times as likely not to be treated with beta-blocker therapy when compared to those seniors aged 66 to 74. Moreover, older seniors who received the beta-blockers were often prescribed doses that were lower than what is considered medically acceptable (Arnold 1999).

Living Arrangements

The elderly live in a variety of contexts, depending on their marital status, health, and financial status. In 2001, the elderly comprised over a third of Canada's one-person households, with women more likely than men to be divorced/widowed and living on their own. For example, for women between 75 and 84, 42.8 percent live on their own while 38.5 percent of women ages 85 and older live in one-person households (Dube 2002). In contrast, the majority of Canadian men between the ages of 50 and 89 are legally married and living with a spouse. Indeed, it is only among men age 90 and over that less than 60 percent of men are married and living with a partner (Reidmann et al. 2003: 483). The death of a spouse and encroaching poverty often necessitates that women sell their family home and move to rental or institutional settings (National Council of Welfare 1998).

Most elderly do not want to be institutionalized but prefer to remain in their own homes or in the homes of others, such as families and relatives. Some require elder care or assistance with daily living activities (see this chapter's *Social Problems Research Up Close* feature). However, they represent only a small proportion of the elderly population. According to the 2001 census, although the population aged 80 and older has increased 41 percent since 1996, the proportion of the total population aged 15 and over which devoted some time to providing unpaid care for a senior was relatively small, at 18.2 percent. In 2001, approximately 20 percent of women and 15 percent of men reported providing care or assistance to a senior. However, less than 4 percent of women and 2 percent of men reported devoting over 10 hours to providing such care in the week preceding census day (Statistics Canada 2002: 35). While well-to-do seniors may opt to live in retirement communities that offer various amenities and activities, there are many other living arrangements, including shared housing, modified independent living arrangements, and nursing homes. With shared housing, people of different ages live together in the same house or apartment; they have separate bedrooms but share a common kitchen and dining area. In modified living arrangements, the elderly live in their own house, apartment, or condominium within a planned community where special services such as meals, transportation, and home repairs are provided. Skilled or semiskilled health care professionals are available on the premises, and call buttons are installed so help can be summoned in case of an emergency.

In 2001, 287 480 seniors lived in health care institutions, including 9.2 percent of senior women and 4.9 percent of senior men (Dube 2002). Nursing

Children and Grand-children as Primary Caregivers

The single most significant demographic change of the next several decades will be the dramatic increase in the number of elderly worldwide. The increase in the elderly is associated with a variety of concerns, including who will care for the growing number of the old. The present study by Dellman-Jenkins, Blankemeyer, and Pinkard (2000) examines a recent trend in caregiving—young adult children and grandchildren as primary caregivers.

Sample and Methods

The present research focuses on three areas: (1) characteristics of young caregivers and the assistance they provide, (2) the consequences of being a primary caregiver for the individual, and (3) caregivers' social support. Specifically, the researchers "compared the caregiving motivations, experiences and support needs of young adult grandchildren providing assistance to grandparents with those of young adult children caring for their older parents" p. 178). Participants were recruited from a variety of sources including social service agencies, hospitals, and assisted living facilities. An open-ended interview was used in conjunction with a 65-item questionnaire. The final sample was composed of 43 caregivers— 20 daughters, 2 sons, 19 grand-daughters, and 2 grandsons (N=43). Eighty-one percent of the sample was white, 53 percent married, and 54 percent lived with the care-recipient; the remainder lived in a separate residence.

Findings and Conclusions

Caregiver Role and Assistance Given. Children, compared with grandchildren, were significantly more likely to respond that they were caring for their parents because no one else would. Grandchildren were most likely to respond that they were caring for their grandparent(s) out of a sense of duty and the desire to avoid nursing home care. Grandchildren also reported volunteering to care for grandparent(s) to help their parents.

> When Alzheimer's became apparent, my parents weren't coping well with it and were mean to her (not physically). I couldn't stand it...I told them I would take her to my house. My dad told me it would be the biggest mistake I ever made. Three years later...I still disagree.

The modal category for length of caregiving for both grandchildren and children was one to five years, with approximately equal proportions of both providing a round-the-clock (47 percent) versus daily assistance (53 percent). Both sets of caregivers provided transportation,

home residents are not typical of the elderly—they are more likely to be widowed or quite ill or over 80, or without family to take care of them (Kinsella and Taeuber 1993). An estimated 7 percent of Canada's 3 795 121 seniors currently require institutional care, and 10.3 percent require some form of home care. In Canada, seniors are the "largest consumers of publicly funded home-care services"; in 1996–97, 5 percent of seniors aged 65 to 75 and 17 percent of those aged 75 and over used home-care services (Health Canada 1999: 166). However, the demand for both publicly funded long-term care beds and home care exceeds their supply.

Victimization and Abuse

Although abuse may take place in private homes by family members, the elderly, like children, are particularly vulnerable to abuse when they are institutionalized. Pillemer and Hudson (1993) conducted interviews with a random sample of nursing home staff and found that 40 percent admitted that during the previous year, they had abused patients psychologically and 10 percent admitted to abusing them physically.

companionship and emotional support, personal care, and household support (e.g., cleaning house, paying bills, making appointments).

Consequences of Role. Caretakers in general, and single caretakers in particular, reported that caretaking activities interfered with their social life. All caretakers reported spending at least three hours a day in the caretaker role. One 20-year-old granddaughter commented that, "I sometimes get mad because I think I'm doing too much for my grandpa and I don't have a life of my own... then I feel selfish for having such thoughts" (p. 184). Caretakers also reported strained family relations, particularly with spouse and children.

> I would like to go camping with my husband once in a while, but I can't just get up and go away, because of taking care of my grandparents. Even though they have the medical alert, I'm afraid they won't use it if something goes wrong.

Further, careers were negatively affected as relocating, job performance, and achievement of long-term goals became difficult because of the demands of caregiving. Both groups also reported increases in stress, although this was significantly higher for grandchildren (81 percent) than children (59 percent). Positive outcomes were also expressed, with over 97 percent of respondents identifying some benefit or reward. Grandchildren were most likely to note maintaining a strong relationship with the care-recipient, whereas children more often listed prevention of nursing home placement as the primary benefit.

Sources of Support. All respondents reported seeking informal assistance from some source. Children most often turned to their siblings for help, whereas grandchildren most often turned to their spouse or dating partner. Formal support, although seldom sought, most often came from nursing/home health care providers or community support groups.

The two generations of caregivers, children and grandchildren, differ little in their caregiving activities, behaviours, and strains. They do, however, differ in their motivation to assist, with grandchildren more often noting attachment rather than need or obligation as the primary reason for becoming a caregiver. Further, the authors conclude, grandchildren are "more likely to report personal rewards (e.g., greater closeness, positive memories), while children were more apt to report instrumental rewards (e.g., providing quality home-care and avoiding nursing home placement)" (p. 185).

SOURCE: Dellman-Jenkins, Mary, Maureen Blankemeyer, and Odessa Pinkard. 2000. "Young Adult Children and Grandchildren in Primary Caregiver Roles to Older Relatives and their Service Needs." *Family Relations* 49: 177–87.

The emerging profile of the abused or neglected elderly person is of a female, 70 years or older, who has physical, mental, and/or emotional impairments and is dependent on the abuser-caregiver for both companionship and help with daily activities. Studies have found that the neglected elderly are older than elder abuse victims are, and have more physical and mental difficulties (Wittaker 1995). Most often, the abuser tends to be an adult child or spouse of the victim who misuses alcohol (Anetzberger et al. 1994). Some research suggests that the perpetrator of the abuse is more often an adult child who is financially dependent on the elderly victim (Boudreau 1993). Whether the abuser is an adult child or a spouse may simply depend on whom the elder victim lives with.

Many of the problems of the elderly are compounded by their lack of interaction with others, loneliness, and inactivity. This is particularly true for the old-old. The elderly are also segregated in nursing homes and retirement communities, separated from family and friends, and isolated from the flow of work and school. A cycle is perpetuated—being poor and old results in being isolated and engaging in fewer activities. Such withdrawal affects health, which makes the individual less able to establish relationships or participate in activities.

Quality of Life

Although some elderly do suffer from declining mental and physical functioning, many others do not. Consider that nearly half a million of Canadians aged 65 or over regularly provide temporary or ongoing childcare to their grandchildren, 7 percent spend at least five hours a week helping other seniors (with some providing over 15 hours a week), about one in four works as a formal volunteer, while six in ten participate in informal volunteer activities (Vanier Institute of the Family 2000: 172).

It should be evident that being old does not mean being depressed, poor, and sick. Indeed, some research indicates that the elderly may be less depressed than the young are, with several studies concluding that the elderly may have the lowest depression rates of all age groups (Health Canada 1999). Other research suggests that depression is "curvilinear" with age, that is, highest at the extremes of the age continuum (DeAngelis 1997). One study suggests that depression of the elderly is better treated by exercise than medication alone, or by medication and exercise combined (Livni 2000).

Among the elderly who are depressed, two social factors tend to be in operation. One is society's negative attitude toward the elderly. Words and phrases such as "old," "useless," and "a has-been" reflect cultural connotations of the aged that influence feelings of self-worth. The roles of the elderly also lose their clarity. How is a retiree supposed to feel or act? What does a retiree do? As a result, the elderly become dependent on external validation that may be weak or absent.

The second factor contributing to depression among the elderly is the process of growing old. This process carries with it a barrage of stressful life events all converging in a relatively short period. These events include health concerns, retirement, economic instability, loss of significant other(s), physical isolation, job displacement, and increased salience of the inevitability of death due to physiological decline. All of these events converge on the elderly and increase the incidence of depression and anxiety, and may increase the decision not to prolong life (see the *Focus on Technology* feature in this chapter).

Strategies for Action: Growing Up and Growing Old

Activism by or on behalf of children or the elderly has been increasing in recent years and, as the number of children and elderly grow, such activism is likely to escalate and to be increasingly successful. For example, global attention to the elderly led to 1999 being declared the "International Year of Older Persons" (DHHS 1998), while "the first nearly universally ratified human rights treaty in history" deals with children's rights (UNICEF 1998). Activism takes several forms, including collective action through established organizations and the exercise of political and economic power.

Collective Action

Countless organizations work on behalf of children, some of which we have already noted. Others include Aboriginal Family Services, Adoption Council of Canada, Alateen, Boys and Girls Club of Canada, Canadian Child Care Federa-

I am old enough to know that nothing I want will ever happen. I might get a faded facsimile.

ELIZABETH SMART
The Assumption of the Rogues and Rascals

All would live long, but none would be old.

BENJAMIN FRANKLIN
Inventor

I guess the time you learn you're going to die is the time you really understand you are human.

W.O. MITCHELL
Writer

tion, Defence for Children International, Global Alliance on the Sexual Exploitation of Youth, Save the Children-Canada, and UNICEF. Many successes take place at the local level where parents, teachers, corporate officials, politicians, and citizens join together in the interests of children.

Similarly, more than a thousand organizations work toward realizing political power, economic security, and better living conditions for the elderly. These organizations include the Seniors Computer Information Project (Manitoba), Saskatchewan Seniors Mechanism, Alberta Senior Citizens Sport and Recreation Association, Council on Aging of Ottawa-Carleton, Alberta Council on Aging, Assemblée des aînés francophones du Canada, National Advisory Council on Aging, Golden Age Association (Montreal), Society for the Retired and Semi-Retired (Edmonton), and the Canadian Association of Retired Persons (CARP).

One of the earliest and most radical groups in North America was the Gray Panthers, founded in 1970 by Margaret Kuhn. The Gray Panthers in the United States were responsible for revealing the unscrupulous practices of the hearing aid industry, persuading the National Association of Broadcasters to add "age" to "sex" and "race" in the Television Code of Ethics statement on media images, and eliminating the mandatory retirement age. In view of these successes, it is interesting to note that the Gray Panthers, with only 50 000 to 70 000 members, is a relatively small organization when compared with the Canadian Association of Retired Persons (CARP).

CARP is Canada's largest 50-plus lobby group with more than 400 000 members. A nonprofit association that does not accept funding from any government body, CARP speaks out on a wide range of issues important to those over 50. Its mandate is "to protect what we have and improve our lifestyle." Services of CARP include discounted mail-order drugs, investment opportunities, travel information, volunteer opportunities, a *Spamhunter's Resource Guide* offering practical advice for dealing with unwanted advertising offers, and news updates on issues of concern to those 50 and older. One of their most recent projects, in collaboration with the PRIME television channel, is a one-hour documentary about ageism titled, "What's Age Got to Do With It" (CARP 2002). The goal of GLARP, the Gay and Lesbian Association of Retiring Persons, is to raise money to develop gay and lesbian retirement communities and retirement resorts (GLARP 2000).

Political and Economic Power

Children are unable to hold office or to vote. Nevertheless, child advocates, acting on behalf of children, have wielded considerable political influence in such areas as childcare, education, health care reform, and crime prevention. At the same time, aging baby boomers may be particularly well situated, because of their numbers, to advance their concerns. Indeed, demographer David Foote has argued that by 2005 the concerns of aging baby boomers "will dominate Canada...as much as their thirty-something angst mirrored the economic woes of the 1980s and their forty-something prudence reflected the government cost cutting of the 1990s" (Nikiforuk 1999). Indeed, one economist, noting that the elderly's economic power is considerable, has referred to the elderly as a "revolutionary class." (Thurow 1996). By 2030, almost half of all adults in developed countries and two-thirds of all voters will be near or at retirement age. The growing political power of the aged is already becoming evident; The Netherlands has a new political party called the Pension Party.

A World Fit for Children is one in which all children get the best possible start in life...we will promote the physical, psychological, spiritual, social, emotional, cognitive and cultural development of children as a matter of national and global priorities.

"A World Fit For Children"— Plan of Action Signatories to the United Nations General Assembly Special Session on Children, May 2002

For age is opportunity, no less than youth itself; although in another dress.

And as the evening twilight fades away

The sky is filled with stars Invisible by day.

Henry Wadsworth Longfellow
Poet

Physician-Assisted Suicide and Social Policy

Given the dramatic increase in the number of elderly and the technological ability to extend life, the debate over physician-assisted suicide (PAS) is likely to continue. When 2000 doctors of terminally ill patients were surveyed, 6 percent said they had assisted in patient suicides and 33 percent said they would prescribe lethal amounts of drugs if permitted to by law (Finsterbusch 2001). Further, in a study of pharmacists in Great Britain, 70 percent agreed that it was the patient's right to choose to die, and 57 percent responded that it was also the patient's right to involve the physician in the decision-making process (Hanlon et al. 2000). However, while the "Canadian Medical Association's ethical guidelines state that physicians need not take heroic measures to keep incurable patients alive in the final stages of a disease, a physician might still want court direction in some cases" (Dranoff 2001: 323).

It is a fundamental principle of Canadian law that every adult who is capable of decision-making has the right to consent to or refuse medical treatment, even if the result of the decision is life-threatening. For example, the courts have held that adult Jehovah witnesses can refuse a blood transfusion even if doing so means certain death (Dranoff 2001: 322). Refusing treatment, or discontinuing treatment once in progress is an option as long as individuals are mentally competent. Nevertheless, the 1992 case of *Nancy B.* in Quebec alerted Canadians to the dilemma faced by some mentally aware patients with incurable diseases who are kept alive by modern technologies.

Nancy B., a young woman in her early 20s, was stricken with Guillain-Barre syndrome, which, in her case, proved unusually debilitating. After two years of being bedridden, unable to breathe without a respirator and paralyzed from the neck down, Nancy B. petitioned the Quebec Superior Court to direct her physician to discontinue treatment. A judge was called to her bedside to hear her submission and, ultimately, granted her request. The respirator was turned off and she died under mild sedation. The action of her doctor was considered palliative in nature and, as such, it was concluded that no contravention of the criminal code had occurred. However, despite the court's ruling in this case, to "counsel, aid, or abet" suicide is a criminal offence in Canada, punishable by a maximum penalty of 14 years imprisonment. Suicide and attempted suicide are not criminal offences. Had Nancy been able to disconnect her own respirator, she would have committed no offence. However, to avoid another being charged, she was forced to appeal to the court.

Even though prosecution is rare against those who have assisted terminally ill patients who expressed the wish to die, anyone who assists another to commit suicide has committed a criminal offence. In cases where a person—whether a doctor, spouse, family member, or friend—has assisted another who is not at death's door to commit suicide, the potential penalties are additionally severe. Under Canadian law, the helper "could face murder or manslaughter charges and be liable to life imprisonment, even if the help was requested and the helper acted out of compassion" (Dranoff 2001: 323).

The issue of physician-assisted suicide was also raised in the case of Sue Rodriguez, a 42-year-old Vancouver woman suffering with amyotrophic lateral sclerosis. ALS is a degenerative nerve disease that is also known as "Lou Gehrig's disease." Rodriguez sought a court declaration that she was entitled to receive assistance in committing suicide when her condition made it physically impossible for her to

I want to ask you gentleman, if I cannot give consent to my own death, then whose body is this? Who owns my life?

SUE RODRIGUEZ

Understanding the Young and the Old

What can we conclude about youth and aging in Canadian society? Age is an ascribed status and, as such, is culturally defined by role expectations and implied personality traits. Society regards both the young and the old as dependent and in need of the care and protection of others. Society also defines the young and old as physically, emotionally, and intellectually inferior. Because of commit suicide on her own. Both the trial court as well as the B.C. Court of Appeal dismissed her application. When the case reached the Supreme Court of Canada in 1993, her life expectancy was between 2 and 14 months. In November 1992, in a videotaped presentation to a House of Commons justice subcommittee, Rodriguez urged amendments to the section of the Criminal Code that makes it a crime for one person to assist another's suicide. Her request for physician-assisted suicide was denied in a decision that was split almost down the middle; five judges held that her appeal should be dismissed while four judges dissented for various reasons. Despite their ruling, Rodriquez committed suicide, aided by an unknown doctor, in February 1994.

The controversy surrounding patient-assisted suicide continues. In 1996, Nancy Morrison, a Halifax respirologist, was charged with homicide after she administered drugs to hasten the death of one of her terminally ill patients. Although "thousands of people signed a petition urging the province to drop the case...[and] a provincial court judge threw the case out in February 1998, saying no jury would convict Morrison, the Crown did not give up until...after its appeal to the Nova Scotia Supreme Court was dis-missed" (Dranoff 2001: 324). Morrison was, however, reprimanded for her actions by the Nova Scotia College of Physicians and Surgeons after she admitted acting outside of the accepted standards of medical care.

Until such time as Parliament decides to address this issue, the Canadian courts will have to decide each case on its own. Elsewhere, however, legislatures have already acted. For example, the state of Oregon recognizes the right of PAS with its Death with Dignity Act. Two physicians must agree that the patient is terminally ill and is expected to die within six months, the patient must ask three times for death both orally and in writing, and the patients must swallow the barbiturates themselves rather than be injected with a drug by the physician (Annual Report 2000). In 2000, the Netherlands passed a law that legalized PAS. The law requires that three conditions be met: that (1) there be unbearable suffering, (2) the case be clinically hopeless, and (3) a voluntary request for assistance be made (Weber 2000).

One argument against PAS is that the practice is subject to abuses—an overburdened family pressuring a vulnerable loved one, a depressed patient making a hasty decision. Concern also exists that legalizing PAS may disproportionately end the lives of minority, ethnic, or psychiatrically disturbed individuals (Allen 1998). Some would argue, however, that ultimately the decision should reside with the patient. As one elderly person said:

> I came into this world as a human being and I wish to leave in the same manner. Being able to walk, to communicate, to take care of my own needs, to think, to feel....There is no need for me to re-experience my first few months of life through my last months in this world...I do not wish to be once again in a diaper. Just the thought of me losing control over my body frightens me. (Leichtenritt and Rettig 2000: 3)

SOURCES: Allen, F. C. L. 1998. "Euthanasia: Why Torture Dying People When We Have Sick Animals Put Down?" *Australian Psychologist*, 33: 12–15. Annual Report. 2000. "Oregon's Death with Dignity Act: The Second Year Experience." *Oregon's Death with Dignity Act Annual Report, 1999.* Center for Health Statistics. Oregon Health Division. Dranoff, Linda Silver. 2001. *Everyone's Guide to the Law.* Toronto: HarperCollins Publishers Ltd. Finsterbusch, Kurt. 2001. *Clashing Views on Controversial Social Issues.* Guilford, CT: Dushkin Publishing. Hanlon, Timothy, Marjorie Weiss, and Judith Rees. 2000. "British Community Pharmacists' View of Physician-Assisted Suicide." *Journal of Medical Ethics*, 26: 363–70. Leichtentritt, R. D., and K. D. Rettig. 2000. "Conflicting value considerations for end-of-life decisions." Poster session at 62nd Annual Meeting of National Council on Family Relations. Minneapolis, Minnesota, November 12. Weber, Kim. 2000. "Dutch Euthanasia Law Passed by Parliament." *Lancet*, 356: 1911. Weber, Kim. 2000. "Netherlands Proposal for Comprehensive Euthanasia Legislation." *Lancet* 356: 1666.

these and other attributions, both age groups are sociologically a minority with limited opportunity to obtain some or all of society's resources.

Although both the young and the old are treated as minority groups, different meanings are assigned to each group. In general, however, the young are more highly valued than the old are. Functionalists argue that this priority on youth reflects the fact that the young are preparing to take over important statuses while the elderly are relinquishing them. Conflict theorists emphasize that in a capitalist society, both the young and the old are less valued than more productive members of society are. Conflict theorists also point out the importance of propagation, that is, the reproduction of workers, which may account for the greater value placed on the young than the old. Finally, symbolic interactionists describe the way images of the young and the old intersect and are socially constructed.

The collective concern for the elderly and the significance of defining ageism as a social problem have resulted in improved economic conditions for the elderly. Currently, they are one of society's more powerful minorities. Research indicates, however, that despite their increased economic status, the elderly are still subject to discrimination in such areas as housing, employment, and medical care and are victimized by systematic patterns of stereotyping, abuse, and prejudice.

In contrast, the position of children, while improving in some ways, remains tragic in others. Wherever there are poor families, there are poor children (see Chapters 10 and 11). Further, age-based restrictions limit their entry into certain roles (e.g., employee) and demand others (e.g., student). While most of society's members would agree that children require special protections, concerns about quality-of-life issues and rights of self-determination are only recently being debated.

Age-based decisions are potentially harmful. If budget allocations were based on indigence rather than age, more resources would be available for those truly in need. Further, age-based decisions may encourage intergenerational conflict. Government assistance should not be thought of as a zero-sum relationship—the more resources one group gets, the fewer resources another group receives. Nevertheless, some predict the emergence of a new "generation gap" in the next decade between aging boomers concerned with their pensions and personal security, and their younger cohorts who will be forced to bear some of the burden for the boomers' support. Indeed, an Organisation for Economic Co-operation and Development (OECD) study of member countries already notes "growing evidence of disaffection among the young in communities with larger proportions of wealthy retired people" (Purvis 1999). This finding must be considered of especial concern within Canada due to the relatively large size of our baby boom generation and their approaching departure from the labour force. "Retiring baby boomers will have a significant impact on the size of the labour market, especially as relatively small cohorts of young people will be entering it. Boomers, those aged 37 to 55 in 2001, made up 47 percent of the labour force. Ten years from now, half of them will be 55 or over, and 18 percent of them will be over the age of 60" (Statistics Canada 2002: 10).

Social policies that allocate resources based on need rather than on age would shift the attention of policymakers to remedying social problems rather than serving the needs of special interest groups. Age should not be used to negatively affect an individual's life any more than race, ethnicity, gender, or sexual orientation. While eliminating all age barriers or requirements is unrealistic, a movement toward assessing the needs of individuals and their abilities would be more consistent with the ideal of equal opportunity for all.

Critical Thinking

1 In many ways, society discriminates against children. Children are segregated in schools, in a separate justice system, and in the workplace. Identify everyday examples of the ways in which children are treated like "second-class" citizens in Canada.

2 Age pyramids pictorially display the distribution of people by age. How do different age pyramids influence the treatment of the elderly?

3 Regarding children and the elderly, what public policies or programs from other countries might be beneficial to incorporate in Canada? Do you think policies from other countries would necessarily be successful here?

4 The meanings and experiences of the aging process are interwoven with social interpretations. Some maintain that our society is characterized by a double standard of aging wherein women "grow old" and contravene standards of physical attractiveness at an earlier chronological age than do men. What examples can you think of to support or contradict this position?

Key Terms

activity theory	gerontophobia	secondary aging
age grading	infantilizing elders	senescence
age pyramids	minority	senilicide
ageism	modernization theory	sex ratio
dependency ratio	primary aging	
disengagement theory	sandwich generation	

7 Gender Inequality

Outline

The Global Context: The Status of Women and Men

Sociological Theories of Gender Inequality

Gender Stratification: Structural Sexism

The Social Construction of Gender Roles: Cultural Sexism

Social Problems and Traditional Gender Role Socialization

Strategies for Action: Toward Gender Equality

Understanding Gender Inequality

Is It True?

1. Worldwide, men are less likely to be able to read and write than women.

2. In general, women are socialized into expressive roles and men into instrumental roles.

3. Since 1961, the greatest single change to the face of the Canadian labour force has been the substantial growth in the number of employed women in general and, in particular, employed women with children.

4. In Canada, nine out of ten persons diagnosed as suffering from eating disorders are women.

5. Women in Canada occupy a greater percentage of legislative positions than do women in any other country in the world.

Answers: 1 = F, 2 = T, 3 = T, 4 = T, 5 = F

Only a radical transformation of the relationship between women and men to one of full and equal partnership will enable that world to meet the challenges of the twenty-first century.

BEIJING DECLARATION AND PLATFORM FOR ACTION

In July of 2002, a young woman was sentenced by a village tribunal court in Meerwala, Pakistan to be gang-raped as punishment for the alleged misdeeds of her brother. Reportedly, the sentence was ordered to purposefully shame the girl's family after her younger brother was seen walking un-chaperoned with a girl from a higher-class tribe. "The girl was raped by four adult men as hundreds of villagers stood outside laughing and cheering, and was then forced to return home naked while dozens of villagers watched" (Bell 2002). In September of that year, an Islamic court in Nigeria upheld a sentence that a 31-year-old woman be stoned to death. Her crime: having had sex and bearing a child out of wedlock. The court ordered that the sentence should be carried out as soon as the woman's infant child was weaned (Maclean's 2002).

The term "gender inequality" begs the question, "Unequal in what way?" Depending on the issue, both women and men are victims of inequality. When income, career advancement, and sexual harassment are the focus, women are most often disadvantaged. But when life expectancy, mental and physical illness, and access to one's children following divorce are considered, it is often men who are disadvantaged. In this chapter, we seek to understand inequalities for both genders.

In the previous chapter, we discussed the social consequences of youth and aging. This chapter looks at **sexism**—the belief that innate psychological, behavioural, and/or intellectual differences exist between women and men and that these differences connote the superiority of one group and the inferiority of the other. As with age, such attitudes often result in prejudice and discrimination at both the individual and the institutional levels. The physician who will not hire a male nurse because he or she believes that women are more nurturing and empathetic and are, therefore, better nurses, reflects individual discrimination. Institutional discrimination, that is, discrimination built into the fabric of society, is exemplified by the difficulty some women experience in finding employment; they may have no work history and few job skills as a consequence of living in traditionally defined marriage roles.

Discerning the basis for discrimination is often difficult because gender, age, sexual orientation, and race intersect. For example, First Nations people, members of visible minorities, and men and women with disabilities generally earn yearly incomes that are well below the Canadian average (Nelson and Robinson 2002). Consider, for example, that in 1995 (the most recent census year for which statistics were available at the time this book went to press) women of colour earned just over half (51 percent) of what White men earned and only 60 percent of what men of colour earned (Figure 7.1). Such **double** or **triple**

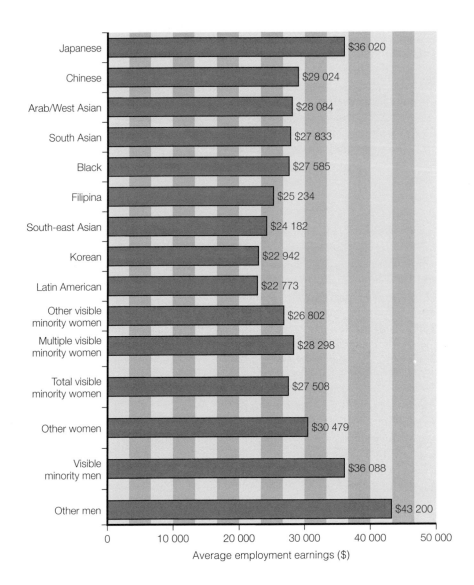

Figure 7.1 *Average Employment Earnings For Women Aged 15–64, by Visible Minority Group, 1995*

SOURCE: Statistics Canada. 1996. 1996 Census of Canada.

(or **multiple**) **jeopardy** occurs when a person is a member of two or more minority groups. In this chapter, however, we emphasize the impact of gender inequality. **Gender** refers to the social definitions and expectations associated with being female or male and should be distinguished from **sex**, which refers to one's biological identity.

The Global Context: The Status of Women and Men

Although societies vary in the degree to which they regard men and women as equals, "no society treats its women as well as its men" (United Nations Development Report 1997: 39). A recent United Nations Report finds that, despite some progress, millions of women around the world remain victims of violence, discrimination, and abuse (Leeman 2000; Austin 2000). For example, worldwide:

- Over 60 million young girls, predominantly in Asia, are listed as "missing" and are likely the victims of infanticide or neglect.
- Two million girls between the ages of 5 and 15 are forced into the sex trade each year.
- Half a million women each year die of complications from childbirth.
- Two-thirds of the world's 876 million women are illiterate.
- One in three women has been abused, beaten, or coerced into sex.

One specific type of violence suffered by millions of women is female genital mutilation (FGM), also known as female circumcision. Clitoridectomy and infibulation are two forms of FGM. In a clitoridectomy, the entire glans and shaft of the clitoris and the labia minora are removed or excised. With infibulation the two sides of the vulva are stitched together shortly after birth, leaving only a small opening for the passage of urine and menstrual blood. After marriage, the sealed opening is reopened to permit intercourse and delivery. After childbirth, the woman is often reinfibulated. Although some progress is being made, worldwide about 100 to 140 million women and girls have undergone genital mutilation (WHO 2001).

> In childhood, a woman must be subject to her father, in youth, to her husband; when her husband is dead, to her sons. A woman must never be free of subjugation.
>
> HINDU CODE

The societies that practise clitoridectomy and infibulation do so for a variety of economic, social, and religious reasons. A virgin bride can inherit from her father, thus making her an economic asset to her husband. A clitoridectomy increases a woman's worth because a woman whose clitoris is removed is thought to experience less sexual desire and therefore less likely to be tempted to have sex before or outside marriage. Older women in the community also generate income by performing the surgery so its perpetuation has an economic function (Kopelman 1994: 62). Various cultural beliefs also justify FGM. In Muslim cultures, for example, female circumcision is justified on both social and religious grounds. Muslim women are regarded as inferior to men: they cannot divorce their husbands, but their husbands can divorce them; they are restricted from buying and inheriting property; and they are not allowed to have custody of their children in the event of divorce. Female circumcision is one expression of the inequality and low social status women have in Muslim society.

Inequality in Canada

Although attitudes toward gender equality are becoming increasingly liberal, Canada has a long history of gender inequality. (You can assess your own beliefs about gender equality in this chapter's *Self and Society* feature). Women have had to fight for equality: the right to vote, equal pay for comparable work, quality education, entrance into male-dominated occupations, and legal equality. Even today, most Canadians would agree that our society does not treat women and men equally. As discussed later, many national statistics support the belief that men and women are not treated equally: women have lower incomes; hold fewer prestigious jobs; remain concentrated in traditionally female-dominated fields of study at universities, community colleges, and trade apprenticeship programs; and are more likely than men are to live in poverty.

The Beliefs About Women Scale (BAWS)

INSTRUCTIONS: The statements listed below describe different attitudes toward men and women. There are no right or wrong answers, only opinions. Indicate how much you agree or disagree with each statement, using the following scale:

A = Strongly Disagree; B = Slightly Disagree; C = Neither Agree nor Disagree; D = Slightly Agree; E = Strongly Agree

_____ 1. Women are more passive than men.

_____ 2. Women are less career-motivated than men.

_____ 3. Women don't generally like to be active in their sexual relationships.

_____ 4. Women are more concerned about their physical appearance than men are.

_____ 5. Women comply more often than men do.

_____ 6. Women care as much as men do about developing a job career.

_____ 7. Most women don't like to express their sexuality.

_____ 8. Men are as conceited about their appearance as women are.

_____ 9. Men are as submissive as women are.

_____ 10. Women are as skillful in business-related activities as men are.

_____ 11. Most women want their partner to take the initiative in their sexual relationships.

_____ 12. Women spend more time attending to their physical appearance than men do.

_____ 13. Women tend to give up more easily than men do.

_____ 14. Women dislike being in leadership positions more than men do.

_____ 15. Women are as interested in sex as men are.

_____ 16. Women pay more attention to their looks than most men do.

_____ 17. Women are more easily influenced than men are.

_____ 18. Women don't like responsibility as much as men do.

_____ 19. Women's sexual desires are less intense than men's.

_____ 20. Women gain more status from their physical appearance than men do.

The Beliefs About Women Scale (BAWS) consists of fifteen (15) separate sub-scales; only four are used here. The items for these four sub-scales and coding instructions are as follows:

Sub-Scales:

1. Women are more passive than men. (Items 1, 5, 9, 13, 17)

2. Women are interested in careers less than men. (Items 2, 6, 10, 14, 18)

3. Women are less sexual than men. (Items 3, 7, 11, 15, 19)

4. Women are more appearance conscious than men (Items 4, 8, 12, 16, 20)

Items 1–5, 7, 11–14, and 16–20 should be scored as followed: Strongly Agree = + 2, Slightly Agree = +1, Neither Agree nor Disagree = 0, Slightly Disagree = –1, and Strongly Disagree = –2.

Items 6, 8, 9, 10, and 15 are scored so that: Strongly Agree = –2, Slightly Agree = –1, Neither Agree Nor Disagree = 0, Slightly Disagree = +1, and Strongly Disagree = + 2. Scores range from –40 to + 40; sub-scale scores range from –10 to +10. The higher your score the more traditional your gender beliefs about men and women.

SOURCE: Snell, William E. Jr., Ph.D. 1997.

Increasingly, however, society recognizes that men are also the victims of gender inequality. When university students were asked to list the best and worst things about being the opposite sex, the same qualities, although in opposite categories, emerged (Cohen 2001). For example, what males list as the best things about being female (e.g., free to be emotional), females list as the worst thing about being male (e.g., not free to be emotional). Similarly, what females list as the best thing about being male (e.g., higher pay), males listed as the worst thing about being female (e.g., lower pay). As Cohen (2001: 3) notes, although "some differences are exaggerated or oversimplified...we identif[ied] a host of ways in which we 'win' or 'lose' simply because we are male or female."

Sociological Theories of Gender Inequality

Both structural-functionalism and conflict theory concentrate on how the structure of society and, specifically, its institutions contribute to gender inequality. However, these two theoretical perspectives offer opposing views of the development and maintenance of gender inequality. Symbolic interactionism, on the other hand, focuses on the culture of society and how gender roles are learned through the socialization process.

Structural-Functionalist Perspective

Structural-functionalists argue that preindustrial society required a division of labour based on gender. Women, out of biological necessity, remained in the home performing such functions as bearing, nursing, and caring for children. Men, who were physically stronger and could be away from home for long periods, were responsible for providing food, clothing, and shelter for their families. This division of labour was functional for society and, over time, became defined as both normal and natural.

Industrialization rendered the traditional division of labour less functional, although remnants of the supporting belief system persist. Today, because of daycare facilities, lower fertility rates, and the less physically demanding and dangerous nature of jobs, the traditional division of labour is no longer as functional. Thus, modern conceptions of the family, to some extent, have replaced traditional ones—families have evolved from extended to nuclear, authority is more egalitarian, more women work outside the home, and there is greater role variation in the division of labour. Functionalists argue, therefore, that as the needs of society change, the associated institutional arrangements also change.

> When I hear men talk about women being the angel of the home I always, mentally at least, shrug my shoulders in doubt. I do not want to be the angel of any home; I want for myself what I want for other women: absolute equality. After that is secured, then men and women can take turns at being angels.
>
> AGNES MACPHAIL
> *Canada's first woman M.P.*

Conflict Perspective

Many conflict theorists hold that the relationship men and women have to the production process shapes male dominance and female subordination. During the hunting and gathering stage of development, males and females were economic equals, each controlling their own labour and producing needed subsistence. As society evolved to agricultural and industrial modes of production, private property developed and men gained control of the modes of production while women remained in the home to bear and care for children. Inheritance laws that ensured that ownership would remain in their hands furthered male domination. Laws that regarded women as property ensured that women would remain confined to the home.

As industrialization continued and the production of goods and services moved away from the home, the male–female gap continued to grow—women had less education, lower incomes, fewer occupational skills and were rarely owners. World War II necessitated the entry of large numbers of women into the labour force, but in contrast to previous periods, many did not return home at the end of the war. They had established their own place in the workforce and, facilitated by the changing nature of work and technological advances, now competed directly with men for jobs and wages (Figure 7.2).

Conflict theorists also argue that the continued domination of males requires a belief system that supports gender inequality. Two such beliefs are that (1) women are inferior outside the home (e.g., they are less intelligent, less reliable, and less rational), and (2) women are more valuable in the home (e.g., they have maternal instincts and are naturally nurturing). Thus, unlike functionalists, conflict theorists hold that the subordinate position of women in society is a consequence of social inducement rather than the biological differences that led to the traditional division of labour.

Symbolic Interactionist Perspective

Although some scientists argue that gender differences are innate, symbolic interactionists emphasize that through the socialization process, both females and males are taught the meanings associated with being feminine and masculine. Gender assignment begins at birth, when a child is classified as either female or male. However, the learning of gender roles is a lifelong process whereby individuals acquire society's definitions of appropriate and inappropriate gender behaviour.

Gender roles are taught in the family, the school, and peer groups, and by media presentations of girls and boys, and women and men. Most important, however, gender roles are learned through symbolic interaction as the messages others send us reaffirm or challenge our gender performances. As Lorber (1998: 213) notes:

> Gender is so pervasive that in our society we assume it is bred into our genes. Most people find it hard to believe that gender is constantly created and recreated out of

> We live in a state of gender warfare...there is a growing public awareness that many women are abused, discriminated against, and hindered in their personal development.
>
> **DANIEL J. LEVINSON**
> *Psychologist*

Figure 7.2 *Percentage of Employed Adults Aged 25 and Older, Canada: 1946–1999*

SOURCE: Crompton, Susan, and Micheal Vickers. 2000. "One Hundred Years of Labour Force." Canadian Social Trends, Summer: 2–6.

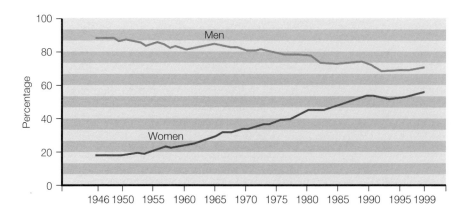

human interaction, out of social life, and is the texture and order of social life. Yet gender, like culture, is a human production that depends on everyone constantly "doing gender."

Conceptions of gender are, thus, socially constructed as societal expectations dictate what it means to be female or what it means to be male. Although race and class variations exist, in general, women are socialized into **expressive roles** or nurturing and emotionally supportive roles and males are more often socialized into **instrumental** (or task-oriented) **roles**. These roles are then acted out in countless daily interactions as the boss and the secretary, the doctor and the nurse, and the football player and the cheerleader "do gender."

■ The country has enfranchised you, but it cannot emancipate you; that is done by your own processes of thought.

NELLIE L. McCLUNG
Suffragette

Gender Stratification: Structural Sexism

As structural-functionalists and conflict theorists argue, the social structure underlies and perpetuates much of the sexism in society. **Structural sexism**, also known as "institutional sexism," refers to the ways in which the organization of society, and specifically its institutions, subordinate individuals and groups based on their sex classification. Structural sexism has resulted in gender differences in educational attainment, income levels, and occupational and political involvement.

Education and Structural Sexism

Literacy rates worldwide indicate that women are less likely to be able to read and write than men, with millions of women being denied access to even the most basic education (Leeman 2000; Population Reference Bureau 1999). For example, on average women in South Asia have only half as many years of education as men (World Bank 2001). In some areas of the world, however, conditions are improving. In Iran, for example, between 1990 and 2000, the number of women entering universities tripled. Today, more than 60 percent of all university entrants in Iran are women (Sachs 2000).

In Canada, the proportionate number of women enrolled full-time at universities has increased noticeably over the past decades. While in 1964–65 less than one-third (31 percent) of full-time undergraduates were women, in the 1997–98 academic year 55 percent of all full-time university students were female (Normand 2000; Statistics Canada 2000). "In 1991, almost three million [Canadian] women aged 25 to 64, or 41% of the total, had a trade, college, or university education. By 2001, this had jumped to almost 4.4 million, or 53%" (Statistics Canada 2003c: 9). While some traditionally male-dominated fields are no longer male dominated, women's participation levels in mathematics, engineering, and the physical and applied sciences remain relatively low (Table 7.1). For example, in 1997–98, only 29 percent of all university students in mathematics and physical sciences, and 22 percent of those in engineering and the applied sciences were women (Normand 2000: 87). In addition, while women's proportional participation remains constant at the master's degree level, they remain underrepresented among doctoral students. While women account for well over half of full-time doctoral students in both education (66 percent) and the fine/applied arts (59 percent) and about half of those in the social sciences (52 percent) and humanities (50 percent), they make up only 23 percent of doctoral candidates in mathematics and the physical sciences and 16 percent of doctoral students in engineering and the applied sciences.

One explanation for why women earn fewer doctoral degrees than men is that women are socialized to choose marriage and motherhood over long-term career preparation (Olson et al. 1990). From an early age, women are exposed to images and models of femininity that stress the importance of domestic family life. When 821 undergraduate women were asked to identify their lifestyle preference, less

Table 7.1 *University and College Graduates, Top Ten Subjects of Study, by Sex, Canada, 2001*

University Graduates, 2001		College Graduates, 2001	
Men		**Men**	
Engineering	15.38%	Electronic and electrical technologies	10.03%
Business and commerce	9.99	Data processing and computer science technologies	9.38
Elementary, secondary, pre-primary teaching	8.22	Mechanical engineering technologies	8.70
Financial management	7.16	Business and commerce	7.28
Computer science and applied mathematics	4.48	Financial management	6.66
Economics	3.49	Building and construction technologies	5.08
Law and jurisprudence	3.36	General and civil engineering technologies	4.90
Medicine	2.98	Social work and social services	4.55
Psychology	2.16	Industrial engineering technologies	3.45
History	1.96	Marketing, merchandising, retail trade, and sales	3.25
All other subjects	40.84	All other subject areas	36.71
Total	100.00	Total	100.00
Women		**Women**	
Elementary, secondary, pre-primary teaching	20.08%	Office administration and secretarial sciences	17.04
Nursing	6.49	Nursing	13.35
Business and commerce	6.06	Financial management	9.40
Financial management	5.19	Business and commerce	7.07
Psychology	4.83	Elementary, secondary, pre-primary teaching	5.84
Medical related subjects	3.20	Social work and social services	4.52
English language and literature	3.01	Data processing and computer science technologies	4.34
Social work and social services	2.80	Nursing assistance	3.93
Sociology	2.68	Marketing, merchandising, retail trade, and sales	2.61
Engineering	2.36	Medical treatment technologies	2.30
All other subjects	43.30	All other subject areas	29.61
Total	100.00	Total	100.00

SOURCE: Adapted from Statistics Canada. 2003. "Education in Canada: Raising the Standard." Catalogue 96FOO30. March 2003.

than 1 percent selected being unmarried and working full-time. In contrast, 53 percent selected "graduation, full-time work, marriage, children, stop working at least until youngest child is in school, then pursue a full-time job" as their preferred lifestyle sequence (Schroeder et al. 1993: 243). Only 6 percent of 535 undergraduate men selected this same pattern.

Structural limitations also discourage women from advancing in the educational profession itself. In 1996, women outnumbered men in elementary and kindergarten teaching positions by approximately four to one and were approximately equal in number to male teachers at the postsecondary level, but men as university professors outnumbered them by about two to one (Statistics Canada 1998). Women seeking academic careers may also find that promotion in higher education is more difficult than it is for men. Long et al. (1993) examined the promotions of 556 men and 450 women with Ph.D.s in biochemistry. They found that women were less likely to be promoted to associate or full professor, were held to a higher standard than men, and were particularly disadvantaged in more prestigious departments. Throughout Canada, women are less likely than men are to be full professors (the highest rank) and when employed as full professors, earn less on average than men who are full professors (*CAUT Bulletin* 2002).

Income and Structural Sexism

When data were first collected in 1967 in Canada on female-to-male earnings, the ratio stood at 58.4 percent. Since that time, it has increased notably. "Earnings have...evolved very differently by gender over the last two decades. They have been stagnant for men, increasing in 2000 for the first time since 1980. In contrast, earnings have increased steadily in each decade for women" (Statistics Canada 2003b) (Figure 7.3). More women are working, and more women are working longer hours. In addition, they are more qualified; since 1980, the proportion of women workers with a university degree has almost tripled, and the proportion of women earners with a university degree now exceeds that of

> Girls should be educated to fit them for the sphere of life for which they are destined—that of the homemaker.
>
> **ADELAIDE HOODLESS**
> *Founder of the Women's Institute in 1897*

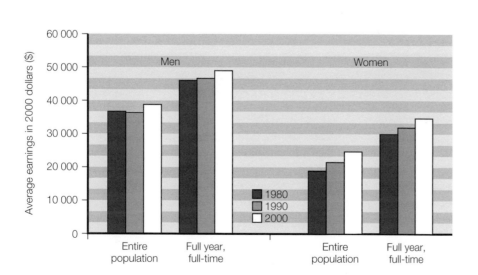

Figure 7.3 *Average Earnings, Men and Women, 1980–2000*

SOURCE: Adapted from Statistics Canada. 2003. "Earnings of Canadians: Making a Living in the New Economy." http://www12.statcan.ca/english/census01/Products/Analytic/companion/earn/charts/menwom.cfm.

men. However, "[d]espite substantial gains in earnings during the past two decades, women still earn less than men" (Statistics Canada 2003b).

In general, the higher one's education, the higher one's income. Yet, even when men and women have identical levels of educational achievement and both work full-time, women, on the average, earn less than men (Table 7.2). For example, although women with a university degree earn substantially more than women with lower levels of education, women university graduates who were employed full-time, full-year earned simply 74 percent as much as their male counterparts in 1997. Moreover, while gender differences are less pronounced for younger than older women, women aged 25 to 29 who were university educated and who worked full-year, full-time in 2000 earned 81 cents for every 1 dollar earned by their male counterparts. Among those with only a high school education, women earned 77 cents to the dollar. The persistent wage gap among these young men and women is partially explained by their different occupational choices, rooted in different fields of study.

> In general, the most common occupations held by young women paid less than those that men most commonly pursued. However, while the wage gap narrows when women pursue occupations that are most commonly chosen by men, a gap still exists. For example, in 2000, university-educated women aged 25 to 29 who worked in the 10 most common occupations chosen by men of the same age group and qualifications earned about 89 cents for every dollar their male counterparts made. (Statistics Canada 2003b)

The wage gap is widespread and exists in all occupational categories (Table 7.3). For example, even though women in professional and related occupations enjoy considerably higher income than women in other occupational groups, the 1997 earnings ratio for women and men employed full-time, full year "ranged from just over 80 percent among professionals employed in the natural sciences and teachers to close to 65 percent for those in management and administration, as well as professionals in social science and religious occupations" (Lindsay 2000: 143).

Tomaskovic-Devey (1993) examined the income differences between males and females and found that the percentage of females in an occupation was the

Table 7.2 *Annual Average Earnings of Persons Employed Full-Time, Full-Year, by Educational Attainment, 1997*

Educational Attainment	Women	Men	Women's Earnings as a % of Men's
Less than Grade 9	$21 403	$30 731	69.6%
Some secondary school	22 846	35 367	64.6
Secondary school graduate	27 525	37 705	73.0
Some postsecondary	28 360	37 812	75.0
Postsecondary certificate/diploma	29 539	41 868	70.6
University degree	42 661	57 930	73.6
Total Average	$30 915	$42 626	72.5%

SOURCE: Statistics Canada, Catalogue no. 13-217-XIB.

■ **Table 7.3** *Average Annual Earnings, by Occupation, 1997*

	Full-time, Full-year workers		
	Women	Men	Earning ratio[1]
Managerial/administrative	$37 092	$56 640	65.5%
Professionals			
Natural sciences	41 221	49 962	82.5
Social sciences/religion	37 280	55 767	66.8
Teaching	40 888	50 305	81.3
Medicine/health	35 407	62 354	56.8
Artistic/recreational	29 324	41 251	71.1
Clerical	28 151	34 863	80.7
Sales	28 843	39 475	73.1
Service	21 516	33 225	64.8
Agriculture	18 366	28 126	73.1
Processing	26 886	40 655	66.1
Product assembly/fabrication/repair	24 384	38 111	64.0
Transport equipment operation	30 253	38 396	78.8
Material handling	22 810	35 821	63.7
Total	30 915	42 626	72.5

[1] Represents women's earnings as a percentage of those of men.

SOURCE: Statistics Canada, Catalogue no. 13-217-XIB.

best predictor of an income gender gap—the higher the percentage of females, the lower the pay. Supporting this observation, a team of researchers (Kilbourne et al. 1994) analyzed data from the National Longitudinal Survey that included more than 5000 women and more than 5000 men. They concluded that occupational pay is gendered and that "occupations lose pay if they have a higher percentage of female workers or require nurturant skills" (p. 708).

The literature frequently cites two hypotheses to explain why the income gender gap continues to exist. One is called the **devaluation hypothesis**. It argues that women are paid less because the work they perform is socially defined as less valuable than the work performed by men. The other hypothesis, the **human capital hypothesis**, argues that female–male pay differences are a function of differences in women's and men's levels of education, skills, training, and work experience.

Tam (1997), in testing these hypotheses, concludes that human capital differences are more important in explaining the income gender gap than the devaluation hypothesis is. A second study, based on data obtained from the Survey of Labour and Income Dynamics, also finds that women's lower amount of actual work experience appears to have a significant bearing on the persistent wage gap between men and women (Statistics Canada 1998). This research reports that about 18 percent, or almost one-fifth, of the wage gap reflected the fact that women generally have less experience than their male counterparts, supervise other employees less often, and are involved in administrative decisions less frequently. Several other factors were also associated with the wage gap, including differences in job tenure and the fact that men are more likely to graduate from programs leading to higher-paying jobs and earnings. Marini and Fan (1997) additionally found support for the human capital hypothesis, although their research supports a third category of variables as well. They found that organizational variables (characteristics of the business, corporation, or industry) explain, in part, the gender income gap. For example, on career entry, employers channel women and men into sex-specific jobs that carry different wage rates.

Work and Structural Sexism

Women now make up one third of the world's labour force. Worldwide, women tend to work in jobs that have little prestige and low or no pay, where no product is produced, and where women are the facilitators for others. Women are also more likely to hold positions of little or no authority within the work environment and to have more frequent and longer periods of unemployment (United Nations 2000c).

No matter what the job, if a woman does it, it is likely to be valued less than if a man does it. For example, in the early nineteenth century, 90 percent of all clerks were men, and being a clerk was a very prestigious profession. As the job became routine, in part because of the advent of the typewriter, the pay and prestige of the job declined and the number of female clerks increased. Today, female clerks predominate, and the position is one of relatively low pay and low prestige.

The concentration of women in certain occupations and men in other occupations is referred to as **occupational sex segregation**. In Canada, "the majority of employed women continue to work in occupations that have traditionally been concentrated" (Ghalam 2000). In 1999, 70 percent of employed women (versus 29 percent of employed men) worked in teaching, nursing, and related health occupations, clerical or other administrative positions, and sales and service occupations. Women tend to be more highly concentrated within fewer occupations while men are more evenly distributed across a larger range of occupations (Table 7.4).

In some occupations, sex segregation has decreased in recent years. Data from the 2001 census indicates that women are "making inroads in many 'non-traditional' areas, particularly in highly skilled occupations" (Statistics Canada 2003a: 8). Women accounted for over one-half of the growth during 1991–2001 in high-skilled occupations (i.e., occupations which normally require a university education) and their numbers doubled in information technology occupations. The number of women more than doubled in professional occupations in business and finance. Over the last decade, the number of women managers has also increased by more than 40 percent. Despite these and other changes, however, women are still heavily represented in low-prestige, low-wage, **pink-collar jobs** that offer few benefits. A **glass ceiling**—an invisible barrier that prevents women and other minorities from moving into top corporate positions—often victimizes even those women in higher-paying jobs. A study of Fortune 500 companies found that women held less than 11 percent of all seats on the Fortune 500 company boards (Klein 1998). Interestingly, Cianni and Romberger's investigation (1997) of visible minority women and men in Fortune 500 companies indicates that gender has more of a role in "organizational treatment" than race.

■ **Table 7.4** *Distribution of Employment, by Occupation, 1987, 1994, and 1999*

	1987 Women as a % of total employed in occupation	1994 Women as a % of total employed in occupation	1999 Women as a % of total employed in occupation
Managerial			
Senior management	16.9	19.8	26.8
Other management	30.6	36.9	35.7
Total management	28.9	35.1	35.1
Professional			
Business and finance	40.7	44.6	49.4
Natural sciences/engineering/mathematics	16.7	17.0	19.6
Social sciences/religion	47.8	56.5	58.2
Teaching	57.3	59.4	62.1
Doctors/dentists/other health	44.1	48.7	47.1
Nursing/therapy/other health-related	87.3	87.1	86.5
Artistic/literary/recreational	50.4	53.6	54.8
Total professional	49.8	52.2	51.8
Clerical and administrative	74.4	74.9	75.3
Sales and service	55.7	56.4	58.7
Primary	20.0	21.3	21.6
Trades, transport, and construction	5.3	5.4	6.2
Processing, manufacturing, and utilities	30.2	29.2	29.8
Total[1]	43.0	45.3	45.9

[1] Includes occupations that are not classified.

SOURCE: Statistics Canada, Labour Force Survey.

Sex segregation in occupations continues for several reasons (Martin 1992; Williams 1995). First, cultural beliefs about what is an "appropriate" job for a man or a woman still exist. Cejka and Eagley (1999) report that the more undergraduate students believed that an occupation was male- or female-dominated, the more they attributed success in that occupation to masculine or feminine characteristics. Further, in an examination of gender-role orientations and attitudes toward women as managers among a sample of 194 Canadian business students (71 female and 123 male undergraduate and graduate students), Burke (1994) reports that the men exhibited significantly more negative attitudes toward women as managers than did the women. He suggests that this "augurs badly" for women in at least three ways: (1) as colleagues, these men would be unlikely to endorse initiatives to develop women's careers or, perhaps, actively endorse "backlash" strategies, (2) these men are unlikely to provide women with mentorship or sponsorship and may act as poor role models for other men, and (3) these individuals are unlikely to support the career aspirations of their spouse or female partner.

■ We'll have true equality when we have as many incompetent women in senior positions as incompetent men.

SHEELAGH WHITTAKER
CEO

It doesn't matter what my qualifications are, all some people will see are my pierced ears.

ROBERTA BONDAR
Physician and astronaut

I get jolly well tired of managing a multinational public company by day and doing the ironing when I get home at night.

LYNNE STETHEM
Founder of Angoss Software Corp.

In addition, because of gender socialization, men and women learn different skills and acquire different aspirations. Opportunity structures for men and women and the expectations placed on them also vary. For example, male employers may exclude women, as may employees who fear the prestige of their profession will be lessened with the entrance of women, or who simply believe that "the ideal worker is normatively masculine" (Martin 1992: 220). Finally, since family responsibilities primarily remain with women, working mothers may feel pressure to choose professions that permit flexible hours and career paths, sometimes known as "mommy tracks." Thus, for example, women dominate the field of elementary education, which permits them to be home when their children are not in school. Nursing, also dominated by women, often offers flexible hours.

Politics and Structural Sexism

In 1868, when the first federal general election was held, only men who owned a specified amount of property were allowed to vote; in 1885, the *Electoral Franchise Act* defined a "person" who was eligible to vote as a male who was of other than Mongolian or Chinese origin. While the 1917 *Wartime Election Act* granted wives, sisters, and mothers of servicemen the right to vote, it was not until 1918 that Canadian women won the right to vote in federal elections (Frank 1994). Women over the age of 21 were granted the right to vote in provincial elections in 1916 in Manitoba, Saskatchewan, and Alberta; in 1917 in British Columbia and Ontario; in 1918 in Nova Scotia; in 1919 in New Brunswick; in 1922 in Prince Edward Island; in 1925 in Newfoundland (where initially this right was limited to women over the age of 25); and in 1940 in Quebec (Whitla 1995: 320–2). These rights were first granted to White women; women from certain other ethnic groups did not receive the franchise until later years. For example, Mossman (1998: 181) observes that "prior to 1960, aboriginal women (and men) in Canada were entitled to vote only if they gave up their Indian status, a status defined by the federal *Indian Act*." While an Aboriginal woman became automatically "enfranchised" if she married a White man, "it was only in the 1970s that aboriginal women's claims to equality under the *Indian Act* were tested in the Supreme Court of Canada."

Worldwide, the percentage of legislative seats held by women ranges from 30 to 40 percent in Scandinavian countries to less than 1 percent in several Middle Eastern and African countries (Kenworthy and Malami 1999). Further, in no developing country do women hold more than 8 percent of ministerial positions (World Bank 2001: 5). In response to the underrepresentation of women in the political arena, some countries have institutionalized quotas. In India, a 1993 amendment held one-third of all seats in local contests for women. The result? Eight hundred thousand women were elected. A 1996 law in Britain requires a minimum of 20 percent of each party's candidates be women. Countries with similar policies include Finland, Germany, Mexico, South Africa, and Spain (Sheehan 2000).

There are some signs that Canada is on the road to achieving gender equality in politics. For example, in June 1993, Kim Campbell was elected Conservative Party leader and, by ascension shortly after, became Canada's first female Prime Minister (for an admittedly limited term of less than six months). Some years earlier, in December 1989, the election of Audrey MacLaughlin as leader of the

NDP signalled the first time a Canadian women had been elected as the leader of a national political party. Nevertheless, in general, the more important the political office, the lower the probability a woman will hold it. Running for office requires large sums of money, the political backing of powerful individuals and interest groups, and a willingness of the voting public to elect women. Hunter and Denton (1984) note that Canadian political parties have shown a marked tendency to nominate women only after they have suffered losses at the polls or to nominate women in "lost cause" ridings where another party enjoys the overwhelming support of voters. It is, then, political party-elites who hamper women "in securing nominations in the first place, and beyond this, in gaining nominations which carry a reasonable prospect of victory" (Stark 1992: 454). Moreover, minority women have even greater structural barriers to election and, not surprisingly, represent an even smaller percentage of elected officials.

Consider, for example, that while Mary Ellen Smith became, in 1918, the first woman to be elected to the Legislative Assembly in British Columbia and the first woman in the British Empire to serve as a cabinet minister, it was not until 1972 that a Black woman, Rosemary Brown, won a seat in that province. Brown was the first Black woman elected to any Canadian legislature. In 1991, Zanana Akande was the first Black woman to be elected to the Ontario legislature and also the first Black woman to become a cabinet minister in that province (Mandell 1995: 347).

Human Rights and Structural Sexism

In 2001, the United Nations Development Programme ranked Canada third among 162 nations surveyed, for such "quality of life" variables as health, education levels, life expectancy, and standard of living. However, when the UNDP employed the *Gender Empowerment Measure*, which focuses directly on women's advancement within a nation in terms of its political, economic, and professional life, our national rating declined from third to fifth place (behind Norway, Iceland, Sweden, and Finland) (United Nations Development Programme 2001: 214).

The status of women in Canada was addressed early by the 1970 Report of the Royal Commission on the Status of Women. The Report directed many of its recommendations to legislative reforms in the areas of the criminal law, tax and childcare allowances, social assistance, immigration, and family law. These recommendations were guided by the principle that women and men "having the same rights and freedoms, share the same responsibilities...[and] should have an equal opportunity to fulfil their obligation....[T]here should be equality of opportunity to share the responsibility to society as well as its privileges and prerogatives." However, while advocating, in general, that men and women should be treated identically (i.e., the "sameness standard" of equality), the Report acknowledged that, on occasion, equality might demand or necessitate "special" or "different treatment" of women. For example, because women can become pregnant, the "special needs" created by pregnancy might demand acknowledgment of difference (e.g., maternity leave), or a shift from "equality of treatment" (formal equality) to "equality of outcome" (substantive equality).

In various ways, Canadian laws have not always benefited men and women in equal fashion. Consider, for example, that until 1983, most women were denied the right to claim pregnancy benefits under the old *Unemployment Insurance Act* (Atcheson et al. 1984: 20–21); that until 1983, husbands who raped

> Forgive me for saying this, but what would happen if we were all PMSed the same week? Can you imagine what the Parliament of Canada would be like?
>
> **DEBORAH GREY**
> *M.P.*

> The price of inequality is just too high.
>
> **NASFIS SADIK**
> *United Nations Population Fund*

their wives were exempt from prosecution and conviction; and that before 1989, women could be fired from their jobs simply because they became pregnant. Consider as well, that while the courts have permitted "businessmen to deduct club fees because men like to conduct business with each other over golf," have held the purchase of a Rolls Royce "to be an incident of a professional expense" (because it enhances professional image), and have sustained claims that "making charitable contributions to enhance one's reputation in a community inheres in the business of manufacturing boxes" (Macklin 1992), Canada's *Income Tax Act* refuses to regard the cost of childcare as a legitimate "business deduction." Childcare costs are viewed officially as part of the process of parenting and, in particular, mothering.

Moreover, attempts to "de-gender" the law have not always proven to be fully effective. For example, in the case of *Murdoch v. Murdoch*, Irene Murdoch claimed that, based on her contribution of money and labour during 25 years of marriage, she was entitled to one-half of the property owned by her husband when they divorced. It was noted that her tasks while married had included "haying, raking, swathing, mowing, driving trucks and tractors and teams, quieting horses, taking cattle back and forth to the reserve, dehorning, vaccinating, branding, anything that was to be done...just as a man would" (Dranoff in Mossman 1998: 187). The denial of Mrs. Murdoch's claim in the Supreme Court of Canada generated activism by groups concerned with women's rights and, by 1980, every Canadian province, with the exception of Quebec, had enacted legislation amending the arrangements for the distribution of property between spouses at the time of separation or divorce. Men and women were to be treated "equally."

Although the notion of "equal treatment" sounds fair, does treating those who are unlike the same result in equality? As Mossman (1998: 187) observes, "With the benefit of hindsight, many feminists now recognize that the reform legislation in common law provinces was fundamentally flawed, since it assumed that men and women had equal access to economic self-sufficiency." In the vast majority of cases, it is women who become the custodial parents of dependent children following marital breakdown. The constraints on full-time employment posed by the parental role, coupled with the wage gap, may continue to create substantive hardship for women upon divorce.

> What feminists do in the legal system is to expose its previously unseen maleness and attempt to deconstruct it, in order to make room for the viewpoints, the concerns, and the experiences of women.
>
> **MARY EBERTS**
> *Lawyer and feminist*

The Social Construction of Gender Roles: Cultural Sexism

As symbolic interactionists note, structural sexism is supported by a system of cultural sexism that perpetuates beliefs about the differences between women and men. **Cultural sexism** refers to the ways in which the culture of society—its norms, values, beliefs, and symbols—perpetuates the subordination of an individual or group because of the sex classification of that individual or group.

For example, the *belief* that females are less valuable than males has serious consequences. In one study in Bombay, India, of 8000 abortions performed after amniocentesis, 7900 were of female fetuses (Anderson and Moore 1998). Cultural sexism takes place in a variety of settings, including the family, the school, and the media, as well as in everyday interactions.

Family Relations and Cultural Sexism

From birth, males and females are treated differently. For example, the toys male and female children receive convey different messages about appropriate gender roles. Recently, retail giant Toys "R" Us, after much criticism, removed store directories labelled "Boy's World" and "Girl's World." Similarly, toy manufacturer Mattel came under fire after producing a pink, flowered Barbie computer for girls, and a blue Hot Wheels computer for boys. The social significance of the gender-specific computers and the public criticism came after it was revealed that the accompanying software packages were different—the boys' package had more educational titles (Bannon 2000). This chapter's *Focus on Technology* feature documents the negative consequences of such seemingly harmless differences.

Household Division of Labour Girls and boys work within the home in approximately equal amounts until the age of 18, when the female to male ratio begins to change (Robinson and Bianchi 1997: 4). In a recent study of household labour in 10 Western countries, Bittman and Wajcman (2000) report that "women continue to be responsible for the majority of hours of unpaid labour" ranging from a low of 70 percent in Sweden to a high of 88 percent in Italy (p. 173). The fact that women, even when working full time, contribute significantly more hours to home care than men is known as the "second shift" (Hochschild 1989). The 2001 Census, the second census to include questions on unpaid work, found that women "still had the lion's share of the number of hours devoted to unpaid household work" (Statistics Canada 2003a: 17). Approximately 21 percent of women—but only 8 percent of men—devoted 30 hours or more to unpaid household work during the week prior to the census. While 13.3 percent of men reported that they did not devote any hours to household unpaid work, only 7.5 percent of women reported likewise (Table 7.5).

Three explanations for the continued traditional division of labour emerge from the literature. The first explanation is the "time-availability approach." Consistent with the structural-functionalist perspective, this position emphasizes that role performance is a function of who has the time to accomplish certain tasks. Because women are more likely to be at home, they are more likely to perform domestic chores.

A second explanation is the "relative resources approach." This explanation, consistent with a conflict perspective, suggests that the spouse with the least power is relegated the most unrewarding tasks. Since men often have more education, higher incomes, and more prestigious occupations, they are less responsible for domestic labour.

"Gender role ideology," the final explanation, is consistent with a symbolic interactionist perspective. It argues that the division of labour is a consequence of traditional socialization and the accompanying attitudes and beliefs. Females and males have been socialized to perform various roles and to expect their partners to perform other complementary roles. Women typically take care of the house, men the yard. This division of labour is learned in the socialization process through the media, schools, books, and toys. A recent test of the three positions found that although all three had some support, gender role ideology was the weakest of the three in predicting work allocation (Bianchi et al. 2000).

> Economists could get a very sudden increase in the GNP by discovering and including the unpaid labour of women.
>
> JOHN KENNETH GALBRAITH
> *Economist and essayist*

> Men kinda have to choose between marriage and death. I guess they figure at least with marriage they get meals. Then they get married and find out we don't cook anymore.
>
> RITA RUDNER
> *Comedian*

Women, Men, and Computers

Technology has changed the world in which we live. The technological revolution has brought the possibility of greater gender equality for, unlike tasks dominating industrialization, sex differences in size, weight, and strength are less relevant. Although feminists have long decried the gendering of technology (see Chapter 14), surely computers and other information technologies are gender neutral—or are they?

Girls spend less time playing video games (to wit, "Game Boy") and, consequently, software that appeals to girls is less likely to be manufactured (O'Neal 1998; Children Now 2001). In a recent study of the 10 top-selling video games for each of three major systems (Sony PlayStation, Sega Dreamcast, and Nintendo 64), 54 percent of the games contained female characters whereas 92 percent contained male characters. Of the female characters displayed, over one third had signif-

icantly exposed breasts, thighs, stomachs, midriffs, or bottoms, and 46 percent had "unusually small" waists. Further, despite evidence that girls, contrary to boys, prefer video games that are nonviolent, over half of the female characters were portrayed engaging in violent behaviour (Children Now 2000).

Although young Canadian women aged 15–19 are slightly more likely than their male counterparts to report using a computer, in other age categories, men are more likely to do so (Normand 2000: 91) (Figure 7.4). Some research finds that girls are not as interested in computers as boys and, that when they are interested, they define computers as a tool to accomplish a task, a kind of homework helper (in contrast to boys who define it as a toy to explore). Says Jane Margolis, a researcher at Carnegie Mellon (quoted in Breidenbach 1997: 69):

> Girls want to do something constructive with computers, while boys get into hacking and using computers for their own sake...Computers are just one interest of many for girls, while they become an object of love and fascination for boys.

For significant changes to take place in reference to women, men, and computers we must recognize that computers specifically, and technology in general, are not gender neutral and, in fact, have emerged and flourished within the context of a male-dominated industry. However, if women do not pursue computer-based information technologies, they will have an "intellectual and workplace handicap that can only get worse as technology grows more prevalent" (Currid 1996: 114).

SOURCES: Breidenbach, Susan. 1997. "Where Are All the Women?" *Network World* 14(41): 68–69. Currid, Cheryl. 1996. "Bridging the Gender Gap: Women Will Lose Out Unless They Catch Up with Men in Technology Use." *Informationweek*, April 1: 114. Children Now. 2001. "Girls and Gaming: Gender and Video Game Marketing." *Media Now* (Winter). http://www. childrennow.org/media/medianow. Children Now. 2000. "Top Selling Video Games 'unhealthy' for Girls, Research Show." News Release, December 12. http://www.childrennow.org/newsroom. Normand, Josee. 2000. "Women and Education." *Women in Canada 2000: A Gender-Based Statistical Report*, pp. 85–96. Ottawa: Statistics Canada, Catalogue no. 89-503-XPE. O'Neal, Glenn. 1998. "Girls Often Dropped from Computer Equation." *USA Today*, March 10: D4.

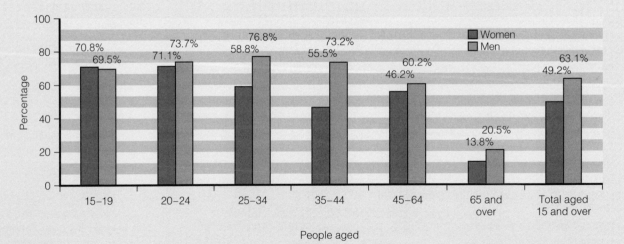

Figure 7.4 *Percentage Using Computers, by Age, 1998*

SOURCE: Statistics Canada, General Social Survey.

■ Table 7.5 *Percentage of Persons Aged 15 and Over, by Number of Unpaid Hours Doing Housework, Canada, 2001**

Women	
No hours	7.5
Less than 5 hours	17.4
5 to 14 hours	29.7
15 to 29 hours	23.9
30 or more hours	21.4

Men	
No hours	13.3
Less than 5 hours	30.0
5 to 14 hours	33.5
15 to 29 hours	15.4
30 or more hours	7.8

*Refers to the week preceding Census Day.

SOURCE: Adapted from Statistics Canada. 2003. 2001 Census: Analysis Series. "The Changing Profile of Canada's Labour Force." Catalogue no. 96F0030XIE2001009 (released February 11, 2003), p. 36.

The School Experience and Cultural Sexism

Sexism is also evident in the schools. It can be found in the books students read, the curricula and tests they are exposed to, and the different ways teachers interact with students.

Textbooks The bulk of research on gender images in textbooks and other instructional materials documents the way male and females are portrayed stereotypically. For example, Purcell and Stewart (1990) analyzed 1883 storybooks used in schools and found that they tended to depict males as clever, brave, adventurous, and income producing and females as passive and as victims. Females were more likely to be in need of rescue, and were also depicted in fewer occupational roles than males. Witt (1996), in a study of third grade textbooks from six publishers, reports that little girls were more likely to be portrayed as having both traditionally masculine and feminine traits whereas little boys were more likely pictured as having masculine characteristics only. These results are consistent with research that suggests that boys are much less free to explore gender differences than females, and with Purcell and Stewart's conclusion that boys are often depicted as having "to deny their feelings to show their manhood" (1990: 184). Although some evidence suggests that the frequency of male and female textbook characters is increasingly equal, portrayals of girls and boys largely remain stereotypical (Evan and Davies 2000).

Teaching-Student Interactions Sexism is also reflected in the way teachers treat their students. After interviewing 800 adolescents, parents, and teachers in three school districts in Kenya, Mensch and Lloyd (1997) report that teachers were more likely to describe girls as lazy and unintelligent. "And when the girls do badly," the researchers remark, "it undoubtedly reinforces teachers' prejudices, becoming a vicious cycle." Similarly, in the United States Sadker and Sadker (1990) observed that elementary-school and secondary-school teachers pay more attention to boys than to girls. Teachers talk to boys more, ask them more questions, listen to them more, counsel them more, give them more extended directions, and criticize and reward them more frequently. However, a recent book by philosopher Christina Sommers (2000) entitled *The War Against Boys* argues that it is boys, not girls, who are "on the weak side of the educational gender gap" (p.14). Noting that boys are at a higher risk for learning disabilities and lag behind in reading and writing scores, Sommers argues that the belief that females are educationally shortchanged is untrue (see Chapter 12).

> In the school room, more than any other place, does the difference of sex, if there is any, need to be forgotten.
>
> SUSAN B. ANTHONY
> *Feminist*

Can the differing expectations and/or encouragement that females and males receive also contribute to their varying abilities, as measured by standardized tests, in such disciplines as math and science? In an experiment at the University of Waterloo, male and female university students, all of whom said they were good in math, were shown either gender-stereotyped or gender-neutral advertisements. When, subsequently, female students who had seen the female stereotyped advertisement took a math test, they performed not only lower than women who had seen the gender-neutral advertisements but lower than their male counterparts (Begley 2000). Research also indicates that standardized tests themselves are biased, almost exclusively being timed, multiple-choice tests—a format that, some argue, favours males (Smolken 2000).

Media, Language, and Cultural Sexism

One concern voiced by social scientists in reference to cultural sexism is the extent to which the media portrays females and males in a limited and stereotypical fashion, and the impact of such portrayals.

Signorielli (1998) analyzed gender images presented in six media: television, movies, magazines, music videos, TV commercials, and print media advertisements. The specific items selected from each medium were those most often consumed by 12- to 17-year-old girls, for example, the 25 most-watched television shows. The results indicate:

- In general, media content stresses the importance of appearance and relationships for girls/women and of careers and work for boys/men.
- Across the six media, 26 to 46 percent of women are portrayed as "thin or very thin" in contrast to 4 to 16 percent of men; 70 percent of girls wanted to look like, fix their hair like, or dress like a character on television, compared with 40 percent of boys.
- In a survey of boys and girls, both agreed that "worrying about weight, crying or whining, weakness, and flirting" are characteristics associated more with girls than with boys, and that "playing sports, being a leader, and wanting to kiss or have sex..." are more often characteristic of male characters.

Like media images, both the words we use and the way we use them can reflect gender inequality. The term nurse carries the meaning of "a woman who..." and the term engineer suggests "a man who...". Terms like "broad," "old maid," and "spinster" have no male counterpart. Language is so gender-stereotyped that the placement of male or female before titles is sometimes necessary, as in the case of "female police officer" or "male prostitute." Further, as symbolic interactionists note, the embedded meanings of words carry expectations of behaviour.

Virginia Sapiro (1994) has shown how male-female differences in communication style reflect the structure of power and authority relations between men and women. For example, women are more likely to use disclaimers ("I could be wrong but...") and self-qualifying tags ("That was a good movie, wasn't it?"), reflecting less certainty about their opinions. Communication differences between women and men also reflect different socialization experiences. Women are more often passive and polite in conversation; men are less polite, interrupt more often, and talk more (Tannen 1990).

Social Problems and Traditional Gender Role Socialization

Cultural sexism, transmitted through the family, school, media, and language, perpetuates traditional gender role socialization. Gender roles, however slowly, are changing. As one commentator observed (Fitzpatrick 2000: 1), "...the hard lines that once helped to define masculine [and feminine] identity are blurring. Women serve in the military, play pro basketball, run corporations, and govern. Men diet, undergo cosmetic surgery, bare their souls in support groups and cook...."

Despite this "**gender tourism**" (Fitzpatrick 2000), most research indicates that traditional gender roles remain dominant, particularly for males who, in general, have less freedom to explore the gender continuum. Social problems that result from traditional gender socialization include the feminization of poverty, social-psychological and health costs, and conflict in relationships.

The Feminization of Poverty

Globally, the percentage of female households is increasing dramatically, with approximately 25 percent of all households in Africa, North America, the Caribbean, and parts of Europe headed by women (Population Reference Bureau 1999). Often living in poverty, many of these households are headed by young women with dependent children and older women who have outlived their spouses. More than 900 million women, worldwide, live on less than $1 a day (United Nations 2000b).

In addition to individual and institutional discrimination, traditional gender role socialization also contributes to poverty among women. Women are often socialized to put family ahead of their education and careers. Women are expected to take primary responsibility for child care, which contributes to the alarming rate of female-headed lone-parent families in Canada. In 1997, when compared to children in two-parent families, children in female-headed lone-parent families were almost five times more likely to be in a low-income situation. In that year, more than half (56 percent) of non-elderly females lived below the "poverty line" (i.e., spent more than 54.7 percent of their income on food, shelter, and clothing) (Statistics Canada 1999). Further, a study of the relationship between marital status, gender, and poverty in Canada, the United States, Australia, and France indicates that never-married women—compared to ever-married women in all four countries—are more likely to live in poverty (Nichols-Casebolt and Krysik 1997).

Social-Psychological Costs

Many of the costs of traditional gender socialization are social-psychological in nature. Reid and Comas-Diaz (1990) noted that the cultural subordination of women results in women having low self-esteem and being dissatisfied with their roles as spouses, homemakers or workers, mothers, and friends. In a study of self-esteem among more than 1160 students in grades 6 through 10, girls were significantly more likely to have "steadily decreasing self-esteem," whereas boys were more likely to fall into the "moderate and rising" self-esteem group (Zimmerman et al. 1997).

Not all researchers have found that women have a more negative self-concept than men do. Summarizing their cross-cultural research on the self-concepts of women and men, Williams and Best (1990) found "no evidence of an appreciable difference" (p. 153). They also found no consistency in the self-concepts of women and men in 14 countries: "[I]n some of the countries the men's perceived self was noticeably more favourable than the women's, whereas in others the reverse was found" (p. 152). More recent research also documents that women are becoming more assertive and desirous of controlling their own lives rather than merely responding to the wishes of others or the limitations of the social structure (Burger and Solano 1994).

Men also suffer from traditional gender socialization. Men experience enormous cultural pressure to be successful in their work and earn a high income. Research indicates that men who have higher incomes feel more "masculine" than those with lower incomes (Rubenstein 1990). Not surprisingly, males are more likely than females to value materialism and competition over compassion and self-actualization (Beutel and Marini 1995; Cohen 2001; McCammon et al. 1998). Traditional male socialization also discourages males from expressing emotion—part of what Pollock (2000a) calls the "boy code." This chapter's *The Human Side* feature describes the problems and pressures of being male in our society.

On the average, men in Canada die earlier than women, although gender differences in life expectancy have been shrinking (Statistics Canada 2001). Traditional male gender socialization is linked to males' higher rates of heart disease, cirrhosis of the liver, most cancers, AIDS, homicide, drug- and alcohol-induced deaths, suicide, and firearm and motor vehicle accidents (Wilkins 1996). Females, however, after the age of 15, are twice as likely to suffer from depression as males (Kalb 2000) and much more likely to suffer from anorexia or bulimia. Seven million women and girls suffer from eating disorders (Wilmot 1999).

Are gender differences in morbidity and mortality a consequence of socialization differentials or physiological differences? Although both nature and nurture are likely to be involved, social rather than biological factors may be dominant. As part of the "masculine mystique," men tend to engage in self-destructive behaviours—heavy drinking and smoking, poor diets, a lack of exercise, stress-related activities, higher drug use, and a refusal to ask for help. Men are also more likely to work in hazardous occupations than women are. For example, men are more likely to be miners than are women—an occupation with one of the highest mortality rates in Canada. Women's higher rates of depression are also likely to be

I learned from my father how to work. I learned from him that work is life and life is work, and work is hard.

PHILIP ROTH
Author

Real Boys' Voices: The "Boy Code"

Brad, 14

Guys aren't supposed to be weak or vulnerable. Guys aren't supposed to be sweet. A friend of mine died in the hospital...I knew that, as a guy, I was supposed to be strong and I wasn't supposed to show any emotion...I was supposed to be tough...when I went home, I just sat by myself and let myself cry. (p.17)

Sam, 16

I think most of the macho stuff guys do is stupid...like the kids who do wrestling moves in the hall. At the same time, there are things that I wouldn't do because I'm a guy. I've never gone to a guy friend, for example, and said, "I'm feeling hurt right now and let's talk about it." (p. 31)

Gordon, 18

All the men in my family...have been the epitome of negativity. Some have become wrapped up in infidelity, some abuse, some alcoholism. I don't want to become a man, because I don't want to become this. (p. 53)

Jeff, 16

Your virginity is what determines whether you're a man or a boy in the eyes of every teenage male. Teenage men see sex as a race: the first one to the finish line wins. (p. 69)

Brett, 17

I think most guys are kind of isolated because it's thought of as weird if you have any really close guy friends. To get around it, guys will go fishing or hunting or bowling or something else "masculine," and then talk about personal or serious things while they're doing that activity. (p. 116)

Jesse, 17

From the girls I've spoken to about relationships, one of their biggest complaints is that they're doing all the giving and the guy is doing all the taking. Girls also tend to be better able to understand social situations. Girls can look at someone and tell what they're feeling. They have more social intuitiveness, more than we clueless guys do. I think that makes them more aware of what's happening in a relationship than we are. (p. 253)

Graham, 17

We would live in a better society if guys could share their feelings more easily. But guys still hear mixed messages from our society. On the one hand they hear that it's OK now to talk about their feelings, but on the other hand they still hear that they have to be tough and that only girls get emotional. My friend who talked to me and cried about his girlfriend was on the football team. His teammates would laugh at him if he tried to talk to them about that sort of stuff. (p. 272)

Jake, 16

Ever since I've played Little League the word "win" has been forced into my mind. When I was eight years old, the coach would tell us at the beginning of the season that we were just out there for fun, but I knew that it wasn't true. Every day that there was a game, my day would be ruined. (p. 280–281)

Dylan, 17

If I get in shape, if I develop a more attractive body, I'd be more popular. It's like the way life is around here, what society shows you. It's a problem to be naturally skinny like me. You're not as athletic or muscular or attractive; you're not as good as the other kids are. (p. 302)

Kirk, 18

I think it's hard growing up in the year 2000. It's definitely hard for a guy. Going through high school is tough. I have pressures in sports, school, life all rolled into one. My parents pressure me to do well in school, do well in sports, and I pressure myself to do well in life....I worry about life a lot. I feel that everything is going to work out for everybody except me, that I'll be left in the dust. (p. 341)

SOURCE: From *Real Boys: Rescuing Our Sons from the Myths of Boyhood* by William Pollock, copyright © 1998 by William Pollock. Used by permission of Random House, Inc.

rooted in traditional gender roles. The heavy burden of childcare and household responsibilities, the gender gap and occupation gap, and fewer socially acceptable reactions to stress (e.g., it is more acceptable for males than females to drink alcohol), contribute to gender differences in depression (Klein 1997).

Conflict in Relationships

Gender inequality also has an impact on relationships. For example, negotiating work and home life can be a source of relationship problems. While men in traditional versus dual-income relationships are more likely to report being satisfied with household task arrangements, women in dual-income families are the most likely to be dissatisfied with household task arrangements (Baker et al. 1996). Further, the belief that one's partner is not performing an equitable portion of the housework is associated with a reduction in the perception of spousal social support (Van Willigen and Drentea 1997).

We must consider also the practical difficulties of raising a family, having a career, and maintaining a happy and healthy relationship with a significant other. In a recent survey, over 80 percent of both men and women responded that changing gender roles make it more difficult to have a successful marriage (Morin and Rosenfeld 2000). Successfully balancing work, marriage, and children may require a number of strategies, including (1) a mutually satisfying distribution of household labour, (2) rejection of such stereotypical roles as "supermom" and "breadwinner dad" (see this chapter's *Social Problems Research Up Close* feature), (3) seeking outside help from others (e.g., childcare givers, domestic workers), and (4) a strong commitment to the family unit.

Finally, violence in intimate relationships is gendered (see Chapters 4 and 5). Although men are more likely to be victims of violent crime, women are more likely to be victims of sexual assault and domestic violence that results in physical harm. Violence against women reflects male socialization that emphasizes aggression and dominance over women. Male violence is a consequence of gender socialization and a definition of masculinity which holds that "as long as nobody is seriously hurt, no lethal weapons are employed, and especially within the framework of sports and games—football, soccer, boxing, wrestling—aggression and violence are widely accepted and even encouraged in boys" (Pollock 2000b: 40).

Strategies for Action: Towards Gender Equality

Efforts to achieve gender equality have been largely fuelled by the feminist movement. Despite a conservative backlash, feminists, and to a lesser extent men's activist groups, have made some gains in reducing structural and cultural sexism in the workplace and in the political arena.

Grassroots Movements

Feminism Feminism is the belief that women and men should have equal rights and responsibilities. However, in its early incarnation, the suffrage movement in Canada, or the "first wave" of feminism, "was less a 'woman's movement' than an attempt on the part of particular men and women, predominantly urban professionals and entrepreneurs, to supervise [the moral development of] society" (Bacchi 1983: 13). First at the local level, and later at the national and provincial levels, thousands of upper- and middle-class women sought to ameliorate a host

Our discontents are passing. We may yet live to see the day when women will be no longer news! And it cannot come too soon. I want to be a peaceful, happy human, pursuing my unimpeded way through life, never having to explain, defend or apologize for my sex.

NELLIE L. McCLUNG
Suffragette

Family, Gender Ideology, and Social Change

One of the most important questions concerning gender is the extent to which gender ideologies affect family roles. An investigation by Zuo and Tang (2000) addresses this issue by focusing on two research questions: (1) are men less likely than women to believe in the equality of roles and, (2) is the male "breadwinner" status predictive of beliefs about gender ideology?

Sample and Methods

Data for this investigation came from a randomly selected national U.S. sample of married persons collected by the Bureau of Sociological Research at the University of Nebraska. As part of a larger longitudinal study, respondents (N=400 married men and 640 married women) were interviewed in 1980, 1983, and 1992. All were between the ages of 18 and 55, 95 percent were white, and 67 percent had 1992 annual incomes between $25 000 and $45 000. The proportion of a husband's income to the total family income measured the independent variable, *breadwinner status*. For example, a husband who provided 90 percent of the total family income received a higher score than a husband who provided 50 percent of the total family income. The higher a respondent's score, the higher their breadwinner status and the lower the bread-

winner status of their spouse. *Gender ideology*, the dependent variable, was measured by the extent to which a respondent agreed or disagreed with statements concerning: (1) the wife's economic role (e.g., "a woman should not be employed if jobs are scarce"), (2) the provider role (e.g., "a husband should be the main breadwinner even if his wife works"), and (3) the women's maternal role (e.g., "a woman's most important task in life is being a mother"). In combination, these three variables indicated the extent to which respondents adhered to a traditional or egalitarian (i.e., equal partners) gender ideology.

Findings and Conclusions

The results signify that over the years studied, both men and women have shifted toward a more egalitarian gender role ideology. The shift, however, is greater for women than for men. One notable exception is in reference to beliefs about a woman's maternal role. Here, men held more egalitarian beliefs than women. The authors caution, however, that this result does not necessarily indicate that women hold more traditional beliefs about motherhood than men. It may be, for example, that women's stress over the lack of childcare facilities outside of the home is responsible for gender differences on this indicator.

Results also indicate that the higher a husband's breadwinner status, that is, the more he con-

tributes to household finances, the more likely he is to hold traditional gender beliefs. Conversely, the lower a husband's breadwinner status, the more likely he is to hold egalitarian gender beliefs. Similarly, the higher a wife's breadwinner status, that is, the more she contributes to household finances, the more likely she is to hold egalitarian beliefs, and the lower her breadwinner status, the more likely she is to hold traditional beliefs.

The authors conclude that the results of their study support what is called the *benefits hypothesis*. The benefits hypothesis holds that men whose wives earn high wages, that is, men who have lower breadwinner statuses, are likely to embrace rather than be threatened by role equality. Given the empirical support for this hypothesis, the authors predict a continued narrowing in male–female differences in gender role ideology.

> The present trend is that men's breadwinner status continues to decline; more and more individuals perform non-gendered family roles. Based on these facts, it may be predicted that the movement toward egalitarianism for both men and women will continue and a further decrease in the gender gap in gender ideology is down the road. (2000: 36)

SOURCE: Zuo, Jiping, and Shengming Tang. 2000. "Breadwinner Status and Gender Ideologies of Men and Women Regarding Family Roles." *Sociological Perspectives* 43: 29–44.

of social ills and became active in the temperance movement, in campaigns for religious instruction, better workplace conditions, improvements in public health and child welfare, and in the development of living facilities for single women. Women's early activism in these areas was often linked to "women's auxiliaries, institutes and missionary societies to spread the word of God" (Errington 1993: 73) established by Christian churches and forwarded as the philanthropic extension of women's "natural" expertise as wives, mothers, and "guardians" of moral virtue.

In 1876, Dr. Emily Howard Stowe founded the Toronto Women's Literary Club, an organization that "in 1883…took a name more revealing of its politics: the Toronto Women's Suffrage Association" (Adamson et al. 1988: 33). Stowe's organization launched a campaign to demand the franchise for women at every political level and for women's rights to education and entrance into the prestigious occupations. However, when compared to their counterparts in the United States and England, early Canadian feminists were more likely to engage in a war of words than in firebrand tactics.

In the decades between the first and second waves of the feminist movement, the position of women did improve in Canadian society. Moreover, as Wine and Ristock (1991: 1) have suggested, "[p]erhaps the most impressive impact of the [women's] movement is the massive shift in the consciousness of the Canadian public in terms of affirmation of women's right to equality, including reproductive freedom, equal treatment in the workplace, and freedom from violence." However, it has been acknowledged that the second wave of the women's movement did not always nor consistently recognize, include, or champion the needs of all Canadian women equally. For example, women with disabilities often found their needs excluded or marginalized (Driedger 1993). Similarly, Wine and Ristock (p. 13) have observed that "though women's organizations provided some support,…[t]he activist work of Native women to change section 12(b) of the *Indian Act*, and its denial of treaty rights to Native women who married non-Native men…[was a] battle fought almost entirely by Native women." As Cassidy et al. (1998: 26) acknowledge in their discussion of "silenced and forgotten women"—First Nations women, Black women, immigrant women, women with disabilities, and poor women—it is only recently that the second wave of the women's movement "has finally begun to address criticisms that White, middle-class feminists have denied, dismissed, and denigrated the experiences of differently raced, abled, and classed women."

The Men's Movement As a consequence of the women's rights movement, men began to re-evaluate their own gender status. In *Unlocking the Iron Cage*, Michael Schwalbe (1996) examines the men's movement as both participant and researcher. For three years, he attended meetings and interviewed active members. His research indicates that participants, in general, are White middle-class men who feel they have little emotional support, who question relationships with their fathers and sons, and who are overburdened by responsibilities, unsatisfactory careers, and what is perceived as an overly competitive society.

As with any grassroots movement, several factions co-exist in the men's movement. Some men's organizations advocate gender equality; others developed to oppose "feminism" and what was perceived as male bashing. For example, the Promise Keepers are part of a Christian men's movement that has often been criticized as racially intolerant, patriarchal, and antifeminist. However, one female researcher and author who attended meetings incognito, that is, as a man, reports: "I'm struck with how close it all sounds like feminism" (Leo 1997).

> As long as a flag waves over a person disenfranchised on account of sex, that flag is not big enough for me.
>
> FLORA MACDONALD DENISON
> *First wave feminist*

Today, issues of custody and fathers' rights headline the men's rights move-ment and have led to increased visibility (Goldberg 1997). Many members of such groups argue that society portrays men as "disposable," and that as fathers and husbands, workers and soldiers, they feel that they can simply be replaced by other men willing to do the "job." They also hold that there is nothing male-affirming in society and that the social reforms of the last 30 years have "been the deliberate degradation and disempowerment of men economically, legally and socially" (NCFM 1998: 7). Still other men's advocates concentrate less on men's rights and more on personal growth, advocating "the restoration of ear-lier versions of masculinity" (Cohen 2001: 393).

Public Policy

The introduction of policy changes and programs designed to eliminate gender inequality have not been without controversy. Here we direct attention to sexual harassment and employment equity and note some of the debates these issues have inspired on Canadian campuses in recent years.

Sexual Harassment Canadian case law has recognized that sexual harass-ment is a multifaceted phenomenon that may include sexual assault; unwanted touching or patting; leering, sexually suggestive gestures; demands for sexual favours; derogatory or degrading remarks; repeated and unwelcome sexual flir-tations, advances, or propositions; the use of sexually degrading words to describe a person; sexist jokes that cause embarrassment; and displaying sexu-ally offensive material. The Law Society of Canada notes that "[w]hether a par-ticular type of conduct constitutes sexual harassment is sometimes difficult to determine" and that although "the severity of the conduct may be the most con-clusive factor...what is determinative is a combination of frequency, severity and persistence" (in Mossman 1997: 244). In 1998, complaints of sexual harass-ment accounted for one-fifth of new complaints brought to the Canadian Human Rights Commission (Dranoff 2001: 73).

There are two types of **sexual harassment**: (1) *quid pro quo*, in which an employer requires sexual favours in exchange for a promotion, salary increase, or any other employee benefit, and (2) the existence of a hostile environment that unreasonably interferes with job performance, as in the case of sexually explicit comments or insults being made to an employee. Sexual harassment occurs at all occupational levels, and some research suggests that the number of incidents of sexual harassment is inversely proportional to the number of women in an occupational category (Fitzgerald and Shullman 1993). Female doctors (Schneider and Phillips 1997) and lawyers (Rosenberg et al. 1997) report high rates of sexual harassment, in the first case by male patients and in the second by male colleagues. Sexual harassment is also a worldwide phe-nomenon. Seventy percent of female government employees in Japan report being sexually harassed at work (Yamaguchi 2000). Finally, sexual harassment is not exclusively a "women's problem." Research suggests that approximately 15 percent of men are subject to sexual harassment (Henslin and Nelson 1997).

Employment Equity The passage of the *Canadian Human Rights Act* in 1977 provided the legal foundation for **employment equity**. Section 16(1) of the *Canadian Human Rights Act* asserts that it is not a discriminatory practice to adopt or carry out a special program, plan, or arrangement designed to prevent, eliminate, or reduce disadvantages suffered by persons or groups because of race, national or ethnic origin, skin colour, religion, age, sex, family status, marital status, or disability by improving their opportunities in respect to goods, services, facilities, accommodations, or employment. Thus, the Act implicit asserts that "employment equity" does not constitute "reverse discrimination." Rather, under the terms of reference of the Canadian Human Rights Commission, charged with administering the Act, an employment equity program may be required as part of the settlement of a complaint of discrimination, as a strategic attempt to forestall the future recurrence of discriminatory practices.

The federal *Employment Equity Act* (1985) required the federal public service, federally regulated companies (e.g., banks and Crown corporations) and all private-sector employers with 100 or more employees that did over $200 000 worth of business with the federal government to have employment equity plans and to ensure that their procedures for hiring, firing, promotion, and training were equitable to all groups. The goal was to redress discrimination against women, visible minorities, people with disabilities, and First Nations people. However, the only penalties that could be imposed were for the organization's failure to file yearly progress reports. In 1996, legislative changes were made to the Act that made it practically potent. For example, the disadvantaged groups to be protected under this legislation were more precisely defined. Employers were required to identify and eliminate barriers to employment, implement positive policies and practices, prepare a plan defining short-term (under three years) and long-term goals, and establish a timetable for the implementation of these plans. The Act is now enforced by the Canadian Human Rights Commission, which has the authority to conduct compliance audits to ensure that "numerical goals (not quotas) are met, to hold tribunals and to levy fines of up to $50 000 for noncompliance with the law" (Dranoff 2001: 57).

Opponents of employment equity argue that, despite the good intentions of its creators, employment equity will not quell discrimination, may well lead us back to the degrading colour/racial/gender consciousness of the past, and may latently function to create resentment of and hostility toward those groups that it seeks to help. Consider, for example, that in August 1999, academics from across Canada wrote letters to officials at Wilfrid Laurier University to protest a job posting for a psychology professor that specified that only women would be considered. "Obviously, at Laurier the commitment to...fairness and the pursuit of academic excellence takes a back seat to social goals like achieving a gender balance in departments. This bodes...ill for your institution, which has gone down in my estimation, as I'm sure it has in that of many academics," read one letter received by the institution. The gender-specific job posting was described by the chairperson of the psychology department at Laurier as an attempt to "address a gender imbalance" in the psychology department at that university; at the time of the posting, the department had 18 male professors and only four women professors.

Nevertheless, academics protesting the job posting also submitted numerous queries to the Ontario Human Rights Commission, questioning the university's use of Section 14 of the Ontario Human Rights Code, which stipulates that a special program may be implemented as long as it does not infringe on other rights—such as freedom from discrimination—and "is designed to relieve hard-

> Canadians have financed an increasingly destructive agenda whose outcome is not unity, equality, or fairness but division.
>
> Martin Loney
> *Political scientist*

ship or economic disadvantage." Although conceding that women have suffered job discrimination at universities in the past, critics of the gender-specific posting argued that women academics were "hardly a disadvantaged group" (*National Post* 1999: A4).

International Efforts

The Convention to Eliminate All Forms of Discrimination Against Women (CEDAW), also known as the International Women's Bill of Rights, was adopted by the United Nations in 1979. CEDAW establishes rights for women not previously recognized internationally in a variety of areas, including education, politics, work, law, and family life. Over 166 countries have ratified the treaty, including every country in the Western Hemisphere and every industrialized nation in the world with the exception of Switzerland and the United States (United Nations 2000a; Rabin 2000).

In addition to many other global efforts, individual countries have instituted programs or policies designed to combat sexism and gender inequality. For example, Japan has implemented the Basic Law for a Gender-Equal Society, a "blueprint for gender equality in the home and workplace" (Yumiko 2000: 41). The new South African Bill of Rights prohibits discrimination on the basis of, among other things, gender, pregnancy, and marital status (IWRP 2000), and China has recently established a Programme for the Development of Chinese Women, which focuses on empowering women in the areas of education, human rights, health, child care, employment, and political power (*WIN News* 2000).

Understanding Gender Inequality

Gender roles and the social inequality they create are ingrained in our social and cultural ideologies and institutions, and are, therefore, difficult to alter. For example, in almost all societies women are primarily responsible for child care and men for military service and national defence (World Bank 2001). Nevertheless, as we have seen in this chapter, growing attention to gender issues in social life has spurred some change. Women who have traditionally been expected to give domestic life first priority are now finding it acceptable to be more ambitious in seeking a career outside the home. Men who have traditionally been expected to be aggressive and task-oriented are now expected to be more caring and nurturing. Women seem to value gender equality more than men do, however, perhaps because women have more to gain. For instance, 84 percent of 600 adult women said that the ideal man is caring and nurturing; only 52 percent of 601 adult men said that the ideal woman is ambitious (Rubenstein 1990: 160).

However, men also have much to gain by gender equality. Eliminating gender stereotypes and redefining gender in terms of equality does not mean simply liberating women, but liberating men and our society as well. "What we have been talking about is allowing people to be more fully human and creating a society that will reflect that humanity. Surely that is a goal worth striving for" (Basow 1992: 359). Regardless of whether traditional gender roles emerged out of biological necessity as the functionalists argue or out of economic oppression as the conflict theorists hold, or both, it is clear today that gender inequality carries a high price: poverty, loss of human capital, feelings of worthlessness, violence, physical and mental illness, and death. Surely, the costs are too high to continue to pay.

Critical Thinking

1 Some research suggests that "[men] and women with more androgynous gender orientations—that is to say, those having a balance of masculine and feminine personality characteristics—show signs of greater mental health and more positive self-images." (Anderson 1997: 34). Do you agree or disagree? Why or why not?

2 The chapter indicates that there is a "gender gap" in the number of men and women obtaining doctoral degrees. Why might this be?

3 What have been the interpersonal costs, if any, of sensitizing Canadian society to the "political correctness" of female–male interactions?

4 Why are women more likely to work in traditionally male occupations than men are to work in traditionally female occupations? Are the barriers that prevent men from doing "women's work" cultural, structural, or both? Explain.

Key Terms

cultural sexism	gender tourism	pink-collar jobs
devaluation hypothesis	glass ceiling	sex
double jeopardy	human capital hypothesis	sexism
employment equity	instrumental roles	sexual harassment
expressive roles	multiple jeopardy	structural sexism
feminism	occupational sex segregation	triple jeopardy
gender		

Race and Ethnic Relations

8

Is It True?

1. Many anthropologists and other scientists have concluded that "races" do not really exist.

2. Canada holds the dubious distinction of being one of the world's largest mailing centres for hate literature.

3. Only in Australia is the proportion of the population born outside the country higher than it is in Canada.

4. When asked whether Canada's cultural diversity tends to enhance or erode the Canadian identity, a majority of Canadians responded that it "erodes Canadian identity."

5. In Sweden, it is against the law to give the Nazi salute.

Answers: 1 = T, 2 = T, 3 = T, 4 = F, 5 = T

We make a great mistake by associating the inheritance of physical characteristics with far more complex traits of human personality and behaviour.

DAVID SUZUKI
Scientist and author

In November 1999, five British Columbian skinheads entered guilty pleas to charges of manslaughter in a B.C. courtroom. The five had beaten an elderly caretaker to death at a Sikh temple in Surrey, B.C. The judge presiding at the sentencing hearing, Judge William Stewart of the provincial court, referred to the five as "social misfits," and noted that the victim, Nirmal Singh Gill, had been singled out for attack and "died simply because he was Indo-Canadian." Although the Crown had demanded that life terms be imposed upon the five men, Judge Stewart sentenced the convicted killers to 12 to 15 year terms of imprisonment (Maclean's 1999a: 33).

Canada is becoming increasing diversified in the racial and ethnic composition of its population. Consider that "Canadians listed more than 200 ethnic groups in answering the 2001 Census question on ethnic ancestry, reflecting a varied, rich cultural mosaic as the nation started the new millennium" (Statistics Canada 2003a: 5). In that year, almost four million individuals identified themselves as visible minorities (Statistics Canada 2003b). Many Canadians might be startled to realize that, amidst such diversity, there are individuals in Canada who would wilfully kill another human being simply because of skin colour or ethnicity. However, many others would not be surprised.

In this chapter, we discuss the nature and origins of prejudice and look "under the rug" to uncover the extent of discrimination and its consequences for both racial and ethnic minorities. We also discuss strategies designed to reduce prejudice and discrimination. We begin by examining racial and ethnic diversity worldwide and in Canada, emphasizing first that the concept of race is based on social rather than biological definitions.

The Global Context: Diversity Worldwide

A first-grade teacher asked the class, "What is the colour of apples?" Most of the children answered red. A few said green. One boy raised his hand and said "white." The teacher tried to explain that apples can be red, green, or sometimes golden, but never white. The boy insisted his answer was right and finally said, "Look inside" (Goldstein 1999). Like apples, human beings may be similar on the "inside," but are often classified into categories according to external appearance. After examining the social construction of racial categories, we review patterns of interaction among racial and ethnic groups and overview racial and ethnic diversity in Canada.

The Social Construction of Race

The concept of **race** refers to a category of people who are believed to share distinct physical characteristics that are deemed socially significant. Racial groups are sometimes distinguished based on such physical characteristics as skin colour, hair texture, facial features, and body shape and size. Some physical variations among people are the result of living for thousands of years in different geographical regions (Molnar 1983). For example, humans living in regions with hotter climates developed darker skin from a natural skin pigment, melanin, which protects the skin from the sun's rays. In regions with moderate or colder climates, people had no need for protection from the sun and thus developed lighter skin.

Cultural definitions of race have taught us to view race as a scientific categorization of people based on biological differences between groups of individuals. Yet, racial categories are based more on social definitions than on biological differences. Anthropologist Mark Cohen (1998) explains that distinctions among human populations are graded, not abrupt. Skin colour is not black or white, but rather ranges from dark to light with many gradations of shades. Noses are not either broad or narrow, but come in a range of shapes. Physical traits such as these, as well as hair colour and other both visible and invisible characteristics, come in an infinite number of combinations. For example, a person with dark skin can have any blood type and can have a broad nose (a common combination in West Africa), a narrow nose (a common trait in East Africa), or even blond hair (a combination found in Australia and New Guinea).

The science of genetics also challenges the notion of race. Geneticists have discovered that "the genes of black and white...[North Americans] probably are 99.9 percent alike" (Cohen 1998: B4). Furthermore, genetic studies indicate that genetic variation is greater within racially classified populations than between racial groups (Keita and Kittles 1997). Classifying people into different races fails to recognize that over the course of human history, migration and intermarriage have resulted in the blending of genetically transmitted traits. Identifying a person as belonging to a specific "race"—or ethnicity—is not a simple task. For example, if you went back in your family history as far as the Norman Conquest of 1066, you would find yourself claiming 41 000 000 ancestors (Fitzhugh 1991: 290). With the passage of time, fewer if any individuals can claim that their racial or ethnic ancestry is "pure." Thus, there are no "pure" races; people in virtually all societies have genetically mixed backgrounds.

The American Anthropological Association has passed a resolution stating that "differentiating species into biologically defined 'race' has proven meaningless and unscientific" (Etzioni 1997: 39). Scientists who reject the race concept now speak of **populations** when referring to groups that most people would call races (Zack 1998).

Clear evidence that race is a social, rather than biological concept is the fact that different societies construct different systems of racial classification, and that these systems change over time (Niemonen 1999). Leggon (1999) explains, "The major significance of race is not biological but social and political, insofar as race is used as the primary line of demarcation separating 'we' from 'they' and, consequently, becomes a basis for distinctive treatment of a group by another" (p. 382). Despite the increasing acceptance that race is not a valid biological categorization, its social significance continues to be evident throughout the world.

Patterns of Racial and Ethnic Group Interaction

When two or more racial or ethnic groups come into contact, one of several patterns of interaction may occur, including genocide, expulsion or population transfer, slavery, colonialism, segregation, acculturation, assimilation, pluralism, and amalgamation. These patterns of interaction may occur when two or more groups exist in the same society or when different groups from different societies come into contact. Although not all patterns of interaction between racial and ethnic groups are destructive, author and Mayan shaman Martin Prechtel reminds us that "Every human on this earth, whether from Africa, Asia, Europe, or the Americas, has ancestors whose stories, rituals, ingenuity, language, and life ways were taken away, enslaved, banned, exploited, twisted, or destroyed..." (quoted in Jensen 2001: 13).

- **Genocide** refers to the deliberate, systematic annihilation of an entire nation or people. The European invasion of the Americas, beginning in the sixteenth century, resulted in the decimation of most of the original inhabitants of North and South America. For example, labelling Aboriginal peoples as "savages" allowed early Canadian settlers and visiting fishermen to commit "atrocities of a most barbaric kind" upon the Beothuks of Newfoundland (Rowe 1977: 146). Indeed, some scholars have claimed that the eventual extinction of the Beothuk resulted from the "sport of Indian hunting": murder committed "for fun" (Horwood 1969) and for the payment of a bounty for each Beothuk killed (Such 1978: 62). Although some Native groups were intentionally killed, others fell victim to diseases brought by the Europeans. In the twentieth century, Hitler led the Nazi extermination of more than 12 million people, including more than six million Jews, in what has become known as the Holocaust. More recently, ethnic Serbs have attempted to eliminate Muslims from parts of Bosnia—a process they call "ethnic cleansing."

- **Expulsion** or **population transfer** occurs when a dominant group forces a subordinate group to leave the country or to live only in designated areas of the country. During World War II, approximately 22 000 Japanese-Canadians were stripped of their rights, had their homes, property, and businesses confiscated, and were evacuated from British Columbia and resettled in internment camps. In addition, the "Deemed Suspect," refugees from Germany and Austria, were deported from England to Canada and interned here as "enemy aliens." Between 1940 and 1943, 2300 individuals "deemed suspect" were interned in Canada within eight camps (Columbo 1986).

- **Slavery** exists when one group treats another group as property to exploit for financial gain. The dominant group forces the enslaved group to live a life of servitude, without the basic rights and privileges enjoyed by the dominant group. In early American history, slavery was tolerated and legal for three centuries. In what is now Canada, slavery was practised by several Indian tribes on the Northwest Coast and by Europeans, beginning in 1500 in Newfoundland. By 1608, Black slaves were introduced by the French with the first slave transported directly from Africa sold in 1629. In New France, there were 3604 recorded slaves by 1759, 1132 of whom were Black, the remainder of whom were "panis" (Indians). The "right" of Canadians to own and sell Native people as slaves was declared on May 29, 1733. Canada prohibited the importation of slaves in 1793; that same year, an act of the Upper Canada legislature ruled that all children in its jurisdiction born to slaves after that year were to be free upon reaching the age of 25 and proposed the gradual emancipation of slaves. Although the last slave auction in Canada was held in 1797 in Montreal, slavery remained technically legal in most of Canada until 1834 when it was abolished for the entire British Empire (Winks 1999).

- **Colonialism** occurs when a racial or ethnic group from one society takes over and dominates the racial or ethnic group(s) of another society. The European invasion of North America, the British occupation of India, and the Dutch presence in South Africa before the end of apartheid are examples of outsiders taking over a country and controlling the native population. As a territory of the United States, Puerto Rico is essentially a colony whose residents are U.S. citizens but who cannot vote in presidential elections unless they move to the mainland.

- **Segregation** refers to the physical separation of two groups in residence, workplace, and social functions. Segregation may be **de jure** (Latin meaning "by law") or **de facto** ("in fact"). For example, Blacks across Canada were treated as inferior from the time they began to settle here, prohibited from entering restaurants, hotels, and recreational facilities, and barred from most professions. In provinces such as Nova Scotia and Ontario, where Blacks were most concentrated, Blacks were often forced into segregated schools. The last segregated school in southwestern Ontario closed in 1956; however, it was 1975 before Windsor, Ontario, became the last municipality to desegregate its public facilities (Henry and Tator 1985: 321–22). In like fashion, because of a range of discriminatory legislation in B.C. "where anti-Asian sentiment was endemic from the 1850s to the 1950s" (Dreidger 1999: 1889), "Chinese, Japanese and South Asians could not vote, practise law or pharmacy, be elected to public office, serve on juries or work in public works, education or the civil service." Consider as well that in the 1920s and 1930s, Jews were automatically excluded from employment in major institutions such as banks and the police and were barred from elite social clubs, beaches, and holiday resorts in Montreal, Toronto, and Winnipeg. Universities set limits on Jewish enrolment (Henry et al. 1995).

- **Acculturation** refers to learning the culture of a group different from the one in which a person was originally raised. Acculturation may involve learning the dominant language, adopting new values and behaviours, and changing the spelling of the family name. In some instances, acculturation may be forced. For example, the 1977 passage of the French Language Charter (Bill 101) established French as the official language of Quebec and made French the legal language of work and the public sector. It also resulted in a situation in which educational instruction takes place almost exclusively in French, with English granted "secondary language status." Similarly, the Canadian government's policy of "aggressive civilization," which was designed to destroy all aspects of Aboriginal culture and which found expression in the creation of native residential schools, is discussed in detail in Chapter 12.

> I do not look back fondly to my college days at McGill University, either. That may have something to do with the then prevailing entrance rules: 750 points for Jews and 600 for everyone else.
>
> JUDITH N. SHKLAR
> *Political Scientist*

> I lost my talk
>
> The talk you took away.
>
> Let me find my talk
>
> So I can teach you about me.
>
> RITA JOE
> *"Men of Peace"*

- **Assimilation** is the process by which formerly distinct and separate groups merge and become integrated as one. There are two types of assimilation: secondary and primary. **Secondary assimilation** occurs when different groups become integrated in public areas and in social institutions, such as neighbourhoods, schools, the workplace, and in government. **Primary assimilation** occurs when members of different groups are integrated in personal, intimate associations such as friends, family, and spouses. The degree of acculturation and assimilation that occurs between majority and minority groups depends in part on (1) whether minority group members have voluntary or involuntary contact with the majority group and (2) whether majority group members accept or reject newcomers or minority group members. Groups that *voluntarily immigrate* and that are *accepted* by "host" society members will experience an easier time acculturating and assimilating than those that are forced (through slavery, frontier expansion, or military conquest) into contact with and are rejected by the majority group.

- **Pluralism** refers to a state in which racial and ethnic groups maintain their distinctness, but respect each other and have equal access to social resources. In Switzerland, for example, four ethnic groups—French, Italians, Germans, and Romansch—maintain their distinct cultural heritages and group identities in an atmosphere of mutual respect and social equality. Similarly, a policy of cultural pluralism, or **multiculturalism**, is evidenced in the description of Canada as a "mosaic" of peoples, which dates back to 1922. Unlike the United States, which, since 1908, has been described by some as a unicultural "**melting pot**," Canada encourages the expression of ethnic and other differences. Indeed, one of the most important recommendations of the Royal Commission on Bilingualism and Biculturalism, appointed in 1963, was that Canada's multicultural heritage be preserved. In a speech given in the House of Commons on October 8, 1971, then–Prime Minister Pierre Trudeau committed his government to "a policy of multiculturalism within a bilingual framework…as the most suitable means of assuring the cultural freedom of Canadians" (in Columbo 1986: 353). When launching its multicultural policy in 1971, the Canadian government confirmed its commitment to an ideal that acknowledged that Canada, while officially bilingual, had no "official" culture—that is, that none of the distinguishable cultures took precedence over the others.

Multiculturalism attempts to foster a society in which diversity is viewed as valuable. In July 1988, the Conservative government passed a bill to introduce the *Canadian Multiculturalism Act*. This act sets forth the government's multiculturalism policy: to wit, "to recognize all Canadians as full and equal participants in Canadian society." Since 1972, there has been a minister responsible for multiculturalism and, since 1973, a Canadian Multiculturalism Council and a Multiculturalism Directorate within the Department of the Secretary of State. In 1991, a Department of Multiculturalism and Citizenship was established to emphasize that multiculturalism empowers minorities to pursue the dual goals of ethnicity and equality.

Currently, Canada's Multicultural Program, which is based on the goals of the Multicultural Policy and the Canadian *Multicultural Act*, has three fundamental goals: (1) identity: fostering a society that recognizes, respects, and reflects a diversity of cultures such that people of all backgrounds feel a sense of belonging and attachment to Canada; (2) civic participation:

I want to get rid of the Indian problem.…Our objective is to continue until there is not a single Indian in Canada that has not been absorbed into the body politic and there is no Indian question, and no Indian Department, that is the whole object of this Bill.

DUNCAN CAMPBELL SCOTT
Then–deputy superintendent general of Indian Affairs

For although there are two official languages, there is no official culture, nor does any ethnic group take precedence over any other. No citizen or group of citizens is other than Canadian, and all should be treated fairly.

PIERRE ELLIOTT TRUDEAU
Former prime minister

developing active citizens with both the opportunity and the capacity to participate in shaping the future of Canada and its communities; (3) social justice: building a society that ensures fair and equitable treatment and that respects the dignity of and accommodates peoples of all origins.

• **Amalgamation**, also known as **marital assimilation**, occurs when different ethnic or racial groups become married or pair-bonded and produce children. Although in most societies, the norm of **endogamy** influences individuals to marry within their social group, there is no doubt that miscegenation or interracial marriages have become more acceptable in Canada in the past few decades. The Project Canada national surveys of adults, which have examined attitudes in this country since 1975, report increases in the percentages of those expressing approval towards racial intermarriage (Bibby 2001: 216) (Table 8.1). Moreover, data from the 2001 census suggests that while the vast majority of Canadian couples marry or cohabit with another from the same ethnic or cultural group, an increasing number of unions involve individuals from different groups. In 2001, there were 217 500 mixed unions (marriages and common-law unions) involving either persons from two different visible minority groups or one person from a visible minority group and one who is not. The proportion of mixed unions was most common in certain census metropolitan areas and higher than the national average (3.1 percent) in both Vancouver (7 percent) and Toronto (6 percent) (Table 8.2).

I liken Canada to a garden. A mosaic is a static thing with each element separated and divided from the others. Canada is not that kind of country. Neither is it a "melting pot" in which the individuality of each element is destroyed in order to produce a new and totally different element. It is rather a garden into which have been transplanted the hardiest and brightest of flowers from many lands, each retaining in its new environment the best of the qualities for which it was loved and prized in its native land.

JOHN G. DIEFENBAKER
Former prime minister

Visible Minorities in Canada

Before 1996, the Canadian census derived indirect information on the numbers and characteristics of persons who were visible minorities from responses to

Table 8.1 *Approval of Intergroup Marriage, 1975–1995*

	1975	1980	1985	1990	1995
Whites and Native peoples	75%	80%	83%	84%	84%
Whites and Asians	66	75	78	82	83
Whites and East Indians/Pakistanis	58	66	72	77	80
Whites and Blacks	57	64	72	79	81

SOURCE: Bibby, Reginald W. 1995. *The Bibby Report: Social Trends Canadian Style*. Toronto: Stoddart, p.54.

Table 8.2 *Couples (Married and Common-law) by Visible Minority Status, Canada, 2001 and 1991*

	Percentage of all couples	
	1991	2001
Total intermarried couples	2.6	3.1
Two different visible minority groups	0.3	0.4
One visible minority and one non–visible-minority	2.3	2.7

SOURCE: Adapted from Statistics Canada. 2003. "Canada's Ethnocultural Portrait: The Changing Mosaic." 2001 Census: Analysis Series. Catalogue 96F0030XIE2001008, p. 45.

questions on ethnic or cultural origin. However, beginning in 1996, the Canadian census introduced a new question that asked respondents directly if they were members of one of the population groups defined by the *Employment Equity Act* as "visible minorities," that is, "persons, other than Aboriginal peoples, who are non-Caucasian in race or non-White in colour." Included under this definition are: Chinese, South Asians, Blacks, Arabs and West Asians, Filipinos, Southeast Asians, Latin Americans, Japanese, Koreans, and Pacific Islanders. Census respondents were asked to indicate their population group by checking one or more of ten mark-in categories.

According to Statistics Canada (2003a), in 2001, 13.4 percent of Canada's total population identified themselves as members of a visible minority. Since 1981, there has been a three-fold increase in Canada's visible minority population and, based on current trends, it is expected that by 2016, visible minorities will account for one-fifth of Canada's population (Statistics Canada 2003a). In 2001, the three largest visible minority populations in Canada—Chinese, South Asians, and Blacks—accounted for two-thirds of Canada's visible minority population. In that year, Chinese were the single largest visible minority population with over one million individuals (3.5 percent of the total national population and 26 percent of the visible minority population) (Statistics Canada 2003a).

Approximately three out of every ten individuals who identified themselves as members of a visible minority were born in Canada, and the rest were immigrants. Some visible minority groups, such as Blacks and Japanese, have long histories in this country, and are more likely to be Canadian-born than others. For example, in 2001, "[a]bout 65 percent of the Japanese were born in Canada, the highest proportion of all visible minority groups, followed by 45 percent of Blacks, 29 percent of South Asians, 25 percent of Chinese, 21 percent of Arabs and West Asians, 20 percent of Latin Americans, and 17 percent of Koreans" (Statistics Canada 2003a: 10). In recent decades, the biggest contributor to the rapid growth of the visible minority population has been immigration (Statistics Canada 2003a: 10). While in the past, immigrants to Canada were likely to be of European descent, this is no longer the case (Table 8.3).

Table 8.3 *Top 10 Countries of Birth, Canada, 2001*

Immigrated before 1961		Immigrated 1991–2001	
United Kingdom	24.3	People's Republic of China	10.8
Italy	16.5	India	8.5
Germany	10.8	Philippines	6.7
Netherlands	8.9	Hong Kong, Special Administrative Region	6.5
Poland	5.0	Sri Lanka	3.4
United States	3.9	Pakistan	3.2
Hungary	3.1	Taiwan	2.9
Ukraine	2.4	United States	2.8
Greece	2.3	Iran	2.6
People's Republic of China	1.8	Poland	2.4

SOURCE: Adapted from Statistics Canada. 2003. "Canada's Ethnocultural Portrait: The Changing Mosaic." 2001 Census: Analysis Series. Catalogue 96F0030XIE2001008.

Almost three-quarters (73 percent) of those who immigrated to Canada during the 1990s were members of a visible minority group (compared with 68 percent of those arriving in the 1980s and 52 percent of those who came in the 1970s) (Statistics Canada 2003a: 10).

Considerable variation exists in the proportion of visible minorities within Canada's provinces and territories. Ontario and British Columbia, which contain half our country's total population, account for almost three-quarters of the visible minority population. In 2001, visible minorities accounted for 22 percent of the population in British Columbia (the highest proportion of any province), 19 percent in Ontario and 11 percent in Alberta, but less than 1 percent in Newfoundland and Labrador, Prince Edward Island, and Nunavut. The majority of visible minorities live in one of Canada's 25 census metropolitan areas (CMAs). The term "census metropolitan area" refers to a very large urban area whose principal or central city has a population of at least 100 000. In 2001, the majority of Ontario's and B.C.'s visible minority populations lived in the census metropolitan areas of Toronto and Vancouver, respectively, representing almost 47 percent of the total population in each.

Aboriginality

The *Constitution Act, 1981* defines "aboriginal peoples of Canada" as belonging to four major groups:

1. *Status Indians.* Persons whose names appear on the Indian Register maintained by the Department of Indian and Northern Affairs Canada under the *Indian Act* and who are registered as Indians for the purpose of special entitlements.

2. *Nonstatus Indians.* Those whose Indian status has been extinguished for a variety of reasons and whose names do not appear on the Indian Register. In former times, Indians gave up their official status when they wanted to vote, to drink alcohol off the reserve, or (if they were women) to marry a non-Indian. In 1985, the federal government introduced Bill C-31, which enabled Indian women to regain their legal status if they had lost it by marrying men who did not possess Indian status. The bill also allowed all first-generation children of such marriages and any Indian who had been disenfranchised to regain their legal status as Indian. In consequence, the number of nonstatus Indians has dwindled.

3. *Métis.* The descendants of Indian and non-Indian unions (principally between Indians and Europeans and, prior to Confederation, between Indians and the French). Previously regarded as "halfbreeds," the Métis have sought to establish their status within Canadian society, past and present. For example, they have suggested that Louis Riel be regarded as the Métis' "Father of Confederation," and argued that Riel "intuitively sensed the future for Canada and wanted to guarantee a place for Métis people in that future" (Kilgour 1988: 48).

4. *The Inuit.* This term, meaning "the people," replaced "Eskimos," an Algonquian word meaning "eaters of raw flesh" that is now considered derogatory. The Inuit became the first Aboriginal group in Canada to achieve at least partial self-determination with the creation of Nunavut (Inuktitut for "our land"). First proposed in 1976 as an Inuit homeland by the Inuit Tapirisat (an association of Inuit leaders), and established by the *Nunavut Act*

of June 1993, Nunavut became a constitutional entity on April 1, 1999. About 80 percent of Nunavut's total population (approximately 27 000) is Inuit (Crauford-Lewis 1999: 1686).

In census years before 1996, the numbers of Aboriginal persons in Canada were ascertained from a question that asked respondents about their ancestry. For example, in the 1991 Canadian census, the question posed was, "To which ethnic or cultural group(s) did this person's ancestor's belong?" and respondents asked to report as many of their ethnic or cultural origins (e.g., English, French, German, and North American Indian) as applicable. In 1996, however, the census included both an ancestry and an identity question. The identity question was: "Is this person an Aboriginal person, that is North American Indian, Métis, or Inuit (Eskimo)?"

In 2001, 976 300 individuals said they were members of at least one of three aboriginal groups: North American Indian, Métis, or Inuit (Figure 8.1). In that year, 1 319 890 reported native ancestry. Overall, native peoples made up 3.3 percent of the Canadian population in 2001, up from 2.8 in 1996. The increase in the Aboriginal population stems from their high birthrate, an increased tendency of people to identify themselves as Aboriginal, and fewer incompletely enumerated reserves. In 2001, children 14 years of age and under accounted for one-third of the Aboriginal population; Aboriginal children represent 5.6 percent of all Canadian children.

The status of Canada's Native peoples reflects the strains of almost 400 years of cultural domination, exploitation, and exclusion. The consequences are not surprising. Native people suffer the lowest levels of education, income, health, and employment in Canada. Social conditions on many Native reserves, the lands set aside for the exclusive use of status Indians, reflects the historical and political neglect that Canada has shown toward its Indigenous peoples. On many reserves, housing fails to meet the most basic structural standards. Less than half of on-reserve homes have sewer or water hook-ups and half can best be described as overcrowded (Frideres 1993). Native men on reserves die, on average, seven years sooner than other Canadians, and the life expectancy for Native women remains six years lower than the national norm (Health Canada

---

Aboriginal peoples are not racial groups; rather they are organic political and cultural entities.

RECONSTRUCTING THE RELATIONSHIP: VOLUME 2, PART 1: REPORT OF THE ROYAL COMMISSION ON ABORIGINAL PEOPLES **(1996)**

Figure 8.1 *Aboriginal Makeup, 2001*

SOURCE: Adapted from Statistics Canada. 2003. "Census of Population: Immigration, Birthplace and Birthplace of Parents, Citizenship, Ethnic Origin, Visible Minorities and Aboriginal Peoples." *The Daily*, January 21.

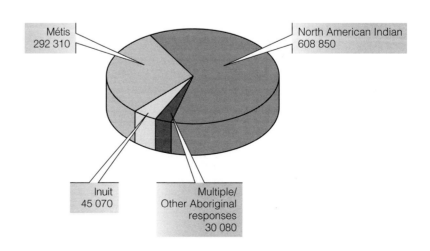

Métis 292 310

North American Indian 608 850

Inuit 45 070

Multiple/ Other Aboriginal responses 30 080

1999). It has been estimated that the suicide rate among the Aboriginal population averages two to seven times that of the Canadian population as a whole (Health Canada 1999).

Native people do not consider themselves simply part of the Canadian multicultural mosaic; rather, they seek recognition of their sovereign status as the ancestral occupants of Canada. In support of this position, the main conclusion of the 1996 Royal Commission on Aboriginal Peoples "was the need for a complete restructuring of the relationship between aboriginal and non-aboriginal peoples in Canada." Doerr (1999: 3) notes that their recommendations included:

> Governmental commitment to a new set of ethical principles…which acknowledged and respected aboriginal cultures and values, the historical origins of aboriginal nationhood and the inherent right to aboriginal self-determination.
>
> That the further development of aboriginal governments should focus on aboriginal nations rather than single communities…[and] the establishment of an aboriginal parliament which would comprise aboriginal representatives and advise Parliament on matters affecting aboriginal peoples.
>
> The need to significantly increase land holdings for First Nations in southern Canada…[and] a recommendation for an independent lands and treaties tribunal to oversee negotiations among federal, provincial and aboriginal governments on land issues.
>
> Adoption of aboriginal health and healing strategies, an aboriginal peoples international university, educational programs to support aboriginal self-government and public education initiatives to promote cultural sensitivity and understanding among non-aboriginals.

However, in its response to the Report, the federal government limited itself to pursuing four objectives: "renewing partnerships; strengthening aboriginal governance; developing a new fiscal relationship; and supporting strong communities, people and economies" (Doerr 1999: 4). The federal government also issued a Statement of Reconciliation, which expressed regret for past errors and a determination to learn from these errors, and committed $350 million to support community-based healing.

Ethnic Diversity in Canada

Ethnicity refers to a shared cultural heritage or nationality. Ethnic groups may be distinguished based on language, forms of family structures and roles of family members, religious beliefs and practices, dietary customs, forms of artistic expression such as music and dance, and national origin.

Two individuals with the same racial identity may have different ethnicities. For example, a Black Canadian and a Black Jamaican have different cultural, or ethnic, backgrounds. Conversely, two individuals with the same ethnic background may identify with different races. Consider for example, that while Jews in China may look Asian, some Jews in Sweden may be blue-eyed blondes, and Jews in Ethopia may be Black.

Canadians come from a variety of ethnic backgrounds. "Ethnic origin," as defined in the 2001 Canadian census, refers to ethnic or cultural ancestry and should not be confused with place of birth, citizenship, or nationality. Before 1996, the census question "To which ethnic or cultural group(s) did this person's

I am a chief, but my quiver has no arrows and my bow is slack. My warriors have been lost among the white man's cities. They have melted away into the crowds as once they did amid the forests. But this time they will not return. Yes, my quiver is empty, my bow is slack.

CHIEF DAN GEORGE
Chief, Native elder, actor

We advocate recognition of Aboriginal nations within Canada as political entities through which Aboriginal people can express their distinctive identity within the context of their Canadian citizenship.

RENEWAL: VOLUME 5: REPORT OF THE ROYAL COMMISSION ON ABORIGINAL PEOPLES **(1996)**

Sadly, our history with respect to the treatment of Aboriginal people is not something in which we can take pride. Attitudes of racial and cultural superiority led to a suppression of Aboriginal culture and values.

JANE STEWART
Then-minister of Indian Affairs

ancestors belong" was accompanied by a list of the 15 most frequent ethnic origins. Respondents, in turn, were asked to mark as many from this list as applicable and were provided with two blank spaces in which they could indicate other ethnic origins that were not included on the list. However, beginning with the 1996 census, the format of the ethnic origin question has been modified. Rather than providing respondents with a list of answer categories, respondents were given four blank spaces in which to indicate single or multiple ethnic origins. In recognition of the fact that "Canadian" was the fifth most frequently reported ethnic origin in the 1991 census, "Canadian" was included, for the first time in 1996, among the examples given of how this question might be answered.

As might be expected, the inclusion of this example "resulted in a major change in the way ethnic origin origins were reported" (Statistics Canada 1998). In 2001, 6.7 million people (23 percent of Canada's total population) reported their ethnic origin as simply "Canadian." In 1991, when "Canadian" was not listed as an option, only 3 percent identified their ethnic origin solely as Canadian, with an additional 1 percent listing it in combination with one or more other ethnic origins. Most of those people who reported themselves as "Canadian" in 2001 were Canadian-born, had both parents Canadian-born, and had French or English as their first language. With the exception of Saskatchewan (where German was the most frequently reported origin) and British Columbia (where English was the most frequent origin), "Canadian" was the most frequently reported origin in almost all provinces. Evidence also suggests that those who identified themselves as Canadian were those who had, on earlier censuses, identified their ethnic origins as English or French. After Canadian, the most frequently reported ethnic origins, whether alone or in combination with other origins, were English (6 million), French (4.7 million), Scottish (4.2 million), and Irish (3.8 million) (Table 8.4).

Statistics Canada's decision to include the ethnic category of "Canadian" has not been without controversy and researchers, government departments, and ethnic groups continue to debate the usefulness of the designation. Some have

Table 8.4 *Top 10 Ethnic Origins, Canada, 2001*

	Percent
Canadian	39.4
English	20.2
French	15.8
Scottish	14.0
Irish	12.9
German	9.3
Italian	4.3
Chinese	3.7
Ukrainian	3.6
North American Indian	3.4

SOURCE: Adapted from Statistics Canada. 2003. "Canadian's Ethnocultural Portrait: The Changing Mosaic." Census 2001: Analysis Series. Catalogue 96F0030XIE2001008, p. 45.

argued that the category should be dropped from the next census because it makes it difficult to obtain reliable information on the ethnic backgrounds of Canadians. According to Jack Jedwab, the head of the Association for Canadian Studies, injecting nationalism into the census only frustrates the work of researchers. "The sheer number of people who identify themselves as Canadians makes it difficult to determine how many people are not indicating their ethnic background" (*National Post* 1999a: A1). More recently, there has been considerable debate over whether the ethnicity question itself ought to be deleted from the Canadian census.

The Québécois In Canada, we have traditionally spoken of the English and the French as "**charter groups**," a term that reflects the historical importance of these groups in Canada's history. Although the *British North America Act* of 1867 acknowledged and enshrined the rights and privileges of the French and the British as the founding or charter groups of Canadian society, "the history of English–French relations in Canada is one of competition between two collectivities engaged in constructing and maintaining a society" (Breton 1988: 557). Indeed, Lord Durham's 1839 description of this relationship as "two nations warring in the bosom of a single state" may still strike some as apt. As Behiels (1999: 909) has commented, "Observers of the continuing debate over Quebec's role within Confederation, and particularly the contemporary Québécois secessionist movement, might be tempted to believe that Durham's assessment can be applied as a general principle to the entirety of the Canadian experience." However, he emphasizes that this would be a gross simplification of the situation and stresses that the character of francophone–anglophone relations has, in fact, "ebbed and flowed in response to changing socioeconomic, political and ideological factors as well as to the commitment of Canada's majority and minority francophone communities to survival and equality."

During the period between Confederation and World War II, institution-building in Canada largely favoured the English. The development of the Canadian collective identity, Breton (1988) has argued, was not modelled on something uniquely "Canadian," but rather was decidedly "British" and "Protestant." Although in the English collectivity, immigration was pursued as the central means for ensuring the growth of the English-speaking population, in Quebec, the concern that French Catholics would be drowned in a British Protestant sea found expression in a natality policy that encouraged childbearing. Nevertheless, with the influx of English-speaking merchants and settlers into Quebec, the English, although a statistical minority, gradually assumed power. Over time, this former minority transformed itself into an elite that dominated the economic cartels that emerged in the areas of finance, transportation, and staples. English-speaking groups came to dominate the Quebec economy and the politico-bureaucratic groups that strongly influenced the federal government.

Urban migration, a postwar industrial expansion, and reforms made during Quebec's Quiet Revolution in 1960 and 1966 encouraged a strong rise in Quebec nationalism. Under the leadership of Jean Lesage, the provincial government of Quebec initiated a broad range of structural and ideological reforms that increased the role of the state and reduced the authority and role of the Catholic Church. A steeply declining birthrate and an increase in the number of non-francophone immigrants (many of whom chose to use English

> We Quebecers are uncertain of our identity and haunted by the fear of a tragic destiny.
>
> LÉON DION
> *Political scientist*

> We are not a small people. Perhaps we come close to being a great people.
>
> RÉNÉ LEVESQUE
> *Former Quebec premier*

> How can you expect the federal government to represent the Québécois people when it pretends that a Québécois people does not exist?
>
> LUCIEN BOUCHARD
> *Former Quebec premier*

at work and for the schooling of their children) reinforced the belief among francophones in Quebec that to survive as a French-speaking society, the French language would have to be aggressively promoted. Francophones became increasingly likely to equate their collective identity with the empowerment of Quebec itself. Those who had formerly referred to themselves as "canadien" or "canadien-français" increasing began to use the name "Québécois" and to assert their belief that Quebec was capable of directing and controlling its own future.

The victory of the Parti Québécois, a party dedicated to Quebec's achievement of independent nationhood, in the 1976 Quebec provincial election notified Canadians of both the strength of French nationalism within that province and the depth of French-Canadian dissatisfaction. Neither the 1969 passage of Canada's *Official Languages Act*, nor the passage in 1977 of the French Language Charter (Bill 101) in Quebec, which established French as the only official language of education, work, and the public sector in that province, extinguished the perceived threat of assimilation.

Since then, "French Canada's attempt to redefine its role within Canada has produced vigorous public debate and considerable political turmoil" (Behiels 1999: 911). The desire to create a French homeland that is predominantly French in character is not, strictly speaking, a "new" idea but one that has circulated since at least the time of Confederation. However, it gained a sense of immediacy in the early 1990s when Lucien Bouchard's secessionist Bloc Québécois won 54 of the province's 75 seats. In 1994, the leader of the Parti Québécois, Jacques Parizeau, announced that a referendum on the concept of sovereignty-partnership would be held the following year. It was maintained that should Canada refuse "to negotiate an economic association with an independent Quebec following a majority vote…[that] Quebec would unilaterally declare its independence from Canada" (p. 912).

With polls suggesting a victory for secessionist forces, Prime Minister Jean Chrétien promised the Québécois a veto over all major constitutional changes and recognition of Quebec as a distinct society. When the referendum vote was held, just more than 50 percent voted "No" to secession and just less than 50 percent voted "Yes"—a wafer-thin rejection of sovereignty that Parizeau blamed on "money and the ethnic vote." A poll conducted in 1995 reported that one in three Canadians and one in two Quebecers believed that "the country…[would] cease to exist by the end of the decade" (*Maclean's* 1999b: 28).

In the aftermath of the referendum, the federal government passed a bill granting all five regions of Canada, including Quebec, a veto over future constitutional changes, and a resolution supporting the concept of Quebec as a distinct society. The federal government also agreed to refer the question of whether or not Quebec had the absolute right to secede unilaterally from Canada to the Supreme Court of Canada. The Supreme Court of Canada later issued the unanimous ruling that Quebec did not have this right under Canadian constitutional law nor under international law. However, it was also the opinion of the Supreme Court that

> if Quebec voters demonstrated a clear, and not just a simple, majority on a straightforward question on outright secession, then Ottawa and the other provinces would have an obligation to enter into negotiations with the government of Quebec. They also pointed out that there was no guarantee that such negotiations would succeed or that the territory of the province of Quebec would remain intact if the negotia-

tions succeeded since the rights of the majority had to respect those of the various minorities. (Behiels 1999: 912)

The problem, however, was that the Supreme Court did not define what it meant by "clear" or "substantial." In November 1999, Prime Minister Jean Chrétien announced that his cabinet had agreed that the federal government would have to act to ensure these terms were clearly defined and tabled a draft bill, the *Clarity Act*, that set out the conditions under which Ottawa would negotiate the break-up of the country following a referendum win by Yes forces. Although the draft bill declared that a simple majority of 50 percent plus one would not be enough to trigger separation, it did not spell out exactly what percentage would be considered sufficient.

In response to this move by the federal government, Joseph Facal, Quebec's intergovernmental affairs minister announced that only Quebec's National Assembly could decide the wording of the referendum and the terms for leaving Canada. According to Facal, "Ottawa, inspired by a Soviet-style law, is trying to impose a real straitjacket on Quebec's political future. It's an assault without precedent on the democratic rights of the people of Quebec to choose the political future it wants to choose" (*National Post* 1999b: A11). For their part, the Bloc Québécois labelled the move "a crime against history"; Quebec premier Lucien Bouchard called Ottawa's move "a strain on Canada's democratic reputation in the eyes of the international community" (*Maclean's* 1999b: 83).

An Angus Reid Survey of Quebec residents, released on December 14, 1999, found that 80 percent of those polled agreed that a clear referendum question was needed and 59 percent said that a clear majority—more than 50 percent plus one—was needed before Quebec could negotiate separation. A second poll, conducted by Ekos Research Associates in December 1999, found that only 30 percent of Quebecers would vote for outright independence in a referendum while 64 percent favoured the status quo. Only 17 percent of Quebecers, the lowest level ever reported in a survey, stated that they expected that Quebec would be a country in five years' time (*National Post* 1999c: A7).

Canadian Immigration

Immigration is, arguably, the area of public policy that has had the greatest impact on Canada's history, economy, multicultural identity, and regional diversity. The growing racial and ethnic diversity of Canada is largely attributable to immigration. However, the history of Canada's immigration policies is far from exemplary. In the 1870s and 1880s, the active attempt to recruit immigrants to Canada for labour-intensive industries was accompanied by the emergence of regulations that sought to preserve Canada's "English stock" by restricting or denying entry to certain groups. These regulations reflected the sentiment that, while useful as labourers, certain groups were "undesirable" as permanent residents of Canada. For example, hostility toward Asians and a fear of the "yellow peril" is clear in the statement by Sir John A. Macdonald, Canada's first prime minister, that "a Mongolian or Chinese population in our country…would not be a wholesome element in this country" (in Sher 1983: 33). Later, Canada's 1910 *Immigration Act* gave the government the formal power to "prohibit for a stated period, or permanently, the landing in Canada…of immigrants belonging to any race unsuited to the climate or requirements of Canada." Amendments

It is true that we were beaten by the power of money and the ethnic vote. That only means that the next time instead of getting 60 percent of the [francophone] votes we will get 63 or 64 percent….We will get our country.

JACQUES PARIZEAU
Former Quebec premier

outlawing the landing of anyone who did not come directly to Canada from their country of origin effectively eliminated the entry of people from India, "who had no choice but to book passages on ships through a third country because no direct routes existed to Vancouver" (Bricker and Greenspon 2001: 287). Regulations imposed in 1919 explicitly prohibited Doukhobors, Mennonites, and Hutterites.

In 1923, Canada's *Chinese Immigration Act* completely barred the Chinese from entering Canada and Chinese persons already in Canada were not allowed to sponsor family or relatives. In the same year, the federal government listed Poland, Yugoslavia, Hungary, and Romania as "non-preferred" countries for the purposes of immigration. Abella and Troper (1998: 108) emphasize that Canada's refusal to accept Jewish refugees from Hitler's Europe reflected the pervasive anti-Semitism of pre-war Canada. They note that when a senior Canadian official was asked by journalists how many Jewish refugees would be admitted after the war, his response was: "None is too many." "It is perhaps no surprise therefore that Canada had by far the worst record of any Western country for providing sanctuary to the Jews of Europe in the 1930s and 1940s" (Abella 1999: 90).

In 1947, Prime Minister William Lyon Mackenzie King pledged to remove "objectionable discrimination" from the *Immigration Act*. Certain blatantly discriminatory features of the Act were removed, but Canada's immigration policy still included "selective restriction." Preferred candidates were those who were British, Irish, French, or American. The Ministry of Citizenship and Immigration was to determine the suitability of other would-be immigrants in light of "the climate, educational, social, industrial, labour, and other requirements in Canada." A person applying to immigrate to Canada could be declared "undesirable" because of "his peculiar customs, habits, modes of life, methods of holding property or his general inability to assimilate."

In the 1950s, the Canadian government, under pressure from other countries of the Commonwealth, began to relax its immigration policies. However, it was not until the 1960s that Canada's immigration determinations became colour-blind. The White Paper of 1966 and the Regulations of 1967 called for the abolishment of discrimination based on race, colour, religion, national origin, or gender (it would not be until 1978 that homosexuality was officially removed as a prohibited category). Immigration was to respond to Canada's need for workers, and cultural enrichment was added as part of Canada's immigration objectives. In addition, the White Paper noted Canada's commitment to the plight of international refugees.

"As of May 15, 2001, 5.4 million people, or 18.4 percent of the total population, were born outside of Canada" (Statistics Canada 2003b). Only in Australia is the proportion of the population born outside of the country higher than it is in Canada (Statistics Canada 2003a: 5). Of those immigrating to Canada in the 1990s, 58 percent were born in Asia (including the Middle East), 20 percent in Europe, 11 percent in the Caribbean and Central and South America, 8 percent in Africa and 3 percent in the United States. Among those who immigrated to Canada during the 1990s, the leading country of birth was the People's Republic of China (Statistics Canada 2003a). Quebec is also being transformed by immigration. "Immigrants make up about 10 percent of the population of Quebec, less than many other provinces, but the fastest growing segment of the population nonetheless" (Bricker and Greenspon 2001: 294).

History is the social memory of human experience.

NORTHROP FRYE
Cultural critic

We Canadians had a terrible record. Little Dominican Republic, which fits into most of Toronto, took as many Jews in as all of Canada [before and during World War II].

W. GUNTHER PLAUT
Rabbi

In 2001, Canada welcomed over a quarter of a million permanent residents and, based on current targets, will accept anywhere from 220 000 to 245 000 immigrants in 2003. Canada divides its immigration intake into three categories: (i) economic immigrants, who accounted for about 153 000 of those who arrived in 2001; (ii) family-status immigrants (a parent, child, spouse and so on of a Canadian resident), who comprised 66 000 new immigrants; and (iii) refugees, who numbered 27 800. Recent changes to our immigration law emphasize the desirability of attracting skilled workers with the selection system placing considerable weight on an applicant's education or trade skills, language proficiency, and "adaptability" (which includes the education of an applicant's spouse) (Janigan 2002). (See this chapter's *Self and Society* feature.)

Canada is a signatory to the 1951 United Nations Convention Relating to the Status of Refugees. The *Immigration Act, 1976* and the 1992 amendments introduced by Bill C-86 additionally provide for the admission of "designated classes" on humanitarian grounds. A UN Convention refugee is defined as a person who "owing to a well-founded fear of being prosecuted for reasons of race, religion, nationality, membership in a particular social group or political opinion, is outside the country of his nationality and is unable, or owing to such fear, is unwilling to avail himself of the protection of that country." The term "designated classes" is used to refer to "a variety of refugee-like situations including mass outflows...disproportionate punishment for violation of strict exit controls (self-exiles) and, for specific countries, the internally displaced (political prisoners and oppressed people)" (Boyd 2000: 84).

Some notable differences are apparent between the immigrant population and the Canadian-born population. While over four in ten (44 percent) who arrived in 2001 spoke neither English nor French, almost 60 percent of those who were adults had a post-secondary degree (compared with 43 percent of the existing population) (Janigan 2002). Compared to those who are Canadian-born, recent immigrants, regardless of their country of birth, tend to be in better health—a tendency that reflects the demands of our immigration requirements (Health Canada 1999).

In other ways, however, recent immigrants are less fortunate. For example, the 2001 Canadian census found that "[t]he average earnings in 2000 of male immigrants age 25 to 54 who arrived in Canada between 1990 and 1999 was $33 900, almost 25 percent lower than that of the Canadian-born...[and] well below the average of $40 100 among recent male immigrants who arrived in Canada two decades earlier" (Statistics Canada 2003d). A comparable situation was found for female immigrants of the same age, with average earnings of $21 959, 24 percent lower than those of the Canadian-born. Compared to the Canadian-born, "the earnings of recent immigrants...have deteriorated sharply. In 2000, male immigrants who had been in this country one full year made 63 cents for every dollar made by those born in Canada," while those who had been in this country for ten years made 80 cents for each dollar earned by workers who were Canadian-born. In contrast, while in 1990 recent male immigrants started out earning 63 cents for every dollar earned by Canadian-born workers, those who had been in this country for ten years earned over 90 cents. In addition, "[t]he earnings gain associated with immigrant skills, among them language and university education, has fallen" (Statistics Canada 2003d).

Reactions towards immigration are mixed. For example, while data from a 1999 survey indicates that six out of ten Canadians feel that cultural diversity

Becoming a Canadian Citizen: Could You Pass the Test?

Canadian citizenship is a relatively new concept. It was not until after World War II that an independent Canadian citizenship was introduced. Before then, Canadians were considered British subjects residing in Canada, rather than Canadian "citizens." Generally, those who are born in Canada automatically become Canadian citizens. In addition, those who were born in another country after February 15, 1977, and who have at least one parent who was a Canadian citizen at the time of their birth, are Canadian citizens. However, others may apply to become Canadian citizens.

To apply for Canadian citizenship, you must be 18 years of age or older, a permanent resident, and in Canada legally as a "permanent resident." You must have lived in Canada for at least three out of the four years right before the day you apply (this three-year residency requirement is waived in the case of children who are under the age of 18). Any time spent in Canada before becoming a resident is counted as half time if it falls within this four-year period; all the time spent in Canada since becoming a permanent resident counts as full time. An individual cannot become a Canadian citizen if that individual is or was in prison, on parole, or on probation in the past four years; convicted of an indictable offence in the past three years; charged with an indictable offence; under a deportation order and not currently allowed to be in Canada; currently facing charges under the *Citizenship Act;* or under investigation for a war crime or a crime against humanity, or if that individual has had his or her Canadian citizenship revoked in the past five years.

To become a Canadian citizen you must be proficient enough in either of Canada's official languages, English or French, to understand others and have them understand you. This translates into the ability to speak and understand spoken English or French or to read and write in simple English or French. You must pass a written test that asks general questions about Canada's system of governance, its geography, history, and people, and the rights and responsibilities of citizenship. This citizenship test includes specific questions about the economy, geography, and history of the region in which the applicant resides. For those who are visually impaired, oral examinations are available. To pass the citizenship test, applicants must answer at least 12 out of 20 questions correctly.

Those who apply for and meet all the requirements for Canadian citizenship are sent a Notice to Appear to Take the Oath of Citizenship, which tells them when and where their citizenship ceremony will take place. At the ceremony, individuals take the Oath of Citizenship; those who wish to swear the oath of citizenship on their holy book are invited to bring it to the ceremony. At the citizenship ceremony, new Canadians receive a certificate of citizenship and a commemorative document that shows the date on which they became a Canadian citizen.

The following questions, taken from a larger list of sample questions that appear on the Web site of Citizenship and Immigration Canada, www.cic.gc.ca, are typical of those appearing on the written examination. Could you pass the test?

SAMPLE QUESTIONS

1. Who are the Aboriginal peoples of Canada?
2. From whom are the Métis descended?
3. Who were the United Empire Loyalists?
4. When did the *British North America Act* come into effect?
5. Which four provinces first formed Confederation?
6. List each province and territory and when each joined Confederation.
7. When is Canada Day and what does it celebrate?
8. Name two fundamental freedoms protected by the Canadian Charter of Rights and Freedoms.
9. List four rights Canadian citizens have.
10. Which legal document recognizes the cultural diversity of Canadians?

enhances Canadian identity, "[o]nly 14 percent...[said] they would like to see more immigration in future versus 43 percent who like the current levels and 41 percent who would like us to scale down" (Bricker and Greenspon 2001: 297). A poll conducted in the wake of the terrorist attacks on the United States on September 11, 2001 suggests a hardening of attitudes towards both immigrants and refugees (Figure 8.2). For example, this survey found that almost one in two Canadians (49 percent) supported restricting immigration from Muslim countries (*Maclean's* 2001/2002). A second survey, conducted shortly before the first anniversary of the tragedy of "9/11" found that over a third of respondents (35 percent) wanted our immigration laws and quotas tightened significantly, while 34 percent wanted them tightened somewhat; only 3 percent wanted immigration rules relaxed (Granatstein 2002).

Managing Canada's increasing diversity has also become a challenge for the federal government and municipal governments, for school boards, and for businesses. According to research conducted by the Privy Council Office, federal efforts will be required to fill an expanding gap in providing English training for the young and to match the skills of new immigrants to job openings. At the municipal level, there will be a challenge to deliver services to a multilingual population. The problem of figuring out who needs what is also essential. For example, immigrants from Vietnam have difficulty with the school system and, while 47 percent of new immigrants fall into a low-income bracket, those from Mexico and Central American suffer from unusually high rates of unemployment. Immigration also poses many challenges to those who experience the process (see this chapter's *The Human Side* feature).

> ■ Canada, of course, is a nation of refugees. Except for the aboriginals, we are nearly all boat people.
>
> PETER C. NEWMAN
> *Writer*

■ Strongly support □ Somewhat support ▨ Neutral ■ Little support ☐ No support

Introducing personal-identity cards for all Canadian residents with a photo and a thumb print

| 53 | 22 | 5 | 10 | 9 |

Sending anybody who claims refugee status without valid ID back to where they arrived from

| 44 | 21 | 8 | 13 | 13 |

Having a common security perimeter around North America that would include allowing U.S. customs and immigration officials at all entry points into Canada

| 31 | 28 | 9 | 14 | 15 |

Keeping all refugee claimants in secure locations with no contact with Canadian society until their cases have been heard

| 31 | 28 | 12 | 15 | 11 |

Making Canadian and American immigration and refugee policy the same

| 27 | 26 | 10 | 16 | 16 |

Restricting the number of immigrants from Muslim countries

| 26 | 21 | 12 | 20 | 19 |

■ **Figure 8.2** *A Hardening of Attitudes towards Immigrants and Refugees*

SOURCE: *Maclean's*. 2001/2002. "Since Sept.11: The Responses Show how Terrorism and War Have Left Their Mark." December 31– January 7: 39.

Immigrant Youth in Canada: In Their Own Words

Between 1996 and 1998, approximately 230 000 immigrant children and youth came to Canada. Almost half came from Asia and the Pacific region. Upon their arrival, many had little knowledge of English or French. Like adult immigrants, immigrant children were primarily located in Canada's large urban centres, such as Toronto, Vancouver, and Montreal. To understand the experiences of these young people more fully, the Canadian Council on Social Development commissioned focus groups of young immigrants to ask them about their lives here. The full text of their report can be found on the World Wide Web at http://www.ccsd.ca/subsites/cd/docs/iy.words.htm. Here, we present some highlights.

Learning the language was the primary challenge cited by most of the young people....Although the majority of participants seemed well adapted to Canada, it was apparent that their sense of belonging to the country was weak, undermined by a strong sense of attachment to their country of origin. Typically, participants described Canada in positive, yet dispassionate tones, emphasizing the economic advantage it offered while describing how they missed their family and friends "back home." "It's just so different here. Everything is different." The vast majority of young immigrants felt that they would never "feel Canadian." For some, this was a conscious decision. "I don't want to give up being Chinese; it's who I am." Others felt that speaking with an accent and the fact that they were not born in Canada meant that they could never feel truly Canadian....

General Perceptions of Canada

Focus group participants most often identified "freedom" and "opportunity" as the "best things" about living in Canada. For some young immigrants, freedom meant the increased liberation from their parents which they had gained by moving to a more permissive society. "In my country, people my age don't date, but here it's normal. My mother doesn't like it, but she understands that we are in Canada now." For others, freedom related more to human rights and freedom from state-sponsored oppression. "Here you can do whatever you want and nobody bothers you. You won't be persecuted for your beliefs or opinions."...Participants also liked what they described as Canada's multicultural and relatively tolerant society, one in which immigrants were not pressured to abandon their roots. "When I want to be Indian, I can be Indian, and when I want to be Canadian, I can be that too...."

There was one aspect of Canadian society that most participants did not like: the consumer culture and the unrestrained pursuit of wealth and status symbols. "Here's it's all about money. At my school, if you have money and the right clothes you are cool."...

Integration

The majority of young immigrants indicated that their first year in Canada was "very difficult." In addition to the severe challenge that

Sociological Theories of Race and Ethnic Relations

Some theories of race and ethnic relations suggest that individuals with certain personality types are more likely to be prejudiced against or to direct hostility toward minority group members. Sociologists, however, concentrate on the impact of the structure and culture of society on race and ethnic relations. Three major sociological theories lend insight into the continued subordination of minorities.

many faced in not being able to speak the language well—or often, not at all—participants said that they were often homesick and they felt socially isolated in Canada. "I remember the first year was very tough. I left all my friends and when I came here, I stayed in the house a lot. I didn't know anybody. I remember wanting to go back, but I couldn't because my parents had decided that we would live in Canada now." "I'm still ashamed of the way I speak English. I know I have an accent and that makes me shy to talk to people."...In some cases, participants described how they gravitated to other youth who came from their country of origin. "The first day my brother and I went to school, word got around that there were some new Russian kids in the school, so all the Russian kids came to my class to see who I was. I started to hang around with them immediately."...

We're Always Terrorists in the Movies

Many young immigrants felt that people from their country were often negatively depicted in films, television, and in the news media. Black and Hispanic people, they said, were portrayed as gangsters and criminals, and Russians as "lovers of vodka" and arms dealers. Immigrants from Algeria felt that Muslims and North Africans were portrayed as terrorists; Haitians and Africans were stereotyped as impoverished and uneducated. "You would think that everyone in Africa is starving to death and living in huts. That's not the case. In the cities, for example, we have things like mass transit systems." Indo-Pakistani people were said to be depicted as grovelling shopkeepers. "Well, there's Apu on the Simpsons."...

Racism

The issue of racism was raised spontaneously in all of the focus groups....Some participants felt that the police "hassled" them because they were "dark-skinned." "My friend and I get stopped all the time, for nothing. He looks like me, he's tall, dark and has 'dreads.'"...Participants agreed that it was difficult to tell whether the discrimination they perceived to be coming from authority figures was based on the fact that they were immigrants or because they were members of visible minority groups. "I think it's probably both."...While most focus group participants—and almost all of those who were members of visible minority groups—had experienced racism or bigotry in Canada,...the majority were rather philosophical about the issue, noting that racism and bigotry are found in all countries and cultures....Many also pointed out that, compared to other countries, Canada's multicultural makeup likely made racism less of a problem here. In terms of solutions, several participants felt that efforts to promote tolerance and understanding should be focused on schools and aimed at both teachers and students.

SOURCE: Abridged from Canadian Council on Social Development. 2001. *Immigrant Youth in Canada: In Their Own Words*. http://www.ccsd.ca/subsites/cd/docs/iy/words.htm. Reprinted by permission of Canadian Council on Social Development.

Structural-Functionalist Perspective

Functionalists emphasize that each component of society contributes to the stability of the whole. In the past, inequality between majority and minority groups was functional for some groups in society. For example, in the United States, the belief in the superiority of one group over another provided moral justification for slavery, supplying the South with the means to develop an agricultural economy based on cotton. Further, southern Whites perpetuated the belief that emancipation would be detrimental for Blacks, who were highly dependent upon their "White masters" for survival (Nash 1962).

Functionalists recognize, however, that racial and ethnic inequality is also dysfunctional for society (Schaefer 1998; Williams and Morris 1993). A society that practises discrimination fails to develop and utilize the resources of minority members. Prejudice and discrimination aggravate social problems such as crime and violence, war, poverty, health problems, unemployment, and drug use—problems that cause human suffering and financial burdens for individuals and society.

Conflict Perspective

Conflict theorists emphasize the role of economic competition in creating and maintaining racial and ethnic group tensions. Majority group subordination of racial and ethnic minorities reflects perceived or actual economic threats by the minority. For example, although 15 000 Chinese were allowed to enter Canada as a pool of inexpensive labour for the building of the transcontinental railway, on its completion, they were treated as unwelcome guests. In 1885, the infamous "head tax" was imposed on every Chinese immigrant to Canada. Initially set at $50, the head tax was increased to $100 in 1900, and three years later to $500—an astronomical amount at that time—in an obvious attempt to restrict the entrance of Chinese and other Asians to Canada.

Further, conflict theorists suggest that capitalists profit by maintaining a surplus labour force, that is, having more workers than are needed. A surplus labour force ensures that wages remain low, because someone is always available to take a disgruntled worker's place. Minorities who are disproportionately unemployed serve the interests of the business owners by providing surplus labour, keeping wages low, and, consequently, enabling the owners to maximize profits.

Conflict theorists also argue that the wealthy and powerful elites foster negative attitudes toward minorities to maintain racial and ethnic tensions among workers. As long as workers are divided along racial and ethnic lines, they are less likely to join forces to advance their own interests at the expense of the capitalists. In addition, the "haves" perpetuate racial and ethnic tensions among the "have-nots" to deflect attention away from their own greed and exploitation of workers.

Struggles over political power also affect race and ethnic relations. When the first free elections were held in South Africa, the Black African National Congress (ANC) led by Nelson Mandela had campaigned on a platform that promised several plans of affirmative action to reverse the four decades of apartheid that barred Black South Africans from political participation and denied them many basic human rights. The White Nation Party, which was trying to maintain the position of political power it had held during apartheid, also promised affirmative action in the 1994 election campaign, but it did not announce this change in platform until two months before the election, when polls began to predict a landslide victory for the African National Congress (Guillebeau 1999).

Symbolic Interactionist Perspective

The symbolic interactionist perspective focuses on how meanings and definitions contribute to the subordinate position of certain racial and ethnic groups. The different connotations of the colours white and black are a case in point.

The white knight is good, and the black knight is evil; angel food cake is white, devil's food cake is black. Other negative terms associated with black include black sheep, black plague, black magic, black mass, blackballed, and blacklisted. The continued use of such derogatory terms as Jap, Gook, Spic, Frog, Kraut, Coon, Chink, Wop, and Mick also confirms the power of language in perpetuating negative attitudes toward minority group members.

For example, research by Donakowski and Esses (1996) concludes that the labels used to refer to minority groups play a role in the attitudes that are expressed toward them. In their research, 108 Canadian university students responded to a questionnaire that assessed attitudes toward Native peoples, as well as three components of attitudes: stereotypes (characteristics attributed to the group), symbolic beliefs (beliefs that the group promotes or threatens cherished values, customs, and traditions), and emotions. Five different labels were used for the group: Aboriginal peoples, First Nations people, Native Canadians, Native Indians, and Native peoples. Among non-Native students, the term Aboriginal peoples was associated with the most positive attitude, followed by Native peoples, Native Indians, First Nations people, and Native Canadians.

Noting that attitudes toward Native peoples were less favourable when the labels Native Canadians and First Nations were used, the researchers conclude that this stemmed, in part, from the symbolic beliefs that came to mind in response to these labels. When labelled Native Canadians or First Nations people, Native peoples were viewed as more likely to threaten national unity than when the three other labels were used. The researchers conclude that "it is possible that when the label First Nations People is used, individuals may be more likely to base their attitudes toward the group on beliefs about the political role of Natives in Canada (a Native activist organization in Canada goes by a similar name: 'Assembly of First Nations'…[and] remind people that Natives are now working within Canadian society toward more autonomy and political power" (p. 90).

The labelling perspective directs us to consider the role that negative stereotypes play in race and ethnicity. **Stereotypes** are exaggerations or generalizations about the characteristics and behaviour of a particular group. Negative stereotyping of minorities leads to a self-fulfilling prophecy. As Schaefer (1998: 17) explains,

> Self-fulfilling prophecies can be devastating for minority groups. Such groups often find that they are allowed to hold only low-paying jobs with little prestige or opportunity for advancement. The rationale of the dominant society is that these minority individuals lack the ability to perform in more important and lucrative positions. Training to become scientists, executives, or physicians is denied to many subordinate group individuals, who are then locked into society's inferior jobs. As a result, the false definition becomes real. The subordinate group has become inferior because it was defined at the start as inferior and was therefore prevented from achieving the levels attained by the majority.

Prejudice and Racism

Prejudice refers to an attitude or judgment, usually negative, about an entire category of people. Prejudice may be directed toward individuals of a particular religion, sexual orientation, political affiliation, age, social class, sex, race, or

> It is never too late to give up your prejudices.
>
> HENRY DAVID THOREAU
> *Writer, activist*

ethnicity. **Racism** is a belief system, or ideology, that includes three basic ideas (Marger 2000):

1. Humans are divided naturally into different physical types.
2. The physical traits associated with each human type are innately related to the culture, personality, and intelligence of each type.
3. One the basis of their genetic inheritance, some groups are innately superior to others.

The perception that certain groups have inferior traits serves to justify subordination and mistreatment of those groups.

Aversive and Modern Racism

Compared with traditional, "old-fashioned" prejudice which is blatant, direct, and conscious, contemporary forms of prejudice are often subtle, indirect, and unconscious. Two variants of these more subtle forms of prejudice include aversive racism and modern racism.

Aversive Racism **Aversive racism** represents a subtle, often unintentional form of prejudice exhibited by many well-intentioned people who possess strong egalitarian values and who view themselves as nonprejudiced. The negative feelings that aversive racists have toward minority groups are not feelings of hostility or hate, but rather, feelings of discomfort, uneasiness, disgust, and sometimes fear (Gaertner and Dovidio 2000). Aversive racists may not be fully aware that they harbour these negative racial feelings; indeed, they disapprove of individuals who are prejudiced and would feel falsely accused if they were labelled as prejudiced. "Aversive racists find Blacks 'aversive,' while at the same time find any suggestion that they might be prejudiced 'aversive' as well" (Gaertner and Dovidio 2000: 14).

Another aspect of aversive racism is the presence of so-called "pro-White" attitudes, as opposed to, for example, "anti-Black" attitudes. In several studies, respondents did not indicate that Blacks were worse than Whites, only that Whites were better than Blacks (Gaertner and Dovidio 2000). For example, Blacks were not rated as being lazier than Whites, but Whites were rated as being more ambitious than Blacks. Gaertner and Dovidio (2000) explain that "aversive racists would not characterize Blacks more negatively than Whites because that response could readily be interpreted by others or oneself, to reflect racial prejudice" (p. 27). Compared with anti-black attitudes, pro-white attitudes reflect a more subtle prejudice that, although less overtly negative, is still racial bias.

Modern Racism Like aversive racism, **modern racism** involves the rejection of traditional racist beliefs, but a modern racist displaces negative racial feelings onto more abstract social and political issues. The modern racist believes that serious discrimination in Canada no longer exists, that any continuing racial inequality is the fault of minority group members, and that demands for employment equity for minorities are unfair and unjustified. "Modern racism tends to 'blame the victim' and place the responsibility for change and improvements on the minority groups, not on the larger society" (Healey 1997: 55). Like the aversive racist, modern racists tend to be unaware of their negative racial feelings and do not view themselves as prejudiced.

Learning To Be Prejudiced: The Role of Socialization, Stereotypes, and the Media

Psychological theories of prejudice focus on forces within the individual that give rise to prejudice. For example, the **frustration-aggression theory** of prejudice (also known as the **scapegoating theory**), suggests that prejudice is a form of hostility that results from frustration. According to this theory, minority groups serve as convenient targets of displaced aggression. The **authoritarian-personality theory** of prejudice suggests that prejudice arises in people with a certain personality type. According to this theory, people with an authoritarian personality—who are highly conformist, intolerant, cynical, and preoccupied with power—are prone to being prejudiced.

Rather than focus on the individual, sociologists focus on social forces that contribute to prejudice. Earlier we explained how intergroup conflict over wealth, power, and prestige give rise to negative feelings and attitudes that serve to protect and enhance dominant group interests. In the following discussion, we explain how prejudice is learned through socialization, stereotypes, and the media.

Learning Prejudice through Socialization
In the socialization process, individuals adopt the values, beliefs, and perceptions of their family, peers, culture, and social groups. Prejudice is taught and learned through socialization, although it need not be taught directly and intentionally. Parents who teach their children to not be prejudiced, yet live in an all-White neighbourhood, attend an all-White church, and have only White friends may be indirectly teaching negative racial attitudes to their children. Socialization may also be direct, as in the case of a parent who uses racial slurs in the presence of her children, or forbids her children to play with children from a certain racial or ethnic background. Children may also learn prejudicial attitudes from their peers. The telling of racial and ethnic jokes among friends, for example, perpetuates stereotypes that foster negative racial and ethnic attitudes.

> We are not born with hatred; we learn to hate.
>
> *Holocaust survivor*

Stereotypes
Prejudicial attitudes toward racial and ethnic groups are based on false or inadequate group images known as **stereotypes.** Consider, in this context, Toronto mayor Mel Lastman's "joke" about travelling to Africa, "What the hell do I want to go to a place like Mombasa?...I just see myself in a pot of boiling water with all these natives dancing around me" (Deziel and Cameron 2001/2002: 21). As noted earlier, stereotypes are exaggerations or generalizations about the characteristics and behaviour of a particular group. Shipler (1998) suggests that negative stereotyping of minorities enhances the self-esteem of majority group members. "If Blacks are less intelligent, in Whites' belief, then it follows that Whites are more intelligent. If Blacks are lazier, Whites are harder working. If Blacks would prefer to live on welfare, then Whites would prefer to be self-supporting" (p. 3).

Prejudice and the Media The media contribute to prejudice by portraying minorities in negative and stereotypical ways, or by not portraying them at all. For example, Mosher (1998) notes that the racialization of crime has a long history in Canada, with the Canadian news media displaying an increasing tendency to attribute the social problem of crime to Blacks and Asians. Research by Claxton-Oldfield and Keefe (1999) on stereotypes about the Innu of Davis Inlet, Labrador, also suggests the potency of the media in shaping public opinion about different racial and ethnic groups. In the first part of their research, a sample of 22 male and 56 female Newfoundland college students (aged 18 to 23) were asked to list the characteristics that came to mind about the Innu and to indicate where these impressions came from. At least 20 percent of the students described the Innu as being uneducated, alcoholic, poor, and isolated, and as gas-sniffers. The two most important sources for the students' impressions of the Innu were television and newspapers. In the second phase of their investigation, the researchers examined the image of the Innu in a daily Newfoundland newspaper for one year (January to December 1996). Headline analysis revealed that conflict and deviance words (e.g., gas-sniffing, sexual abuse, protest) appeared in 44 percent of the headlines of newspaper items about the Innu. The researchers conclude that stereotypes of the Innu mirror the images that are portrayed of them in the media.

Consider as well that in the 1999–2000 television season, a majority (61 percent) of prime time shows had more than one minority character when the entire casts of characters were considered. However, when only main characters were considered, nearly half (48 percent) of the shows had all-White casts (Children Now 2000a). Another analysis of the 1999–2000 prime time television season revealed evidence of progress in the ways minority characters were portrayed: characters of colour were more likely than White characters to be shown as "good," competent at work, and law-abiding (Children Now 2000b). However, stereotyping remained rampant. For example, stereotypes of Asians on prime time television programs included the nerdy student, the martial arts master, the seductive "Dragon Lady," and the "clueless immigrant."

Negative, stereotypical views of minorities are also found on the Internet. "Mr. Wong," an Internet cartoon series appearing on Icebox.com, features a buck-toothed, yellow-faced Chinese servant and his white socialite boss, Miss Pam, who is always insulting him. Finding the portrayal of Mr. Wong offensive, many Asians have demanded that the cartoon be discontinued (Liu 2000). The Internet also spreads messages of hate toward minority groups through the Web sites of various white supremacist and hate group organizations (see this chapter's *Focus on Technology* feature).

Another media form that contributes to hatred of minority groups is "white power music": music with racist lyrics and titles such as *Coon Hunt, Race Riot,* and *White Revolution.* Consider the following music lyrics from the band Berserkr:

> ... Niggers just hit this side of town, watch my property values go down. Bang, gang, watch them die, watch those niggers drop like flies....

Resistance Records, a company that sells "white power" music, sells 50 000 compact discs a year in Canada, Europe, South Africa, South America, and the United States (Intelligence Report 1998). "Skinhead" music, which contains anti-Semitic, racist, and homophobic lyrics, has become a leading recruitment tool for white supremacist groups ("Intelligence Briefs" 2000).

A frightening reality is that every child...is just a mouseclick away from hate.

MORRIS DEES
Co-founder of the Southern Poverty Law Center

Hate on the Web

The Internet provides access to a wide range of information for the over 250 million people worldwide using the World Wide Web. Unfortunately, many Web sites promote hate and intolerance toward various minority groups. In Chapter 9, for example, we refer to a Web site that promotes antigay sentiments: www.godhatesfags.com. Here, we focus on the use of Internet technology to promote hatred toward racial and ethnic groups.

One non-profit organization that combats hate, intolerance, and discrimination has tracked over 400 hate Web sites, many of which are designed to lure children and teenagers into the ideologies and organizations that promote hate (Dees 2000). According to their investigations, "the gospel of hate is being projected worldwide, more cheaply and effectively than ever before, and it is attracting a new demographic of youthful followers..." (*SPLC Report* 2000).

Those who live in countries where laws prohibit the wilful promotion of hatred or associated activities have embraced the Internet. For example, many German neo-Nazi white supremacist groups now use U.S.-based Internet servers. German intelligence officials report that 70 percent of the nearly 400 German neo-Nazi sites are on U.S. servers, and about a third of those would be illegal under German law (Kaplan and Kim 2000). One U.S.-based Web page posted in German offered a $7500 reward for the murder of a young, left-wing activist, giving his home address, job, and phone number.

Although the Internet is used as a vehicle for spreading messages of hate, it is also used to combat such messages. Although it is now offline, for six years the Web site of "HateWatch" (www.hatewatch.org) was devoted to educating the public about the proliferation of hate on the Internet. In conjunction with the release of a documentary, "HATE.COM: Extremists on the Internet," which premiered on Home Box Office in October 2000, HBO developed on its Web site (www.hbo.com) a special cyber-campaign called "Hate Hurts," about the impact of hate on individuals, families, and communities.

The corporate sector can also play a role in the fight against hate on the Web. In January 2001, Yahoo announced it would actively try to keep hateful material out of its auctions, classified sections, and shopping areas. This policy came shortly after a French court ordered Yahoo to pay fines of about $13 000 a day if the company did not install technology that would shield French Web users from seeing Nazi-related memorabilia in its auction site (French law prohibits the display of such material).

SOURCES: Dees, Morris. 2000 (Dec. 28). Personal correspondence. Morris Dees, co-founder of the Southern Poverty Law Center. 400 Washington Avenue, Montgomery, AL 36104. Kaplan, David E., and Lucien Kim. 2000. "Nazism's New Global Threat." *U.S. News Online.* September 25. http://www.usnews.com/ usnews/issue/000925/nazi.htm. *SPLC Report.* 2000 (September). "HBO, Center Document Hate on Net." 30(3):1. Southern Poverty Law Center. 400 Washington Ave. Montgomery, AL 36104.

Discrimination against Racial and Ethnic Minorities

Whereas prejudice refers to attitudes, **discrimination** refers to actions or practices that result in differential treatment of categories of individuals. Although prejudicial attitudes often accompany discriminatory behaviour or practices, one may be evident without the other.

Individual versus Institutional Discrimination

Individual discrimination occurs when individuals treat persons unfairly or unequally because of their group membership. Individual discrimination may be overt or adaptive. In **overt discrimination** the individual discriminates

> Canada is as blatantly racist as the United States. We know it exists. People who don't appear to be Canadian—people of colour—don't get the same treatment. They associate you with your parents' birthplace or your birthplace....It's an issue.
>
> **DONOVAN BAILEY**
> *Athlete*

because of his or her own prejudicial attitudes. For example, a White landlord may refuse to rent to a First Nations family because of her own prejudice against Aboriginal peoples.

Suppose a Vietnamese-Canadian family wants to rent an apartment in a predominantly White neighbourhood. If the landlord is prejudiced against the Vietnamese and does not allow the family to rent the apartment, that landlord has engaged in overt discrimination. However, what if the landlord is not prejudiced against the Vietnamese but still refuses to rent to a Vietnamese family? Perhaps that landlord is engaging in **adaptive discrimination**, or discrimination that is based on the prejudice of others. In this example, the landlord may fear that if he rents to a Vietnamese-Canadian family, other renters who are prejudiced against the Vietnamese may move out of the building or neighbourhood and leave the landlord with unrented apartments. Overt and adaptive individual discrimination may coexist. For example, a landlord may not rent an apartment to a Vietnamese family because of her own prejudices *and* the fear that other tenants may move out.

> Canadians, even when they are racist, realize that it's not a nice thing to be.
>
> NEIL BISSOONDATH
> *Novelist, social critic*

Institutional discrimination occurs when normal operations and procedures of social institutions result in unequal treatment of minorities. Institutional discrimination is covert and insidious and maintains the subordinate position of minorities in society. As conflict theorists emphasize, majority group members make rules that favour their own group.

Although discrimination may have become more subtle and less overt, racial and ethnic minorities continue to experience discrimination and its effects in almost every sphere of social life (Noh and Belser 1999; Stodolska and Jackson 1998). For example, Kunz et al. (2000) finds that:

- foreign-born visible minorities experience greater discrepancies between education and occupation than other groups (less than half of those with a university education have high skill level jobs);
- even with post-secondary education, unemployment rates are higher for racial minorities, especially foreign-born visible minorities (12 percent) and Aboriginal peoples (23 percent) compared to Whites (7 percent) and Canadian-born visible minorities (8 percent);
- given the same level of education, Whites, whether foreign or Canadian-born, are three times as likely as Aboriginal peoples and about twice as likely as foreign-born visible minorities to be in the highest income quintile;
- Canadian-born visible minorities are still less likely than Whites (Canadian and foreign-born) to be in the top 20 percent of the income distribution (Weiner 2001).

Next, we look at the extent and brutality of hate crimes against minorities.

> Bad things happen when good people sit on their hands. Good things happen when everyone tries to make a difference. These clichés are true.
>
> BOB RAE
> *Former Ontario premier*

Hate Crime Victimization

A **hate crime** is an act of violence motivated by prejudice or bias against racial, ethnic, religious, and sexual-orientation groups. The brutal murder of Nirmal Singh Gill described in the opening of this chapter is one example of hate crimes or **bias-motivated crimes**. Others include intimidation (e.g., threats), destruction/damage of property, physical assault, and murder. Section 718.2 of the *Criminal Code* provides that "evidence that [an offence] was motivated by bias, prejudice or hate based on race, national or ethnic origin, colour, religion, sex, age, mental or physical disability, sexual orientation or any other similar factor" is to be considered an aggravating circumstance in sentencing convicted offenders. For example, in the case of *R. v. Ingram and Grimsdale* (1977), it was held that "an assault which is racially motivated renders the offence more heinous. Such assaults, unfortunately, invite imitation and repetition by others and incite retaliation. The danger is even greater in a multicultural, pluralistic urban society." In addition, Section 319 of the *Criminal Code* defines the wilful promotion of hatred against any identifiable group (i.e., "any section of the public distinguished by colour, race, religion, or ethnic group") and advocating genocide as criminal offences, punishable by up to two years' imprisonment. Perhaps the best-known prosecution under the latter section of the Code is that of James Keegstra, a former Alberta high-school teacher who was accused of fomenting hatred against the Jews in his classroom lectures. Keegstra was subsequently charged under the subsection of Canada's *Criminal Code* that prohibits hate propaganda other than in private conversations. The case was later appealed to the Supreme Court of Canada. In 1996, the Supreme Court ruled that although hate propaganda "formed part of protected freedom of expression pursuant to subsection 2(b) of the Canadian Charter of Rights and Freedoms" its prohibition was reasonable and "supported by international documents to which Canada is a party and sections 15 (equality) and 27 (multiculturalism) of the Charter" (Beaudoin 1999: 1237).

In other cases, however, the attempt to curtail the spread of hate propaganda has been less successful. For example, after publishing a brochure entitled "Did Six Million Really Die?" that claimed that the Holocaust was a myth propagated by a worldwide Jewish conspiracy, Ernst Zundel was charged under section 181 of the *Criminal Code*, which makes the wilful dissemination of false news a criminal offence. However, the Supreme Court of Canada ruled that this section of the code denied Zundel the right to freedom of expression, as guaranteed under the Canadian Charter of Rights and Freedoms, and that section 181 was not justified in a free and democratic society.

Canada's 1999 General Social Survey produced, for the first time, estimates of self-reported hate crime victimization at the national level. It concluded that there were 272 000 crimes where the victim felt that hate was the motive with over four of ten (43 percent) believing that hatred of race or ethnicity was involved (Blackwell 2002). However, while the United States has systematically compiled statistics on hate crimes since the 1990 passage of the *Hate Crimes Statistics Act*, Canada lacks a national system for collecting hate-crime statistics, and "there has been little systematic research in Canada upon the nature and incidence of hate crimes" (Roberts 1995). There is also considerable variation in Canada in the definitions of "hate crimes" employed by various Canadian police departments. Some police services, however, such as Montreal's, do not gather any information on hate crimes at all.

The Canadian Arab Federation, the Canadian chapter of the Council on American Islamic Relations, the Canadian Jewish Congress, and B'Nai Brith Canada all report a surge in hate crimes since the September 11, 2001 terrorist attacks. For example, B'Nai Brith Canada, which compiles an annual audit of anti-Semitic incidents, reports that by June of 2002, there had been over 180 such offences, ranging from the burning of synagogues to bomb threats and assaults, compared to 286 in all of 2001 (Blackwell 2002). Six months after the tragedy of September 11, a report prepared by the Council on American-Islamic relations

> ■ Racists are like cockroaches: When you turn the lights on them, they scatter.
>
> **IAN KAGEDAN**
> *Spokesperson, League for Human Rights of B'Nai Brith Canada*

> ■ It cost me $40 000 in lost work—but I got a million dollars' worth of publicity for my cause. It was well worth it.
>
> **ERNST ZUNDEL**
> *Race activist, Holocaust denier*

noted 120 anti-Muslim incidents across Canada, including 10 death threats, 13 cases of physical violence and 12 attacks on mosques and Islamic centres (Ray 2002). The 2001 annual report of the hate crimes unit of the Toronto Police Services reports 338 incidents in 2001 (up from 204 the previous year) and suggests that approximately "90 percent of the increase can be linked to the terrorist attacks...with Muslims being the group most frequently targeted" (*KW Record* 2002).

Levin and McDevitt (1995) found that the motivations for hate crimes were of three distinct types: thrill, defensive, and mission. Thrill hate crimes are committed by offenders who are looking for excitement and attack victims for the "fun of it." Defensive hate crimes involve offenders who view their attacks as necessary to protect their community, workplace, or campus from "outsiders." Perpetrators of defensive hate crimes are trying to send a message that their victims do not belong in a particular community, workplace, or campus and that anyone in the victim's group who dares "intrude" could be the next victim. Mission hate crimes are perpetrated by offenders who have dedicated their lives to bigotry. In Levin and McDevitt's study of hate crimes in Boston, the most common type of hate crime was thrill hate crime (58 percent) followed by defensive hate crime (41 percent).

The least common, but most violent, type of hate crime is mission hate crime. Mission hate crimes are often committed by members of White supremacist organizations that endorse racist beliefs and violence against minority group members. The following message is typical of one received by calling a White Aryan Resistance phone number (Kleg 1993: 205):

> This is WAR hotline. How long, White men, are you going to sit around while these non-white mud races breed you out of existence? They have your jobs, your homes, and your country. Have you stepped outside lately and looked around while these Niggers...hep and jive to this Africanized rap music? While these Gooks and Flips are buying up the businesses around you?...This racial melting pot is more like a garbage pail. Just look at your liquor stores. Most of them are owned by Sand Niggers from Iraq, Egypt, or Iran. Most of the apartments are owned by the scum from India, or some other kind of Raghead....[Jews] are like maggots eating off a dead carcass. When you see what these Jews and their White lackeys have done, the gas chambers don't sound like such a bad idea after all. For more information write us at...

Other racist groups known to engage in hate crimes are the Aryan Nations, Heritage Front, Canadian Liberty Net, Church of the Creator, the Identity Church Movement, neo-Nazis, and skinheads. Not all skinheads are racists, however. Many youth have adopted the skinhead "look" and lifestyle but do not endorse racism or violence. One nonracist skinhead remarks: "Being a skinhead does not mean being a Nazi. I happen to have no hair, a black leather jacket, and army boots, and I get stopped all the time by people trying to preach nonviolence to me. I am a pacifist." (Quoted in Landau 1993: 43)

Strategies for Action: Responding to Prejudice, Racism, and Discrimination

Next, we look at various strategies that address problems of prejudice, racism, and discrimination. These include multicultural education, political strategies, employment equity programs, and diversity training in the workplace.

Multicultural Education In Schools and Communities In schools across the nation, **multicultural education**, which encompasses a broad range of programs and strategies, works to dispel myths, stereotypes, and ignorance about minorities, promotes tolerance and appreciation of diversity, and includes minority groups in the school curriculum (see also Chapter 12). With multicultural education, the school curriculum reflects the diversity of Canadian society and fosters an awareness and appreciation of the contributions of different racial and ethnic groups to Canadian culture.

Many colleges and universities have made efforts to promote awareness and appreciation of diversity by offering courses and degree programs in racial and ethnic studies, and multicultural events and student organizations. Evidence suggests a number of positive outcomes for both minority and majority students who take such courses, including increased racial understanding and cultural awareness, increased social interaction with students who have backgrounds different from their own, improved cognitive development, increased support for efforts to achieve educational equity, and higher satisfaction with their experience of higher education (Humphreys 1999). This chapter's *Social Problems Research Up Close* feature presents a study that identifies various factors that influence first-year students' openness to diversity.

Efforts to recruit and admit historically disadvantaged groups in institutions of higher education have also been found to foster positive relationships among diverse groups and enrich the educational experience of all students. Gurin (1999) found that students with the most exposure to diverse population during university had the most cross-racial interactions five years after leaving university. A poll of law students at two universities also found that nearly 90 percent of the students said that diversity in the classroom provided them with a better educational experience. About nine in ten students also said that the contact they had with students of different racial or ethnic backgrounds influenced them to change their view on some aspect of human rights (*Race Relations Reporter* 1999).

Diversity Training in the Workplace Increasingly, corporations have begun to implement efforts to reduce prejudice and discrimination in the workplace through an educational approach known as **diversity training**. Broadly defined, diversity training involves "raising personal awareness about individual 'differences' in the workplace and how those differences inhibit or enhance the way people work together and get work done" (Wheeler 1994: 10). Diversity training may address such issues as stereotyping and cross-cultural insensitivity, as well as provide workers with specific information on cultural norms of different groups and how these norms affect work behaviour and social interactions.

In a survey of 45 organizations that provide diversity training, Wheeler (1994) found that for 85 percent of the respondents, the primary motive for offering diversity training was to enhance productivity and profits. In the words of one survey respondent, "The company's philosophy is that a diverse work force that recognizes and respects differing opinions and ideas adds to the creativity, productivity, and profitability of the company" (p. 12). Only 4 percent of respondents said they offered diversity training out of a sense of social responsibility.

Political Strategies Various political strategies have been implemented or suggested to reduce prejudice and discrimination. However, although it is readily apparent that strategies such as employment equity (see Chapter 7) can

> If we can dream it...we can do it.
>
> JEFF MacINNIS
> *Arctic adventurer*

What Influences Students' Openness to Diversity?

A study by Pascarella et al. (1996) sought to determine how students' openness to diversity is influenced by four different sets of factors: student background characteristics, environmental emphases of the institution attended, measures of the students' academic experience, and measures of students' social involvement.

Sample and Methods

The researchers collected data from 2290 first-year students at 18 colleges and universities. The dependent variable was a scale designed to measure openness to diversity (see scale). This scale not only assesses an individual's openness to cultural, racial, and value diversity, it also measures the extent to which an individual enjoys being challenged by different ideas, values, and perspectives.

Openness to Diversity/Challenge Scale

(Scored on a Likert-type scale: 5=strongly agree to 1=strongly disagree)

1. I enjoy having discussions with people whose ideas and values are different from my own.
2. The real value of a college/university education lies in being introduced to different values.
3. I enjoy talking with people who have values different from mine because it helps me understand myself and my values better.
4. Learning about people from different cultures is a very important part of my university/college education.
5. I enjoy taking courses that challenge my beliefs and values.
6. The courses I enjoy the most are those that make me think about things from a different perspective.
7. Contact with individuals whose background (e.g., race, national origin, sexual orientation) is different from my own is an essential part of my college/ university education.
8. I enjoy courses that are intellectually challenging.

Four sets of independent variables were developed, each of which consisted of numerous measures. These included (1) precollege/preuniversity variables (including a measure of precollege/preuniversity openness to diversity and precollege/preuniversity academic ability), (2) environmental emphasis of the college/university (including a measure of the degree of racial discrimination at the institution), (3) student academic experiences (including number of social science courses taken and self-reported number of hours spent studying per

prevent or reduce discriminatory practices, their effects are complex. For example, legal policies that prohibit discrimination can actually increase modern forms of prejudice, as in the case of individuals who conclude that because laws and policies prohibit discrimination, any social disadvantages of minorities must be their own fault. On the other hand, any improvements in the socioeconomic status of minorities that result from legal/political policies may help to replace negative images of minorities with positive ones. For example, it has been suggested that employment equity provides minority role models. "Nonwhites in educational and professional positions where they were previously not present function as models for other, especially younger, members of their racial group who can identify with them and form realistic goals to occupy the same roles themselves" (Zack 1998: 51).

Understanding Race and Ethnic Relations

After considering the material presented in this chapter, what understanding about racial and ethnic relations are we left with? First, we have seen that racial categories are socially constructed with no scientific validity. Racial and ethnic categories are largely arbitrary, imprecise, and misleading. Although some week), and (4) student social/ nonacademic experiences (including involvement in clubs and organizations and assessment of students' peer interactions and topics of conversation).

Findings

The precollege/preuniversity measure of openness to diversity/ challenge had the strongest effect on openness to diversity/challenge after the first year of attendance. Women and non-White students had higher levels of openness to diversity/challenge than men and White students.

The extent to which students perceived their institution as having a nondiscriminatory racial environment had a positive impact on openness to diversity. Hours spent studying had a small positive effect, while the number of mathematics courses taken during the first year of college had a small negative impact.

Living on campus, participating in a racial or cultural awareness workshop, and hours worked per week had positive effects on openness to diversity/challenge, while joining a fraternity or sorority had a negative effect. In addition, "the more students interact with diverse peers and the greater the extent to which such interactions focus on controversial or value-laden issues that may engender a change in perspective or opinion, the greater one's development of openness to diversity and challenge" (p. 188).

The findings of this study suggest that colleges and universities that offer racial or cultural awareness workshops can foster students' appreciation and acceptance of cultural, racial, and value diversity. Encouraging openness to diversity may also be achieved by the institution establishing policies and programs that sensitize students and personnel to racial discrimination and demonstrate that such discrimi-

nation is not acceptable. Colleges and universities may also consider interventions to counteract the negative influence of membership in fraternities or sororities on openness to diversity.

Finally, the fact that precollege/ preuniversity openness to diversity had the largest effect on openness to diversity among first-year students points to the need to foster openness to diversity in the elementary-school and secondary-school grades. This may be achieved through multicultural programs, educational approaches, and school policies that discourage and sanction prejudice and discrimination.

SOURCE: Based on Pascarella, Ernest T., Marcia Edison, Amaury Nora, Linda Serra Hagedorn, and Patrick T. Terenzini. 1996. "Influences on Students' Openness to Diversity and Challenge in the First Year of College." *Journal of Higher Education* 67(2): 174–93. Copyright 1996 by Ohio State University Press. All rights reserved. Used by permission.

scholars suggest we abandon racial and ethnic labels, others advocate adding new categories—multiracial and multiethnic—to reflect the identities of a growing segment of the Canadian population.

Conflict theorists and functionalists agree that prejudice, discrimination, and racism have benefited certain groups in society. But racial and ethnic disharmony has created tensions that disrupt social equilibrium. Symbolic interactionists note that negative labelling of minority group members, which is learned through interaction with others, contributes to the subordinate position of minorities.

Prejudice, racism, and discrimination are debilitating forces in the lives of minorities. In spite of these negative forces, many minority group members succeed in living productive, meaningful, and prosperous lives. But many others cannot overcome the social disadvantages associated with their minority status and become victims of a cycle of poverty (see Chapter 10). Thus, alterations in the structure of society that increase opportunities for minorities—in education, employment and income, and political participation—are crucial to achieving racial and ethnic equality. In addition, policy makers concerned with racial and ethnic equality must find ways to reduce the racial/ethnic wealth gap and foster wealth accumulation among minorities (Conley 1999). As noted earlier, access to wealth affects many dimensions of well-being.

Human rights activist Lani Guinier (1998) suggests that "the real challenge is to...use race as a window on issues of class, issues of gender, and issues of fundamental fairness, not just to talk about race as if it's a question of individual bigotry or individual prejudice. The issue is more than about making friends— it's about making change." But, as Shipler (1998) argues, making change requires that members of society recognize that change is necessary, that there is a problem that needs rectifying.

> One has to perceive the problem to embrace the solutions. If you think that racism isn't harmful unless it wears sheets or burns crosses or bars blacks from motels and restaurants, you will support only the crudest anti-discrimination laws and not the more refined methods....(p. 2)

Finally, it is important to consider the role of class in race and ethnic relations. bell hooks (2000) warns that focusing on issues of race and gender can deflect attention away from the larger issue of class division that increasingly separates the "haves" from the "have-nots." Addressing class inequality must, suggests hooks, be part of any meaningful strategy to reduce inequalities suffered by minority groups.

Critical Thinking

1 At colleges and universities around North America, a number of professors are endorsing race-based theories of intelligence, Holocaust denial, and other racist ideas. For example, Professor J. Philippe Rushton of the University of Western Ontario and Professor Glayde Whitney of Florida State have both described Blacks as having smaller brains. Professor Edward M. Miller of the University of New Orleans has concluded that Blacks are "small-headed, over-equipped in genitalia, oversexed, hyper-violent and...unintelligent" ("Hate on Campus" 2000: 9). Associate Professor Arthur Butz of Northwest University publicly rejects the claim that millions of Jews were exterminated in the Holocaust ("Hate on Campus" 2000). How should institutions of higher learning respond to such claims by faculty members? What role does the right to free speech and academic freedom play?

2 Burnet (1999) has noted that government policies of multiculturalism have been attacked "as a means of buttressing Anglo-Saxon dominance, by diverting the efforts of the non-French and the non-English from political and economic affairs into cultural activities." Do you agree with this criticism? Why or why not?

3 Lieberman (1997) asked university faculty members in five disciplines (biology, biological anthropology, cultural anthropology, psychological anthropology, and developmental psychology) to indicate agreement or disagreement with the statement "There are biological races in the species Homo sapiens." In each of the disciplines, women were more likely than men to reject race as a biological reality. Why do you think women in Lieberman's study were more likely than men to reject the concept of race?

4 Should race be a factor in adoption placements? Should people be discouraged from adopting a child who is of a different race than the adoptive parents are? Why or why not?

5 Under Swedish law, giving Nazi salutes is a crime (Lofthus 1998). Do you think that the social benefits of outlawing racist expressions outweigh the impingement on free speech? Do you think such a law should be proposed in Canada? Why or why not?

Key Terms

acculturation

adaptive discrimination

amalgamation

assimilation (primary and secondary)

authoritarian-personality theory

aversive racism

bias-motivated crimes

charter groups

colonialism

de facto segregation

de jure segregation

discrimination

diversity training

endogamy

ethnicity

expulsion

frustration-aggression theory

genocide

hate crime

individual discrimination

institutional discrimination

marital assimilation

melting pot

modern racism

multicultural education

multiculturalism

overt discrimination

pluralism

population transfer

populations

prejudice

race

racism

scapegoating theory

segregation

slavery

stereotype

9

Sexual Orientation

Is It True?_____

1. In some countries, homosexual behaviour is punishable by the death penalty.

2. People who believe that gay individuals are born that way tend to be more tolerant of gays than are people who believe that gay individuals choose their sexual orientation.

3. Most countries throughout the world have laws that protect gay individuals from discrimination because of sexual orientation.

4. Homosexuality is classified as a mental disorder.

5. Worldwide, most laws prohibiting homosexual behaviour apply to female rather than male homosexuality.

Answers: 1 = T, 2 = T, 3 = F, 4 = F, 5 = T

I have friends. Some of them are straight....Year after year I continue to realize that the facts of my life are irrelevant to them and that I am only half listened to, that I am an appendage to the doings of a greater world, a world of power and privilege...a world of exclusion. "That's not true," argue my straight friends. There is only one certainty in the politics of power; those left out beg for inclusion, while the insiders claim that they already are. Men do it to women, whites do it to blacks, and everyone does it to queers.

GAY PRIDE PARADE FLIER

On November 17, 2001, 42-year-old Aaron Webster was beaten to death in a vicious attack in a parking lot in Stanley Park, Vancouver, in what is believed to have been British Columbia's first lethal incident of "gay bashing." Webster had been bludgeoned with either a baseball bat or a pool cue by a group of three to four men and left to die. At a memorial service for Webster that drew more than 1500 participants, Vancouver Police Inspector Dave Jones referred to Webster as the victim of a "hate crime, pure and simple" and promised that his department would "do everything in our power" to find the perpetrators and "bring them to justice" (Associated Press 2001; Nagle 2001).

Of the many issues raised by Aaron Webster's death, one was the adequacy of the definition of a "hate crime" under Canada's Criminal Code (Bush and Sainz 2001). Although identified by Inspector Jones as such, the Criminal Code of Canada defines hate crimes as criminal acts motivated by a victim's race, religion, or ethnicity. Under this definition, crimes committed against sexual orientation minorities are not, technically speaking, "hate crimes" (Wetzel 2001). Although in 1999, following the gay bashing of a Fredericton student, Justice Minister Anne McLellan announced that she would introduce amendments to the Code to protect lesbians and gays from hate crimes, she did not do so.

A second question raised by Webster's death was how seriously society responds to crimes against gays and lesbians. Amendments to the Criminal Code made in 1996 do specify sentencing enhancement principles where "there is evidence that the offence was motivated by bias, prejudice or hate based on race, national or ethnic origin, language, colour, religion, sex, age, mental or physical disability, sexual orientation, or any other similar factor." As a result, assaulting a person during an argument generally carries a lighter sentence than assaulting a person because he is gay or Jewish or Black. However, in spite of this provision, "gay-bashers are often able to rely on the discredited 'homosexual panic' defence, claiming they were justified in committing murder because the victim 'came on' to them" (EGALE 2001).

In this chapter we examine prejudice and discrimination toward homosexual (or gay) women (also known as lesbians), homosexual (or gay) men, and bisexual individuals. It is beyond the scope of this chapter to explore how sexual diversity and its cultural meanings vary throughout the world. Rather, this chapter focuses on Western conceptions of diversity in sexual orientation. The term "**sexual orientation**" refers to the classification of individuals as hetero-sexual, bisexual, or homosexual, based on their emotional and sexual attrac-tions, relationships, self-identity, and lifestyle. **Heterosexuality** refers to the predom-inance of emotional and sexual attraction to persons of the other sex. **Homo-sexuality** refers to the predominance of emotional and sexual attraction to persons of the same sex, and **bisexuality** to emotional and sexual attraction to members of both sexes. Lesbians, gays, and bisexuals, sometimes referred to col-lectively as **lesbigays**, are considered to be part of a larger population referred to as the transgendered community. **Transgendered individuals** include per-sons who do not fit neatly into either the male or female category, or their behaviour is not congruent with the roles and expectations for their sex in the society in which they live (Bullough 2000; Gilbert 2000; Herdt 2001). Trans-gendered individuals include not only homosexuals and bisexuals, but also cross-dressers (individuals who occasionally dress in the clothing of the oppo-site sex), transsexuals (individuals who have undergone hormone treatment and sex reassignment surgery to achieve a new identity as a member of the bio-logically opposite sex), and shemales, a term used to refer to those that who, while setting out on the road to sexual reassignment, have stopped "on the safety island in the middle of the boulevard" (e.g., a man who has "used artifi-cial hormones—and perhaps surgery—to develop breasts, buttocks, and hips but retains male genitalia" (Fulford 2002: 64). Much of the current literature on the treatment and political and social agendas of the lesbigay population includes other members of the transgendered community; hence the term **LGBT** is often used to refer collectively to lesbians, gays, bisexuals, and transgendered individ-uals (Craig 2002; Goldie 2001).

We begin by summarizing the legal status of lesbians and gay men around the world. Then, we discuss the prevalence of homosexuality, heterosexuality, and bisexuality, review biological and environmental explanations for sexual orien-tation diversity, and apply sociological theories to better understand societal reactions to sexual diversity. The chapter ends with a discussion of strategies to reduce antigay prejudice and discrimination.

The Global Context: A World View of Laws Pertaining to Homosexuality

Homosexual behaviour has existed throughout human history and, in most, perhaps all, human societies (Kirkpatrick 2000). A global perspective on laws and social attitudes regarding homosexuality reveals that countries vary tremendously in their treatment of homosexuals—from intolerance and crimi-nalization to acceptance and legal protection. A global overview of laws that criminalize sexual behaviour between consenting adults indicates that such behaviour is illegal in 85 countries ("Sodomy Fact Sheet: A Global Overview" 2000). In 52 of these countries, laws criminalizing same-sex sexual behaviour apply to both female and male homosexuality. In 33 of these countries, laws criminalizing same-sex sexual behaviour apply to male homosexuality only (see also Brown 2000). Legal penalties for violating laws that prohibit homosexual sexual acts vary. In 10 countries, individuals found guilty of engaging in same-sex sexual behaviour may receive the death penalty (see Table 9.1). For example, a Somali lesbian couple were sentenced to death for "exercising

■ **Table 9.1** *Countries in which Homosexual Acts Are Subject to the Death Penalty*

Mauritania	Sudan
Afghanistan	Pakistan
Chechen Republic	Iran
Saudi Arabia	United Arab Emirates
Yemen	Somalia

SOURCES: The International Lesbian and Gay Association. 1999. "World Legal Survey, 1999." www.liga.irg; "Jail Death Sentences in Africa." 2001 (February 21). PlanetOut.com. http://www.planetout.com/news/article-print.html?2001/02/21/2.

unnatural behaviour" ("Jail, Death Sentences in Africa" 2001). Although executions in this region are performed by firing squads, religious tradition dictates that those convicted of homosexuality should either have a wall pushed over onto them or be thrown off a roof or other high place.

In general, countries throughout the world are moving toward increased legal protection of sexual orientation minorities. Between 1984 and 1995, 86 countries changed their policies regarding sex between men, sex between women, or both, and nearly every change was toward increased liberalization of policies regarding same-sex sexual behaviour (Frank and McEneaney 1999). According to the International Gay and Lesbian Human Rights Commission (1999), 22 countries have national laws that ban various forms of discrimination against gays, lesbians, and bisexuals. In 1996 South Africa became the first country in the world to include in its constitution a clause banning discrimination based on sexual orientation. Canada, Fiji, and Ecuador also have constitutions that ban discrimination based on sexual orientation ("Constitutional Protection" 1999).

In Brazil, a gay, lesbian, bisexual, or transgendered individual is murdered on the average of every two days. However, the brutal gay-bashing murder of Edson Neris da Silva by a gang of about 30 people resulted in what some believe is Brazil's first trial and convictions in an antigay hate crime ("Brazilian Killers Sentenced" 2001). The first two gang members tried for this murder were sentenced to 21 years in prison.

In recent years legal recognition of same-sex relationships has become more widespread. In June 2000, Canada enacted a bill that extends to same-sex couples and unmarried heterosexual couples who have lived together for at least a year all the benefits and obligations of married couples (*LAWbriefs* 2000) (more recent changes are discussed later in this chapter). In the same month, Brazil extended to same-sex couples the right to inherit each other's pension and social security benefits. The law represents the first time a Latin American country has legally recognized gay relationships (*LAWbriefs* 2000). Also in 2000, the Netherlands enacted a law allowing same-sex marriages. Just after the stroke of midnight on the day the Dutch law went into effect (April 1, 2001), the world's first fully legal same-sex civil marriages took place in Amsterdam (Drinkwater 2001). Same-sex married couples and opposite-sex married couples in the Netherlands will be treated identically, with two exceptions. Unlike opposite-sex marriages, same-sex couples married in the Netherlands are unlikely to have their marriages recognized as fully legal abroad. Regarding children, parental rights will not automatically be granted to the non-biological spouse in gay couples. To become a fully legal parent, the spouse of the biological parent must adopt the child.

In addition, countries that recognize gay and lesbian partnerships include Denmark, Norway, Sweden, Iceland, Greenland, France, and Portugal (Alsdorf 2001; Gay and Lesbian International Lobby 2000). Other European countries are considering same-sex partnership laws include Finland, Switzerland, Germany, Luxembourg, Belgium, and Spain. In the United States, only one state—Vermont—gives legal recognition to a same-sex "**civil union**." As of January 2001, 35 U.S. states had antigay-marriage laws, declaring that they will *not* recognize same-sex marriages (National Gay and Lesbian Task Force 2001).

Clearly, public legitimation of same-sex relations is occurring in the global society. Human rights treaties and transnational social movement organizations have increasingly asserted the rights of persons to engage in same-sex relations. International organizations such as Amnesty International, which resolved in 1991 to defend those imprisoned for homosexuality, the International Lesbian and Gay Association (founded in 1978), and the International Gay and Lesbian Human Rights Commission (founded in 1990), continue to fight prejudice and discrimination against lesbians and gays. Despite the worldwide movement toward increased acceptance and protection of homosexual individuals, the status and rights of lesbians and gays in Canada continues to be one of the most divisive issues in Canadian society.

Homosexuality and Bisexuality: Prevalence and Explanations

In early research on sexual behaviour, Kinsey and his colleagues (1953) found that a substantial proportion of respondents reported having had same-sex sexual experiences. The data revealed that 37 percent of men and 13 percent of women had at least one homosexual experience since adolescence. Yet, very few of the individuals in Kinsey's research reported exclusive homosexual behaviour. These data led Kinsey to conclude that most people are not exclusively heterosexual or homosexual. Rather, Kinsey suggested an individual's sexual orientation may have both heterosexual and homosexual elements. In other words, Kinsey suggested that heterosexuality and homosexuality represent two ends of a sexual orientation continuum, and that most individuals are neither entirely homosexual nor entirely heterosexual, but fall somewhere within the continuum. Kinsey's early sex research demonstrated the difficulty of classifying individuals as heterosexual, homosexual, or bisexual, as the distinctions between these classifications are not as clear-cut as some people believe. While Canadian data is lacking, recent research conducted in the United States has confirmed Kinsey's finding that sexual behaviour, desire, and sexual orientation identity do not always match. In a national study of U.S. adults aged 18 to 59, researchers focused on three aspects of homosexuality: sexual attraction to persons of the same sex, sexual behaviour with people of the same sex, and homosexual self-identification (Michael et al. 1994). This survey found that 4 percent of women and 6 percent of men said they are sexually attracted to individuals of the same sex, and 4 percent of women and 5 percent of men reported that they had sexual relations with a same-sex partner after age 18. Yet less than 3 percent of men and less than 2 percent of women identified themselves as homosexual or bisexual (Michael et al. 1994). What these data tell us is that first, "those who acknowledge homosexual desires may be far more numerous than those who actually act on those desires" (Black et al. 2000: 140). Second, not all people who are sexually attracted to or have had sexual relations with individuals of the same sex view themselves as homosexual or bisexual.

Other data suggest that the percentage of women and men reporting same-sex sexual partnering in the past five years increased from 0.2 percent in 1988 to 2.8 percent in 1998 (Butler 2000). These increases may have resulted from declining social and legal constraints against same-sex sexual behaviour, as well as more positive images of gay men and lesbians in the media, which have made it easier for people to recognize and act on their sexual attraction to others of their same sex. This research also notes that

> These estimates of same-gender sex partnering should not be taken as estimates of the proportion of the population that is gay or lesbian. Some people may engage in same-gender sexual activity and yet identify as heterosexual, whereas other people may identify as gay or lesbian but may not have been sexually active in recent years. (Butler 2000: 342)

Origins of Sexual Orientation Diversity: Nature or Nurture?

One of the prevailing questions raised regarding homosexuality and bisexuality centres on its origin or "cause." However, questions about the "causes" of sexual orientation are typically concerned with the origins of homosexuality and bisexuality. Because heterosexuality is considered normative and "natural," causes of heterosexuality are rarely considered.

Despite the growing research on this topic, a concrete cause of sexual orientation diversity has yet to be discovered. Many researchers believe that an interaction of biological and environmental forces is involved in the development of one's sexual orientation (De Cecco and Parker 1995).

Environmental Explanations of Sexual Orientation According to Doell (1995), "...we all probably develop, from infancy, the capacity to have heterosexual, homosexual, or bisexual relationships" (p. 352). Environmental theories propose that such factors as availability of sexual partners, early sexual experiences, and sexual reinforcement influence subsequent sexual orientation. The degree to which early sexual experiences have been negative or positive has been hypothesized as influencing sexual orientation. Having pleasurable same-sex experiences would be likely to increase the probability of a homosexual orientation. By the same token, early traumatic sexual experiences have been suggested as causing fear of heterosexual activity. However, a study that compared sexual histories of lesbian and heterosexual women found no differences in the incidence of traumatic experiences with men (Brannock and Chapman 1990).

Biological Origins of Sexual Orientation Biological explanations of sexual orientation diversity usually focus on genetic or hormonal differences between heterosexuals and homosexuals. In an overview of genetics research on homosexual and heterosexual orientations, Pillard and Bailey (1998) conclude that genes account for at least half of the variance in sexual orientation. Their review of family, twin, and adoptee studies indicate that homosexuality (and thus heterosexuality) runs in families. However, the actual empirical research attempting to isolate a biological-cause basis for sexuality is less than convincing in its findings.

For example, science has yet to identify a "homosexuality" gene despite the assertion of some researchers, such as Hamer et al. (1993), who claim to have discovered *statistical* evidence for its existence. In their examination of 40 pairs of gay brothers, Hamer et al. note a significantly higher number (33 out of 40) than expected (20 out of 40) of the pairs shared matching DNA in a region called Xq28 at the tip of the X chromosome, a chromosome males genetically inherit from their biological mothers. The researchers focused on this chromosome after noting in previous research that more gay male relatives appear to be found on the mother's side of the family. Hamer and his research team did not actually isolate a specific gene, or even a specific set of genes, existing within that chromosomal region; they only provided the statistics-based suggestion that such genes must be there. Nor do they specifically account for the homosexuality of those brothers who do not possess the matching DNA. Nor have Hamer et al. examined heterosexual brothers for the existence or nonexistence of matching DNA in the Xq28 region to determine whether heterosexual brothers are similar to or different from homosexual brothers (Peele and DeGrandpre 1995). Consider as well that the results of a recent Canadian study (Rice et al. 1999), based on 62 gay male sibling pairs that analyzed the microsatellite markers at position Xq28 did not support Hamer's suggestion of a X-linked gene underlying homosexuality. Nevertheless, while the evidence for any link among humans between genes, hormones (e.g., such as testosterone), and sexual behaviour is very unclear, researchers continue in the quest to isolate a biological cause for human sexuality. This chapter's *Social Problems Research Up Close* feature highlights one such recent effort.

Most gays and gay rights advocates believe that homosexuality is an inherited, inborn trait. One study of homosexual men reported that 90 percent believed that they were born with their homosexual orientation; only 4 percent believed that environmental factors were the sole cause (Lever 1994). There is also evidence that members of the general population increasingly subscribe to the notion that homosexuality is something that a person is "born with" (Gallup Organization 2000).

Can Homosexuals Change Their Sexual Orientation? Individuals who believe that homosexuality is biologically based tend to be more accepting of homosexuality. In contrast, "those who believe homosexuals choose their sexual orientation are far less tolerant of gays and lesbians and more likely to conclude homosexuality should be illegal than those who think sexual orientation is not a matter of personal choice" (Rosin and Morin 1999: 8). Individuals who believe that homosexuals choose their sexual orientation also tend to think that homosexuals can and should change their sexual orientation. Various forms of **reparative therapy** or conversion therapy are dedicated to changing homosexuals' sexual orientation. Some religious organizations sponsor ex-gay ministries, which claim to "cure" homosexuals and transform them into heterosexuals through prayer and other forms of "therapy." Ex-gay ministries attract new recruits by claiming that there is a "cure" for people who are unhappy being gay. Critics of ex-gay ministries take a different approach:

> The cure for unhappiness is not the "ex-gay" ministries—but coming out with dignity and self-respect. It is not gay men and lesbians who need to change...but nega-

What Next? Sexual Orientation and Penis Size

A Canadian professor studying an apparent relationship between penis size and sexual orientation says gay men have longer members than heterosexual men. "If size matters, it may give us clues to sexual development," said Anthony Bogaert, a sexologist in the health studies department at Brock University in St. Catherines, Ont....A study co-written by Prof. Bogaert and published in the June edition of the international journal *Archives of Sexual Behaviour* concluded the average erect penis size of homosexuals is 16.64 cm (6.46 inches) but only 15.6 cm (6.14 inches) for heterosexuals.

The difference in length may suggest that biological factors, such as fluctuations in the levels of testosterone or other pre-natal hormones in the mother's womb, could influence the size of the penis and sexual orientation, the article says. "It may suggest some sort of biological factors involved in sexual orientation development, but the data are open to interpretation at this point," said Prof. Bogaert, who co-authored *The Relation Between Sexual Orientation and Penile Size* with California State University psychology professor Scott Hershberger. "It's rather an interesting, titillating finding."

But Dr. Miriam Kaufman, a pediatrician at the Hospital for Sick Children in Toronto and an associate professor at the University of Toronto, questions why society needs studies that try to determine the reasons for homosexuality. "Any gay man will tell you that he has a longer penis than a straight man," laughed Dr. Kaufman, an expert in sexuality. "To start getting into things like measuring penis size is ridiculous. It's another group of people who will say, 'See, penis size is important.'"

The study relied on data collected between 1938 and 1963 by the Indiana-based Kinsey Institute for Research in Sex, Gender and Reproduction, which asked 4187 heterosexuals and 935 homosexuals to measure themselves with a ruler at home and mail in the lengths. The Kinsey data has been used for many research projects, but this appears to be the first attempt to determine sexual orientation based on penis size.

Dr. Kaufman called the data suspect, questioning the reliability of the participants' sexual orientations and their self-measurements. "Penis size is not exactly a value-neutral matter in our culture." Prof. Bogaert allowed there may be problems with people misrepresenting their size but he argued the Kinsey material has stood up to other medical studies and believes any exaggeration would come equally from gay

and straight men—so the results can be relied upon. The study also reported that factors such as education, height, and weight did not play a significant role in penis size, noting the circumference of the erect organ was also found to be larger for homosexuals (12.6 cm) than heterosexuals (12.2 cm). A more conclusive study would require clinical measurements, but Prof. Bogaert added it would take years to collect data from such a large sample size.

Prof. Bogaert argued that studies tracking the biological reasoning behind sexual orientation also give credence to those who insist that being gay is not a choice. [However] Alison Kemper, executive director of the 519 Church Street Community Centre, a Toronto organization for gays and lesbians, called the study far-fetched and silly....She doubted the penis-length results would give gay men something to cheer about....[Nevertheless] Prof. Bogaert said some gay publications have contacted him about the study. "I think they're likely interested because in this small, little realm, gay men win," said Prof. Bogaert, whose research has also included probing sexual orientation according to birth order. "But I don't think there has been a lot of rallying around the flag."

SOURCE: Abridged from Culbert, Lori. 1999. "Gays' Manhood Surpasses that of Straight Men: Study." *National Post*, September 28: A1, A10.

tive attitudes and discrimination against gay people that need to be abolished. (Besen 2000: 7)

The Canadian Psychiatric Association, Canadian Psychological Association, and the Canadian Medical Association agree that sexual orientation cannot be changed, and that efforts to change sexual orientation do not work and may, in fact, be harmful (Human Rights Campaign 2000a). It is additionally reported that close scrutiny of reports of "successful" reparative therapy reveal that (1) many claims come from organizations with an ideological perspective on sexual orientation, rather than from unbiased researchers; (2) the treatments and their outcomes are poorly documented; and (3) the length of time that clients are followed after treatment is too short to evaluate their success or failure (Human Rights Campaign 2000a). In addition, at least 13 ministries of one reparative therapy group, Exodus, have closed because their directors reverted to homosexuality (Fone 2000).

Sociological Theories of Sexual Orientation

Although sociological theories do not explain the origin or "cause" of sexual orientation diversity, they help explain societal reactions to homosexuality and bisexuality. In addition, the symbolic interaction perspective sheds light on the process of adopting a gay, lesbian, or bisexual identity.

Structural-Functionalist Perspective

In an ultimate sense, the function of human sexuality is to maintain the bonds of mutual affection and nurturance. This is essential to the peaceful survival of our race. Instead of causing shame, caring and sensual tenderness must be accepted as vital forces in our lives.

CYRIL GREENLAND
Psychiatric social worker

Structural-functionalists, consistent with their emphasis on institutions and the functions they fulfill, emphasize the importance of monogamous heterosexual relationships for the reproduction, nurturance, and socialization of children. From a functionalist perspective, homosexual relations, as well as heterosexual relations, are defined as "deviant" because they do not fulfill the family institution's main function of producing and rearing children. Clearly, this argument is less salient in a society in which (1) other institutions, most notably schools, have supplemented the traditional functions of the family; (2) reducing (rather than increasing) population is a societal goal; and (3) same-sex couples can and do raise children.

Some functionalists argue that antagonisms between heterosexuals and homosexuals may disrupt the natural state, or equilibrium, of society. Durkheim, however, recognized that deviation from society's norms might also be functional. As Durkheim observed, deviation "...may be useful as a prelude to reforms which daily become more necessary" ([1938] 1993: 66). Specifically, the gay rights movement has motivated many people to re-examine their treatment of sexual-orientation minorities and has produced a sense of cohesion and solidarity among members of the gay population (although bisexuals and the transgendered have often been excluded from gay and lesbian communities and organizations). Gay activism has been instrumental in advocating for more research on HIV and AIDS, more and better health services for HIV and AIDS patients, protection of the rights of HIV-infected individuals, and HIV/AIDS public education. Such HIV/AIDS prevention strategies and health services benefit the society as a whole.

Finally, the structural-functionalist perspective is concerned with how changes in one part of society affect other aspects. With this focus on the interconnectedness of society, we note that urbanization has contributed to the formation of strong social networks of gays and bisexuals. Cities "acted as magnets, drawing in gay migrants who felt isolated and threatened in smaller towns and rural areas" (Button et al. 1997: 15; Goldie 2001). Given the formation of gay communities in large cities, it is not surprising that the gay rights movement first emerged in large urban centres.

Other research has demonstrated that the worldwide rise in liberalized national policies on same-sex relations and the lesbian and gay rights social movement has been influenced by three cultural changes: the rise of individualism, increasing gender equality, and the emergence of a global society in which nations are influenced by international pressures (Frank and McEneaney 1999). Individualism "appears to loosen the tie between sex and procreation, allowing more personal modes of sexual expression" (p. 930).

Whereas once sex was approved strictly for the purpose of family reproduction, sex increasingly serves to pleasure individualized men and women in society. This shift has involved the casting off of many traditional regulations on sexual behaviour, including prohibitions of male-male and female-female sex (Frank and McEneaney 1999: 936).

Gender equality involves the breakdown of sharply differentiated sex roles, thereby supporting the varied expressions of male and female sexuality. Globalization permits the international community to influence individual nations. For example, when Zimbabwe president Robert Mugabe pursued antihomosexual policies in 1995, many international organizations and human rights associations joined to protest his actions and to ask that he halt his antihomosexual campaign. The pressure of international opinion led Zimbabwe's Supreme Court to rule in favour of lesbian and gay groups' right to organize.

Conflict Perspective

Conflict theorists, particularly those who do not emphasize a purely economic perspective, note that the antagonisms between heterosexuals and nonheterosexuals represent a basic division in society between those with power and those without power. When one group has control of society's institutions and resources, as in the case of heterosexuals, they have the authority to dominate other groups. The recent battle over gay rights is just one example of the political struggle between those with power and those without it.

A classic example of the power struggle between gays and straights took place in 1973 when the American Psychiatric Association (APA) met to revise its classification scheme of mental disorders. Homosexual activists had been appealing to the APA for years to remove homosexuality from its list of mental illnesses but with little success. The view of homosexuals as mentally sick contributed to their low social prestige in the eyes of the heterosexual majority. In 1973, the APA's board of directors voted to remove homosexuality from its official list of mental disorders. The board's move encountered a great deal of resistance from conservative APA members and was put to a referendum, which reaffirmed the board's decision (Bayer 1987).

More currently, gays and lesbians in many countries are waging a political battle to gain human rights protections in the form of laws prohibiting discrimination based on sexual orientation. Conflict theory helps to explain why many business owners and corporate leaders oppose such rights protection for gays and lesbians. Employers fear that such protections would result in costly lawsuits if they refused to hire homosexuals, regardless of the reason for their decision. Business owners also fear that granting human rights protections to homosexual employees would undermine the economic health of a community by discouraging the development of new businesses and even driving out some established firms (Button et al. 1997).

In recent years, many organizations have recognized that implementing antidiscrimination policies that include sexual orientation is good for the bottom line. Over half (51 percent) of Fortune 500 companies and 82 percent of Fortune 1000 companies have included sexual orientation in their nondiscrimination policies and employers are increasingly offering benefits to domestic partners of LGBT employees (Human Rights Campaign 2000b). Gay-friendly workplaces help employers maintain a competitive edge in recruiting and maintaining a talented and productive work force. In some settings, however, the changes that have occurred have not always been wholly or even primarily voluntary. Gay rights activists have pursued their quest for equal treatment to Canadian courtrooms and human rights tribunals, successfully employing the equality provision of the Canadian Charter of Rights and Freedoms. As a result of their activities, some Canadian workplaces have been transformed as "[g]overnments have changed legislation and policies either because courts have ordered them to do so or because of threats of court cases" (Dranoff 2001: 133).

In summary, conflict theory frames the gay rights movement and the opposition to it as a struggle over power, prestige, and economic resources. Recent trends toward increased social acceptance of homosexuality may, in part, reflect the corporate world's competition over the gay and lesbian consumer dollar.

Symbolic Interactionist Perspective

Symbolic interactionism focuses on the meanings of heterosexuality, homosexuality, and bisexuality and how these meanings are socially constructed. The meanings we associate with same-sex relations are learned from society—from family, peers, religion, and the media. Freedman and D'Emilio (1990) observed that "...sexual meanings are subject to the forces of culture. Human beings learn how to express themselves sexually, and the content and outcome of that learning vary widely across cultures and across time" (p. 485).

Historical and cross-cultural research on homosexuality reveals the socially constructed nature of homosexuality and its meaning. Although many North Americans may assume that same-sex romantic relationships have always been taboo in our society, during the nineteenth century, "romantic friendships" between women were encouraged and regarded as preparation for a successful marriage. The nature of these friendships bordered on lesbianism. President Grover Cleveland's sister Rose wrote to her friend Evangeline Whipple in 1890: "...It makes me heavy with emotion...all my whole being leans out to you....I dare not think of your arms" (Goode and Wagner 1993: 49).

The symbolic interactionist perspective also points to the effects of labelling on individuals. Once individuals become identified or labelled as lesbian, gay, or bisexual, that label tends to become their **master status**. In other words, the dominant heterosexual community tends to view "gay," "lesbian," and "bisexual" as the most socially significant statuses of individuals who are identified as such. Esterberg (1997) notes that "unlike heterosexuals, who are defined by their family structures, communities, occupations, or other aspects of their lives, lesbians, gay men, and bisexuals are often defined primarily by what they do in bed. Many lesbians, gay men, and bisexuals, however, view their identity as social and political as well as sexual" (p. 377).

We want to attract the brightest talent that values and embraces diversity in the workplace. The competition for talent is tough out there and we view this move as an important step to keep attracting people.

KATHLEEN OSWALD
Senior vice-president for human resources at Daimler-Chrysler, commenting on the automaker's decision to extent health coverage to partners of lesbian and gay employees

I made the choice that my personal liberty and the emancipation that I felt about coming out was definitely more important than my career at that point.

K.D. LANG
Musician

That would be something. Svend Robinson as Minister of Defence.

BRIAN MULRONEY
Former prime minister, ridiculing the NDP's homosexual defence critic

Heterosexism, Homophobia, and Biphobia

Canada, along with many other countries throughout the world, is predominantly heterosexist. **Heterosexism** refers to "an ideological system that denies, denigrates, and stigmatizes any nonheterosexual form of behaviour, identity, relationship, or community" (Herek 1990: 316). Heterosexism is based on the belief that heterosexuality is superior to homosexuality, and it results in prejudice and discrimination against homosexuals and bisexuals. Prejudice refers to negative attitudes, whereas discrimination refers to behaviour that denies individuals or groups equality of treatment. Before reading further, you may wish to complete this chapter's *Self and Society* feature: The Homophobia Scale.

Homophobia

The term **homophobia** is commonly used to refer to negative attitudes and emotions toward homosexuality and those who engage in it. Homophobia is not necessarily a clinical phobia (that is, one involving a compelling desire to avoid the feared object in spite of recognizing that the fear is unreasonable). Other terms that refer to negative attitudes and emotions toward homosexuality include "homonegativity" and "antigay bias."

In 1996, the year in which "sexual orientation" became a prohibited ground for discrimination under the *Canadian Human Rights Act*, a national survey reported that just over one-third of Canadians (34 percent) agreed with the statement, "Gays should have the same rights as others" (*Maclean's* 1996). A more recent survey of Canadians conducted in 2000 found that almost one in three Canadians believed same-sex relations were "always wrong." While this figure is discouraging to some, acceptance of homosexuality in Canada has grown over the past three decades. For example, in 1975, 63 percent of Canadians viewed homosexuality as "always wrong" (*Maclean's* 2002: 12).

In general, certain categories of people are more likely to have negative attitudes toward homosexuals. Persons who are older, less educated, living in lightly populated rural areas, and Protestant are the most likely to have negative attitudes. In contrast, people who are younger, more educated, never married, living in the West, living in heavily populated urban areas, and Jewish are least likely to have antigay attitudes (Klassen et al. 1989). Also, positive contact with homosexuals or having homosexuals as friends is associated with less homophobia (Simon 1995). Public opinion surveys also indicate that men are more likely than women are to have negative attitudes toward gays (Moore 1993). However, many studies on attitudes toward homosexuality do not distinguish between attitudes toward gay men and attitudes toward lesbians (Kite and Whitley 1996). Research that has assessed attitudes toward male versus female homosexuality has found that heterosexual women and men hold similar attitudes toward lesbians, but men are more negative toward gay men (Louderback and Whitley 1997; Price and Dalecki 1998).

In a study of undergraduates (101 men, 98 women) attending a Canadian university where the majority of students were of working-class or middle-class families of European descent, Schellenberg et al. (1999) found that attitudes toward gay men were more negative than toward lesbians. When compared to science or business students, students in the faculties of arts and social sciences had more positive attitudes toward gay men, and women were more positive than men were. Attitudes toward gay men improved with time spent at university but

> Homophobia alienates mothers and fathers from sons and daughters, friend from friend, neighbour from neighbour....As long as it is legitimated by society, religion, and politics, homophobia will spawn hatred, contempt, and violence, and it will remain our last acceptable prejudice.
>
> BYRNE FONE
> *Activist*

The Homophobia Scale

Directions: Indicate the extent to which you agree or disagree with each statement by placing a check mark on the appropriate line.

	Strongly Agree	Agree	Undecided	Disagree	Strongly Disagree
1. Homosexuals contribute positively to society.	_____	_____	_____	_____	_____
2. Homosexuality is disgusting.	_____	_____	_____	_____	_____
3. Homosexuals are just as moral as heterosexuals are.	_____	_____	_____	_____	_____
4. Homosexuals should have equal civil rights.	_____	_____	_____	_____	_____
5. Homosexuals corrupt young people.	_____	_____	_____	_____	_____
6. Homosexuality is a sin.	_____	_____	_____	_____	_____

SCORING

Assign scores of 0, 1, 2, 3, and 4 to the five choices respectively ("strongly agree" through "strongly disagree") for items 1, 3, and 4. Assign scores of 0, 1, 2, 3, and 4 to the five choices in reverse order ("strongly disagree" through "strongly agree") for items 2, 5, 6, and 7. All items are summed for the total score. The possible range is 0 to 28; high scores indicate greater homophobia.

COMPARISON DATA

The Homophobia Scale was administered to 524 students enrolled in introductory psychology courses at the University of Texas. The mean score for men was 15.8; for women, it was 13.8. The difference was statistically significant.

SOURCE: Bouton, Richard A., P. E. Gallagher, P. A. Garlinghouse, T. Leal, et al. 1987. "Scales for Measuring Fear of AIDS and Homophobia." *Journal of Personality Assessment* 67(1): 609. Copyright © 1987 by Lawrence Erlbaum Associates, Inc. Reprinted by permission.

> There is a difference between being attracted to a person of the same sex and acting on those feelings. It is not sinful to have homosexual tendencies, but sexual acts between people of the same sex are morally wrong because they do not respect the law of God in creating us male and female.
>
> **ALOYSIUS AMBROZIC**
> *Archbishop of Toronto*

only for male students. Although attitudes toward lesbians also improved with time at university, this was not associated with students' gender or faculty of enrolment. Schellenberg et al. conclude that university education may encourage a reduction in antihomosexual prejudice among young people, particularly among young men.

Cultural Origins of Homophobia

Why is homosexuality viewed so negatively in North America? Antigay bias has its roots in various aspects of our culture.

1. *Religion.* Most individuals who view homosexuality as unacceptable say they object on religious grounds (Rosin and Morin 1999). Although some religious groups accept homosexuality, many religions teach that homosexuality is sinful and prohibited by God. The Roman Catholic Church rejects all homosexual expression and resists any attempt to validate or sanction the homosexual orientation. Some fundamentalist churches have endorsed the death penalty for homosexual people and teach the view that AIDS is God's punishment for engaging in homosexual sex (Nugent and Gramick 1989). In

June 1999, an American Baptist preacher from Topeka, Kansas, announced that he and a group of his followers would be leading a demonstration on the steps of the Supreme Court of Canada to protest its decision to extend the definition of "spouse" to same-sex couples. Mr. Phelps, who on previous occasions has picketed gay funerals, same-sex unions, and even Girl Scout meetings brandishing signs that read, "AIDS cures fags," had announced, "We're coming to spread the gospel to you sinners." Phelps referred to Canada as the "sperm bank of Satan" and vowed that he and his supporters would burn Canadian flags in protest. In the end, Mr. Phelps did not appear and his group blamed the unwillingness of Canadian police, "who are as blackhearted as the perverts" to provide him with the level of protection he sought as the reason for the group's absence (Anderssen 1999).

Some religious groups, such as the Quakers, are accepting of homosexuality, and other groups have made reforms toward increased acceptance of lesbians and gays. In the United States, some Episcopal priests perform "ceremonies of union" between same-sex couples; some Reform Jewish groups sponsor gay synagogues and the United Church of Christ allows homosexuals to be ordained (Fone 2000). The United Church of Canada has ignited conflict by declaring that "all persons, regardless of their sexual orientation, are welcome to become full members of the church and are eligible for ordination as ministers" (in Dawson 1993: 323).

2. *Marital and procreative bias.* Many societies have traditionally condoned sex only when it occurs in a marital context that provides for the possibility of producing and rearing children. However, science continues to challenge the necessity of opposite-sex parents. For example, in September 2000, newspaper headlines reported that gay male couples may, in the near future, be able to sire "motherless" children through cell nuclear replacement, a technique originally seen as a way to treat infertility and metabolic disorders. "Under cell nuclear replacement, scientists replace the nucleus from the egg of a female donor with the nucleus from a sperm cell. The resulting 'male egg,' containing only male DNA, is then fertilized in vitro by sperm from another man" (Honore 2000). Even though already-available assisted reproductive technologies make it possible for gay individuals and couples to have children, many people believe that only heterosexual married couples should use these advances (Franklin 1993).

3. *Concern about HIV and AIDS.* Although most cases of HIV and AIDS worldwide are attributed to heterosexual transmission, the rates of HIV and AIDS in Canada are much higher among gay and bisexual men than among other groups. Because of this, many people associate HIV and AIDS with homosexuality and bisexuality. Lesbians, incidentally, have a very low risk for sexually transmitted HIV—a lower risk than heterosexual women do.

4. *Threat to the power of the majority.* Like other minority groups, the gay minority threatens the power of the majority. Fearing loss of power, the majority group stigmatizes homosexuals as a way of limiting their power.

5. *Rigid gender roles.* Antigay sentiments also stem from rigid gender roles. When Cooper Thompson (1995) was asked to give a guest presentation on male roles at a suburban high school, male students told him that the most humiliating put-down was being called a "fag." The boys in this school gave Thompson the impression that they were expected to conform to rigid, narrow standards of masculinity to avoid being labelled in this way.

> How can we expect the church to deal with homosexuality, when it hasn't even dealt with sexuality?
>
> NANCY RADCLYFFE
> *Pastor, Metropolitan Community Church, Toronto*

From a conflict perspective, heterosexual men's subordination and the devaluation of gay men reinforces gender inequality. "By devaluing gay men…heterosexual men devalue the feminine and anything associated with it" (Price and Dalecki 1998: 155–56). Negative views toward lesbians also reinforce the patriarchal system of male dominance. Social disapproval of lesbians is a form of punishment for women who relinquish traditional female sexual and economic dependence on men. Not surprisingly, research findings suggest that individuals with traditional gender role attitudes tend to hold more negative views toward homosexuality (Louderback and Whitley 1997).

6. *Psychiatric labelling.* As noted earlier, before 1973 the APA defined homosexuality as a mental disorder. Treatments for the "illness" of homosexuality included lobotomies, aversive conditioning, and, in some cases, castration. The social label of mental illness by such a powerful labelling group as the APA contributed to heterosexuals' negative reactions to gays. Further, it created feelings of guilt, low self-esteem, anger, and depression for many homosexuals. Thus, the psychiatric care system is now busily treating the very conditions it, in part, created.

7. *Myths and negative stereotypes.* Prejudice towards homosexuals may also stem from some of the unsupported beliefs and negative stereotypes regarding homosexuality. One negative myth about homosexuals is that they are sexually promiscuous and lack "family values" such as monogamy and commitment to relationships. While some homosexuals do engage in casual sex, as do some heterosexuals, many homosexual couples develop and maintain long-term committed relationships.

Another myth that is not supported by data is that homosexuals, as a group, are child molesters. The ratio of heterosexual to homosexual child molesters is approximately 11 to 1 (Moser 1992). Most often, the abuser is a father, stepfather, or heterosexual relative of the family. When a father sexually assaults his daughter, the media do not report that something is wrong with heterosexuality or with traditional families, but when a homosexual is reported to have molested a child, it is viewed as confirmation of "the way homosexuals are" (Mohr 1995: 404). "The Heterosexual Questionnaire" (Table 9.2) parodies the different ways in which we respond to heterosexuals and homosexuals in our society.

Biphobia

Just as the term "homophobia" is used to refer to negative attitudes toward gay men and lesbians, **biphobia** refers to "the parallel set of negative beliefs about and stigmatization of bisexuality and those identified as bisexual" (Paul 1996: 449). Although heterosexuals often reject both homosexual- and bisexual-identified individuals, bisexual-identified women and men also face rejection from many homosexual individuals. Thus, bisexuals experience "double discrimination."

Biphobia includes negative stereotyping of bisexuals; the exclusion of bisexuals from social and political organizations of lesbians and gay men; and fear and distrust of, as well as anger and hostility toward, people who identify themselves as bisexual (Firestein 1996). Individuals who are biphobic often believe that bisexuals are really homosexuals afraid to acknowledge their real identity or homosexuals maintaining heterosexual relationships to avoid rejection by the heterosexual mainstream. Bisexual individuals are sometimes viewed as heterosexuals who are looking for exotic sexual experiences.

■ **Table 9.2** *The Heterosexual Questionnaire*

1. What do you think caused your heterosexuality?
2. When and how did you decide you were a heterosexual?
3. Is it possible that your heterosexuality is just a phase you may grow out off?
4. Is it possible that your heterosexuality stems from a neurotic fear of others of the same sex?
5. If you have never slept with a person of the same sex, is it possible that all you need is a good gay lover?
6. Do you parents know that you are straight? Do your friends and/or roommate(s) know? How did they react?
7. Why do you insist on flaunting your heterosexuality? Can't you just be who you are and keep it quiet?
8. Why do heterosexuals place so much emphasis on sex?
9. Why do heterosexuals feel compelled to seduce others into their lifestyle?
10. A disproportionate majority of child molesters are heterosexual. Do you consider it safe to expose children to heterosexual teachers?
11. Just what do men and women do in bed together? How can they truly know how to please each other, being so anatomically different?
12. With all the societal support marriage receives, the divorce rate is spiralling. Why are there so few stable relationships among heterosexuals?
13. Statistics show that lesbians have the lowest incidence of sexually transmitted diseases. Is it really safe for a woman to maintain a heterosexual lifestyle and run the risk of disease and pregnancy?
14. How can you become a whole person if you limit yourself to compulsive, exclusive heterosexuality?
15. Considering the menace of overpopulation, how could the human race survive if everyone were heterosexual?
16. Could you trust a heterosexual therapist to be objective? Don't you feel she or he might be inclined to influence you in the direction of his or her own leanings?
17. There seem to be very few happy heterosexuals. Techniques have been developed that might enable you to change if you really want to. Have you considered trying aversion therapy?
18. Would you want your child to be heterosexual, knowing the problems that she or he would face?

SOURCE: Rochlin, M. 1982. "The Heterosexual Questionnaire." *Changing Men* (Spring).

Lesbians seem to exhibit greater levels of biphobia than do gay men, probably because many lesbian women associate their identity with a political stance against sexism and patriarchy. Some lesbians view heterosexual and bisexual women who "sleep with the enemy" as traitors to the feminist movement.

One negative stereotype that encourages biphobia is the belief that bisexuals are, by definition, nonmonogamous. However, many bisexual women and men prefer and have long-term committed monogamous relationships.

Effects of Homophobia and Heterosexism on Heterosexuals

The homophobic and heterosexist social climate of our society is often viewed in terms of how it victimizes the gay population. However, heterosexuals are also victimized by homophobia and heterosexism. "Hatred, fear, and ignorance are bad for the bigot as well as the victim" (*Homophobia 101* 2000).

Due to the antigay climate, heterosexuals, especially males, are hindered in their own self-expression and intimacy in same-sex relationships. "The threat of victimization (i.e., antigay violence) probably also causes many heterosexuals to conform to gender roles and to restrict their expressions of (nonsexual) physical affection for members of their own sex" (Garnets et al. 1990: 380). Homophobic epithets frighten youth who do not conform to gender role expectations, leading some youth to avoid activities that they might otherwise enjoy and benefit from (arts for boys, athletics for girls, for example) (*Homophobia 101* 2000).

Some sexual assaults are related to homophobia and compulsory heterosexuality. For example, some men who participate in gang rape, also known as "pulling train," entice each other into the act "by implying that those who do not participate are unmanly or homosexual" (Sanday 1995: 399). Homonegativity also encourages early sexual activity among adolescent men. Adolescent male virgins are often teased by their male peers, who say things like "You mean you don't do it with girls yet? What are you, a fag or something?" Not wanting to be labelled and stigmatized as a "fag," some adolescent boys "prove" their heterosexuality by having sex with girls.

Antigay cultural attitudes also affect family members and friends of homosexuals, who often fear that their lesbian or gay friend or family member will be victimized by antigay prejudice and discrimination. Youth with gay and lesbian family members are often taunted by their peers.

As we have already noted, extreme homophobia can lead to instances of physical violence against homosexuals. But "gay bashings" are crimes of perception, meaning that victims of antigay violence may not be homosexual; they may just be perceived as being homosexual. Many heterosexuals have been victims of antigay physical violence because the attacker(s) perceived the victim to be gay. Antigay harassment has also been a factor in at least some recent cases of school violence. One study concluded that "For boys, no other type of harassment provoked as strong a reaction on average; boys in this study would be less upset about physical abuse than they would be if someone called them gay" (Dozetos 2001).

Discrimination against Sexual-Orientation Minorities

Like other minority groups in Canadian society, homosexuals and bisexuals have experienced and continue to experience various forms of discrimination. From 1952 to 1977, immigration laws prohibited homosexuals from entering Canada and subjected those who were homosexual to the threat of deportation if their sexual orientation became known. From 1892 to 1969, Canadian criminal law made certain forms of sexual conduct engaged in by gay men illegal and rendered gay men vulnerable to indefinite incarceration as "dangerous sexual offenders."

Next, we look at sexual-orientation discrimination in the workplace, in family matters, and in violent expressions of hate. This chapter's *Focus on Technology* feature discusses the discriminatory effects of Internet filtering and monitoring technology on sexual orientation minorities.

Discrimination in the Workplace

In recent years, the percentage of Canadians who express approval of equal employment rights for homosexuals has increased. Nevertheless, many Canadians still feel that homosexuals should not be entitled to the same rights and privileges as others in our society. While support levels for gays working in a variety of different occupations increased between 1988 and 2001, certain occupations are still considered "more suitable" than others. For example, the vast majority of Canadians find it acceptable for gays to work as salespersons (94 percent vs. 72 percent in 1988), Members of Parliament (86 percent vs. 62 percent in 1988), members of our Armed Forces (82 percent vs. 60 percent in 1988), physicians (82 percent vs. 52 percent in 1988) or prison officers (75 percent vs. 44 percent in 1988). However, there is less support for gays working as junior school teachers (67 percent vs. 45 percent in 1988) or members of the clergy (63 percent vs. 44 percent in 1988) (Bricker and Greenspon 2001: 267–68).

Only a few decades ago, there were few legal protections for homosexual individuals who experienced discrimination in employment. Hostility towards gays in the workplace in the 1960s led to more than 8000 gay men being investigated by the RCMP; as a result, approximately 150 gay federal civil servants resigned or were dismissed from their employment positions without just cause. It was only in 1992 that the Canadian Armed Forces, facing a court challenge, agreed to stop discrimination against gays. At the time of writing, discrimination on the basis of sexual orientation was prohibited everywhere in Canada except for the Northwest Territories and Nunavut. While Alberta's legislation does not state this prohibition specifically, the Supreme Court of Canada declared in the 1998 case of *Vriend v. Alberta* that Alberta's human rights legislation "would be interpreted to include sexual orientation as a prohibited ground—whether or not it is specified in the legislation....This marked the first time the Supreme Court of Canada amended legislation on constitutional grounds by reading into law new rights that elected politicians had expressly refused to grant" (Dranoff 2001: 134).

Discrimination in Family Relationships

In addition to discrimination in the workplace, sexual-orientation minorities in Canada have also experienced discrimination in policies concerning marriage, child custody and visitation, and adoption.

Same-Sex Marriage In June of 1999, the Canadian House of Commons voted overwhelmingly in favour of a motion, introduced by MP Eric Lowther, the Reform Party critic on "Children and Families," opposing same-sex marriages. The motion, which signalled the first time same-sex marriage was the subject of a vote in the House of Commons, affirmed the exclusion of gays and lesbians from the institution of marriage and committed Parliament to "take all necessary steps" to preserve legal marriage as an opposite-sex institution. Although passing the motion had no immediate legal impact, it might be presumed that as an official declaration of the Parliament's position on the matter, the "necessary steps" could include invoking the "notwithstanding" clause within the Constitution that allows governments to opt out of the Charter of Rights and Freedoms and to deny equality to some of their citizens, in this case, lesbians and gay men. In total, 216 MPs from all parties voted in favour of the motion,

The Impact of Internet Filtering and Monitoring on Sexual-Orientation Minorities

Joan Garry is the Executive Director of the Gay and Lesbian Alliance Against Defamation (GLAAD) and a mother of three children. When her 10-year-old daughter Sarah approached her for information about COLAGE (Children of Lesbians and Gays Everywhere), a support organization for the children of lesbian and gay parents, they signed on to America Online to look up the Web site. The COLAGE site was "Web Restricted": Sarah could not access the site because her computer was equipped with AOL's filtering software called Kids Only. In fact, when Joan tried to look up various family, youth, and national organization Web sites with lesbian and gay content, most sites came up "Web Restricted" as well (Garry 1999). For example, the Kids Only software blocked access to several youth-oriented gay and lesbian resource sites, including PFLAG (Parents, Family and Friends of Lesbians and Gays), Family Pride, !OutProud!, GLSEN (Gay, Lesbian and Straight Education Network), and Oasis Magazine, a gay and lesbian youth Webzine (Javier 1999).

An explosion of filtering technologies to help maintain "decency" and "community standards" on the Internet has occurred. Examples of filtering technologies include those that block key words or URLs. For example, the search engine Jayde.com, which marketed itself as being able to filter out pornographic material, decided to block the word "lesbian" in its search engine. The filtering software "CYBERsitter" automatically filters out words and phrases like "gay," "lesbian," "gay rights," and "gay community" (Javier 1999). Filtering technologies are promoted as tools to help parents, schools, libraries, and communities prevent children's access to sexually explicit and pornographic material on the Internet. However, some filtering software also denies users access to several lesbian, gay, and bisexual youth resource sites.

Schneider (1999) presents the following scenario:

> Imagine a teenager seeking information about his or her sexual orientation whose attempts to go to gay-related Web sites are met with a warning that tells him or her "Bess doesn't want you to go there." In an unfiltered environment...the teen could be expected to privately retrieve all kinds of information in a discreet, nonjudgmental environment. But place a filter on that computer, and...the teen gets the message that he or she is somehow..."inappropriate." (p. 13)

Given the impact of Internet filtering on the gay community, some gay rights groups oppose the use of filtering software. Instead, they advocate parental oversight, school supervision, and training of young Internet users (Bowes 1999).

Another concern of sexual orientation minorities is the use of monitoring software that allows parents, teachers, and other authority figures to track sites a Web surfer tries to access. The monitoring software industry markets its products by claiming that they allow for parental awareness without censorship, and that parental use of monitoring software encourages open family communication. But for youth who are not ready to reveal their sexual orientation to their family, "such software could potentially 'out' them before they are ready, leading to strained family relations and deeper isolation" (Javier 1999: 8).

In addition, Internet service providers may record every click of your mouse, including personal information you exchange in chat rooms, emails, and instant messages.

Say you visit a Web magazine: the time and date of your visit are recorded. You conduct a search for all articles containing the word "gay." Your inquiry is recorded. You click on an article about new AIDS drugs. Your request for that article is recorded. While reading the article, you click on an ad about online dating services, and that choice is recorded....You decide to enter a gay-oriented chat-room and see if you can make any new friends, or even get a date. You chat with a number of people, and finally connect with one special person, with whom you share instant messages, pictures, and perhaps even a virtual date. Depending on...the Internet provider in question, that date could have just been recorded (Aravosis 1999: 30).

Web sites also record information about your Internet usage. When you visit a free news Web site, you may be required to "subscribe" by giving them your name and email address. After subscribing, you read a few articles. But unbeknownst to you, the news Web site has put a "cookie," or piece of computer code, on the hard drive of your computer. This cookie contains a unique identifier permitting the news site to recognize you when you return to that site. Cookies can do helpful things like remember your password for accessing that site, and tailor Web pages for preset preferences. But they can also contain a record of what you did on that site, including what searches you made and what articles you read (Aravosis 1999). According to one study, of the 7500 busiest servers on the Web, 93 percent of the sites collect personal information from consumers, yet only 66 percent post any disclosure about their information practices (Bowes 1999).

Although some Web sites have strict privacy policies, others sell information about site visitors. One company boasts on its Web site that it is "the world's oldest and largest mailing list manager and broker for Gay, Lesbian, and HIV-related names, currently managing almost two million names, which we estimate to be about 65 percent of all those commercially available in this segment" (Aravosis 1999: 33). Databases containing the names of gay consumers are valuable because gays are perceived as a "wealthy and wired market." A 1998 study found that the average household income of lesbians and gay men on the Internet was $57 300, slightly higher than the $52 000 for the general Internet population. Another study by Computer Economics predicts that within the next few years, the worldwide gay and lesbian Internet population will increase from 9.2 million to 17.1 million (Aravosis 1999).

The Internet has been a useful tool for gays, lesbians, and bisexuals. Going online has allowed the gay community to create safe places for support and information. However, Internet filtering and monitoring software that has been installed on computers in homes, schools, libraries, and workplaces throughout the country represents a threat to the gay community. Filtering and monitoring technologies make it impossible or dangerous for a closeted gay or lesbian to seek out support and information about their community.

We live in an age in which the Internet has become an extremely important part of the coming out process for many gay and lesbian youth. In many cases, it can be a lifeline to those in geographically isolated areas. To deny basic educational and support resources to lesbian and gay youth could seriously endanger their physical and emotional well being. (Appendix A 1999: 46)

SOURCES: Appendix A. 1999. "Frequently Asked Questions." In *Access Denied Version 2.0, The Continuing Threat Against Internet Access and Privacy and its Impact on the Lesbian, Gay, Bisexual and Transgender Community*. New York: Gay and Lesbian Alliance Against Defamation, pp. 45–48. Aravosis, John. 1999. "Privacy: The Impact on Lesbian, Gay, Bisexual and Transgender Community." In *Access Denied Version 2.0, The Continuing Threat Against Internet Access and Privacy and its Impact on the Lesbian, Gay, Bisexual and Transgender Community*. New York: Gay and Lesbian Alliance Against Defamation, pp. 30–33. Bowes, John. 1999. "Conclusions." In *Access Denied Version 2.0, The Continuing Threat Against Internet Access and Privacy and its Impact on the Lesbian, Gay, Bisexual and Transgender Community*. New York: Gay and Lesbian Alliance Against Defamation, pp. 38–44. Garry, Joan M. 1999. "Introduction: How Access and Privacy Impact the Lesbian, Gay, Bisexual and Transgender Community." In *Access Denied Version 2.0, The Continuing Threat Against Internet Access and Privacy and its Impact on the Lesbian, Gay, Bisexual and Transgender Community. New York: Gay and Lesbian Alliance Against Defamation*, pp. 3–5. Javier, Loren. 1999. "The World Since Access Denied." In *Access Denied 2.0, The Continuing Threat Against Internet Access and Privacy and its Impact on the Lesbian, Gay, Bisexual and Transgender Community*. New York: Gay and Lesbian Alliance Against Defamation, pp. 6–9. Schneider, Karen G. 1999. "*Access: The Impact on the Lesbian, Gay, Bisexual and Transgender Community.*" In *Access Denied Version 2.0, The Continuing Threat Against Internet Access and Privacy and its Impact on the Lesbian, Gay, Bisexual and Transgender Community*. New York: Gay and Lesbian Alliance Against Defamation, pp. 10–15.

including the overwhelming majority of the Liberal caucus (all but 11), all Reform Party MPs, and a number of those from the New Democratic Party, Bloc Québécois, and Progressive Conservative Party. Only 55 MPS voted against the motion. Although it was expected that a "free vote" would be held, with MPs asked to "vote their conscience" rather than follow a party line, in the end the Liberal government adopted a government position that supported the Reform Party (EGALE 1999).

In that year, various provincial governments also grappled with the issues presented by same-sex marriages. In May 1999, the Supreme Court of Ontario ruled that an Ontario law that excluded gays and lesbians from a definition of common-law couples was unconstitutional. Shortly after, the Ontario government passed on omnibus bill that amended 67 of its laws to include same-sex couples. Although the Supreme Court's ruling was only binding on the Ontario government, several other provinces quickly announced plans to make similar changes. For example, in June of that year, when the Quebec National Assembly unanimously passed Bill 32, the Quebec government became the first Canadian province to ensure that same-sex couples would receive all the benefits and responsibilities of opposite-sex couples. Bill 32 changed the definition of "spouse" within that province and committed the Quebec government to making changes in 39 provincial laws and regulations. A month later, the British Columbia government introduced the "Definition of Spouse Amendment," which expanded the definition of "spouse" in that province to include "a person who has lived and cohabited with another person, for a period of at least two years immediately before the other person's death, in a 'marriage-like' relationship, including a marriage-like relationship between persons of the same gender." In that province, same-sex couples who meet this definition have the same spousal rights and responsibilities as heterosexual couples, including a right to contract into property and pensions, and to inherit from their partner as a spouse if the partner dies without a will. In 2000, legislation in Nova Scotia revised the definition of a "spouse" to include both opposite and same-sex couples who have lived together in a conjugal relationship for at least one year. In that year, "for the first time in the seven years it had been asking the question, less than half of Canadians [48 percent] opposed same-sex marriage" (Bricker and Greenspon, 2001: 267).

Over the last decade, "courts have 'rewritten' legislation to include same-sex couples or opposite-sex couples into the definition of 'spouse' for various purposes. As well, courts have creatively applied non-family laws, including the law of contract, property and restitution, to cohabiting couples [both same-sex and opposite sex]...who were [formerly] excluded" (Bailey 2000: 3). Most recently, in July 2002, three Ontario Superior Court judges ruled that the federal law prohibiting same-sex marriages was unconstitutional—a decision that is being appealed by the federal government (see this chapter's *The Human Side*).

Advocates of same-sex marriage maintain that as long as same-sex couples cannot be legally married, they will not be regarded as legitimate families by the larger society. However, their opponents do not want to legitimate homosexuality as a socially acceptable lifestyle. Opponents of same-sex marriage who view homosexuality as unnatural, sick, and/or immoral do not want their children to learn that homosexuality is an accepted and acceptable lifestyle. The most common argument against same-sex marriage is that it subverts the stability and integrity of the heterosexual family. However, Sullivan (1997) points out that gays and lesbians are already part of heterosexual families:

"It's about Love": A Canadian Couple Fighting for Recognition of Same-Sex Unions

Kevin Bourassa, 44, and Joe Varnell, 32, were one of two Canadian same-sex couples married on July 14, 2001, at Toronto's Metropolitan Community Church. When the provincial government of Ontario refused to grant them a wedding licence, Bourassa and Varnella turned to the courts. In mid-July of 2002, three Ontario Superior Court judges ruled that the federal law that prohibits same-sex couples from marrying was unconstitutional—a ruling that Ottawa is appealing. In the following extract from an interview which originally appeared in Maclean's in August, 2002, Bourassa and Varnell, co-authors of *Just Married: Gay Marriage and the Expansion of Human Rights*, discuss their fight for the right to marry.

Were you expecting the federal government to appeal the court's decision?

Varnell: When we started, we knew there was a strong possibility that a positive decision would be appealed. But because of the overwhelmingly strong wording of the judgment, telling the government its laws were unconstitutional, we were a little surprised.

Bourassa: Various things led us to be hopeful. The polls, the provincial Conservatives saying they wouldn't appeal the ruling, the federal government floating the trial balloon about getting out of the marriage business, fueled our hope that Ottawa would honour the Charter.

What do you think of the proposal that there should be no more state-sanctioned marriages, just religious ceremonies or civil arrangements?

Varnell: It's an extremely radical step—far more radical than simply extending the definition of marriage to include gays and lesbians. But it would be a disappointing option for us because they would be saying that rather than pollute the institution of marriage with same-sex couples, they'd prefer to pick up their toys and go home.

Why is marriage so important for gay and lesbian couples?

Bourassa: First, it's about the government being allowed to treat one group that is otherwise protected by the Charter differently. It's important to send a message that gays and lesbians are not second-class citizens. But on a personal level, marriage is about love. We should be able to experience that love in the manner we choose, in a manner available to all Canadians.

Is marriage something you think other gay couples should do?

Varnell: Marriage isn't for every couple. Relationships have to be protected in law. But the formalization of those relationships has to be an individual choice.

How has being married affected your personal lives?

Bourassa: Over the past 12 months, I've gone from a banking career to working full time at advocacy. I couldn't do that if it wasn't for Joe. Marriage is like that—it's sharing resources and complementing one another.

And what have you personally, emotionally, got out of marriage?

Bourassa: It's brought us closer and closer together. If you can work together through stress and you can also find that you're building something together that's bigger than the two of you could do alone, that's great. And I think we're doing that.

How have people reacted when you tell them you're married?

Bourassa: Most people respond positively. It's usually not confrontational unless you're dealing with a situation such as when we were watching fireworks on a blanket, and a bunch of kids heckled us from a car. People will do it from a distance. It's much more difficult to do to your face....

Varnell: It's fine to have protection in law, but until you have acceptance in your community, the protection in law can be very cold comfort.

SOURCE: Abridged from *Maclean's*. 2002. "'It's About Love': A Pioneering Gay Couple Defends Same-Sex Unions." August 12, 2002: 46–47. Reprinted by permission of *Maclean's* Magazine.

[Homosexuals] are sons and daughters, brothers and sisters, even mothers and fathers, of heterosexuals. The distinction between "families" and "homosexuals" is, to begin with, empirically false; and the stability of existing families is closely linked to how homosexuals are treated within them. (p. 147)

According to the 2001 Canadian census, 13 percent of female same-sex couples have children living with them and 3 percent of same-sex male couples are also parenting children (Arnold 2002).

Child Custody, Visitation, and Reproductive Rights Another milestone for gay activists was attained in 2001 when, for the first time, a Canadian survey reported majority support for gay adoption (Bricker and Greenspon 2001: 267). In 1995, an Ontario provincial judge ruled that gay and lesbian couples have the right to apply to adopt a child under that province's Child and Family Services Act. In 1998, British Columbia passed amendments to its Adoption Act and Family Relations Act that provided same-sex couples who cohabit continuously for two years with the same right to apply to adopt a child. In 1999, Alberta joined with these provinces in permitting same-sex couples to adopt.

Little was known until relatively recently about the nature of gay and lesbian family life. Many published accounts were nonempirical and saturated with a heterosexist bias that framed gay and lesbian families as "deviant" and "pathological." Even though research on gay and lesbian families expanded dramatically in the 1990s (e.g., Arnup 1995; Benkov 1994; Stone 1990; Weston 1991), generalizable information still remains sparse due to nonrandom sampling, limited sample sizes, and the diversities of these families occasioned by ethnicity, class, age of parents and offspring, and circumstances leading to family formation. However, in a recent review of research on family relationships of lesbians and gay men, Patterson (2001) concludes that "the greater majority of children with lesbian or gay parents grow up to identify themselves as heterosexual" and that "concerns about possible difficulties in personal development among children of lesbian and gay parents have not been sustained by the results of research" (p. 279). Patterson (2001) additionally notes that the "home environments provided by lesbian and gay parents are just as likely as those provided by heterosexual parents to enable psychosocial growth among family members" (p. 283).

At least in theory, custody and access orders in Canada are equally available to members of same-sex unions and opposite-sex unions, with decisions made in "the best interests of the child." However, while "[n]othing in Canadian law stops a homosexual parent from applying for custody, the courts will often take judicial notice (that is, recognize that it could easily be proved) of the fact that some harm might arise from living with a homosexual parent" (Yogis et al. 1996: 56). They note that Canadian case law suggests that "custody is awarded to discreet, non-militant homosexual parents who do not flaunt their sexual orientation" (p. 56).

In addition, while technological change may stimulate social change, the introduction of any device or set of procedures does not always result in changed social attitudes or behaviours. For example, in 1993, a lesbian couple in Vancouver, B.C. sought artificial insemination and were refused by the only local doctor whose practice made available the artificial insemination of frozen sperm. The couple, a lawyer and a doctor, then complained to the B.C. College of Physicians and Surgeons. Their appeal was rejected in a letter stating that since "the service you sought was not urgent nor emergent," the doctor's refusal to take them as patients was justified. In drawing media attention to their experience, the couple stated that they sought to draw attention to discrimination against lesbians as potential users of the new reproductive technology. In 1995, the B.C. Council of Human Rights found the doctor guilty of discrimination on the basis of sexual orientation.

Hate Crimes against Sexual-Orientation Minorities

In eighteenth-century North America, where laws against homosexuality often included the death penalty, violence against gays and lesbians was widespread and included beatings, burnings, various kinds of torture, and execution (Button et al. 1997). Although such treatment of sexual-orientation minorities is no longer legally condoned, gays, lesbians, and bisexuals continue to be victimized by hate crimes. Surveys indicate that as many as one-fourth of lesbians and gay men report having been victims of physical attacks because of their sexual orientation (Herek 1989). A survey of more than 3000 high-school students found that students who reported having engaged in same-sex relations were more than three times as likely to report not going to school because they felt unsafe and more than twice as likely to report having been threatened or injured with a weapon at school (Faulkner and Cranston 1998). These students were also significantly more likely to report that their property was deliberately damaged or stolen at school.

Hate-motivated violence toward sexual-orientation minorities can be brutal. The following example is given in *Reaching Out: A Report on Lesbian, Gay, and Bisexual Youth Issues in Canada*, prepared for the United Church of Canada by John Fisher (1999), executive director of Equality for Gays and Lesbians Everywhere (EGALE).

> When Christian Hernandez was 14 and a Grade 9 student at Notre Dame College High School in Niagara Falls, Ontario, he screwed up his courage and told his best friend that he was gay. That was his first mistake. "He told me he couldn't accept it," recalls Hernandez. "And he began to spread it around." Over the next two years, Hernandez was teased and harassed almost daily. One day, a group of boys waited for him after school. Their leader had a knife, and, says Hernandez, "He told me he didn't accept faggots, that we brought AIDS into the world." The boy then cut Hernandez on the neck, putting him in the hospital for a week. When Hernandez told his parents about the attack, his father, who has since moved back to his native El Salvador, said he would "rather have a dead son than a queer son."

Next, we highlight some of the strategies for reducing and responding to prejudice and discrimination toward sexual-orientation minorities.

Strategies for Action: Reducing Antigay Prejudice and Discrimination

Many of the efforts to change policies and attitudes regarding sexual-orientation minorities have been spearheaded by organizations such as Equality for Gays and Lesbians Everywhere (EGALE), Canada's only national equal rights organization advocating for lesbians, gays, and bisexuals with members in every province and territory; Parents, Family, and Friends of Lesbians and Gays (PFLAG); the Foundation for Equal Families (FFEF); Victoria Youth Pride Society; Pink Triangle Services Youth Group in Ottawa; Lesbian and Gay Health Services in Saskatoon; and the British Columbia Civil Liberties Association. These organizations are politically active in their efforts to achieve equal rights for gays, lesbians, and bisexuals. For example, the mandate of the Foundation for Equal Families is to achieve equality and recognition of same-sex relationships and associated family rights through legal action and education. In January 1999, the Foundation launched an omnibus challenge of 58 federal laws affecting the rights of lesbian and gay couples. The omnibus challenge affected laws as diverse as the *Income Tax Act*, the *Canadian Pension Plan Act*, the *Criminal Code*, the *Immigration Act*, the *Evidence Act*, the *Judges' Act*, the *Old Age Security Act*, the *Veterans Allowance Act*, and the Royal Canadian Mounted Police's *Superannuation Act*. The gay rights movement is also active in promoting HIV/AIDS research, adequate health care for AIDS victims, and the rights of HIV-infected individuals. Other target areas include providing programs and services for gay and lesbian students.

In addition, demonstrative and cultural expressions of gay activism, such as "gay pride" celebrations, marches, demonstrations, or other cultural activities promoting gay rights are important in organizing gay activists. However, it has been noted that

> Too many people have seen the cultural activity as a substitute for democratic political participation. In too many cases over the past decades we have left the political arena to our most dedicated opponents [of gay rights], whose letter writing, phone calling, and lobbying have easily triumphed over our marching, demonstrating, and dancing. The most important lesson…is that politics—conventional, boring, but essential politics—will ultimately have a major impact on the extent to which we can rid our lives of prejudice. (Frank 1997: xi)

In Canada, the various political parties have shown different levels of support for gay rights issues. For example, despite a caucus of 175 members, no Member of Parliament who is a Liberal has identified himself or herself as gay, lesbian, or bisexual and some, such as Roseanne Stoke and Tom Wappel, have shown a willingness to consistently refer to homosexuality as "unnatural," "immoral," and a "perversion." The prime minister, in turn, when confronted with such reactions by members of his party has only seen fit to comment that "We give our members the freedom to express themselves." In the Bloc Québécois, Réal Ménard is the only openly gay Member of Parliament, but the party has, to date, voted consistently in favour of gay rights' issues. In the NDP, another openly gay MP, Svend Robinson, has also consistently demonstrated strong support for lesbian and gay equality, as has the leader of the federal New Democratic Party. In contrast, members of the Alliance Party, and its precursor, the Reform Party, have almost invariably voted against bills seeking to advance the rights of lesbians and gays (EGALE 2001).

Although in the late 1990s Winnipeg elected its first openly gay mayor, Glen Murray, it would seem presumptuous to suppose that the issue of a candidate's sexual orientation is not considered relevant by at least some voters. It seems undeniable that the Christian right, religious and church groups, conservative family groups, and other conservative organizations and their political allies will continue to crusade against gay rights. Nevertheless, opposition groups are up against an increasingly powerful progay rights movement.

Educational Strategies: Policies and Programs in the Schools

A survey of youths' risk behaviour found that 30 percent of gay teens attempted suicide in the previous year, compared with 7 percent of their straight peers (reported in Platt 2001). Forty percent of gay youth report schoolwork being negatively affected by conflicts around sexual orientation and over one-quarter of gay youth drop out of school (Chase 2000; *Homophobia 101* 2000). Recent research conducted in Calgary also reports that gay and bisexual males were "almost 14 times more likely to have made a serious suicide attempt at some point in their lives than their heterosexually oriented counterparts" and that lesbian, gay, and bisexual youth of colour were dramatically overrepresented in attempted suicide statistics. According to one of the authors of this research, Pierre Tremblay, "This is the fallout of living with no guidance and no support. It's a problem every teacher knows about, but too often the attitude is, 'we would like to help, but we don't want to promote homosexuality.' It is a total abdication" (in Fisher 1999).

All of these findings suggest that if schools are to promote the health and well-being of all students, they must address the needs of gay, lesbian, and bisexual youth and promote acceptance of sexual orientation diversity within the school setting (Flowers and Bustin 2001; Murphy 2001). One strategy for promoting tolerance for diversity among students involves establishing and enforcing a school policy prohibiting antigay behaviour. Another strategy for addressing the needs of homosexual and bisexual youth is having school-based support groups. Such groups can help students increase self-esteem, overcome their sense of isolation, provide information and resources, and provide a resource for parents. In-service training for teachers and other staff is also important and may include examining the effects of antigay bias, dispelling myths about homosexuality, and brainstorming ways to create a more inclusive environment (Mathison 1998). However, most public schools offer little to no support and education regarding sexual-orientation diversity. Most schools have no support groups or special counselling services for gay and lesbian youth, and the majority of schools do not have any policies prohibiting antigay harassment (Button et al. 1997).

Nevertheless, some progress is being made. For example, in February 1997, the Calgary board of education approved an "Action Plan on Gay/Lesbian/Bisexual Youth and Staff Safety" that requires guidance counsellors to provide "comprehensive information to students" when discussing sexual orientation and to "encourage students to discuss the issue with their parents." In Toronto, the Triangle Program offers gays who have been harassed at school an alternative place to study for up to 18 months and a curriculum that emphasizes the contributions of gays and lesbians in various fields. Various Canadian school boards and teaching institutes have adopted policies or initiatives that promote the equal treatment of gays and lesbians. For example, the Vancouver School Board's Statement of Mission and Beliefs states that "We believe in equitable treatment for all individuals, regardless of race, culture, gender, religion, socioeconomic status, sexual orientation or physical or mental ability." In addition, the federal government has launched a national initiative, the "Safe Spaces Project," funded by the federal Department of Health, to help produce educational materials for both heterosexual and lesbian and gay youth on lesbian, gay, and bisexual issues, and to create safe spaces for lesbian, gay, and bisexual youth.

Campus Policies Regarding Homosexuality

Student groups have been active in the gay liberation movement since the 1960s. Numerous gay student groups are organized in community colleges and universities across Canada.

D'Emilio (1990) suggests that colleges and universities have the ability and the responsibility to promote gay rights and social acceptance of homosexual people:

> For reasons that I cannot quite fathom, I still expect the academy to embrace higher standards of civility, decency, and justice than the society around it. Having been granted the extraordinary privilege of thinking critically as a way of life, we should be astute enough to recognize when a group of people is being systematically mistreated. We have the intelligence to devise solutions to problems that appear in our community. I expect us also to have the courage to lead rather than follow. (p. 18)

In addition to including sexual orientation in discrimination policies, colleges and universities have also taken more proactive measures to support the lesbigay student population. Such measures have included offering gay and lesbian studies programs, social centres, and support groups, and sponsoring events and activities that celebrate diversity. "These programs serve as both a refuge for lesbians and gay men on campus, and common ground from which to launch educational projects that foster respect for difference" (Lambda Legal Defense and Educational Fund 2000: 10).

Strategies for reducing antigay prejudice and discrimination are influenced largely by politicians, religious leaders, courts, and educators who will continue to make decisions that either promote the well-being of sexual orientation minorities or hinder it. Ultimately, however, each individual must decide to embrace either an inclusive or exclusive ideology; collectively, those individual decisions will determine the future treatment of sexual orientation minorities.

In addition, lesbigay individuals must find their own strategies for living in a homophobic, and biphobic society. They may find encouragement in the following:

> If you dream of a world in which you can put your partner's picture on your desk, then put his picture on your desk...and you will live in such a world.
>
> If you dream of a world in which there are more openly gay elected officials, then run for office...and you will live in such a world.
>
> And if you dream of a world in which you can take your partner to the office party...then take her to the party. I do, and now I live in such a world.
>
> Remember, there are two things that keep us oppressed—them and us. We are half of the equation. (Baldwin 2000)

Understanding Sexual Orientation

As both functionalists and conflict theorists note, alternatives to a heterosexual lifestyle are threatening because they challenge traditional definitions of family, childrearing, and gender roles. The result is economic, social, and legal discrimination by the majority. Gay, lesbian, and bisexual individuals are also victimized by hate crimes. In some countries, homosexuality is formally sanctioned, with penalties ranging from fines to imprisonment and even death.

In the past, homosexuality was thought to be a consequence of some psychological disturbance. More recently, some evidence suggests that homosexuality, like handedness, may have a biological component. The debate between biological and social explanations is commonly referred to as the "nature versus nurture" debate. Research indicates that both forces affect sexual orientation, although debate over which is dominant continues. Sociologists are interested in society's response to sexual-orientation diversity and how that response affects the quality of life of society's members. Because individuals' views toward homosexuality are related to their beliefs about what "causes" it, the question of the origins of sexual-orientation diversity has sociological significance.

Prejudice and discrimination toward sexual-orientation minorities are rooted in various aspects of culture, such as religious views, rigid gender roles, and negative myths and stereotypes. Hate crimes against homosexuals and bisexuals are blatant examples of the discrimination that sexual orientation minorities continue to experience.

Attitudes towards lesbians and gays have become more accepting in recent years. One explanation for these changing attitudes is that personal contact with openly gay individuals has increased in recent years as more gay and lesbian Canadians are coming out to their family and friends. "This is likely to increase support for gay and lesbian equality because contacts with openly gay individuals reduce negative stereotypes and ignorance" (Wilcox and Wolpert 2000: 414). Another explanation for changing attitudes toward homosexuality is the positive depiction of gays and lesbians in the popular media. In 1992 *Roseanne* and *Melrose Place* had gay and lesbian characters, in 1998 Ellen DeGeneres came out on her sitcom *Ellen*, and by 2000 there were gay and lesbian characters in many television shows, including *Dawson's Creek*, *Will and Grace*, *Buffy the Vampire Slayer*, *Friends*, *ER*, *Spin City*, *Normal, Ohio* and a gay million-dollar winner on *Survivor* (Deziel 2000).

But as one scholar expressed, "the new confidence and social visibility of homosexuals...have by no means conquered homophobia. Indeed it stands as the last acceptable prejudice" (Fone 2000: 411). Although the gay rights movement has made significant gains in the last few decades, it has also suffered losses and defeat due to gay rights opposition groups and politicians. Many strategies for promoting gay rights have been successful and the Canadian public is becoming increasingly supportive of gay rights. But, as Yang (1999) points out, as the antigay minority diminishes in size, "it often becomes more dedicated and impassioned" (p. ii). For those who believe that all Canadians, regardless of sexual orientation, should be treated equally,

> Our task in the coming years is to get...[those] who support our cause to feel as passionately outraged by the injustices we face and to be as strongly motivated to act in support of our rights as our adversaries are in their opposition to our rights. (p.iii)

Critical Thinking

1 How do you think the legalization of same-sex marriages in Canada would affect public attitudes toward homosexuals?

2 Through the use of the Internet, sexual-orientation minorities today can readily gain access to support organizations and networks. How do you think this use of the Internet has affected the gay rights movement?

3 How is the homosexual population similar to and different from other minority groups?

4 Do you think that social acceptance of homosexuality leads to the creation of laws that protect lesbians and gays? Or does the enactment of laws that protect lesbians and gays help to create more social acceptance of gays?

Key Terms

biphobia	homophobia	reparative therapy
bisexuality	homosexuality	sexual orientation
civil union	lesbigays	transgendered individuals
heterosexism	LGBT	
heterosexuality	master status	

Section 3

Problems of Inequality and Power

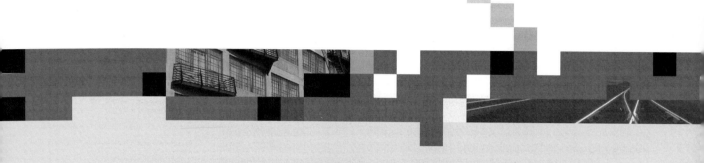

The story of Harrison Bergeron is set in a futuristic society where absolute equality is rigidly enforced (Vonnegut 1968). If people can run faster, they must wear weights in their shoes; if they are brighter, disruptive transistors are implanted in their brains; if they have better vision, blinders are placed over their eyes. The point of the story is that equality, although a cultural ideal, in reality is not always the optimal way to live. The quality of life becomes so unbearable for Harrison Bergeron that he decides that it is better to commit one courageous act of grace and beauty and be killed than to live in a society where everyone is equal.

Differences between people in and of themselves are not what is meant by inequality as a social

Chapter 10
The Haves and the Have-Nots

Chapter 12
Problems in Education

Chapter 11
Work and Unemployment

problem, for few would want to live in a society where everyone was the same. Rather, problems of inequality concern inequities in the quality of life—between the haves and the have-nots (Chapter 10). Social inequality affects the opportunity to work and prosper (Chapter 11) and to attain higher education (Chapter 12).

The chapters in Section 3—"The Haves and the Have-Nots," "Work and Unemployment," and "Problems in Education"—are highly interrelated and speak to the need for examining both the cultural and the structural underpinnings of the social problems described.

10

The Haves and The Have-Nots

Outline

The Global Context: Poverty and Economic Inequality around the World

Sociological Theories of Poverty and Economic Inequality

Wealth, Economic Inequality, and Poverty in Canada

Consequences of Poverty and Economic Inequality

Strategies for Action: Antipoverty Programs, Policies, and Proposals

Understanding the Haves and the Have-Nots

Is It True?

1. Canada has the lowest poverty rate of all industrialized nations.

2. Nearly half of the world's population live on less than $2 a day.

3. Unmarried teenagers make up most of the single-parent mothers on welfare.

4. Many single-parent mothers have many kids to boost their welfare cheques.

5. The age group with the highest poverty rate in Canada is individuals aged 65 and older.

Answers: 1 = F, 2 = T, 3 = F, 4 = F, 5 = F

If all of the afflictions of the world were assembled on one side of the scale and poverty on the other, poverty would outweigh them all.

RABBA, MISHPATIM 31:14

Mable Ditlhakanyane stares into a huge iron pot filled with steaming corn porridge, which is being served with small dollops of chicken, carrots, and potatoes to 5000 landless people who have struck up a muddy protest camp south of the Earth Summit in Johannesburg. "We are starving and our children are dying of AIDS," said the 39-year-old mother of three, who has no job and says she is grateful for the meal. Donated by an American foundation, the food on her chipped plate looks nothing like the oysters, lobsters, and steaks being served to government delegates 25 kilometres away at the Sandton Convention Centre in plush northern Johannesburg, where the marbled floors echo with soothing strands of live African jazz.

The Johannesburg World Summit Company, which organized the biggest UN summit in history, has tried to escape the avalanche of criticisms that has accompanied champagne-and-caviar global meetings before it—notably the recent Food Summit in Rome where delegates gorged on gourmet meals while discussing global starvation....But juggling the demands of kings and presidents with those of a critical public aware that poverty is a major summit theme is proving difficult. The summit's primary hotel indicates that "money is no object" when it comes to the 120 or so national leaders and VIPS....Shipments are arriving daily...about 5000 oysters, 1000 kilograms each of filet beef and chicken breast, 500 kilograms of shellfish, 200 kilograms of salmon, 500 kilograms of bacon and sausages, piles of caviar and paté de fois gras to accompany an extensive wine cellar....

However, even the poorest participants agree they are living better at the summit. "At least we are eating," said Julia Phakathi, a poor villager who came from a remote tribe in Mpumalanga to tell the world that, "we need help"(MacGregor 2002).

This chapter examines the extent of poverty globally and in Canada, focusing on the consequences of poverty for individuals, families, and societies. Theories of poverty and economic inequality are presented and strategies for rectifying economic inequality and poverty are considered.

The Global Context: Poverty and Economic Inequality around the World

Who are the poor? Are rates of world poverty increasing, decreasing, or remaining stable? The answers depend on how we define and measure poverty.

Defining and Measuring Poverty

Poverty has traditionally been defined as the lack of resources necessary for material well-being—most importantly food and water, but also housing, land,

and health care. This lack of resources that leads to hunger and physical deprivation is known as **absolute poverty**. **Relative poverty** refers to a deficiency in material and economic resources compared with some other population. Consider, for example, that while many Canadians are poor, they still have resources and a level of material well being that millions of people living in absolute poverty can only dream of.

Governments, researchers, and organizations use various measures of poverty. Next, we describe international and Canadian measures of poverty.

International Measures of Poverty The World Bank sets a "poverty threshold" of $1 per day to compare poverty in most of the developing world; $2 per day in Latin American; $4 per day in Eastern Europe and the Commonwealth of Independent States (CIS); and $14.40 per day in industrial countries. An estimated 2.8 billion people, nearly half of the world's population, survive on less than $2 per day and a fifth of the world's population (1.2 billion people), live on less than $1 per day (Flavin 2001).

Another poverty measure used by the World Health Organization (WHO) is based on a household's ability to meet the minimum calorie requirements of its members. According to this poverty measure, a household is considered poor if it cannot meet 80 percent of the minimum caloric requirements (established by WHO), even when using 80 percent of its income to buy food.

In industrial countries, national poverty lines are sometimes based on the median household income of a country's population. According to this relative poverty measure, members of a household are considered poor if their household income is less than 50 percent of the median household income in that country.

Research on poverty concludes that poverty is multidimensional and includes such dimensions as food insecurity; poor housing; unemployment; psychological distress; powerlessness; hopelessness; lack of access to health care, education, and transportation; and vulnerability (Narayan 2000). To capture the multidimensional nature of poverty, the United Nations Development Programme (1997) developed a composite measure of poverty: the **Human Poverty Index (HPI)**. Rather than measure poverty by income, three measures of deprivation are combined to yield the Human Poverty Index: (1) deprivation of a long, health life, (2) deprivation of knowledge, and (3) deprivation of decent living standards. As shown in Table 10.1, the Human Poverty Index for developing countries (HPI) is measured differently than for industrialized countries (HPI-2). Among the 17 industrialized countries for which the HPI-2 was calculated in 2001, Sweden has the lowest level of human poverty (6.8 percent), followed by Norway (7.5 percent), and the Netherlands (8.5 percent). The Human Poverty Index is a useful complement to income measures of poverty and "will serve as a strong reminder that eradicating poverty will always require more than increasing the income of the poorest" (United Nations Development Programme 1997: 19).

Measures of poverty tell us how many, or what percentage of, people are living in poverty in a given year. Another way to assess poverty is to note the degree to which those who are poor stay in poverty from year to year. This can be done by calculating the average annual poverty exit rate—the share of the poor in one year that have left poverty by the following year. One study followed the same families over a five-year period in six countries—Canada, Germany, Netherlands, Sweden, United Kingdom, and the United States (reported

Human poverty is more than income poverty—it is the denial of choices and opportunities for living a tolerable life.

UNITED NATIONS DEVELOPMENT PROGRAMME
Human Development Report 1997

■ **Table 10.1** *Measures of Human Poverty in Developing and Industrialized Countries*

	Longevity	Knowledge	Decent Standard of Living
For developing countries	Probability at birth of not surviving to age 40	Adult illiteracy	A composite measure based on: 1. Percentage of people without access to safe water 2. Percentage of people without access to health services 3. Percentage of children under five who are underweight
For Industrialized countries	Probability at birth of not surviving to age 60	Adult functional illiteracy rate	Percentage of people living below the income poverty line, which is set at 50 percent of median disposable income

SOURCE: Adapted from the United Nations Development Programme. 2000. *Human Development Report 2000*. New York: Oxford University Press.

in Mishel et al. 2001). The results indicated that, with the exception of the Netherlands, the poor in Canada were more likely than the poor elsewhere to leave poverty from one year to the next. According to this research, 44 percent of the poor in the Netherlands and 42 percent of the poor in Canada escape poverty each year, compared with 28.6 percent of the poor in the United States, 29.1 percent in the United Kingdom, 36 percent in Sweden, and 37 percent in Germany.

Canadian Measures of Poverty

Statistics Canada developed the **low-income cutoff (LICO)** as a measure of poverty in 1968. Estimating that poor families or individuals spent approximately 34.7 percent or more of their pre-tax income on such basic needs as food, shelter, and clothing, they then added 20 percentage points to determine the cutoff. In consequence, it was arbitrarily established as a standard that families or individuals who spent 54.7 percent of their pre-tax income on food, clothing, and shelter would be in financial difficulty. Recognizing that the minimum income level necessary to avoid financial hardship also varies according to changes in the cost of living, family size, and place of residence, Statistics Canada calculates different low-income cutoffs for different communities and for families of varying sizes within these communities. For example, in 2001, the low-income cutoff for a family of four living in an urban area with a population of half a million or more was $35 471. For a family of four living in a rural area, it was $24 513 (Table 10.2).

Poverty lines might be drawn in several other ways. For example, the poverty line established by a special Senate committee on poverty used post-tax or disposable income. This method produces a poverty line that is set at approximately 56 percent of the level of average Canadian family income. Another way of measuring poverty is by employing the "market basket measure"—a measure that Human Resources Development Canada has been developing at the request of the federal and provincial governments. This measure is based on

■ **Table 10.2** *Low Income Cut-Off Lines, 2001*[1]

Family size[2]	Population				
	30 000	**30 000 to 99 999**	**100 000 to 499 999**	**500 000+**	**Rural Areas**
1 person	$14 940	$16 055	$16 167	$18 849	$13 026
2 persons	18 674	20 070	20 209	22 561	16 283
3 persons	23 224	24 958	25 134	29 303	20 251
4 persons	28 113	30 214	30 424	35 471	24 513
5 persons	31 425	33 773	34 010	39 651	27 402
6 persons	34 737	37 333	37 595	43 830	30 292
7+ persons	38 049	40 893	41 181	48 010	33 181

[1]National Council of Welfare Estimates of Statistics Canada's Before-Tax Low Income Cut-Offs (1992 base) for 2001 based on 2.6 percent inflation in 2001.

[2]Does not distinguish between adults and children as family members.

SOURCE: National Council of Welfare. 2002. "Fact Sheet: Poverty Lines 2001." March 2002. On the World Wide Web at http://www.ncwcnbes.net/htmdocument/principales/povertyline.htm. Reproduced with the permission of the Minister of Public Works and Government Services Canada, 2003.

the concept of "necessaries" as defined by the eighteenth-century economist Adam Smith: "Whatever the custom of the country renders it indecent for creditable people, even of the lowest order, to be without." While the market basket concept is used by the provinces to set welfare rates, defining what, exactly, are "necessaries" is not easy. The concept, as used by Smith, implies that necessaries are broader than what is needed for mere subsistence.

Another way of defining low income or the "poverty line" is to employ the **Low-Income Measure (LIM)**. To assess low income using this measure, Statistics Canada has established a figure for the needs of one adult and proceeded on the assumption that family needs increase in proportion to the size of the family, with each additional adult increasing the family needs by 40 percent of the first adult and each additional child increasing the family's needs by 30 percent. To calculate how many Canadians, individuals, or family members, lack sufficient income to cover their basic needs for food, clothing, shelter, and other necessities, Statistics Canada compares these income figures with the actual incomes of families and individuals.

It is evident that estimating the numbers of Canadians who are poor is no simple task. The writings of Christopher Sarlo (1992; 1996) have repeatedly drawn attention to what he perceives to be the inadequacies of employing the LICO as a measure of poverty in Canada. For example, he notes that the LICO does not include benefits in kind, or capital gains, or, of course, unreported income. Sarlo additionally claims that "of all households below the LICO in 1990, almost one in five owned their homes, mortgage free...97 percent, had colour television...53 percent owned a car—the same rate as for those above the poverty line" (in Coyne 1997). According to Sarlo, "poverty, as it has been traditionally understood, has been virtually eliminated" (1992: 2). However, this claim is based on the assumptions that non-nutritious consumables such as coffee, ketchup, and jam are unnecessary, that $245 a year is sufficient to provide an individual with a year's supply of clothing and footwear, and that hairdressing services can be adequately performed by family members on each other. For those who experience trouble with their vision or experience toothaches, Sarlo "assumes that dental societies will provide free dental services to low-income families and that Lions Clubs will provide free eyeglasses" (Krahn 1994: 2.8).

Ross et al. (1994) emphasize that in employing the LICO "Statistics Canada does not claim to measure poverty; rather, it defines a set of income cutoffs below which people may be said to live in straitened circumstances." However, as we have noted, the way in which poverty is defined does have serious practical consequences—it determines who will receive help and who will not and, what types of social policies and programs are thought necessary.

The Extent of Global Poverty and Economic Inequality

The *Global Poverty Report* (2000) finds that globally, the proportion of people living on less than $1 per day fell from 29 percent in 1987 to 26 percent in 1998. Social indicators have also improved over the last three decades. In developing countries, life expectancy rose from 55 years in 1970 to 65 years in 1998 and infant mortality rates have fallen from 107 per 1000 live births to 59. However, sub-Saharan Africa, Central Asia, and Eastern Europe have not shared in this progress (*Global Poverty Report* 2000). South Asia has the greatest number of people affected by poverty and sub-Saharan Africa has the highest proportion of people in poverty. Indeed, in every region of the world except Africa, the share of the population that is hungry is diminishing (Brown 2001). Recent estimates of world hunger and malnourishment vary from 830 million (Wren 2001) to 1.1 billion people worldwide (Flavin 2001). In some Africa countries, such as Kenya, Zambia, and Zimbabwe, as much as 40 percent of the population is malnourished (Flavin 2001).

The 1997 *Report on the World Social Situation* notes that "infant mortality has fallen almost steadily in all regions and life expectancy has risen all over the globe. Educational attainment is rising, health care and living conditions are improving in most countries, and the quantity, quality, and range of goods and services available to a large majority of the world's population is increasing" (United Nations 1997: 80). But the report goes on to say that "not everyone has shared in this prosperity. Economic growth has been slow or non-existent in many of the world's poorest countries....The plight of the poor stands in stark contrast to the rising standards of living enjoyed by those favoured by growing abundance" (p. 80).

Global economic inequality has reached unprecedented levels. Consider that in 1998, the combined wealth of the world's 200 richest people was $1 trillion. In the same year, the combined incomes of the 582 million people living in the 43 least developed countries was $146 billion (United Nations Development Programme 2000). And global economic inequality widening the gap between the haves and the have-nots is likely to increase, if past trends continue. In 2000, the average income of the richest 20 countries was 37 times that of the poorest 20 countries—a gap that has doubled in the past 40 years (World Bank 2001). As the global gap between the rich and the poor increases, wealthy populations increase their consumption. As we discuss in Chapter 13, overconsumption by the rich is a significant environmental problem. The wealthiest

25 percent of the world population consumes 85 percent of the world's resources and produces 90 percent of its wastes (Cracker and Linden 1998).

Sociological Theories of Poverty and Economic Inequality

The three main theoretical perspectives in sociology—structural-functionalism, conflict theory, and symbolic interactionism—offer insights into the nature, causes, and consequences of poverty and economic inequality. Before reading further, you may want to take the "Attitudes towards Economic Opportunity" survey in this chapter's *Self and Society* feature.

Structural-Functionalist Perspective

According to the structural-functionalist perspective, poverty and economic inequality serve a number of positive functions for society. Decades ago, Davis and Moore (1945) argued that because the various occupational roles in society require different levels of ability, expertise, and knowledge, an unequal economic reward system helps to ensure that the person who performs a particular role is the most qualified. As people acquire certain levels of expertise (e.g., B.A., M.A., Ph.D., M.D.), they are progressively rewarded. Such a system, argued Davis and Moore, motivates people to achieve by offering higher rewards for higher achievements. If physicians were not offered high salaries, for example, who would want to endure the arduous years of medical training and long, stressful hours at a hospital?

The structural-functionalist view of poverty suggests that a certain amount of poverty has positive functions for society. Although poor people are often viewed as a burden to society, having a pool of low-paid, impoverished workers ensures that there will be people willing to do dirty, dangerous, and difficult work that others refuse to do. Poverty also provides employment for those who work in the "poverty industry" (such as welfare workers) and supplies a market for inferior goods such as older, dilapidated homes and automobiles (Gans 1972).

The structural-functionalist view of poverty and economic inequality has received a great deal of criticism from contemporary sociologists, who point out that many important occupational roles (such as childcare workers) are poorly paid, whereas many individuals in nonessential roles (such as professional sports stars and entertainers) earn astronomical sums of money. Functionalism also accepts poverty as unavoidable and ignores the role of inheritance in the distribution of rewards.

Conflict Perspective

Conflict theorists regard economic inequality as resulting from the domination of the **bourgeoisie** (owners of the means of production) over the **proletariat** (workers). The bourgeoisie accumulate wealth as they profit from the labour of the proletariat, who earn wages far below the earnings of the bourgeoisie. The educational institution furthers the ideals of capitalism by perpetuating the belief in equal opportunity and the value of the work ethic. The proletariat, dependent on the capitalistic system, continue to be exploited by the wealthy and accept the belief that poverty is a consequence of personal failure rather than of a flawed economic structure.

Conflict theorists note how laws and policies benefit the wealthy and contribute to the gap between the haves and the have-nots. Laws and policies that favour the rich—sometimes referred to as **wealthfare** or **corporate welfare**—include low-interest government loans to failing businesses, special subsidies and tax breaks to corporations, and other laws and policies that benefit corporations and the wealthy. Between 1994 and 1999, federal handouts to businesses topped $14 billion (Canadian Centre for Policy Alternatives Monitor 1999). Corporate "tax breaks" or "loopholes" cost the Canadian treasury billions. "Businesses are still permitted to deduct from the money they owe in taxes 20 percent of their expenses for meals and entertainment—such as luxury boxes at the SkyDome and escort services—from their taxable income" (Barlow and Campbell 1995: 174–75). In addition, "generous tax subsidies to oil and gas companies for their exploration and development costs" divert half a billion a year from Canada's treasury. Indeed,

> So many tax loopholes are available to corporations that each year tens of thousands of profitable companies pay not a penny in income taxes. The result is that corporate income tax paid in Canada is in the bottom half of industrialized countries….Canada has the second worst record in the industrialized world (after Australia) for taxing wealth, making it a tax haven for wealthy individuals. (175–76)

Conflict theorists also note that throughout the world, "free-market" economic reform policies have been hailed as a solution to poverty. Yet, while such economic reform has benefited many wealthy corporations and investors, it has also resulted in increasing levels of global poverty. As companies relocate to countries with abundant supplies of cheap labour, wages decline. Lower wages lead to decreased consumer spending, which leads to more industries closing plants, going bankrupt, or laying off workers (downsizing). This results in higher unemployment rates and a surplus of workers, enabling employers to lower wages even more. Chossudovsky (1998) suggests that "this new international economic order feeds on human poverty and cheap labour" (p. 299).

Symbolic Interactionist Perspective

Symbolic interactionism focuses on how meanings, labels, and definitions affect and are affected by social life. This view calls attention to ways in which wealth and poverty are defined and the consequences of being labelled as "poor." Individuals who are viewed as poor—especially those receiving public assistance (i.e., welfare)—are often stigmatized as lazy, irresponsible, and lacking in abilities, motivation, and moral values. Indeed, the phrase "poor but honest" implicitly suggests that we view honesty and low income as an unlikely combination and must single out those who are both as exceptions to the rule. Wealthy individuals, on the other hand, tend to be viewed as capable, motivated, hard working, and deserving of their wealth.

The symbolic interaction perspective also focuses on the meanings of being poor. A qualitative study of over 40 000 poor women and men in 50 countries around the world explored the meanings of poverty from the perspective of those who live in poverty (Narayan 2000). Among the study's findings is that the experience of poverty involves psychological dimensions such as powerlessness, voicelessness, dependency, shame, and humiliation.

Although I have made a fortune in the financial markets, I now fear that the untrammeled intensification of laissez-faire capitalism and the spread of market values into all areas of life is endangering our open and democratic society.

George Soros
Financier

In many of the companies that are corporate welfare bums, receptionists pay more in income tax than the companies do.

Cameron Smith
Author

Attitudes towards Economic Opportunity

After responding to the questions below, compare your answers with the results obtained from a Gallup poll of 5001 U.S. adults.

1. Using a one-to-five scale, where "1" means not at all important, and "5" means extremely important, indicate how important each of the following is as a reason for a person's success.

Item	Ranking (1 = not at all important; 5 = extremely important)				
a. Hard work and initiative	1	2	3	4	5
b. Member of a particular race/ethnic group	1	2	3	4	5
c. Getting right education and training	1	2	3	4	5
d. Dishonesty and willingness to take whatever one can get	1	2	3	4	5
e. Parents and family	1	2	3	4	5
f. Willingness to take risks	1	2	3	4	5
g. Gender (whether one is male or female)	1	2	3	4	5
h. Connections/knowing the right people	1	2	3	4	5
i. Money inherited from family	1	2	3	4	5
j. Ability or talent one is born with	1	2	3	4	5
k. Good luck/in right place at right time	1	2	3	4	5
l. Physical appearance/good looks	1	2	3	4	5

2. For the following two questions, indicate your answer from the choices provided:

   a. Why are some people poor?

   _____ lack of effort   _____ circumstances beyond their control

   _____ both   _____ don't know

   b. Why are some people rich?

   _____ strong effort   _____ circumstances beyond their control

   _____ both   _____ don't know

Meanings and definitions of wealth and poverty vary across societies and across time. For example, the Dinka are the largest ethnic group in the sub-Saharan African country of Sudan. By global standards, the Dinka are among the poorest of the poor, being among the least modernized peoples of the world. In the Dinka culture, wealth is measured in large part according to how many cattle a person owns. But, to the Dinka, cattle have a social, moral, and spiritual value as well as an economic value. In Dinka culture, a man pays an average "bridewealth" of 50 cows to the family of his bride. Thus, men use cattle to obtain a wife to beget children, especially sons, to ensure the continuity of their ancestral lineage and, according to Dinka religious beliefs, their linkage with

3. Complete the following sentence with one of the two choices provided:

The economic system in this country:

_____ is basically fair, since all individuals have an equal opportunity to succeed.

_____ is basically unfair, since all individuals do not have an equal opportunity to succeed.

HOW DO YOUR ANSWERS COMPARE WITH A NATIONAL SAMPLE OF U.S. ADULTS?*

1. This figure reveals the percentages of U.S. adults who rated the items in question #1 as important for success.

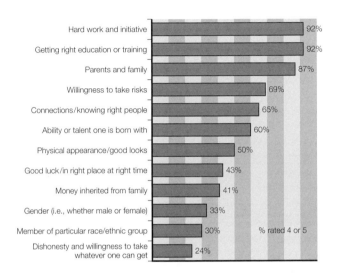

Hard work and initiative	92%
Getting right education or training	92%
Parents and family	87%
Willingness to take risks	69%
Connections/knowing right people	65%
Ability or talent one is born with	60%
Physical appearance/good looks	50%
Good luck/in right place at right time	43%
Money inherited from family	41%
Gender (i.e., whether male or female)	33%
Member of particular race/ethnic group	30%
Dishonesty and willingness to take whatever one can get	24%

% rated 4 or 5

2a. In explaining why some people are poor, 43 percent of respondents indicated "lack of effort," 41 percent indicated "circumstances beyond their control," and 16 percent indicated "both" or "don't know."

2b. In explaining why some people are rich, 53 percent of respondents indicated "strong effort," 12 percent indicated "circumstances beyond their control," and 15 percent indicated "both" or "don't know."

3. Sixty-eight percent of respondents indicated that they believe their nation's economic system is basically fair; 29 percent believe it is basically unfair; and three percent had no opinion.

*The percentages given were obtained in a 1998 Gallup poll of 5001 U.S. adults.

SOURCE: Adapted from Gallup News Service Social Audit. 1998. (April 23 to May 31). http://www.gallup.com/poll/socialaudits/have_havenot.asp (used by permission).

God. Although modernized populations might label the Dinka as poor, the Dinka view themselves as wealthy.

Definitions of poverty also vary within societies. For example, in Ghana men associate poverty with a lack of material assets, whereas for women poverty is defined as food insecurity (Narayan 2000).

The symbolic interactionist perspective emphasizes that norms, values, and beliefs are learned through social interaction and that social interaction influences the development of one's self-concept. Lewis (1966) argued that, over time, the poor develop norms, values, beliefs, and self-concepts that contribute to their own plight. According to Lewis, the **culture of poverty** is characterized

In today's economy a woman is considered lazy when she's at home taking care of her children. And to me that's not laziness.... Let some of these men that work in the government, let some of them stay home and do that. They'll find that a woman is not lazy when she's taking care of her family.

DENISE TURNER
Welfare recipient

by female-centred households, an emphasis on gratification in the present rather than in the future, and a relative lack of participation in society's major institutions. "The people in the culture of poverty have a strong feeling of marginality, of helplessness, of dependency, of not belonging....Along with this feeling of powerlessness is a widespread feeling of inferiority, of personal unworthiness" (Lewis 1998: 7). Early sexual activity, unmarried parenthood, joblessness, reliance on public assistance, illegitimate income-producing activities (e.g., selling drugs) and substance use are common among the **underclass**—people living in persistent poverty. The culture of poverty view emphasizes that the behaviours, values, and attitudes exhibited by the chronically poor are transmitted from one generation to the next, perpetuating the cycle of poverty. Critics of the culture of poverty approach point out that behaviours, values, and attitudes of the underclass emerge from the constraints and blocked opportunity that have resulted largely from the disappearance of work (Van Kempen 1997; Wilson 1996) (see also Chapter 8).

> In an environment...where families with a steady, employed breadwinner have become the exception rather than the rule, the chance to contact families and institutions that represent conventional role models is small. Hence, people are not introduced into jobs, and they do not learn from experience about the behaviour and norms that belong to steady work and stable family life. Being surrounded by people who have to rely on other, often illegal strategies to survive, these strategies come to be seen as a way of life. (Van Kempen 1997: 434)

Money to us is of no value, and to most of us unknown; and as no consideration whatever can induce us to sell our lands, on which we get sustenance for our women and children, we hope we may be allowed to point out a mode by which your settlers may be removed, and peace thereby obtained.

JOSEPH BRANT
Mohawk leader

Wealth, Economic Inequality, and Poverty in Canada

Canada is a nation of tremendous economic variation ranging from the very rich to the very poor. Signs of this disparity are visible everywhere, from opulent mansions to squalid rooming houses, from those who drive or are driven in luxury cars to those who cannot afford the price of a monthly bus pass.

Wealth in Canada

Wealth refers to the total assets of an individual or household, minus liabilities (mortgages, loans, and debts). Wealth includes the value of a home; investment real estate; cars; an unincorporated business; life insurance (cash value); stocks, bonds, mutual funds, trusts; chequing and savings accounts; retirement savings plans; and valuable collectibles. As of May 2002, publishing magnate Kenneth Thomson was the richest Canadian with a net worth of $27.71 billion (see Table 10.3). However, the United States leads the world in countries with the greatest number of billionaires followed, in order, by Japan and Germany (Ash 2001: 202).

For real wealth and real power in Canada, inherit it, marry it, or forget it.

WALTER STEWART
Journalist

A 2001 Statistics Canada study reveals that Canada is an "increasingly polarized country, with the top 20 percent of families gaining a whopping 39 percent in accumulated wealth since 1984, while the average wealth of the bottom 20 percent actually shrunk" (Centre for Social Justice 2001). While in 1984, the average wealth of the top 20 percent of households was $291 200, by 1999, the average was $439 000. In contrast, the bottom 20 percent saw their average

■ Table 10.3 *Wealthiest 10 Canadians, 2002*

Individual or Family	Estimated Wealth	Assets and Notes
Kenneth Thomson	$27.71 billion	Former Chairman, Thomson Corp., moving from a newspaper empire to an e-information and solutions company; chairman and director, Woodbridge Company Limited (the Thomson family holding company); http://www.thomson.com
Galen Weston	$10.24 billion	George Weston Ltd., founded 1882; Loblaws; President's Choice; Zehrs; Connors Seafood; owns more than 20 salmon farms; Holt Renfrew; http://www.weston.ca
Bombardier family	$4.65 billion	Bombardier Aerospace; Ski-doo snowmobiles; production sites in Canada, United States, Mexico, Austria, Germany, Switzerland, etc.; http://www.bombardier.com
James Pattison	$3.81 billion	Auto sales; food; media
Jeff Skoll	$3.43 billion	e-Bay
Eugene Melnyk	$3.3 billion	Pharmaceuticals (Biovail Corp.)
Irving family	$3.2 billion	Irving Oil; JD Irving Ltd; reputed to have revenues as large as the province of New Brunswick; http://www.irvingoil.com or http://www.jdirving.com
Paul Desmarais, Sr.	$2.79 billion	Financial services (Great West Lifeco, Investors Group); publishing (La Presse, Power Corp.)
Bernard Sherman	$2.73 billion	Pharmaceuticals (Apotex)
Charles Bronfman	$2.38 billion	Entertainment; telecommunications

SOURCE: Brieger et al. Wealth Report (May 25, 2002). *National Post*, WR4.

wealth decline by about $800. In addition, the top 10 percent of families accounted for more than half (53 percent) of all personal wealth in 1999—up from 51.3 percent in 1984.

Economic Inequality in Canada

The three decades after the end of World War II were a time of unprecedented economic prosperity and stability in Canada. Throughout the 1950s and 1960s, unemployment and inflation were low and a steady increase in personal incomes financed the growth of the social safety net, including universal health care, the Canadian Pension Plan, unemployment insurance, and inexpensive postsecondary education. By the 1970s however, "stagflation" had set in, with increases in both consumer prices and unemployment levels and a halt in the growth of real income. During this period, many Western countries, including Canada, were pushed into the steepest recession since the time of the Great Depression. Because of economic downturns, economic inequality—the gap between the haves and the have-nots—grew significantly. Since the 1970s, much has changed, beginning with the government's introduction of various tax measures and policy decisions, such as deregulation, privatization, free trade, and monetarism, which reflected a "corporate agenda." These measures have most obviously benefited corporations and those whom economist John Kenneth Galbraith has dubbed the "contented classes."

Barlow and Campbell (1995: 76) point out that income inequality in Canada has not only been growing in the past decades "but it has been picking up speed." While high-income families have reaped benefits from very high interest rates on their savings, and tax breaks, lower income tax rates, and an increase in both the numbers of those employed within professional and managerial groups and the level of executive earnings, others have fared more poorly. Declines in family income and median real wages, rising unemployment, increases in part-time, temporary, and low-paying jobs, and the accelerated pace of social cuts (designed to make Canada's system of social security more "affordable" and to level the free-trade playing field) have had a huge impact on Canada's poor. According to research conducted by the Toronto Centre for Social Justice, the average incomes of the top 10 percent of families with children in 1973 were 8.5 times those of the bottom 10 percent; by 1996, this ratio had increased to 10.2 (Yalnizyan 1998).

The gap between the richest and poorest families increased after 1995, when the federal government made drastic cuts in social program spending. Cuts to public programs at both the provincial and federal levels have hit poorest families the hardest (Bricker and Greenspon 2001; Daub and Young 1999; National Council of Welfare 2000). While in 1989, the top quintile of families with the highest incomes received 41.9 percent of total market income, this proportion rose to 45.2 percent in 1998. In contrast, the share of the market income going to the 20 percent of families with the lowest incomes decreased from 3.8 percent to 3.1 percent over the same time period. Moreover, "[d]espite the equalizing role played by transfers and taxes, the gap between the two ends of the income scale widened slightly during the 1990s, even on an after-tax basis" (Statistics Canada 2000).

I'm an optimist in the long run, but what I don't know—and I don't think politicians know—is how we are going to make it through the night, with the rich getting richer and the poor poorer.

MATTHEW BARRETT
Former CEO, Bank of Montreal

Patterns of Poverty in Canada

Although poverty is not as widespread or severe in Canada as it is in many less developed countries, it nevertheless represents a significant social problem. According to the National Council of Welfare (2000), "[i]n 1999, there were 1 025 000 families and 1 677 000 unattached individuals living in poverty in Canada." However, poverty is not equally distributed. Poverty rates vary according to age, education, gender, family structure, disability, race/ethnicity, and labour force participation.

Age and Poverty Despite a political landscape "littered with political rhetoric about children," Canada has had little success in reducing child poverty (see Chapter 6). In 1989, when the House of Commons passed a unanimous resolution to eliminate child poverty in Canada by the year 2000, the child poverty rate was 15.2 percent—representing about one million poor children. While the child poverty rate in Canada peaked in 1996 (at 21.6 percent) and has declined since that time, the child poverty rate in 1999 was 18.7 percent (about 1.3 million children). The child poverty rate in Canada remained higher than the average poverty rate (16.2 percent). Moreover, in 1999, "most Canadian poor families with children needed, on average, more than $8000 before taxes and more than $5000 after taxes just to meet the poverty line" (National

Council of Welfare 2000). During the time period of 1993 to 1998, children under the age of six were the most likely of all age groups to have lived in poverty for all six years.

Government programs and policies (see Chapter 6) have led to an improvement in the poverty rate among Canada's seniors. Between 1980 and 1999, the poverty rate for Canada's seniors was almost halved, from 34 percent in 1980 to 17.7 percent in 1999 (National Council of Welfare 2000). However, while the poverty rate among senior couples is low (4.7 percent in 1999), unattached seniors continue to experience high rates of poverty. Moreover, while the poverty rate of senior unattached men decreased from 35.1 percent in 1998 to 31.9 percent in 1999, the poverty rate of unattached senior women rose from the already high rate of 47.9 percent in 1998 to an even higher rate of 48.5 percent in 1999.

Education and Poverty Education is one of the best insurance policies to protect against an individual living in poverty. In general, the higher a person's level of educational attainment, the less likely that person is to be poor (see also Chapter 12). For example, Canadian families in which the principal income earner had at least a university degree had a poverty rate of 6 percent in 1999. In contrast, single-parent mothers with less than a high school diploma had a poverty rate of 82.3 percent in that year. However, "[a]lthough level of education and poverty rates are somewhat inversely related, education is not always a guarantee against poverty" (National Council of Welfare 2000: 7). More than half (52 percent) of the 1 667 000 poor unattached individuals in 1999 had at least a high school diploma.

Gender and Poverty Women are more likely than men are to live below the poverty line—a phenomenon referred to as the **feminization of poverty**. As discussed in Chapter 7, women are less likely than men are to pursue advanced educational degrees in nontraditional areas of study. They also tend to be more heavily concentrated in a narrower range of jobs than men are, and within lower-paying jobs, such as service and clerical work (Statistics Canada 2002). Women who are minorities or who are single mothers are at increased risk of being poor. In 1999, the pre-tax poverty rates of Canadian women surpassed men's in almost all categories (National Council of Welfare 2000).

Family Structure and Poverty Poverty is much more prevalent among female-headed single-parent households than among other types of family structures. The relationship between family structure and poverty helps to explain why women and children have higher poverty rates than men (see also Chapter 5). While the poverty rate for families headed by single-parent families fluctuated between 51.8 percent and 61.8 percent between 1980 and 1999, in 1999, "single-mother families were the only family type with a majority of its members still living below the poverty line" (National Council of Welfare 2000: 15). In comparison, the poverty rate in 1999 for families headed by single-parent fathers was 18 percent (down from 25.4 percent in 1980).

Disability and Poverty According to data compiled by the Canadian Council on Social Development (Fawcett 1999), disability is a strong indicator of poverty. In 1995, more than one third (36.2 percent) of women with disabilities versus 18.5 percent of Canadians without disabilities aged 15 to 64 were poor. This pattern also holds for men with disabilities. In 1996, while the national poverty rate for men without disabilities was 15.6 percent, among men with disabilities it was 34.1 percent (Figure 10.1). As one might expect, there are significant differences in the poverty rates between men with disabilities and particularly women with disabilities who have full-time, full-year employment and those who do not (Figure 10.2). However, a substantial proportion of people with disabilities do not participate in the paid labour force at all.

Obtaining employment and remaining employed often poses a considerable challenge to both men and women who have disabilities. First, employment discontinuities are common due to the cyclical nature of some disabilities and a tendency for those with disabilities to be the "last hired and the first fired." In addition, while many income support programs, including social assistance and disability pensions, provide support for disability-related expenses (e.g., medication, transportation), such supports disappear when individuals with disabilities become employed. Accordingly, if one's employment income is insufficient to cover such expenses, one cannot truly "afford to work." As Fawcett (1999) points out, "persons with disabilities who look for work face a dilemma: in their attempts to convince potential employers that they are capable of working, they may disqualify themselves from the social assistance and disability supports they need in order to survive."

Compared to their counterparts without disabilities, both women and men with disabilities are more likely to be the sole providers of family income. However, the situation is particularly bleak among women with disabilities because they are more likely than other groups to live as lone parents. In 1996, almost one in ten (9.7 percent) women with a disability was a lone parent (compared

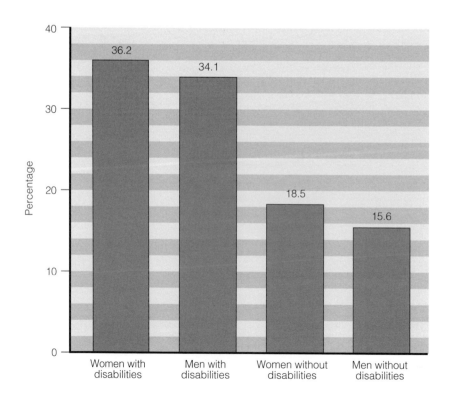

■ **Figure 10.1** *Poverty Rates for Working-age Women and Men with and without Disabilities, Canada 1995*

SOURCE: Prepared by the Canadian Council on Social Development using data from Statistics Canada's 1996 Census.

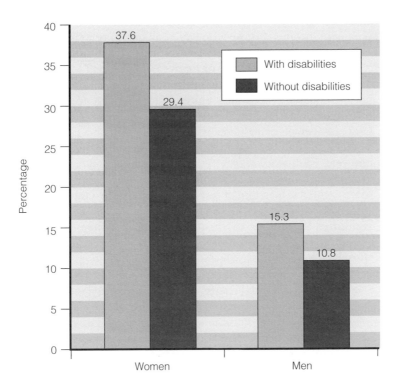

Figure 10.2 *Women and Men Employed Full Year, with Earnings under $15 640, by Disability Status, Canada, 1996*

SOURCE: Prepared by the Canadian Council on Social Development using Statistics Canada's Survey of Labour and Income Dynamics, 1993–1994.

with 7.6 percent of women without disabilities, 2.8 percent of men with disabilities, and 1.1 percent of men without disabilities). Women with disabilities who obtain full-time, full-year employment typically earn less than either women without disabilities or men with disabilities. As Fawcett (1999) has observed, "with these earnings prospects, many women with disabilities would not be able to earn the 'premium' required to support themselves and their families, *and* pay the extra costs of disability-related supports. For many women with disabilities, the safest choice is to remain out of the labour market."

Race and Ethnicity and Poverty Based on the findings of the 1996 Canadian census, the incidence of low income is high among visible minorities in Canada and among its Aboriginal people (Figure 10.3). Canada's visible minority population, of which the largest proportion were recent immigrants, had below average employment incomes and an incidence of low income that

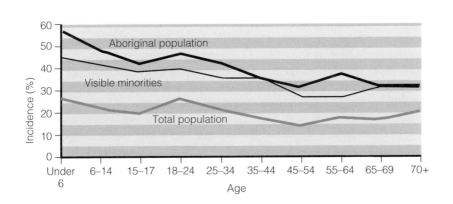

Figure 10.3 *Incidence of Low Income by Age, Canada, 1995*

SOURCE: Statistics Canada. 1998. *The Daily*, May 12.

was significantly above average (36 percent versus 20 percent). In 1995, the average employment income of those who were Canadian-born visible minority earners was almost 30 percent below the level reported by all other Canadian-born earners (Statistics Canada 1998b). In that year, almost half (45 percent) of the children under the age of six in the visible minority population lived in low-income families (compared with 26 percent of all children). Among those who were 65 years of age or older, the incidence of low income was 32 percent (compared to a national average of 19 percent). Between 1993 and 1998, approximately 42.5 percent of Canada's immigrant visible minorities lived in poverty for at least one year, compared to 29.5 percent of the total population. In addition, "15.6 percent of immigrant visible minorities lived in poverty for all six years, compared with five percent of persons who are not visible minorities (National Council on Welfare 2002b: 6).

A study conducted by Michael Ornstein on poverty levels among racialized minorities in Toronto that was based on data from the 1996 Canadian census found that "[w]hile 14 percent of European families live below the Low Income Cut Off, the percentage is much higher for non-Europeans: 32.1 percent for Aboriginals; 35 percent for South Asians; 45 percent for Africans, Blacks and Caribbeans; and 45 percent for Arabs and West Asians" (Centre for Social Justice 2001b). The study also notes that the unemployment rate among racialized groups was up to six times higher than Toronto's average unemployment rate.

A recent analysis of the economic performance of racialized group members and other Canadians over the period 1996–98 (Galabuzi 2001) also finds evidence of "economic apartheid," or the economic segregation and social marginalization of racialized groups, particularly in urban areas. Among her findings:

- There is a persistent and sizeable (double digit) gap between the economic performance of racialized group members and other Canadians....In 1998 there was a 24 percent gap in average before tax income and a 20 percent gap in after tax income.
- [A] racialized labour market is an endemic feature of the Canadian economy. Characteristic of the racial and gender labour market segmentation is the overrepresentation of racialized (particularly women) members in low paid, low-end occupations and low income sectors, and also temporary work. They are especially over-represented in low-end service sector jobs and precarious and unregulated temporary or contingent work....
- Income inequalities are a significant contributor to racialized group members' persistent above average poverty rates across the nation, and particularly in...urban areas where they are concentrated. The patterns suggest that a process of racialization of poverty is underway.

Aboriginal people also experience heightened risk of poverty (see also Chapters 2 and 8). Excluding the Aboriginal population who lived on reserves, in the Yukon, or Northwest Territories (where income is generally lower than for the Aboriginal population living off reserve), 44 percent of the Aboriginal population in 1995 was below Statistics Canada's low-income cutoffs. Among those who identified themselves as North American Indians, almost half (48 percent) were in a low-income situation. Among the Métis (the second largest group), almost four in ten (39 percent) were in a low-income situation. In that year, three out of five Aboriginal children under the age of six were in low-income families. Among those aged 6 to 14, the incidence of low income was

48 percent, or more than twice the national rate of 22 percent (Statistics Canada 1998b) (see Figure 10.3).

Between 1993 and 1999, 49.4 percent of Aboriginals persons living off reserve lived in poverty in at least one of the six years; an estimated 12.6 percent lived in long-term poverty during this six-year period (National Council of Welfare 2002b: 6).

Labour Force Participation and Poverty A common image of the poor is that they are jobless and unable or unwilling to work. Although the Canadian poor are primarily children and adults who are not in the labour force, many poor are classified as "**working poor.**" Consider that in 1999, over 40 percent of the more than one million Canadian families who lived in poverty were headed by persons who were employed. "Single-parent mothers working full-time, full-year still had a poverty rate of 19.7 percent" (National Council of Welfare 2002b: 7).

Labour force attachment does, to be sure, offer a buffer against poverty. In 1999, the poverty rate for unattached individuals under the age of 65 and for their families decreased as their weeks of paid employment increased. Specifically, among unattached individuals, the poverty rate for persons with no paid work was 80.1 percent versus 18.4 percent for those who worked 49 to 52 weeks. For families, the poverty rate for those with no paid work was 56 percent versus 3 percent among families with 103 or more weeks of paid work (i.e., two full-year workers).

> On this continent, indigenous and indigent are synonymous.
>
> MAURUS E. MALLON
> *Aphorist*

Consequences of Poverty and Economic Inequality

Poverty is associated with health problems, problems in education, problems in families and parenting, and housing problems. These various problems are interrelated and contribute to the perpetuation of poverty across generations, feeding a cycle of intergenerational poverty. In addition, poverty and economic inequality breed social conflict and war.

Health Problems and Poverty

In Chapter 2, we noted that poverty has been identified as the world's leading health problem. Persistent poverty is associated with higher rates of infant mortality and childhood deaths and lower life expectancies among adults. Although access to universally insured health care remains largely unrelated to income in Canada, many low-income and moderate-income Canadians have limited or no access to such health services as eye care, dentistry, mental health counselling, and prescription drugs (Health Canada 1999).

Economic inequality also affects psychological and physical health. "[P]erceptions of inequality translate into psychological feelings of lack of security, lower self-esteem, envy and unhappiness, which, either directly or through their effects on life-styles, cause illness" (Streeten 1998: 5). People who live in areas with the greatest gap between the rich and the poor are much more likely to rate their own health as poor or fair than people who live in areas where income is more equitably distributed (Kennedy et al. 1998).

There are doubtless things money won't buy, but one can't think of them at a moment's notice.

RICHARD NEEDHAM
Newspaper columnist

■ **Educational Problems and Poverty**

Research indicates that children living in poverty are more likely to suffer academically than are children who are not poor. "Overall, poor children receive lower grades, receive lower scores on standardized tests, are less likely to finish high school, and are less likely to attend or graduate from university than are nonpoor youth" (Seccombe 2001: 323). The various health problems associated with childhood poverty contribute to poor academic performance (see Chapter 12). In addition, because poor parents have less schooling, on average, than do nonpoor parents, they may be less able to encourage and help their children succeed in school. However, research suggests that family income is a stronger predictor of ability and achievement outcomes than are measures of parental schooling or family structure (Duncan and Brooks-Gunn 1997). Poor parents have fewer resources to provide educational experiences (such as travel), private tutoring, books, and computers for their children. Not surprisingly, parental wealth strongly influences university enrollment (Conley 2001).

Poverty also presents obstacles to educational advancement among poor adults. Women and men who want to further their education in order to escape poverty may have to work while attending school or may be unable to attend school because of unaffordable childcare, transportation, and/or tuition/fees/books.

Family and Parenting Problems Associated with Poverty

In some cases, family problems contribute to poverty. For example, domestic violence causes some women to flee from their homes and live in poverty without the economic support of their husbands. Poverty also contributes to family problems. The stresses associated with poverty contribute to substance abuse, domestic violence, child abuse, divorce, and questionable parenting practices. For example, poor parents unable to afford childcare expenses are more likely to leave children home without adult supervision. Poor parents are more likely than other parents are to use harsh disciplinary techniques, such as physical punishment, more likely to value obedience, and less likely to be supportive of their children (Mayer 1997; Seccombe 2001).

The National Longitudinal Survey of Children and Youth reports that the capacity of parents to care for children and their children's developmental outcomes are better at each step up the income ladder. Low social support, family dysfunction, and parental depression, all of which have significant negative effects on children, are all also more common in low-income households. According to this study, 18 percent of children living in low-income households (versus 8 percent of children in middle-income households and 5 percent of children in higher-income families) lived with parents who had many symptoms of depression (National Council of Welfare 1999c).

Another family problem associated with poverty is teenage pregnancy. Poor adolescent girls are more likely to have babies as teenagers or to become young single mothers. Early childbearing is associated with numerous problems, such as increased risk of premature or low birth-weight babies, dropping out of school, and lower future earning potential due to lack of academic achievement.

Luker (1996) notes that "the high rate of early childbearing is a measure of how bleak life is for young people who are living in poor communities and who have no obvious arenas for success" (p. 189). For poor teenage women who have few employment opportunities and are disillusioned with education, "childbearing...is one of the few ways...such women feel they can make a change in their lives..." (p. 182).

Housing and Homelessness

According to the National Council of Welfare (1998: 53), finding decent and affordable housing that is suitable to a family's needs "is one of the biggest financial burdens for people on welfare and for low-income people in general." The provision of housing for lower-income Canadians has been an area of continuing governmental concern since the first Canadian social-housing legislation, the 1938 *National Housing Act*, made provision for the construction of low-rent housing.

The majority of low-income families and unattached individuals are renters rather than homeowners. For example, as of March 1997, 68.2 percent of all those living on welfare lived in rental housing; only a small portion lived in their own home (6.9 percent) or in subsidized housing (6.8 percent). Among couples with children, 71.3 percent were renters, 16.2 percent were home owners, 8.2 percent lived in subsidized housing, and 4.2 lived in other forms of housing (e.g., were boarding or living with relatives). Among single-parent families, 76.6 percent were renters, 6.3 percent lived in their own homes, 11 percent lived in subsidized housing, and 6.1 percent lived in other forms of housing. In general, single parents on welfare made proportionately more use of subsidized housing and were far less likely to board or to live with relatives.

While poor individuals are more likely than the nonpoor are to have spartan accommodations in high-crime neighbourhoods (Mayer 1997), even substandard housing would be a blessing to many people who live without conventional housing—the homeless.

Homelessness is a growing problem in Canada. It is estimated that as many as 200 000 Canadians are homeless, including increasing numbers of women and children, Aboriginal people, adolescents, and people with mental illnesses (Health Canada 1999). Some homeless individuals have been forced out of their houses or apartments by rising rents or the inability to pay the mortgage. The homeless population also includes runaway or "throw away" youths, and individuals who have been released from mental hospitals because of the movement to deinstitutionalize individuals with psychiatric disorders. For these individuals, life is especially uncertain, danger-filled, and precarious.

Intergenerational Poverty

As we have seen, problems associated with poverty, such as health and educational problems, create a cycle of poverty from one generation to the next. Poverty that is transmitted from one generation to the next is called **intergenerational poverty**.

Intergenerational poverty creates a persistently poor and socially disadvantaged population sometimes referred to as the underclass. The term underclass usually refers to impoverished individuals who have low educational attainment, have criminal records, are unmarried mothers on welfare, or are ghetto

I hope to see a time of much greater concern for the welfare of others—a time when no one ignores the man or woman sleeping on the sidewalk.

JUNE CALLWOOD
Humanitarian

residents. Although the underclass is stereotyped as being composed of minorities living in inner-city ghetto communities, the underclass is actually a far more heterogeneous population (Alex-Assensoh 1995).

Mead (1992) argues that intergenerational poverty may be caused by welfare dependency. According to Mead, when poor adults rely on welfare, the stigma of welfare fades, and welfare recipients develop poor work ethics that are passed on to their children. William Julius Wilson attributes intergenerational poverty and the underclass to a variety of social factors, including the decline in well-paid jobs and their movement out of urban areas, the resultant decline in the availability of marriageable males able to support a family, declining marriage rates and an increase in out-of-wedlock births, the migration of the middle class to the suburbs, and the impact of deteriorating neighbourhoods on children and youth (Wilson 1987; 1996).

Using income tax information reported by a cohort of approximately 285 000 young men and women aged 28 in 31 in 1994, Corak (1998) related the total market income of these young adults to the incomes of their fathers and mothers in 1982 (when his participants were 16 to 19 years of age and still living at home). Among his findings: the adult sons and daughters of very low-income fathers (i.e., those in the bottom 10 percent of income earners) were overrepresented in the lowest income decile. A detailed description of Corak's findings is contained within this chapter's *Social Problems Research Up Close*.

War and Social Conflict

Poverty is often the root cause of conflict and war within and between nations as "the desperation of the poor is never quiet for long" (Speth 1998: 281). Not only does poverty breed conflict and war, but also war contributes to poverty. For example, war contributes to homelessness as individuals and families are forced to flee from their homes. Military and weapons spending associated with war diverts resources away from economic development and social spending on health and education.

Briggs (1998) suggests that the widening inequalities between the haves and the have-nots present a threat to social order. He asks how long a country can maintain social order "when increasing numbers of persons are left out of the banquet while a few are allowed to gorge?" (p. 474). Although Karl Marx predicted that the have-nots would revolt against the haves, Briggs does not foresee a revival of Marxism; "the means of surveillance and the methods of suppression by the governments of industrialized states are far too great to offer any prospect of success for such endeavors" (p. 476). Instead, Briggs predicts that capitalism and its resulting economic inequalities will lead to social anarchy—a state of political disorder and weakening of political authority.

Would that wars rather than men went unwaged.

MAURUS E. MALLON
Aphorist

Strategies for Action: Antipoverty Programs, Policies, and Proposals

In Canada, federal, provincial, and local governments have devoted considerable attention and resources to antipoverty programs since the 1960s. In 1964, "the United States launched its 'war against poverty' and Canada began a more quiet campaign of study and legislation in an effort to understand better the causes of and remedies for poverty" (Ross and Lochhead 1999: 1881).

The 1960s and 1970s saw the introduction of several significant pieces of antipoverty legislation in Canada. Recognition that the private pension system failed to provide adequate support for retired low-income workers and their families led to the introduction of the Canada and Quebec pension plans and to the Guaranteed Income Supplement Program for those elderly individuals with little or no income other than Old Age Security. In 1966, the Canada Assistance Plan (CAP) was introduced. The CAP replaced the "many piecemeal cost-shared programs that the federal and provincial governments had begun entering into as far back as 1927" with a comprehensive social-assistance program that provided a major source of funds for people with disabilities who were unemployed, offered assistance to others in low-income circumstances, and brought a wide array of social services (e.g., daycare, family counselling, homemaker and child-welfare services) under federal cost sharing (Ross and Lochhead 1999: 1888). At least in theory, the CAP was designed not only to respond to the problem of poverty, but also to prevent it. In 1968, the *Medical Care Act* (Medicare) provided free access to basic health care for all Canadians. The *Unemployment Insurance Act* (1940), which had ushered in Canada's first national social-insurance program, was amended in 1971 to provide greater coverage to the unemployed as well as to the sick by extending its coverage and liberalizing its benefits. Today, these efforts are considered by many to distinguish Canada as a nation. Consider, for example, that in 1999, a *Maclean's* and CBC survey reported that almost six out of ten Canadians believe that "the way we treat the poor and disadvantaged" is an important part of what makes us Canadian (*Maclean's* 1999).

In this section, we describe some national and international responses to poverty and note the role of charity and the nonprofit sector in the alleviation of poverty.

Government Public Assistance and Welfare Programs in Canada

Under the *Constitution Act*, social and welfare services are the responsibility of the provincial and territorial governments. However, the federal government is also involved in the provision of these services through its cost-sharing agreements with the provinces and territories. Before April 1996, the federal government provided financial support for social services to the provinces and territories through a 50–50 cost-sharing scheme called the Canada Assistance Plan. The CAP was aimed at improving standards of provincial social-assistance programs ("welfare") and introduced national standards into public welfare for the first time. In place of "a confusing mix of program categories based on the poor law practice of separating the 'worthy' [e.g., people with disabilities] from the 'unworthy' poor…one program [was to be established by each province and territory in exchange for federal funding] to meet financial need—provincial social assistance. An appeal procedure, a striking innovation in public assistance, was also a stipulation under the Canada Assistance Plan" (Guest 1999a: 2203).

However, beginning in the 1970s and in response to rising unemployment and inflation, claims were made that Canada's economic prosperity was best assured by decreasing government expenditures, particularly for social programs. Since that time, Moscovitch (1999: 2496) notes that both the federal and

Getting Ahead in Life: Does Your Parents' Income Count?

Parents hope their children will become successful and self-sufficient adults. But raising children is a complicated affair, and a child's fortune in life is determined not only by parenting strategies, but also by the support available in the community, the resources offered by the State, and sometimes just plain luck. That being said, a prime role in the eventual labour market outcomes of children is often attributed to money.... But...a dollar is not a dollar is not a dollar...and...the sources of a parent's income influence the employment outcomes of their adult children (see table)....

The source of the father's income is strongly associated with the adult incomes of children. Children had significantly higher market incomes as adults if their fathers had self-employment income than if they did not—almost $1200 for sons and $850 for daughters in 1994. If fathers had received Unemployment Insurance (UI) benefits, the effect was just as dramatic but in the opposite direction: sons' incomes were $1400 and daughters' $870 lower than those of children whose fathers had not received UI.

A father with asset income [net income from interest and investments, real estate, dividends from Canadian corporations, and taxable capital gains or losses] provided the most significant advantages for his children. After accounting for all other factors, sons whose fathers

had some income from assets earned over $3100 more than those whose fathers had no assets did, and daughters earned almost $2700 more. These are very substantial amounts, but what may be even more significant is that the actual dollar amount of the father's asset income seems much less important than its presence. In fact, children's adult incomes rise by only an average $28 for every $1000 increase in their father's asset income; for example, someone whose father had $10 000 in asset income would enjoy a market income that was only $252 higher ($280 – $28) than a person whose father had $1000 in asset income....

Not only do varying sources of income have different effects on an adult child's labour market success, but so too does the parent who earns it. For every $1000 increase in the father's income, the adult child's market income increased by about $91 for sons and about $47 for daughters. In contrast, sons and daughters did equally well as the mother's income rose—about $80 to $90 per $1000 increase. There are two possible explanations for this finding. The first focuses on the father's role and suggests that a high-earner father has a stronger effect on sons than on daughters by encouraging the pursuit of income. The second keys on the mother's role and suggests that mothers may be more likely to treat children of each gender equally when making spending decisions, and if women have higher incomes, they probably have greater discretion over spending....

The affluence of the neighbourhood in which children, especially boys, spend their early teens is positively associated with their incomes as adults. For every $1000 increase in the median income of the neighbourhood, adult incomes increased by about $370 for sons, and by $72 for daughters. There are a number of reasons why high-income neighbourhoods may improve the labour market outcomes of children. They may offer a more-developed physical infrastructure—higher quality schools, recreational facilities, and social institutions—as well as the kind of network or peer group effects that are sometimes called "social capital"—that is, the set of norms or standards that exist at the community level and help to reinforce the parents' goals for their children. An alternative interpretation is that parents will select a neighbourhood with the qualities they prefer if they can afford to choose the community where they raise their children. The type of neighbourhood may thus reflect the parents' choices and priorities for their children's future, rather than being a causal factor in its own right....

Clearly, different dollars produce different effects for the "average kid." Does the same hold true for low-income children?...In a world of equal opportunity, the labour market outcomes of adult children would not depend upon their family background. Ideally, a child with a very low-income father (bottom 10 percent of the income distribution) would have an equal chance of entering any income decile; that is, the child would be just as likely to become a very high-income earner (10 percent) as a very low-income earner (also 10 percent).

However, in fact, children of very low-income fathers were more likely to follow their father's example than to improve their own position in the income distribution. About 15 percent of sons also found themselves in the bottom decile, and another 14 percent moved up by only one decile. The figures for daughters were very similar, at 14 percent and 11 percent respectively. Only about six percent of sons and daughters of very low-income fathers managed to reach the top 10 percent of the income rankings. (In contrast, over 20 percent of sons and daughters born to fathers in the top decile also occupied the top decile, and less than 7 percent fell

all the way to the bottom.) These patterns suggest that low-income in one generation is associated with low-income in the next, with children of very low-income families most likely to end up at the bottom of the income hierarchy.

A father's source of income had a clear effect on their adult children's incomes (see table). Children were less likely (12 to 13 percent) to remain in the bottom income decile if their father had some self-employment income than if he did not (15 to 16 percent) while children whose father received UI benefits were more likely to remain there (15 to 16 percent) than if he did not (13 to 14 percent). However, the most striking result is the improvement in income mobility if a father reported some asset income: only 12 percent of sons remained in the bottom decile,

compared with over 17 percent of those whose fathers had no income from assets. For daughters, the pattern was very similar, at 11 percent compared with 17 percent....

The community has as great an effect on a low-income child as on the average child. Children of very low-income fathers living in high-income neighbourhoods tended to do better. This was especially true in the case of sons; only 12 percent remained in the bottom income decile if they grew up in a high-income community, compared with 16 percent if they were raised in a low-income neighbourhood. For daughters, the difference was slight, at 14 percent and 15 percent respectively....

SOURCE: Abridged from Corak, Miles. 1998. "Getting Ahead in Life: Does Your Parents' Income Count?" *Canadian Social Trends* 49 (Summer): 6–15.

Children's Increase in Income Based on Parent's Sources of Income

	Market Income of Adult Child Changed by $__	
	Sons	**Daughters**
Father's income if father reported income from		
Self-employment	1157	850
Assets	3107	2698
Unemployment Insurance	−1442	−865
For every $1000 increase in father's income from		
Paid work	91	47
Self-employment	76	50
Assets	28	28
Unemployment Insurance	−10	−23
For every $1000 increase in		
Mother's income	90	82
Median income of neighbourhood	368	72

SOURCE: Corak, Miles. 1988. "Getting Ahead in Life: Does Your Parents' Income Count?" *Canadian Social Trends* 49 (Summer): 6–15.

the provincial governments have used the following methods to control social expenditures: "changing eligibility and benefits, particularly under unemployment insurance and social assistance; 'privatizing' provincial social programs by contracting out responsibility for social services (particularly those relating to children and the aged); provincial attempts to raise revenues through Medicare premiums and user fees; decreasing social-program budgets relatively if not absolutely; imposing an eroding level of assistance benefits; and termination of some social programs." In an attempt to reduce expenditures on social programs, between 1984 and 1993, the federal Conservative governments further reduced old-age security benefits at middle-income levels and above, decreased the range of workers who were covered by Unemployment Insurance and the benefits available to them, and imposed spending limits on Canada's three richest provinces, Ontario, British Columbia, and Alberta, effectively forcing these provinces to absorb up to 70 percent of the costs. In its 1997 report, *Another Look at Welfare Reform*, the National Council of Welfare noted that provincial and territorial governments also implemented cuts to most welfare programs, with the most extreme example occurring in Ontario in 1995, with a 21.6 percent cut to welfare recipients. The depth of this cut, the report emphasizes, "was completely arbitrary, with no assessment of how people who depended on welfare would be able to afford adequate food, clothing and shelter, let alone the impact of these cuts on young children and their families." While those with disabilities were exempted from the cuts, families with children were not.

In February 1995, the federal budget introduced the *Canada Health and Social Transfer* (CHST) (which became effective in April of 1996) and eliminated two federal transfer programs: Established Programs Financing, which provided for the consolidation of hospital, Medicare, and postsecondary education funding, and the Canada Assistance Plan. The CHST combined federal transfer payments for social assistance (previously under the CAP) with those for Medicare and postsecondary education into a single "block" transfer made up of cash payments and tax points. As a result, Canada's social safety net was fundamentally altered. Among the changes: "the new arrangement included a significant cut in federal support for these programs and a significant change in the way the provinces and territories account for the money they receive" (National Council of Welfare 1999b: 79).

Under the CHST, the provinces now have greater discretion in deciding how to apportion their share of the reduced federal transfer. At least theoretically, provincial and territorial governments could elect to use all of the federal money they receive for Medicare and devote none to the other areas. Guest (1999a: 2203) points out that "Some have already made the decision to cut social-assistance programs to Canada's poorest families and individuals—Ontario and Alberta—while British Columbia has imposed a residence requirement of three months on all new applications for social assistance." It is also evident that not all groups affected by spending cuts are equally vocal nor are all voices equally heard. As Guest additionally reports, "One concern by welfare advocates is that money will be siphoned from welfare to cool the anger of health and higher education supporters" (p. 2203).

Family Allowance and Child Benefits Canada's first universal welfare program, introduced in 1945, was **family allowance**, a monthly allowance paid to families with children. The term "universal" here refers to the fact that such benefits flowed from the principle of entitlement and were available without reference to a recipient's income or assets. In contrast, when benefits are directed at particular groups within the population, they are termed **demogrants.**

Following a failed attempt by the federal government in 1972 to replace the universality of family allowances with selectivity related to income, the government introduced a new *Family Allowance Act* that made family allowances taxable. In 1978, further restructuring occurred with the government's establishment of a Refundable Child Tax Credit, which offered $200 per year for families with incomes under $18 000, and which taxed away benefits entirely for those whose incomes reached $26 000. The tax credit was financed through scaling back the amount of monthly family allowance payments (from an average of $28 per month to $20) and through the reduction or elimination of other tax exemptions for children. Beginning in 1985, family benefits were further restructured with the partial indexing of family allowances and child tax credits. As well, the number of families qualifying for the tax credit was reduced when the maximum income for receipt of the credit was decreased from $26 300 to $23 500. Guest (1999b: 815) reports that by 1991, these changes "represented a spending cut in family benefits [of] $550 million...with only a token increase" in the net family benefits received by Canada's poorest families.

In 1989, the universality of family allowances disappeared, with the federal government requiring parents with upper-incomes to repay all of their benefits at the time they paid their yearly taxes. In 1991, family allowances, the Refundable Child Tax Credit, and a nonrefundable child tax credit were consolidated into a new **Canada Child Tax Benefit (CCTB)**. The CCTB is a tax-free monthly payment made to eligible families to help them with the cost of raising children under the age of 18. Benefits are calculated for a 12-month period based on the number of children in a family and their ages, the applicant's province or territory of residence, the family's net income, and the applicant's (or his or her spouse's) deduction for childcare expenses. Except in Alberta, the basic benefit in 2002 was $95.91 a month for each child under age 18 plus $6.66 a month for a third or additional child, plus $19.00 for each child under age 7. In Alberta, the basic monthly benefit rate was $87.91 for children under 7, $93.83 for children aged 7–11, $105.00 for children 12–15 and $111.25 for children 16–17 (Canada Customs and Revenue Agency 2002). The CCTB is based on net family income reported on the tax return of the previous year and is gradually reduced as family income reaches an "income ceiling" ($32 960 in 2002).

The federal government increased the Canada Child Tax Benefit in July of 1998 for low-income families by adding a **National Child Benefit Supplement (NCBS)**. This tax-free monthly benefit for low-income families with children under age 18 is the federal government's contribution to the **National Child Benefit (NCB)**. In 2002, the NCBS amounts were $1293 a year for a one-child family and $2380 for a two-child family. Families with three or more children receive $2380 for the first two children plus $1009 a year for the third or each additional child. The maximum NCBS is paid only to those families with a net incomes of under $22 397 (Canada Customs and Revenue Agency 2002). It is reduced by a percentage amount (which depends on the number of children within a family) when the family net income exceeds this amount. In most of Canada's provinces and territories, the NCBS is considered income and will affect the amount of social assistance families are eligible to receive.

The NCB is a joint initiative of federal, provincial, and territorial governments designed to help prevent and reduce the depth of child poverty and to promote parental attachment to the workforce by improving available benefits and services. According to the *National Child Benefit Progress Report 1999*, "key to the NCB is the effort to move child benefits out of the welfare system so that when parents leave social assistance for work, these benefits go with them, helping to ensure their children's well-being during this transition" (Government of Canada 1999).

Employment Insurance Benefits   In January 1997, the *Employment Insurance (EI)* Act was implemented in Canada, replacing the former Unemployment Insurance (UI) Program. Individuals may receive regular benefits if they lose a job through no fault of their own and cannot find work. Those who quit their job without just cause or who are fired for misconduct are ineligible to receive EI benefits. Similarly, those affected by a strike, lockout, or other forms of labour dispute are ineligible unless they are not taking part in the dispute, are not giving money to support the dispute, and are not directly interested in the dispute (i.e., their wages or working conditions are not affected by the outcome of the dispute).

To be eligible for EI benefits, individuals must apply; have paid into the EI account; have been without work and pay for at least seven consecutive days; have worked for the required number of hours based on where they live and the unemployment rate in their area; be available for work but unable to find it; and be in Canada. The current system is based on hours of paid work and responds to variations in work situations such as part time, extended hours, or compressed weeks. Whether one works full time, part time, or on a seasonal basis, the hours a person works for pay are accumulated toward eligibility for EI benefits. These hours include overtime (which is calculated on an hour-for-hour rate) and paid leave (which is insured for the number of hours that normally would be worked in that period).

To qualify for EI, most individuals will need to have worked between 420 and 700 hours during the last 52 weeks or since the start of their last claim, whichever is shorter. The specific number of hours of insurable employment in the past 52 weeks needed to qualify for EI depends on the unemployment rate in the region where each person lives. For example, in an area where the regional rate of unemployment is 0 percent to 6 percent, 700 hours of insurable employment are necessary; in an area with a regional unemployment rate of 9.1 percent to 10 percent, 560 hours are needed. In an area with a regional unemployment rate of 13.1 percent or higher, 420 hours are needed. In some instances, however, individuals will need a great number of insurable employment in the past 52 weeks to qualify. For example, among those who are in the workforce for the first time, a minimum of 910 hours of insurable work in the past 52 weeks is required. Those who apply for sickness, maternity, or parental benefits will need 700 hours of insurable work. Those who have previously committed EI violations may also face increases in the number of hours they are required to possess before qualifying for EI benefits.

The length of time for which benefits can be received depends on the regional unemployment rate and how long an individual has worked in the last 52 weeks or since their last claim (whichever is shorter). Depending on the amount of insurable hours, benefits can be received from 14 to a maximum of

45 weeks. The basic benefit rate is 55 percent of average insured earnings up to a maximum payment of $413 per week. However, those who have drawn regular benefits in the past may have their benefits adjusted and reduced under the "intensity rule." Under this rule, benefit rates are reduced by 1 percent for every 20 weeks of regular benefits claimed since June 30, 1996, to a maximum of 5 percent if that person has more than 100 weeks of benefits over that five-year period. Individuals receiving regular benefits can earn up to 25 percent of their weekly benefits or $50 (whichever is higher) without changing the weekly amount they receive. However, all earnings above this limit are deducted dollar for dollar from their weekly benefits. Other sources of money that can affect the amount of EI benefits include such things as Canada Pension Plan or Quebec Pension Plan retirement income, self-employment earnings, or monies received in damages for wrongful dismissal. (Payments from private RRSPs, disability pensions, survivor's pensions, or dependent's pensions does not affect the calculation of EI payments.) Depending on net income and past-claim history, all or some of the EI benefits received may have to be repaid at income tax time.

Families with children in a low-income situation (i.e., having a family net income under $25 921 a year) who receive the Canada Child Tax Benefit (CCTB) automatically receive the **Family Supplement** with a rate based on family net income and the number and ages of children in the family. If both spouses claim EI at the same time, only one can receive the Family Supplement.

Over time, the percentage of unemployed Canadians who are eligible for UI or EI benefits has fallen. Since the 1970s, the federal government has also steadily trimmed away the benefits available to unemployed workers. For example, while in the early 1970s, weekly benefits were as high as 75 percent of a person's maximum weekly insurable earnings while employed, they are now, as earlier noted, 55 percent. Similarly, while in the early 1970s the maximum length available for regular benefits was 51 weeks, it is now 45 weeks. While some of those who are unemployed are able to locate and obtain employment quickly, for others, their unemployment will last far longer than the benefit coverage that EI provides.

Guest (1999a: 2203) emphasizes that we should be concerned about the separation of claimants into "normal" and "frequent user" categories. He observes that frequent users "may suffer benefit reductions and possibly be subject to an income test, and receipt of benefit might be contingent on the claimant's willingness to take part in community work projects or training programs." As a result, he argues, "This is no longer social insurance but a form of 'workfare.'"

Educational Assistance In Canada, public education is free until the end of secondary school (or "high school"). However, the costs associated with higher education have long been recognized to pose special problems to those of low income. Until 1939 and the federal government's passage of the **Dominion Provincial Student Aid Program (DSAP)**, economic assistance for low-income persons wanting to attend postsecondary institutions was limited to those high scholastic achievers who could obtain privately funded assistance from universities and colleges. The encroachment of the federal government into the area of education (which, under the *Constitution Act* of 1867, is the exclusive domain of provincial legislatures) was legitimated with reference to economic growth, labour training, and labour mobility—areas that fell under federal jurisdiction. From this vantage point, the DSAP was simply a subset of the *Youth*

Training Act or another part of national economic policy. By 1944, all of Canada's provinces had joined the plan; however, in 1954, Quebec opted out of the arrangement, "citing constitutional reasons of provincial primacy and autonomy in higher education" (Orlikow 1999: 2265). DSAP was discontinued in 1967.

In 1964, the **Canada Student Loans Program (CSLP)** was established. Under this plan, the federal government guarantees loans to all full-time students demonstrating financial need to a provincial or territorial government. These loans must be repaid over a period that does not exceed 9.5 years at a rate of interest that is set annually. Students are not required to begin making payments until six months after they have ceased to be a full-time student, but interest on the monies owed begins to accrue as soon as they leave full-time studies. In 1994, the *Canada Student Financial Assistance Act (CSFA Act)* revised the CSLP, increasing the amounts of the maximum loans available to full-time and part-time students, establishing a national program of grants for students with permanent disabilities, part-time students with high financial need, students with dependents, and women in doctoral programs in certain fields, and expanding interest relief for unemployed borrowers and those of low income. In 1998, the government also introduced new measures to assist students in loan repayment.

Most recently, the introduction of Registered Education Saving Plans (RESP) represents an attempt to assist families who can afford to set monies aside for the future costs of their children's education. Family members can contribute up to $4000 a year (up to a maximum of $20 000) into RESPs on behalf of a particular beneficiary. The Canada Education Saving Grant (CESG) is added to the monies invested. The CESG is a federal government grant paid directly in a beneficiary's RESP, which provides 20 percent to the first $2000 in contributions made into an RESP per eligible beneficiary on an annual basis. RESPs grow tax-free until such time as the beneficiary is ready to attend any eligible post-secondary educational institution (Human Resources Development Canada 2001).

Nevertheless, the rising cost of tuition (up 115 percent since 1980) will continue to make the costs of postsecondary education difficult for many and prohibitive for some (see also Chapter 12).

Maternal and Parental Benefits In Canada, maternity and parental leave is part of our federal employment insurance system. Under Canada's current EI rules, new mothers receive a maximum of 15 weeks (the first two of which are nonpayable) of pregnancy benefits *only* if they have worked at least 600 hours in the 52 weeks prior and then they only receive 55 percent of their normal weekly pay to a maximum of $413 a week. Employment Insurance additionally provides for a maximum of 35 weeks of parental leave (to either a natural or adoptive parent) that is payable up to one year after the birth of an infant or the placement of an adopted child.

Under provincial and territorial legislation, all Canadian provinces and territories provide either 17 or 18 weeks of unpaid maternity leave. "In every jurisdiction, the laws guarantee an employee reinstatement after the leave period to at least a comparable job with the same or similar wages and benefits, without loss of seniority" (Dranoff 2001: 44). However, not all employees (e.g., domestics) are protected under most employment standards legislation.

Child Support Enforcement In February 1997, Bill C-41 received Royal assent and became law in May of that year. This legislation included amendments to the *Divorce Act* to establish a framework for the use of child support guidelines; amendments to the *Family Orders and Agreements Enforcement Assistance Act* (FOAEA) that added Revenue Canada to the list of federal departments whose databanks can be searched to locate persons who have breached family support orders; new provisions in the FOAEA Act to establish a new federal licence denial scheme that will also authorize the suspension of passports and certain federal transport licences when a payer of child support has persistently breached support obligations; amendments to the *Garnishment, Attachment and Pension Diversion Act* to expand access to federal public service employee pension benefits to satisfy support arrears, and amendments to the *Shipping Act* to allow the wages of a person working at sea to be garnished to support a family obligation. All Canadian provinces now have their own programs to protect against the nonpayment of child support.

Under the *Divorce Act*, either spouse or former spouse may be ordered to pay child support; child support is not taxable for the parent who receives the support nor is it deductible for the parent who pays the support on agreements made after May 1, 1997. (Child support agreements made before this date are not affected by this ruling.) Child support is also completely protected against bankruptcy claims.

Welfare in Canada: Myths and Realities

Public attitudes toward welfare assistance and welfare recipients are generally negative. Rather than view poverty as the problem, many Canadians view welfare as the problem. What are some of the common myths about welfare that perpetuate negative images of the welfare and welfare recipients?

MYTH 1 People receiving welfare are lazy and have no work ethic.

Reality First, single parents on welfare already do work—they do the work of parenting. Albelda and Tilly (1997) emphasize that "raising children is work. It requires time, skills, and commitment. While we as a society do not place a monetary value on it, it is work that is invaluable—and indeed, essential to the survival of our society" (p. 111). Single parents and people with disabilities tend to have longer spells on welfare and those who are *able to work* tend to have shorter spells. Second, it should be evident that not all persons who would prefer to work are able to find jobs, particularly those in low-skill job categories. For example, Newfoundland has long had very high rates of unemployment, a fact that helps to explain why its welfare caseload is heavily laden with long-term welfare recipients. The National Council of Welfare (1999b: 17) notes that "Canada has seen a decline in the number of secure, full-time, well-paying jobs and an increase in the number of short-term, part-time jobs with low wages, few benefits and little or no security." As they emphasize, "For those individuals with low levels of education, 'bad' jobs are often the only real possibilities of employment, yet they cannot eliminate child and family poverty, no matter how hard a parent works. When lay-offs come, parents fall still further behind." Some provinces, such as Ontario, have incorporated "workfare" into its welfare system, which requires able-bodied people to do specific jobs as a condition of welfare. However, most of the workfare jobs created are menial, dead-end jobs that are unlikely to lead to permanent employment.

Rather than disparage the work ethic of those on welfare, the National Council of Welfare (1998: 62) emphasizes that it might be well to recognize that "everyone is at risk of falling on welfare at some point in their lives. The numbers speak for themselves: an estimated 1 910 900 people in Canada were on welfare as of March 31, 2001" (National Council of Welfare 2002a). As they observe, "Losing a job, losing a spouse, and losing good health are some of the reasons that people go on welfare. The biggest myth of all would be to assume that most of us are immune to any of these personal tragedies or the many other misfortunes that can lead to reliance on welfare."

MYTH 2 Welfare benefits are granted to many people who are not eligible to receive them and welfare fraud is rampant.

Reality Although some people obtain welfare benefits through fraudulent means, it is much more common for people who are eligible to receive welfare to not receive benefits. A main reason for not receiving benefits is lack of information; people do not know they are eligible. Some people who are eligible for public assistance do not apply for it because they do not want to be stigmatized as lazy people who just want a "free ride" at the taxpayers' expense—their sense of personal pride prevents them from receiving public assistance. Others want to avoid the administrative hassles involved in obtaining it.

Nevertheless, the impression that welfare fraud is widespread is undoubtedly suggested by government statistics on welfare "fraud and misuse." For example, in December 1999, Ontario's Community and Social Service Minister John Baird boasted that $35 million in "fraud savings" had occurred because of increased government vigilance in policing welfare recipients. However, what the ministry figures show is not truly welfare "fraud" on the part of claimants at all but rather, overpayments resulting from administrative errors as well as a notable vigour in relation to the disqualification of vulnerable individuals from receiving assistance. While in 1997–98, 61 653 cases were investigated for "welfare fraud," in fewer than one in four cases (23.9 percent) did the Ministry reduce the amount of the benefit or terminate the benefit altogether; only 1.2 percent (or 1100) of the cases investigated resulted in a criminal conviction for fraud. In addition, in more than 90 percent of the 14 771 cases in which the Ministry reduced the amount of the benefit or terminated benefits altogether, such actions were the result of an administrative error, not fraud. Reductions in benefits or termination of benefits can occur in the absence of any wrongdoing on the part of welfare recipients. For example, should the Consolidated Verification Project (CVP) investigation reveal that a document is missing from a welfare recipient's file, the recipient is required to provide the necessary paperwork (whether it is two days or 20 years old) or face termination of benefits.

MYTH 3 Most welfare parents are teenagers.

Reality According to the National Council of Welfare (1998), teenage single parents accounted for only 3 percent of single parents on welfare in March 1997. Parents in their 20s to 40s accounted for 87 percent of couples with children on welfare and 91 percent of single parents on welfare.

MYTH 4 Most welfare mothers have large families with many children.

Reality Mothers receiving welfare have no more children, on average, than mothers in the general population.

MYTH 5 Unmarried women have children so they can receive benefits. If single mothers already receive benefits, they have additional children to receive increased benefits.

Reality Research consistently shows that receiving welfare does not significantly increase out-of-wedlock births (Albelda and Tilley 1997).

MYTH 6 Most people on welfare also have income from part-time work or Employment Insurance or government pensions.

Reality According to the National Council of Welfare (1998), only 29 percent of welfare cases in March 1997 had outside income from work, government pensions, support payments, Employment Insurance, or other sources. Among couples with children, wages were the most common form of outside income; among single parents with children, child support or alimony was the most common source of outside income, with wages a close second. While transfer payments and wages were the main sources of outside income both for couples without children and for unattached persons, the percentage of unattached persons receiving either form of outside income was extremely low.

MYTH 7 Almost all the people on welfare are adults.

Reality According to the National Council of Welfare (1998: 31), in March 1997, dependent children accounted for nearly 1.1 million of the people on welfare in Canada.

Despite the public perception that welfare benefits are too generous, cash and other forms of assistance to the poor do not meet the basic needs for many individuals and families who receive such benefits (see this chapter's *The Human Side* feature).

Minimum Wage Increase

As noted earlier, many families that leave welfare for work are still living in poverty because of involuntary part-time work and low wages. One strategy for improving the standard of living for low-income individuals and families is to increase the minimum wage (Schenk 2001). As the National Council of Welfare (1999b: 18) has noted, "Nowhere in Canada are minimum wages high enough to allow even full-time workers to escape poverty...[and] [t]he situation is much worse when a minimum wage worker has children to support."

In Winnipeg in 1999, a single parent with one child had to work 80 hours a week simply to get to the poverty line. A two-parent family with two children in Winnipeg had to work 118 hours a week to reach the poverty line (and there are only 168 hours in a week). In Vancouver, where the minimum wage is the highest in the country, a single parent had to work 61 hours a week and a couple with two children had to work 89 hours a week to reach the poverty line. Clearly, minimum wages comes nowhere near to covering the costs of living.

Canadians don't hate unemployment but they hate the unemployed.

REUBEN BAETZ
Executive director, Canadian Council on Social Development

Remembering Kimberly Rogers

The following is an extract of an article by Jennifer Keck that first appeared in Perception, *vol. 25, #3/4 (Winter/ Spring 2002). The unabridged version of this article can be found on the World Wide Web at www.ccsd.ca/ perception/ 2534/kimberly.htm.*

Kimberly Rogers...died alone and eight months pregnant, in her sweltering apartment in Sudbury, Ontario, while under house arrest for welfare fraud....Kimberly Rogers was charged with welfare fraud after collecting both social assistance and student loans to help cover the costs of attending four years of community college. She was convicted in April 2001 and the penalty was stiff: six months under house arrest (with the right to be allowed out of her hot apartment three hours per week); a requirement to repay more than $13 000 in benefits; 18 months probation and loss of the right to have part of her student loan forgiven. At the time of Rogers' conviction, Ontario Works' regulations specified that anyone convicted of welfare fraud would be automatically suspended from receiving benefits for three months. This stipulation has since been made tougher. Anyone convicted of welfare fraud in the province of Ontario will be banned for life from ever being able to collect social assistance. In Rogers' case the three-month suspension meant that she was confined to house arrest with no source of income to cover her rent, food, or other expenses. On May 14, 2001, Kimberly Rogers became the first Ontario resident to launch a case under the Charter of Rights and Freedoms that challenged the constitutional validity of Ontario works regulations that suspended benefits. She did this with the help of the Sudbury Community Legal Clinic. In her charter case, Rogers argued: (i) the law that allowed welfare authorities to disqualify her from receiving assistance contravened the Charter rights to life, liberty, and security of the person (she had no source of income); (ii) cutting off her assistance after she had already been severely punished constituted "cruel and unusual punishment"; and (iii) as a pregnant woman with a diagnosed disability, the automatic suspension infringed the Charter's guarantee of equality....Judge Gloria Epstein granted a constitutional exemption to the law for Rogers while Rogers' legal team prepared her case. In making her decision, the judge pointed to Canada's human rights commitments: "In the unique circumstances of this case, if [Ms. Rogers] is exposed to the full three months suspension of her benefits, a member of our community carrying an unborn child may well be homeless and deprived of basic sustenance. Such a situation would jeopardize the health of Ms. Rogers and the fetus, thereby adversely affecting not only mother and child but also the public—its dignity, its human rights commitments, and its health care resources. For many reasons there is overwhelming public interest in protecting a pregnant woman in our community from being destitute."... Even with Ontario Works benefits...[Rogers] was unable to support herself and her unborn child. After a deduction of 10 percent (towards repayment to Ontario Works), Rogers received $468 per month. With $450 going towards paying the rent, Rogers was left with $18 per month to cover all other necessities....Tragically, while still under house arrest, Kimberly Rogers died just weeks after the Ontario Superior Court of Justice released its exceptional decision....

The coroner's verdict in the case of Kimberly Rogers was delivered in October 2002 and found her death to be a suicide as a result of an overdose of anti-depressant medication.

SOURCE: Keck, Jennifer. 2002. "Remembering Kimberly Rogers," vol. 25, #3/4 (Winter/ Spring 2002).

For this reason, they argue that both the federal and provincial governments must ensure that minimum wages in their jurisdictions provide adequate incomes and that minimum wages must be indexed so that they rise each year with increases in the average industrial wage.

Those opposed to increasing the minimum wage argue that such an increase would result in higher unemployment and fewer benefits for low-wage workers; businesses would reduce wage costs by hiring fewer employees and providing fewer benefits. However, research has failed to find any systematic significant job loss associated with minimum wage increases (Economic Policy Institute 2000).

The National Council of Welfare has recommended that

- The federal government must provide wage supplements to parents in the labour force to cover the additional costs of raising children.
- Governments must provide job training that prepares workers for new jobs.
- Governments must ensure that postsecondary educational opportunities are open to everyone, not just students who are lucky enough to have families able to afford to pay their tuition fees and living expenses.
- Governments must ensure that legislation governing unpaid maternity and parental leave in their jurisdictions adequately covers the time that parents are required to care for young children. Existing parental leaves cover the first months of children's lives, but parents also need time to care for sick children and take them to medical appointments when their children are much older.
- Governments must ensure that employment and pay equity laws are strengthened and enforced.

Equal Pay for Women

On paper, Canadian women have had the "right" to equal pay for equal work since the 1950s. Unfortunately, while early laws enunciated lofty goals, they failed to result in fair wages. Because of occupational sex segregation, few men and women were doing precisely the same work. Two decades later, some Canadian provinces amended their laws to require that women be paid the same as men for performing "substantially the same work." Once again, however, such laws proved ineffective. Enforcement mechanisms were meagre and employers found various ways of arguing that unequal wages did not signal discrimination on the basis of sex.

In the 1980s, researchers found women earn less than men partly because jobs in which women are concentrated are valued less than jobs in which men are concentrated. They therefore tried to establish gender-neutral standards by which they could judge the dollar value of work. These standards include such factors as the education and experience required to do a particular job and the level of responsibility, amount of stress, and working conditions associated with it. Researchers felt that, by using these criteria to compare jobs in which women and men are concentrated, they could identify pay inequities. The underpaid could then be compensated accordingly. In other words, women and men would receive equal pay for jobs of "comparable worth," even if they did different jobs. In consequence, during the mid-1980s, some governments amended the law to state that women should be paid equally for work of equal value. This amendment required employers to compare the rates of pay for women and men in dissimilar jobs that nevertheless involved the same skill, effort, responsibility, and working conditions.

In 1985, Manitoba became the first Canadian province to demand that its public sector be pro-active and implement plans for "equal pay for work of equal value"—or **pay equity**, as it came to called. With the exception of Alberta, Saskatchewan, and the Northwest Territories, pay equity is now official policy in 10 of 13 Canadian jurisdictions, although provisions vary widely. While undoubtedly a significant step towards achieving gender equality, inequity remains, as evidenced by both the persistence of the wage gap between working men and women and women's heightened susceptibility to poverty.

Charity, Nonprofit Organizations, and Nongovernmental Organizations

Various types of aid to the poor are provided through individual and corporate donations to charities and nonprofit organizations. In 1996, the average charitable donation declared by tax filers was $730. Four billion dollars in donations was declared in that year. Those residing in Canada's richer provinces were not more likely to donate to charities nor were they the most generous donors. Rather, those residing in Manitoba and Prince Edward Island were the most likely to donate, and residents of Newfoundland, the province with the lowest total median income, made the highest median donation. Corporations also donate to charitable causes. In 1982, they contributed some $200 million; in 1995, they contributed $500 million to charities (Statistics Canada 1998a).

Charity involves giving not only money, but also time and effort in the form of volunteering. In Canada, those who reside in the Prairie provinces and the well educated are particularly likely to be volunteers. Women are slightly more likely than men are to be volunteers and rural and small-town residents more likely than city dwellers to be involved in volunteer activity. Nevertheless, high rates of volunteerism are found in cities such as Saskatoon (44 percent), Calgary (38 percent), and Edmonton (Statistics Canada 1998a).

Nongovernmental organizations (NGOs) address many issues related to human rights, social justice, and environmental concerns. The number of international NGOs grew from fewer than 400 in 1900 to 26 000 in the year 2000—more than four times as many as existed just 10 years earlier (Knickerbocker 2000; Paul 2000). At the Millennium Forum meeting in 2000, representatives from over 1000 NGOs called for a UNI Global Poverty Eradication Fund to ensure that poor people have access to credit (Deen 2000). The NGOs declared that poverty is the most widespread violation of human rights and called upon governments around the world to make poverty alleviation a priority.

> Giving money requires even more prescience, more imagination, more executive skill, than making it.
>
> FRANCIS WINSPEAR
> *Investor and philanthropist*

International Responses to Poverty

Alleviating worldwide poverty continues to be a major concern for both developing and developed countries. Approaches to poverty reduction include promoting economic growth and investing in "human capital." Conflict resolution and the promotion of peace are also important for reducing poverty worldwide.

Promoting Economic Growth Economic growth, over the long term, generally reduces poverty (United Nations Development Programme 1997). An expanding economy creates new employment opportunities and increased goods and services. In 1998, 150 million of the world's workers were unemployed (United Nations Development Programme 2000). As employment prospects improve, individuals are able to buy more goods and services. The increased demand for goods and services, in turn, stimulates economic growth. As emphasized in Chapter 14, economic development requires controlling population growth and protecting the environment and natural resources, which are often destroyed and depleted in the process of economic growth.

However, economic growth does not always reduce poverty; in some cases, it increases it. For example, growth resulting from technological progress may reduce demand for unskilled workers. Growth does not help poverty reduction when public spending is diverted away from meeting the needs of the poor and instead is used to pay international debt, finance military operations, and support corporations that do not pay workers fair wages. The World Bank loans about $30 billion a year to developing nations to pay primarily for roads, bridges, and industrialized agriculture that mostly benefit corporations. "Relatively little attention or money has been given to developing basic social services, building schools and clinics, and building decent public sanitation and clean water systems in some of the world's poorest countries" (Mann 2000: 2). Thus, "economic growth, though essential for poverty reduction, is not enough. Growth must be pro-poor, expanding the opportunities and life choices of poor people" (United Nations Development Programme 1997: 72–73). Because three-fourths of poor people in most developing countries depend on agriculture for their livelihoods, economic growth to reduce poverty must include raising the productivity of small-scale agriculture. Not only does improving the productivity of small-scale agriculture create employment, it also reduces food prices. The poor benefit the most because about 70 percent of their income is spent on food (United Nations Development Programme 1997). This chapter's *Focus on Technology* examines agricultural biotechnology as a strategy for alleviating global hunger.

Investing in Human Capital Promoting economic development in a society requires having a productive workforce. Yet, in many poor countries, large segments of the population are illiterate and without job skills, or are malnourished and in poor health. Thus, a key feature of poverty reduction strategies involves investing in human capital. The term **human capital** refers to the skills, knowledge, and capabilities of the individual. Investments in human capital involve programs and policies that enhance the individual's health, skills, knowledge, and capabilities. Such programs and policies include those that provide adequate nutrition, sanitation, housing, health care (including reproductive health care and family planning), and educational and job training. Nobel Laureate Gary Becker has concluded that "the case is overwhelming that investments in human capital are one of the most effective ways to raise the poor to decent levels of income and health" (reported in Hill 1998: 279).

Poor health is both a consequence and a cause of poverty; improving the health status of a population is a significant step toward breaking the cycle of poverty. Increasing the educational levels of a population better prepares individuals for paid employment and for participation in political affairs that affect poverty and other economic and political issues. Improving the educational level and overall status of women in developing countries is also associated with lower birth rates, which in turn fosters economic development.

Trying to eradicate hunger while population continues to grow rapidly is like trying to walk up a down escalator.

LESTER R. BROWN
World Watch Institute

Whether there is proved to be life on Mars, and whether you may conduct your affairs electronically without leaving your armchair, the new century is not going to be a new century at all in terms of progress of humanity if we take along with us acceptance of the shameful shackles of the past. The shackles of poverty are not just a metaphor.

NADINE GORDIMER
Writer, speaking at the United Nations on the occasion of International Day for the Eradication of Poverty

Global Hunger: Is Agricultural Biotechnology the Solution?

Biotechnology is any technique that uses living organisms or substances from those organisms to make or modify a product or develop microorganisms for specific uses (see also Chapter 13). Agricultural biotechnology involves the application of biotechnology to agricultural crops and livestock; however, our discussion here focuses on crops. Various terms refer to products that have been created or modified through agricultural biotechnology, including genetically modified organisms (GMOs), genetically improved organisms (GIOs), and genetically engineered foods (GE foods).

In 1999, over 70 genetically modified varieties of crops were registered for commercial cultivation worldwide (Persley 2000). Such crops include cotton, potato, pumpkin, corn, soybean, tobacco, papaya, squash, tomato, and canola (rapeseed). An estimated 30 000 products in our supermarkets today—from ice cream to cantaloupes to corn flakes—contain genetically engineered ingredients (Environmental Defense 2000). Global areas planted with GM crops grew from 1.7 million hectares in 1996 to nearly 40 million in 1999; 72 percent of this area was in the United States, followed by Argentina (17 percent) and Canada (10 percent) (Serageldin 2000).

Scientists, academics, environmentalists, public health officials, policy makers, corporations, farmers, and citizens throughout the world are deeply divided over the use of agricultural biotechnology. Not surprisingly, supporters of agricultural technology emphasize its potential benefits, while critics focus on the potential risks. A number of ethical and other issues are also at the centre of the controversy concerning biotechnology.

Health and Environmental Benefits

- *Alleviation of Poverty, Hunger, and Malnutrition.* Worldwide, 70 percent of poor and food-insecure people live in rural areas, and most of these poor depend on agriculture for their livelihood (Pinstrup-Andersen and Cohen 2000). Any technology that improves agricultural productivity can potentially alleviate the poverty and hunger among the rural poor. Agricultural biotechnology can enable farmers to produce more food with higher nutritional value. Some GMOs are designed to have a higher yield and earlier maturation. Others are engineered to be more durable during harvest or transportation. Some crops have improved tolerance to drought and poor soil conditions. Other crops are designed to resist herbicides (chemicals used to kill weeds), insects, and diseases.

  Genes that increase vitamin A production and iron have been incorporated experimentally in rice. This could enhance the diets of the 180 million children who suffer from vitamin A deficiency—a deficiency that causes two million deaths annually and 14 million cases of eye damage. Iron deficiency, which affects one billion people in the developing world, leads to anemia—a condition that can diminish learning capacity and contributes to illness and death (Persley 2000).

- *Reduction in Pesticide Use.* Because some GMOs are designed to repel insects, they could replace chemical (pesticide) control and reduce the excessive use of pesticides that poisons field workers and contaminates land, water, and animals.

- *Less Deforestation.* As farmers have access to less land on which to plant crops, they are forced to clear forest area. As discussed in Chapter 13, deforestation contributes to environmental problems. GMOs enable farmers to reap higher yields from crops, and to plant crops on soil that otherwise would not be usable in farming. Thus, GMOs can potentially reduce deforestation.

Health and Environmental Risks

"Although no clear cases of harmful effects on human health have been documented from new genetically improved food, that does not mean that risks do not exist" (Persley 2000: 12). One potential health risk is food allergens in GM foods. Other health concerns are related to possible toxicity, carcinogenicity, food intolerance, antibiotic resistance buildup, and decreased nutritional value.

Another potential environmental risk is the spread of traits from GM plants to other plants, the effects of which are unknown. Additionally, insect populations can potentially build up resistance to GM plants with insect-repelling traits. Another potential threat to biodiversity is posed by the widespread uniformity of GM crops.

Ethical Issues and Other Concens

- *"Playing God."* To some, the use of agricultural biotechnology is offensive because it involves "tinkering with the natural order" and "playing God." Leisinger (2000) answers that criticism by saying "If God created humans as intelligent creatures, it should be compatible with God's intentions that they use their intelligence to improve living conditions" (p. 175).
- *Intellectual Property Rights.* Corporations that develop biotechnologies may obtain intellectual property rights, such as patents for their biotechnological inventions. A patent is a monopoly granted to the owner of an invention for a limited period of up to 20 years. Critics suggest that such rights result in increased prices, as other companies cannot offer the same technology at a competitive price. In response to this concern, Richer (2000) points out that intellectual property rights enable companies to recoup their investment in developing new technologies (the average cost of developing a GM plant is about $150 million).

  Others are concerned that intellectual property rights give corporations ownership of life forms—an idea that is intuitively unappealing. Yet, we already accept ownership rights of plants and animals. Serageldin (2000) asks how owning a "building block of life" is different from owning the actual living thing itself.

Finally, critics are concerned about the "terminator gene"— the first patented technology aimed at protection of intellectual property rights regarding biotechnology. The terminator gene is designed to genetically switch off a plant's ability to germinate a second time. The terminator gene prevents farmers from planting seeds that are harvested from GMO crops and forces them to buy a fresh supply of seeds each year (if they want GMO seeds). Seeds with the terminator gene are not appropriate for small farmers in developing countries because the existing production process may not keep fertile and infertile seeds apart. If farmers accidentally planted infertile seeds, their losses could be devastating (Pinstrup-Andersen and Cohen 2000). In response to protests against terminator technology, Monsanto announced it would not market it (Shah 2001). But other approaches to property rights protection are under development. GE seeds are being developed that can only be activated through chemical treatment. Otherwise, the seed maintains its normal characteristics (without genetic modifications), but is still fertile. The farmer would have the choice to plant the seed as is, or to activate the genetically modified traits by applying the chemical (which is also made and sold by the same corporation that makes the seeds).

- *Corporate Greed.* Corporations that develop agricultural biotechnology do so in hopes of earning profit. However, according to

Pinstrup-Andersen and Cohen (2000), corporations are not the only economic beneficiaries of GMOs. They cite a study of the distribution of the economic benefits of herbicide-tolerant soybean seed in 1997: the patent-holding company, Monsanto, received 22 percent of the economic benefits, seed companies gained 9 percent, consumers gained 21 percent, and farmers worldwide obtained 48 percent.

- *Neglect of the Needs of Developing Countries.* The development of GMOs to meet specific needs of developing countries is not likely to be profitable; consequently, relatively little biotechnology research has focused on the needs of poor farmers and consumers in developing countries. Those concerned with this neglect of the needs of developing countries call for stronger public sector involvement in the research and development of GMOs (Pinstrup-Andersen and Cohen 2000). Globally, 80 percent of biotechnology research is done by the private sector (Persley 2000).
- *Increased Poverty and Economic Inequality.* A criticism of agricultural biotechnology is that it is too expensive and inaccessible to small farmers. Persley (2000) suggests that unless countries have policies to ensure that small farmers have access to GM crop seeds and markets, agricultural biotechnology could lead to increased inequality of income and wealth if large farmers reap most of the benefits.

(continued)

- *Scientific Apartheid*. Biotechnological knowledge and research is skewed to the potential markets of the affluent, excluding the concerns of the poor. This contributes to **scientific apartheid**—the growing gap between the industrial and developing countries in the rapidly evolving knowledge frontier (Serageldin 2000). To address this concern, poor farmers and other low-income populations in developing countries must have a voice in the development of and policies concerning agricultural biotechnology.

- *Insufficient Safeguards and Regulatory Mechanisms*. In 2000, Taco Bell taco shells, made by Kraft Foods, were recalled after traces of a genetically engineered variety of corn that had not been approved for human consumption were found in the taco shells (Union of Concerned Scientists 2001). No one—from farmers to grain dealers to Kraft—could explain how it got mixed into corn meant for taco shells. Further, Genetically Engineered Food Alert—a coalition of biotech

skeptics and foes—discovered the traces of unapproved corn.

This widely publicized incident raised disturbing questions about the regulatory oversight of GE foods. Indeed, there is widespread agreement that the pursuit of agricultural biotechnology requires regulatory systems to govern food safety, assess risks, monitor compliance, and enforce regulations. But such safeguards are nonexistent in some countries and, as the Taco Bell incident suggests, even when regulatory systems are in place, they are not foolproof. However, some progress toward improving biotechnology safeguards was made in February 2000 when the landmark Biosafety Protocol was signed in Montreal by 130 nations. (Signing the protocol indicates general support for the Protocol and the intention to become legally bound by it. However, the Protocol does not become legally binding until a country ratifies the treaty by submitting a letter of acceptance to the

United Nations.) The Biosafety Protocol includes the requirement that producers of a GMO must demonstrate it is safe before it is widely used. The Biosafety Protocol also allows countries to ban the import of GM crops based on suspected health, ecological, or social risks.

Concluding Remarks

Many citizens have clearly taken a stand either for or against agricultural biotechnology. However, many more are uncertain and struggle to make sense out of the competing claims of the benefits and safety versus the potential hazards of GMOs, and the complex ethical and sociopolitical implications of using these technologies.

As we strive to make sense of these issues, is it helpful to consider that many technologies with known risks have broad social acceptance? Consider the automobile—a technology that contributes to pollution and global warming and kills thousands of people each year (Serageldin 2000). Yet, few individuals would agree to ban the automobile.

One way to help poor countries invest in human capital and reduce poverty is to provide debt relief. If African countries were relieved of their national debts, they would have funds that would save the lives of millions of children and provide basic education to millions of girls and women. Providing debt relief to the 20 worst affected countries would cost between $5.5 billion and $7.7 billion—roughly the cost of building the Euro-Disney theme park in France (United Nations Development Programme 1997).

Understanding the Haves and the Have-Nots

As we have seen in this chapter, economic prosperity has not been evenly distributed; the rich have become richer, while the poor have become poorer.

Is it helpful to consider the role of the media in shaping public views and opinions on biotechnology? Some have charged the media with biased reporting on biotechnology that fuels anti-biotech sentiments. For example, according to Leisinger (2000), when the Federal Institute of Technology in Zurich informed the world in 1999 of the possibility of genetically modifying rice to contain vitamin A and iron—a major health benefit to the 250 million poor malnourished who subsist on rice—the media had little reaction. Four months later when news broke that larvae of the monarch butterfly were damaged in a GM crop experiment, the media picked up on the story and focused on the potential harm of biotechnology to biodiversity.

Lester Brown (2001) of the World Watch Institute suggests that "perhaps the largest question hanging over the future of biotechnology is the lack of knowledge about the possible environmental and human health effects of using genetically modified crops on a large scale over the long term" (p. 52).

This lack of knowledge calls for more research to answer questions about the potential risks of GM crops. But efforts to conduct such research are impeded by anti-biotechnology activists who have destroyed test sites and research offices. "Open debate about the issues involved is essential, but physical attacks on research and testing efforts contribute little to the free exchange of ideas or the formulation of policies that will advance food security" (Pinstrup-Andersen and Cohen 2000: 168).

Finally, even supporters of agricultural biotechnology remind us that such technology is not a "silver bullet" that will end poverty and hunger. Rather, "it is critical that biotechnology be viewed as one part of a comprehensive sustainable poverty alleviation strategy, not a technological 'quick-fix' for world hunger and poverty" (Persley 2000: 16).

SOURCES: Brown, Lester R. 2001. "Eradicating Hunger: A Growing Challenge." In *State of the World 2001*, eds. Lester R. Brown, Christopher Flavin, and Hilary French, pp. 43–62. New York: W.W. Norton and Co. Environmental Defense. 2000. "*Annual Report 2000*." http://www.environmentaldefense.org/pub/AnnualReport/2000/AR00.pdf. Leisinger, Klaus M. 2000. "Ethical Challenges of Agricultural Biotechnology for Developing Countries." In *The Use of Agricultural Biotechnology to Feed the Poor*, eds. G. J. Persley and M. M. Lantin, pp. 173–80. Washington DC: Consultive Group on International Research. The World Bank. Persley, G. J. 2000. "Agricultural Biotechnology and the Poor: Promethean Science." In *The Use of Agricultural Biotechnology to Feed the Poor*, eds. G. J. Persley and M. M. Lantin, pp. 3–21. Washington DC: Consultive Group on International Research. The World Bank. Pinstrup-Andersen, Per, and Marc J. Cohen. 2000. "Modern Biotechnology for Food and Agriculture: Risks and Opportunities for the Poor." In *The Use of Agricultural Biotechnology to Feed the Poor*, eds. G. J. Persley and M. M. Lantin, pp. 159–68. Washington DC: Consultive Group on International Research. The World Bank. Richer, David L. 2000. "Intellectual Property Protection: Who Needs It?" In *The Use of Agricultural Biotechnology to Feed the Poor*, eds. G. J. Persley and M. M. Lantin, pp. 159–68. Washington DC: Consultive Group on International Research. The World Bank. Serageldin, Ismail. 2000. "The Challenge of Poverty in the 21st Century: The Role of Science." In *The Use of Agricultural Biotechnology to Feed the Poor*, eds. G. J. Persley and M. M. Lantin, pp. 25–32. Washington DC: Consultive Group on International Research. The World Bank. Shah, Anup. 2001. "Terminator Technology." *Genetically Engineered Food*. January 1: http://www.globalissues.org/EnvIssues/GEFood/Terminator.asp?Print5True. Union of Concerned Scientists. 2001. http://www.ucsusa.org/agriculture/0biotechnology.html.

Meanwhile, Canada has implemented measures that essentially weaken the safety net for the most impoverished segment of the population—largely, children. The decrease in assistance to the poor is a major reason poverty rates have remained high, despite the economic prosperity of the country. Many families leaving welfare report struggling to get food, shelter, medical care, childcare, and transportation. The effects of poverty on children perpetuate the cycle of poverty. Larin (1998) notes that "while it always has been possible for individuals to move up the economic ladder, the odds against it are high for individuals who suffer from the ill effects of poverty during childhood" (p. 26). Given the association between poverty and poor health and low educational attainment, poor children often grow up to be poor adults who are unable to escape poverty.

Our lives are short, and we all end in the grave. But we *can* abolish poverty, ignorance, sexism, racism, and the other social evils. They are our own creations. Are we even trying to do that anymore?

SILVER DONALD CAMERON
Writer

I'm a dreamer. But what's the alternative?

OVIDE MERCREDI
Native activist and lawyer

A common belief among Canadians is that the rich are deserving and the poor are failures. Blaming poverty on individuals rather than on structural and cultural factors implies not only that poor individuals are responsible for their plight, but also that they are responsible for improving their condition. If we hold individuals accountable for their poverty, we fail to make society accountable for making investments in human capital that are necessary to alleviate poverty. Such human capital investments include providing health care, adequate food and housing, education, childcare, and job training. Economist Lewis Hill (1998) believes that "the fundamental cause of perpetual poverty is the failure of...people to invest adequately in the human capital represented by impoverished children" (p. 299). Blaming the poor for their plight also fails to recognize that there are not enough jobs for those who want to work and that many jobs fail to pay wages that enable families to escape poverty. Lastly, blaming the poor for their condition diverts attention away from the recognition that the wealthy—individuals and corporations—receive far more benefits in the form of wealthfare or corporate welfare, without the stigma of welfare.

Ending or reducing poverty begins with the recognition that doing so is a worthy ideal and an attainable goal. Imagine a world where everyone had comfortable shelter, plentiful food, adequate medical care, and education. If this imaginary world were achieved, and absolute poverty were effectively eliminated, what would the effects be on such social problems as crime, drug abuse, family problems (such as domestic violence, child abuse, and divorce), health problems, prejudice and racism, and international conflict? It would be too costly to eliminate poverty—or would it? According to one source, the cost of eradicating poverty worldwide would be only about 1 percent of global income—and no more than 2 to 3 percent of national income in all but the poorest countries (United Nations Development Programme 1997). Certainly the costs of allowing poverty to continue are much greater than that.

Critical Thinking

1 Is it possible for a decline in Canada's "poverty rates" to be accompanied by an increase in the numbers of individuals experiencing economic hardships?

2 Should someone receiving welfare benefits be entitled to spend some of his or her money on "nonessentials" such as cigarettes, eating out, lottery tickets, and cable TV? Why or why not?

3 According to the National Council of Welfare (1999c: 8), "Many social programs support families but childcare is the backbone of them all." However, many groups that proclaim the need to promote and strengthen "family values" oppose the implementation of a national system of childcare and early childhood education. What reasons might underlie their opposition to this recommendation?

4 The poor have low rates of voting and thus have minimal influence on elected government officials and the policies they advocate. What strategies might be effective in increasing voter participation among the poor?

5 Oscar Lewis (1998) noted that "some see the poor as virtuous, upright, serene, independent, honest, secure, kind, simple, and happy, while others see them as evil, mean, violent, sordid, and criminal" (p. 9). Which view of the poor do you tend to hold? How have various social influences, such as parents, peers, media, social class, and education, shaped your views toward the poor?

Key Terms

absolute poverty

bourgeoisie

Canada Child Tax Benefit (CCTB)

Canada Student Financial Assistance Act (CSFA Act)

Canada Student Loans Program (CSLP)

corporate welfare

culture of poverty

demogrant

Dominion Provincial Student Aid Program (DSAP)

family allowance

Family Supplement

feminization of poverty

human capital

Human Poverty Index (HPI)

intergenerational poverty

low-income cutoff (LICO)

Low-Income Measure (LIM)

National Child Benefit (NCB)

National Child Benefit Supplement (NCBS)

pay equity

poverty

proletariat

relative poverty

scientific apartheid

underclass

wealth

wealthfare

working poor

11

Work and Unemployment

Is It True?

1. In 1999, at least 140 trade unionists around the world were assassinated, disappeared, or committed suicide after they were threatened as a result of their labour advocacy.

2. Compared to male workers, Canadian women workers are more likely to be unionized.

3. The world's top 200 corporations control more than one-fourth of all sales in the global economy but employ less than 1 percent of the world's workforce.

4. Women in Canada are more likely than men to face a boom-and-bust job environment.

5. There are as many people in Canada who believe they could lose their jobs in the next few years as feel secure in their jobs.

Answers: 1 = T, 2 = F, 3 = T, 4 = F, 5 = T

Promises of better things to come, repeated for years and years, are a cruel hoax on those who are hoping and waiting....

DAVID LEWIS

Politician, key architect of the New Democratic Party, labour lawyer, and university professor

By now, she's used to the juggling act. For the past four years, Martha Jane Robbins, 22, has been a high-achieving international studies student at the University of Saskatchewan. Since 1999, she also served as national youth president for the National Farmers Union. The dual roles allow Robbins to pursue two of her passions: speaking up on behalf of Canadian farmers, while reaching out to help those in less prosperous countries help themselves. "We have a tendency to assume problems in the Third World are theirs alone and have nothing to do with us," says Robbins. "But that's not so."...

She has visited Costa Rica as part of a farmer's exchange program and, in the winter of 2001, studied for four months in Guatemala, where she witnessed how deforestation has driven peasant farmers off their traditional lands. After pursuing further studies, Robbins hopes to work in some social justice capacity, most likely with a non-governmental organization. In the longer run, she does not rule out a return to farming. "For young people, it's getting tougher all the time to stay on the land," says Robbins. "But it's a way of life that's definitely worth preserving" (Aubin et al. 2002: 22. Reprinted by permission of Maclean's *Magazine).*

Martha Jane Robbins, like thousands of other students, is concerned with the issues of work and worker's rights. In this chapter, we examine problems of work and unemployment, including child and sweatshop labour, job dissatisfaction and alienation, work–family concerns, and labour strength and representation. We begin by looking at the global economy.

Before reading further, you may want to complete the "Attitudes Towards Corporations" survey in the *Self and Society* feature of this chapter. It might be interesting to retake this survey after reading this chapter and see how your attitudes may have changed.

The Global Context: The Economy in the Twenty-first Century

In 1999, 11 of the 15 European Union nations began making the transition from their national currency to a new common currency—the euro—that will lock them together financially. The euro will replace German marks, French francs, and Italian lire. The adoption of the euro reflects the increasing globalization of economic institutions. The term **economic institution** refers to the structure and means by which a society produces, distributes, and consumes goods and services.

Attitudes towards Corporations

Part One

How good a job do you think corporations are doing these days? Using letter grades like those in school, give corporations an A, B, C, D, or F in:

Letter Grade

1. Paying their employees good wages   _____

2. Being loyal to employees   _____

3. Making profits   _____

4. Keeping jobs in Canada   _____

Part Two

Here are some things some large corporations are doing that some people think are serious problems, while others think they are not serious problems. For each of the following practices, indicate whether you think this is a serious problem or not.

	Serious Problem	Not a Problem	Don't Know
5. Not providing health care and pension to employees	_____	_____	_____
6. Not paying employees enough so that they and their families can keep up with the cost of living	_____	_____	_____
7. Paying CEOs 200 times what their employees make	_____	_____	_____
8. Laying off large numbers of workers even when the company is profitable	_____	_____	_____

Part Three

Which of the following statements comes closer to your view? (check one)

9A. Two major problems with the economy today are government waste and inefficiency. Excessive government spending and high taxes burden middle-class families and slow economic growth. Our government debt drives up interest rates, making it much harder for businesses to invest and create jobs.

OR

9B. A major problem with the economy today is politicians catering to the interests of powerful corporations and wealthy campaign contributors at the expense of working families. That is why politicians are not doing anything to stop large corporations from laying off large numbers of employees, denying health benefits, moving jobs overseas, and raiding pension funds.

9A. _____   9B. _____

10A. Wasteful and inefficient government is preventing the middle class from getting ahead and doing better. Excessive government spending and high taxes burden working families and slow economic growth. The budget deficit drives up interest rates and taxes, hurts consumers and business, and reduces job-creating investments. Red tape and excessive regulation are hurting business.

OR

10B. Corporate greed is preventing the middle class from getting ahead and doing better. In the past, when people did their jobs well, they could earn a decent wage and provide a better life for their children. Now, corporate Canada is squeezing their employees—cutting wages, downsizing jobs, and eliminating pensions and health benefits. Companies say they cannot afford to treat employees better, but many have growing profits, record stock prices, and huge salaries for their executives.

10A. _____   10B. _____

11A. Large corporations are laying people off, cutting benefits, and moving jobs overseas mainly because they have gotten greedy and are squeezing employees to maximize profits.

OR

11B. Large corporations are laying people off, cutting benefits, and moving jobs overseas mainly because they have to stay in business and provide jobs.

11A. _____   11B. _____

FOR COMPARISON

You may want to compare your answers to this survey with responses from a national sample of American adults. (Note: In Question 4, survey respondents were asked about keeping jobs in America. Question 10B referred to corporate America).

Part One
(Percentages do not total 100 due to individuals who responded "Don't know.")

1.		2.		3.		4.	
A:	11%	A:	10%	A:	52%	A:	12%
B:	26%	B:	16%	B:	26%	B:	16%
C:	36%	C:	28%	C:	9%	C:	31%
D:	12%	D:	23%	D:	3%	D:	20%
F:	7%	F:	19%	F:	2%	F:	18%

Part Two

	Serious	Not Serious	Don't Know
5.	82%	15%	3%
6.	76%	19%	5%
7.	79%	14%	7%
8.	81%	14%	5%

Part Three

9A. 33%	9B. 40%	(21% answered "Both," and 6% answered "Don't know")
10A. 28%	10B. 46%	(22% answered "Both," and 4% answered "Don't know")
11A. 70%	11B. 22%	(7% answered "Don't know")

SOURCE: Adapted from "Corporate Irresponsibility: There Ought to be Laws." 1996. EDK Poll, Washington, DC: Preamble Center for Public Policy, December 12, 1998 www.preamble.org/polledk.html. Used by permission.

In recent decades, innovations in communication and information technology have spawned the emergence of a **global economy**—an interconnected network of economic activity that transcends national borders and spans the world. The globalization of economic activity means that increasingly our jobs, the products and services we buy, and our nation's political policies and agendas influence and are influenced by economic activities occurring around the world. After summarizing the two main economic systems in the world—capitalism and socialism—we look at the emergence of corporate multinationalism. Then we describe how industrialization and postindustrialization have changed the nature of work.

Capitalism and Socialism

The principal economic systems in the world are capitalism and socialism. Under **capitalism**, private individuals or groups invest capital (money, technology, machines) to produce goods and services to sell for a profit in a competitive market. Capitalism is characterized by economic motivation through profit, the determination of prices and wages primarily through supply and demand, and the absence of governmental intervention in the economy. More people are working today in a capitalist economy than ever before in history (Went 2000). Critics of capitalism argue that it creates too many social evils, including alienated workers, poor working conditions, near-poverty wages, unemployment, a polluted and depleted environment, and world conflict over resources.

Pure capitalism (known as "hands off" capitalism) exists only when market forces can operate without interference from the government. However, in Canada, many restraints to the laissez-faire model have traditionally existed. *State capitalism* is a form of capitalism in which private citizens own the means of production and pursue profits but do so within a vast system of laws designed to protect the welfare of the population. In Canada, state capitalism also refers to public or state investment in sectors of the economy that could be private. Canada's economy was once described as "a strange mix of interventionism and free-market policies" (Hallsworth 1993: 445); however, since the 1980s, the state has begun to withdraw from the private sector by selling off public assets (e.g., Petro-Canada, Air Canada) and through an ongoing process of deregulation (e.g., the North American Free Trade Agreement, the reduction of interprovincial trade barriers, and the "open skies" agreement with the United States).

Socialism emphasizes public rather than private ownership. Theoretically, goods and services are equitably distributed according to the needs of the citizens. Whereas capitalism emphasizes individual freedom, socialism emphasizes social equality.

Advocates for capitalism and socialism claim that the one they support results in economic well-being for society and for its members. In reality, both capitalist and socialist countries have been unable to fulfill their promises. Although the overall standard of living is higher in capitalist countries, so is economic inequality. Some theorists suggest that capitalist countries will adopt elements of socialism and socialist countries will adopt elements of capitalism. This idea, known as the **convergence hypothesis**, is reflected in the economies of Germany, France, and Sweden, which are sometimes called "integrated economies" because they have elements of both capitalism and socialism.

Capitalism is the extraordinary belief that the nastiest of men, for the nastiest of reasons, will somehow work for the benefit of us all.

JOHN MAYNARD KEYNES
Economist

Is the new capitalism fertile ground for the extension of human freedom? Hardly.

JAMES LAXER
Political scientist

Corporate Multinationalism

Corporate multinationalism is the practice of corporations having their home base in one country and branches, or affiliates, in other countries. Corporate multinationalism allows businesses to avoid import tariffs and costs associated with transporting goods to another country. Access to raw materials, cheap foreign labour, and the avoidance of government regulations also drive corporate multinationalism. "By moving production plants abroad, business managers may be able to work foreign employees for long hours under dangerous conditions at low pay, pollute the environment with impunity, and pretty much have their way with local communities. Then the business may be able to ship its goods back to its home country at lower costs and bigger profits" (Caston 1998: 274–75).

Although multinationalization provides jobs for managers, secures profits for investors, and helps Canada compete in the global economy, it also has "far-reaching and detrimental consequences" (Epstein et al. 1993: 206). Corporate multinationalization must take its share of the blame for an array of social problems such as poverty resulting from fewer jobs, urban decline resulting from factories moving away, and racial and ethnic tensions resulting from competition for jobs. In addition, as Maule (1999: 1536) points out, "[l]ess developed countries argue that they have traded political independence for economic and cultural dependence. Politically, there remains concern over the extent to which multinational corporations are used as instruments of foreign policy by the governments of countries where parent companies are located. Culturally, the concern is over the loss of national identity." Noting that the rapid increase of foreign ownership in the Canadian economy after World War I was linked to the rise of multinational corporations, economic nationalists have also expressed concern over "the special problems created by this type of investment, particularly the stunted and distorted pattern of economic development" and the broader impact of multinationals on Canadian society, identity, and sovereignty (Rotstein 1999: 717). For example, Bellan (1999) points out that

> Huge and increasing amounts of money have to be remitted to U.S. owners in the form of dividends on their investment and contributions by branch plants toward head office costs of administration, research, product development and advertising. A large proportion of these payments must be made in U.S. dollars....The consequence is that a very large fraction of the U.S. dollars that Canada earns by its exports must be used to make interest and dividend payments and branch plant remittances to U.S. firms. (p. 884–85)

Second, Bellan charges that multinational corporations have "carried on their Canadian operations to serve their own best interests, not those of Canada," with industrial research and development that are "essential to industrial innovation and growth" generally conducted in their U.S. facilities rather than at their Canadian branch plants. Third, he notes that multinationals show no particular loyalty to Canada when the demand for their products falls or a cheaper source of supplies or labour is found in another country.

Industrialization, Postindustrialization, and the Changing Nature of Work

The nature of work has been shaped by the **Industrial Revolution**, the period between the mid–eighteenth century and the early nineteenth century when

■ Corporate welfare bums.

DAVID LEWIS
Former leader of the New Democratic Party, referring to those corporations which avoided paying their fair share of business taxes as well as those businesses which pressed all levels of government for additional grants, concessions, subsidies, deferrals, remissions, depreciations, and incentives

■ I do not understand how nine million people can enter into such arrangements as are proposed with ninety million strangers on an open frontier of four thousands miles, and at the same time preserve their own national integrity....Whatever the United States may gain, I see nothing for Canada in Reciprocity except a little money which she does not need, and a long repentance.

RUDYARD KIPLING
Author and imperialist, in a cable sent in support of the anti-reciprocity movement, September 8, 1911

■ The more Canada's economy is tied to that of our powerful neighbour, the more Canada operates as a branch plant of the American military-industrial complex in a high-tech nuclear age.

REMI J. DE ROO
Bishop of Victoria

the factory system was introduced in England. Industrialization dramatically altered the nature of work: machines replaced hand tools; and steam, gasoline, and electric power replaced human or animal power. Industrialization also led to the development of the assembly line and an increased division of labour as goods began to be mass-produced. The development of factories contributed to the emergence of large cities where the earlier informal social interactions dominated by primary relationships were replaced by formal interactions centred on secondary groups. Instead of the family-centred economy characteristic of an agricultural society, people began to work outside the home for wages.

Postindustrialization refers to the shift from an industrial economy dominated by manufacturing jobs to an economy dominated by service-oriented, information-intensive occupations. Postindustrialization is characterized by a highly educated workforce, automated and computerized production methods, increased government involvement in economic issues, and a higher standard of living (Bell 1973). Like industrialization before it, postindustrialization has transformed the nature of work.

The three fundamental work sectors (primary, secondary, and tertiary) reflect the major economic transformation in society—the Industrial Revolution and the Postindustrial Revolution. The **primary work sector** involves the production of raw materials and food goods. In developing countries with little industrialization, about 60 percent of the labour force works in agricultural activities; in Canada less than 3 percent of the workforce is in farming (Bracey 1995; *Report on the World Social Situation* 1997; Statistics Canada 1998a). The **secondary work sector** involves the production of manufactured goods from raw materials (e.g., paper from wood). The **tertiary work sector** includes professional, managerial, technical-support, and service jobs. The transition to a postindustrial society is marked by a decrease in manufacturing jobs and an increase in service and information-technology jobs in the tertiary work sector. For example, even though the high-tech sector was struggling on a number of fronts in 2000, the demand for computer specialists led the growth in the Canadian labour force during the 1990s, most notably in the latter half of the decade (Statistics Canada 2003: 8). Between 1991 and 2001, almost one-half of the growth in the Canadian labour force "occurred in highly skilled occupations that normally require university qualifications, while low skilled occupations requiring high-school or less accounted for only a quarter of the increase" (Statistics Canada 2003: 5). Consider as well that, in 2001, the "top 10 disappearing jobs" in Canada were, in order: typist; typesetter; watch/clock repairer; statistical clerk; fisher; bank teller; telephone operator; tool and die maker; farmer; and locomotive operator. In that year, the "top 10 growth careers" in Canada were, in order: in-home nurse; nurse practitioner; physician; teacher, special education; pharmacist; programmer; psychiatrist; radiology technician; registered nurse; and physiotherapist (Ash 2001: 194).

In a postindustrial society, highly skilled and technological personnel are needed, but many workers, particularly women and minorities, are not educated and skilled enough for many of these positions (Koch 1998). Data from the 2001 census indicate that Canada has increasingly looked to immigration as a source of skills and knowledge. The latest census "showed a dramatic increase in the proportion of recent immigrants working in high skilled occupations—those that normally require a university education" (Statistics Canada 2003: 13). While immigrants who arrived between 1986 and 1990 accounted for 13 percent of the

Canada's prosperity essentially rests on its ability to export modern technology, expertise, and information.

FRANK FEATHER
Futurologist

workforce in highly skilled occupations in 1991, in 2001, recent immigrants aged 25 to 64 who arrived during the 1990s represented almost one-quarter (24 percent) of the workforce in highly skilled occupations. Recent immigrants have played an important role in the growth of highly skilled occupations in Canada over the 1990s, particularly in computer-related occupations and accounting. The proportion of new immigrants aged 25 to 44 who worked in information technology occupations rose from about three percent in 1991 to 12 percent in 2001. New immigrants were also overrepresented in engineering and natural sciences occupations. "In 2001, three percent of recent immigrants aged 25 to 44 in the labour force were in engineering compared to only one percent of the Canadian born. Similarly, 1.2 percent of recent immigrants were in natural sciences occupations compared to 0.6 percent of the Canadian born" (Statistics Canada 2003: 14). In developing countries, many individuals with the highest level of skill and education leave the country in search of work abroad, leading to the phenomenon known as the **brain drain** (see also Chapter 12). Although employers in developed countries benefit, developing countries lose valuable labour.

> ◼ A nation that sends an important segment of its young people abroad, for lack of options at home, risks losing them forever. It has chosen provincialism as a way of life, and thereby called into question its reason for existence.
>
> JOHN C. POLANYI
> *Scientist and Nobel laureate*

Sociological Theories of Work and the Economy

Numerous theories in economics, political science, and history address the nature of work and the economy. In sociology, structural-functionalism, conflict theory, and symbolic interactionism serve as theoretical lenses through which we may better understand work and economic issues and activities.

Structural-Functionalist Perspective

According to the structural-functionalist perspective, the economic institution is one of the most important of all social institutions. It provides the basic necessities common to all human societies, including food, clothing, and shelter. By providing for the basic survival needs of members of society, the economic institution contributes to social stability. After the basic survival needs of a society are met, surplus materials and wealth may be allocated to other social uses, such as maintaining military protection from enemies, supporting political and religious leaders, providing formal education, supporting an expanding population, and providing entertainment and recreational activities. Societal development is dependent on an economic surplus in a society (Lenski and Lenski 1987).

Although the economic institution is functional for society, elements of it may be dysfunctional. For example, before industrialization, agrarian societies had a low division of labour in that few work roles were available to members of society. Limited work roles meant that society's members shared similar roles and thus developed similar norms and values (Durkheim [1893] 1966). In contrast, industrial societies are characterized by many work roles, or a high division of labour, and cohesion is based not on the similarity of people and their roles but on their interdependence. People in industrial societies need the skills and services that others provide. The lack of common norms and values in industrialized societies may result in **anomie**—a state of normlessness—which is linked to a variety of social problems including crime, drug addiction, and violence (see Chapters 3 and 4).

Conflict Perspective

According to Karl Marx, capitalism is responsible for the inequality and conflict within and between societies. The ruling class controls the economic system for its own benefit and exploits and oppresses the working masses. While structural-functionalism views the economic institution as benefiting society as a whole, conflict theory holds that capitalism benefits an elite class that controls not only the economy but other aspects of society as well—the media, politics and law, education, and religion.

For example, corporate power is reflected in the policies of the International Monetary Fund (IMF) and the World Bank, which pressure developing countries to open their economies to foreign corporations, promoting export production at the expense of local consumption, encouraging the exploitation of labour as a means of attracting foreign investment, and hastening the degradation of natural resources as countries sell their forests and minerals to earn money to pay back loans. Ambrose (1998) asserts that "for some time now, the IMF has been the chief architect of the global economy, using debt leverage to force governments around the world to give big corporations and billionaires everything they want—low taxes, cheap labour, loose regulations—so they will locate in their countries" (p. 5). Treaties such as the North American Free Trade Agreement (NAFTA), the General Agreement on Tariffs and Trade (GATT), and the proposed Multilateral Agreement on Investments (MAI) also benefit corporations at the expense of workers by providing corporations with greater access to foreign markets. "These laws increasingly allow corporations to go anywhere and do anything they like, and prohibit workers and the governments that supposedly represent them from doing much about it" (Danaher 1998: 1).

According to the conflict perspective, work trends that benefit employees, such as work site health promotion programs and work–family policies (discussed later in this chapter) are not the result of altruistic or humanitarian concern for workers' well-being. Rather, corporate leaders recognize that these programs and policies result in higher job productivity and lower health care costs and are thus good for the bottom line.

Symbolic Interactionist Perspective

According to symbolic interactionism, the work role is a central part of a person's identity. When meeting someone new, one of the first questions we usually ask is, "What do you do?" The answer largely defines for us who that person is. For example, identifying a person as a truck driver provides a different social meaning than identifying someone as a physician. The title of a person's work status—maintenance supervisor or prime minister of Canada—also gives meaning and self-worth to the individual. An individual's job is one of his or her most important statuses; for many, it is a master status, that is, the most significant status in that person's social identity.

As symbolic interactionists note, definitions and meanings influence behaviour. Meanings and definitions of child labour (discussed later) contribute to its perpetuation. In some countries, children learn to regard working as a necessary and important responsibility and rite of passage, rather than as an abuse of human rights. Some children look forward to becoming bonded to a master "in the same way that…children [in our society] look forward to a communion or getting a driver's license" (Silvers 1996: 83).

Our principal motivations in world affairs have been largely economic.

RICHARD C. CASTON
Sociologist

What is prosperity? The fact that a bank manager, a railway president, or an industrialist states at an annual meeting that his business has had a prosperous year is no indication as to conditions throughout the country. Prosperity reflects itself in the general conditions of the masses and when they are prosperous, only then can we say we are in a state of prosperity.

A. A. HEAPS
Socialist Member of Parliament, 1928

The important ethical question here is: Who do you stand with and why? The men in suits who say free trade has been good or the unemployed people who say it has cost them their livelihood?

TIMOTHY FINDLEY
Novelist

Symbolic interactionism emphasizes that attitudes and behaviours are influenced by interaction with others. The applications of symbolic interactionism in the workplace are numerous—employers and managers are concerned with using interpersonal interaction techniques that achieve the attitudes and behaviours they want from their employees; union organizers are concerned with using interpersonal interaction techniques that persuade workers to unionize; and job training programs are concerned with using interpersonal interaction techniques that are effective in motivating participants.

> Free trade is desirable depending on where you sit—and whether you have a job.
>
> ROBERT MACNEIL
> *Broadcaster and author*

Problems of Work and Unemployment

Next, we examine unemployment and other problems associated with work. The problem of discrimination in the workplace based on gender, age, race and ethnicity, and sexual orientation is addressed in other chapters. Minimum wage issues are discussed in Chapter 10. Here we discuss problems concerning child labour, health and safety hazards in the workplace, job dissatisfaction and alienation, work–family concerns, unemployment and underemployment and labour unions and their struggle for workers' rights.

Child Labour: A Global Problem

Child labour involves children performing work that is hazardous, that interferes with a child's education, or that harms a child's health or physical, mental, spiritual, or moral development (U.S. Department of Labor 1995). Even though virtually every country in the world has laws that limit or prohibit the extent to which children can be employed, child labour persists throughout the world.

An estimated 250 million children between 5 and 14 work for a living (Human Rights Watch 2001). Child labourers work in factories, workshops, construction sites, mines, quarries, and fields, on deep-sea fishing boats, at home, and on the street. They make bricks, shoes, soccer balls, fireworks, matches, furniture, toys, rugs, and clothing. They work in manufacturing of brass, leather goods, and glass. They tend livestock and pick crops. In Egypt, over one million children ages seven to 12 work each year in cotton pest management. When they are perceived to be slowing down, they endure routine beatings with wooded switches by their supervisors. They face exposure to heat and pesticides ("Underage and Unprotected" 2001). Children typically earn the equivalent of $1 per day and work 7:00 a.m. to 6:00 p.m. with one midday break, seven days a week.

Children as young as five or six also work in domestic service. In one Latin American country, an estimated 22 percent of all working children are employed as servants (International Labour Organization 2000). This form of child labour is difficult to monitor, because of the hidden nature of the practice. Children additionally number among the millions of people worldwide who work in **sweatshops**—work environments that are characterized by less-than-minimum wage pay, excessively long hours of work (often without overtime pay), unsafe or inhumane working conditions, abusive treatment of workers by employers, and/or the lack of worker organizations aimed at negotiating better working conditions. Sweatshop labour conditions occur in a wide variety of industries, including garment production, manufacturing, mining, and agriculture. The dangerous conditions of sweatshops result in high rates of illness, injury, and death. The International Labour Organization estimates 1.4 million workers worldwide die on the job or from occupational disease each year (*Multinational Monitor* 2000). In one tragic example of death resulting from sweatshop conditions, at least 53 workers, including 10 children, were burned to death in a fire at a Sagar Chowdury garment factory in Bangladesh (Hargis 2001). The fire, caused by an electrical short circuit, engulfed the entire factory with 900 workers who were *locked inside*. Local residents and firefighters broke open the locked gates of the building and rescued survivors.

Child labour is most prevalent in Africa, Asia, and Central and South America. India has the largest child labour force in the world, with between 20 and 80 million working children (Parker 1998). This chapter's *The Human Side* feature depicts child labour in Pakistan.

Bonded labour—an extreme form of child labour—refers to the repayment of a debt through labour. Typically, an employer loans money to parents, who then give the employer their children as labourers to repay the debt. Sometimes the child is taken far away from the family to work; other times the child works in the same village and continues to live at home. The children are unable to work off the debt because of high interest rates, low wages, and wage deductions for meals, lodging, and mistakes made at work (U.S. Department of Labor 1995). Bonded labour is like slavery; a bonded worker is not free to leave the workplace. Between 10 and 20 million children in the world are forced to work as bonded labourers (Parker 1998). Bonded labour is most common in India, Nepal, Bangladesh, and Pakistan.

Child Prostitution and Trafficking

One of the worst forms of child labour is child prostitution and child trafficking. Although it is impossible to identify how prevalent child prostitution is, research estimates suggest that the problem is widespread. For example, surveys have identified 3000 child prostitutes in Montreal, 2930 in Athens, and up to 300 000 in the United States (Dorman 2001). Child prostitution occurs throughout the world and is particularly prevalent in Asia and Central and South America. In poor countries, families often sell the sexual services of their children in an attempt to get money. Some children are kidnapped or lured by traffickers with promises of employment, only to end up in a brothel. An estimated one-quarter of all visitors using child prostitutes in Asia are North American businessmen or military personnel (Kennedy 1996).

Causes of Child Labour Poverty, economic exploitation, social values, and lack of access to education are factors contributing to the persistence of child labour. One mother in Bangladesh whose 12-year-old daughter works up to 14 hours a day in a garment sweatshop explained, "Children shouldn't have to work....But if she didn't, we'd go hungry" (Parker 1998: 47). The economic advantages to industries that profit from child labour also perpetuate the practice. Traditional social values have also contributed to child labour. In the words of one employer in Pakistan who uses child labour, "Child labour is a tradition the West cannot understand and must not attempt to change" (Silvers 1996: 86). Finally, child labour results from failure to provide education to all children. The education system in Pakistan, for example, can only accommodate about one-third of the country's school-age children, leaving the remainder to join the child labour pool.

Child Labour in Pakistan

Like most other countries, Pakistan has laws prohibiting child labour and indentured servitude. However, these laws are largely ignored, and about 11 million children aged 4 to 14 work under brutal and squalid conditions. Children make up about a quarter of the unskilled work force in Pakistan and can be found in virtually every factory, field, and workshop. They earn on average a third of the adult wage. The following excerpt from an Atlantic Monthly *report describe child labour in Pakistan (Silvers 1996).*

Soon after I arrived in Pakistan, I arranged a trip to a town whose major factories were rumored to enslave very young children. I found myself hoping during the journey there that the children I saw working in fields, on the roads, at the marketplaces, would prepare me for the worst. They did not. No amount of preparation could have lessened the shock and revulsion I felt on entering a sporting-goods factory in the town of Sialkot...where scores of children, most of them aged 5 to 10, produce soccer balls by hand for 40 rupees, or about $1.20, a day. The children work 80 hours a week in near-total darkness and total silence. According to the foreman, the darkness is both an economy and a precautionary measure; child-rights activists have difficulty taking photographs and gathering evidence of wrongdoing if the lighting is poor. The silence is to ensure product quality: "If the children speak, they are not giving their complete attention to the product and are liable to make errors." The children are permitted one 30-minute meal break each day; they are punished if they take longer. They are also punished if they fall asleep, if their workbenches are sloppy, if they waste material or miscut a pattern, if they complain of mistreatment to their parents or speak to strangers outside the factory....Punishments are doled out in a storage closet at the rear of the factory....Children are hung upside down by their knees, starved, caned, or lashed....The punishment room is a standard feature of a Pakistani factory, as common as a lunchroom at an...assembly plant.

The town's other factories are no better, and many are worse. Here are brick kilns where five-year-olds work hip-deep in slurry pits, where adolescent girls stoke furnaces in 160-degree heat. Here are tanneries where nursing mothers mix vats of chemical dye, textile mills where eight-year-olds tend looms and breathe air thick with cotton dust.... A carpet workshop...was...about the size of a subway car, and about as appealing. The long, narrow room contained a dozen upright looms. On each rough-hewn workbench between the looms squatted a carpet weaver. The room was dark and airless. Such light as there was came from a single ceiling fixture, two of its four bulbs burned out. A thermometer read 105 degrees, and the mud walls were hot to the touch....

Of the 12 weavers, five were 11 to 14, and four were under 10. The two youngest were brothers named Akbar and Ashraf, aged eight and nine. They had been bonded to the carpet master at age five, and now worked six days a week at the shop. Their workday started at 6:00 a.m. and ended at 8:00 p.m., except, they said, when the master was behind on his quotas and forced them to work around the clock. They were small, thin, malnourished, their spines curved from lack of exercise and from squatting before the loom. Their hands were covered with calluses and scars, their fingers gnarled from repetitive work. Their breathing was laboured, suggestive of tuberculosis. Collectively these ailments, which pathologists call *captive-child syndrome*, kill half of Pakistan's working children by age 12....

A hand-knotted carpet is made by tying short lengths of fine colored thread to a lattice of heavier white threads. The process is labour-intensive and tedious: a single four-by-six-foot carpet contains well over a million knots and takes an experienced weaver four to six months to complete....Each carpet...would retail....[in North America] for about $2000—more than the boy would earn in 10 years. Abkar revealed that, "the master screams at us all the time, and sometimes he beats us....We're slapped often. Once or twice he lashed us with a cane. I was beaten 10 days ago after I made many errors of colour in a carpet. He struck me with his fist quite hard on the face....I was fined 1000 rupees and made to correct the errors by working two days straight."...The fine was added to Akbar's debt, and would extend his "apprenticeship" by several months....

Akbar declared that "staying here longer fills me with dread. I know I must learn a trade. But my parents are so far away, and all my friends are in school. My brother and I would like to be with our family. We'd like to play with our friends. This is not the way children should live."

SOURCE: Silver, Jonathan. 1996. From "Child Labor in Pakistan." © 1996 by Jonathan Silvers as first published in *The Atlantic Monthly*, February 1996. Reprinted by permission.

Consequences of Child Labour Child labourers are at risk for a variety of health problems such as injuries, stunted growth, and many diseases. Child carpet weavers develop gnarled fingers from the repetitive work, and their spines are curved from sitting at looms all day. Young brickworkers breathe in dust from the dry bricks and sand, causing scarring of the lungs and early death. Child farmworkers are exposed to harmful pesticides. In rural areas, more child workers in agriculture die from pesticide poisonings than from all of the most common childhood diseases put together (UNICEF 2000). Child prostitutes are often physically abused by their pimps and customers, are at high risk for acquiring HIV and other sexually transmitted infections, and suffer the emotional scars of their exploitation. Child labourers are fed inadequate diets and must endure harsh punishment from their employers. One girl who was forced into prostitution in Bangkok said, "One time I refused to sleep with a man and they slapped me, hit me with a cane and bashed my head against the wall. One of my friends tried to run away but unfortunately she was caught and very badly beaten" (Parker 1998: 42).

Child labour also increases poverty by depressing already low wages. Parker (1998) explains,

> For every child who works, there may be an adult who cannot find a job. Children are usually paid less than adult workers—sometimes only one-third of what adults earn. As a result, adult workers' wages stay low or go down. When parents cannot find jobs, they are more likely to send their children to work. They have more children in the hope of increasing their income. Each generation of poor, uneducated child workers becomes the next genre of poor parents who must send their kids to work. Then the cycle of poverty and illiteracy continues. (Parker 1998: 48)

Health and Safety Hazards in the Workplace

Accidents at work and hazardous working conditions contribute to illnesses, injuries, and deaths. Globally, an estimated 1.1 million workers die on the job or from occupational disease every year (*Multinational Monitor* 2000). Some occupational health and safety hazards are attributed to wilful disregard of information and guidelines concerning worker safety. For example, the dangers of asbestos were known as early as 1918, when insurance companies stopped selling life insurance policies to asbestos workers. Nevertheless, the asbestos industry took little action until the 1960s. Of the half-million workers exposed to "significant doses of asbestos," 100 000 will die from lung cancer, 35 000 from mesothelioma, and 35 000 from asbestosis (Coleman 1994: 79). In 1999, the Ontario Federation of Labour (OFL) launched a campaign to push the government for stricter limits on the exposure to toxic substances in workplaces and to demand that enough inspectors be put in place to ensure those limits are adhered to in all companies. In support of these demands, the OFL produced documents, obtained by the Canadian Auto Workers union through Freedom of Information requests, that showed a blatant disregard for the health and well-being of workers. For example, even though company and government officials knew that workers at the Holmes Insulation plant in Sarnia were being poisoned and exposed to amounts of asbestos that were far beyond the allowable limits, no one did anything to stop it. The OFL has compiled a top 12 dangerous workplace materials list that includes asbestos, benzene, cadmium, diesel exhaust emissions, fibreglass, formaldehyde, lead, met-alworking fluids (used in coolants and lubricants in cutting, drilling, and machining metal), nickel, silica, styrene, and vinyl chloride (Simone 1999). Insulating occupations remain classified as the seventh most dangerous occu-pation in Canada because of the dangers associated with long-term exposure to asbestos (Statistics Canada 1998a).

In an average year in the 1970s, approximately 11 workers for every 100 000 workers died in the course of, or because of, their employment. In the 1990s, the fatality rate fell to seven deaths for every 100 000 workers. The three most dangerous occupations in Canada are, in order, the cutting and loading of rock, general mine labouring, and operating small engines (Statis-tics Canada 1998a).

Workplace Illnesses and Injuries The rate of reported time-loss work injuries has been decreasing steadily, from 49 injuries for every 1000 workers in 1987 to slightly less than 28 per 1000 workers in 1996. However, according to data collected by Statistics Canada on behalf of the Association of Workers' Com-pensation Boards of Canada, in 1996 there were still more than 377 000 time-loss work injuries in Canada. The definition of a "time-loss injury" is an injury that results in compensation for lost wages because of time off work or for a per-manent disability, regardless of the time lost. In that year, men's rate of time-loss injury was more than two and a half times that of women (Figure 11.1).

The rate of injuries per 1000 workers was highest among those aged 15 to 29; among this age cohort, the injury rate was 43.4 per 1000 (more than 57 percent above the average for all ages and both sexes). The rate of compensated injuries was far higher in forestry and logging than in any other industry, although rates in transportation, wholesale trade, manufacturing, and construction were also well above average (Figure 11.2) (Health Canada 1999). Among white-collar industries, government and the health care sectors had the two highest rates of time-loss injuries in 1996 (Health Canada 1999).

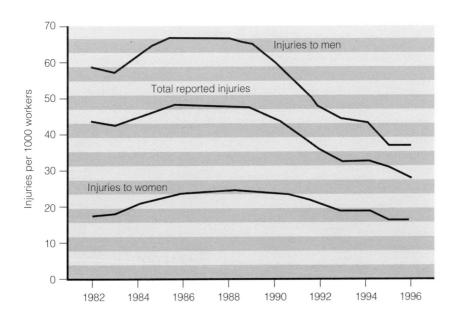

Figure 11.1 *Time-loss Work Injuries, Employed Persons 15+, Canada, 1982–1996*

SOURCE: Statistics Canada, Health Statistics Division, special tabulation of data from the Association of Workers' Compensation Boards of Canada (collected by Statistics Canada) and the Labour Force Survey subdivision of Statistics Canada.

Figure 11.2 *Time-loss Work Injuries, by Industry, Employed Persons Aged 15+, Canada, 1992–1996*

SOURCE: Statistics Canada, Health Statistics Division, special tabulation of data from the Association of Workers' Compensation Boards of Canada (collected by Statistics Canada and the Labour Force Survey subdivision of Statistics Canada.

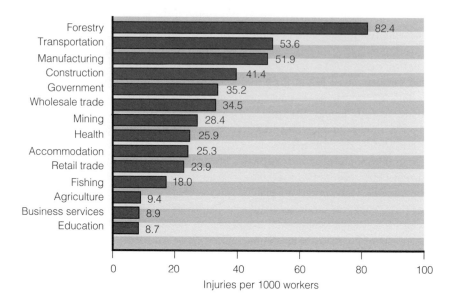

Among the most common types of workplace illnesses are disorders associated with repeated trauma, such as carpal tunnel syndrome (a wrist disorder that can cause numbness, tingling, and severe pain), tendonitis (inflammation of the tendons) and noise-induced hearing loss. Such disorders—referred to by a number of terms, including **cumulative trauma disorders**, **repetitive strain disorders**, and **repeated trauma disorders**—are muscle, tendon, vascular, and nerve injuries that result from repeated or sustained actions or exertions of different body parts. Jobs that are associated with high rates of upper body cumulative trauma disorders include computer programming, manufacturing, meatpacking, poultry processing, and clerical/office work (National Safety Council 1997). Cumulative trauma disorders are classified as illnesses, not as injuries, because they are not sudden, instantaneous traumatic events.

Job Stress and Chronic Fatigue Another work-related health hazard is job stress and chronic fatigue. To measure work stress, the 1996–97 National Population Health Survey used a scale composed of 12 questions describing working conditions that were answered on a five-point scale of agree or disagree. The minimum score on the scale was 0 and the maximum was 45; "high stress" was defined as a score of 30 or higher. Using this scale, the survey found that more women reported high work stress levels than men did in every age category, with women aged 20 to 24 almost three times as likely to report high work stress as the average Canadian worker. Notable differences in high work stress also existed among persons in different types of households. Single parents were twice as likely as Canadians in couple relationships without children were to report high work stress (Health Canada 1999).

Prolonged job stress, also known as **job burnout**, can cause physical problems, such as high blood pressure, ulcers, and headaches, as well as psychological problems. Although an international survey reports that employees in Canada logged fewer hours than those in 28 countries logged (Figure 11.3), many Canadian workers report feeling exhausted and emotionally drained at the end of the day.

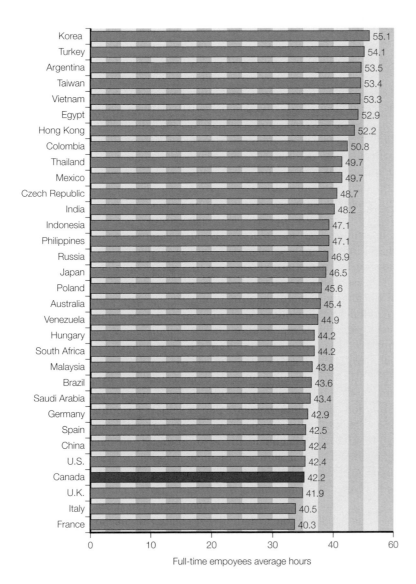

■ **Figure 11.3** *The Work Week: Full-time Employee's Average Hours*

SOURCE: © Roper ASW, LLC.

A survey of 2000 Canadian men and women, 18 years of age and over, who worked at least 20 hours a week outside the home found that about one in three respondents agreed with the statement that "my job often is so stressful that I feel burned out"; an additional 23 percent said they sometimes felt that way. Women were more likely than men to report feeling burned out (63.8 percent and 51.5 percent, respectively). In addition, this survey found that susceptibility to burnout varied by industry, with those employed in government, education, and health care significantly more likely like to say they often felt burned out. Those in occupations with high susceptibility to burnout were also likely to feel that they lacked the resources they needed to perform their job well (Table 11.1).

Dissatisfaction and Alienation

If you read the classified ad section of any newspaper, you are likely to find job advertisements that entice applicants with claims such as "discover a rewarding

■ **Table 11.1** *The Perceptions of Workers by Sector*

By, sector, the percentage who agreed with the following statements	High tech	Finance/Insurance	Government/ health/education	Service	Manufacturing/ construction	Transportation/ Communication/ utilities	Agriculture
1. I have the resources I need to do my job well	61.1	64.2	50.7	62.4	71.2	62.7	66.7
2. My organization satisfies our customers' needs	68.6	68.8	60.8	71.1	75.9	71.3	76.9
3. My job often is so stressful that I feel burned out	29.6	31.8	43.8	33.0	35.0	30.2	15.4

SOURCE: *Maclean's*. 1999. "The Best and Worst Jobs." May 31: 18–23.

Clearly the most unfortunate people are those who must do the same thing over and over again, every minute, or perhaps 20 to the minute. They deserve the shortest hours and the highest pay.

JOHN KENNETH GALBRAITH
Economist

Without work, all life goes rotten, but when work is soulless, life stifles and dies.

ALBERT CAMUS
Philosopher

and challenging career..." and "we offer opportunities for advancement and travel...". Unfortunately, most jobs do not allow workers to "be all that they can be." In reality, most employers want you to be all you can be for them, with limited concern for your career satisfaction. This chapter's *Social Problems Research Up Close* examines jobs in industries that produce knowledge-based technologies, products, and services with those in the rest of the private sector.

Factors that contribute to job satisfaction include income, prestige, a feeling of accomplishment, autonomy, a sense of being challenged by the job, opportunities to be creative, congenial coworkers, the feeling that one is making a contribution, fair rewards (pay and benefits), promotion opportunities, and job security (Bavendam 2000; Robie et al. 1998). These factors often overlap—for example, high-paying jobs tend to have more prestige, be more autonomous, provide more benefits, and permit greater creativity. However, many jobs lack these qualities, leaving workers dissatisfied. Moreover, many Canadians are worried that they may lose their jobs in the next few years. In 2001, one in five Canadians told pollsters that they were concerned that someone in their household would lose a job (Bricker and Greenspon 2001: 18). "Unsurprisingly, older workers, single parents, and those with less than high school education are the least confident of finding a new job if they were ever to lose the existing one" (Bricker and Greenspon 2001: 125).

One form of job dissatisfaction is a feeling of **alienation**. A high division of labour and specialization of work roles characterize work in industrialized societies. As a result, workers' tasks are repetitive and monotonous and often involve little or no creativity. Limited to specific tasks by their work roles, workers are unable to express and utilize their full potential—intellectual, emotional, and physical. According to Marx, when workers are merely cogs in a machine, they become estranged from their work, the product they create, other human beings, and themselves. Marx called this estrangement "alienation."

Alienation usually has four components: powerlessness, meaninglessness, normlessness, and self-estrangement. Powerlessness results from working in an environment in which workers have little or no control over the decisions that affect their work. Meaninglessness results when workers do not find fulfillment in their work. Workers may experience normlessness if workplace norms are unclear or conflicting. For example, many companies that have family leave policies informally discourage workers from using them, or workplaces that officially promote nondiscrimination in reality practise discrimination. Alienation also involves a feeling of self-estrangement, which stems from the workers' inability to realize their full human potential in their work roles and from a lack of connections to others. In general, traditional "women's work" is more alienating than "men's work" (Ross and Wright 1998). "Homemaking exposes women to routine, unfulfilling, isolated work; and part-time employment exposes them to routine, unfulfilling work, with little decision-making autonomy" (p. 343).

Work–Family Concerns

As a result of a combination of social forces, including economic pressures, changing gender ideologies, improved contraception, increased life expectancy, and the marked trend toward smaller families, the dual-earner family has become the "new norm" in Canada (Figure 11.4). Understandably, for many employed parents, balancing work and family demands is a daily challenge. When Hochschild (1997) asked a sample of employed parents, "Overall, how well do you feel you can balance the demands of your work and family?" only 9 percent said "very well" (pp. 199–200). (Work–family concerns are also discussed in Chapters 5, 7, and 10.)

The lack of affordable, quality child care is one stressor that many Canadian parents confront. Although "[c]hild care is a fact of life for Canadian children and their families very little regulated child care even exists in Canada" (National Council of Welfare 1999b: 17). While the costs of child care in general, and for preschoolers in particular, are high and rising, the federal, provincial, and territorial governments have cut funding for social programs, cut or frozen subsidies to low-income families, and made eligibility criteria for subsidies more restrictive. In addition, parents of children with special needs as well as those parents who work irregular hours or shift work may find it impossible to obtain child care.

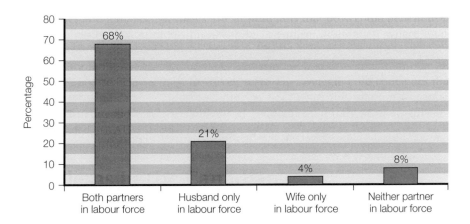

■ Figure 11.4 *Labour Force Status of Couples with Children, 1996*

SOURCE: Statistics Canada. 1996. 1996 Census, The Nation Series, CD-ROM, 93F0020XCB96004.

Labour force status measured for the week prior to Census day in May, 1996. Couples include married and common-law partners with never-married children of any age living at home.

Workplace and Employee Survey: Better Jobs in the New Economy?

Sample and Methods

The 1999 Workplace and Employee Survey (WES), conducted by Statistics Canada, compared jobs in industries that produce knowledge-based technologies, products, and services with those in the rest of the private sector. The WES covers the private sector (i.e., all industries with the exception of farming, fishing, hunting, trapping and public administration). Within this study, the term "knowledge-based industries" refers to "industries that spend a relatively large amount of resources on research and development and have professionals, such as scientists and engineers, as a substantial proportion of their workforce" (Statistics Canada 2002). In addition, it is limited to jobs in research and development-based firms that produce knowledge-based technologies, products, and services. Included here would be most, although not all, industries within the information and communication technology sector, including telecommunications, data processing, and computer systems design, as well as the pharmaceutical and chemical manufacturing industries.

Within this study, industries were classified into five mutually exclusive groups: (1) knowledge-based in the goods sector; (2) knowledge-based in the service sector; (3) other goods producing; (4) retail trade and consumer services; and (5) other professional and other services. The study examined job characteristics such as work hours, hourly wages, pension coverage, stock options, personal and family support programs, teamwork, performance appraisal, grievance systems, and job satisfaction.

Findings and Conclusions

Workers in knowledge-based industries receive relatively high wages, have good fringe benefits, and often profit from fitness and recreation services as well as employee assistance programs. However, many work fairly long hours, and those employed in the service sector rarely have access to a formal grievance system in their workplace....

1. *Workers in knowledge-based industries receive relatively high wages.* On average, employees in knowledge-based industries earned $24.09 per hour in 1999, 32 percent more than the $18.19 received by employees in other industries. The wage gap between knowledge-based industries and other industries was 14 percent for university graduates, compared with 31 percent for other workers with some postsecondary education. Employees in knowledge-based workplaces earn relatively high wages for a number of reasons. They are generally better educated than other workers and tend to be employed in larger establishments, which generally pay higher wages. They may also receive higher wages to compensate for the relatively high costs of living in larger areas, where such workplaces tend to be located. Many of these employees are in high-paying professional occupations such as engineering and science. Lastly, some, such as university graduates, could receive higher wages as compensation for relatively long hours....

2. *Workers often have stock options.* Employees in knowledge-based industries were not necessarily better covered by a registered pension plan than other workers. For instance, 40 percent of employees in service-producing, knowledge-based workplaces had a pension plan in 1999, compared with 48 percent of their counterparts in professional

Unemployment and Underemployment

The International Labour Organization (2001) reports that one-third of the world's workforce is unemployed or underemployed. Poor countries tend to suffer high rates of unemployment. For example, recent unemployment rates in South Africa and Lesotho (a southern African country) were 23 percent and 42 percent, respectively (International Labour Organization 2001).

and other services. However, 31 percent of employees in service-producing knowledge-based workplaces received stock options, five times the proportion (6 percent) in professional and other services. On average, employees in knowledge-based industries were more likely to be covered by life or disability insurance, supplemental medical insurance, and dental plans. They were also more likely to have profit-sharing plans....

3. *Employees often benefit from fitness services and assistance programs.* Roughly 25 percent of employees in knowledge-based industries were in workplaces that provided fitness and recreation services (on- or off-site). The corresponding numbers for other goods-producing industries, professional and other services, and retail trade and consumer services were 15 percent, 17 percent and 5 percent, respectively. In addition, 40 percent of workers in knowledge-based workplaces were offered employee assistance programs (counselling, substance abuse control, financial assistance, legal aid). Such programs were available to 35 percent, 29 percent and 8 percent of employees in professional and other services,

other goods-producing industries, and retail trade and consumer services, respectively....

4. *University graduates in knowledge-based industries work fairly long hours.* Compared to their counterparts in the rest of the economy, university graduates employed full time in knowledge-based industries worked either longer hours or more hours of unpaid overtime. Their total workweek, including unpaid overtime, averaged 46.6 hours per week. This was at least two hours more than in professional and other services (44.3) or in retail trade and consumer services (44.4)....

5. *In the service sector, few have access to a formal grievance system.* In 1999, 20 percent of employees in knowledge-based industries were unionized. This compares with 13 percent in consumer services and retail trade, and 33 percent in professional and other services or in other goods-producing industries. However, there were substantial differences within the knowledge-based sector. About 14 percent of employees in service-producing workplaces were unionized, compared with 25 percent in goods-producing workplaces. As a result, only 18 percent of workers in service-

producing, knowledge-based industries reported having access to a formal grievance system such as a labour-management committee or an outside arbitrator. In contrast, access to such a system was reported by 46 percent of those in goods-producing, knowledge-based industries, 41 percent in professional and other services, and 38 percent in other goods-producing industries....

6. Performance appraisal is more frequent in knowledge-based industries. At least 65 percent of employees in knowledge-based industries had their job performance evaluated through a standard process, compared with only 45 percent to 58 percent of workers in other industries. Furthermore, employees in knowledge-based industries were almost twice as likely as other workers to have their level of pay or benefits directly affected by job evaluation results. Thus, work evaluation was more systematic in the knowledge-based sector than in other industries.

SOURCE: Adapted and abridged from Statistics Canada. 2002. "Workplace and Employee Survey: Better Jobs in the New Economy?" *The Daily*, July 18. Available on the World Wide Web at http://www.statcan.ca/Daily/English/020718/d020718b.htm and on the July 2002 online issue of *Perspectives on Labour and Income*, vol.3 no. 7 (75-001-XIE).

Measures of **unemployment** consider an individual to be unemployed if he or she is currently without employment, is actively seeking employment, and is available for employment. Unemployment figures do not include "discouraged workers," who have given up on finding a job and are no longer looking for employment. **Underemployment** is a broader term that includes unemployed workers, discouraged workers, and those working part-time but who wish to work full-time. For example, although the overall size of the Canadian labour force has grown significantly in the past three decades, much of the growth has been in part-time jobs and self-employment, neither of which provides benefits and pensions. In 1998, about 30 percent of adult women working part-time were doing so involuntarily because they could not obtain full-time employment (Statistics Canada 1999).

Compared with other industrialized countries, Canada has a low rate of unemployment (see Table 11.2). However, unemployment rates vary across Canada with, traditionally, the picture improving from east to west. For example, in 2000, unemployment rates in Canada ranged from a high of 16.7 in Newfoundland to 4.9 in Manitoba (*Canadian Global Almanac* 2002: 206). While the gap has narrowed in recent years, unemployment rates for Canadian men have been higher than for women (Statistics Canada 1998b).

Types and Causes of Unemployment Unemployment can be either discriminatory or structural. **Discriminatory unemployment** involves high rates of unemployment among particular social groups, such as racial and ethnic minorities and women (see Chapters 7 and 8). **Structural unemployment** exists when there are not enough jobs available for those who want them. Structural unemployment is the result of social factors rather than personal inadequacies of the unemployed or discrimination.

For example, unemployment can result from **corporate downsizing**—the corporate practice of discharging large numbers of employees. Simply put, the term "downsizing" is a euphemism for mass firing of employees (Caston 1998). Another cause of unemployment is **job exportation**, the relocation of Canadian jobs to other countries where products can be produced more cheaply. Job exportation has had a particularly profound effect on garment workers and the Canadian garment industry over the past decade (Yanz and Jeffcott 1997). **Automation**, or the replacement of human labour with machinery and equipment, is another feature of the work landscape that contributes to unemployment (see also Chapter 13). For example, recorded phone trees, automated teller machines (ATMs), and automatic car washes do jobs that otherwise would be performed by workers.

Table 11.2 *Unemployment Rates in Nine Countries, 2000*

Country	Unemployment Rate
United States	4.0%
Canada	5.8%
Australia	6.6%
Japan	4.8%
France	9.7%
Germany	8.3%
Italy	10.7%
Sweden	5.8%
United Kingdom	5.5%

SOURCE: Bureau of Labor Statistics. 2001. "Unemployment Rates in Nine Countries, 1990–2001." Washington, DC: U.S. Department of Labor.

Because of the changing nature of work, displaced workers may find themselves unable to obtain satisfactory employment. Consider, for example, that since 1989, the number of employed clerical workers in Canada has dropped from 2.2 million to 1.9 million while the number of manufacturing jobs has declined from 1.8 million to 1.7 million. It is evident that not all Canadians possess the credentials that are increasingly necessary to climb out of the ranks of the unemployed and underemployed (Statistics Canada 1998a; 2003). Data from the 2001 census indicate that while highly skilled occupations—those normally requiring a university education—accounted for almost one half of the total labour force growth over the last decade, skilled occupations—those requiring a community college diploma or apprenticeship training—"grew at less than a third of the pace of the labour force as a whole...[and] there was a 3.8 percent decline in the number of people in occupations normally requiring apprenticeship training, such as skilled trades" (Statistics Canada 2003: 7). In certain construction trades, for example, the number has fallen by between 40 and 60 percent. In low-skill occupations (i.e., those requiring a high school diploma at most), the rate of growth was much slower than total labour force growth.

Effects of Unemployment and Underemployment The personal consequences of unemployment (and in some cases, underemployment) include anxiety, depression, alcohol abuse, and lowered self-esteem and confidence (Feather 1990; Liem and Liem 1990; Tremblay et al. 2002). Unemployment has consequences for families and communities as well, and has been linked to increased family violence (Reidmann et al. 2003). Unemployment may also mean losing supplemental health care benefits for workers and their families, and underemployed individuals rarely get health care benefits from their employers. Unemployment and underemployment result in a decline in an individual's standard of living.

Strategies for Action: Responses to Workers' Concerns

Government, private business, human rights organizations, and labour organizations play important roles in responding to the concerns of workers. Next we look at responses to child labour, health and safety regulations, work site programs, work–family policies and programs, efforts to strengthen labour, and workforce development programs.

Responses to Child Labour

The International Programme on the Elimination of Child Labour has been working to remove child labourers from oppressive work conditions, provide them with education, and provide their parents with jobs or income. Since the program began in 1992, it has grown from six participating countries to more than 200 participating countries in 2000 (Human Rights Watch 2001).

In 1999, 174 nations adopted the new Convention on the Worst Forms of Child Labour, and by September 2000, 37 countries had ratified the convention (Human Rights Watch 2001). This represents a global consensus to end the most severe forms of child labour and requires nations to take immediate measures to abolish child slavery, trafficking, debt bondage, child prostitution and pornography, and forced labour. Human rights organizations such as the International Labour Organization, UNICEF, and the Child Labour Coalition, are also active in the campaign against child labour. Another organization, the Bonded Labour Liberation Front (BLLF) has led the fight against bonded and child labour in Pakistan, freeing 30 000 adults and children from brick kilns, carpet factories, and farms, and placing 11 000 children in its own primary school system (Silvers 1996). However, employers in Pakistan have threatened workers with violence if they talk with "the abolitionists" or possess "illegal communist propaganda." Human rights activists campaigning against child labour have also been victims of threats and violence.

The United Nations Children's Fund recommends that national and international corporations adopt codes of conduct guaranteeing that neither they nor their subcontractors will employ children in conditions that violate their rights (UNICEF 1997). Some industries, including rug and clothing manufacturers, use labels and logos to indicate that child labourers do not make their products. A recently formed Fair Labour Association (FLA) involves six leading apparel and footwear companies who voluntarily participate in a monitoring system to inspect their overseas factories and require them to meet minimum labour standards, such as not requiring workers to work more than 60 hours a week. However, critics point out a number of problems with the Fair Labour Association, including (1) standards are too low (allows below-poverty wages and excessive overtime); (2) only 10 percent of companies' factories must be monitored yearly; (3) companies can influence which factories are inspected and who does the inspection; and (4) FLA does not uphold workers' right to organize (Benjamin 1998). Critics charge that companies use their participation in FLA as a marketing tool. Once "certified" by FLA, companies can sew a label into their products saying they were made under fair working conditions.

Pressure from students and other opponents of child and sweatshop labour along with consumer boycotts of products made by child and sweatshop labour have resulted in some improvements. Factories that make goods for companies, such as Nike and Gap, have cut back on child labour, use less dangerous chemicals, and require fewer employees to work 80-hour weeks (Greenhouse 2000; Klein 2000). At many factories, supervisors have stopped hitting employees, have improve ventilation, and have stopped requiring workers to obtain permission to use the toilet. But improvements are not widespread and oppressive forms of labour continue throughout the world. According to the National Labour Committee, two areas where "progress seems to grind to a halt" are efforts to form unions and efforts to achieve wage increases (Greenhouse 2000).

Efforts to eliminate child labour cannot succeed unless the impoverished conditions that contribute to its practice are alleviated. A living minimum wage must be established for adult workers so they will not need to send their children to work. One labour rights advocate said, "We will not end child labour merely by attacking it in the export sector in poor nations. If children's parents in all countries around the world are not earning a living wage…, children will be driven into working in dangerous informal sector jobs. Labour rights for adults are essential if we truly want to eliminate child labour" (Global March against Child Labor 1998).

Efforts to Strengthen Labour

International norms established by the United Nations and the International Labour Organization declare the right of workers to organize, negotiate with management, and strike (Human Rights Watch 2000). In European countries, labour unions are generally strong (Mishel et al. 2001). However, in many less developed countries and countries undergoing economic transition, workers and labour unions struggle to have a voice in matters of wages and working conditions. A survey of 113 countries by the International Confederation of Free Trade Unions (ICFTU) found that both corporations and governments repressed union efforts ("Global Labor Repression" 2000). Among the survey's findings are:

- At least 140 trade unionists around the world in 1999 were assassinated, disappeared, or committed suicide after they were threatened as a result of their labour advocacy. Columbia was found to be the most dangerous country for union activists. In 1999, 76 trade unionists in Columbia were assassinated or reported missing.
- Nearly 3000 people were arrested, more than 1500 were injured, beaten, or tortured, and at least 5800 were harassed because of their trade union activities. Another 700 trade unionists received death threats.
- About 12 000 workers were unfairly dismissed or refused reinstatement, sometimes with the complicity of the government, because they were active members of a trade union. Governments, sometimes with the support of employers using strikebreakers, repressed at least 140 strikes or demonstrations; 80 of the 113 countries surveyed restrict the right to strike.

In spite of these repressive actions, labour unions have played an important role in fighting for fair wages and benefits, healthy and safe work environments, and other forms of worker advocacy. In Canada, about 3.7 million paid workers belonged to unions during the first half of 2000, with workers in Newfoundland the most likely to be union members (with just under 40 percent of all paid employees union members). In that year, the average hourly earnings of unionized workers exceeded those of non-unionized workers for both full-time and part-time workers (Statistics Canada 2002). Almost all of Canada's nurses and teachers, about one-third of Canada's white-collar workers, half of Canada's professional and managerial workers, and four in ten blue-collar workers were union members (Statistics Canada 1998a; Statistics Canada 2002).

Although Canadian women workers are less likely than their male counterparts to be unionized, unionization among women has risen considerably over the past three decades (Figure 11.5). In 1999, women accounted for 46 percent of all union members in Canada (Ghalam 2000: 106). The growth in unionization among women stems from several factors including, "most notably, their growing presence in the heavily unionized public sector" (Ghalam 2000: 106). In 2001, the largest labour unions in Canada were the Canadian Union of Public Employees (486 000 members), the National Union of Public and General Employees (325 000 members), Canadian Auto Workers (245 000), United Food and Commercial Workers (220 000), United Steel Workers (187 000), Public Service Alliance (150 000), Communications, Energy and Paperworkers

Figure 11.5 *Percentage of Workers Unionized, 1966–1999*

SOURCE: Statistics Canada, Labour Force Survey; and CALURA.

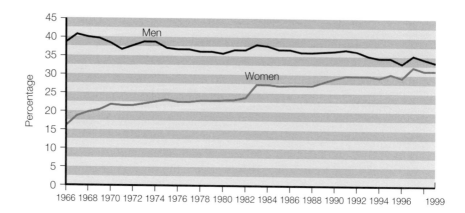

(150 000), Teamsters (95 000), Fédération des affaires sociales inc. (95 000), and Service Employees (80 000) (Ash 2001: 195).

Workforce Development and Job-creation Programs

The International Labour Organization (2001) estimates that over 500 million new jobs are needed by 2010 to accommodate new entrants to the workforce and to reduce current unemployment levels by half. Developing a workforce and creating jobs involves far-reaching efforts, including those designed to improve health and health care, alleviate poverty and malnutrition, develop infrastructures, and provide universal education.

In Canada, workforce development programs have provided a variety of services, including assessment to evaluate skills and needs, career counselling, job search assistance, basic education, occupational training (classroom and on-the-job), public employment, job placement, and stipends or other support services for childcare and transportation assistance (Levitan et al. 1998). Numerous studies have looked at the effectiveness of workforce development programs. In general, "evaluations indicate that employment and training programs enhance the earnings and employment of participants, although the effects vary by service population, are often modest because of brief training durations and the inherent difficulty of alleviating long-term deficiencies, and are not always cost effective" (Levitan et al. 1998: 199). However, funding for federal job training programs is insufficient to reach more than a small fraction of the workforce and even those who complete training and retraining programs do not always find new jobs at comparable wages.

Efforts to prepare high school students for work include the establishment of technical and vocational high schools and school-to-work programs. School-to-work programs involve partnerships between business, labour, government, education, and community organizations that help prepare high school students for jobs (Leonard 1996). Although school-to-work programs vary, in general, they allow high school students to explore different careers, and they provide job skill training and work-based learning experiences, often with pay (Bassi and Ludwig 2000). Nevertheless, for many young Canadians, finding employment continues to be elusive, with "McJobs"—dead-end jobs in the service industry—the only option. Consider, in this context, that from 1986 to 1996, the percentage of 25-to 34 year-old Canadians living in their parental homes "shot up from 23 percent of females and 28 percent of males to 33 percent of females and 40 percent of males" (Bricker and Greenspon 2001: 32). Many Canadians are finding it difficult to leave their parental nests.

Although more than 1.5 million jobs were created in Canada between 1997 through 2000 (Bricker and Greenspon 2001: 15), efforts to create jobs must consider where the jobs are being created. The Canadian economy can be described as a **split labour market** (or dual economy), because it is made up of two labour markets. The *primary labour market* refers to jobs that are stable, economically rewarding, and come with benefits. These jobs are usually occupied by the most educated and trained individuals (e.g., a corporate attorney, teacher, or accountant). The *secondary labour market* refers to jobs that involve low pay, no security, few benefits, and little chance for advancement. Domestic servants, clerks, and food servers are examples of these jobs. These workers often have no union to protect them and are more likely to be dissatisfied with their job than workers in the primary labour market.

Responses to Worker Health and Safety Concerns

Over the past few decades, health and safety conditions in the workplace have improved because of media attention, regulations, demands by unions for change, and more white-collar jobs. Canadian governments have expanded workplace protection through human rights laws, which prohibit discrimination in hiring, promotion, and working conditions, and workers' compensation programs, which pay partial lost wages to sick or injured workers. However, Krahn and Lowe (1993: 280–81) point out that "[t]he Canadian state's involvement in occupational health [actually] goes back to the *Factory Acts* of the 1800s…, [which] required fencing around machines, reasonable ventilation, lunchrooms, and lavatories." They note that "the first major initiative to involve workers directly in health and safety was the 1972 *Saskatchewan Occupational Health Act*…, [which] established workplace health and safety programs premised on the right of workers to participate in the identification and regulation of hazards" through their participation in joint health and safety committees. Since that time, they observe, "[o]ther provinces and the federal government have followed Saskatchewan's legislative lead, to varying degrees, and now most jurisdictions have elements of what is known as the 'internal responsibility system' (IRS)." The *Canada Labour Code*, in 1986, established the right of workers to be told about the potential hazards of workplace materials, with this "right to know" buttressed by the national Workplace Hazardous Materials Information System. Worker health and safety committees are also a standard feature of companies in many industrialized countries and are mandatory in most of Europe. These committees are authorized to inspect workplaces and cite employers for violations of health and safety regulations.

Maximizing the health and safety of workers involves more than implementing, monitoring, and enforcing regulations. Increasingly, businesses and corporations are attempting to maximize workers' health (and corporate profits) by offering work-site health promotion programs. Work-site health promotion consists of health education, screening, and interventions designed to achieve better health among workers. Programs range from single interventions (such as screening for high blood pressure) to comprehensive health and fitness programs, aerobic exercise and fitness, nutrition and weight control, stress management, smoking cessation, cancer-risk screening, drug and alcohol abuse prevention, accident prevention, and health information (Conrad 1999). Some workplaces have nap rooms, allowing workers to take naps (Bettelheim 1998). Many companies have employee assistance programs to help employees and their families with substance abuse, family discord, depression, and other mental health problems.

At the same time, one highly controversial health and safety strategy used by business management is behavioural-based safety programs. Instead of examining how work processes and conditions compromise health and safety on the job, **behavioural-based safety programs** direct attention to workers themselves as the problem. Behaviour-based safety programs claim that 80 to 96 percent of job injuries and illnesses are caused by workers' own carelessness and unsafe acts (Frederick and Lessin 2000). These programs focus on teaching employees and managers to identify, "discipline," and change unsafe worker behaviours that cause accidents, and to encourage a work culture that recognizes and rewards safe behaviours.

Critics contend that behaviour-based safety programs divert attention away from the employer's failure to provide safe working conditions. For example, when a worker slipped and fell on the ice in the parking lot of a tire manufacturing company,

> the official accident report...stated, "Worker's eyes not on path," as the cause of the injury. The report did not mention the need to have ice and snow removed from the parking lot. It did not mention that the sidewalk had not been cleared of snow and ice for several weeks, even though workers were required to use the sidewalk periodically. (Frederick and Lessin 2000)

Critics also say that the real goal of behaviour-based safety programs is to discourage workers from reporting illness and injuries. Workers whose employers have implemented behaviour-based safety programs describe an atmosphere of fear in the workplace, such that workers are reluctant to report injuries and illnesses for fear of being labelled an "unsafe worker." At one factory that had implemented a behavioural safety program, when a union representative asked workers during shift meetings to raise their hands if they were afraid to report injuries, about half of the 150 workers raised their hands (Frederick and Lessin 2000). Worried that some workers feared even raising their hand in response to the question, the union representative asked a subsequent group to write "yes" on a piece of paper if they were afraid to report injuries. Seventy percent indicated they were afraid to report injuries. Asked why they would not report injuries, workers said, "we know that we will face an inquisition," "we would be humiliated," and "we might be blamed for the injury."

Work–Family Policies and Programs

The influx of women into the workplace has been accompanied by an increase in government and company policies designed to help women and men balance their work and family roles. In 2001, Canada doubled the length of its paid maternity/parental leave to eligible claimants through the Employment Insurance (EI) program from six months to one year. Employment Insurance (EI) allows 15 weeks (the first two of which are unpaid) of *maternity benefits*, provided that the pregnant woman has worked at least 600 hours during the previous year. These benefits provide women with 55 percent of their normal weekly pay to a maximum amount of $413 dollars a week (gross). Fathers or mothers may also apply for *parental benefits* for an additional 35 weeks following the birth or adoption of a child. While women who claim maternity benefits are prohibited from employment, those who receive parental benefits are allowed to work part-time and earn 25 percent of their wage up to a set minimum.

Results from the longitudinal Survey of Labour and Income Dynamics (SLID) indicate self-employment and the absence of maternity leave are linked to quick returns to the paid workplace. "The odds of the mother's returning to work by the end of the first month [following a child's birth] were almost six times higher when she did *not* receive maternity leave benefits. Also, the odds of returning early were almost eight times higher for the self-employed than for employees" (Marshall 1999: 22). In general, however, mothers evidenced a strong attachment to participation in the paid labour force: only 7 percent of all Canadian women who gave birth in the early 1990s did not return to paid work after two years. Compared to those who returned to paid work, non-returnees were more likely to have been employed in part-time work, and less likely to have held, prior to giving birth, a unionized job or a professional job. In addition, non-returnees had, on average, spent less time at their last job than those who returned and earned lower median salaries ($16 700 versus $25 000). Non-returnees were also younger and more likely to be unmarried. Those who return to paid employment quickly after childbirth may perceive that they have more to gain and more to lose than those who do not.

Women in Canada today are less likely to interrupt their paid work and, when interruptions do occur, return to gainful employment more quickly than women did in the past. Most mothers in Canada, even those with very young children, are employed in the paid work force (Figure 11.6). Reflecting this, the 2001 census counted over 136 000 childcare workers—an increase of 87 percent over the past decade—with gains particularly notable in Quebec (Statistics Canada 2003: 8). Yet, not all Canadian provinces and territories have shown

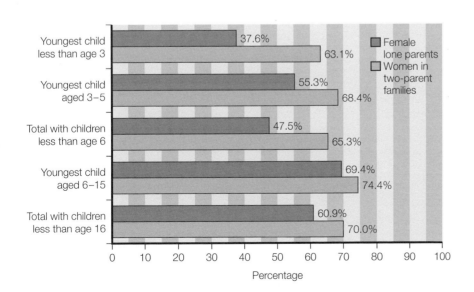

Figure 11.6 *Employment of Mothers, by Age of Youngest Child and Family Status, 1999*

SOURCE: Statistics Canada: Labour Force Survey, 1999.

equal commitment to providing Canada's workers with access to safe, affordable and accessible child care.

In 1997, Quebec introduced a comprehensive family policy that attempts to integrate family benefits, paid parental level, child care, and kindergarten. Its child care component heralded universally available, affordable child care in that province. The aim was to make every child in Quebec, by 2001, able to receive child care for $5 a day (and for as little as $2 a day for certain low-income families). This nominal fee was to entitle a child to a maximum of 10 hours a day of child care, one meal, two snacks, and use of all educational materials. In September 1997, all five-year-olds in Quebec whose families desired it became entitled to receive full-time kindergarten with $5-a-day after school care organized by the educational authorities. Similarly, all four-year-olds have part-time or full-time junior kindergarten or child care for $5 a day, with additional free early intervention services available for those whose parents receive welfare. In September 1998, all three-year-olds became eligible for $5-a-day child care. In 2000, Quebec additionally launched 10 pilot projects offering evening, weekend, and even overnight childcare—all available at the same $5-a-day rate (Doherty 2001). While the costs of providing such a comprehensive child care system are significant, Quebec's family policy has been lauded by some as "a pioneering approach to family supports in North America" (National Council of Welfare 1999a: 44).

In March 2000, the provincial budget of British Columbia committed that government to working towards the creation of publicly funded child care. In doing so, the province of B.C. became the second jurisdiction in North America to move towards publicly funded child care for all families "rich, poor, and the large majority in between" (Canadian Council on Social Development 2001: 6). From January 1, 2001, families in British Columbia who seek before- and after-school care for their children became able to access licensed spaces on and off school sites at a cost to parents of $7 a day during the school year and $14 a day during school holidays. However, elsewhere in Canada, the provision of child care "continues to be provided with no clear sense of direction" and is "severely compromised on three fronts: the availability of spaces to meets the needs of children and their families, the affordability of care and the quality of services provided" (National Council of Welfare 1999b: 44).

Offering employees greater flexibility in their work hours could also help parents to balance their work and family demands. Flexible work arrangements, which benefit childfree workers as well as employed parents, include flextime, job sharing, a compressed workweek, and telecommuting. **Flextime** allows employees to begin and end the workday at different times, as long as 40 hours per week are maintained. For example, workers may begin at 6 a.m. and leave at 2 p.m. instead of the traditional 9 a.m. to 5 p.m. With **job sharing**, two workers share the responsibility of one job. In Canada, job-sharers are most likely to be well-educated individuals in good jobs (e.g., nurses, teachers). About half have a college or university education and about four of ten are professionals; nurses and teachers are most likely to participate in job sharing (Statistics Canada 1998a).

A **compressed workweek** allows employees to condense their work into fewer days (e.g., four 10-hour days each week). **Telecommuting** allows employees to work part-time or full-time at home or at a satellite office (see this chapter's *Focus on Technology*). A study of U.S. companies found that the more women and minorities a company has in managerial positions, the more likely that company is to offer flexible work options (Galinsky and Bond 1998).

Fran Rodgers, president of Work/Family Directions explains the need for work–family policies:

> For over 20 years we at Work/Family Directions have asked employees in all industries what it would take for them to contribute more at work. Every study found the same thing: They need aid with their dependent care, more flexibility and control over the hours and conditions of work, and a corporate culture in which they are not punished because they have families. These are fundamental needs of our society and of every worker. (Galinsky et al. 1993: 51)

Challenges to Corporate Power and Globalization

Challenges to corporate power have also taken root in Canada and throughout the world. Antiglobalization activists have targeted the World Trade Organization (WTO), the International Monetary Fund (IMF), and World Bank as forces that advance corporate-led globalization at the expense of social goals like justice, community, national sovereignty, cultural diversity, ecological sustainability, and workers' rights.

In 1999, 50 000 street protesters and Third World delegates demonstrated in opposition to the policies of the World Trade Organization that promoted corporate-led globalization. Another confrontation between pro-globalization and anti-globalization forces occurred at the 2000 meeting of the International Monetary Fund (IMF) and the World Bank in Washington and, most recently, at the 2002 meetings of the G-8 leaders in Kananaskis, Alberta. Media attention to such protests contributes to the growing worldwide awareness of the forces of corporate globalization and its social, environmental, and economic effects.

Understanding Work and Unemployment

On December 10, 1948, the General Assembly of the United Nations adopted and proclaimed the Universal Declaration of Human Rights. Among the articles of that declaration are the following:

> Article 23. Everyone has the right to work, to free choice of employment, to just and favourable conditions of work and to protection against unemployment.

> Everyone, without any discrimination, has the right to equal pay for equal work.

> Everyone who works has the right to just and favourable remuneration ensuring for himself [sic] and his [sic] family an existence worthy of human dignity, and supplemented, if necessary, by other means of social protection.

> Everyone has the right to form and to join trade unions for the protection of his [sic] interests.

> Article 24. Everyone has the right to rest and leisure, including reasonable limitation of working hours and periodic holidays with pay.

More than half a century later, workers around the world are still fighting for these basic rights as proclaimed in the Universal Declaration of Human Rights.

Telework: The New Workplace of the Twenty-first Century

The ever-widening use of modern technology in the workplace, such as computers, the Internet, e-mail, fax machines, copiers, mobile phones, and personal digital assistants, makes it possible for many workers to perform their jobs at a variety of locations. The term **telework** (also known as "telecommuting") refers to flexible and alternative work arrangements that involve use of information technology. There are four types of telework (Pratt 2000): (1) homebased telework; (2) satellite offices where all employees telework for one employer; (3) telework centres, which are occupied by employees from more than one organization; and (4) mobile workers. Most (89 percent) teleworkers are homebased (Bowles 2000). Some people telework full-time, but a larger number telework one or two days a week. Nevertheless, predictions are that there will be 137 million teleworkers worldwide by 2003. If current trends hold, the largest fraction of teleworkers will be professionals (over a third), followed by clerical and sales.

Telework holds potential benefits for employers, workers, and the environment. After presenting some of these benefits, we discuss concerns related to telework.

Benefits of Telework for Employers

Attracts and Helps Retain Employees. Companies regard telework and other flexible work arrangements as important in recruiting and maintaining good employees. Telework can also lower turnover, and thus save companies expenses associated with hiring and training replacement employees. However, Bowles (2000) reports that companies are beginning to express dissatisfaction with telework "because they believe that it causes resentment among office-bound colleagues and weakens corporate loyalty" (p. 2).

Reduces Costs. Telework eliminates offices that teleworkers don't need, allows employers to consolidate others, and reduces related overhead costs (Lovelace 2000).

Increases Worker Productivity. Several studies of managers and employees at large companies conclude that telework increases worker productivity (Lovelace 2000).

Benefits of Telework for Employees

Increases Job and Life Satisfaction. Studies have shown that employee satisfaction among teleworkers is higher than for their non-teleworking counterparts (Lovelace 2000). Much of the job satisfaction among telecommuters is related to the job flexibility that enables them to balance work and family demands.

Helps Balance Work/Family Demands. Telework can provide flexibility to working parents and adults caring for aging parents, thus reducing role conflict and strengthening family life. One father of three children described his being home when his children came back from school as being "the most significant impact" of his telecommuting (Riley, Mandavilli, and Heino 2000: p. 5). He also took time during the day to take his children to school, to the doctor's office, and to run errands. However, a study of children whose parents work at home found that older children (grades 7 to 12) were more likely to agree that "my father does not have the energy to do things with me because of his job" and "my father has not been in a good mood with me because of his job" than the children of fathers who work in an office (Galinsky and Kim 2000). The effects of telework on parent/child relationships seems to depend then on how each parent interacts with his or her children.

Expands Work Opportunities for Canadians Outside the Economic Mainstream. Telework may expand

To understand the social problems associated with work and unemployment, we must first recognize the power and influence of governments and corporations on the workplace. We must also be aware of the role that technological developments and postindustrialization have on what we produce, how we produce it, where we produce it, and who does the producing. Canada is moving away from producing manufactured goods toward producing services. The labour-intensive job opportunities for rural job seekers who lack local employment opportunities, and for low-income urban job seekers who lack access to suburban jobs (Kukreja and Neely 2000). Telework can also bring work opportunities to individuals with disabilities. Some of the technologies that have been developed for individuals with serious disabilities include "Eye Gaze" (a communication system that allows people to operate a computer with their eyes); "Magic Wand Keyboard" (for people with limited or no hand movement); and "Switched Adapted Mouse and Trackball" (that allows clicking the mouse with other parts of the body) (Bowles 2000).

Avoids the Commute. Telework allows individuals to reduce or eliminate daily commutes. Consider that eliminating a 50-minute daily commute allows an individual to gain almost 5 weeks per year in time (Lovelace 2000).

Environmental Benefits of Telework

Telework can reduce pollution by reducing the need for transportation to the workplace, thus reducing the pollution associated with vehicle emissions. Indeed, some maintain that "telecommuting presents a non-coercive way for corporations to help the nation achieve environmental goals and improve quality of life" (quoted in Lovelace 2000: 3).

Concerns about Telework

Blurred Boundaries between Home and Work. People who work at home may find themselves on call around the clock, responding to e-mail, pagers, faxes, and voice mail. Without clear boundaries between home and work, teleworkers may feel that they are unable to escape the work environment and mindset (Pratt 2000). Questions about overtime pay may arise when work spills over into personal time. Having a separate office within the home and a routine work schedule may help create the psychological boundary between work and family/leisure. But for some teleworkers, learning to "log off" is a challenge.

Zoning Regulations. Teleworkers who work at home full time must contend with zoning regulations that may prohibit residents from having an "office" in their home.

Losing Benefits as a Contract Employee. Some employers attempt to convert the teleworker into a contract worker. This type of worker lacks job protections and benefits (Bowles 2000).

Social Isolation. Does telework lead to social isolation for those who live and work at home? Evidence suggests that teleworkers are able to maintain personal relationships with co-workers and are included in office networks. However, for rural and disabled individuals, telework may contribute to social isolation.

Exclusion of the Disenfranchised. Lower socioeconomic groups are less likely than more affluent populations to have access to and skills in the Internet and other modern forms of information technology. Bowles (2000) suggests that "the eventual success of telework programs in the future must...account for the masses of people left behind...All must be included in the new economy; it is not a luxury, but a must" (p. 9).

SOURCES: Bowles, Diane O. 2000. "Growth in Telework." Paper presented at the symposium *Telework and the New Workplace of the 21st Century,* Xavier University, New Orleans, October 16, 2000. Galinsky, Ellen, and Stacy S. Kim. 2000. "Navigating Work and Parenting by Working at Home: Perspectives of Workers and Children Whose Parents Work at Home." Paper presented at the symposium *Telework and the New Workplace of the 21st Century,* Xavier University, New Orleans, October 16, 2000. Lovelace, Glenn. 2000. "The Nuts and Bolts of Telework." Paper presented at the symposium *Telework and the New Workplace of the 21st Century,* Xavier University, New Orleans, October 16, 2000. Kukreja, Anil, and George M. Neely, Sr. 2000. "Strategies for Preventing the Digital Divide." Paper presented at the symposium *Telework and the New Workplace of the 21st Century,* Xavier University, New Orleans, October 16, 2000. Pratt, Joanne H. 2000. "Telework and Society—Implications for Corporate and Societal Cultures." Paper presented at the symposium *Telework and the New Workplace of the 21st Century,* Xavier University, New Orleans, October 16, 2000. Riley, Patricia, Anu Mandavilli, and Rebecca Heino. 2000. "Observing the Impact of Communication and Information Technology on 'Net-Work.'" Paper presented at the symposium *Telework and the New Workplace of the 21st Century,* Xavier University, New Orleans, October 16.

blue-collar assembly line is declining in importance, and information-intensive white-collar occupations are increasing. Because of increasing corporate multinationalization, Canadian jobs are being exported to foreign countries where labour is cheap, regulations are lax, and raw materials are available. Finally, the workforce is becoming more diverse in terms of gender and racial and ethnic background and is including more contingent workers than in the past.

Decisions made by Canadian corporations about what and where to invest influence the quantity and quality of jobs available in Canada. As conflict theorists argue, such investment decisions are motivated by profit, which is part of a capitalist system. Profit is also a driving factor in deciding how and when technological devices will be used to replace workers and increase productivity, but if goods and services are produced too efficiently, workers are laid off and high unemployment results. When people have no money to buy products, sales slump, a recession ensues, and social welfare programs are needed to support the unemployed. When the government increases spending to pay for its social programs, it expands the deficit and increases the national debt. Deficit spending and a large national debt make it difficult to recover from the recession, and the cycle continues.

> What the public wants is called "politically unrealistic." Translated into English, that means power and privilege are opposed to it.
>
> NOAM CHOMSKY
> *Academic and activist*

What can be done to break the cycle? Those adhering to the classic view of capitalism argue for limited government intervention on the premise that business will regulate itself via an "invisible hand" or "market forces." For example, if corporations produce a desired product at a low price, people will buy it, which means workers will be hired to produce the product, and so on.

Ironically, those who support limited government intervention also sometimes advocate that the government should intervene to bail out failed banks and lend money to troubled businesses (or hockey teams). Such government help benefits the powerful segments of our society. Yet, when economic policies hurt less powerful groups, such as minorities, there has been a collective hesitance to support or provide social welfare programs. It is also ironic that such bailout programs, which contradict the ideals of capitalism, are needed because of capitalism. For example, the profit motive leads to multinationalization, which leads to unemployment, which leads to the need for government programs. The answers are as complex as the problems. The various forces transforming our economy are interrelated—technology, globalization, capital flight through multinationalization, and the movement toward a service economy (Eitzen and Zinn 1990). For the individual worker, the concepts of work, job, and career have changed forever.

Critical Thinking

1 In 1999, 10 years after Canada and the United States signed a free trade accord that bound their economies ever more tightly, the C.D. Howe Institute released a study that argued the merits of Canada using the same currency as the United States. If Canadian nationalists reacted to the suggestion of a common currency with predictions of Canada's imminent demise, the issue of "dollarization"—instituting the American dollar for local currencies—has found considerable support in such countries as Argentina and Mexico. What would be the advantages and disadvantages of Canada establishing a currency union with the United States?

2 Foreigners (chiefly Americans) control a considerable fraction of the Canadian economy. Indeed, Bellan (1999: 884) notes that "[t]his large foreign presence in the economy [is] quite unparalleled elsewhere in the world [and] has deep historic roots." Identify some of the consequences of having a very large part of the Canadian economy controlled by American interests.

3 Besides the strategies discussed in this chapter, what other strategies might assist Canada's working parents as they attempt to balance work and family concerns?

Key Terms

alienation

anomie

automation

behavioural-based safety programs

bonded labour

brain drain

capitalism

child labour

compressed workweek

convergence hypothesis

corporate downsizing

corporate multinationalism

cumulative trauma disorders

discriminatory unemployment

economic institution

flextime

global economy

Industrial Revolution

job burnout

job exportation

job sharing

postindustrialization

primary work sector

repeated trauma disorders

repetitive strain disorders

secondary work sector

socialism

split labour market

structural unemployment

sweatshop

telecommuting

telework

tertiary work sector

underemployment

unemployment

work sectors (primary, secondary, tertiary)

12

Problems in Education

Is It True?

1. In 2001, more than half of Canada's population had less than a Grade 9 education.

2. Among the 29 OECD countries, Canada ranks fourth in the proportion of its working-age population with a university degree.

3. Among immigrants arriving in the 1990s, both sexes tended to be highly educated.

4. More than half of the people living in developing nations are illiterate.

5. IQ is the best predictor of school success.

Answers: 1 = F, 2 = T, 3 = T, 4 = T, 5 = F

A nybody who cares about the matter knows that the intellect requires constant attention and renewal.

ROBERTSON WILLIAM DAVIES
Man-of-letters

One year to the day after Eric Harris and Dylan Klebold opened fire on classmates at Columbine High School, a Grade 10 student at an Ottawa-area high school staged a bloody attack, stabbing four students and a staff member with a kitchen knife he brought from home. The 15-year-old student...was also wounded before the school's principal convinced him to surrender the weapon....

Students...said the boy who wielded the knife was a loner who was frequently teased. They recounted kidding him about his severe acne, and called him "pubic head" because of his kinked hair. Police said the boy's injury was self-inflicted, and students said he had previously tried to slit his wrists. "In Grade 9, I used to make fun of him a lot. I just went along with what everyone else said," said Katelyn Thijssen, who was in Grade 10 with [the boy] (MacKinnon et al. 2000).

Education is often claimed as a panacea—the cure-all for poverty and prejudice, drugs and violence, war and hatred—yet, daily, it seems, we are reminded of problems that exist in Canada's educational system. Some have charged that our educational system is encumbered by seniority and indifference to absolute educational outcomes, which hamper Canada's ability to compete. Others direct attention to the ravages of budget cuts, increasing tuition costs and staggering levels of student debt. Others highlight funding "reforms" that have triggered dramatic cuts to special education programs and the allied services of speech pathologists and psychologists (Schofield 1999).

Can one institution, riddled with obstacles, be a solution for other social problems? In this chapter, we focus on this question and what is being called one of the major sociopolitical issues of the century—the educational crisis (Associated Press 1998). We begin with a look at education around the world.

The Global Context: Cross-Cultural Variation in Education

Looking only at the Canadian educational system might lead to the conclusion that most societies have developed some method of formal instruction for their members. After all, there are almost 16 000 elementary and secondary schools in Canada, employing a full-time teaching force of almost 300 000, and some 300 colleges and universities, employing an additional 60 000 full-time educators (Statistics Canada 1998). In reality, many societies have no formal mechanism for educating the masses. As a result, worldwide, over 120 million children do not attend school—42 million in sub-Saharan Africa alone—and over 880 million adults are illiterate. In 2000, the World Education Forum met in Dakar, Senegal, where over 1000 leaders from 145 countries recommitted their energies to improving basic education in developing countries (U.S. Newswire 2000).

At the other end of the continuum are societies that emphasize the importance of formal education. Public expenditures on education in developed countries are 25 times higher than in less-developed countries (Population Reference Bureau 1999). In Japan, students attend school on Saturday and the school calendar is 57 days longer than in Canada (243 days in comparison to 186 days). China (with a school year of 251 days), South Korea (220 days), Israel (215 days), Germany (210 days), Russia (210 days), Switzerland (207 days), the Netherlands (200 days), Scotland (200 days), and Thailand (200 days) also have more mandatory school days than Canada (Ash 2001: 102).

Some countries additionally empower professionals to organize and operate their school systems. Japan, for example, hires professionals to develop and implement a national curriculum and to administer nationwide financing for its schools. In contrast, "Canada is unique among developed countries in having no federal office or ministry of education" (Orlikow and Peters 1999: 738) at either the public school level or postsecondary level. Our country lacks a coordinated education policy and, because of historical, cultural, and demographic differences between the various regions in Canada, we are unlikely to see the development of such a policy in the future.

Under the terms of the *British North America Act*, education is a provincial responsibility, and each province has the constitutional authority to develop its own educational organization. Although education in Yukon, the Northwest Territories, and Nunavut is funded by the federal government, it is governed by ordinances of the assemblies of these regions. In consequence, Canada has 13 unique school systems that fund and administer public, private, denominational, and linguistic schools somewhat differently. The issues of religion and language are two of the differences that exist within our system of education.

Consider, for example, that our Constitution, unlike that of the United States, protects denominational or "separate" schools. However, "[a]s each province joined Confederation, it brought its own approach to religious schools and Canadians are still dealing with the legacy of this process" (Statistics Canada 1998: 146). In Canada, free public education in a nondenominational public school system is available for all Canadians. Separate schools, denominational schools operated by the Catholic Church, receive public support in Alberta, Ontario, Saskatchewan, Yukon, and the Northwest Territories; elsewhere, where available, separate schools are privately funded. Until 1997, Newfoundland had an entirely denominational system of education. However, in 1997, almost three-quarters (73 percent) of the citizenry of Newfoundland voted to abolish its 277-year-old system of church-run schools.

"In 1982, Canada's Charter of Rights and Freedoms gave English- and French-speaking minorities the right to educate their children in their mother tongue and the courts have consistently supported this right for these two minority groups across Canada" (Statistics Canada 1998: 146). *Minority language education* is designed to offer the minority group in a province (anglophones in Quebec, francophones outside Quebec) education in their mother tongue. *Second language education* is designed to offer instruction in the minority language

> Education is an indispensable tool for the improvement of the quality of life.
>
> **United Nations**
> *Conference on Population and Development*

> We should try to get our money's worth out of the schools. It's ridiculous having them standing idle 12 months of the year.
>
> **Richard Needham**
> *Columnist*

for children. In recognition of Canada's status as a multicultural society, heritage language programs now allow for education in the traditional languages of ethnic minorities where the numbers so warrant.

Although the BNA Act of 1867 made the federal government responsible for the education of Aboriginal people, over the past few decades, the growing demand that Aboriginal peoples be allowed to run their own schools has led to a reduction in the direct involvement of the Department of Indian Affairs. Because of agreements made between First Nations bands and the Department of Indian Affairs, the role of the federal government has increasingly been reduced to that of a funding source for programs controlled by the Native community. Generally, decisions regarding the distribution of resources, staffing, curriculum, language of instruction, and length of school year are now made by band education authorities in most areas.

Canadians hold a strong belief in the importance of education—and with good reason. Consider that in 2001, Statistics Canada reported that while the average family headed by a high school graduate enjoyed a net worth of approximately $65 000, this rose to $120 000 for a family headed by a university graduate and about $320 000 for those with a professional degree in law, medicine, dentistry, and the like (Bricker and Greenspon 2001: 158). At the same time, however, Canadians are increasingly likely to raise questions about the quality of education in this country. One recent survey reported that "a staggering 82 percent of parents worried about the quality of education received by their children," while a second found that over one in three Canadians (37 percent) thought that education was in worse shape than 25 years earlier (Bricker and Greenspon 2001: 156, 162). At present, it seems that Canadians "have only a moderate level of confidence in the job being done by the public education sector as a whole" (Canadian Council on Social Development 1999). Many perceive there is considerable room—and need—for improvement.

Sociological Theories of Education

The three major sociological perspectives—structural-functionalism, conflict theory, and symbolic interactionism—are important in explaining different aspects of Canadian education.

Structural-Functionalist Perspective

According to structural-functionalism, the educational institution accomplishes important tasks for society, including instruction, socialization, the provision of custodial care, and the sorting of individuals into various statuses. Many social problems, such as unemployment, crime and delinquency, and poverty, may be linked to the failure of the educational institution to fulfill these basic functions (see Chapters 4, 10, and 11). Structural-functionalists also examine the reciprocal influences of the educational institution and other social institutions, including the family, political institution, and economic institution.

Instruction A major function of education is to teach students the knowledge and skills necessary for future occupational roles, self-development, and social functioning. Although some parents teach their children basic knowledge and skills at home, most parents rely on schools to teach their children to read, spell, write, tell time, count money, and use computers. The failure of schools to instruct students in basic knowledge and skills both causes and results from many other social problems.

Socialization The socialization function of education involves teaching students to respect authority—behaviour that is essential for social organization (Merton 1968). Students learn to respond to authority by asking permission to leave the classroom, sitting quietly at their desks, and raising their hands before asking a question. Students who do not learn to respect and obey teachers may later disrespect and disobey employers, police officers, and judges.

The educational institution also socializes youth into the dominant culture. Schools attempt to instill and maintain the norms, values, traditions, and symbols of the culture in a variety of ways, such as celebrating holidays (Remembrance Day, Thanksgiving); requiring students to speak and write in English and French; displaying the Canadian flag; and discouraging violence, drug use, and cheating.

As the number and size of racial and ethnic minority groups have increased, Canadian schools are faced with a dilemma: should public schools promote only one common culture, or should they emphasize the cultural diversity reflected in the Canadian population? Consider that "[o]ver the next 20 years, an increasing proportion of children in schools will be immigrants and members of visible minority groups," and that of the 200 000 immigrants who enter Canada each year, almost 45 000 are school-aged children who enroll in Canada's elementary and secondary schools (Canadian Council on Social Development 1999).

Sorting Individuals into Statuses Schools sort individuals into statuses by providing credentials for individuals who achieve various levels of education, at various schools, within the system. These credentials sort people into different statuses—for example, "high school graduate," "Rhodes scholar," and "Ph.D." Further, schools sort individuals into professional statuses by awarding degrees in such fields as medicine, nursing, and law. The significance of such statuses lies in their association with occupational prestige and income—in general, the higher one's education, the higher one's income (Ghalam 2000) (see Figure 12.1). Further, unemployment rates are tied to educational status (Chard 2000).

Custodial Care The educational system also serves the function of providing custodial care (Merton 1968), which is particularly valuable to single-parent and dual-earner families, and the likely reason for the increase in enrollments of three- and four-year-olds. The school system provides free supervision and care for children and adolescents until they complete secondary or "high school"—almost 13 000 hours per pupil. Some school districts are experimenting with offering classes on a 12-month basis, Saturday classes, and/or longer school days. Working parents, the hope that increased supervision will reduce delinquency rates, and higher educational standards that require longer hours of study are some of the motivations behind the "more time" movement (Wilgoren 2001).

I just got involved more or less gradually. But when I realized that Canada must be the only country in the world where high school kids aren't taught their own literature, then I had to tell them and their teachers about it. I had to tell them what they're missing.

JAMES (JIM) FOLEY
Teacher, organizer of the first Canada Day to celebrate Canadian writing

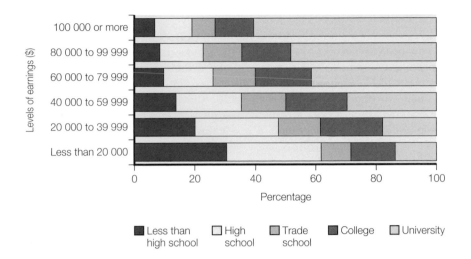

Figure 12.1 *Most Low Earners Had High School or Less While Most High Earners Had a University Degree, Canada, 2001*

SOURCE: Statistics Canada. 2003. "Earnings of Canadians: Making a Living in the New Economy," Catalogue 96FOO3OXIE2001013. Adapted from the Statistics Canada Web site, http://www12.statcan.ca/english/census01/Products/Analytic/companion/earn/charts/earnedu.cfm.

Conflict Perspective

Conflict theorists emphasize that the educational institution solidifies the class positions of groups and allows the elite to control the masses. Although the official goal of education in society is to provide a universal mechanism for achievement, in reality educational opportunities and the quality of education are not equally distributed.

Conflict theorists point out that the socialization function of education is really indoctrination into a capitalist ideology. In essence, students are socialized to value the interests of the state and to function to sustain it. Such indoctrination begins in kindergarten. Rosabeth Moss Kanter (1972) coined the term "the organization child" to refer to the child in nursery school who is most comfortable with supervision, guidance, and adult control. Teachers cultivate the organization child by providing daily routines and rewarding those who conform. In essence, teachers train future bureaucrats to be obedient to authority.

Further, to conflict theorists, education serves as a mechanism for **cultural imperialism**, or the indoctrination into the dominant culture of a society. When cultural imperialism exists, the norms, values, traditions, and languages of minorities are systematically ignored. For example, in his analysis of the development of the educational system in Ontario in the mid-1800s, Neil McDonald emphasized how education was conceived of as crucial for maintaining dominant ideologies. He notes that the chief architect of the Ontario school system, Egerton Ryerson, purposefully set out to create a system in which "young people would remain loyal to the Crown...never participate in the kind of rebellion which had been put down in Upper Canada in 1837, and...cooperate with one another, regardless of their social class backgrounds." Through education, the working class were to be persuaded that "their interests were also those of the middle and upper classes and that, as a collectivity, there was a 'common' or 'public good' towards which all must work" (McDonald, as cited in Curtis and Lambert 1994: 12). As Curtis and Lambert (1994: 12) remark, "In short, Ryerson's objective was social control, and he charged the schools with the responsibility of inculcating the beliefs and attitudes of mind that would accomplish it."

Traditionally, the school curriculum has not given voice to the perspective of minority groups, including women. Lessons in history, for example, are given from the perspective of the victors—not the vanquished. Moreover, the cultural genocide promoted within the residential schools for Canada's indigenous people must be recognized as one of the bleakest notes in the history of Canadian education (see this chapter's *The Human Side*.) As only one example, Native students who dared to speak their own language were routinely punished by having a sewing needle pushed through their tongue in a practice known as the "needle torture."

Finally, the conflict perspective focuses on what Kozol (1991) calls the "savage inequalities" in education that perpetuate racial inequality. As the Canadian Council of Social Development (1999) has emphasized, "Lower educational results among particular groups perpetuate their social exclusion and lower economic outcomes, raising serious doubts about how the educational system can be changed to serve the needs of these students."

Comparisons among individuals aged 25 to 64 who identified themselves as a member of an Aboriginal group in 1996 and 2001 does suggest that progress has occurred. For example, the proportion of Aboriginal people with a high school diploma rose from 21 percent in 1996 to 23 percent in 2001. The share of those with post-secondary qualifications also increased from 33 percent to 38 percent over this time period. In consequence, the gap between the educational profile of the Aboriginal and non-Aboriginal populations has narrowed somewhat, particularly in relation to the proportions with a trade certificate (16 percent of the working-age Aboriginal population and 13 percent of the working-age non-Aboriginal population) or college qualifications (15 percent among Aboriginal people and 18 percent among non-Aboriginal people). "However, the gap in university graduates remained wide. In 1996, 6 percent of Aboriginal people aged 25 to 64 had a university education. This increased to 8 percent in 2001" (Statistics Canada 2003: 16).

Symbolic Interactionist Perspective

Whereas structural-functionalism and conflict theory focus on macro-level issues such as institutional influences and power relations, symbolic interactionism examines education from a micro perspective. This perspective is concerned with individual and small group issues, such as teacher–student interactions, the students' self-esteem, and the self-fulfilling prophecy.

Teaching is a passing on, *an act of future.* The expert may expand the range of what is possible, but the teacher expands the range of who can do the possible.

KEN DRYDEN
Hockey legend and student of education

Teacher–Student Interactions Symbolic interactionists have examined the ways in which students and teachers view and relate to each other. For example, children from economically advantaged homes may be more likely to bring social and verbal skills into the classroom that elicit approval from teachers. From the teachers' point of view, middle-class children are easy and fun to teach: they grasp the material quickly, do their homework, and are more likely to "value" the educational process. Children from economically disadvantaged homes often bring fewer social and verbal skills to those same middle-class teachers, who may, inadvertently, hold up social mirrors of disapproval. Teacher disapproval contributes to the lower self-esteem among disadvantaged youth.

Education as Cultural Genocide

The province of Canada in 1847 published a report...which formed the basis for future directions in policy for Indian Education. Clearly expressed is the perception of the superiority of the European culture, the need "to raise [aboriginal people] to the level of the whites," and the ever-increasing pressure to take control of land out of Indian hands....The general recommendations of the report were that the Indians remain under the control of the Crown rather than the provincial authority, that efforts to Christianize the Indians and settle them in communities be continued, and finally that schools, preferably manual labour ones, be established under the guidance of missionaries....Cultural oppression was becoming written policy. Within the discussion of the recommendations is the following comment:

> Their education must consist not merely of the training of the mind, but of a weaning from the habits and feelings of their ancestors, and the acquirements of the language, arts and customs of civilized life.

What clearer statement of an effort to destroy a culture could exist?...

Following the establishment of the Indian Act of 1876, a consolidation of existing legislation, the government commissioned N.F. Davin to report on industrial schools established for native people in the United States. Out of his report came the strong recommendations which resulted in the establishment of many residential schools across Canada...In the introduction to the report, Davin made references to President Grant's policy on the Indian question: "The industrial school is the principal feature of the policy known as aggressive civilization...." While positively endorsing the notion of residential schools for Indians in Canada, Davin's final comment is, "If anything is to be done with the Indian, we must catch him very young..."

By 1920 amendments to the Indian Act included compulsory school attendance of Indian children and industrial or boarding schools for Indians....[I]n 1920 the House of Commons....Deputy Superintendent General Duncan Campbell Scott stated clearly the idea that Indian cultures as such were to be eliminated:

> Our object is to continue until there is not a single Indian in Canada that has not been absorbed into the body politic and there is no Indian question, and no Indian department, that is the whole object of the Bill.

Not until 1946 was there serious possibility for change in this attitude and in the expressed intent of Department of Indian Affairs policy....[In that year,] Andrew Paull, President of the North American Indian Brotherhood, appeared before the Special Joint Committee. He was highly critical of the committee's lack of Indian representation. He condemned the existing Act as "an imposition, the carrying out of the most bureaucratic and autocratic system that were ever imposed upon any people in this world of ours." He spoke strongly of Indian self-government, and finally he commented that what was needed was

> to lift up the morale of the Indians in Canada. That is your first duty. There is no use in passing legislation about this or that if you do not lift up the morale of the people. The only way you can lift up the morale of any people is to let the members look after themselves and look after their people.

His words fell upon deaf ears.

SOURCE: Adapted from Haig-Brown, Celia. 1993. *Resistance and Renewal: Surviving the Indian Residential School*. Vancouver: Arsenal Pulp Press.

Self-Fulfilling Prophecy The **self-fulfilling prophecy** occurs when people act in a manner consistent with the expectations of others. For example, a teacher who defines a student as a slow learner may be less likely to call on that student or to encourage the student to pursue difficult subjects. As a consequence of the teacher's behaviour, the student is more likely to perform at a lower level.

An early study by Rosenthal and Jacobson (1968) provided empirical evidence of the self-fulfilling prophecy in the public school system. Five elementary school students were selected at random and identified for their teachers as "spurters." Such a label implied that they had superior intelligence and academic ability. In reality, they were no different from the other students in their classes. At the end of the school year, however, these five students scored higher on their intelligence quotient (IQ) tests and made higher grades than their classmates who were not labelled as spurters. In addition, the teachers rated the spurters as more curious, interesting, and happy and more likely to succeed than the "nonspurters." Because the teachers expected the spurters to do well, they treated the students in a way that encouraged better school performance.

Who Succeeds? The Inequality of Educational Attainment

The 1996 census was the first Canadian census to record a higher number of university graduates than of people reporting less than a Grade 9 education. Most recently, the 2001 census declared Canada a "world leader in education" and noted that, in 2000, 20 percent of Canada's population aged 25 to 64 had a university education (Statistics Canada 2003: 10). Among the 29 countries surveyed by the Organisation for Economic Co-operation and Development in 2000, only three countries had higher proportions of their working-age population with a university degree—the United States (28 percent), Norway (26 percent), and the Netherlands (21 percent) (Statistics Canada 2003: 10). However, "[i]f university and college are combined, no other OECD nation had a higher proportion than Canada" in that year (Statistics Canada 2003: 10) (Table 12.1). Yet not all Canadians are equally likely to attain higher levels of education. As noted earlier, conflict theory focuses on inequalities in the educational system. Educational inequality is based on social class and family back-

■ **Table 12.1** *Education Standings, College or University, OECD Member Countries, 2000*

Rank	Country	College or University
1.	Canada	41%
2.	United States	37
3.	Ireland	36
4.	Japan	34
5.	Finland	32
6.	Sweden	32
7.	Australia	29
8.	New Zealand	29
9.	Norway	29
10.	Belgium	27

SOURCE: Adapted from Statistics Canada. 2003. "Education in Canada: Raising the Standard." Catalogue 96F0030, March 2003.

ground, race and ethnicity, and gender. Each of these factors influences who succeeds in school.

Social Class and Family Background

One of the best predictors of educational success and attainment is socioeconomic status (Lam 1997). Children whose families are in middle and upper socioeconomic brackets are more likely to perform better in school and to complete more years of education than children from lower socioeconomic families. For example, Muller and Schiller (2000) report that students from higher socioeconomic backgrounds are more likely to enroll in advanced mathematics course credits, and to graduate from high school—two indicators of future educational and occupational success. Table 12.2 shows that in 1998, young people from high-income families were 1.5 times more likely than those from low-income families to have been enrolled in a postsecondary institution (71.0/48.8 = 1.5) and about 2.5 times more likely to have gone to university in 1998 (39.6/16.3 = 2.4). It is evident that class determines whether one gets a post-secondary education in Canada, and it even more strongly determines whether one will get a university education.

While noting that "[p]oor children are not always disadvantaged and disadvantaged children are not always poor" (Health Canada 1999: 73), the 1996–1997 National Longitudinal Survey of Children and Youth (NLSCY) found that household income was clearly associated with school readiness—an important indicator of developmental maturity and future success at school (Doherty 1997). Figure 12.2 shows the relationship between school readiness and parents' education—iteslf associated with income, as shown in Figure 12.1. In addition, as family income decreases, the likelihood that children will experience a host of other problems that will negatively influence their school performance increases. For example, poor health, hyperactivity, and delayed vocabulary development are all higher among children in low-income families than among children in middle- and higher-income families (Ross 1998). Children who score low on school readiness are also more likely to have mothers with low levels of education and to be living in neighbourhoods that their mothers characterize as unsafe or as lacking in social cohesiveness (Health Canada 1999: 79).

■ **Table 12.2** *Participation in Post-secondary Education and Family Income, 1998*

Highest level of education in which the student participated	Family Income		
	Bottom Quartile	Middle Half	Top Quartile
College	26.7%	29.5%	28.2%
University	16.3	26.1	39.6
All post-secondary	48.8	61.4	71.0

SOURCE: Statistics Canada. 2001. "Participation in Post-secondary Education and Family Income, 1998." *The Daily*, December 7. On the World Wide Web at http://www.statcan.ca/Daily/English/011207/d011207c.htm.

■ **Figure 12.2** *School Readiness, by Parents' Education, Age Four–Five, Canada, 1994–1995*

SOURCE: Human Resources Development Canada and Statistics Canada. 1996. *Growing Up in Canada: National Longitudinal Survey of Children and Youth.* Ottawa: Statistics Canada, November 1996 (Statistics Canada Cat. No. 89–55–MPE, No. 1).

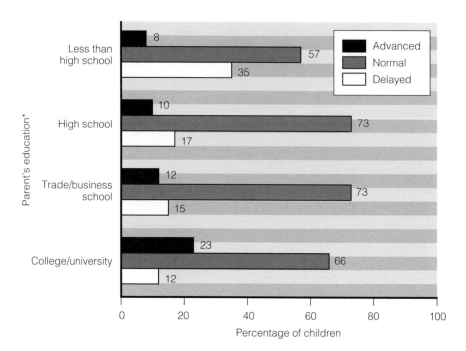

*Education of most-schooled parent

Low-income families have less money to buy books, computers, tutors, and lessons in activities such as dance and music and are less likely to take their children to museums and zoos. For example, in 1998, the majority of Canadian parents who owned a home computer reported buying it for educational purposes; 90 percent said that having a computer had positively affected their children's learning ability and 79 percent claimed that it had improved the quality of their child's homework. However, in that year, three out of four households (74 percent) in the highest-income group had computers, compared with less than one in five of households (18 percent) in the lowest income group (Canadian Council on Social Development 2001).

Parents in low-income brackets are also less likely to expect their children to go to college or university, and their behaviour may lead to a self-fulfilling prophecy. "Only half of children aged 12 and 13 in families with incomes of less than $20 000 per year hoped to go to university. The figure was 71 percent for children from families with incomes over $80 000" (Canadian Council on Social Development 2001). As we have noted, disproportionately, children from low-income families do not go on to institutions of higher learning (Levinson 2000).

Low-income parents are also less involved in their children's education. Yet parental involvement is crucial to the academic success of the child. Although working-class parents may value the education of their children, in contrast to middle- and upper-class parents, they are more likely to feel intimidated by their child's schools and teachers and to lack the time or job flexibility to attend teacher conferences (Lareau 1989).

Because low-income parents are often themselves low academic achievers, their children are exposed to parents who have limited language and academic skills. Children learn the limited language skills of their parents, which restricts their ability to do well academically. Low-income parents may be unable to help their children with their math, science, and language homework because they themselves lack the academic skills to do the assignments. Call et al. (1997) report that even among impoverished youths, parental education is one of the best predictors of a child's academic success.

Children from poor families are also more likely to have lower functioning vision, hearing, speech, mobility, dexterity, and cognition (Campaign 2000 2001). However, services to assist children with special needs are often lacking in Canada's schools (see this chapter's *Social Problems Research Up Close*). Poor children also experience a heightened likelihood of health problems and nutritional deficiencies (Campaign 2000 2001). It is obvious that children cannot learn when they are sick, in pain, hungry, or malnourished. Consider, in this context, that food bank use has risen more than 92 percent since 1989 and that the number of children relying on donated food has increased more than 85 percent. "Inadequate nutrition threatens children's overall well being as it has been linked to a variety of physical, cognitive, social and emotional problems" (Covell 2001: 25).

It has been suggested that early developmental programs can decrease the chances of developmental problems in children and enhance their performance within schools. For example, **Head Start** programs are based on the belief that to assist children, the entire family must be helped (Fact Sheet 2000). Evaluations of Head Start programs in Canada and the United States report such benefits as: "more students completing school and with better grades; fewer young people needing mental health services; fewer parents abusing alcohol with concurrent reductions of alcohol's impact on children; a reduction in family violence; [and] fewer students with preventable disabilities and reduced demand for medical services" (Government of Canada 2001; Summary Report 2001). In Edmonton, for example, Head Start programs have existed for 25 years.

Head Start programs have been identified as particularly important in increasing the educational success of Aboriginal students. Canada introduced the Aboriginal Head Start Program in 1995 and the First Nations Head Start in 1998. In 1998, the federal government announced that it would provide permanent funding for the aboriginal Head Start programs that already existed in Canada at the time as well as additional funds for the establishment of new Head Start programs on reserves. However, it is estimated that existent programs only reach about 5 percent of the Aboriginal children who could potentially benefit from their availability (George 1998). Admittedly, the costs of providing early childhood intervention programs are not insignificant. For example, in 1998, Health Canada spent approximately $22.5 million a year on Head Start programs that served approximately 4000 Northern and urban Aboriginal children—or merely 5 percent of those who required such programs. However, to reach its target audience would require spending 10 to 20 times that amount. Nevertheless, it has been argued that the investments we make in the critical early years of a child's life not only benefit Canada's children but our economy as well. Indeed, one Canadian study reports that "every dollar spent in early intervention can save seven dollars in future expenditures in health and social spending" (Health Canada 1999: 88).

Racial and Ethnic Minorities

Socioeconomic status interacts with race and ethnicity. Because race and ethnicity are so closely tied to socioeconomic status, it appears that race or ethnicity

> Over the world, let us be clear: there is no literate population that is poor; no illiterate population that is other than poor.
>
> JOHN KENNETH GALBRAITH
> *Economist and essayist*

Special Education

Special education is designed to help children who require special educational help due to "low intelligence, visual or auditory impairment, or emotional or specific learning difficulties, disabilities or problems" (Brown 1999: 741). Special education is a critical community resource. However, it is one that is too often lacking.

Sample and Methods

In order to investigate the educational resources available for children with special needs in Canada, Angela Kierstead and Louise Hanvey (2001) conducted key informant interviews in each province with experts in the field of special education. During the summer of 2000, 17 experts from across Canada in the field of special education were interviewed. The survey was divided into three main sections: general context of special education services; assessment of how well children's needs are met; and special education resources.

Findings and Conclusions

An overwhelming majority of respondents (88 percent) reported that their educational systems have gone through major restructuring over the last five years. However, when asked if the educational system in their province was meeting the needs of children with special needs, only 19 percent said "yes." When asked if their educational system was able to identify all those children who would benefit from special education, about six in ten said, "yes."

The majority of respondents believed that there was substantial inequality in the delivery of services to children in rural and urban areas, with children in urban centres far more likely to receive a better level of service. When asked if the need for special education services had increased, decreased, or remained constant in recent years, 94 percent of respondents reported an increase. When asked to account for why the dramatic increase had occurred, respondents attributed at least part of the increase to growing parental awareness of learning disabilities. In addition, they noted that some provinces, such as Newfoundland, have systems in place to determine what the needs of a child are and whether or not the child requires supplemental special education services.

Respondents in this survey believed that children with physical disabilities were the group most likely to receive an acceptable level of service, regardless of whether they lived in an urban or rural area. Children with hearing impairments were felt to receive very different levels of service, depending on where they lived. While 71 percent of respondents believed that children with hearing impairments who lived in cities were completely or adequately served, only 28 percent felt that this group of children in rural areas received adequate levels of service. The services provided to children with Attention Deficit Disorder (ADD) or Attention Deficit Hyperactivity Disorder (ADHD) were generally viewed as poor, regardless of where children lived: "87 percent of respondents reported that the needs of children with ADD/ADHD living in urban areas were being met only somewhat or not at all; for children...in rural areas, an overwhelming 93 percent of respondents stated that students' needs were met only somewhat or inadequately" (p. 3).

Respondents identified the lack of qualified personal to provide such services as a key factor in explaining the inadequacy of services for ADD/ADHD children. They noted that, in many provinces, classroom teachers are not required to take courses in special education. In addition, the majority (88 percent) believed that there were not enough special education teachers available; over half (53 percent) believed that the number of special education teachers had decreased over the past five years. The overwhelming majority of respondents also felt that there were not nearly enough teachers' aides and assistants available. Finally, when asked about the level of funding for special education in their province or territory, 82 percent felt that it was inadequate. Complexities in provincial funding formulas, stringent guidelines, and an increase in the paperwork required of teachers in completing special education claims forms were all identified as factors that negatively affected the provision of services to children with special needs.

SOURCE: Kierstead, Angela, and Louise Harvey. 2001. "Special Education in Canada." *Perception* 25(2), Fall.

alone can determine school success. While race and ethnicity also have independent effects on educational achievement (Bankston and Caldas 1997; Jencks and Phillips 1998), their relationship is largely due to the association between race and ethnicity, and socioeconomic status.

One reason why some minority students have academic difficulty is that they did not learn English as their native language. As previously noted, there are growing numbers of immigrant children of school-age who do not speak either of Canada's official languages upon arrival—a fact which suggests the growing importance of such programs as English as a Second Language (ESL). Another factor that may have a negative impact upon both immigrant and minority students is the use of tests to assess academic achievement and ability that are biased against minorities. For example, questions on standardized tests often require students to have knowledge that is specific to the white middle-class majority culture. For example, it has been noted that IQ tests measure not only intelligence but also culturally acquired knowledge. The cultural bias built into the IQ tests used in schools makes it more likely that children from some backgrounds—and not others—will score high results. Consider as well, that in 2000, it was reported that the Ontario Human Rights Commission had been asked to investigate the charge that the Law School Admission Test (LSAT), a test used by North American law schools to rank applicants, was biased against racial minorities (Vago and Nelson 2003).

In addition to being hindered by speaking a different language and being from a different cultural background, minority students may also be disadvantaged by overt racism and discrimination. It has been noted, for example, that "[m]any visible minorities, such as native people and blacks, continue to have much greater school dropout rates" (Livingstone 1999: 743). Moreover, while research conducted by the Toronto Board of Education (1993) suggests that immigrant children, in general, tend to do well at school after a period of acclimatization, a notable exception exists with respect to Afro-Canadian children "who experience lower rates of integration into the educational system and have lower levels of educational attainment."

An on-going debate in Canada is whether or not students, at all levels, are better served by a faculty whose composition is less singular and reflects the diversity of our population. It has been noted that while the composition of Canada's student population is becoming increasingly multicultural, this is less true of Canada's teachers at present and in the foreseeable future. According to the Canadian Council of Social Development (1999), "[r]esearch suggests that teachers will continue to be mainly white, middle-aged women." Moreover, as the number and size of racial and ethnic minority groups increase, some have additionally suggested the need for more inclusive curricula to promote multicultural education. One might consider in this context that at least some school boards have perceived the need to modify the courses they offer in light of Canada's changing composition. Edmonton, for example, already offers children such alternatives to French as Arabic, German, Ukrainian, and Mandarin; in 2001, the number of students enrolled in these programs (2250) exceeded the number enrolled in French immersion (1895). School boards in both Calgary and Edmonton have also recently launched publicly funded Spanish bilingualism programs (Bricker and Greenspon 2001: 284).

In addition, it has been argued that **multicultural education**, education that includes all racial and ethnic groups in the school curriculum, is necessary to promote awareness and appreciation for cultural diversity (Conciatore 2000; Henry et al. 2000). For example, Ken Osborne (1988) maintains that, at present, "There can be no doubt that existing curricula are biased, both in what they include and in what they omit, nor that for many...students they have little appeal." In consequence, some recommend that "the experiences of women (and of First Nations people, working-class people, visible minorities and other disadvantaged groups) must be incorporated into the curriculum....The purpose of schooling must be to 'empower'...them, to give them the ability to participate fully in struggles, large and small, to gain respect, dignity and power."

Not all, however, agree with this position. For example, Thomas Sowell (1994) maintains that "most of the arguments" for an inclusive curricula "are so flimsy, inconsistent, and downright silly that it is hard to imagine that they would have been taken seriously if they were not backed up by shrill rhetoric, character assassination, and the implied or open threat of organized disruption and violence on campus." In his opinion, the limited amount of class time available makes it impossible for educators to include the experiences of non-dominant groups. Those who would attempt to do so, he maintains, are "just kidding...[themselves] that...[they] are educating anybody....[A]ll you are really doing is teaching them to accept superficiality." Similarly, he maintains that the absence of information on the historic achievements and contributions of minority groups occurs for a reason:

> [H]ow can a people's achievements be unaffected by their oppression? One of the many reasons to be against oppression is that it keeps people from achieving all that they could have had they been treated more decently....The past is many things, but one thing it is, is irrevocable. A past to your liking is not an entitlement.

All of these opposing viewpoints reflect the "culture wars" that surround education today. There can be no doubt that the field of education has "become increasingly politicized over issues involving curriculum, admission of minority students (and respect for minority cultures), women's rights, and other cultural debates" (Bender and Leone 1994: 72). However, as John Wilson (in Whitehead 1994: 13) has suggested, these debates may well provide educators with a unique opportunity to contemplate and reassess "the questions of what should be taught and how we ought to teach."

> The examined life makes a virtue of uncertainty. It celebrates doubt.
>
> JOHN RAULSTON SAUL
> *Writer*

Gender

Worldwide, women receive less education than men. Two-thirds of the world's 920 million illiterate people are women (United Nations Population Fund 1999).

Historically, schools have discriminated against women. When Martha Humm Lewis gained entrance to a training school for teachers in New Brunswick in 1849, the principal of the school cautioned her to "enter the classroom ten minutes before the male students, sit alone at the back of the room, always wear a veil, leave the classroom five minutes before the end of the lesson and leave the building without speaking to any of the young men" (MacLellan 1972, in Schaefer et al. 1996: 282). Although Canadian schools are not typically segregated by sex any longer, a look at the elementary schools within your community that were built prior to 1960 will likely yield a large number with the designations "Girls" and "Boys" over separate entrances, reflecting past attempts to keep the sexes apart.

Since the 1960s, the women's movement has sought to end sexism in education. For example, the 1970 Canadian Royal Commission on the Status of Women made the following recommendations: "adoption of textbooks that portray both sexes in diversified roles and occupations; provision of career information about the broad field of occupational choice for girls; improved availability of sport programs for both sexes; development of educational programs to meet the special needs of rural and immigrant women and of Indian and Inuit girls and young women; and the continuing education of women with family responsibilities" (as cited in Mackie 1991: 158). Three decades later, textbooks using gender-neutral language and images are increasingly being adopted and there has been a trend towards a more integrated curriculum in which boys and girls learn, for example, both auto mechanics and cooking.

Traditional gender roles account for many of the differences in educational achievement and attainment between women and men. As noted in Chapter 7, schools, teachers, and educational materials reinforce traditional gender roles in several ways. Some evidence suggests, for example, that teachers provide less attention and encouragement to girls than to boys and that textbooks tend to stereotype females and males in traditional roles (Evans and Davies 2000).

Most of the research on gender inequality in the school focuses on how female students are disadvantaged in the educational system. But what about male students? As discussed in Chapter 7, the arguments that girls have been educationally shortchanged has recently come under attack as some academicians charge that it is boys, not girls, who have been left behind (Sommers 2000).

The problems that boys bring to school may indeed require schools to devote more resources and attention to them. More than 70 percent of students with learning disabilities such as dyslexia are male, as are 75 percent of students identified as having serious emotional problems. Boys are also more likely than girls to have speech impairments, to be labelled as mentally retarded, to exhibit discipline problems, to drop out of school, and to feel alienated from the learning process (this chapter's *Self and Society* feature assesses student alienation) (Bushweller 1995; Goldberg 1999; Sommers 2000).

Some educational reformers have suggested a return to single-sex schools for both males and females. For males, the argument is that boys could benefit from the masculine environment provided by all-male academies where male teachers serve as positive role models. For females, the argument is that same-sex schools minimize the stereotyping, harassment, and discrimination that can exist in mixed-sex classrooms. However, researcher Maggie Ford concludes that the evidence indicates "...that separating by sex is not the solution to gender inequity in education. When elements of good education are present, girls and boys succeed" (AAUW 1998).

Problems in the Canadian Educational System

Let us examine some of the major problems that have been identified within Canadian education today—and several potential solutions.

> ▪ A recent investigation reveals that five million Canadian adults are 'functionally illiterate.' But why, one wonders, do so many of these seek, and achieve, election?
>
> ROBERTSON WILLIAM DAVIES
> *Man-of-letters*

Student Alienation Scale

Indicate your agreement to each statement by selecting one of the responses provided:

1. It is hard to know what is right and wrong because the world is changing so fast.
   _____ Strongly agree _____ Agree _____ Disagree _____ Strongly disagree

2. I am pretty sure my life will work out the way I want it to.
   _____ Strongly agree _____ Agree _____ Disagree _____ Strongly disagree

3. I like the rules of my school because I know what to expect.
   _____ Strongly agree _____ Agree _____ Disagree _____ Strongly disagree

4. School is important in building social relationships.
   _____ Strongly agree _____ Agree _____ Disagree _____ Strongly disagree

5. School will get me a good job.
   _____ Strongly agree _____ Agree _____ Disagree _____ Strongly disagree

6. It is all right to break the law as long as you do not get caught.
   _____ Strongly agree _____ Agree _____ Disagree _____ Strongly disagree

7. I go to ball games and other sports activities at school.
   _____ Always _____ Most of the time _____ Some of the time _____ Never

8. School is teaching me what I want to learn.
   _____ Strongly agree _____ Agree _____ Disagree _____ Strongly disagree

9. I go to school parties, dances, and other school activities.
   _____ Strongly agree _____ Agree _____ Disagree _____ Strongly disagree

10. A student has the right to cheat if it will keep him or her from failing.
    _____ Strongly agree _____ Agree _____ Disagree _____ Strongly disagree

11. I feel like I do not have anyone to reach out to.
    _____ Always _____ Most of the time _____ Some of the time _____ Never

12. I feel that I am wasting my time in school.
    _____ Always _____ Most of the time _____ Some of the time _____ Never

13. I do not know anyone that I can confide in.
    _____ Strongly agree _____ Agree _____ Disagree _____ Strongly disagree

14. It is important to act and dress for the occasion.
    _____ Always _____ Most of the time _____ Some of the time _____ Never

Low Levels of Academic Achievement

Worrisome evidence that suggested the inferiority of the Canadian school system appeared throughout the 1990s. One study of the math, science, and literacy scores of students in 29 countries in the Organisation for Economic Co-operation and Development found that, in 1994, Canadian students hovered near the middle, well behind students in such countries as the Netherlands and South Korea (Barlow and Robertson 1994). For some social commentators, such results proved the inadequacy of our educational system and, in particular, the aftermath of **grade inflation** (the awarding of As to students whose work warrants lower grades) and **social promotion** (the practice of passing students from one

15. It is no use to vote because one vote does not count very much.

_____ Strongly agree _____ Agree _____ Disagree _____ Strongly disagree

16. When I am unhappy, there are people I can turn to for support.

_____ Always _____ Most of the time _____ Some of the time _____ Never

17. School is helping me get ready for what I want to do after university.

_____ Strongly agree _____ Agree _____ Disagree _____ Strongly disagree

18. When I am troubled, I keep things to myself.

_____ Always _____ Most of the time _____ Some of the time _____ Never

19. I am not interested in adjusting to Canadian society.

_____ Strongly agree _____ Agree _____ Disagree _____ Strongly disagree

20. I feel close to my family.

_____ Always _____ Most of the time _____ Some of the time _____ Never

21. Everything is relative and there just aren't any rules to live by.

_____ Strongly agree _____ Agree _____ Disagree _____ Strongly disagree

22. The problems of life are sometimes too big for me.

_____ Always _____ Most of the time _____ Some of the time _____ Never

23. I have lots of friends.

_____ Strongly agree _____ Agree _____ Disagree _____ Strongly disagree

24. I belong to different social groups.

_____ Strongly agree _____ Agree _____ Disagree _____ Strongly disagree

INTERPRETATION

This scale measures four aspects of alienation: powerlessness, or the sense that high goals (e.g., straight A's) are unattainable; meaninglessness, or lack of connectedness between the present (e.g., school) and the future (e.g., job); normlessness, or the feeling that socially disapproved behaviour (e.g., cheating) is necessary to achieve goals (e.g., high grades); and social estrangement, or lack of connectedness to others (e.g., being a "loner"). For items 1, 6, 10, 11, 12, 13, 15, 18, 19, 21, and 22, the response indicating the greatest degree of alienation is "strongly agree" or "always." For all other items, the response indicating the greatest degree of alienation is "strongly disagree" or "never."

SOURCE: Adapted from Mau, Rosalind Y. 1992. "The Validity and Devolution of a Concept: Student Alienation." *Adolescence* 27: 107, pp. 739–40. Used by permission of Libra Publishers, Inc., 3089 Clairemont Drive, Suite 383, San Diego, California 92117.

grade to the next even though they have not mastered the necessary grade-level skills). Canadians schools, critics charged, churned out **functional illiterates**: people who cannot "read basic signs or maps, complete simple forms, or carry on many of the tasks required of an adult" (Literacy 2000: 1).

In response to the disappointing performance of Canadian students on international tests, many Canadians began to clamour for the administration of province-wide standardized tests for both students and teachers. Such tests, it was argued, would allow school performance to be independently and objectively assessed. Indeed, a May 2000 poll reported that more than eight in ten of those surveyed supported province-wide tests for students. A similar proportion believed that high school students should be required to pass both a compulsory

> Everyone knows that every other country's kids know twice as much as our kids at half their age.
>
> MAUDE BARLOW
> HEATHER-JANE ROBERTSON
> *Social activists*

literacy test and standardized, province-wide knowledge test prior to graduation (Bricker and Greenspon 2001: 165–66). However, some analysts emphasized that the results of international tests are misleading for various reasons (Barlow and Robertson 1994; Bracey 1998; Schrag 1997).

In the first place, most of the countries that participated in the study did not follow sampling guidelines. Specifically, many excluded those students whom educational administrators thought would perform badly on the exam. As a result, these countries artificially inflated their scores. Second, different countries have different kinds of secondary school systems. For instance, some keep students in school for 14 years, while others, like Canada, have 12-year systems (13 years in Ontario until 2001). Some countries have higher dropout rates than Canada has and/or siphon off poor academic performers to trades schools and job-training programs before they graduate from high school. As a result, only the top academic performers are left by the last year of high school. In contrast, Canada attempts to ensure that as many students as possible graduate from high school since this enhances the quality of democracy, increases social cohesion in a culturally diverse society, and may improve economic performance. However, for all of these reasons, international comparisons can be misleading.

Despite the limitations of international comparisons, many Canadians still felt buoyed when the results of the most recent international tests in reading, math, and science were released in 2001. Among 32 countries, Canada ranked second overall in reading and fifth in math and science. When provincial results were analyzed separately, students in Alberta, Quebec, and British Columbia ranked among the best in the world. Indeed, Alberta students obtained the highest scores in the world in reading and placed third in both science and math. Quebec came second in math with scores that almost rivalled those obtained by students in Japan and placed fourth in reading and science. Other provinces, however, most notably those in the Atlantic region, did not fare as well (Sokoloff 2001a).

Some observers claimed that Alberta's success stemmed from a provincial formula of frequent testing, standardized curriculum, financial support for disadvantaged schools, and high expectations conveyed to students from teachers and parents. On a national scale, Canada's improved performance was seen to signify the narrowing of the achievement gap between poor and well-off students. Canada, it was noted, was one of six countries (the others being Finland, Iceland, Japan, South Korea, and Sweden) singled out as providing good education to students from all socioeconomic classes.

Nevertheless, it would premature to think that we can simply now rest on our laurels. The 2001 international study also found that, throughout the world, students from wealthier backgrounds outperformed students from poorer families. Family structure also contributes to student performance. Students from two-parent families fared better than those from single-parent families in half of the countries surveyed. While students at private schools outscored their public school counterparts in every province in Canada and every country examined, it is the socioeconomic status of those who attend private schools rather than the type of schools that seems responsible for the performance difference. Compared to students in the public system, students attending private schools in Canada are more likely to have parents with higher education and income. Predictably, students with such parents also perform well in the public system (Sokoloff 2001b).

School Dropouts

According to the latest available figures, approximately one-quarter of Canadian youth drop out of high school, "the second-worst record among the seven largest industrialized countries" (Bricker and Greenspon 2001: 159). However, even though the stereotype of the dropout is that of a poorly motivated under-achiever who prefers to live on social assistance and use drugs, a Statistics Canada survey presents a different picture. Indeed, recognizing the negative connotation associated with "dropout," the study discarded this term and replaced it with the more neutral-sounding term, "school leaver."

In their summary of this research, Sid Gilbert and Bruce Orok (1993: 3) report that, in contrast to the stereotype, many school leavers come from intact, two-parent homes, were doing well at school, and were either not working or working only moderate hours prior to leaving school. Upon leaving school, school leavers were generally employed, worked long hours, and planned to continue with further education or job training. "Among male school leavers aged 18–20, the two most important reasons for leaving were that they preferred work to school (28 percent) and boredom (19 percent)....Female leavers aged 18–20 cited boredom (22 percent) and problems with schoolwork (13 percent) as the top two reasons for leaving school." Nine percent of male respondents mentioned the need to work for financial reasons, while eight percent mentioned problems with teachers. Among female school leavers, 10 percent reported that they preferred work to school while 9 percent reported that pregnancy was important in their leaving school.

According to survey research conducted by Paul Grayson and Michael Hall on the characteristics of dropouts:

> students who have the greatest probability of being dropouts are those who are dis-
> abled; have dependent children; have fathers who have not completed high school;
> have changed schools a number of times; live with friends or alone rather than with
> their families; work while attending high school; are male; are married, live
> common-law, or have been separated or divorced; and, have parents and friends
> who do not consider completing high school to be important. (As summarized in
> Barlow and Robertson 1994: 30)

According to the School Leavers Survey, compared with graduates, more school leavers lived with lone-parent families or with no parent during their last year in school; had at least one parent with a low level of education; reported that they did not enjoy school; expressed dissatisfaction with the courses offered and their utility; reported that they had skipped school; did not get along with their teachers or felt they did not "fit in" at school; had experienced failure in elementary school; had grade averages of C or lower before leaving school; consumed alcohol on a regular basis; had experienced trouble with the law during their last year of school; and had worked long hours for paid employment.

A closer analysis of the relationship between school, work, and dropping out, conducted by the same survey, shows that while working moderate work hours is associated with a reduced risk of dropping out for both male and female students, intensive work involvement appears to substantially increase the likelihood of dropping out among young men. In contrast, lack of employment is associated with the highest risk of dropping out for young women (Sunter

1993). It may be that such aspects of work as punctuality, initiative, and so on increase success-oriented behaviours as well as a student's self-esteem. Moreover, in that the bulk of working students are employed in low-skill, low-paying jobs, Sunter (1993: 51) suggests that the work experiences of students "may convince many that high school graduation is essential to gaining access to more interesting employment with greater earnings potential."

The economic and social consequences of dropping out of school are significant. Dropouts are more likely than those who complete high school to be unemployed and to earn less when they are employed (*Digest of Educational Statistics* 2001). Individuals who do not complete high school are also more likely to engage in criminal activity, have poorer health and lower rates of political participation, and require more government services such as welfare and health care assistance (Natriello 1995). There are, however, some hopeful signs: "thanks to the success of programs aimed at giving dropouts a second chance, the percentage of 25 to 29 year-olds without a high school diploma fell from 20 percent to 13 percent between 1990 and 1998. One-quarter of the dropouts identified in a 1991 study had gone back and completed high school when revisited four years later" (Bricker and Greenspon 2001: 159).

Student Violence

On April 28, 1999, just eight days after the shooting rampage at Columbine High School in Littleton, Colorado, where two students killed 13 others (12 students and one teacher) before taking their own lives, a 15 year-old boy in Taber, Alberta gunned down one teen and wounded another in a school hallway. The boy's mother told reporters that her son was a depressed and lonely social misfit who had become fixated on the Columbine massacre and "got into a fantasy that he just could not get out of" (Harrington 1999: A4). In February 2000, three Toronto teenagers were wounded in a gun battle in a high school parking lot; the same day, at another Toronto high school, a 13 year-old boy was charged with choking and sexually assaulting a 17 year-old girl. Concealed in his inside jacket pocket at the time was a bored-out starter's pistol, loaded with .22 calibre bullets and ready to fire (Appleby 2000).

While we might prefer to think of aggression or violence in school as exceptional, evidence suggests that they are not (Table 12.3). A 1999 survey of 2000 Alberta students in Grades 7 to 12 reports that violence was highest among students in Grades 8 and 9. Approximately 16 percent of students in this survey acknowledged bringing weapons to school, with illegal knives and replica weapons the most common (Canadian Press 2000). The 2000 Project Canada Survey on teens finds that one in two Canadian teens view violence in schools as a "very serious" problem. Female teenagers were especially likely to view violence in schools as a very serious problem (59 percent of female teens vs. 40 percent of males) (Bibby 2001: 81). About one in three teenagers (32 percent) reported having a close friend who had been physically attacked at school. Male teens were especially likely to report having a friend who experienced physical violence while at school (39 percent of males vs. 25 percent of females) (Bibby 2001: 82). In addition, it should be noted that aggressive acts by students do not always entail physical violence. Consider here that in 2002, in a landmark case that was reputedly the first to hold schoolyard bullies to account, a 16-year-old girl was found guilty of criminal harassment for her role in bullying a Grade 9

■ **Table 12.3** *Weapons Offences, Incidents Reported in Toronto Schools During 1999*

Possession of weapon, dangerous to public	24
Carrying a concealed weapon	18
Assault with weapon, causing bodily harm	17
Dangerous use/storage of firearm	15
Robbery, mugging	8
Robbery, swarming	6
Uttering threats	5
Possession of unregulated restricted weapon etc.	4
Use of firearm in commission of offence	4
Aggravated assault	2
Assault	2
Extortion by threats, violence	2
Mischief	1
Others	2
Total offences	110

SOURCE: Appleby, Timothy. 2000. "Weapons turn up more often at schools: police." *Globe and Mail*, February 18: A18.

Abbotsford, B.C. student, Dawn-Marie Wesley. Wesley was so tormented that she committed suicide in November 2000 (*Maclean's* 2002).

Various attempts have been made to redress the problem of violence, bullying, and harassment in schools. "In what is believed to be the first measure of its kind in Canada," the city of Edmonton passed a by-law in March 2003 that bans harassment of people under the age of 18 (Mahoney 2003: A8). The by-law, which took effect in May 2003, defines "bullying" as "repeated intimidation of others" including "real or threatened infliction of various types of abuse, including physical, verbal, emotional, or written," and covers bullying in public places. Those who bully can be given a $250 ticket—and it's anticipated that the use of this by-law will be heaviest in schools. Some schools have installed security systems, hired security guards, shortened school days to eliminate free time, and expelled troublemakers. "Zero tolerance" policies have also attempted to discourage violence by making any misbehaviour grounds for immediate suspension. Others, however, advocate a quite different approach to the problem of anti-social and aggressive behaviour in schools.

For example, after experiencing several incidents of racially charged violence, Cole Harbour High School in Nova Scotia, introduced a "Student of the Week" program, designed to encourage students learn respect for the cultures of others, and implemented a system of peer mediators. Peer mediators are students who are given special training in mediation techniques under the supervision of a staff person, in order to work at the front line in conflict between small numbers of students. It is believed that these mechanisms allow students to develop "a sense of responsibility for the condition of their school; they feel they have control over events in the school; and the program creates an environment where a minor conflict can be handled without the principal's intervention."

Alberta's Safe and Caring Schools project advocates that the problem of school violence is best dealt with through community-wide efforts to encourage responsible behaviour. According to the Safe and Caring Schools project, early intervention and prevention are needed.

Consistent with this approach, Dan Offord, head of child psychiatry at McMaster University, has argued that attempts to reduce violent behaviour in schools must begin with screening programs directed at children in early grades who display antisocial behaviour. He suggests that as many as 20 percent of school-aged children and teens suffer "from some type of emotional disorder" and that "at least 12 percent" could benefit from individual attention. Moreover, he maintains that while many find a "get tough" approach appealing, "there has to be a place for everyone in schools...you can't just push kids out of the school system. Where do they go?" (as cited in Crane 1999: A2)

The High Costs of Education

As Table 12.4 suggests, Canada compares favourably to many other countries in terms of various indicators of education. For example, compared to most other

■ **Table 12.4** *How We Compare: Education Spending by G7 Countries, 1996*

	Canada	U.S.	France	U.K.	Germany	Italy	Japan
Education spending as a percentage of total public expenditures	13.6	14.4	11.1	n.a.	9.5	9.0	9.8
Public spending as a percentage of GDP	5.8	8.0	5.8	4.6	4.5	4.5	3.6
Participation rate in formal education (percentage)[1]	68.2	68.8	64.5	66.8	61.8	53.8	57.0
Ratio of secondary school graduates to population (percentage)	73	72	85	n.a.	86	79	99
Ratio of first university degree to population (percentage)	32	35	n.a.	34	n.a.	1	23
Labour Force Participation by Education Attainment (Percentage)							
Secondary education							
Men	89	88	90	89	85	80	n.a.
Women	72	72	76	74	69	61	n.a.
University education							
Men	92	93	92	94	93	92	n.a.
Women	85	82	83	86	83	81	n.a.
Unemployment Rate by Level of Educational Attainment (Percentage)							
Upper secondary education							
Men	9	6	8	8	8	6	n.a.
Women	9	4	12	6	10	11	n.a.
University education							
Men	5	2	6	4	5	5	n.a.
Women	6	2	9	3	5	10	n.a.

[1]Total number of students enrolled in formal education as a percentage aged 5–29. (n.a.) Not available.

SOURCE: Statistics Canada. 1998. *Canada Yearbook 1999*. Ottawa: Minister of Industry.

Western countries, we tend to spend a higher proportion of our GDP on education. The salaries of our teachers additionally suggest the value we place on education. "Today...Canada's teachers average about $57 600 a year compared to national income average for full-time workers of $36 235" (Statistics Canada 1998: 145). Moreover, unlike the majority of countries worldwide, we encourage those who are imprisoned in Canada's penitentiaries to enroll in secondary, vocational, and postsecondary courses on site or through correspondence. At the same time however, problems exist.

Reduced funding for public and post-secondary education and an increased reliance at the college and university level on student fees has led, in turn, to soaring increases in tuition costs for Canadian postsecondary students, demands for postsecondary institutions to accept more students (without additional funding), less academic hiring, rising student-faculty ratios, and dwindling resources. It is conservatively expected that university enrolment will increase by 20 percent by 2010. It is also expected, however, that over 20 000 of Canada's 33 000 aging faculty will have retired or departed for greener vistas. As Johnston (1999: 51) observes:

> [T]he fallout has been huge. The number of lab assistants has been dwindling for years; lab equipment is outdated; library journals have been cancelled. And in many cases, what is known as the "physical plant"—the bricks and mortar—is crumbling.

Would-be and current postsecondary students and their families are increasingly forced to confront the financial burdens posed by higher education—and the costs are considerable.

Although the cost of post-secondary education in Canada "has always been a responsibility shared by society through tax dollars, and by parents and children through personal savings," soaring tuitions (up 115 percent since 1980) contrast sharply with the 1 percent rise in average family income (after adjusting for inflation) (Clark 1999: 24). Using data from the National Graduates Survey of 1995, Clark (1999) examined the extent of student debt and the impact of high debt on postsecondary graduates who had used government loans to finance their studies. He reports that both college and bachelor's degree graduates were most likely to finance their education through employment earnings (59 percent college, 69 percent bachelor's) and student loans (41 percent college, 42 percent bachelor's). While parents ranked third for those who acquired bachelor's degrees, neither college nor university students identified scholarships, fellowships, prizes, grants or bursaries as a significant source of funding. Students from families with lower parental education (i.e., whose fathers had not completed high school) were more likely to use student loans than those students with higher parental education. As well, students in their late 20s were more likely to borrow from government student loan programs and to borrow the most.

The financial burden assumed by graduates from the class of 1995 were often significant. Clark (1999: 25) notes:

> Compared with the class of 1982, college and bachelor's graduates from the class of 1995 owed between 130 percent and 140 percent more to government student loan programs at graduation (after adjusting for inflation). On average, the 1995 graduates owed $9 600 (college) and $13 000 (bachelor's) when they graduated.

Among the class of 1995, 7 percent of college graduates and 22 percent of bachelor's graduates owed more than $20 000 at graduation. In Quebec, where undergraduate tuition fees for resident students are the lowest in Canada, graduates had one of the lowest debt levels at graduation ($11 600 in student loans). Students in Saskatchewan had the highest debt level at graduation ($16 200) (p. 28).

It is not surprising, perhaps, that those who borrowed from student loan programs often faced difficulty in paying back the monies they had received. Clark reports that "during the two years following graduation, one-sixth of 1995 college and bachelor's borrowers indicated they were already having difficulty making payments on their government student loans." Women with bachelor's degrees were more likely than men with bachelor's degrees to experience difficulty repaying their loans; however, among college graduates, there were only marginal differences in repayment difficulties between women and men. Moreover, Clark notes that "[b]ecause their earnings did not keep pace with these increasingly large loans, many graduates experienced repayment difficulties...[and] [w]ithin two years of graduation, one in 20 borrowers ended up defaulting on their loan" (p. 28).

For those who pursue professional degrees, the burden may be even more oppressive. Consider, for example, that since 1998, when the Ontario government deregulated tuition fees for professional and graduate programs, allowing institutions to set tuition fee levels, tuition fees have soared. At the University of Toronto's law school, for example, tuition fees have risen 380 percent since 1995. Since 1998, the increase has been particularly steep, climbing from $3808 in 1997–98 to $12 000 in 2001. In addition, in December 2001 the school announced that it was considering a five-year plan that would more than double its current yearly tuition fees to $25 000 (Schmidt 2001).

A 2000 Angus Reid poll found that eight in ten respondents opposed increasing tuition fees. Canadians are increasingly conscious that the cost of higher education may prove prohibitive for many bright and able students. "In a world in which education matters more than ever, Canadians view reasonable access to higher learning as a social must" and "overwhelmingly believe that merit should be the only criterion in determining access to higher learning, not financial means" (Bricker and Greenspon 2001: 172–73).

Inadequate School Facilities and Personnel

We have previously noted that special education programs for children with learning disabilities are unavailable for many of those who could benefit from them. More broadly, however, since the early 1990s, the Canadian school system has experienced budgets cuts and the message to "do more with less." With the proclaimed intent of improving school standards, provincial governments have often removed resources from the educational system, centralized control of schools by imposing standardized testing and new curricula, and reduced the power of school boards. In theory, these measures allow provincial governments to balance their budgets, stimulate economic growth, and offer taxpayers tax cuts.

However, decreasing educational resources obviously reduces the number of jobs available for principals, teachers, and support staff and increases educational inequality. With fewer teachers, a pared back curriculum, and increasing costs being shouldered by families rather than the state, the prospects of children from lower socioeconomic strata may be grim. As we have seen, the Canadian educational system has generally acted to reproduce the country's stratification system. Since the early 1990s, however, it has acted to help increase the degree of social stratification in Canadian society (Johnston 2001).

According to Michael Fullan (Fullan [1982] 2001; Hammonds 2002), we must reinvest and reinvent our system of education. He argues that education must become a "meaningful learning community," a setting in which all participants engage in education because it brings them substantial moral benefits. For example, he maintains that students learn best when engaged in achieving mastery of subjects that they deem relevant to their needs and backgrounds. Similarly, he argues that teachers teach best when they feel empowered by having the autonomy, resources, peer support, and "professional development" they require.

Strategies for Action: Trends and Innovations in Canadian Education

Canadians rank improving education as one of their top priorities. In 2000, when an Angus Reid Group survey asked Canadians to volunteer their "top-of-mind" priority issues, education was mentioned by 29 percent of Canadians as a national priority, surpassed only by health care (Bricker and Greenspon 2001: 150). In addition, it is evident that education plays a critical role in Canadian society. Education has been referred to "as the one truly proactive public investment we make. It is not designed to address a problem, but rather to build the society we want for the future by investing in the creation of human and social capacity" (Canadian Council on Social Development 1999). Yet, at the same time, our educational system must be reactive, responsive to Canada's changing demography—changes in the age composition of our population, its ethnoracial mix and family structures—as well as to trends in the labour market, the economy, and the development of information and communications technology. To be sure, these are formidable challenges.

There is no shortage of suggestions on how we can improve our educational system. Here we review but a few.

> Changing human to humane takes one letter and most of a lifetime.
>
> MAURIUS E. MALLON
> *Aphorist*

Moral and Interpersonal Education

Most school curricula neglect the human side of education—the moral and interpersonal aspects of developing as an individual and as a member of society. Proponents of character education argue that students should "be engaged in a general education that guides them in caring for self, intimate others, global others, plants, animals, the environment, objects and instruments, and ideas" (Noddings 1995: 369). For example, service learning programs are community-based initiatives in which students volunteer in the community and receive academic credit for doing so. Studies on student outcomes have linked service learning to enhanced civic responsibility and moral reasoning, increased tolerance of diversity and promotion of racial equality, and a strong commitment to volunteerism (Zlotkowski 1996; Waterman 1997; Aberle-Grasse 2000). Character education also occurs to some extent in schools that have peer mediation and conflict resolution programs. Such programs teach the value of nonviolence, collaboration, and helping others, as well as skills in interpersonal communication and conflict resolution.

Computer Technology in Education

Computers in the classroom allow students to access large amounts of information (see this chapter's *Focus on Technology*). The proliferation of computers both in school and at home may mean that teachers will become facilitators and coaches rather than sole providers of information. Not only do computers enable students to access enormous amounts of information, including that from the World Wide Web, but they also allow students to progress at their own pace.

Canada was one of the first countries to link its student body to the information superhighway. In 1995, Newfoundland became the first province with full Internet access. By 1997, almost all Canadian schools had Internet access through the SchoolNet electronic network. In that year, Industry Canada's "Computers in the Schools" program had placed over 20 000 computers and 40 000 pieces of software in Canadian schools and libraries (Canadian Council on Social Development 1999). The attempt to make educational settings inclusive also suggests the benefits of computer technology in education. Software that reads aloud what is on the screen, large-screen monitors, voice-input software, and scanners are among the technologies used by differently abled students in Canada (Fichten et al. 1999).

Alternative School Choices

Traditionally, children have gone to school in the district where they live. However, alternative schools, charter schools, home schooling, and private schools provide parents with alternative school choices for their children. **Alternative schools** began in Canada in the 1970s. According to Chernos (1998: 13), "Perhaps the one element that unifies alternative schools is their diversity. Each operates within school board and education ministry guidelines, yet maintains a unique character. Like snowflakes, no two are exactly alike." However, this diversity may encourage students who might otherwise fall through the cracks of the educational system to remain in school and/or to reenter the mainstream system at some later time.

For example, in London, Ontario, Richmond Centre and Dundas Centre Schools "are intended as an interim measure for students experiencing social, emotional, psychological, behavioral or academic troubles"(Chernos 1998: 15). The London board also maintains other alternative schools for Native Youth, Annishnabe and Wiingashk, both of which incorporate Native culture and traditions within a core curriculum of basic Grade 9 to 12 subjects. In Toronto, the focus of Horizon Alternative Senior School in Toronto "is on creating a caring community" and on balancing "core subjects...with an outward world-view that emphasizes self-expression, debate, role playing dialogue and conflict resolution" (Chernos 1998: 13). In Ontario alone there are several dozen elementary and secondary schools that bill themselves as alternative schools.

Alternative schools typically offer a variety of innovative and experimental programs. They generally have low student populations ranging from 70 to 250, with small, informal classes, and place emphasis on close interaction between students and teachers. In many alternative high schools, student representatives join teachers, parents, and, sometimes, community members on the school's board of directors. According to Levin (1999: 732), alternative schools can be distinguished by "the sense of ownership, autonomy and control that teachers, parents, and students feel towards their school even as governments and school boards move to assert and maintain stronger administrative control" upon them. Indeed, he suggests that "alternative schools may be forerunners of a more decentralized, pluralistic, community-based education system."

In complementary fashion, **charter schools** are public schools that function as semiautonomous units but derive their special character from a charter that declares the school's specialized purpose and reason for being. Currently, Alberta is the only province in Canada with charter schools. In that province, they were established to provide students and their parents with greater choice and to encourage educational innovation. "Some of the specific characteristics of these schools are that they cannot deny access to students as long as space is available, they must require students to write provincial examinations, they may exist in present school buildings, they must employ certified teachers, and they are subject to annual audits" (Brown 1999: 440).

Some parents are choosing not to send their children to school at all but to teach them at home. For some parents, **home schooling** is part of a fundamentalist movement to protect children from perceived non-Christian values in the public schools. Other parents are concerned about the quality of their children's education and their safety. How does being schooled at home instead of attending public school affect children? Some evidence suggests that home-schooled children perform as well or better than their institutionally schooled counterparts (Webb 1989; Winters 2000).

Another choice parents may make is to send their children to a private school. The primary reason parents send their children to private schools is for religious instruction. The second most frequent reason is the belief that private schools are superior to public schools in terms of academic achievement. Research suggests, however, that when controlling for parents' education and income, there are few differences in private and pubic school educational outcomes (Shanker 1996; Ascher et al. 1997; Cohen 1998). Parents also choose private schools for their children in order to have greater control over school policy, or to obtain a specific course of instruction such as dance or music.

Understanding Problems in Education

What can we conclude about the state of the educational system in Canada? Any criticism of education must take into account that over a century ago, many children did not receive even a primary school education. Instead, they worked in factories and on farms to help support their families. Whatever education they received came from the family or the religious institution. It is evident that Canada has come a long way since that time. From humble beginnings, education in Canada has grown into a massive industry with total expenditures now exceeding $61 billion a year (*Canadian Global Almanac* 2000: 82).

At the same time, it is evident that problems exist. While public schools are supposed to provide all Canadian children with the academic and social foundations necessary to participate in society in a productive and meaningful way, some remain marginalized and do not enjoy its benefits as much as others. As conflict theorists note, the educational institution can perpetuate a downward

Distance Learning and the New Education

Imagine never having an eight o'clock class or walking in to the lecture room late. Imagine no room-and-board bills, and not having to eat your roommate's cooking one more time. Imagine going to class when you want, even three o'clock in the morning. Imagine not worrying about parking! The future of higher education? Maybe. It's possible that the World Wide Web and other information technologies have so revolutionized education that the above scenarios are a *fait accompli*.

What is distance learning? **Distance learning** separates, by time or place, the teacher from the student. They are, however, linked by some communication technology: video-conferencing, satellite, computer, audiotape or videotape, real-time chat room, closed-circuit television, electronic mail, or the like. Examples of distance learning abound. "In 1997, New Brunswick's TeleEducation NB launched TeleCampus— one of the world's first virtual campuses—on the World Wide Web" (Statistics Canada 1998: 159), an electronic school which allows students to enroll, study, and pay for courses via the Internet. Athabasca University, in northern Alberta, is Canada's leading open university and considered a leader in developing electronic courseware. It offers students access to courses through tele-conferencing, videoconferencing, and other electronic means and offers many courses over the World Wide Web. Wasja, run by the Northern Nishnawbe Education Council, uses radio to provide educational opportunities to students in the Sioux Lookout area in Ontario. Kayas Cultural College runs the Little Red River Cree Nation in northeast Alberta and uses videoconferencing to provide academic upgrading and college courses. The University of Waterloo offers over 270 distance education courses and has approximately 10 000 registrants (Haughey 1999: 672).

Distance education has been available in Canada for over a century. It was first used in 1889 "to provide opportunities for teachers who were unable to attend McGill University in the winter months to study for their degree" (Haughey 1999: 672). However, since that time its scope and clientele has vastly expanded. At present, a minimum of half a million people in Canada study through distance education and programs. The available courses range from those at the elementary level through to university level.

Across Canada, over 65 percent of colleges offer at least one distance education course with over 60 000 students enrolled. Over 35 universities offer distance education courses. Many government departments and over 35 percent of large companies in Canada are already using some form of distance edu-

cycle of failure, alienation, and hopelessness. Breaking the cycle requires providing adequate funding for teachers, school buildings, equipment, and educational materials. In addition, jobs must be provided for those who successfully complete their education. Students with little hope of job success will continue to experience low motivation as long as job prospects are bleak and earnings in available jobs are low. Ray and Mickelson (1993) explain:

> ...School reforms of any kind are unlikely to succeed if...students cannot anticipate opportunity structures that reward diligent efforts in school. Employers are not apt to find highly disciplined and motivated young employees for jobs that are unstable and low paying. (pp. 14–15)

Moreover, Canada's "**brain drain**" suggests the lack of career opportunities that exist in our country. Although a study conducted by Statistics Canada that tracked 43 000 individuals who graduated from Canadian post-secondary institutions in 1995 reported that relatively few (only 1.5 percent of the total graduating class) moved to the United States after graduation, nearly half of those cation. Commercial suppliers as well as industrial, trade, and professional organizations are also providing distance learning courses and resources. (Haughey 1999: 672)

The benefits of distance learning are clear. It provides a less expensive, accessible, and often more convenient way to complete a degree. There are even pedagogical benefits. Research suggests that "students of all ages learn better when they are actively engaged in a process, whether that process comes in the form of a sophisticated multimedia package or a low-tech classroom debate on current events" (Carvin 1997). Distance education also benefits those who have historically been disadvantaged in the classroom. A review of research on gender differences suggests that females outperform males in distance learning environments (Koch 1998).

But all that glitters is not gold. There is evidence that students feel more estranged from their distance learning instructors than from teachers in conventional classrooms (Freitas et al. 1998).

Additionally problematic is the proliferation of "virtual degrees." An elementary school teacher enrolled in an online university to complete a master's degree in special education. After paying $800 of a total $2000 bill, she was sent a book to summarize as part of her degree requirements. Shortly after returning her summary, she was sent not only a master's degree, but a Ph.D. and transcripts of courses she had never taken with a recorded 3.9 grade point average (GPA) (Koeppel 1998). In spite of such problems, however, distance education continues to grow, in part because it is a moneymaker. Indeed, many commercial sites now offer "educational" courses while many educational sites increasingly carry advertising banners, consumer discounts, and so on.

Will distance learning solve all the problems facing education today? The answer is clearly no. While not the technological fix some are looking for, distance education, from digital libraries to "virtual" charter schools, does provide a provocative and financially lucrative alternative to traditional education providers.

SOURCES: Carvin, Andy. 1997. *EdWeb: Exploring Technology and School Reform.* http://www.ed-web.gsn.org. Freitas, Frances Anne, Scott Meyers, and Theodore Avtgis. 1998. "Student Perceptions of Instructor Immediacy in Conventional and Distributed Learning Classrooms." *Communication Education* 47(4): 366–72. Haughey, Margaret. 1999. "Distance Learning." In *The Canadian Encyclopedia: Year 2000 Edition*, edited by James H. Marsh, pp. 672–73. Toronto: McClelland and Stewart, Inc. Koch, James V. 1998. "How Women Actually Perform in Distance Education." *Chronicle of Higher Education* 45: A60. Koeppel, David. 1998. "Easy Degrees Proliferate on the Web." *New York Times*, August 2: 17. Statistics Canada. 1998. *Canada Yearbook 1999.* Ottawa: Minister of Industry.

who relocated ranked near the top of their graduating class in their field of study and those who left were more likely to have received scholarships or other academic awards than their counterparts. The group that left also included a disproportionate number of Ph.D. holders and master's graduates. Fifteen percent of those who moved had a master's degree and 8 percent held a doctorate. Among graduates who stayed in Canada, 7 percent had a master's degree and 1 percent had a doctorate. About one-third of those who emigrated to the United States were either nurses or doctors; the next largest occupations were engineers and computer specialists.

The research reported that the most common reason for leaving Canada was career opportunity. Over one-half of those who moved to the U.S. did so for career opportunity; few moved to take advantage of the lower taxes in the United States. While approximately 18 percent of the graduates who left in 1995 had returned to Canada by March 1999 (mostly to advance their careers or for personal reasons), the majority of those who remained in the United States indicated that they planned to remain there (Waldie 1999).

Finally, "if we are to improve the skills and attitudes of future generations of workers, we must also focus attention and resources on the quality of the lives children lead outside the school" (Murnane 1994: 290). We must provide support to families so children grow up in healthy, safe, and nurturing environments. Children are the future of our nation and of the world. Whatever resources we provide to improve the lives and education of children are sure to be wise investments in our collective future.

Critical Thinking

1 Clearly, there are both advantages and disadvantages to home schooling. After making a list of each, consider whether you would want your child to be home schooled. Why or why not?

2 As discussed in Chapter 6, the proportion of elderly in Canada is increasing dramatically as we move into the twenty-first century. Since the elderly are unlikely to have children in public schools, how will the allocation of needed school funds be affected by this demographic trend?

3 One response to school violence is primarily defensive, that is, expelling students, installing metal detectors, etc. Other than such defensive tactics, what violence prevention techniques should be instituted?

4 Students who drop out of school are often blamed for their lack of motivation. How may a teenager's dropping out of high school be explained as a failure of the educational system rather than as a "motivation" problem?

Key Terms

alternative schools	functional illiterates	self-fulfilling prophecy
brain drain	grade inflation	social promotion
charter schools	Head Start	special education
cultural imperialism	home schooling	
distance learning	multicultural education	

Section 4

Problems of Modernization

Section 4 focuses on problems of modernization—the cultural and structural changes that occur as a consequence of society changing from traditional to modern. Both Durkheim and Marx were concerned with the impact of modernization. Each theorized that as societies moved from "mechanical" to "organic solidarity" (in Durkheimian terms) or from "production for use" to "production for exchange" (in Marxian terms), fundamental changes in social organization would lead to increased social problems. Although modernization has contributed to many of the social problems we have already discussed, it is more directly related to the three prob-lems we examine in this section—technology, popu-lation, and the environment.

One of the difficulties in understanding social problems involves sorting out the numerous social forces that contribute to social problems. Every social problem is related, in some way, to many other social problems. Nowhere is this more appar-ent than in these final chapters. For example, even though scientific and technological advances are designed and implemented to enhance the quality and conditions of social life, they contribute to other social problems. Science and technology have extended life through various medical advances and

Chapter 13
Science and Technology

Chapter 14
Population and Environmental Problems

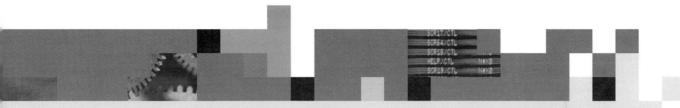

have successfully lowered the infant mortality rate in many developing nations. However, these two "successes" (fewer babies dying and an increased life expectancy), when coupled with a relatively high fertility rate, lead to expanding populations. Many nations struggle to feed, clothe, house, and provide safe drinking water and medical care for their increased numbers. Further, in responding to problems created by overpopulation, science and technology have contributed to the growing environmental crisis. For example, many developing countries use hazardous pesticides to increase food production for their growing populations; overuse land, which leads to desertification; and, out of eco-nomic necessity, agree to deforestation by foreign investors.

Developed countries also contribute to the environmental crisis. Indeed, modernization itself, independent of population problems, exacerbates environmental concerns as the fragile ecosystem is overburdened with the by-products of affluent soci-eties and scientific and technological triumphs: air pollution from the burning of fossil fuels, ground-water contamination from chemical runoff, nuclear waste disposal, and destruction of the ozone layer by chlorofluorocarbons. Thus, science and technology (Chapter 13) and population and the environment (Chapter 14) are inextricably related.

13

Science and Technology

Is It True?

1. Although the birth control pill has been commonly used in the West for the past three decades, it was not until 1999 that women in Japan won the right to use it.

2. Non-English speakers constitute the fastest-growing group of Internet users.

3. Many Canadians believe that social problems can be resolved through a technological fix rather than through social engineering.

4. Capitalist industrialists invented the clock as a means of controlling the time workers spent on the job.

5. Computer industry estimates put the number of computers in the world at 98 million in 2000.

Answers: 1 = T, 2 = T, 3 = F, 4 = F, 5 = F

M ost of the consequences of technology that are causing concern at the present time— pollution of the environment, potential damage to the ecology of the planet, occupational and social dislocations, threats to the privacy and political significance of the individual, social and psychological malaise...are with us in large measure because it has not been anybody's explicit business to foresee and anticipate them.

EMMANUEL MESTHENE
Former Director of the Harvard Program on Technology and Society

Mitch Maddox was a 26-year-old computer systems manager when, on January 1, 2000, he moved into an empty house with little more than a laptop and the clothes on his back. After legally changing his name to DotComGuy, the former Mr. Maddox pledged to "live off the Internet for a year and never leave the apartment" (quoted in Brand 2000: 1). Financed by advertisers, including United Parcel Services, his former employer, Mr. DCG then went about furnishing his new apartment—shopping online, of course. Throughout his year of confinement, DotComGuy relied completely on the Internet for all of life's basic needs: groceries (Peapod.com, a grocery delivery service), entertainment (online games, CDs, videos), companionship (chat rooms and dating services), recreation (online golf lessons), and of course pet supplies for his beagle, DotComDog.

Mr. DCG "made internet and marketing history" with the "first 24-hour-365 day uninterrupted multi-camera production" including a live Net concert performed by 70s rock group Kansas (DotComGuy, Inc. 2001; Witt 2000). DotComGuy, however, doesn't want to be known as an entertainer; he wants to "show the ease of e-commerce [and] how it can simplify your life" (Stenger 2000: 1). He also wants to provide a service to the online community—a cyber Consumer Reports *if you will. As a very, very regular online shopper, Mr. DCG visits hundreds of sites daily and ranks them from one to five based on their "usability, reliability, value, selection, and customer support" (Witt 2000). What's next for DotComGuy? He'll continue to help surfers find the right product at the right price. A comic strip may even be on the horizon, or should we say a DotComStrip.*

Living in an apartment for a year with your only means of communication being a computer, a monitor, and a modem is a little futuristic. But, like DotComGuy, virtual reality, cloning, and teleportation are no longer just the stuff of popular sci-fi movies such as *The Cell, Star Trek,* and *The Matrix.* Virtual reality is now used to train workers in occupations as diverse as medicine, engineering, and professional football. The ability to genetically replicate embryos has sparked worldwide debate over the ethics of reproduction, and just as the telephone, the automobile, the television, and countless other technological innovations have forever altered social life, so will more recent technologies (see this chapter's *Focus on Technology* feature).

Science and technology go hand in hand. **Science** is the process of discovering, explaining, and predicting natural or social phenomena. A scientific approach to understanding AIDS, for example, might include investigating the

New Technological Inventions

Here are some of the finalists from *Discovery* magazine's annual awards for technological innovation.

- *Micro Disks.* Size does matter. The size of a disk determines storage, i.e., the capacity for memory— one of the most important characteristics in selecting a personal appliance, whether it be a digital camera or a hand-held computer. Researchers have recently created a microdrive, a drive as powerful as those in full size desktop computers but made for a disk the size of a quarter. Such an innovation is likely to lead to the further miniaturization of electronic appliances.
- *Tendon-activated Hand.* Prosthetics are generally clumsy and not very responsive to fine-tuned actions. However, a new "tendon-activated hand" connects sensors in the artificial hand to remnant tendons, providing flexible and natural movement in the prosthetic. One recent accident victim has even returned to playing the piano!
- *Lego Mindstorms.* Researchers have developed computer controlled building blocks. Described as half robot and half Lego, the custom designed software helps children write computer programs by piecing together instructions on a computer screen that are transmitted to a robot. The robot then carries out the instructions— whether it be dealing a hand of gin rummy or playing a game of hide-and-seek. Besides being fun, children learn the elementary principles of programming.

- *Talking Lights.* Imagine you are visually impaired and in search of the "Main Street" exit of a building. As you walk through a door the badge you are wearing says, "This is the Main Street exit." Designed by electrical engineers, talking lights transform ordinary fluorescent light bulbs into "global positioning satellites" that can be used to guide people around malls, senior centres, hospitals, and the like. The lights simply emit information to a decoder that then translates it to verbal messages. The unit is wireless, inexpensive, and consumes no more energy than a regular light bulb.
- *Recodable Lock.* One of the biggest concerns of the twenty-first century is computer security— Internet privacy, virus-free computer environments, secure e-mail, etc. Although software security continues to be a multibillion dollar industry, two researchers may have discovered a way to secure a computer from the inside out. This new microscopic lock is almost impossible to crack and may do to electronic snoopers what software programs have failed to do—put a lock on cyberspace.
- *Microsystems Jini.* All of us have spent hours pouring over the manuals of our latest high tech purchases trying to figure out the operating instructions of each new gadget. *Jini*, however, is a new software package that once installed allows your computer to talk to other "intelligent" appliances installed into the *Jini* system. From the *Jini* Web page simply click on an icon to warm your coffee, retrieve pictures from a digital camera, or toast a Pop Tart.

- *Toyota Prius.* For years, car manufacturers have tried to find the perfect balance of economy, efficiency, and comfort. Toyota's Prius, as one of the finalist in the transportation category, may be the perfect mix. The new automobile combines a conventional gasoline engine with a nickel-metal hydride battery resulting in an attractive, roomy, economy size car.
- *Virtual Touch.* Using a computer is a multisensory experience—bright lights, moving images, and real life audio but, until recently, no tactile stimuli. Researchers have now created what they call a haptic interface, that is, a joystick, which gives the computer user a sense of touch. The advantages of such an innovation are unlimited, allowing doctors to actually feel tissue during cybersurgery or engineers to experience the goodness of fit of parts just designed.
- *Breaking Through.* That all too familiar sound of a jackhammer may be a thing of the past. In trying to design a quiet way to break up concrete, researchers have developed RAPTOR, a lightweight "gun" that fires penny nails at speeds of 1500 m per second. When the nails are fired into the concrete in consecutive lines, stress fractures occur and even the thickest of concrete begins to crumble. Because RAPTOR can be fitted with a silencer, the firing of nails not only breaks up the concrete it does so quietly and with much less effort on the part of the operator.

SOURCES: D'Agnese, Joseph. 2000. "The 11th Annual Discover Awards." *Discover* 21(7): July. http://www.discover.com/jul_00featawards.htm. "1999 Emerging Technology Finalists." http://www.discover.com/awards/awards_emerging.shtml.

molecular structure of the virus, the means by which it is transmitted, and public attitudes about AIDS. **Technology**, "the skills, tools and machines used by members of a society to convert material objects (e.g., natural resources) into products useful to themselves" (Richardson 1999: 2297), is intended to accomplish a specific task—in this example, the development of an AIDS vaccine.

Societies differ in their level of technological sophistication and development. In agricultural societies, which emphasize the production of raw materials, **mechanization**, or the use of tools to accomplish tasks previously done by hand, dominates. As societies move toward industrialization and become more concerned with the mass production of goods, automation prevails. **Automation** involves the use of self-operating machines, as in an automated factory where autonomous robots assemble automobiles. Finally, as a society moves toward post-industrialization, it emphasizes service and information professions (Bell 1973). At this stage, technology shifts toward **cybernation**, whereby machines control machines—making production decisions, programming robots, and monitoring assembly performance.

What are the effects of science and technology on humans and their social world? How do science and technology help to remedy social problems and how do they contribute to social problems? Is technology, as Postman (1992) suggests, both a friend and a foe to humankind? This chapter addresses each of these questions.

The Global Context: The Technological Revolution

Less than 50 years ago, travelling across Canada was an arduous task, a long-distance phone call was a memorable event, and mail carriers brought belated news of friends and relatives from far away. Today, travellers journey between continents in a matter of hours, and for many, e-mail, faxes, video-conferencing, and electronic fund transfers have replaced conventional means of communication.

The world is a much smaller place than it used to be and will become even smaller as the technological revolution continues. The Internet is projected to have over 750 million users in over 100 countries by the year 2003 (Global Reach 2000). Americans constitute the largest share of Internet users, followed by the Japanese. English-speakers comprise the largest language group online (48 percent), but non-English speakers constitute the fastest growing group on the Internet. For example, Brazil, China, and South Korea were recently added to the list of the top 10 online countries—edging out several European nations. Although 87 percent of all Internet users live in industrialized countries, there is some movement toward the Internet becoming a truly global medium as Africans and Latin Americans increasingly "get online" (Sampat 2000; World Employment Report 2001).

The movement toward the globalization of technology is, of course, not limited to the use and expansion of the Internet. The world robot market continues to expand (IFR 1997); Latin America's computer industry is dominated by Texas-based manufacturer Compaq; Microsoft's Internet platform and support products are sold overseas; "globe-trotting scientists" collect skin and blood

The revolutionary element is built into contemporary society everywhere. A technological revolution makes the world more uniform: one cannot take off in a jet plane and expect a radically different way of life in the place where the plane lands.

NORTHROP FRYE
Cultural critic

samples from remote islanders for genetic research (Shand 1998); and a global treaty regulating trade of genetically altered products between over a hundred nations has been signed (Pollack 2000).

To achieve such scientific and technological innovations, sometimes called research and development (R&D), countries need material and economic resources. Research entails the pursuit of knowledge; development refers to the production of materials, systems, processes, or devices directed toward the solution of a practical problem. In 1999, $14.9 billion was spent on research and development in Canada (up from $14.4 billion in 1998). As in most other countries, Canadian funding sources in that year were primarily from the business sector (63 percent), colleges and universities (24 percent), and the federal government (11 percent). At 1.6 percent of Gross Domestic Product, Canada's R&D spending was lower than that of all other G-7 countries except for Italy (1.1 percent) (Statistics Canada 2003c). In 2001, a United Nations technology index, which combined ratings for technology creation, diffusion of recent innovations, diffusions of old innovations, and human skills, positioned Canada eighth—ahead of Germany (11th), Ireland (13th), and France (17th), but well-behind Finland (ranked first), the United States, Sweden, Japan, South Korea, the Netherlands, and the United Kingdom (Edwards 2001).

Scientific discoveries and technological developments also require the support of a country's citizens and political leaders. For example, although abortion has been technically possible for years, millions of the world's citizens live in countries where abortion is either prohibited or permitted only when the life of the mother is in danger. Similarly, although the birth control pill has been available in most countries in the West for more than three decades, it was only in the summer of 1999 that Japan's national pharmaceutical regulatory board recommended approval of the pill to the government's ministry of health. Critics of the birth control pill had long claimed that its use would damage the nation's morals and cause a variety of social ills, including environmental harm from the hormones of women who took it. Nevertheless, women's groups in Japan intensified their campaign for the pill's approval after the Japanese government gave their swift approval to Viagra, the male anti-impotence pill, in January of 1999 (*Maclean's* 1999a: 53). It is evident that the degree to which science and technology are considered good or bad, desirable or undesirable, is largely socially constructed.

Postmodernism and the Technological Fix

Many people believe that social problems can be resolved through a **technological fix** (Weinberg 1966) rather than through social engineering. For example, a social engineer might approach the problem of water shortages by persuading people to change their lifestyle: use less water, take shorter showers, and wear clothes more than once before washing. A technologist would avoid the challenge of changing people's habits and motivations and instead concentrate on the development of new technologies that would increase the water supply. Social problems may be tackled through both social engineering and technological fixes. In recent years, for example, social engineering efforts to reduce drunk driving have included imposing stiffer penalties for drunk driving and disseminating public service announcements such as "Friends Don't Let Friends Drive Drunk."

An example of a technological fix for the same problem is the development of car air bags, which reduce injuries and deaths from car accidents.

Not everyone, however, agrees that science and technology are good for society. **Postmodernism**, an emerging worldview, holds that rational thinking and the scientific perspective have fallen short in providing the "truths" they were once presumed to hold. During the industrial era, science, rationality, and technological innovations were thought to pave the way to a better, safer, and more humane world. Today, postmodernists question the validity of the scientific enterprise, often pointing to the unforeseen and unwanted consequences of resulting technologies. Automobiles, for example, began to be mass-produced in the 1930s in response to consumer demands. However, the proliferation of automobiles also led to increased air pollution and the deterioration of cities as suburbs developed; today, traffic fatalities are the number one cause of death from all accidents. Examine Table 13.1 and consider the positive and negative consequences of each of these modern-day technologies.

Table 13.1 *Home Electronics and Appliances Owned by Canadians, Selected Years, 1965–1998*

	1965	1975	1985	1995	1998
Air conditioners	2.2	12.4	18.0	29.3	29.1*
Automobiles	75.0	78.9	77.3	73.9	79.0
Camcorders	n.a.	n.a.	n.a.	16.1	17.7
Cellular phones	n.a.	n.a.	n.a.	14.1	26.0
Clothes dryers	25.2	48.1	68.4	76.5	79.0
Compact disc players	n.a.	n.a.	n.a.	53.4	67.0
Computer modems	n.a.	n.a.	n.a.	15.5	32.0
Dishwashers	2.7	15.2	37.1	47.7	51.0
Electric stoves	69.0	85.1	92.3	93.7	93.5*
Electric washers	86.2	76.9	77.3	79.6	80.0*
Freezers	22.6	41.8	57.0	57.1	53.9*
Gas barbecues	n.a.	n.a.	19.9	57.1	59.0
Home computers	n.a.	n.a.	n.a.	31.6	45.0
Microwave ovens	n.a.	0.8	23.0	85.2	89.0
Radios	96.1	98.3	98.7	98.6	98.7*
Refrigerators	95.8	99.3	99.2	99.6	99.8*
Smoke detectors	n.a.	n.a.	n.a.	95.7	98.6*
Telephones	89.4	96.4	98.2	98.7	98.6*
Television, cable	n.a.	40.4	62.5	74.0	73.0
Television	92.6	96.8	98.3	99.1	99.0
Television, colour	n.a.	53.4	91.4	98.5	99.0
Videocassette recorders	n.a.	n.a.	23.5	83.5	88.0

*1997 data.

SOURCES: Based on *Canadian Global Almanac*. 2000. Edited by Susan Girvan. Toronto: Macmillan Canada; Statistics Canada 1999. *Science Statistics* 23(6), November, Catalogue 88-001-XIB.

Sociological Theories of Science and Technology

Each of the three major sociological frameworks helps us to better understand the nature of science and technology in society.

Structural-Functionalist Perspective

Functionalists view science and technology as emerging in response to societal needs—that "[science] was born indicates that society needed it" (Durkheim [1925] 1973). As societies become more complex and heterogeneous, finding a common and agreed-on knowledge base becomes more difficult. Science fills the need for an assumed objective measure of "truth" and provides a basis for making intelligent and rational decisions. In this regard, science and the resulting technologies are functional for society.

If society changes too rapidly because of science and technology, however, problems may emerge. When the material part of culture (i.e., its physical elements) changes at a faster rate than the nonmaterial (i.e., its beliefs and values), a **cultural lag** may develop (Ogburn 1957). For example, the typewriter, the conveyor belt, and the computer expanded opportunities for women to work outside the home. With the potential for economic independence, women were able to remain single or to leave unsatisfactory relationships or establish careers. But although new technologies have created new opportunities for women, beliefs about women's roles, expectations of female behaviour, and values concerning equality, marriage, and divorce have "lagged" behind.

Robert Merton (1973), a functionalist and founder of the subdiscipline sociology of science, also argued that scientific discoveries or technological innovations may be dysfunctional for society and create instability in the social system. For example, the development of timesaving machines increases production, but also displaces workers and contributes to higher rates of employee alienation. Defective technology can have disastrous effects on society. In 1994, a defective Pentium chip was discovered to exist in more than two million computers in aerospace, medical, scientific, and financial institutions, as well as schools and government agencies. Replacing the defective chip was a massive undertaking, but was necessary to avoid thousands of inaccurate computations and organizational catastrophes.

> I've got gigabytes. I've got megabytes. I'm voice-mailed. I'm e-mailed. I surf the Net. I am a Cyber-Man. So how come I feel so out of touch?"
>
> VOLKSWAGEN TELEVISION COMMERCIAL

Conflict Perspective

Conflict theorists, in general, emphasize that science and technology benefit a select few. For some conflict theorists, technological advances occur primarily as a response to capitalist needs for increased efficiency and productivity and thus are motivated by profit. As McDermott (1993) notes, most decisions to increase technology are made by "the immediate practitioners of technology, their managerial cronies, and for the profits accruing to their corporations" (p. 93). The Dalkon Shield and silicone breast implants are examples of technological advances that promised millions of dollars in profits for their developers. However, the rush to market took precedence over thorough testing of the products' safety. Subsequent lawsuits filed by consumers who argued that both products had compromised the physical well-being of women resulted in large damage awards for the plaintiffs.

Science and technology also further the interests of dominant groups to the detriment of others. The need for scientific research on AIDS was evident in the early 1980s, but the required large-scale funding was not made available as long as the virus was thought to be specific to homosexuals and intravenous drug users. Only when the virus became a threat to all North Americans were millions of dollars made available for AIDS research. Hence, conflict theorists argue that granting agencies act as gatekeepers to scientific discoveries and technological innovations. Powerful interest groups and the marketability of the product influence these agencies rather than the needs of society.

Finally, conflict theorists as well as feminists argue that technology is an extension of the patriarchal nature of society that promotes the interest of men and ignores the needs and interests of women. For example, washing machines, although time-saving devices, disrupted the communal telling of stories and the resulting friendships among women who gathered together to do their chores. Bush (1993) observes that in a "society characterized by a sex-role division of labour, any tool or technique...will have dramatically different effects on men than on women" (p. 204).

Symbolic Interactionist Perspective

Knowledge is relative. It changes over time, over circumstances, and between societies. We no longer believe that the world is flat or that the earth is the centre of the universe, but such beliefs once determined behaviour as individuals responded to what they thought to be true. The scientific process is a social process in that "truths"—socially constructed "truths"—result from the interactions between scientists, researchers, and the lay public.

Kuhn (1973) argues that the process of scientific discovery begins with assumptions about a particular phenomenon (e.g., the world is flat). Since unanswered questions about a topic always exist (e.g., why don't the oceans drain?), science works to fill these gaps. When new information suggests that the initial assumptions were incorrect (e.g., the world is not flat), a new set of assumptions or a framework emerges to replace the old one (e.g., the world is round). It then becomes the dominant belief or paradigm.

Symbolic interactionists emphasize the importance of this process and the impact social forces have on it. Conrad (1997), for example, describes the media's contribution to framing societal beliefs that alcoholism, homosexuality, and racial inequality are genetically determined. Social forces also affect technological innovations, and innovations' success is, in part, dependent on the social meaning assigned to any particular product. If a product is defined as impractical, cumbersome, inefficient, or immoral, it is unlikely to gain public acceptance. Consider, for example, that when Segolene Royal, the French deputy education minister, announced that, beginning in 2000, schoolgirls in France would be provided with the morning-after contraceptive pill in "cases of distress and extreme urgency," she also noted that this decision was likely to "cause uproar among conservative church groups." However, she emphasized that teen pregnancies caused a "huge problem of distress amid adolescents in France," with 6700 of 10 000 pregnancies ending in abortion, and she justified this move as an "emergency" measure (*National Post* 1999: A11).

> New technologies alter the structure of our interests: the things we think about. They alter the character of our symbols: the things we think with. And they alter the nature of community: the arena in which thoughts develop.
>
> NEIL POSTMAN
> *Philosopher of technology*

Not only are technological innovations subject to social meaning but who becomes involved in what aspects of science and technology is also socially defined. As we note in Chapter 7, men outnumber women in earning computer science degrees. Men also score higher on measures of computer aptitude and report higher computer use than do women (Lewin 1998; Papadakis 2000; AAUW 2000). Societal definitions of men as being rational, mathematical, scientifically minded, and having greater mechanical aptitude than women are, in part, responsible for these differences. This chapter's *Social Problems Research Up Close* highlights one of the consequences of the masculinization of technology, as well as the ways in which computer hacker identities and communities are socially constructed.

Technology and the Transformation of Society

A number of modern technologies are considerably more sophisticated than technological innovations of the past. Nevertheless, older technologies have influenced the social world as profoundly as the most astonishing modern inventions. Postman (1992) describes how the clock—a relatively simple innovation that is taken for granted in today's world—profoundly influenced not only the workplace but the larger economic institution:

> The clock had its origin in the Benedictine monasteries of the twelfth and thirteenth centuries. The impetus behind the invention was to provide a more or less precise regularity to the routines of the monasteries, which required, among other things, seven periods of devotion during the course of the day. The bells of the monastery were to be rung to signal the canonical hours; the mechanical clock was the technology that could provide precision to these rituals of devotion....What the monks did not foresee was that the clock is a means not merely of keeping track of the hours but also of synchronizing and controlling the actions of men. And thus, by the middle of the fourteenth century, the clock had moved outside the walls of the monastery, and brought a new and precise regularity to the life of the workman and the merchant....In short, without the clock, capitalism would have been quite impossible. The paradox...[is] that the clock was invented by men who wanted to devote themselves more rigorously to God; it ended as the technology of greatest use to men who wished to devote themselves to the accumulation of money. (pp.14–15)

Technology has far-reaching effects not only on the economy but on every aspect of social life. The following sections discuss societal transformations resulting from various modern technologies, including workplace technology, computers, the information highway, and science and biotechnology.

Technology in the Workplace

All workplaces, from doctors' offices to factories and from supermarkets to real estate corporations, have felt the impact of technology. Technology can make workers more accountable by gathering information about their performance. Through such timesaving devices as personal digital assistants and battery-powered store shelf labels, technology can enhance workers' efficiency. Technology is also changing the location of work and allowing some employees to

Technology is not something you can put back in the black box and return to Radio Shack. It's the vaccinations you've had and all that metal in your teeth. It's everything, the whole thing that makes us what we are. There is absolutely no option. Whatever it is, we're going there. We can't say, 'Oh no, back to nature!' because nature no longer exists. We messed with it too much.

WILLIAM GIBSON
Novelist

telework—that is, complete all or part of their work away from the workplace (Carey 1998).

Information technologies are also changing the nature of work. Lilly Pharmaceutical employees communicate via their own "intranet," on which all work-related notices are posted. Federal Express not only created a FedEx network for their 30 000 employees, but allowed customers to enter their package-tracking database, saving that company $2 million a year. It is estimated that one-fifth of all corporations are now using such telecommunication devices, offering the potential of a paperless workplace (GIP 1998).

Robotic technology, sometimes called computer-aided manufacturing (CAM), has also revolutionized work, particularly in heavy industry such as automobile manufacturing. An employer's decision to use robotics depends on direct (e.g., initial investment) and indirect (e.g., unemployment compensation) costs, the feasibility and availability of robots performing the desired tasks, and the increased rate of productivity. Use of robotics may also depend on whether there is union resistance to the replacement of workers by machines.

The Computer Revolution

Early computers were much larger than the small machines we have today and were thought to have only esoteric uses among members of the scientific and military communities. In 1951, only about half a dozen computers existed (Ceruzzi 1993). The development of the silicon chip and sophisticated microelectronic technology allowed tens of thousands of components to be imprinted on a single chip that was smaller than a dime. The silicon chip led to the development of laptop computers, mini-television sets, cellular phones, electronic keyboards, and singing birthday cards. The silicon chip also made computers affordable. Although the first personal computer (PC) was developed only 20 years ago, computer industry estimates put the number of computers in the world at 98 million in 1990, 222 million in 1995, and 579 million in 2000 (Ash 2001: 213) (Table 13.2).

Today, computers form the backbone of universities, government agencies, corporations, and businesses. Statistics Canada (1998) notes that the federal, provincial, and municipal governments in Canada are the "prime customers for

Table 13.2 *Countries with the Most Computers*

Country	Percentage of World Total	Computers
1. U.S.	28.32	164 100 000
2. Japan	8.62	49 900 000
3. Germany	5.28	30 600 000
4. U.K.	4.49	26 000 000
5. France	3.77	21 800 000
6. Italy	3.02	17 500 000
7. Canada	2.76	16 000 000
8. China	2.75	15 900 000
9. Australia	1.82	10 600 000
10. South Korea	1.82	10 600 000

SOURCE: Ash, Russell. 2001. *The Top 10 of Everything: Canadian Edition 2002.* Toronto: Dorling Kindersley Limited. Reprinted by permission of Dorling Kindersley.

The Social Construction of the Hacking Community

Cyberstalking, pornography on the Internet, identity theft—crimes almost unheard of before the computer revolution and the enormous growth of the Internet. One such "high tech" crime, computer hacking, ranges from childish pranks to costly viruses that shut down corporations. Below Jordan and Taylor (1998) enter the world of hackers, analyzing the nature of this activity, hackers' motivations, and the social construction of the "hacking" community.

Sample and Methods

Jordan and Taylor (1998) researched computer hackers and the hacking community through 80 semi-structured interviews, 200 questionnaires, and an examination of existing data on the topic. As is often the case in crime, illicit drug use, and other similarly difficult research areas, a random sample of hackers was not possible. **Snowball sampling** is often the preferred method in these cases; that is, one respondent refers the researcher to another respondent, who then refers the researcher to another respondent, and so forth. Through their analysis, the authors lend insight into this increasingly costly social problem and the symbolic interactionist notion of "social construction"—in this case, of an online community.

Findings and Conclusions

Computer hacking, or "unauthorized computer intrusion," is an increasingly serious problem, particularly in a society dominated by information technologies. Unlawful entry into computer networks or databases can be achieved by several means including (1) guessing someone's password, (2) tricking a computer about the identity of another computer (called "IP spoofing"), or (3) "social engineering," a slang term referring to getting important access information by stealing documents, looking over someone's shoulder, going through their garbage, and so on.

Hacking carries with it certain norms and values because, according to Jordan and Taylor, the hacking community can be thought of as a culture within a culture. The two researchers identify six elements of this socially constructed community:

- *Technology*. The core of the hacking community is the technology that allows it to occur. As one professor interviewed stated, the young today have "…lived with computers virtually from the cradle, and therefore have no trace of fear, not even a trace of reverence."
- *Secrecy*. The hacking community must, on the one hand, commit secret acts since their "hacks" are

> But the essence of the new technological society is that it's not an infrastructure outside our lives. Increasingly, it's the infrastructure within which we live.
>
> HEATHER MENZIES
> *Sociologist*

services" and account for 17 percent of computer and computer-related services (closely followed by the finance and insurance sector). In addition, "[t]he demand for computer specialists led the growth in the labour force during the 1990s, although almost all of it occurred in the latter half of the decade" (Statistics Canada 2003a: 8). According to the 2001 census, over 406 000 persons (2.6 percent of the total labour force) worked in computer-related occupations in Canada (e.g., analysts, consultants, programmers, Web site developers, and software writers). Approximately three-quarters of this group were in occupations that demanded a university education. Compared to others providing business services, those employed in computer and computer-related services tend to earn higher-than-average salaries. According to the 2001 Census, young men, aged 20 to 34, account for one-third of the total growth in information technology occupations (Statistics Canada 2003a: 9).

Computers and computer software are also big business (Table 13.3)—and in some cases, too big. In 2000, a U.S. federal judge found that Microsoft Corporation was in violation of antitrust laws, which prohibit unreasonable restraint of trade. At issue were Microsoft's Windows operating system and the vast array of Windows-based applications (e.g., spreadsheets, word processors, tax software) i.e., applications that *only* work with Windows. The court held that the 70 000 illegal. On the other hand, much of the motivation for hacking requires publicity to achieve the notoriety often sought. Further, hacking is often a group activity that bonds members together. As one hacker stated, hacking "can give you a real kick some time. But it can give you a lot more satisfaction and recognition if you share your experiences with others...."

- *Anonymity.* While secrecy refers to the hacking act, anonymity refers to the importance of the hacker's identity remaining anonymous. Thus hackers and hacking groups take on names such as, for example, Legion of Doom, the Inner Circle I, Mercury, and Kaos, Inc.
- *Membership Fluidity.* Membership is fluid rather than static, often characterized by high turnover rates, in part as a response to law enforcement pressures. Unlike more structured organizations, there are no formal rules or regulations.
- *Male Dominance.* Hacking is defined as a male activity and, consequently, there are few female hackers. Jordan and Taylor also note, after recounting an incident of sexual harassment, that "...the collective identity hackers share and construct...is in part misogynist" (p. 768).
- *Motivation.* Contributing to the articulation of the hacking communities' boundaries are the agreed-on definitions of acceptable hacking motivations, including: (1) addiction to computers, (2) curiosity, (3) excitement, (4) power, (5) acceptance and recognition, and (6) community service through the identification of security risks.

Finally, Jordan and Taylor note that hackers also maintain group boundaries by distinguishing between their community and other social groups, including "an antagonistic bond to the computer security industry (CSI)" (p. 770). Ironically, hackers admit a desire to be hired by the CSI, which would not only legitimize their activities but give them a steady income as well.

The authors conclude that the general fear of computers and of those who understand them underlies the common although inaccurate portrayal of hackers as pathological, obsessed computer "geeks." When journalist Jon Littman asked hacker Kevin Mitnick if he was demonized because of increased dependence on and fear of information technologies, Mitnick replied, "Yeah....That's why they're instilling fear of the unknown. That's why they're scared of me. Not because of what I've done, but because I have the capability to wreak havoc" (Jordan and Taylor 1998: 776).

SOURCE: Jordan, Tim, and Paul Taylor. 1998. "A Sociology of Hackers." *Sociological Review* (November): 757–78.

■ Table 13.3 *Ten Largest Computer Companies*

Company/Country	Annual Sales (U.S.$)*
1. IBM, U.S.	88 396 000 000
2. Hewlett-Packard, U.S.	48 782 000 000
3. Fujitsu, Japan	47 196 000 000
4. Compaq Computer, U.S.	42 383 000 000
5. Dell Computer, U.S.	31 888 000 000
6. Canon, Japan	23 062 000 000
7. Xerox, U.S.	18 632 000 000
8. Sun Microsystems, U.S.	15 721 000 000
9. Ricoh, Japan	12 997 000 000
10. Gateway, U.S.	9 601 000 000

* In latest year for which figures available.

SOURCE: Ash, Russell. 2001. *The Top 10 of Everything: Canadian Edition 2002*. Toronto: Dorling Kindersley Limited. Reprinted by permission of Dorling Kindersley.

programs written exclusively for Windows made "competing against Microsoft impractical" (Markoff 2000). In an agreement reached between the U.S. Department of Justice and Microsoft Corporation, Microsoft will be divided into two companies—an operating-systems company and an applications company.

The Information Highway

Information technology, or IT for short, refers to any technology that carries information. Most information technologies were developed within a 100-year span: photography and telegraphy (1830s), rotary power printing (1840s), the typewriter (1860s), transatlantic cable (1866), telephone (1876), motion pictures (1894), wireless telegraphy (1895), magnetic tape recording (1899), radio (1906), and television (1923) (Beniger 1993). The concept of an "information society" dates back to the 1950s when an economist identified a work sector he called "the production and distribution of knowledge."

The **Internet** is an international information infrastructure—a network of networks—available through universities, research institutes, government agencies, and businesses. Between 1996 and 1997 alone, Internet access in Canadian workplaces more than doubled; one in four Canadian workers now uses a wide variety of cyberspace tools (Statistics Canada 1998). The successful implementation of the SchoolNet program also made Canada the first nation in the world to connect its schools and libraries to the information superhighway (Fenna 1999).

In 2000, Canada ranked among the top 10 countries with the most Internet users (Table 13.4). Among Canadians 15 years of age and over, about one in four women and one in three men uses the Internet in Canada on an average day (Normand 2000: 92). Canadians use the Internet for a variety of purposes (Table 13.5)—including **e-commerce**, or the buying or selling of goods and services over the Internet (Table 13.6). Interestingly, online consumerism may actually help the environment. A team of energy experts report that e-commerce may substantially prevent the release of greenhouse gases by reducing the need for energy-consuming office buildings and malls (Sampat 2000: 94).

■ **Table 13.4** *Countries with the Most Internet Users*

Country	Percentage of Population	Internet Users*
1. U.S.	54.7	153 840 000
2. Japan	30.5	38 640 000
3. Germany	24.4	20 100 000
4. U.K.	33.9	19 940 000
5. China	1.3	16 900 000
6. South Korea	35.0	16 400 000
7. Italy	23.4	13 420 000
8. Canada	42.6	13 280 000
9. Brazil	5.8	9 840 000
10. Russia	6.3	9 200 000
World total	6.7	407 100 000

* Estimates for weekly usage as of end of 2000.

SOURCE: Ash, Russell. 2001. *The Top 10 of Everything: Canadian Edition 2002*. Toronto: Dorling Kindersley Limited. Reprinted by permission of Dorling Kindersley.

■ **Table 13.5** *Uses of the Internet in Canada*

Purpose of Use	% Internet Users*
1. E-mail	91.7
2. Other specific information#	85.1
3. General browsing	84.7
4. Medical/health information	54.2
5. Government information	44.1
6. Playing games	42.7
7. Formal education/training	32.0
8. Electronic banking	27.7
9. Obtaining/saving music	27.1
10. Chat groups	26.2

* Regular home-use households, 1999.

Other than medical/health or government information.

Other common uses of the Internet identified in the poll were listening to the radio (17.5 percent) and purchasing goods and services (19 percent).

SOURCE: Statistics Canada.

Science and Biotechnology

While recent computer innovations and the establishment of an information highway have led to significant cultural and structural changes, science and its resulting biotechnologies have led to not only dramatic changes, but also hotly contested issues. Here we will look at some of the issues raised by developments in genetics and reproductive technology.

Genetics Molecular biology has led to a greater understanding of the genetic material found in all cells—DNA (deoxyribonucleic acid)—and with it the ability for **genetic screening**. Currently, researchers are trying to complete genetic maps that will link DNA to particular traits (Lemonick 1999). Already, specific

■ **Table 13.6** *Items Most Purchased Online in Canada*

Item	Percentage*
1. Computers and computer-related products	68
2. Books	54
3. CDs, recorded music	40
4. Clothing and accessories (women's)	29
5. Electronic products (small)	20
6. Magazines	20
7. Hotel reservations	19
8. Air travel reservations	17
9. Videos, filmed entertainment	16
10. Clothing and accessories (men's)	14

* Percentage of purchasers who have bought item online one or more times.

SOURCE: Reprinted by permission of Ernst and Young.

strands of DNA have been identified as carrying such physical traits as eye colour and height, as well as increased risk of such diseases as breast cancer, cystic fibrosis, prostate cancer, and Alzheimer's.

The Human Genome Project, a 10-year effort to map human DNA, was completed in 2000. The decoding entailed "identifying and placing in order the 3.1 billion-unit long sequence that make up human DNA" (Potter 2001: 1). This information will revolutionize medicine. The hope is that if a defective or missing gene can be identified, it may be possible to get a healthy duplicate and transplant it to the affected cell. This is known as **gene therapy**. Alternatively, viruses have their own genes that can be targeted for removal. Experiments are now under way to accomplish these biotechnological feats.

Genetic engineering is the ability to manipulate the genes of an organism in such a way that the natural outcome is altered. Genetic engineering is accomplished by splicing the DNA from one organism into the genes of another. Often, however, unwanted consequences ensue. For example, through genetic engineering some plants are now self-insecticiding, that is, the plant itself produces an insect-repelling substance. Ironically, the continual plant production of the insecticide, in contrast to only sporadic application by farmers, is leading to insecticide-resistant pests (Ehrenfeld 1998).

The debate over genetically engineered crops is ongoing as advocates note the prospects for expanded food production and opponents question the health and environmental consequences (see Chapter 10).

Reproductive Technologies The evolution of "reproductive science" has been furthered by scientific developments in biology, medicine, and agriculture. At the same time, however, its development has been hindered by the stigma associated with sexuality and reproduction, its link with unpopular social movements (e.g., contraception), and the feeling that such innovations challenge the natural order (Clarke 1990). Nevertheless, new reproductive technologies have been and continue to be developed.

In **in-vitro fertilization** (IVF), an egg and a sperm are united in an artificial setting such as a laboratory dish or test tube. Although the first successful attempt at IVF occurred in 1944, it was not until 1978 that the first test-tube baby, Louise Brown, was born. In Canada, 23 clinics from Halifax to Vancouver offer IVF, which, reportedly, is responsible for thousands of pregnancies a year (Geddes 1999). In the United States, more than 300 fertility clinics provide this procedure, resulting in about 10 000 live births a year. Criticisms of IVF are often based on traditional definitions of the family and the legal complications created when a child can have as many as five potential parental ties—egg donor, sperm donor, surrogate mother, and the one or two people who raise the child (depending on the situation, IVF may not involve donors or a surrogate). Litigation over who are the "real" parents has already occurred.

Perhaps more than any other biotechnology, abortion epitomizes the potentially explosive consequences of new technologies. **Abortion** is the removal of an embryo or fetus from a woman's uterus before it can survive on its own. After amendments to Canada's abortion laws were made in 1969, which allowed for "therapeutic abortions" in hospitals, both the numbers and rates of therapeutic abortions rose significantly, then stabilized beginning in 1983 and continuing for some years (Figure 13.1). The number and rate of abortions began to rise substantially again after 1989, when the Supreme Court struck

It is now a matter of a handful of years before biologists will be able to irreversibly change the evolutionary wisdom of billions of years with the creation of new plants, new animals, and new forms of human and post human beings.

TIM HOWARD

JEREMY RIFKIN

Biotechnology critics

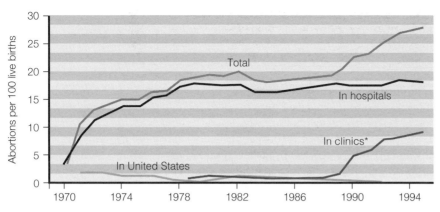

Figure 13.1 *Thera-peutic Abortions, Cana-dian Residents, 1970–95**

SOURCE: Statistics Canada. 1995. *Therapeutic Abortions*, 1995 (Statistics Canada Cat. No. 82-219-XPB), Table 11.

* For 1978–89, information pertains to Quebec only. For 1990, clinics in Newfoundland, Nova Scotia, Quebec, Ontario, Manitoba, and British Columbia are included. Alberta clinics are added in 1991–95 data, and New Brunswick clinics are included in 1994 and 1995.

down the 1969 abortion law. Before 1989, abortion clinics operated only in Quebec; by 1995, abortion clinics outside hospitals operated in all Canadian provinces except Prince Edward Island and Saskatchewan. In 1998, one-third of all therapeutic abortions were performed in clinics and the remaining two-thirds were performed in hospitals. Far fewer Canadian women now obtain abortions in the United States (down from 2757 in 1987 to 297 in 1998). In 1998, 110 331 women obtained therapeutic abortions in Canada. Women in their 20s accounted for half of all those who obtained abortions in that year (Health Canada 1999; Statistics Canada 2000).

Most recent debates concern intact dilation and extraction (D&X) abortions. Opponents refer to such abortions as **partial birth abortions** because the limbs and the torso are typically delivered before the fetus has expired. D&X abortions are performed because the fetus has a serious defect, the woman's health is jeopardized by the pregnancy, or both. Undoubtedly, the controversy over whether a fetus is or is not a child will also be affected by the emergence of recent scanning technology which provides a four-dimensional ultrasound picture or video of a fetus that is "sometimes clear enough to evaluate subtle facial features and judge whether Junior resembles mom or dad" (Abraham 2002).

Abortion is a complex issue for everyone, but especially for women, whose lives are most affected by pregnancy and childbearing. On a global level, women who have abortions are disproportionately poor, unmarried minority members who say they intend to have children in the future. Abortion is also a complex issue for societies, which must respond to the pressures of conflicting attitudes toward abortion and the reality of high rates of unintended and unwanted pregnancy.

Attitudes toward abortion tend to be polarized between two opposing groups of abortion activists—prochoice and prolife. Advocates of the prochoice movement hold that freedom of choice is a central human value, that procreation choices must be free of government interference, and that since the woman must bear the burden of moral choices, she should have the right to make such decisions. Alternatively, prolifers hold that the unborn fetus has a right to live and be protected, that abortion is immoral, and that alternative means of resolving an unwanted pregnancy should be found. You may assess your attitude towards abortion in this chapter's *Self and Society* feature.

In July 1996, Scottish scientist Ian Wilmut successfully cloned an adult sheep named Dolly. To date, cattle, goats, mice, and pigs have also been cloned. This technological breakthrough has caused worldwide concern about the possibility of human cloning. One argument in favour of developing human cloning technology is its medical value; it may potentially allow everyone to have "their own reserve of therapeutic cells that would increase their chance of being cured of various diseases, such as cancer, degenerative disorders and viral or inflammatory diseases" (Kahn 1997: 54). Human cloning could also provide an alternative reproductive route for couples who are infertile and for those in which one partner is at risk for transmitting a genetic disease.

Arguments against cloning are largely based on moral and ethical considerations. Critics of human cloning suggest that, whether used for medical therapeutic purposes or as a means of reproduction, human cloning is a threat to human dignity. For example, cloned humans would be deprived of their individuality and, as Kahn (1997: 119) points out, "creating human life for the sole purpose of preparing therapeutic material would clearly not be for the dignity of the life created." Nonetheless, British physicians recently recommended that therapeutic cloning be permitted. **Therapeutic cloning** entails using stem cells from human embryos. Stem cells can produce any type of cell in the human body and, thus, can be used for "grow-your-own organ transplants and tissue for use in treating medical conditions ranging from paralysis to diabetes" (Reuters 2000: 1). Because the use of stem cells entails the destruction of human embryos, many prolifers are opposed to the practice.

Despite what appears to be a universal race to the future and the indisputable benefits of such scientific discoveries as the workings of DNA and the technology of IVF, some people are concerned about the duality of science and technology. Science and the resulting technological innovations are often life assisting and life giving; they are also potentially destructive and life threatening. The same scientific knowledge that led to the discovery of nuclear fission, for example, led to the development of both nuclear power plants and the potential for nuclear destruction. Thus, we now turn our attention to the problems associated with science and technology.

Societal Consequences of Science and Technology

Scientific discoveries and technological innovations have implications for all social actors and social groups. As such, they also have consequences for society as a whole.

Alienation, Deskilling, and Upskilling

As technology continues to play an important role in the workplace, workers may feel there is no creativity in what they do—they feel alienated (see Chapter 11). The movement from mechanization to automation to cybernation increasingly

Abortion Attitude Scale

This is not a test. There are no wrong or right answers to any of the statements, so just answer as honestly as you can. The statements ask you to tell how you feel about abortion (the voluntary removal of a human fetus from the mother) during the first three months of pregnancy by a qualified medical person. Indicate how you feel about each statement by circling one of the choices beside each sentence. Respond to each statement and circle only one response.

Strongly agree = 5; Agree = 4; Slightly agree = 3; Slightly disagree = 2; Disagree = 1; Strongly disagree = 0

1. Abortion is a good way of solving an unwanted pregnancy.	5	4	3	2	1	0
2. A mother should feel obligated to bear a child she has conceived.	5	4	3	2	1	0
3. Abortion is wrong no matter what the circumstances are.	5	4	3	2	1	0
4. A fetus is not a person until it can live outside its mother's body.	5	4	3	2	1	0
5. The decision to have an abortion should be the pregnant mother's.	5	4	3	2	1	0
6. Every conceived child has the right to be born.	5	4	3	2	1	0
7. A pregnant female not wanting to have a child should be encouraged to have an abortion.	5	4	3	2	1	0
8. Abortion should be considered killing a person.	5	4	3	2	1	0
9. People should not look down on those who choose to have an abortion.	5	4	3	2	1	0
10. Abortion should be an available alternative for unmarried, pregnant teenagers.	5	4	3	2	1	0
11. Persons should not have the power over the life or death of a fetus.	5	4	3	2	1	0
12. Unwanted children should not be brought into the world.	5	4	3	2	1	0
13. A fetus should be considered a person at the moment of conception.	5	4	3	2	1	0

SCORING AND INTERPRETATION

As its name indicates, this scale was developed to measure attitudes towards abortion. It was developed by Sloan (1983) for use with high school and university students. To compute your score, first reverse the point scale for items 2, 3, 6, 8, 11, and 13. Total the point responses for all items. Sloan provided the following categories for interpreting the results:

65–51 Strong proabortion
50–39 Moderate proabortion
38–22 Unsure
21–11 Moderate antiabortion
10–0 Strong antiabortion

RELIABILITY AND VALIDITY

An unmodified Abortion Attitude Scale was administered to high school and university students, Right to Life group members, and abortion service personnel. Sloan (1983) reported a high total test estimate of reliability (0.92). Construct validity was supported in that Right to Life members' mean scores were 16.2; abortion service personnel mean scores were 55.6, and other groups' scores fell between these values.

SOURCE: Adapted from "Abortion Attitude Scale" by L.A. Sloan. Reprinted with permission from the *Journal of Health Education* Vol. 14. No. 3, May/June 1983. The *Journal of Health Education* is a publication of the American Allegiance for Health, Physical Education, Recreation and Dance. 1900 Association Drive, Reston, Virginia 20191.

removes individuals from the production process, often relegating them to flip-ping a switch, staring at a computer monitor, or entering data at a keyboard. For example, many low-paid employees, often women, sit at computer terminals for hours entering data and keeping records for thousands of businesses, corpora-tions, and agencies. The work that takes place in these "electronic sweatshops" is monotonous, solitary and provides little autonomy.

Not only are these activities routine, boring, and meaningless, they promote **deskilling**, that is, "labour requires less thought than before and gives them [workers] fewer decisions to make" (Perrolle 1990: 338). Deskilling stifles development of alternative skills and limits opportunities for advancement and creativity as old skill sets become obsolete. To conflict theorists, deskilling also provides the basis for increased inequality because "throughout the world, those who control the means of producing information products are also able to deter-mine the social organization of the 'mental labour' which produces them" (Perrolle 1990: 337).

Technology in some work environments, however, may lead to **upskilling**. Unlike deskilling, upskilling reduces alienation as employees find their work more rather than less meaningful, and have greater decision-making powers as information becomes decentralized. Futurists argue that upskilling in the work-place could lead to a "horizontal" work environment where "employees do not so much do what they are told to do, but what their expansive knowledge of the entire enterprise suggests to them needs doing" (GIP 1998).

Social Relationships and Social Interaction

Technology affects social relationships and the nature of social interaction. The development of telephones has led to fewer visits with friends and relatives; with the coming of VCRs and cable television, the number of places where social life occurs (e.g., movie theatres) has declined. Even the nature of dating has changed as computer networks facilitate cyberdates and private chat rooms. As technology increases, social relationships and human interaction are transformed.

Technology also makes it easier for individuals to live in a cocoon—to be self-sufficient in terms of finances (e.g., Quicken), entertainment (e.g., pay-per-view movies), work (e.g., telecommuting), recreation (e.g., virtual reality), shopping (e.g., eBay), communication (e.g., Internet), and many other aspects of social life. Ironically, although technology can bring people together, it can also isolate them from each other, leading the Amish to ban any technology that "is seen as a threat to the cohesion of the community or might contaminate the culture's values" (Hafner 1999: 1). For example, some technological innovations replace social roles—an answering machine may replace a secretary, a computer-operated vending machine may replace a salesperson, an automatic teller machine may replace a banker, and closed circuit television, a teacher (Johnson 1988; Schwartz 2001; Winner 1993). These technologies may improve effi-ciency, but they also reduce human contact.

> Men [and women] have become the tools of their tools.
>
> HENRY DAVID THOREAU
> *Writer, social activist*

Loss of Privacy and Security

When professor of media technology Nicholas Negroponte was asked what he feared most in thinking about the digital future he cited the erosion of privacy and security:

When I send you a message in the future, I want you to be sure it is from me; that when that message goes from me to you, nobody is listening in; and when it lies on your desk, nobody is snooping later. (Negroponte 1995: 88)

Schools, employers, and the government are increasingly using technology to monitor individuals' performance and behaviour. Today, through cybernation, machines monitor behaviour by counting a telephone operator's minutes online, videotaping a citizen walking down a city street, or tracking the whereabouts of a needed employee (Quick 1998; White 2000).

Employers and others may subject individuals to drug testing technology (see Chapter 3). Through computers, individuals can obtain access to phone bills, tax returns, medical reports, credit histories, bank account balances, and driving records. Some companies sell such personal information. Unauthorized disclosure is potentially devastating. In response to the possibility of such consequences David Brin (1998), author of *The Transparent Society*, argues that since it is impossible to prevent such intrusions, "reciprocal transparency," or complete openness, should prevail. If organizations can collect the information, then citizens should have access to it and to its uses.

> Online life is rich and rewarding, but it's no substitute for face-to-face interaction.
>
> JACQUES LESLIE
> *Writer*

Unemployment

Some technologies replace human workers—robots replace factory workers, word processors displace secretaries and typists, and computer-assisted diagnostics reduce the need for automobile mechanics. The 2001 census noted that "[w]ith the proliferation of word processing, accounting software, and office automation, the demand for secretaries and accounting clerks declined. The census counted 271 000 secretaries, excluding legal and medical secretaries, 35 percent fewer than there were a decade earlier" (Statistics Canada 2003a: 8). The number of accounting clerks has also fallen by 31 percent. Estimates suggest that, over the next decade, thousands of bank branches will be replaced by automatic teller machines. The cost of a teller transaction is $1.07; an electronic transaction, $0.07 (Fix 1994). In Canada, there are more than 34 million debit cards in use and more than 400 000 merchant terminals and automatic teller machines (*Maclean's* 1999b: 56).

Technology is likely to cause worldwide increases in unemployment, according to activist Jeremy Rifkin, whose book *The End of Work* (1996) predicts a global reduction in service-sector employees. Unlike previous decades, according to Rifkin, when uprooted workers moved from farms to factories to offices, today's technologically displaced workers have no place to go. Whether or not Rifkin is accurate in his predictions, there can be little doubt that technology changes the nature of work and the types of jobs available. For example, fewer semiskilled workers are needed since machines have replaced many of these jobs. The jobs that remain, often white-collar jobs, require more education and technological skills. Technology thereby contributes to the split labour market as the pay gulf between skilled and unskilled workers continues to grow (Pascal 1996). For example, Addison et al. (2000) report that employees who use computers at work are at a lower risk of losing their jobs than non-computer users.

The Digital Divide

One of the most significant social problems associated with science and technology is the increased division between the classes. As Welter (1997) notes,

...it is a fundamental truth that people who ultimately gain access to, and who can manipulate, the prevalent technology are enfranchised and flourish. Those individuals (or cultures) that are denied access to the new technologies, or cannot master and pass them on to the largest number of their offspring, suffer and perish. (p. 2)

The fear that technology will produce a "virtual elite" (Levy 1997) is not uncommon. Several theorists hypothesize that as technology displaces workers, most notably the unskilled and uneducated, certain classes of people will be irreparably disadvantaged—the poor, minorities, and women (Hayes 1998; Welter 1997). There is even concern that biotechnologies will lead to a "genetic stratification," whereby genetic screening, gene therapy, and other types of genetic enhancements are available only to the rich (Mehlman and Botkin 1998).

The wealthier the family, for example, the more likely the family is to have a computer. According to Statistics Canada, in 1998, the 20 percent of households with the highest incomes were four times more likely to have a computer than those in the lowest income group. In that year, almost three in four (74 percent) of those in the highest income group versus fewer than one in five (18 percent) in the lowest income group had a computer. Internet access was six times more common in households in the highest income group (48 percent) than in households in the lowest income group (8 percent) (Statistics Canada 1999).

This situation is not unique to Canada. Consider, for example, that in the United States, inner-city neighbourhoods, disproportionately populated by racial and ethnic minorities, are simply less likely to be "wired," that is, to have the telecommunications hardware necessary for schools to access online services. In fact, cable and telephone companies are less likely to lay fibre optics in these areas—a practice called "information apartheid" or "electronic redlining." Students who live in such neighbourhoods are technologically disadvantaged and may never catch up to their middle-class counterparts (Welter 1997).

The cost of equalizing such differences is enormous, but the cost of not equalizing them may be even greater. Employees who are technologically skilled have higher incomes than those who are not—up to 15 percent higher (World Employment Report 2001). Further, technological disparities exacerbate the structural inequities perpetuated by the split labour force and the existence of primary and secondary labour markets (see Chapter 11).

Mental and Physical Health

Some new technologies have unknown risks. Biotechnology, for example, has promised and, to some extent, has delivered everything from life-saving drugs to hardier pest-free tomatoes. Biotechnologies have also, however, created **technology-induced diseases**, such as those experienced by Chellis Glendinning (1990). Glendinning, after using the pill and, later, the Dalkon Shield IUD, became seriously ill.

> Despite my efforts to get help, medical professionals did not seem to know the root of my condition lay in immune dysfunction caused by ingesting artificial hormones and worsened by chronic inflammation. In all, my life was disrupted by illness for twenty years, including six years spent in bed....For most of the years of illness, I lived in isolation with my problem. Doctors and manufacturers of birth control technologies never acknowledged it or its sources.

Other technologies that pose a clear risk to a large number of people include nuclear power plants, DDT, automobiles, X-rays, food colouring, and breast implants.

The production of new technologies may also place manufacturing employees in jeopardy. For example, the electronics industry uses thousands of hazardous chemicals, including freon, acetone, and sulphuric and nitric acids:

> [Semiconductor] workers are expected to dip wafer-thin silicon that has been painted with photoresist into acid baths. The wafers are then heated in gas-filled ovens, where the gas chemically reacts with the photosensitive chemicals. After drying, the chips are then bonded to ceramic frames, wires are attached to contacts and the chip is encapsulated with epoxy. These integrated circuits are then soldered onto boards, and the whole device is cleaned with solvents. Gases and silicon lead to respiratory and lung diseases, acids to burning and blood vessel damage, and solvents to liver damage. (Hosmer 1986: 2)

Finally, technological innovations are, for many, a cause of anguish and stress, particularly when the technological changes are far-reaching (Hormats 2001). As many as 10 percent of Internet users are "addicted" to being online and, alternatively, nearly 60 percent of workers report being "technophobes," that is, fearful of technology (Boles and Sunoo 1998; Papadakis 2000). Says Dr. Michelle Weil, a clinical psychologist, the key to dealing with technophobia is to decide "which tools make sense in a person's life and will give them more control, and, ultimately, more enjoyment" (Kelly 1997: 4). This chapter's *The Human Side*, "Data Smog Removal Techniques," deals directly with this issue.

The Challenge to Traditional Values and Beliefs

Technological innovations and scientific discoveries often challenge traditionally held values and beliefs, in part because they enable people to achieve goals that were previously unobtainable. Before recent advances in reproductive technology, for example, women could not conceive and give birth after menopause. Technology that allows postmenopausal women to give birth challenges societal beliefs about childbearing and about the role of older women. Macklin (1991) notes that the techniques of egg retrieval, in-vitro fertilization, and gamete intrafallopian transfer (GIFT) make it possible for two different women to each make a biological contribution to the creation of a new life. Such technology requires society to re-examine its beliefs about what a family is and what a mother is. Should custom, law, or the intentions of the parties involved define family?

Medical technologies that sustain life lead us to rethink the issue of when life should end. The increasing use of computers throughout society challenges the traditional value of privacy. New weapons systems challenge the traditional idea of war as something that can be survived and even won. Cloning challenges our traditional notions of family, parenthood, and individuality. Toffler (1970) coined the term **future shock** to describe the confusion resulting from rapid scientific and technological changes that unravel our traditional values and beliefs.

Finally, if the information superhighway allows us to increasingly live in a global village, some have expressed concern that, in the process, we may lose

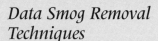
Data Smog Removal Techniques

The following excerpt from David Shenk's Data Smog: Surviving the Information Glut *(1997), outlines techniques for simplifying your life and reducing the stress associated with a "high-tech" lifestyle.*

Most of us have excess information in our lives, distracting us, pulling us away from our priorities and from a much-desired tranquility. If we stop just for a moment to look (and listen) around us, we will begin to notice a series of data streams that we'd be better off without, including some distractions we pay handsomely for.

- *Turn the television off*. There is no quicker way to regain control of the pace of your life, the peace of your home, and the content of your thinking than to turn off the appliance that supplies for all-too-many of us the ambiance of our lives....
- *Leave the pager and cell-phone behind*. It is thrilling to be in touch with the world at all times, but it's also draining and interfering. Are wireless communicators instruments of liberation, freeing people to be more mobile with their lives—or are they more like electronic leashes, keeping people more plugged into their work and their info-glutted lives than is necessary and healthy?
- *Limit your e-mail*. If we're spending too much time each day reading and answering e-mail that has virtually no value, we must take steps to control it. Ask people (nicely) not to forward trivia indiscriminately. "Unsubscribe" to the news groups that you're no longer really interested in. Tell spammers that you have no interest in their product, and ask them to remove you from their customer list.
- *Say no to dataveillance*. With some determination and a small amount of effort, one can also greatly reduce the amount of junk mail and unsolicited sales phone calls. It involves writing just a few letters, requesting to have your name put on "do-not-disturb" lists, which some 75 percent of direct marketers honour.
- *Resist upgrade mania*. Remember: Upgrades are designed to be sales tools, not to give customers what they've been clamouring for.
- *Cleanse your system with "data-fasts."*... Take some time to examine your daily intake and consider whether or not your info diet needs some fine-tuning. Take some data naps in the afternoon, during which you stay away from electronic information for a prescribed period. You could also consider limiting yourself to no more than a certain number of hours on the Internet each week, or at least balancing the amount of time spent online with an equal amount of time reading books....[P]eriodic fasts of a week or month have a remarkably rejuvenating effect. One sure way to gauge the value of something, after all, is to go without it for a while.

SOURCE: Shenk, David. 1997. *Data Smog: Surviving the Information Glut*. pp. 184–89. San Francisco: HarperEdge. Copyright © 1997 by David Shenk. Reprinted by permission of HarperCollins Publishers Inc.

The history of the "rocky road of progress" is made up of apparent technological wonders that turned out to be techno-threats or outright disasters.

ABIGAIL TRAFFORD
ANDREA GABOR
Journalists

our national identity as Canadians (Wallace 1999). According to the *Maclean's* 1999 year-end poll, after noting the pervasiveness of the American media and the impact of U.S. investment in and takeovers of Canadian businesses, "more respondents think the Internet now has a greater impact on drawing us closer to Americans. Only 23 percent of those who think we are becoming more like Americans attribute it to free trade, while 34 percent point to the Internet" (Wallace 1999) (Table 13.7).

■ **Table 13.7** *How Much of an Impact Has Each of the Following Had on Making Us More Like Americans?*
Asked of those who thought that Canadians were becoming more like Americans.

	Major impact	Some impact	Neutral	Not too much impact	No impact at all
American media like TV, magazines, and film	48	36	7	7	2
U.S. investment and takeovers of Canadian businesses	35	44	9	8	4
The Internet and information economy	34	41	11	6	4
The North American Free Trade Agreement	23	42	14	10	4
Canadian government adopting the same kinds of policies as the U.S. government	20	42	18	14	4
Changes in our social programs	15	39	21	18	6

SOURCE: Wallace, Bruce. 1999. "Say It Ain't So.:" *Maclean's*, July 5: 14–19.

Strategies for Action: Controlling Science and Technology

As technology increases, so does the need for social responsibility. Nuclear power, genetic engineering, cloning, and computer surveillance all increase the need for social responsibility: "...technological change has the effect of enhancing the importance of public decision making in society, because technology is continually creating new possibilities for social action as well as new problems that have to be dealt with" (Mesthene 1993: 85). In the following section, we address various aspects of the public debate, including science, ethics, the law, and the role of corporations and government policy.

■ Technological systems are both socially constructed and society shaping.

THOMAS HUGHES
Social scientist

Science, Ethics, and the Law

Science and its resulting technologies alter the culture of society by challenging traditional values. Public debate and ethical controversies, however, have led to structural alterations in society as the legal system responds to calls for action. For example, in 1993 Royal Commission on New Reproductive Technology recommended that the government should criminalize the sale of eggs, sperm, embryos and fetal issue, ban surrogate motherhood as well as the donation of eggs in exchange for in vitro services, eliminate clinics that allow for sex-selection of fetuses, and impose tighter controls on in vitro fertilization. Even these recommendations failed to keep up with what science had made technologically feasible for shortly after the release of the Royal Commission report, a procedure was developed that allowed scientists to surgically extract sperm from the body of a dead man.

In a delayed response to the Royal Commission's recommendations, Canada's federal health minister called for "voluntary restraint" in the commercial use of the new reproductive technologies. The following year, the Liberal government introduced Bill C-47, legislation designed to ban 14 practices including the creation of embryos for research and the sale of human sperm and eggs. However, after the medical community strongly opposed the legislation, the bill did not pass. Although the government has continued to wrestle with the issue,

> it is still legal to engage in the buying and selling of eggs, sperm and embryos, sex-selection for non-medical reasons, commercial surrogacy arrangements, cloning of human embryos, ectogenesis (maintaining an embryo in an artificial womb), creation of animal-human hybrids, retrieval of sperm or eggs from cadavers or fetuses for fertilization and implantation, research involving the maturation of sperm or ova outside the human body, germ-line genetic alteration (manipulation of an embryo's genetic makeup to affect the individual and all descendents), creation of embryos for research purposes, and any offer to pay for prohibited services. (Dranoff 2001: 15)

Are regulations to control such practices necessary? In a society characterized by rapid technological and thus social change—a society where custody of frozen embryos is part of the divorce agreement—many would say yes. Cloning, for example, is one of the most hotly debated technologies in recent years. Bioethicists and the public vehemently debate the various costs and benefits of this scientific technique. Ironically, the Internet provides numerous sites that discuss the benefits and disadvantages of cloning, with one high-tech innovation providing a forum for discussion for another.

Should the choices that we make, as a society, be dependent on what we *can* do or what we *should* do? While scientists and the agencies and corporations who fund them often determine the former, who should determine the latter? Although such decisions are likely to have a strong legal component, that is, they must be consistent with the rule of law and the ethics of scientific inquiry (Eibert 1998; White 2000), legality or the lack thereof often fails to answer the question, what *should* be done? Thus, it is likely that the issues surrounding the most controversial of technologies will continue into the twenty-first century, with no easy answers.

> Prohibiting scientific and medical activities would also raise troubling enforcement issues.... Would they [police] raid research laboratories and universities? Seize and read the private medical records of infertility patients? Burst into operating rooms with their guns drawn? Grill new mothers about how their babies were conceived?
>
> **MARK EBERT**
> *Lawyer*

Technology and the Corporate World

As philosopher Jean-François Lyotard notes, knowledge is increasingly produced to be sold (Powers 1998). The development of genetically altered crops, the commodification of women as egg donors, and the harvesting of regenerated organ tissues are all examples of potentially market-driven technologies. Like the corporate pursuit of computer technology, profit-motivated biotechnology creates several concerns.

Foremost is the concern that only the rich will have access to such life-saving technologies as genetic screening and cloned organs. Such fears are justified. Several "companies with enigmatic names such as Progenitor, Millennium Pharmaceuticals, and Darwin Molecular have been pinpointing and patenting human life with the help of $4.5 billion in investments from pharmaceuticals companies" (Shand 1998: 46). Millennium Pharmaceutical holds the patent on genes associated with melanoma and with obesity; Darwin Molecular controls a gene associated with premature aging, and Progenitor a gene associated with schizophrenia.

These patents result in **gene monopolies**, which could lead to astronomical patient costs for genetic screening and treatment. One company's corporate literature candidly states that its patent of the breast cancer gene will limit competition and lead to huge profits (Shand 1998: 47). The biotechnology industry argues that such patents are the only way to recoup research costs, which, in turn, lead to further innovations. To date, about 1000 genes have been patented and thousands of others are in the process of being claimed (Regalado 2000).

The commercialization of technology causes several other concerns, including the tendency for discoveries to remain closely guarded secrets rather than collaborative efforts, and issues of quality control (Lemonick and Thompson 1999; Rabino 1998). Further, industry involvement has made government control more difficult as researchers depend less and less on governmental funding. Finally, although there is little doubt that profit acts as a catalyst for some scientific discoveries, other less commercially profitable but equally important projects may be ignored. As biologist Isaac Rabino (1998) states, "imagine if early chemists had thrown their energies into developing profitable household products before the periodic table was discovered…" (112).

Runaway Science and Government Policy

Science and technology raise many public policy issues. Policy decisions, for example, address concerns about the safety of nuclear power plants, the privacy of electronic mail, the hazards of chemical warfare, and the legality of surrogacy. In creating science and technology, have we created a monster that has begun to control us rather than the reverse? What controls, if any, should be placed on science and technology? As well, are such controls consistent with existing law? Consider the use of Napster software to download music files and the question of intellectual property rights and copyright infringement.

The government, through regulatory agencies and departments, prohibits the use of some technologies (e.g., assisted-suicide devices) and requires others (e.g., seat belts). To instill consumer trust in Internet commerce, the federal government has engaged in several efforts designed to complement the technological and management security solutions developed by industry. For example, the federal government introduced Bill C-54, the *Personal Information and Electronic Documents Act,* to facilitate e-commerce in Canada by enabling the use of electronic documents and electronic signatures. In addition, the Organisation for Economic Co-operation and Development (OECD) Working Party on Information Security and Privacy has scrambled to keep up with what technology has made it possible to do, issuing a number of reports and policies related to authentication, such as the 1992 *OECD Guidelines for the Security of Information Systems*, the 1997 *OECD Guidelines on Cryptography Policy*, and the 1998 *Declaration on Authentication for Electronic Commerce*. Growing concern with genetically altered crops led, in 2000, to the adoption of a 130-nation treaty that permits countries to "bar imports of genetically altered seeds, microbes, animals and crops that they deem a threat to their environment" (Pollack 2000: 1).

Understanding Science and Technology

What are we to understand about science and technology from this chapter? As functionalists argue, science and technology evolve as a social process and are a natural part of the evolution of society. As society's needs change, scientific discoveries and technological innovations emerge to meet these needs, thereby serving the functions of the whole. Consistent with conflict theory, however, science and technology also meet the needs of select groups and are characterized by political components. As Winner (1993) notes, the structure of science and technology conveys political messages, including "power is centralized," "there are barriers between social classes," "the world is hierarchically structured," and "the good things are distributed unequally" (288).

The scientific discoveries and technological innovations that are embraced by society as truth itself are socially determined. Research indicates that science and the resulting technologies have both negative and positive consequences—a **technological dualism**. Technology saves lives, time, and money; it also leads to death, unemployment, alienation, and estrangement. Weighing the costs and benefits of technology poses ethical dilemmas, as does science itself. Ethics, however, "is not only concerned with individual choices and acts. It is also and, perhaps, above all concerned with the cultural shifts and trends of which acts are but the symptoms" (McCormick 1994: 16).

Thus, society makes a choice by the very direction it follows. Such choices should be made based on guiding principles that are both fair and just (Eibert 1998; Goodman 1993; Winner 1993):

- Scientists and those working in technology should be prudent. Adequate testing, safeguards, and impact studies are essential. Impact assessment should include an evaluation of the social, political, environmental, and economic factors.
- No technology should be developed unless all groups, and particularly those who will be most affected by the technology, have at least some representation "at a very early stage in defining what that technology will be" (Winner 1993: 291). Traditionally, the structure of the scientific process and the development of technologies has been centralized (that is, decisions have been in the hands of a few scientists and engineers); decentralization of the process would increase representation.
- Means should not exist without ends. Each innovation should be directed toward fulfilling a societal need rather than the more typical pattern in which a technology is developed first (e.g., high-definition television) and then a market is created (e.g., "you'll never watch regular TV again!"). Indeed, from the space program to research on artificial intelligence, the vested interests of scientists and engineers, whose discoveries and innovations build careers, should be tempered by the demands of society.

What the twenty-first century will hold, as the technological transformation continues, may be beyond the imagination of most of society's members. Technology empowers; it increases efficiency and productivity, extends life, controls the environment, and expands individual capabilities. But, as Steven Levy (1995) notes, there is a question as to whether society can accommodate such empowerment (p. 26).

Now that we have entered the first computational millennium, one of the great concerns of civilization is the attempt to reorder society, culture, and government in a manner that exploits the digital bonanza, yet prevents it from running roughshod over the checks and balances so delicately constructed in those simpler precomputer years.

> It would be nice if the scientist and the engineer were cognizant of, and deeply concerned about, the potential risks, secondary consequences, and other costs of their creations.
>
> ALLAN MAZUR
> *Sociologist*

Critical Thinking

1 Use of the Internet by neo-Nazi and White supremacist groups has recently increased. Should such groups have the right to disseminate information about their organizations and recruit members through the Internet?

2 A student at the University of Waterloo developed the "V-chip"—a technological device designed to prevent children from watching programs their parents find objectionable. Hollywood executives opposed the V-chip on the grounds that it is intrusive and violates guarantees of freedom of expression. Others have also been critical, pointing to the difficulty of establishing a universal definition of violence, and the impact on advertising revenues (Makris 1996). How might a conflict theorist explain opposition to the V-chip?

3 What currently existing technologies have had more negative than positive consequences for individuals and for society?

4 Some research suggests that productivity actually declines with the use of computers (Rosenberg 1998). Assuming this "paradox of productivity" is accurate, what do you think causes the reduction in efficiency?

Key Terms

abortion	genetic engineering	snowball sampling
automation	genetic screening	technological dualism
cultural lag	information technology	technological fix
cybernation	Internet	technology
deskilling	in-vitro fertilization	technology-induced diseases
e-commerce	mechanization	telework
future shock	partial birth abortion	therapeutic cloning
gene monopolies	postmodernism	upskilling
gene therapy	science	

14

Population and Environmental Problems

Outline

The Global Context: A World View of Population Growth

Sociological Theories of Population and Environmental Problems

Social Problems Related to Population Growth

Strategies for Action: Slowing Population Growth

Environmental Problems

Social Causes of Environmental Problems

Strategies for Action: Responding to Environmental Problems

Understanding Population and Environmental Problems

Is It True?

1. Most of the world's population growth is occurring in the most developed countries.

2. Globally, the 1990s was the warmest decade on record, providing evidence of global warming.

3. Computer monitors contain an average of five to seven pounds of lead, most of which ends up in landfills.

4. At least 1000 plant and animal species become extinct each year.

5. Over half of Canadians report voting for, or against, political candidates or parties based on their stand on environmental issues.

Answers: 1 = F, 2 = T, 3 = T, 4 = T, 5 = F

T he beginning of a new millennium finds the planet Earth poised between two conflicting trends. A wasteful and invasive consumer society, coupled with continued population growth, is threatening to destroy the resources on which human life is based. At the same time, society is locked in a struggle against time to reverse these trends and introduce sustainable practices that will ensure the welfare of future generations.

UNITED NATIONS ENVIRONMENT PROGRAMME

World history changed on September 11, 2001, when a band of fanatical terrorists revealed the vulnerability of the most powerful nation now on earth. As stock markets tumbled, airlines collapsed, and nations tried to find ways of dealing with an unidentified enemy who had no fear of death, the problems facing our environment temporarily retreated from frontline public concern. This new threat to our survival and way of life became our highest priority. But what September 11 has also taught us is that issues of security, stability, and freedom are inseparably linked to those of poverty, equity, justice, and environmental productivity. This was indeed a new kind of war, and the questions it has raised may include an opportunity to step outside our usual definitions and rhetoric in order to reassess our global priorities: our values and the ways we share—or do not share—the resources provided by the earth....

Those concerned with survival—not just about whether our society can keep producing oil and allow trade to flow freely after a terrorist attack, but with the protection of air, water, and food for our long term survival—are unanimous in saying we need to ask straightforward questions about how we live: Is the way we produce, manufacture, buy and sell goods sustainable? Are our methods of extracting and distributing materials safe? Will our current practices bring us a long, healthy future, or are they leading towards even greater problems with our food, water, and air—as well as to fear of our neighbours...? (Suzuki and Dressel 2002: 1–3).

In this chapter, we discuss population and environmental problems. As Hunter (2001) explains:

Global population size is inherently connected to land, air, and water environments because each and every individual uses environmental resources and contributes to environmental pollution. While the scale of resource use and the level of wastes produced vary across individuals and across cultural contexts, the fact remains that land, water, and air are necessary for human survival. (p. 12)

After discussing population growth in the world and in Canada, we view population and environmental problems through the lens of structural-functionalism, conflict theory, and symbolic interactionism. We also explore how population growth contributes to a variety of social problems and examine strategies for limiting population growth. The second half of the chapter focuses on environmental problems, examining their social causes and exploring strategies that attempt to reduce or alleviate environmental problems.

The Global Context: A World View of Population Growth

For thousands of years, the world's population grew at a relatively slow rate. During 99 percent of human history, the size of hunting and gathering societies was restricted by disease and limited food supplies. Around 8000 B.C., the development of agriculture and the domestication of animals led to increased food supplies and population growth, but even then harsh living conditions and disease still put limits on the rate of growth. This pattern continued until the mid-eighteenth century when the Industrial Revolution improved the standard of living for much of the world's population. The improvements included better food, cleaner drinking water, and improved housing, as well as advances in medical technology such as antibiotics and vaccinations against infectious diseases; all contributed to rapid increases in population (see Figure 14.1).

World Population Growth

In the year A.D. 1, the world's population was about 250 million. It took until 1830 for the world population to reach one billion. Since then the population has increased exponentially. The **doubling time**—or time it takes for a population to double in size from any base year—decreases as the population grows. Although the population in A.D. 1 took 1650 years to double, the second doubling took only 200 years, and the third 80 years. In 2000, the doubling time for the world's population was 51 years (Population Reference Bureau 2000a). When world population reached six billion on October 12 1999, "the five billionth baby had not even reached adolescence yet, having been born in 1986" (Population Institute 2000: 8). It took less time—only 12 years—to add this last billion to the world's population than any previous billion, despite an annual population growth rate of only 1.3 percent, which is the lowest growth rate in a half-century (Halwell 2000). Figure 14.2 illustrates world population growth from 1950 projected until 2050.

As much as 97 percent of annual world population growth is occurring in poor developing countries that are already overburdened with economic, environmental, and public health problems (Population Institute 1999). Consider that Africa's share of global population is expected to rise to 20 percent by 2050, as

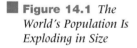**Figure 14.1** *The World's Population Is Exploding in Size*

SOURCE: Weeks, John R. 2001. *Population: An Introduction to Concepts and Issues*, 7th edition. Belmont, CA: Wadsworth Publishing Company, p. 10.

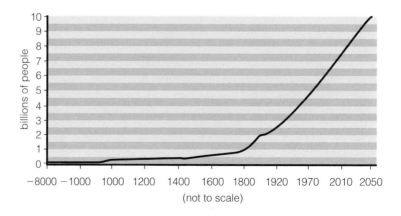

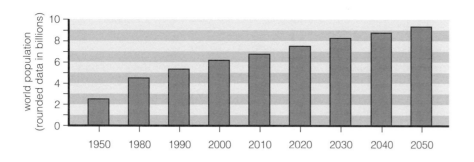

Figure 14.2 *World Population Growth 1950–2050*

SOURCES: Brown, Lester R., Gary Gardner, and Brian Halwell. 1998. *Beyond Malthus: Sixteen Dimensions of the Population Problem.* World Watch Paper 143. Washington, DC: World Watch Institute; *Statistical Abstract of the United States: 1998*, 118th edition. U.S. Bureau of the Census. Washington, DC: U.S. Government Printing Office, Table 1340.

compared to only 9 percent in 1960 (Hunter 2001). Populations of 65 countries are expected to double within 30 years (Population Institute 2000). As shown in Table 14.1, the population doubling time in less developed countries is much shorter than the population doubling time in more developed countries.

Falling Fertility Rates and the "Birth Dearth"

While many countries, especially in the developing world, are experiencing continued population growth, other countries are declining in population. According to the United Nations Population Division (2001), 39 countries, including Japan, Germany, Italy, Hungary, and Russia, are expected to decrease in population size over the next 50 years. In these countries, the **fertility rate**—the average number of children born to each woman—has fallen below 2.1, the **replacement level** required to maintain the population. Declining birthrates in some countries are thought to result from high unemployment and a high cost of living. Spain has the lowest birthrate in the world: each woman has an average of 1.15 children in her lifetime. Falling population levels are also a concern in France, Germany, Greece, Italy, Russia, and Japan. According to Steve Mosher, president of the Population Research Institute, "humanity's long-term problem is not too many children being born but too few....Over time, the demographic collapse will extinguish entire cultures" (Cooper 1998: 612).

One defining characteristic of a civilized society is a sense of responsibility to the next generation. If we do not assume that responsibility, environmental deterioration leading to economic decline and social disintegration could threaten the survival of civilization as we know it.

LESTER R. BROWN
JENNIFER MITCHELL
World Watch Institute

Canadian Population Growth

Based on the census of 1851, the population of Canada was estimated to be 2 436 000, largely (80 percent) concentrated in Ontario and Quebec. Following Confederation, the total combined population of the four provinces (Ontario, Quebec, Nova Scotia, and New Brunswick) reached 3 486 000. However, as

Table 14.1 *Population Doubling Time**

Area	Years to doubling
World	51 years
More developed countries	809 years
Less developed countries	42 years
Less developed countries (excluding China)	36 years

* Based on rates of population growth in 2000.

SOURCE: Population Reference Bureau. 2000. "2000 World Population Data Sheet."

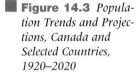

Assuming a fertility rate of 1.7 and net migration (immigration minus emigration) of zero, Canada's population would stop growing in 2022 and then begin a long, lingering decline that would continue until the last Canadian, unable to find a mate anywhere from Victoria to St. John's, died of loneliness in 2786.

DAVID K. FOOT
Demographer
DANIEL STOFFMAN
Journalist

Canada's boundaries expanded to the Hudson's Bay Company territories of Rupert's Land and the North-Western Territory, Manitoba, and British Columbia, its population increased to 3 595 000 in 1871. With the addition of Prince Edward Island in 1873 and the establishment of the provinces of Alberta and Saskatchewan in 1905, Canada continued to increase in population size. Between 1901 and 1931 (and particularly between 1901 and 1911), large-scale immigration helped to almost double the population from 5 371 000 to 10 377 000. However, the 1930s and the years of the Great Depression saw our lowest rate of growth (McVey and Kalbach 1995). Although Canada experienced a high fertility rate during the period of the baby boom (which is generally considered to have occurred in Canada from 1946 to 1959), the birth rate in Canada has been declining since the 1970s.

In 1995–2001, Canada's fertility rate was 1.6 (United Nations 2001). Reasons for this decline include (1) fewer children born to women of child-bearing age following the baby boom (the "baby bust" years), (2) the decline in the size of large families, (3) the increase in the average age of women giving birth for the first time, and (4) the increasing popularity of sterilization as a method of contraception (*Canadian Global Almanac* 2000). It has been estimated that as baby boomers reach old age and the death rate per total population naturally rises, Canada's natural growth in the population will approach zero by 2020 (Figure 14.3). Accordingly, population growth in Canada now depends on immigration.

Sociological Theories of Population and Environmental Problems

The three main sociological perspectives—structural-functionalism, conflict theory, and symbolic interactionism—may be applied to the study of population and environmental problems.

■ **Figure 14.3** *Population Trends and Projections, Canada and Selected Countries, 1920–2020*

SOURCE: Medium variant estimates and projections from United Nations World Population Projections 1992.

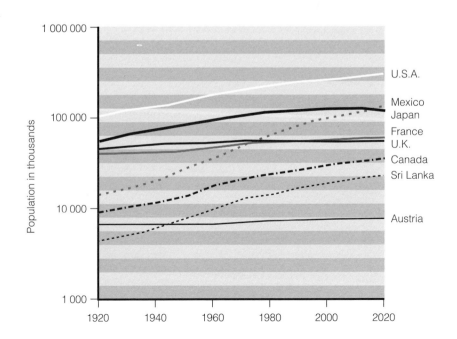

Structural-Functionalist Perspective

Structural-functionalism emphasizes the interdependence between human beings and the natural environment. From this perspective, human actions, social patterns, and cultural values affect the environment and in turn, the environment affects social life. For example, population growth affects the environment, as more people utilize natural resources and contribute to pollution. However, the environmental impact of population growth varies tremendously according to a society's patterns of economic production and consumption (Hunter 2001).

Structural-functionalism focuses on how changes in one aspect of the social system affect other aspects of society. For example, the **demographic transition theory** of population describes how industrialization has affected population growth. According to this theory, in traditional agricultural societies, high fertility rates are necessary to offset high mortality and to ensure continued survival of the population. As a society becomes industrialized and urbanized, improved sanitation, health, and education lead to a decline in mortality. The increased survival rate of infants and children, along with the declining economic value of children, leads to a decline in fertility rates.

Other changes in social structure and culture that affect population include the shift in values toward individualism and self-fulfillment. The availability and cultural acceptability of postnatal forms of family size limitation also affect fertility rates (Mason 1997). In some countries, traditional values permit parents to control family size postnatally by "returning" children at birth (i.e., killing them), selling them to families in need of a child, sending them into bonded labour or prostitution, or marrying them off in early childhood.

The structural-functional perspective is concerned with latent functions—consequences of social actions that are unintended, and not widely recognized. For example, the more than 840 000 dams worldwide provide water to irrigate farmlands and currently supply 19 percent of the world's electricity ("A Prescription for Reducing the Damage Caused by Dams" 2001). Yet dam building has had unintended negative consequences for the environment, including the loss of wetlands and wildlife habitat, the emission of methane (a gas that contributes to global warming) from rotting vegetation trapped in reservoirs, and the altering of river flows downstream killing plant and animal life. Dams have also displaced millions of people from their homes. As philosopher Kathleen Moore points out, "sometimes in maximizing the benefits in one place, you create a greater harm somewhere else...While it might sometimes seem that small acts of cruelty or destruction are justified because they create a greater good, we need to be aware of the hidden systematic costs" (Jensen 2001: 11). Being mindful of latent functions means paying attention to the unintended and often hidden environmental consequences of human activities.

Conflict Perspective

The conflict perspective focuses on how wealth and power, or the lack thereof, affect population and environmental problems. In 1798, Thomas Malthus predicted that population would grow faster than the food supply and that masses of people were destined to be poor and hungry. According to **Malthusian theory**, food shortages would lead to war, disease, and starvation that would eventually slow population growth. However, conflict theorists argue that food

> Big dams did not start out as a cynical enterprise, they began as a dream. They have ended up as a nightmare. It's time to wake up.
>
> ARUNDHATI ROY
> *Author*

shortages result primarily from inequitable distribution of power and resources (Livernash and Rodenburg 1998: 4).

Conflict theorists also note that population growth results from pervasive poverty and the subordinate position of women in many less developed countries. Poor countries have high infant and child mortality rates. Hence, women in many poor countries feel compelled to have many children to increase the chances that some will survive into adulthood. The subordinate position of women prevents many women from limiting their fertility. For example, in 14 countries around the world, a woman must get her husband's consent before she can receive any contraceptive services (United Nations Population Fund 1997). Thus, according to conflict theorists, population problems result from continued inequality within and between nations.

The conflict perspective also emphasizes how wealth, power, and the pursuit of profit underlie many environmental problems. Wealth is related to consumption patterns that cause environmental problems. Wealthy nations have higher per capita consumption of petroleum, wood, metals, cement, and other commodities that deplete the earth's resources, emit pollutants, and generate large volumes of waste (Population Institute 2000). The capitalistic pursuit of profit encourages making money from industry regardless of the damage done to the environment. Further, to maximize sales, manufacturers design products intended to become obsolete. As a result of this **planned obsolescence**, consumers continually throw away used products and purchase replacements. Industry profits at the expense of the environment, which must sustain the constant production and absorb ever-increasing amounts of waste. Industries also use their power and wealth to resist environmental policies that would hurt the industries' profits. For example, to fight the attack on fossil-fuel use (a major polluter and contributor to global warming), petroleum, automobile, coal, and other industries that profit from fossil-fuel consumption created and fund the Global Climate Coalition, an industry-front group that proclaims global warming a myth and characterizes hard evidence of global climate change as "junk science"(Jensen 1999).

A final example of how wealthy and powerful industries pursue profits at the expense of environmental and public health is the "cancer establishment"— organizations and corporations that (1) profit from medical and pharmaceutical products and services designed to detect and treat cancer and/or (2) have a vested interest in keeping public attention on detecting and treating cancer, rather than on preventing it. Rather than focus on preventing cancer by examining the role that environmental pollutants and hazardous substances play in cancer, industries—who are major sources of pollutants and hazardous substances—focus attention on detection and treatment. This approach, some argue, "keep people from understanding 'what is really going on'....While women who detect breast cancer early are better off than those who detect it late, early detection is certainly no guarantee. On the other hand, the focus on detection comes at the expense of any critical questioning about [cancer] causation..." (Barbara Brenner quoted in Mokhiber and Weissman 2000: 11).

Symbolic Interactionist Perspective

The symbolic interaction perspective focuses on how meanings, labels, and definitions learned through interaction affect population and environmental prob-

> Do not live with a vocation that is harmful to humans and nature. Do not invest in companies that deprive others of their chance to live.
>
> THICH NHAT HANH
> *Buddhist monk and teacher*

> Pollution will be recognized as a serious problem when it interferes with TV reception.
>
> HUGH ARSCOTT
> *Aphorist*

lems. For example, many societies are characterized by **pronatalism**—a cultural value that promotes having children. Throughout history, many religions have worshipped fertility and recognized it as being necessary for the continuation of the human race. In many countries, religions prohibit or discourage birth control, contraceptives, and abortion. Women in pronatalist societies learn through interaction with others that deliberate control of fertility is defined as deviant and socially unacceptable. Once some women learn new definitions of fertility control, they become role models and influence the attitudes and behaviours of others in their personal networks (Bongaarts and Watkins 1996).

Meanings, labels, and definitions learned through interaction and the media also affect environmental problems. Whether or not an individual recycles, carpools, or joins an environmental activist group is influenced by the meanings and definitions of these behaviours that the individual learns through interaction with others.

Some businesses and industries have been criticized for attempting to increase profits and increase their public image through a strategy called **greenwashing**. The term greenwashing refers to the way in which environmentally damaging companies portray their corporate image and products as being "environmentally friendly" or socially responsible. As described by Peter Dykstra of Greenpeace, "greenwashing companies depict five percent of environmental virtue to mask 95 percent of environmental vice" (Hager and Burton 2000). Switzer (1997) explains that public relations firms that specialize in damage control for clients whose reputations and profits have been hurt by poor environmental practices commonly use greenwashing. Philip Morris, the infamous cigarette and food producer donated $60 million to charity in 1999, but spent another $180 million in advertising to tell the world about their generosity ("Corporate Spotlight" 2001). DuPont, the biggest private generator of toxic waste in the United States, attempted to project a "green" image by producing a TV ad showing seals clapping, whales and dolphins jumping, and flamingos flying. In an Earth Day event at the National Mall in Washington, D.C., the National Association of Manufacturers (NAM) highlighted renewable and energy-efficient technologies. Yet members of NAM have spent millions of dollars lobbying against use of these very same technologies (Karliner 1998). A logging company facing opposition from environmentalists in New Zealand described their activities as "sustainable harvesting of indigenous production forests"—a phrase that sounds more environmentally friendly than "logging of old growth forests" (Hager and Burton 2000).

Although greenwashing involves manipulation of public perception to maximize profits, many corporations make genuine and legitimate efforts to improve their operations, packaging, or overall sense of corporate responsibility toward the environment (Switzer 1997). For example, in 1990, McDonald's announced it was phasing out foam packaging and switching to a new, paper-based packaging that is partially degradable. Later in this chapter we discuss ways in which industries are participating in alleviating environmental problems.

Social Problems Related to Population Growth

Some of the most urgent social problems today are related to population growth. They include poor maternal and infant health, shortages of food and

> Love has to become a stronger power than the poisons of self-interest and powerlessness or else we will all perish.
>
> ANASTASIA M. SHKILNYK
> *Sociologist*

> The mayor of Elliot Lake, Ontario, Roger Taylor said he had no objection to a permanent dump for radioactive waste being located near his town, because it was not a dump: "It's a containment initiative."
>
> "DOUBLESPEAK"
> The People's Almanac Presents the Twentieth Century

Bottle caps and metal cans do not disintegrate for at least 100 years on the tundra. Fifty to 100 years of plant growth can be snuffed out by a beer can.

ANN H. ZWINGER
Environmental activist

water, environmental degradation, overcrowded cities, and conflict within and between countries. Yet when asked to rate how serious the problem of rapid population growth is on a scale of one to 10 (10 = very serious), only 20 percent of respondents rated rapid population growth as very serious; the average rating was 6.5 (DaVanzo et al. 2000).

Poor Maternal and Infant Health

As noted in Chapter 2, maternal deaths (deaths related to pregnancy and child-birth) are the leading cause of mortality for reproductive-age women in the developing world. Having several children at short intervals increases the chances of premature birth, infectious disease, and death for the mother or the baby. Child-bearing at young ages has been associated with anemia and hemorrhage, obstructed and prolonged labour, infection, and higher rates of infant mortality (Zabin and Kiragu 1998). In developing countries, one in four children are born unwanted, increasing the risk of neglect and abuse. In addition, the more children a woman has, the fewer parental resources (parental income, time, and maternal nutrition) and social resources (health care and education) are available to each child (Catley-Carlson and Outlaw 1998). The adverse health effects of high fertility on women and children are, in themselves, compelling reasons for providing women with family planning services. "Reproductive health and choice are often the key to a woman's ability to stay alive, to protect the health of her children and to provide for herself and her family" (Catley-Carlson and Outlaw 1998: 241).

Increased Global Food Requirements

As populations expand, more food must be grown to feed them. This presents a challenge, especially for countries that have not been able to meet the food needs of their current populations. In 1950, 500 million people (20 percent of the world's population) were considered malnourished; in the late 1990s, more than three billion people (one-half of the world's population) suffered from malnutrition (Pimentel et al. 1998).

The greatest challenge of the coming century is the maintenance of growth in global food production to match or exceed the projected doubling (at least) of the human population.

PAUL EHRLICH
ANNE H. EHRLICH
Demographers
GRETCHEN C. DAILY
Biologist

Countries with large populations, few resources, and limited land are particularly vulnerable to food shortages. An estimated 420 million people live today in countries that have less than 0.7 hectare of cultivated land per person (less than one-seventh the size of a football field)—the minimum parcel capable of supplying a vegetarian diet for one person without costly chemicals and fertilizers (Engelman et al. 2000).

As global food requirements increase with population growth, so do demands on the environment. Agricultural activities contribute to the destruction of forests and the species that inhabit them: nearly one-third of temperate, tropical, and subtropical forests have been converted to agriculture (Wood, et al. 2000). Expanding agricultural activities also deplete water supplies, as agriculture consumes 70 percent of the fresh water used by humans (primarily for irrigation). Pesticides and fertilizers used in agriculture contaminate soil and water. Although genetically modified crops are extolled as providing solutions to some of the environmental problems associated with feeding an expanding population, these crops pose potential environmental problems as well (see the *Focus on Technology* feature in Chapter 10).

Water Shortages and Depletion of Other Natural Resources

Global water use has tripled since 1950. Canadians tend to take fresh water availability for granted, as they water lawns and clean their cars, take long showers, and leave the water running while they brush their teeth. But the authors of *State of the World 1998* suggest that "one of the most underrated issues facing the world as it enters the third millennium is spreading water scarcity" (Brown et al. 1998: 5). About 40 percent of the world population faces water shortages at some time during the year (Zwingle 1998) and 13 countries are expected to have chronic water shortages by 2025 ("Water Wars Forecast if Solutions Not Found" 1999). The number of people living in countries facing severe or chronic water shortages is projected to increase more than four-fold over the next 25 years, from an estimated 505 million people in 2000 to between 2.4 and 3.2 billion people by 2025 (Engelman et al. 2000).

Water shortages are exacerbating international conflict. Jordan, Israel, and Syria compete for the waters of the Jordan River basin. Jordan's King Hussein declared that water was the only issue that could lead him to declare war on Israel (Mitchell 1998). Speaking of the water shortage, General Federico Mayor, director of UNESCO, warned, "[a]s it becomes increasingly rare, it becomes coveted, capable of unleashing conflicts. More than petrol or land, it is over water that the most bitter conflicts of the near future may be fought" ("Water Wars Forecast if Solutions Not Found" 1999).

Population growth also contributes to the depletion of other natural resources such as forests, oil, gas, coal, and certain minerals. Later in this chapter, we discuss environmental problems associated with the use of these natural resources.

> It doesn't matter how much rainfall is received, if it isn't captured, an area can still be short of water. It is unbelievable but true that Cherrapunji, which gets 11 000 mm of annual rainfall, still suffers from serious drinking water shortages.
>
> CENTRE FOR SCIENCE AND ENVIRONMENT, NEW DELHI, INDIA

Urban Crowding and High Population Density

Population growth contributes to urban crowding and high population density. Without economic and material resources to provide for basic living needs, urban populations in developing countries often live in severe poverty. Urban poverty in turn produces environmental problems such as the unsanitary disposal of waste. In Nigerian urban ghettos, for example, the "mounds of refuse (including human wastes) that litter everywhere—gutters, schools, roads, market places and town squares—have been accepted as part of the way of life" (Nzeako, quoted in Agbese 1995). The World Health Organization estimates that half the people in the world do not have access to a decent toilet. Unsanitary disposal of human waste contaminates water supplies. Half the people in the developing world suffer from diseases caused by poor sanitation. Diarrhea caused by many of these diseases is the leading killer of children today (Gardner 1998).

Densely populated urban areas facilitate the spread of disease among people. Infectious diseases cause more than one-third of all deaths worldwide. Crowded conditions in urban areas provide the ideal environment for the culture and spread of diseases such as cholera and tuberculosis (Pimentel et al. 1998).

> Environmental scarcity has insidious and cumulative social impacts, such as population movement, economic decline, and the weakening of states. These can contribute to diffuse and persistent sub-national violence. The rate and extent of such conflicts will increase as scarcities worsen.
>
> THOMAS F. HOMER-DIXON
> *Political Scientist*

Strategies for Action: Slowing Population Growth

In some countries with below-replacement-level birthrates, government policies have attempted to encourage rather than discourage childbearing. For example, Italy, Germany, and France have implemented generous child subsidies, in the form of tax credits for every child born, extended maternal leave with full pay, guaranteed employment on returning to work, and free childcare (Cooper 1998). In Japan, a country with one of the world's lowest birth rates, (1.4 children per woman), a Japanese toy company is offering its employees $10 000 for every baby born after the second child ("Japanese Toy Firm Offers Employees Fertility Incentives" 2000).

Most strategies related to population involve attempts to slow population growth by reducing fertility levels. Strategies for slowing population growth include providing access to birth control methods, improving the status of women, increasing economic development and improving health status, and imposing governmental regulations and policies. However, while industrialized countries provided $2.1 billion in international assistance for reproductive health and population programs in 2000, this is far less than the $5.7 billion suggested by The International Conference on Population and Development (United Nations Population Fund 2000).

Even if every country in the world achieved replacement-level fertility rates (an average of 2.1 births per woman), populations would continue to grow for several decades because of **population momentum**—continued population growth as a result of past high fertility rates which have resulted in large numbers of young women who are currently entering their childbearing years.

Provide Access to Birth Control Methods

The question that society must answer is this: Shall family limitation be achieved through birth control or abortion? Shall normal, safe, effective contraceptives be employed, or shall we continue to force women to the abnormal, often dangerous surgical operation? Contraceptives or abortion—which shall it be?

MARGARET SANGER
Birth control advocate

An estimated 120 million women worldwide do not have access to safe family planning services because such services do not exist or cultural and religious barriers prevent their use (Halwell 2000). Another 350 million women—nearly a third of all women of reproductive age in developing countries—have incomplete or sporadic access to safe family planning services (Halwell 2000). In some countries, methods of birth control are provided only to married women. Family planning personnel often refuse, or are forbidden by law or policy, to make referrals for contraceptive and abortion services for unmarried women. Finally, many women throughout the world do not have access to legal, safe abortion. Without access to contraceptives, many women who experience unwanted pregnancy resort to abortion—even under illegal and unsafe conditions (see also Chapter 2).

Significant gains have been made in increasing contraceptive use in less developed countries. Today, more than half of married women in less developed countries use some form of contraceptive, compared with 10 percent in 1960 (Population Reference Bureau 2000b). But use of contraceptives is still very low in some countries, particularly those in sub-Saharan Africa (see Figure 14.4). In Yemen, only 10 percent of married women use modern contraceptive methods, and only 8 percent do so in Uganda (Hunter 2001).

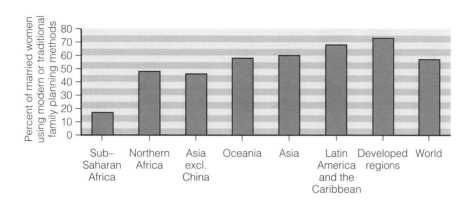

■ **Figure 14.4** *Contraceptive Use in Selected Regions*

SOURCE: Population Reference Bureau. 1999. "1999 World Population Data Sheet." Washington, DC: Population Reference Bureau.

Improve the Status of Women

Throughout the developing world, the status of women is primarily restricted to that of wife and mother. Women in developing countries traditionally have not been encouraged to seek education or employment, but rather to marry early and have children. In some countries, a woman must obtain the consent of her husband before she can receive contraceptive services. In a study in Zambia, one man interviewed said: "I cannot allow my wife to become a whore. Women who use contraceptives cannot be trusted" (quoted in Population Reference Bureau 2000b: 3).

Improving the status of women is vital to curbing population growth. Education plays a key role in improving the status of women and in reducing fertility rates. Educated women are more likely to delay their first pregnancies, to use safe and effective contraception, and to limit and space their children (United Nations Population Fund 2000; Population Institute 2000). Providing employment opportunities for women is also important to slowing population growth; high levels of female labour force participation and higher wages for women are associated with smaller family size (Population Reference Bureau 2000c).

Increase Economic Development and Health Status

Although fertility reduction may be achieved without industrialization, economic development may play an important role in slowing population growth. Families in poor countries often rely on having many children to provide enough labour and income to support the family. Economic development decreases the economic value of children. Economic development is also associated with more education for women and greater gender equality. As previously noted, women's education and status are related to fertility levels. Economic development tends to result in improved health status of populations. Reductions in infant and child mortality are important for fertility decline, as couples no longer need to have many pregnancies to ensure that some children survive into adulthood. Finally, the more developed a country is, the more likely women will be exposed to meanings and values that promote fertility control through interaction in educational settings and through media and information technologies (Bongaarts and Watkins 1996).

Impose Government Regulations and Policies

The higher the educational level and social status of women in a society, the fewer the children. This reverse correlation seems to hold true across economic, cultural, and religious barriers.

David Suzuki
Scientist, environmentalist, and broadcaster
Holly Dressel
Writer

Some countries have imposed strict governmental regulations on reproduction. In the 1970s, India established mass sterilization camps and made the salaries of public servants contingent on their recruiting a quota of citizens who would accept sterilization. The Indian state of Maharashtra enacted compulsory sterilization legislation and in a six-month period sterilized millions of people, many of them against their will (Boland et al. 1994). This policy has since been rescinded.

Governmental population regulations in China are less extreme, but still controversial. In 1979, China developed a one-child family policy whereby parents get special privileges for limiting their family size. Specifically, parents who pledge to have only one child receive an allowance for health care for five years that effectively increases their annual income by 10 percent. Parents who have only one child also have priority access to hospitals and receive a pension when they reach old age. In addition, their only child is given priority enrollment in nursery school and is exempted from school tuition. However, China has begun to phase out its one-child-per-family policy, largely because Chinese officials conclude that there will not be enough adult children to care for aging parents unless the one-child policy is ended ("China Phasing Out One-Child Policy" 2000). To begin the phase-out, the Chinese government now offers exemptions to adults who have no siblings. When two of these adults with no siblings marry, they are allowed to have two children and prevent a second generation in which one couple must be responsible for four elderly parents with no siblings to help.

Environmental Problems

An expanding population is one of many factors that contribute to environmental problems such as land, water, and air pollution and depletion of natural resources. Before reading further, you may want to take the Eco-Quiz in this chapter's *Self and Society* feature.

Air Pollution

I suggest that, as the human population grows and environmental damage progresses, policymakers will have less and less capacity to intervene to keep this damage from producing serious social disruption, including conflict.

Thomas F. Homer-Dixon
Political scientist

Transportation vehicles, fuel combustion, industrial processes (such as the burning of coal and wood), and solid waste disposal have contributed to the growing levels of air pollutants, including carbon monoxide, sulphur dioxide, nitrogen dioxides, and lead. Air pollution levels are highest in areas with both heavy industry and traffic congestion, such as Los Angeles, New Delhi, Jakarta, Bangkok, Tehran, Beijing, and Mexico City. In the mid-1990s, breathing the air in Mexico City was like smoking two packs of cigarettes a day (Weiner 2001).

In Canada, the latest craze of boomers—minivans, sport utility vehicles (SUVs), and other light trucks—has alarmed environmentalists. These vehicles, when compared with the standard passenger car, not only guzzle one-third more gas, but also spew one-third more pollution out their tailpipes. However, recent industry surveys of customer preferences suggest that such vehicle amenities as coffee-cup holders outrank green concerns, and that "[f]uel efficiency is not at the top of consumers' lists in terms of purchasing requirements. It ranks 9th to 15th on their list of criteria, depending on the study. Coffee cups rank higher. Stereos rank higher" (as cited in Speirs 2000: A24). While the

David Suzuki Foundation has remarked that "[t]his light truck category is a moving disaster" (Speirs 2000: A24), sales of light trucks have accounted for more than 50 percent of the passenger vehicle market in recent years.

Indoor Air Pollution When we hear the phrase "air pollution," we typically think of smokestacks and vehicle exhausts pouring grey streams of chemical matter into the air. However, much air pollution is invisible to the eye and exists where we least expect it—in our homes, schools, workplaces, and public buildings. Common household, personal, and commercial products contribute to indoor pollution. Some of the most common indoor pollutants include carpeting (which emits nearly 100 different chemical gases), mattresses (which may emit formaldehyde and aldehydes), drain cleaners, oven cleaners, spot removers, shoe polish, dry-cleaned clothes, paints, varnishes, furniture polish, potpourri, mothballs, fabric softener, and caulking compounds. Air fresheners, deodorizers, and disinfectants emit the pesticide paradichlorobenzene. Potentially harmful organic solvents are present in numerous office supplies, including glue, correction fluid, printing ink, carbonless paper, and felt-tip markers.

In poor countries, fumes from cooking and heating are major contributors to indoor air pollution. About half of the world's population and up to 90 percent of rural households in developing countries rely on wood, dung, and crop residues for fuel (Bruce et al. 2000). These fuels are typically burnt indoors in open fires or poorly functioning stoves, producing hazardous emissions such as soot particles, carbon monoxide, nitrous oxides, sulphur oxides, and formaldehyde. An estimated two million deaths in developing countries each year result from exposure to indoor air pollution (Bruce et al. 2000).

Destruction of the Ozone Layer The use of human-made chlorofluorocarbons (CFCs), which are used in refrigerators, cleaning computer chips, hospital sterilization, solvents, dry cleaning, and aerosols, has damaged the ozone layer of the earth's atmosphere. The depletion of the ozone layer allows hazardous levels of ultraviolet rays to reach the earth's surface. Ultraviolet light has been linked to increases in skin cancer and cataracts, declining food crops, rising sea levels, and global warming. The largest ozone hole is over Antarctica and spans 18.5 million square kilometres (Stiefel 2000). Previously, this ozone hole exposed only ocean and barren land in Antarctica. But now it exposes Puntas Arenas, Chile, a populous city near the southern tip of South America.

Acid Rain Air pollutants, such as sulphur dioxide and nitrogen oxide, mix with precipitation to form **acid rain**. Polluted rain, snow, and fog contaminate crops, forests, lakes, and rivers. Acid rain is a particular threat in Ontario, New Brunswick, Nova Scotia, and Quebec because these provinces are directly in the path of much of the continent's SO_2 and NO_x emissions, and the nonporous granite that composes the majority of the Canadian Shield is less able to absorb acid rain. Roughly 40 percent of Canada's total land area (approximately 4 million square kilometres) is extremely sensitive to acid rain (Statistics Canada 1998). Moreover, because pollutants in the air are carried by the wind, industrial pollution in the midwest United States falls back to Earth as acid rain on southeast Canada and the northeast New England states. However, acid rain is not just a problem in North America; it decimates plant and animal species around the globe.

Environmental Knowledge Survey

Directions: After answering each of the following items, check your answers for items 2 through 11 using the answer key provided. For items 2 through 11, calculate the total number of items you answered correctly.

1. In general, how much do you feel you yourself know about environmental issues and problems—would you say you know a lot, a fair amount, only a little, or practically nothing?
   a. A lot
   b. A fair amount
   c. Only a little
   d. Practically nothing
   e. Don't know

2. How is most of the electricity in Canada generated?
   a. By burning oil, coal, and wood
   b. With nuclear power
   c. Through solar energy
   d. At hydroelectric power plants
   e. Don't know

3. What is the most common cause of pollution of streams, rivers, and oceans?
   a. Dumping of garbage by cities
   b. Surface water running off yards, city streets, paved lots, and farm fields
   c. Trash washed into the ocean from beaches
   d. Waste dumped by factories
   e. Don't know

4. What do you think is the main cause of global climate change, that is, the warming of the planet Earth?
   a. A recent increase in oxygen in the atmosphere
   b. Sunlight radiating more strongly through a hole in the upper ozone layer
   c. More carbon emissions from autos, homes, and industry
   d. Increased activity from volcanoes worldwide
   e. Don't know

5. To the best of your knowledge, what percentage of the world's water is fresh and available for use?
   a. 1%
   b. 5%
   c. 10%
   d. 33%
   e. Don't know

6. The current worldwide reduction in the number of ocean fish is *primarily* the result of which of the following?
   a. Pollution in coastal waters worldwide
   b. Increased harvesting by fishing vessels
   c. Changes in ocean temperature
   d. Loss of fishing shoals and other deep sea habitats
   e. Don't know

7. What is the leading cause of childhood death worldwide?
   a. Malnutrition and starvation
   b. Asthma from dust in the air
   c. Auto and home accidents
   d. Germs in the water
   e. Don't know

8. What is the most common reason that an animal species becomes extinct?
   a. Pesticides are killing them
   b. Humans are destroying their habitats
   c. There is too much hunting
   d. Climate changes are affecting them
   e. Don't know

9. Thousands of waste disposal areas—dumps and landfills—in Canada contain toxic waste. The greatest threat posed by these waste disposal areas is:
   a. Chemical air pollution
   b. Contact with farm animals and household pets
   c. Contamination of water supplies
   d. Human consumption through contaminated food
   e. Don't know

10. Many communities are concerned about running out of room in their community trash dumps and landfills. What is the greatest source of landfill material?
    a. Disposable diapers
    b. Lawn and garden clippings, trimmings, and leaves
    c. Paper products including newspapers, cardboard, and packaging
    d. Glass and plastic bottles and aluminum and steel cans
    e. Don't know

11. Some scientists have expressed concern that chemicals and certain minerals accumulate in the human body at dangerous levels. These chemicals and minerals enter the body primarily through
    a. Breathing air
    b. Living near toxic waste dumps
    c. Household cleaning products
    d. Drinking water
    e. Don't know

Answer Key for Items 2 through 11: 2d, 3b, 4c, 5a, 6b, 7d, 8b, 9c, 10c, 11d

Average Number of Correct Responses in a U.S. national survey: 3.2 (Note: Questions 2 and 9 referred to the United States.)

SOURCE: Adapted with permission of the National Environmental Education and Training Foundation.

Global Warming

A trend of increasing air temperature provides evidence of global warming. Globally, the 1990s was the warmest decade on record. Average global air temperature rose by 0.6 degrees Celsius over the twentieth century and, between 1990 and 2100, is expected to rise another 1.4 to 5.8 degrees Celsius (Intergovernmental Panel on Climate Change 2001a).

Causes of Global Warming The main cause of **global warming** is the accumulation of various gases that collect in the atmosphere and act like the glass in a greenhouse, holding heat from the sun close to the earth and preventing it from rising back into space. **Greenhouse gases** include carbon dioxide, methane, and nitrous oxide. In Canada, more than a third of emissions "come directly from the energy industry, a byproduct of oil, gas, coal, and electricity production. The remaining two-thirds is released by industries and activities that subsequently use that energy. Transportation accounts for 25 percent of all emissions" (Stanford 2002: 12). Due to the heavy pollution caused by oil and gas operations, Alberta is "far and away Canada's leading greenhouse gas polluter, releasing more emissions than Ontario (which has four times the population...[or] in per capita terms, more than three times the Canadian average" (Stanford 2002: 12) (Figure 14.5).

Since 1750, atmospheric concentrations of carbon dioxide have increased by 31 percent; methane by 153 percent, and nitrous oxide by 17 percent (Intergovernmental Panel on Climate Change 2001a). Three-fourths of human-activity-related emission of carbon dioxide during the last 20 years is the result of fossil fuel burning; the rest is predominantly caused by deforestation. Trees and other plant life utilize carbon dioxide and release oxygen into the air. As forests are cut down, fewer trees are available to absorb the carbon dioxide.

Effects of Global Warming Numerous effects of global warming have been observed and are anticipated in the future (Intergovernmental Panel on Climate Change 2001b). As temperature increases, some areas will experience heavier rain, while other regions will get drier. Whereas some regions will experience increased water availability and crop yields, other regions, particularly tropical and subtropical regions, are expected to experience decreased water availability and a reduction of crop yields. Global warming results in shifts of plant and animal habitats and the increased risk of extinction of some species. Regions that experience increased rainfall as a result of increasing temperatures may face increases in waterborne diseases and diseases transmitted by insects. Over time, climate change may produce opposite effects on the same resource. For example, in the short-term, forest productivity is likely to increase in response to higher levels of carbon dioxide in the air, but over the long term, forest productivity is likely to decrease because of drought, fire, insects, and disease.

Global warming also threatens to melt glaciers and permafrost, resulting in a rise in sea level. Global average sea levels rose 0.1 to 0.2 metres during the twentieth century, and are expected to rise by 0.09 to 0.88 metres from 1990 to 2100. As sea levels rise, some island countries, as well as some barrier islands, are likely to disappear and low-lying coastal areas will become increasingly vulnerable to storm surges and flooding (Hunter 2001). In urban areas, flooding can be a problem where storm drains and waste management systems are inadequate. Increased flooding associated with global warming is expected to result in

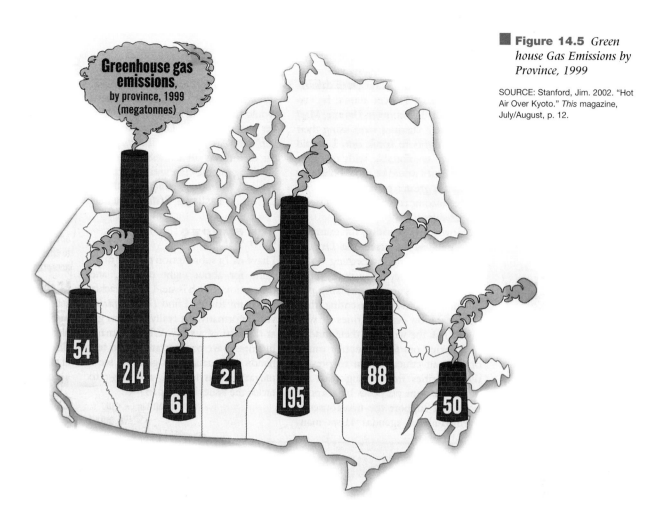

■ **Figure 14.5** *Green house Gas Emissions by Province, 1999*

SOURCE: Stanford, Jim. 2002. "Hot Air Over Kyoto." *This* magazine, July/August, p. 12.

increases in drownings and diarrheal and respiratory diseases. An increase in the number of people exposed to insect- and water-related diseases, such as malaria and cholera, are also expected. Even if greenhouse gases are stabilized, global air temperature and sea level are expected to continue to rise for hundreds of years.

Land Pollution

About 30 percent of the world's surface is land, which provides soil to grow the food we eat. Increasingly, humans are polluting the land with toxic and radioactive waste, solid waste, and pesticides.

Toxic and Radioactive Waste The global community generates more than a million tons of hazardous waste each day (Brown 1995). In the United States alone, decades of nuclear weapons production has polluted more than 2.3 million acres of land in at least 24 U.S. states; cleanup will extend well into the twenty-first century at a cost of more than $200 billion (Black 1999). Radioactive waste from nuclear power plants and major weapons production sites is associated with cancer and genetic defects. Radioactive plutonium, used in both

The question is, when do we all become indigenous people? When do we become native to this place? When do we decide we are not leaving?

BILL MCDONOUGH
Architect and designer

nuclear power and weapons production, has a half-life (the time it takes for its radioactivity to be reduced by half) of 24 000 years (Mead 1998). The disposal of nuclear waste is particularly problematic. The U.S. Nuclear Regulatory Commission licenses nuclear reactors for 40 years. When nuclear reactors reach the end of their 40-year licences, the radioactive waste must be stored somewhere. About 28 000 metric tons of nuclear waste are already stored around the United States. This figure is expected to grow to 48 000 metric tons by 2003 and 87 000 metric tons by 2030 (not including waste from military nuclear operations) (Stover 1995). The United States has also promised to accept nuclear waste from about 40 nations with nuclear research reactors.

In Canada, radioactive waste has been produced since the early 1930s, when the first uranium mine began operating in the Northwest Territories at Port Radium (see Figure 14.6). Radium was refined for medical use and uranium was later processed at Port Hope, Ontario. In the 1940s, research and development on the application of nuclear energy to produce electricity began at the Chalk River Laboratories (CRL) of Atomic Energy of Canada Limited (AECL). Currently, radioactive waste is produced from uranium mining, milling, refining

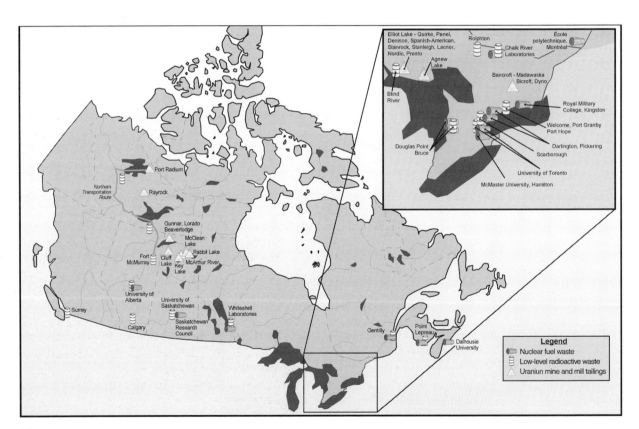

Figure 14.6 *Radioactive Waste Sites in Canada as of December 31, 1998*

Note: These locations relate to the peaceful applications of nuclear energy; national-defence related sites are not included.

SOURCE: Duke Engineering and Services (Canada), Inc. 1999. "Executive Summary." *Inventory of Radioactive Waste in Canada: A Report Prepared for the Low-Level Radioactive Waste Management Office.* Gloucester, Ontario. Low-Level Radioactive Waste Management Office, November.

and conversion; nuclear fuel fabrication; nuclear reactor operations; and nuclear research and radioisotope manufacture and use. Under Canada's Radioactive Waste Policy Framework, producers and owners of radioactive waste are responsible for the funding, organization, management, and operation of disposal and other facilities required for their waste.

The cost of storing radioactive waste and cleaning other hazardous waste sites is immense, but not cleaning these sites is also costly. Brown (1995) remarks that "one way or another, society will pay—either in clean up bills or in rising health care costs" (p. 416). Scientists have proposed several options for disposing of nuclear waste, including burying it in rock formations deep below the Earth's surface or under Antarctic ice, injecting it into the ocean floor, or hurling it into outer space. Each of these options is risky and costly. Recognizing the environmental hazards of nuclear power plants and their waste, Germany has become the first country to order all of its 19 nuclear power plants shut down by 2020 ("Nukes Rebuked" 2000). Nevertheless, at the end of 1999, 431 nuclear reactors were operating around the world (Lenssen 2000).

In addition, the devastation caused by the 1986 accident at the Chernobyl nuclear reactor in the former Soviet Union should serve as a powerful reminder of the devastating toll caused by nuclear mishaps. In 2002, the Canadian Safety Commission announced that it would be funding research to examine the foreseeable consequences should one of Canada's nuclear power plants have a major accident. The study was to provide a calculation of the number of people who would die immediately as well as those who would later suffer from fatal cancers, non-fatal cancers, and early morbidity. The economic consequences, which were anticipated to be "staggering," would include the costs of the farmland, businesses, and homes whose values would be impaired by such an accident, as well as the costs of accommodating those who would be forced to move from adjacent areas (Mittelstaedt 2002).

The infamous tar ponds of Sydney, Nova Scotia are the largest toxic waste dump in North America. For over 50 years, the effluent from the provincially owned steel mills and coke ovens was "dumped without the slightest attempt at containment" (Suzuki and Dressel 2002: 296). As a result,

> It now contaminates the springs, streams, ditches, wells, and the entire estuary of this habour town. The "tar ponds" at the back of the estuary contain 700 000 tons of sludge containing every known polyaromatic hydrocarbon (PAH), including naphthalene, benzene, toluene, and benzopyrene—all recognized carcinogens—plus PCBs. Besides that, more than 125 acres (50 hectares) of land where the coke ovens used to stand are saturated to depths of 25 meters with more PAHS, as well as arsenic, cyanide, lead, and other heavy metals. (Suzuki and Dressel 2002: 296)

Solid Waste According to the Canadian Waste Management Industry Survey, governments and businesses disposed of 20.6 million tons of waste in 1996, the equivalent of approximately 620 kilograms of waste for each Canadian (Statistics Canada 1999). Some of this waste is converted into energy by incinerators; more than half is taken to landfills. However, it has been reported that no less than a trillion litres of raw and partially treated sewage are dumped into Canada's waters every year (CELA 1999). This chapter's *Focus on Technology* feature examines the hazards associated with disposing of computers in landfills (and other environmental and health hazards of computers).

> The high-tech electronics industry uses vast amounts of dangerous chemicals and significantly depletes natural resources to fuel its global expansion and rapidly changing product lines. There are few other products for which the sum of the environmental impacts of raw material extraction, industrial refining and production, use and disposal is so extensive.
>
> SILICON VALLEY TOXICS COALITION

Environmental and Public Health Hazards Associated with Computers

Computers play an important role in improving and protecting the environment in several ways. First, computers are an important part of environmental education, as they provide improved public access to information about environmental issues. Second, through video-conferencing and e-mail, computers help reduce the use of paper. Finally, computers have enabled hundreds of thousands of individuals to participate in on-line activism, which has become a vital part of the environmental movement. Yet, the production and disposal of computers pose significant hazards to public and environmental health.

The Hazards of Computer Manufacturing, Disposal and Recycling

Computer equipment is composed of more than 1000 materials, many of which are highly toxic. Toxic components in computers include lead and cadmium in computer circuit boards, lead oxide and barium in computer monitors' cathode ray tubes, mercury in switches and flat screens, brominated flame retardants on printed circuit boards, cables and plastic casing, polychlorinated biphenyls (PCBs) present in older capacitors and transformers, and polyvinyl chloride (PVC)-coated copper cables and plastic computer casings that release highly toxic dioxins and furans when burned (Silicon Valley Toxic Coalition 2001a).

The average computer now has a lifespan of about two years. Hardware and software companies constantly generate new programs that demand more speed, memory, and power, and it is usually cheaper and more convenient to buy a new machine than it is to upgrade the old. Estimates suggest that over three-quarters of all computers ever bought are currently stored in people's attics, basements, office closets, and pantries (Silicon Valley Toxics Coalition 2001b). Many of these computers are destined for landfills, incinerators, or hazardous waste exports. Only about 14 percent of unwanted computers are recycled or donated. It is estimated that 67 324 tons of information technology equipment (including monitors, notebooks and peripherals, will be disposed of in Canada in 2005 (Enviros 2000).

The toxic materials used in computer manufacturing pose significant hazards for workers in the production of computers. In addition, the toxic **e-waste** (waste from electronic equipment) makes the disposal and recycling of computers a human and environmental hazard.

Hazards of Computer Production. The production of semiconductors, printed circuit boards, disk drives, and monitors uses particularly hazardous chemicals, and workers in chip manufacturing are reporting cancer clusters and birth defects (Silicon Valley Toxics Coalition 2001b).

Hazards of Disposing E-Waste. Most discarded computers end up in landfills, and when we consider that all landfills leak and eventually allow a certain amount of chemical and metal leaching, the mountains of e-waste destined for landfills are particularly disturbing. In many city landfills, cathode ray tubes from computers and TVs are the largest source of lead (Motavalli 2001). Computer monitors (medium size) contain an average of two to four kilograms of lead (Fisher 2000). Lead can cause damage to the central and peripheral nervous systems, endocrine system, circulatory system, and kidneys. Its serious negative effects on children's brain development have been well documented. Lead accumulates in the environment and has high acute and chronic toxic effects on plants, animals, and microorganisms. The main concern in regard to the presence of lead in landfills is the potential for the lead to leach and contaminate water supplies. Other toxic materials that leach into the soil and groundwater from land-filled computers include mercury and cadmium.

Some computer waste is disposed of through incineration (burning). Incineration of scrap computers generates extremely toxic dioxins that are released in air emissions. Incineration of computers also results in high concentration of toxic heavy metals in the flue gas residues, fly ash, and filter cake.

Hazards of Recycling Computers. The presence of toxic polybrominated flame retardants in computers makes recycling dangerous and difficult. High concentrations of these substances have been found in the blood of workers in recycling plants. In addition, a Swedish study found that when computers, fax machines, or other electronic equipment are recycled, dust containing toxic flame retardants is spread in the air (Silicon Valley Toxics Coalition 2001b).

The Exportation of Hazardous E-Waste. Industrialized countries generate the majority of the world's hazardous waste. Exporting this waste to less developed countries has been one way in which the industrialized world has cut costs of waste disposal. In 1989 the world community established the Basel Convention on the Transboundary Movement of Hazardous Waste for Final Disposal to stop industrialized nations from dumping their waste on less developed countries. (The United States, however, has declined to sign the Convention. In the United States, an estimated one million of the 1.7 million monitors recycled in 1997 were shipped abroad for processing (Fisher 2000)).

Over 60 countries have agreed to ban exports of hazardous waste to poor countries. But this ban did not stop the transport of waste that countries claimed was being exported for recycling purposes. China and 77 non-OECD countries supported a ban on the shipping of waste for recycling. As a result, the Basel Ban was adopted, promising to end the export of hazardous waste from rich OECD countries to poor non-OECD countries—even when the waste was exported for recycling. The United States has declined to participate in the ban and has lobbied Asian governments to establish bilateral trade agreements to allow continued exporting of hazardous waste after the Basel Ban came into effect on January 1, 1998. The amount of computer scrap exported from the United States is expected to grow as product obsolescence increases (Silicon Valley Toxics Coalition 2001b).

SomeSoutions to the Problem of Toxic E-Waste

The European Union's WEEE Directive. The European Union (comprising 15 European nations) has proposed legislation on Waste from Electrical and Electronic Equipment (the WEEE directive) that would make producers responsible for taking back their old products and phasing out the use of certain toxic materials in computer manufacturing, and would encourage cleaner product design and less waste generation. This strategy, known as *Extended Producer Responsibility*, is based on the principle that producers bear a degree of responsibility for all the environmental impacts of their products. This includes impacts arising from the choice of materials and from the manufacturing process as well as the use and disposal of products. By making manufacturers financially responsible for waste management of their products, electronic producers will have a financial incentive to design their products with less hazardous and more recyclable materials. Various European countries (the Netherlands, Denmark, Sweden, Austria, Belgium, Italy, Finland, and Germany) have already drafted legislation requiring Extended Producer Responsibility. The WEEE Directive would harmonize all these countries' initiatives to allow industry to operate uniformly throughout Europe. The WEEE Directive calls for the following (Silicon Valley Toxics Coalition 2001b):

- The use of mercury, cadmium, hexavalent chromium, and two classes of brominated flame retardants in electronic and electrical goods must be phased out by the year 2004.
- Producers of electronics must bear full financial responsibility for setting up collection, recycling, and disposal systems.
- Seventy percent of collected computers and monitors must be recycled. "Recycling" does not include incineration, so companies won't be able to meet recycling goals by burning the waste.
- For disposal, incineration with energy recovery is allowed for the 10 percent to 30 percent of waste remaining. However, components containing certain toxic substances (such as lead, mercury, and cadmium) must be removed from any equipment that is destined for landfill, incineration, or recovery.
- Member states shall encourage producers to integrate an increasing quantity of recycled material in new products. Originally the EU stipulated that by 2004 new equipment must contain at least 5 percent of recycled plastic content but this provision was recently dropped because of intense industry lobbying.
- Producers must design equipment that includes labels for recyclers that identify plastic types and location of all dangerous substances.
- Producers can undertake the treatment operation in another country, but this should not lead to shipments of e-waste to non-European Union (EU) countries where no or lower treatment

(continued)

standards than in the EU exist. Accordingly, producers shall deliver e-waste only to those establishments that comply with the treatment and recycling requirements set out in the proposal.

Industry Initiatives. A number of industries have taken steps to alleviate the environmental hazards of computers. Some computer manufacturers such as Dell and Gateway lease out their products, thereby ensuring that they get them back to further upgrade and lease out again. In 1998 IBM introduced the first computer that uses 100 percent recycled resin in all major plastic parts. Hewlett-Packard Company has developed a safe cleaning method for chips using carbon dioxide cleaning as a substitute for hazardous solvents. On July 23, 2002, Hewlett-Packard (Canada)

Ltd. also launched a take-back service that allows Canadian consumers and businesses to recycle unwanted computers and equipment (Hewlett Packard 2002). Toshiba is working on a modular upgradeable and customizable computer to reduce product obsolescence. Pressures to eliminate halogenated flame retardants and design products for recycling have led to the use of metal shielding in computer housings and a range of lead-free solders is now available.

As governments and industries continue to develop strategies for reducing environmental hazards associated with computer manufacturing and disposal, consumers can also make a difference by choosing manufacturers who practise "Product Stewardship" by making products that are less toxic, conserve natural resources, and reduce waste. *A Guide to Environmentally*

Preferable Computer Purchasing is available from the Northwest Product Stewardship Council at http://www.govlink.org/nwpsc/. Information on Hewlett-Packard's take-back service can be accessed via the Web at http://www.hp.ca/recycle.

SOURCES: Enviros RS. 2000 (October). "Information Technology (IT) and Telecommunications (Telecom) Waste in Canada." Ottawa: Prepared for Environment Canada, National Office of Pollution Prevention. Fisher, Jim. 2000. "Poison PCs." September 18. http://www.salon.com/tech/feature/2000/09/18/toxic_pc/: Hewlett-Packard (Canada) Ltd. 2002. "HP Take-Back Program Offers Canadian Businesses and Consumers Convenient and Environmentally Safe Way to Recycle Computers." July 23. http://www.hp.com/hpinfo/newsroom/press23jul02a.htm. Motavalli, Jim. 2001. "Is There an Afterlife for Your Computer?" *Environmental Defence*, XXXII(2), March: 6. Silicon Valley Toxics Coalition. 2001a. "Why Focus on Computers?" http://www.svtc.org/cleancc/focus/htm. Silicon Valley Toxics Coalition. 2001b. *"Just Say No to E-Waste: Background Document on Hazards and Waste from Computers.* http://www.svtc.org.

Pesticides Pesticides are used worldwide in the growing of crops and gardens; outdoor mosquito control; the care of lawns, parks, and golf courses; and indoor pest control. Pesticides contaminate food, water, and air and can be absorbed through the skin, swallowed, or inhaled. Many common pesticides are considered potential carcinogens and neurotoxins. However, even when a pesticide is found to be hazardous and is banned in Canada, other countries may continue to use it. In this chapter's *Social Problems Research Up Close*, we highlight research conducted by the Ontario College of Family Physicians (Environmental Health Committee) and the Canadian Environmental Law Association (CELA), which provides an urgent warning about the health dangers pesticide use poses to children.

Water Pollution

Many harmful substances, including pesticides, industrial waste, acid rain, and oil spills, are polluting our water. Although Canada is home to approximately one-seventh of the world's accessible fresh water, we cannot afford to become complacent. Our experience in relation to the Great Lakes illustrates this point well. The Great Lakes are a major source of fresh water, but

At Risk: Canadian Children and Environmental Toxins

In December 1999, a study by the Ontario College of Physicians (Environmental Health Committee) and the Canadian Environmental Law Association (CELA) concluded that the health of Canadian children was being jeopardized by weaknesses within Canada's regulatory system that governs pesticides and their use and by the failure of the Canadian government to enforce existing laws and policies. The study focused on children because of their particular susceptibility to pesticides. Compared to adults, children are relatively more frequently exposed to pesticides. Exposure to pesticide may come through everyday applications in homes and yards, residues from agricultural applications of pesticides, and through diet.

For example, one study on toxic chemicals in food and on bio-engineered food available in Canada noted that "from paint stripper to pesticides to urinal deodorizers and wood preservatives, the variety of toxic chemicals in food is truly amazing. From conception on, a Canadian child is exposed to toxins in food through the womb, the breast-milk, and the first peanut butter sandwich; children get more toxins from their food than any other way." Pork, for example, was found to contain lindane, dioxins and furans, butyl benzyl phthala pentachlorophenol, lead, selenium, cadmium, di-2-ethythexyl phtalate, PCBs, arsenic, and octochlorodibenzode.

According to Dr. Loren Vanderlinden, co-author of the study, "Our study warns that every parent should be concerned about expo-sure of their children to pesticides. The potential for children's health to be affected by pesticides is undeniable. Although more research needs to be done, this does not exonerate pesticides as human toxins, especially when one considers that children are far more vulnerable to pesticides than are adults. Not only is there potential for harm, but in all likelihood some Canadian children are now enduring the negative effects of pesticides."

In particular, the immune systems of Inuit children are being jeopardized by exposure to many persistent chemicals, including DDE (a by-product of the pesticide DDT) through their mothers' breast-milk and through their traditional diet, which relies heavily on marine mammals, which have relatively high levels of contaminants. Children in agricultural areas may also face heightened risk of cognitive defects (i.e., damage to their nervous systems) without obvious clinical symptoms of pesticide exposure. Children from poorer families, those who live in older housing, and children with chemical sensitivities or immune system problems are also believed to have a heightened vulnerability to the effects of pesticide exposure.

Many commonly used pesticides can be detected in our food supply and frequently at levels that would be unsafe for children. As well, pesticide use in the home puts children, pregnant women, and their potential offspring at risk of such health problems as cancer and reproductive problems in later life. "The sad message is that children's health is being impacted because of our inadequate regulatory system, a system that the federal government promised to fix as far back as 1994. Our study finds that the great majority of prior commitments remain unfulfilled. Cana-dians do not really have a regulator. Rather, industry has a customer services department," said Kathleen Cooper, co-author of the study.

Of the 45 recommendations made by authors of the study, many suggested changes to Canada's regulatory system. These included: (1) changes to the *Pest Control Products Act* to ensure a precautionary approach when the weight of evidence suggests a potentially unacceptable risk of harm; (2) implementation of a Federal Toxic Substances Management Policy to allow for immediate bans on pesticides that stay in the environment for a long time or accumulate in fat cells; (3) revision of the registration process for new products to ensure that their impact on children is taken into account; (4) improved inspection and enforcement by the Pest Management Regulatory Agency (PMRA) to ensure appropriate pesticide use; (5) development and application by PMRA of a sustainable pest management policy to reduce overall pesticide use; and (6) improvements in public access to information that is essential to understanding the risks posed by pesticide exposure. As Cooper observed, "[t]he message is not only that children are being impacted by pesticides but that the federal government is knowingly refusing to act to make legislative changes and spend the necessary resources. What can be more important than the health of young Canadians?"

SOURCE: Adapted from CELA (Canadian Environmental Law Association). 1997. "A Taste of Canada: Toxins in Our Food and Bio-engineering on Supermarket Shelves." Media Release. April 2. http://www.web.net/~cela/mr970402.htm. CELA. 1999. "New Study Warns of Children's Health Risks from Pesticides and Calls for Urgent Changes to Pesticide Regulatory Systems." Media Release. December 1. http://www.web.net/~cela/mr991201.htm.

they are bordered on the Canadian side by land that is both densely populated and heavily farmed. "By the late 1950s, fertilizers from farms and phosphates from household detergents had leached into the lake," encouraging abnormal growth of algae, which in turn choked other life forms out of the lakes (Statistics Canada 1998). Fish that survived the algae problem were poisoned by various substances, particularly PCB (polychlorinated biphenyl). These substances can harm those who eat the contaminated fish. One study reported that pregnant women who had consumed 12 kilograms or more of the contaminated fish from the Great Lakes over a six-year period were more likely than those who had not to give birth prematurely and to have smaller babies (Statistics Canada 1998). In the 1970s, substance controls brought the algae problem within the Great Lakes under control and, currently, the federal government and the provincial government of Ontario are working with the United States to clean up the Great Lakes. This effort includes the federal government's Great Lakes Clean-up Fund, which, since 1994, has seen the investment of more than $35 million in more than 150 projects designed to develop solutions to the problems of pollutants, the development of new technologies, and the rehabilitation of wildlife habitat (Statistics Canada 1998).

> I am wondering when God is going to punish us for Lake Ontario.
>
> ROBERTSON DAVIES
> *Man-of-letters*

Worldwide, however, more diseases and deaths are caused by water contaminated by feces, not by chemicals (Kemps 1998). About 1.2 billion people lack access to clean water. In developing nations, as much as 95 percent of untreated sewage is dumped directly into rivers, lakes, and seas that are used for drinking and bathing (Pimentel et al. 1998). Closer to home, the tragic events at Walkerton, Ontario, where seven people died in 2000 and over 2000 became extremely ill during an outbreak of E. coli 0157:H7 caused by contaminated water, should remind Canadians not to be complacent about the quality of our water.

Depletion of Natural Resources

Overpopulation contributes to the depletion of natural resources, such as coal, oil, and forests. The demand for new land, fuel, and raw materials has resulted in **deforestation**—the conversion of forestland to non-forestland (Intergovernmental Panel on Climate Change 2000b) (Table 14.2). Global forest cover has been reduced by at least 20 percent and as much as 50 percent since pre-agricultural times (World Resources Institute 2000). The major causes of deforestation are the expansion of agricultural land, commercial logging, and road building.

As we explained earlier, deforestation contributes to global warming. Deforestation also displaces people and wild species from their lands. About half of the world's approximately 14 million species live in tropical forests (World Resources Institute 1998). Finally, soil erosion caused by deforestation may lead to flooding.

Deforestation contributes to **desertification**—the degradation of semiarid land, which results in the expansion of desert land that is unusable for agriculture. Overgrazing by cattle and other herd animals also contributes to desertification. The problem of desertification is most severe in Africa (Reese 2001). As more land turns into desert land, populations can no longer sustain a livelihood on the land, and so they migrate to urban areas or other countries, contributing to social and political instability.

■ **Table 14.2** *Deforesting Countries*

Average Annual Forest Loss, 1990–95		
Country	Sq miles	Sq km
1 Brazil	9 863	25 544
2 Indonesia	4 187	10 844
3 Dem. Rep. of Congo	2 857	7 400
4 Bolivia	2 245	5 814
5 Mexico	1 961	5 080
6 Venezuela	1 944	5 034
7 Malaysia	1 545	4 002
8 Myanmar (Burma)	1 496	3 874
9 Sudan	1 361	3 526
10 Thailand	1 271	3 294

Some 47 740 sq km (18 433 sq miles) of tropical forest was lost in South America each year between 1990 and 1995, plus a further 37 480 sq km (14 471 sq miles) in Africa, and 33 280 sq km (12 849 sq miles) in Asia. The total global loss during that five-year period was 563 460 sq km (217 553 sq miles), an area equivalent to twice that of the UK. However, while Brazil tops the list of countries with the highest amount of forest loss, the rate of deforestation is only 0.5 percent.

SOURCE: Ash, Russell. 2001. *The Top 10 of Everything: Canadian Edition 2002*. Toronto: Dorling Kindersley Limited. Reprinted by permission of Dorling Kindersley.

Environmental Illness

Exposure to pollution, toxic substances, and other environmental hazards is associated with numerous illnesses and even death. Worldwide, pesticide poisoning results in about a million deaths and chronic illnesses each year (Pimentel et al. 1998). In 1996, the National Environmental Protection Agency of China reported three million deaths in cities during the preceding two years from chronic bronchitis resulting from urban air pollution (Brown 1998). The destruction of the ozone layer increases ultraviolet B (UVB) radiation, and the incidence of skin cancer has quadrupled over the past 20 years, resulting in nearly 10 000 deaths per year (Pimentel et al. 1998). Since 1969, the rates of melanoma, a serious form of skin cancer, have increased fourfold for men and almost doubled for women in Canada (Statistics Canada 1998). Destruction of the ozone layer also results in increased exposure of the eyes to radiation in sunlight, which increases the risk of cataracts (Bergman 1998).

Many of the chemicals we are exposed to in our daily lives can cause not only cancer, but also other health problems such as infertility and impaired intellectual development in children (McGinn 2000). Persistent organic pollutants (POPs), which accumulate in the food chain and persist in the environment, taking centuries to degrade, contribute to increasing rates of birth defects, fertility problems, greater susceptibility to disease, diminished intelligence, and certain cancers (Fisher 1999). Chemicals in the environment are being investigated as causes of a number of childhood developmental and learning problems (Kaplan and Morris 2000).

Substances found in common household, personal, and commercial products can result in a variety of temporary acute symptoms such as drowsiness, disorientation, headache, dizziness, nausea, fatigue, shortness of breath, cramps, diarrhea,

■ With over 70 000 new chemicals added to our environment since the 1940s, how could anyone say that our food supply is the best it's ever been?

ZOLTAN P. RONA
Physician

and irritation of the eyes, nose, throat, and lungs. Long-term exposure can affect the nervous system, reproductive system, liver, kidneys, heart, and blood ("The Delicate Balance" 1994). Fragrances, which are found in many consumer products, may produce sensory irritation, pulmonary irritation, decreases in expiratory airflow velocity, and possible neurotoxic effects (Fisher 1998). Fragrance products can cause skin sensitivity, rashes, headache, sneezing, watery eyes, sinus problems, nausea, wheezing, shortness of breath, inability to concentrate, dizziness, sore throat, cough, hyperactivity, fatigue, and drowsiness (DesJardins 1997). More and more businesses are voluntarily limiting fragrances in the workplace or banning them altogether to accommodate employees who experience ill effects from them.

Sick building syndrome (SBS) is a situation in which occupants of a building experience symptoms that seem linked to time spent in a building, but no specific illness or cause can be identified (Lindauer 1999). Building occupants complain of symptoms such as headache; eye, nose, and throat irritation; a dry cough; dry or itchy skin; dizziness and nausea; difficulty in concentrating; fatigue; and sensitivity to odours. Although specific causes of SBS remain unknown, contributing factors may include polluted outdoor air that enters a building through poorly located air intake vents, windows, and other openings and indoor air pollution from sources inside the building, such as adhesives, upholstery, carpeting, copy machines, manufactured wood products, cleaning agents, and pesticides.

Sufferers of a controversial condition known as **multiple chemical sensitivity (MCS)** say that after one or more acute or traumatic exposures to a chemical or group of chemicals, they began to experience adverse effects from low levels of chemical exposure that do not produce symptoms in the general public. Some individuals with MCS build houses made from materials that do not contain chemicals that are typically found in building materials. Sufferers of MCS often avoid public places and/or wear a protective breathing filter to avoid inhaling the many chemical substances in the environment.

When scientists tested journalist Bill Moyers' blood as part of a documentary on the chemical industry, they found traces of 84 of the 150 chemicals they had tested for (PBS 2001). Sixty years ago, when Moyers was six years old, only one of these chemicals—lead—would have been present in his blood. Only a small fraction of the chemicals that are commercially used have been properly tested for their health effects on humans (PBS 2001). With more than 1000 new chemicals being introduced to the global market each year (McGinn 2000), the need for testing health effects of chemicals in our environment is clear.

Environmental Injustice

Although environmental pollution and degradation and depletion of natural resources affect us all, some groups are more affected than others. **Environmental injustice**, also referred to as **environmental racism**, refers to the tendency for socially and politically marginalized groups to bear the brunt of environmental ills. Environmental injustice affects marginalized populations around the world, including minority groups, Indigenous peoples, and other vulnerable and impoverished communities such as peasants and nomadic tribes (Renner 1996). These groups are often powerless to fight against government and corporate powers that sustain environmentally damaging industries. For example, in the early 1970s, a huge copper mine began operations on the

South Pacific island of Bougainville. While profits of the copper mine benefited the central government and foreign investors, the lives of the island's inhabitants were being destroyed. Farming and traditional hunting and gathering suffered as mine pollutants covered vast areas of land, destroying local crops of cocoa and bananas, and contaminating rivers and their fish. Indigenous groups in Nigeria, such as the Urhobo, Isoko, Kalabare, and Ogoni, are facing environmental threats caused by oil production operations run by multinational corporations. Oil spills, natural gas fires, and leaks from toxic waste pits have polluted the soil, water, and air and compromised the health of various local tribes. "Formerly lush agricultural land is now covered by oil slicks, and much vegetation and wildlife has been destroyed. Many Ogoni suffer from respiratory diseases and cancer, and birth defects are frequent" (Renner 1996: 57). The environmental injustices experienced by Bougainville and the Ogoni are only the tip of the iceberg. Renner warns that "minority populations and Indigenous peoples around the globe are facing massive degradation of their environments that threatens to irreversibly alter, indeed destroy, their ways of life and cultures" (p. 59).

Threats to Biodiversity

Biodiversity refers to the great variety of life forms on Earth. The diverse forms of life provide food, fibres, and many other products and "natural services." Insects, birds, and bats provide pollination services that enable us to feed ourselves. Frogs, fish, and birds provide natural pest control. Various aquatic organisms filter and cleanse our water and plants and microorganisms enrich and renew our soil. In recent decades, we have witnessed mass extinction rates of diverse life forms. Most estimates suggest that at least one thousand species of life are lost per year (Tuxill 1998). Unlike the extinction of the dinosaurs millions of years ago, humans are the primary cause of disappearing species today. Air, water, and land pollution; deforestation; disruption of native habitats, and overexploitation of species for their meat, hides, horns, or medicinal or entertainment value threaten biodiversity and the delicate balance of nature. The primary cause of species decline is human-induced habitat destruction (Hunter 2001). Most estimates suggest that at least 1000 species of life are lost per year (Tuxill 1998). Biologists expect that at least half of the roughly 10 million species alive today will become extinct during the next few centuries from habitat losses alone, over-harvesting, and global warming (Cincotta and Engelmann 2000). Table 14.3 lists the numbers of species worldwide that are endangered or threatened.

> The faster populations grow, the more environmental problems are aggravated.
>
> **WERNER FORNOS**
> *President, Population Institute*

Social Causes of Environmental Problems

In addition to population growth, various other structural and cultural factors have also played a role in environmental problems.

Industrialization and Economic Development

Many of the environmental problems confronting the world have been caused by industrialization and economic development. Industrialized countries, for example, consume more energy and natural resources than poor countries.

Table 14.3 *Threatened and Endangered Species* Worldwide, 2000*

Item	Mammals	Birds	Reptiles	Amphibians	Fishes	Snails	Clams	Crustaceans	Insects	Arachnids	Plants
Total Listings	339	274	115	27	123	32	71	21	42	6	705
Endangered species,											
Total	314	253	79	18	79	21	63	18	34	6	566
United States	63	77	14	10	68	20	61	18	30	6	565
Threatened species,											
Total	25	21	36	9	44	11	8	3	8	—†	139

* An endangered species is one in danger of becoming extinct throughout all or significant part of its natural range. A threatened species is one likely to become endangered in the foreseeable future.

† — represents zero.

SOURCE: *Statistical Abstract of the United States 2000*, 120th edition. Table 404. Washington DC: U.S. Bureau of the Census.

What good is a house if you don't have a decent planet to put it on?

HENRY DAVID THOREAU
Writer, social activist

The relationship between level of economic development and environmental pollution is not necessarily a linear one. For example, industrial emissions are minimal in regions with low levels of economic development, yet high in the middle-development range as developing countries move through the early stages of industrialization. At more advanced industrial stages, some environmental pressures ease because heavily polluting manufacturing industries decline and "cleaner" service industries increase, and because rising incomes are associated with a greater demand for environmental quality and cleaner technologies (Hunter 2001). However, a positive linear correlation has been demonstrated between per capita income and national carbon dioxide emissions (Hunter 2001) (Table 14.4).

Industrialization and economic development have been the primary cause of global environmental problems such as the ozone hole and global warming (Koenig 1995). In less developed countries, environmental problems are largely the result of poverty and the priority of economic survival over environmental concerns. "Poverty can induce people to behave as if they are myopic, making use of local resources without consideration of global effects or the implications for future generations" (Hunter 2001: 32). Vajpeyi (1995) explains:

> Policymakers in the Third World are often in conflict with the ever-increasing demands to satisfy basic human needs—clean air, water, adequate food, shelter, education—and to safeguard the environmental quality. Given the scarce economic and technical resources at their disposal, most of these policymakers have ignored long-range environmental concerns and opted for short-range economic and political gains. (p. 24)

■ **Table 14.4** *Carbon Dioxide–emitting Countries*

Country	CO₂ Emissions Per Head, 1997 (Tonnes of Carbon)
1 Qatar	18.19
2 United Arab Emirates	9.40
3 Kuwait	7.88
4 Guam	7.04
5 Bahrain	6.95
6 Singapore	6.39
7 US	5.48
8 Luxembourg	5.16
9 Brunei	4.79
10 Australia	4.71
Canada	4.42

CO_2 emissions derive from three principal sources: fossil fuel burning, cement manufacturing, and gas flaring. Since World War II, increasing industrialization has resulted in huge increases in carbon dioxide output, a trend that most are now actively attempting to reverse. The US remains the worst offender in total, with 1 500 million tonnes released in 1997.

SOURCE: Ash, Russell. 2001. *The Top 10 of Everything: Canadian Edition 2002*. Toronto: Dorling Kindersley Limited. Reprinted by permission of Dorling Kindersley.

Measures of economic development and the "health" of economies are based primarily on gross domestic product (GDP) and consumer spending. Until definitions and measurements of "economic development" and "economic health" reflect the social and environmental costs of the production and consumption of goods and services, the pursuit of economic development will continue to contribute to environmental problems.

Cultural Values and Attitudes

Cultural values and attitudes that contribute to environmental problems include individualism, capitalism, and materialism. Individualism puts individual interests over collective welfare. Even though recycling is good for our collective environment, many individuals do not recycle because of the personal inconvenience involved in washing and sorting recyclable items. Similarly, individuals often indulge in countless behaviours that provide enjoyment and convenience at the expense of the environment: long showers, use of dishwashing machines, recreational boating, meat eating, and use of air conditioning, to name just a few.

Finally, the influence of materialism, or the emphasis on worldly possessions, also encourages individuals to continually purchase new items and throw away old ones. The media bombard us daily with advertisements that tell us life will be better if we purchase a particular product. Materialism contributes to pollution and environmental degradation by supporting industry and contributing to garbage and waste.

Strategies for Action: Responding to Environmental Problems

Lowering fertility, as discussed earlier, helps reduce population pressure on the environment. Environmental activism, environmental education, the development of alternative sources of energy, modifications in consumer behaviour, government regulations, sustainable economic development, and international cooperation and assistance can also alleviate environmental problems.

Environmentalist Activism

> I do not feel like a freak. I feel normal. And sometimes I wonder if the rest of the world is normal, especially that part of it that goes round plundering the natural world.
>
> PAUL WATSON
> *Ecologist, environmental activist*

Environmentalist groups exert pressure on the government to initiate or intensify actions related to environmental protection. They also design and implement their own projects, and disseminate information to the public about environmental issues.

In North America, environmentalist groups date back to 1892, with the establishment of the Sierra Club, followed by the Audubon Society in 1905. Other environmental groups include the National Wildlife Federation, World Wildlife Fund, Environmental Defense Fund, Friends of the Earth, Union of Concerned Scientists, Canadian Environmental Law Association, Canadian Environmental Defence Fund, Canadian Environmental Network, Great Lakes United, Common Frontiers, Greenpeace, Environmental Action, Natural Resources Defense Council, World Watch Institute, National Recycling Coalition, Campaign for Nuclear Phase-Out, the New Brunswick Environmental Network, World Resources Institute, Rainforest Alliance, Global Climate Coalition, and Mothers and Others, to name a few. One recent development in the environmental movement is the emergence of **ecofeminism**—a synthesis of feminism, environmentalism, and antimilitarism. Another is online activism, with the Internet and e-mail providing important tools for environmental activism.

Industries are major contributors to environmental problems and often fight against environmental efforts that threaten their products. However, some industries are joining the environmental movement for a variety of reasons, including pressure from consumers and environmental groups, the desire to improve their public image, and genuine concern for the environment. For example, in 1997, British Petroleum (BP) publicly acknowledged that global warming is a threat to human and environmental health and began working with the environmental organization Environmental Defense to develop ways to reduce its greenhouse gas emissions ("Global Corporations Join Us to Reduce Greenhouse Gas Emissions" 2000). This led to the development of the Partnership for Climate Action—a collaboration between Environmental Defense and seven of the world's largest corporations (including companies in the petroleum, aluminum, chemical, and electric power sectors) to take action against global warming. Participating companies have committed to report their emissions publicly, and each has a firm target for emissions reductions. Environmental Defense is working with each company to devise ways to improve energy efficiency, use renewable energy sources, and improve manufacturing processes. BP, along with several other industries, has also withdrawn from membership in the Global Climate Coalition—an industry group that denies global warming and the role that industries play in the emission of greenhouse gases. Other industries that have quit the Global Climate Coalition include Ford, Shell Oil, Dow Chemical, General Motors, and Daimler-Chrysler (Associated Press 2000).

An extreme form of environmental activism is **ecoterrorism**, defined as any crime intended to protect wildlife or the environment that is violent, puts human life at risk, or results in damages of $10 000 or more (Denson 2000). Documented crimes of ecoterrorism include arson, bombings, and mailing letters rigged with razors to primate researchers. Groups known to engage in ecoterrorism include the Earth Liberation Front, the Animal Liberation Front, and a group calling itself the Justice Department. Although critics of ecoterrorism cite the damage done by such tactics, members and supporters of ecoterrorist groups claim that the real terrorists are corporations that plunder the earth.

Environmental Education

One goal of environmental organizations and activists is to educate the public about environmental issues and the seriousness of environmental problems. It is believed that "[i]ncreased knowledge is the key to changing attitudes and behaviours on issues critical to our environmental future" (National Environmental Education and Training Foundation and Roper Starch Worldwide 1999: 41).

A major source of information about environmental issues for most Canadians is the media. However, because corporations and wealthy individuals with corporate ties own media, unbiased information about environmental impacts of corporate activities may not readily be found in mainstream media channels. Indeed, the public must consider the source in interpreting information about environmental issues. Propaganda by corporations sometimes comes packaged as "environmental education." Hager and Burton (2000) explain: "Production of materials for schools is a growth area for public relations companies around the world. Corporate interests realize the value of getting their spin into the classrooms of future consumers and voters" (p. 107).

Technological Innovations in Sources and Uses of Energy

In the 1990s, the world's primary sources of energy were oil (34 percent), coal (24 percent), gas (19 percent), renewables or biomass (e.g., fuel wood, crops, animal wastes) (18 percent), and nuclear (5 percent) (Fridleifsson 2000). Cleaner alternative sources of energy include solar power, geothermal power, ocean thermal power, tidal power, and energy from fuel cells. The fastest developing alternative source of energy is wind power, which could supply 10 percent of the world's electricity by 2020 (Flavin 2000). In addition to developing cleaner forms of energy, efforts are being made to develop products that use energy more efficiently. For example, several car manufacturers have developed eco-friendly cars powered by non-polluting electric motors or "hybrid" gasoline-electric motors (Buss 2001). As well, cars with hydrogen-powered fuel cells are expected to be available within the next decade.

Modifications in Consumer Behaviour

Increasingly, consumers are making choices in their behaviour and in purchases that reflect environmental awareness. For example, consumers are increasingly

My specific thought about garbage sprang from the realization that Canadian society has travelled in my lifetime from returnable glass bottles for milk to throwaway plastic bags. This is not progress. Moreover, in the same lifetime, Canadian cities have abandoned horse-drawn carts doing door-to-door milk routes. This probably isn't progress either.

MICHAEL VALPY
Columnist

Multiply our individual choices that affect our environment five billion times and we can begin to see that, every time we just do what all the others are doing, we are contributing to the stress of the planet in ways that are cumulatively dangerous.

JAMES GEORGE
Former Canadian ambassador

buying energy-efficient compact fluorescent lamps (CFLs) (Scholand 2000). CFLs last about 10 times longer than the more commonly used incandescent light bulb and they use 75 percent less electricity. The 275 million CFLs used in North America in 2000 avoided 3.5 million tons of carbon emissions and 69 000 tons of sulfur emissions during the year (Scholand 2000). According to surveys conducted in Canada by Environics Research Group in the late 1990s, Canadians are increasingly engaging in actions designed to preserve their physical environment or to protect their health against perceived environmental hazards, or both. They are recycling newspapers, cans, and glass, turning off lights and electrical appliances when not in use, and trying to conserve water and to cut down on the amount of trash their household creates (Statistics Canada 1998). Sales of organic foods (that are grown without the use of pesticides) are also increasing—although primarily because of consumers' concern for their own health, rather than for the health of the planet (Lipke 2001).

From credit card and long-distance telephone companies that donate a percentage of their profits to environmental causes, to socially responsible investment services, consumers are increasingly voting with their dollars to support environmentally responsible practices. This chapter's *The Human Side* feature offers some examples of how consumers can resist materialistic urges and reduce waste and overconsumption.

> For decades I have been preaching that we must discard the concept of "waste" to be "disposed of" as obsolete, and replace it by the notion of by-products to be reused and recycled.
>
> HANS BLUMENFELD
> *Architect-planner*

Government Regulations and Funding

Worldwide, governments spend about $700 billion per year subsidizing environmentally unsound practices in the use of water, agriculture, energy, and transportation (World Resources Institute 2000). Yet, through regulations and the provision of funds, governments also play a vital role in protecting and restoring the environment. Governments have responded to concerns related to air and water pollution, ozone depletion, and global warming by imposing regulations affecting the production of pollutants. Governments have also been involved in the preservation of deserts, forests, reefs, wetlands, and endangered plant and animal species.

Sustainable Economic Development: An International Agenda

> It will not be possible for the community of nations to achieve any of its major goals—not peace, not environmental protection, not human rights or democratization, not fertility reduction, not social integration—except in the context of sustainable development.
>
> UNITED NATIONS DEVELOPMENT PROGRAMME Human Development Report 1994

Achieving global cooperation on environmental issues is difficult, in part, because developed countries (primarily in the Northern Hemisphere) have different economic agendas from developing countries (primarily in the Southern Hemisphere). The northern agenda emphasizes preserving wealth, affluent lifestyles, and the welfare state while the southern agenda focuses on overcoming mass poverty and achieving a higher quality of life (Koenig 1995). Southern countries are concerned that northern industrialized countries—having already achieved economic wealth—will impose international environmental policies that restrict the economic growth of developing countries just as they are beginning to industrialize. Global strategies to preserve the environment must address both wasteful lifestyles in some nations and the need to overcome overpopulation and widespread poverty in others.

Development involves more than economic growth, it involves sustainability—the long-term environmental, social, and economic health of societies. **Sustainable development** involves meeting the needs of the present world without endangering the ability of future generations to meet their own needs.

Escape from Affluenza

A 1997 PBS television program, *Affluenza*, explored "the high social and environmental costs of materialism and overconsumption." In a 1998 sequel, *Escape from Affluenza*, people working to reduce waste and overconsumption and live their lives in balance with the environment are profiled. Below is a partial list, by category, of some of the ways you can "Escape from Affluenza."

Shopping

- Biggest shopping trap—it was on sale. If it was not something you identified as a need, you did not save money, you spent money. Learn this mantra: It is not a bargain if I don't need it.
- Mail-order shopping is a great way to save time, fuel, and money. But avoid the companies that make up the cost of glossy catalogues by charging twice as much. About 94 percent of these catalogues go unused into the waste stream: don't be one of the 6 percent who pay more to make this practice profitable!
- The average family of four spends an estimated 10 percent of its annual income on clothing. Using principles you already know (only buying what you need, buying secondhand items that are as good as new, for instance), you can easily cut your clothing expenditures in half.

Waste and Clutter

- A poorly insulated house can easily waste 30 to 50 percent of the energy poured into it... Simple changes around the house: run the dishwasher half

as often as you do now, and save 50 percent in water, energy, and time. Wash only full loads of clothing, and, since 90 percent of the cost of washing clothes is to heat the water, avoid using hot water.
- Half of the average family's household energy goes to heating and cooling, at a cost of about $450 a year. Put a 15 percent dent in this expense by keeping the thermostat set at 65°F [18°C] in the daytime, and 55°F to 60°F [13°C to 16°C] at night.
- Planting a large tree to shade your home can save you an estimated $73 a year in air-conditioning bills.
- An estimated 50 percent of the waste stream is discarded packaging. Be very aware of packaging excess, and when all else is equal, choose the least-packaged. Help raise awareness of this issue by being a packaging activist: ask your grocers to phase out pre-wrapped fruits and vegetables.

Home and Hearth

- When home-hunting, pick the smallest amount of space in which you are comfortable. This will limit the amount of stuff you can accumulate, and take far less of your time and resources to furnish, clean, maintain, insure, and pay for.
- Eighty percent of the dirt in your home is brought in on shoes. Save time and cleaning expenses by starting a no-shoes policy.
- Start a neighbourhood swap of seldom-used tools. Why should a street of 10 houses have 10 lawnmowers, 10 paint-sprayers, and 10 band saws (or 55 Disney videos, for that matter)?

Food

- Eat a local diet as much as possible. This creates jobs in the region, reduces transportation costs and energy consumption, ensures higher nutritional value, and encourages local small-scale agriculture that protects land from development. Ask your grocers to mark foods local. Hint—If it's out of season, you know it's not local.
- To dramatically reduce your ecological footprint, save about 50 percent in food costs, and maximize your prospects for a longer, healthier life: become a vegetarian.

Health and Happiness

- Prevention is the cheapest and best health insurance. Get an annual check-up (even frugal fanatics agree this is worth the money). Take care of your body by eating and sleeping right, and stop smoking.
- Stop equating the amount of fun and pleasure you get with the amount of money you spend to get it. Sit down and make a list of 25 things you like to do that cost little or no money, and keep it where you can see it every day.
- Instead of spending your time and energy buying and taking care of stuff, volunteer to feed the hungry, care for the suffering, visit the lonely, or mentor a child.
- Be happy with what you have. If you make a habit of thinking in terms of what you have, rather than of what you don't, you may well find that you have enough.

SOURCE: Adapted from *100 Ways to Escape from Affluenza* as it appears on www.pbs.org/kcts/affluenza/escape by Vivia Boe. Reprinted by permission. Films are available from bullfrog films, 800-543-FROG or www.bullfrogfilms.com.

"The aim here is for those alive today to meet their own needs without making it impossible for future generations to meet theirs....This in turn calls for an economic structure within which we consume only as much as the national environment can produce, and make only as much waste as it can absorb" (McMichael et al. 2000: 1067).

International Cooperation and Assistance

Global environmental concerns such as global warming and climate change require international governmental cooperation. Since the first U.N. Stockholm Conference on the Human Environment in 1972, about 240 international environmental agreements have been reached (French 2000). For example, the 1992 Earth Summit in Rio de Janeiro brought together heads of state, delegates from more than 170 nations, nongovernmental organizations, representatives of indigenous peoples, and the media to discuss an international agenda for both economic development and the environment. The 1992 Earth Summit resulted in the Rio Declaration—"a nonbinding statement of broad principles to guide environmental policy, vaguely committing its signatories not to damage the environment of other nations by activities within their borders and to acknowledge environmental protection as an integral part of development" (Koenig 1995: 15).

A certain ancient Aboriginal visionary of this country once said: "We have not inherited this land, we have merely borrowed it from our children."

TOMSON HIGHWAY
Playwright

The 1987 Montreal Protocol forged an agreement made by 70 nations to curb the production of CFCs, (which contribute to ozone depletion and global warming) (Koenig 1995). Under the Montreal Protocol, CFC emissions have dropped nearly 90 percent (French 2000). In 1997, delegates from 160 nations met in Kyoto, Japan, and forged the Kyoto Protocol—the first international agreement to place legally binding limits on greenhouse gas emissions from developed countries. However, Canada's ratification of the Kyoto Protocol, which compels this country to reduce greenhouse gas emissions to 6 percent below 1990 levels by 2012, drew stormy protests, especially from energy-rich Alberta. Many industrial countries have yet to ratify the agreement. As well, representatives from 122 countries recently drafted a legally binding agreement to phase out a group of dangerous chemicals known as persistent organic pollutants (POPs) (Cray 2001). However, "even as the number of treaties climbs, the condition of the biosphere continues to deteriorate...The main reason that many environmental treaties have not yet turned around the environmental trends they were designed to address is because the governments that created them permitted only vague commitments and lax enforcement" (French 2000: 135). In addition, some countries do not have the technical or economic resources necessary for implementing the requirements of environmental treaties.

One way developed countries can help less developed countries address environmental concerns is through economic aid. Because industrialized countries have more economic and technological resources, they bear primary responsibility for leading the nations of the world toward environmental cooperation. Jan (1995) emphasizes the importance of international environmental cooperation and the role of developed countries in this endeavour:

> Advanced countries must be willing to sacrifice their own economic well-being to help improve the environment of the poor, developing countries. Failing to do this will lead to irreparable damage to our global environment. Environmental protection is no longer the affair of any one country. It has become an urgent global issue.

Environmental pollution recognizes no national boundaries. No country, especially a poor country, can solve this problem alone. (pp. 82–83)

Understanding Population
and Environmental Problems

Because population increases exponentially, the size of the world's population has grown and will continue to grow at a staggering rate. Given the problems associated with population growth—deteriorating socioeconomic conditions, depletion of natural resources, and urban crowding—most governments recognize the value of controlling population size. Efforts to control population must go beyond providing safe, effective, and affordable methods of birth control. Slowing population growth necessitates interventions that change the cultural and structural bases for high fertility rates. These interventions include increasing economic development and improving the status of women, which includes raising their levels of education, their economic position, and their (and their children's) health.

Globally, the average number of children born to each woman has fallen from five in 1960 to less than three (Engelman et al. 2000), as more women today are using methods of birth control. High mortality rates resulting from HIV/AIDS and war have also contributed to the slowing of population growth in many countries. Although birthrates have decreased in most countries throughout the world, population continues to grow as a result of population momentum. In addition, many African and Middle Eastern nations continue to have high birth rates: 6.9 in Uganda, 7.0 in Somalia, 7.5 in Niger, 6.4 in Saudi Arabia, 6.5 in Yemen, and 7.1 in Oman (Hunter 2001). These factors combined—population momentum and continued high fertility rates in some countries—contribute to escalating world population. Even in the 29 African nations that have been hardest hit by AIDS, overall population is projected to increase by more than half between 1995 and 2015 (Hunter 2001). An estimated 65 countries are expected to double their populations in 30 years or less, and 14 countries will triple or nearly triple their populations by 2050. "The impact of population growth in these fast-growing countries will more than offset the gains of low fertility in 80 other countries" (Population Institute 1998: 3).

Rapid and dramatic population growth, along with expanding world industrialization and patterns of consumption, has contributed to environmental problems. The greater numbers of people make increased demands on natural resources and generate excessive levels of pollutants. Environmental problems result not only from large populations, but also the ways in which these populations live and work. As conflict theorists argue, individuals, private enterprises, and governments have tended to choose economic and political interests over environmental concerns. However, growing evidence of the irreversible effects of global warming and loss of biodiversity, and increased concerns about the health effects of toxic waste and other forms of pollution are making it difficult for even profit-seeking industries to turn their backs on environmental problems.

Many Canadians believe in a "technological fix" for the environment— that science and technology will solve environmental problems. Paradoxically, the same environmental problems that have been caused by technological progress may be solved by technological innovations designed to clean up pollution and preserve natural resources. Although technological innovation is important in resolving environmental concerns, other social changes are needed as well. Addressing the values that guide choices, the economic contexts in which the choices are made, and the governmental policies that encourage various choices is critical to resolving environmental and population problems.

Global cooperation is also vital to resolving environmental concerns, but it is difficult to achieve because rich and poor countries have different economic development agendas: developing poor countries struggle to survive and provide for the basic needs of their citizens; developed wealthy countries struggle to maintain their wealth and relatively high standard of living. Can both agendas be achieved without further pollution and destruction of the environment? Is sustainable economic development an attainable goal? The answer must be yes. But sustainable development will not occur on its own or as the inevitable outcome of current trends. If it is to happen, we must, collectively, make it happen. The motivation for finding and implementing sustainable economies may come from understanding the consequences if we don't. "We must work together to get onto a path of ecological sustainable social and economic development. The level of health attained by the world's population will be the ultimate criterion of how well we succeed" (McMichael et al. 2000: 1067).

Critical Thinking

1 One writer observed that "on a certain November day an obscure woman in Iowa gives birth to seven babies; we marvel and rejoice. On the same day an obscure woman in Nigeria gives birth to her seventh child in a row; we are distressed and appalled" (Zwingle 1998: 38). Why might reactions to these two events be so different?

2 In many developing countries that have strict laws against abortion, the use of child labour is common. Do you think there may be a connection between laws prohibiting abortion and child labour in developing countries? How could you find out if there is a connection?

3 Do you think governments should regulate reproductive behaviour to control population growth? If so, how?

4 Babies eat more, drink more, and breathe more, proportionally, than adults—which means babies are more susceptible to environmental toxins than are adults (Dionis 1999). Yet, federal environmental standards are largely set at levels designed to protect adults. What social forces do you think discourage the government from setting environmental standards based on what is safe for infants and young children?

5 In Chapters 7 and 9, we discussed hate crimes and noted that Canadian law provides for sentencing enhancements for those whose crimes are motivated by hate. Should motives be considered in imposing penalties on persons who are convicted of acts of ecoterrorism? For example, should a person who sets fire to a business to protect against that business' environmentally destructive activities receive a lighter penalty than a person who sets fire to a business for some other reason?

Key Terms

acid rain

biodiversity

deforestation

demographic transition
  theory

desertification

doubling time

ecofeminism

ecoterrorism

environmental injustice

environmental racism

e-waste

fertility rate

global warming

greenhouse gases

greenwashing

Malthusian theory

multiple chemical
  sensitivity (MCS)

planned obsolescence

population momentum

pronatalism

replacement level

sick building syndrome
  (SBS)

sustainable development

Glossary

abortion The intentional termination of a pregnancy.

absolute poverty The chronic absence of the basic necessities of life, including food, clean water, and housing.

acculturation Learning the culture of a group different from the one in which a person was originally raised.

achieved status A status assigned on the basis of some characteristic or behaviour over which the individual has some control.

acid rain The mixture of precipitation with air pollutants, such as sulphur dioxide and nitrogen oxide.

acquaintance rape Rape that is committed by someone known by the victim.

activity theory A theory that emphasizes that the elderly disengage, in part, because they are structurally segregated and isolated with few opportunities to engage in active roles.

acute condition A health condition that can last no more than three months.

adaptive discrimination Discrimination that is based on the prejudice of others.

age grading The assignment of social roles to given chronological ages.

age pyramids Graphlike presentations that show the percentage of a population in various age groups.

ageism The belief that age is associated with certain psychological, behavioural, or intellectual traits.

alienation The concept used by Karl Marx to describe the condition when workers feel powerlessness and meaninglessness as a result of performing repetitive, isolated work tasks. Alien-ation involves becoming estranged from one's work, the products one creates, other human beings, or one's self; it also refers to powerlessness and meaninglessness experienced by students in traditional, restrictive educational institutions.

alternative schools Alternative schools began in Canada in the 1970s. Each operates within school board and education ministry guidelines but is unique in its character.

amalgamation The physical blending of different racial or ethnic groups, resulting in a new and distinct genetic and cultural population; results from the intermarriage of racial and ethnic groups over generations.

anomie A state of normlessness in which norms and values are weak or unclear; results from rapid social change and is linked to many social problems, including crime, drug addiction, and violence.

ascribed status A status that society assigns to an individual on the basis of factors over which the individual has no control.

assimilation The process by which minority groups gradually adopt cultural patterns of the dominant majority group. See also **primary assimilation** and **secondary assimilation**.

authoritarian-personality theory A psychological theory of prejudice that suggests prejudice arises in people with a certain personality type. According to this theory, people with an authoritarian personality, who are highly conformist, intolerant, cynical, and preoccupied with power, are prone to prejudice.

automation A type of technology in which self-operated machines accomplish tasks formerly done by workers; develops as a society moves toward industrialization and becomes more concerned with the mass production of goods.

aversive racism A subtle, often unintentional form of prejudice exhibited by many individuals who possess strong egalitarian values and who view themselves as non-prejudiced.

behavioural-based safety programs A controversial health and safety strategy used by business management that attributes health and safety problems in the workplace to workers' behaviour, rather than to work processes and conditions.

beliefs Definitions and explanations about what is assumed to be true.

bias-motivated crimes See **hate crimes**.

biodiversity The variability of living organisms on earth.

biphobia Negative attitudes toward bisexuality and people who identify as bisexual.

bisexuality A sexual orientation that involves cognitive, emotional, and sexual attraction to members of both sexes.

bonded labour The repayment of a debt through labour.

bourgeoisie The owners of the means of production.

brain drain The phenomenon whereby many individuals with the highest level of skill and education leave the country in search of work abroad.

burden of disease The number of deaths in a population combined with the impact of premature death and disability on that population.

Canada Child Tax Benefit (CCTB) A tax-free monthly payment made to eligible families to help them with the cost of raising children under the age of 18. Benefits are calculated for a 12-month period based on the number of children in a family and their ages, the applicant's province or territory of residence, the family's net income and the applicant's (or the applicant's spouse's) deduction for childcare expenses.

Canada Student Financial Assistance Act (CSFA Act) The CSFA Act of 1994 revised the Canada Student Loans Plan and increased the amounts of the maximum loans available for full-time and part-time students.

Canada Student Loans Program (CSLP) A plan that permits eligible Canadian citizens and permanent residents to finance their postsecondary education with government-sponsored loans. Full-time students, enrolled in a program that lasts for at least 12 weeks, may qualify for a loan that is based on the costs of their program and on the financial resources available to them.

capitalism An economic system in which private individuals or groups invest capital to produce goods and services, for a profit, in a competitive market.

census family A now-married couple (with or without never-married sons and/or daughters of one or other spouses), a couple living common-law (again, with or without never-married sons and/or daughters of either or both parents), or a lone parent of any marital status, with at least one never-married son or daughter living in the same dwelling.

charter groups A term that has been traditionally used in Canada to refer to the English and French and that reflects the historical importance of these groups in Canada's history.

charter schools Public schools founded by parents, teachers, and communities, and maintained by school tax dollars.

chemical dependency A condition in which drug use is compulsive, and users are unable to stop because of physical or psychological dependency or both.

child abuse The physical or mental injury, sexual abuse, negligent treatment, or maltreatment of a child under the age of 18 by a person who is responsible for the child's welfare.

child labour Children performing work that is hazardous, that interferes with a child's education, or that harms a child's health or physical, mental, spiritual, or moral development.

chronic condition A long-term health problem, such as a disease or impairment.

civil union A legal status that entitles same-sex couples who apply for and receive a civil union certificate to nearly all the benefits available to married couples.

classic rape A rape committed by a stranger with the use of a weapon resulting in serious bodily injury.

club drugs A general term used to refer to illicit, often synthetic drugs commonly used at nightclubs or all-night dances called "raves".

colonialism When a racial or ethnic group from one society takes over and dominates the racial or ethnic group(s) of another society.

common couple violence Occasional acts of violence that result from conflict that gets out of hand between persons in a relationship.

compressed workweek Workplace option in which employees work a full week, full-time, but in four rather than five days.

computer crime Any violation of the law in which a computer is the target or means of criminal activity.

conflict perspective A sociological perspective that views society as comprising different groups and interests competing for power and resources.

control theory A theory that argues that a strong social bond between a person and society constrains some individuals from violating norms.

conventional crime Traditional illegal behaviour that most people think of as crime, including such offences as murder, sexual assault, assault, armed robbery, break and enter, and theft.

convergence hypothesis The argument that capitalist countries will adopt elements of socialism and socialist countries will adopt elements of capitalism; that is, they will converge.

corporal punishment The use of physical force with the intention of causing a child to experience pain, but not injury, for the purpose of correction or control of a child's behaviour.

corporate downsizing The corporate practice of discharging large numbers of employees. Simply put, the term "downsizing" is a euphemism for mass firing of employees.

corporate multinationalism The practice of corporations having their home base in one country and branches, or affiliates, in other countries.

corporate murder The label for deaths as a result of unsafe consumer products.

corporate violence The production of unsafe products and the failure of corporations to provide a safe working environment for their employees.

corporate welfare Laws and policies that favour corporations, such as low-interest government loans to failing businesses and special subsidies and tax breaks to corporations.

covenant marriage A type of marriage offered in Louisiana that permits divorce only under condition of fault or after a marital separation of more than two years.

crack A crystallized illegal drug product made by boiling a mixture of baking soda, water, and cocaine.

crime The violation of norms that are written into law.

cultural imperialism The indoctrination into the dominant culture of a society; when cultural imperialism exists, the norms, values, traditions, and languages of minorities are systematically ignored.

cultural lag A condition in which the material part of the culture changes at a faster rate than the nonmaterial part.

cultural sexism The ways in which the culture of society perpetuates the subordination of individuals based on their sex classification.

culture of poverty The set of norms, values, and beliefs and self-concepts that contribute to the persistence of poverty among the underclass.

cumulative trauma disorders The most common type of workplace injury; it includes muscle, tendon, vascular, and nerve injuries that result from repeated or sustained actions or exertions of different body parts. Jobs that are associated with high rates of upper body cumulative stress disorders include computer programming, manufacturing, meat packing, poultry processing, and clerical or office work.

cybernation The use of machines that control other machines in the production process; characteristic of post-industrial societies that emphasize service and information professions.

cycle of abuse Involves a violent or abusive episode, followed by a makeup period where the abuser expresses sorrow and asks for forgiveness and "one more chance." The honeymoon period may last for days, weeks, or even months before the next outburst of violence occurs.

date-rape drugs Drugs that are used to render victims incapable of resisting sexual assaults.

de facto segregation Segregation that is not required by law, but exists "in fact," often as a result of housing and socioeconomic patterns.

de jure segregation Segregation that is required by law.

decriminalization The removal of criminal penalties for a behaviour, as in the decriminalization of drug use.

deforestation The destruction of the earth's rainforests.

demogrant A benefit directed at a particular group within the population.

demographic transition theory A theory that attributes population growth patterns to changes in birthrates and death rates associated with the process of industrialization. In preindustrial societies, the population remains stable because, although the birthrate is high, the death rate is also high. As a society becomes industrialized, the birthrate remains high, but the death rate declines, causing rapid population growth. In societies with advanced industrialization, the birthrate declines, and this decline, in conjunction with the low death rate, slows population growth.

dependency ratio The number of societal members who are under 18 or 65 and over compared to the number of people who are between 18 and 64.

dependent variable The variable that the researcher wants to explain. See also **independent variable.**

deregulation The reduction of government control of, for example, certain drugs.

desertification The expansion of deserts and the loss of usable land due to the overuse of semiarid land on the desert margins for animal grazing and obtaining firewood.

deskilling The tendency for workers in a postindustrial society to make fewer decisions and for labour to require less thought.

deterrence The use of harm or the threat of harm to prevent unwanted behaviours.

devaluation hypothesis The hypothesis that argues that women are paid less because the work they perform is socially defined as less valuable than the work performed by men.

differential association A theory developed by Edwin Sutherland that holds that through interaction with others, individuals learn the values, attitudes, techniques, and motives for criminal behaviour.

disability-adjusted life year (DALY) Years lost to premature death and years lived with illness or disability. More simply, one DALY equals one year lost of healthy life.

discrimination Differential treatment of individuals based on their group membership.

discriminatory unemployment High rates of unemployment among particular social groups such as racial and ethnic minorities and women.

disengagement theory A theory claiming that the elderly disengage from productive social roles to relinquish these roles to younger members of society. As this process continues, each new group moves up and replaces another, which, according to disengagement theory, benefits society and all of its members.

distance learning Learning in which, by time or place, the student is separated from the teacher.

diversity training Workplace training programs designed to increase employees' awareness of cultural differences in the workplace and how these differences may affect job performance.

divorce law reform Policies and proposals designed to change divorce law. Usually, divorce law reform attempts to make divorce more difficult to obtain.

divorce mediation A process in which divorcing couples meet with a neutral third party (mediator) who assists the individuals in resolving such issues as property division, child custody, child support, and spousal support in a way that minimizes conflict and encourages cooperation.

Dominion Provincial Student Aid Program (DSAP) An act passed by the federal government in 1939. Under DSAP, the federal government contributed to each participating province and the province was expected to provide an equal amount of assistance to students.

double jeopardy See **multiple jeopardy**.

doubling time The time it takes for a population to double in size from any base year.

drug Any substance other than food that alters the structure and functioning of a living organism when it enters the bloodstream.

drug abuse The violation of social standards of acceptable drug use, resulting in adverse physiological, psychological, or social consequences.

drug addiction See **chemical dependency**.

ecofeminism A synthesis of feminism, environmentalism, and anti-militarism.

e-commerce The buying and selling of goods and services over the Internet.

economic institution The structure and means by which a society produces, distributes, and consumes goods and services.

ecoterrorism Any violent crime intended to coerce, intimidate, or change public policy on behalf of the natural world.

elder abuse The physical or psychological abuse, financial exploitation, or medical abuse or neglect of the elderly.

emotional abuse Often involves using negative labels (e.g., "stupid," "whore," "bad") to define a partner or family member. Such labels negatively affect the self-concept of abuse victims, often convincing them that they deserve the abuse.

employment equity An attempt to ensure that there is a proportional number of designated target groups (e.g., women, visible minorities, Aboriginal peoples, and people with disabilities) throughout all income and occupational levels at ratios that are consistent with the proportion of these groups within the local or regional workforce.

endogamy The social norm that influences people to marry within their social group and discourages interracial and interethnic marriages.

environmental injustice See also environmental racism. The tendency for socially and politically marginalized groups to bear the brunt of environmental ills.

environmental racism The tendency for hazardous waste sites and polluting industries to be located in areas where the surrounding residential population is an ethnic or racial minority.

epidemiological transition The shift from a society characterized by low life expectancy and parasitic and infectious diseases to one characterized by high life expectancy and chronic and degenerative diseases.

epidemiologist A scientist who studies the social origins and distribution of health problems in a population and how patterns of illness and disease vary between and within societies.

epidemiology The study of the distribution of disease within a population.

ethnicity A shared cultural heritage or national origin.

euthanasia The deliberate taking of an individual's life at her or his request.

e-waste Waste from electronic equipment.

experiment A research method that involves manipulating the independent variable to determine how it affects the dependent variable.

expressive roles Nurturing and emotionally support roles that women are generally socialized into.

expulsion When a dominant group forces a subordinate group to leave the country or to live only in designated areas of the country.

familism A value system that encourages family members to put their family's well-being above their individual and personal needs.

family allowance Canada's first universal welfare program, introduced in 1945, which promised a monthly allowance paid to families with children. The term "universal" here refers to the fact that the benefit flowed from the principle of entitlement and was available without reference to a recipient's income or assets.

family preservation program An in-home intervention for a family who is at risk of having a child removed from the home because of abuse or neglect.

Family Supplement Those families with children in a low-income situation (i.e., having a family net income under $25 921 a year) and who receive the Canada Child Tax Benefit automatically receive the Family Supplement with a rate based on family net income and the number and ages of children in the family.

feminism The belief that women and men should have equal rights and responsibilities.

feminization of poverty The disproportionate distribution of poverty among women.

fertility rate The average number of births per woman.

field research A method of research that involves observing and studying social behaviour in settings in which it naturally occurs; includes participant observation and nonparticipant observation.

flextime An option in work scheduling that allows employees to begin and end the workday at different times as long as they perform a given number of hours of work per week.

folkways The customs and manners of society.

frustration-aggression theory Also known as the "scapegoating theory" of prejudice; a psychological theory of prejudice that suggests prejudice is a form of hostility resulting from frustration. According to this theory, minority groups serve as convenient targets of displaced aggression.

functional illiterates High-school graduates who have difficulty with basic reading and math skills.

future shock The state of confusion resulting from rapid scientific and technological changes that challenge traditional values and beliefs.

gateway drug A drug (e.g., marijuana) that is believed to lead to the use of other drugs (such as cocaine and heroin).

gender The social definitions and expectations associated with being male or female.

gender tourism The recent tendency for definitions of masculinity and femininity to become less clear, resulting in individual exploration of the gender continuum.

gene monopolies Exclusive control over a particular gene as a result of government patents.

gene therapy The transplantation of a healthy duplicate gene to replace a defective or missing gene.

genetic engineering The manipulation of an organism's genes in such a way that the natural outcome is altered.

genetic screening The use of genetic maps to detect predispositions to human traits or diseases.

genocide The systematic annihilation of one racial or ethnic group by another.

gerontophobia Fear or dread of the elderly.

glass ceiling An invisible, socially created barrier that prevents women and other minorities from being promoted into top corporate positions.

global economy An interconnected network of economic activity that transcends national borders.

global warming The increasing average global air temperature, caused mainly by the accumulation of various gases that collect in the atmosphere.

globalization The economic, political, and social interconnectedness among societies throughout the world.

grade inflation Higher grades given than the work warrants; a general increase in student grades without a corresponding increase in learning.

greenhouse gases The collection of increasing amounts of chlorofluorocarbons (CFCs), carbon dioxide, methane, and other gases in the atmosphere, where they act like the glass in a greenhouse, holding heat from the sun close to the earth and preventing the heat from rising back into space.

greenwashing The corporate practice of displaying a sense of corporate responsibility for the environment. For example, many companies publicly emphasize the steps they have taken to help the environment. Another greenwashing strategy is to retool, repackage, or relabel a company's product.

hate crime An act of violence motivated by prejudice.

Head Start A project begun to help preschool children from disadvantaged families.

health A state of complete physical, mental, and social well-being.

heterosexism The belief that heterosexuality is the superior sexual orientation; it results in prejudice and discrimination against homosexuals and bisexuals.

heterosexual monogamy Marriage between two opposite-sex partners.

heterosexuality The predominance of cognitive, emotional, and sexual attraction to persons of the other sex.

home schooling The education of children at home instead of in a public or private school; often part of a fundamentalist movement to protect children from perceived non-Christian values in the public schools.

homophobia Negative attitudes toward homosexuality.

homosexuality The predominance of cognitive, emotional, and sexual attraction to persons of the same sex.

human capital The skills, knowledge, and capabilities of the individual.

human capital hypothesis The hypothesis that female–male pay differences are a function of differences in women's and men's levels of education, skills, training, and work experience.

Human Poverty Index (HPI) A composite measure of poverty based on three measures of deprivation: (1) deprivation of life, which is measured by the percentage of people expected to die before age 40; (2) deprivation of knowledge, which is measured by the percentage of adults who are illiterate; and (3) deprivation in living standards, which is measured as a composite of three variables—the percentage of people without access to health services, the percentage of people without access to safe water, and the percentage of malnourished children under five.

hypothesis A prediction or educated guess about how one variable is related to another variable.

incapacitation A criminal justice philosophy that views the primary purpose of the criminal justice system as preventing criminal offenders from committing further crimes against the public by putting them in prison.

incidence The number of new cases of a specific health problem within a given population during a specified period.

independent variable The variable that is expected to explain change in the dependent variable.

individual discrimination Discriminatory acts by individuals that are based on prejudicial attitudes.

individualism A value system that stresses the importance of individual happiness.

Industrial Revolution The period between the mid-eighteenth and the early nineteenth centuries when machines and factories became the primary means for producing goods.

infant mortality rate The number of deaths of infants under one year of age per one thousand live births in a calendar year.

infantilizing elders The portrayal of the elderly in the media as childlike in terms of clothes, facial expression, temperament, and activities.

information technology Any technology that carries information.

institution An established and enduring pattern of social relationships. The five traditional social institutions are family, religion, politics, economics, and education. Institutions are the largest elements of social structure.

institutional discrimination Discrimination in which the normal operations and procedures of social institutions result in unequal treatment of minorities.

instrumental roles Task-oriented roles that males are generally socialized into.

intergenerational poverty Poverty that is transmitted from one generation to the next.

Internet An international information infrastructure available through many universities, research institutes, government agencies, and businesses; developed in the 1970s as a U.S. Defense Department experiment.

intimate partner violence Actual or threatened violent crimes committed against persons by their current or former spouses, boyfriends, or girlfriends.

intimate terrorism Almost entirely perpetrated by men, a form of violence that is motivated by a wish to control one's partner and involves the systemic use of not only violence, but economic subordination, threats, isolation, verbal and emotional abuse, and other control tactics. This form of violence is more likely to escalate over time and to involve serious injury.

in-vitro fertilization The union of an egg and a sperm in an artificial setting such as a laboratory dish.

job burnout Prolonged job stress; it can cause physical problems, such as high blood pressure, ulcers, and headaches, as well as psychological problems.

job exportation The relocation of jobs to other countries where products can be produced more cheaply.

job sharing A work option in which two people share and are paid for one job.

labelling theory A symbolic interactionist theory that is concerned with the effects of labelling on the definition of a social problem (e.g., a social condition or group is viewed as problematic if it is labelled as such) and with the effects of labelling on the self-concept and behaviour of individuals (e.g., the label "juvenile delinquent" may contribute to the development of a self-concept and behaviour consistent with the label).

latent function Consequence that is unintended and often hidden or unrecognized; for example, a latent function of education is to provide schools that function as babysitters for employed parents.

laws Norms that are formalized and backed by political authority.

legalization Making prohibited behaviour legal; for example, legalizing marijuana or prostitution.

lesbigays A collective term sometimes used to refer to lesbians, gays, and bisexuals.

LGBT A term used to refer collectively to lesbians, gays, bisexuals, and transgendered individuals.

life expectancy The average number of years that a person born in a given year can expect to live.

low-income cutoff (LICO) Developed by Statistics Canada as a measure of poverty in 1968. Estimating that poor families or individuals spend approximately 34.7 percent or more of their pre-tax income on such basic needs as food, shelter, and clothing, 20 percentage points were added to this figure to determine the cutoff. This standard suggests that individuals or families who spent 54.7 percent of their pre-tax income on food, clothing, and shelter would experience financial difficulty. Different low-income cutoff lines are established by Statistics Canada for different communities as well as for families of varying sizes within these communities.

low-income measure (LIM) For the purposes of assessing low income using this measure, Statistics Canada has established a figure for the needs of one adult and proceeded on the assumption that family needs increase in proportion to the size of the family, with each additional adult increasing the family needs by 40 percent of the first adult and each additional child increasing the family's needs by 30 percent.

macro sociology The study of large aspects of society, such as institutions and large social groups.

MADD Mothers Against Drunk Driving. A social action group committed to reducing drunk driving.

Malthusian theory The theory proposed by Thomas Malthus in which he predicted that the population would grow faster than the food supply and that masses of people were destined to be poor and hungry. According to Malthus, food shortages would lead to war, disease, and starvation that would eventually slow population growth.

manifest function A consequence that is intended and commonly recognized; for example, a manifest function of education is to transmit knowledge and skills to youth.

marital assimilation Assimilation that occurs when different ethnic or racial groups become married or pair-bonded and produce children.

master status The status that is considered the most significant in a person's social identity.

maternal mortality rate The numbers of death that result from complications associated with pregnancy or childbirth per one thousand pregnant women.

mechanization The use of tools to accomplish tasks previously done by workers; characteristic of agricultural societies that emphasize the production of raw materials.

medicalization The tendency to define negatively evaluated behaviours or conditions as medical problems in need of medical intervention.

Medicare Canada's health care system, which provides access to universal comprehensive coverage for medically necessary inpatient and outpatient physician services.

melting pot The product of different groups coming together and contributing equally to a new common culture.

mental disorder A behavioural or psychological syndrome or pattern that occurs in an individual and that is associated with present distress or disability, or with a significantly increased risk of suffering, death, pain, disability, or loss of freedom.

mental health The successful performance of mental function, resulting in productive activities, fulfilling relationships with other people, and the ability to adapt to change and to cope with adversity.

mental illness A term used to refer collectively to all mental disorders.

micro sociology The study of the social psychological dynamics of individuals interacting in small groups.

minority A category of people who are denied equal access to positions of power, prestige, and wealth because of their group membership.

modern racism A subtle and complex form of racism in which individuals are not explicitly racist but tend to hold negative views of racial minorities and blame minorities for their social disadvantages.

modernization theory A theory claiming that as society becomes more technologically advanced, the position of the elderly declines.

morbidity The amount of disease, impairment, and accidents in a population.

mores Norms that have a moral basis.

mortality Death.

multicultural education Education that includes all racial and ethnic groups in the school curriculum and promotes awareness and appreciation for cultural diversity.

multiculturalism A philosophy that argues that the culture of a society should represent and embrace all racial and ethnic groups in that society.

multiple chemical sensitivity (MCS) A controversial health condition in which, after one or more acute or traumatic exposures to a chemical or group of chemicals, people experience adverse effects from low levels of chemical exposure that do not produce symptoms in the general public.

multiple jeopardy The disadvantages associated with being a member of two or more minority groups.

mutual violent control A rare pattern of abuse when two intimate terrorists battle for control.

National Child Benefit (NCB) Introduced in July 1998, NCB is a joint initiative of federal, provincial, and territorial governments designed to help prevent and reduce the depth of child poverty and to promote parental attachment to the workforce.

National Child Benefit Supplement (NCBS) A monthly benefit for low-income families with children that is the federal government's contribution to the National Child Benefit (NCB).

new ageism The belief that the elderly are a burden on the economy and, specifically, on the youth of Canada.

no-fault divorce A divorce that is granted based on the claim that there are irreconcilable differences within a marriage (as opposed to one spouse being legally at fault for the marital breakup).

norms Socially defined rules of behaviour, including folkways, mores, and laws.

objective element (of a social problem) Awareness of social condi-tions through one's own life experience and through reports in the media.

occupational sex segregation The concentration of women in certain occupations and of men in other occupations.

operational definition In research, a definition of a variable that specifies how that variable is to be measured (or was measured) in the research.

organized crime Criminal activity conducted by members of a hierarchi-cally arranged structure devoted pri-marily to making money through illegal means.

overt discrimination Discrimination that occurs because of an individual's own prejudicial attitudes.

parental alienation syndrome (PAS) An emotional and psychological disturbance in which children engage in exaggerated and unjustified denigra-tion and criticism of a parent.

partial birth abortion Also called an intact dilation and extraction (D&X) abortion, the procedure may entail delivering the limbs and the torso of the fetus before it has expired.

patriarchy A tradition in which fami-lies are male-dominated.

pay equity Also known as "equal pay for work of equal value"; requires equal pay for women who perform jobs of equal value to men in the same establishment. Requires employers to compare women's and men's jobs on the basis of skill, effort, responsibility, and working conditions to determine their value.

pink-collar jobs Jobs that offer few benefits, often have low prestige, and are disproportionately held by women.

planned obsolescence The manufac-turing of products that are intended to become inoperative or outdated in a fairly short time.

pluralism A state in which racial or ethnic groups maintain their distinct-ness but respect each other and have equal access to social resources.

polyandry The concurrent marriage of one woman to two or more men.

polygamy A form of marriage in which person may have two or more spouses.

polygyny The concurrent marriage of one man to two or more women.

population momentum Continued population growth that occurs even if a population achieves replacement-level fertility (2.1 births per woman) due to past high fertility rates which have resulted in large numbers of young women who are currently entering their childbearing years.

population transfer See expulsion.

populations The word scientists who reject the race concept now use when referring to groups that most people would call races.

postindustrialization The shift from an industrial economy dominated by manufacturing jobs to an economy dominated by service-oriented, infor-mation-intensive occupations.

postmodernism A world view that questions the validity of rational thinking and the scientific enterprise.

poverty Lacking resources for an "adequate" standard of living (see also **absolute poverty** and **relative poverty**).

prejudice An attitude or judgment, usually negative, about an entire cate-gory of people based on their group membership.

prevalence The total number of cases of a condition within a population that exist at a given time.

primary aging Biological changes associated with aging that are due to physiological variables such as cellular and molecular variation (e.g., grey hair).

primary assimilation The integration of different groups in personal, inti-mate associations such as friends, family, and spouses.

primary group A small group charac-terized by intimate and informal inter-action.

primary prevention (strategies) Family violence prevention strategies that target the general population.

proletariat Workers who were often exploited by the bourgeoisie.

pronatalism A cultural value that promotes having children.

race A category of people who are believed to share distinct physical characteristics that are deemed socially significant.

racial profiling The law enforcement practice of targeting suspects based upon race.

racism The belief that certain groups of people are innately inferior to other groups of people based on their racial classification. Racism serves to justify discrimination against groups that are perceived as inferior.

rehabilitation A criminal justice philosophy that views the primary purpose of the criminal justice system as changing the criminal offender through such programs as education and job training, individual and group therapy, substance abuse counselling, and behaviour modification.

relative poverty A deficiency in material and economic resources compared with some other population.

reparative therapy Various therapies that are aimed at changing homosexuals' sexual orientation.

repeated trauma disorders The most common types of workplace illnesses include muscle, tendon, vascular, and nerve injuries that result from repeated or sustained actions or exertions of different body parts. Jobs that are associated with high rates of upper body repeated trauma disorders include computer programming, manufacturing, meat packaging, poultry processing, and clerical/office work.

repetitive strain disorders See **repeated trauma disorders**.

replacement level The average number of births per woman (2.1) in a population, below which the population begins to decline.

restorative justice A philosophy primarily concerned with reconciling conflict between the offender, the community, and the victim.

roles A set of rights, obligations, and expectations associated with a status.

sample In survey research, the portion of the population selected to be questioned.

sanctions Social consequences for conforming to or violating norms. Types of sanctions include positive, negative, formal, and informal.

sandwich generation The generation that has the responsibility of simultaneously caring for their children and their aging parents.

scapegoating theory See **frustration-aggression theory**.

science The process of discovering, explaining, and predicting natural or social phenomena.

scientific apartheid The growing gap between the industrial and developing countries in the rapidly evolving knowledge frontier.

second shift The household work and childcare that employed parents (usually women) do when they return from their jobs.

secondary aging Biological changes associated with aging that can be attributed to poor diet, lack of exercise, and increased stress.

secondary assimilation The integration of different groups in public areas and in social institutions, such as in government, neighbourhoods, schools, and the workplace.

secondary group A group characterized by impersonal and formal interaction.

secondary prevention (strategies) Prevention strategies that target groups that are thought to be at high risk for family violence.

segregation The physical and social separation of categories of individuals, such as racial or ethnic groups.

self-fulfilling prophecy A concept referring to the tendency for people to act in a manner consistent with the expectations of others.

senescence The biology of aging.

senilicide The killing of the elderly.

sex A person's biological classification as male or female.

sex ratio The ratio of men to women in a given society or subgroup of society.

sexism The belief that there are innate psychological, behavioural, or intellectual differences between females and males and that these differences connote the superiority of one group and the inferiority of another.

sexual aggression Sexual interaction that occurs against one's will through the use of physical force, pressure, use of alcohol/drugs, or use of position of authority.

sexual harassment When an employer requires sexual favours in exchange for a promotion, salary increase, or any other employee benefit, or the existence of a hostile environment that unreasonably interferes with job performance, as in the case of sexually explicit remarks or insults being made to an employee.

sexual orientation The identification of individuals as heterosexual, bisexual, or homosexual based on their emotional and sexual attractions, relationships, self-identity, and lifestyle.

sick building syndrome (SBS) A situation in which occupants of a building experience symptoms that seem to be linked to time spent in a building but for which no specific illness or cause can be identified.

slavery A condition in which one social group treats another group as property to exploit for financial gain.

snowball sampling A method of sampling in which one respondent refers the researcher to another respondent, who then refers the researcher to another respondent, and so forth.

social group Two or more people who have a common identity and who interact and form a social relationship; institutions are made up of social groups.

social problem A social condition that a segment of society views as harmful to members of society and in need of remedy.

social promotion The passing of students from grade to grade even if they are failing.

socialism An economic ideology that emphasizes public rather than private ownership. Theoretically, goods and services are equitably distributed according to the needs of the citizens.

sociological imagination A term coined by C. Wright Mills to refer to the ability to see the connections between our personal lives and the social world in which we live.

special education Remedial education designed to help children and adults who are exceptional in some way, including but not limited to, low intelligence, visual or auditory disabilities, and emotional or specific learning difficulties.

split labour market The existence of primary and secondary labour markets. A primary labour market refers to jobs that are stable and economically rewarding and have many benefits; a secondary labour market refers to jobs that offer little pay, no security, few benefits, and little chance for advancement.

status A position a person occupies within a social group.

stereotype An oversimplified or exaggerated generalization about a category of individuals. Stereotypes are either untrue or are gross distortions of reality.

stigma Refers to any personal characteristic associated with social disgrace, rejection, or discrediting.

strain theory A theory that argues that when legitimate means of acquiring culturally defined goals are limited by the structure of society, the resulting strain may lead to crime or other deviance.

street crime Also known as "conventional crime"; those traditional illegal behaviours that most people think of as crime, such as sexual assault, assault, armed robbery, break and enter, and so on.

structural sexism The ways in which the organization of society, and specifically its institutions, subordinate individuals and groups based on their sex classification.

structural unemployment Exists when there are not enough jobs available for those who want them; unemployment that results from structural variables such as government and business downsizing, job exportation, automation, a reduction in the number of new and existing businesses, an increase in the number of people looking for jobs, and a recessionary economy where fewer goods are purchased and, therefore, fewer employees are needed.

structural-functionalism A sociological perspective that views society as a system of interconnected parts that work together in harmony to maintain a state of balance and social equilibrium for the whole; focuses on how each part of society influences and is influenced by other parts.

subcultural theory A theory that argues that certain groups or subcultures in society have values and attitudes that are conducive to crime and violence.

subjective element (of a social problem) The belief that a particular social condition is harmful to society, or to a segment of society, and that it should and can be changed.

survey research A method of research that involves eliciting information from respondents through questions; includes interviews (telephone or face-to-face) and written questionnaires.

sustainable development Societal development that meets the needs of current generations without threatening the future of subsequent generations.

sweatshop A work environment characterized by less than minimum wage pay, excessively long hours of work often without overtime pay, unsafe or inhumane working conditions, abusive treatment of workers by employers, or the lack of worker organizations aimed at negotiating better work conditions.

symbol Something that represents something else.

symbolic interactionism A sociological perspective that emphasizes that human behaviour is influenced by definitions and meanings that are created and maintained through symbolic interaction with others.

technological dualism A term referring to the tendency for technology to have both positive (e.g., time saving) and negative (e.g., unemployment) consequences.

technological fix The use of scientific principles and technology to solve social problems.

technology Activities that apply the principles of science and mechanics to the solution of specific problems.

technology-induced diseases Diseases that result from the use of technological devices, products, or chemicals.

telecommuting A work option in which workers complete all or part of their work at home with the use of information technology.

telemedicine Using information and communication technologies to deliver a wide range of health care services, including diagnosis, treatment, prevention, health support and information, and education of health care workers.

telework A form of work that allows employees to work part- or full-time at home or at a satellite office.

tertiary prevention (strategies) Prevention strategies that target families who have experienced family violence.

therapeutic cloning Therapeutic cloning entails using stem cells from human embryos to produce body cells that can be used to grow needed organs or tissues.

therapeutic communities Organizations in which 35 to 100 individuals reside for up to 15 months to abstain from drugs, develop marketable skills, and receive counselling.

transgendered individuals Persons who do not fit neatly into either the male or female category, or whose behaviour is not congruent with the rules and expectations for their sex in the society in which they live.

transnational crime Crime that, directly or indirectly, involves more than one country.

triad dispute resolution Dispute resolution that involves two disputants and a negotiator.

triangulation The use of multiple methods and approaches to study a social phenomenon.

triple jeopardy See **multiple jeopardy**.

underclass A persistently poor and socially disadvantaged group that disproportionately experiences joblessness, welfare dependency, involvement in criminal activity, dysfunctional families, and low educational attainment.

underemployment Employment in a job that is underpaid; is not commensurate with one's skills, experience, or education; or involves working fewer hours than desired.

under-five mortality rate The rate of deaths among children under age five.

unemployment The unemployed are those who want and are able to work but who have no work at present. For statistical purposes, Statistics Canada defines the unemployed more precisely as those who did not work in the labour market during the survey reference week (but may have done housework, etc.), were available for work and had actively looked for work in the past four weeks, were on temporary layoff for 26 weeks or less and expected to be recalled by their employer, or were waiting for a new job to begin within four weeks.

upskilling The opposite of **deskilling**; upskilling reduces employee alienation and increases decision-making powers.

values Social agreements about what is considered good and bad, right and wrong, desirable and undesirable.

variable Any measurable event, characteristic, or property that varies or is subject to change.

victimless crime An illegal activity, such as prostitution or drug use, that has no complaining party; also called "vice crime."

violent resistance Acts of violence by a partner that are committed in self-defence. Violent resistance is almost exclusively perpetrated by women against a male partner.

wealth The total assets of an individual or household minus liabilities.

wealthfare Governmental policies and regulations that economically favour the wealthy.

white-collar crime Includes both occupational crime, where individuals commit crimes in the course of their employment, and corporate crime, where corporations violate the law in the interest of maximizing profit.

work sectors (primary, secondary, tertiary) The division of the labour force into distinct categories (primary, secondary, and tertiary) based on the types of goods or services produced.

working poor Individuals who work in the labour force, but who nevertheless live in poverty.

References

Preface

Safransky, Sy. 1990. *Sunbeams: A Book of Quotations*. Berkeley, CA: North Atlantic Books.

Chapter 1

Bibby, Reginald W. 1995. *The Bibby Report: Social Trends Canadian Style*. Toronto: Stoddart.
———. 2001. *Canada's Teens: Today, Yesterday, and Tomorrow*. Toronto: Stoddart.
Blumer, Herbert. 1971. "Social Problems as Collective Behavior." *Social Problems* 8(3): 298–306.
Catania, Joseph A., David R. Gibson, Dale D. Chitwook, and Thomas J. Coates. 1990. "Methodological Problems in AIDS Behavioral Research: Influences on Measurement Error and Participation Bias in Studies of Sexual Behavior." *Psychological Bulletin* 108: 339–62.
Coleman, John R. 1990. "Diary of a Homeless Man." In *Social Problems*, pp. 160–69. Englewood Cliffs, NJ: Prentice-Hall.
Dordick, Gwendolyn A. 1997. *Something Left to Lose: Personal Relations and Survival Among New York's Homeless*. Philadelphia: Temple University Press.
Dunn, Jennifer. 2000. "What Love Has to Do With It: The Cultural Construction of Emotion and Sorority Women's Responses to Forcible Interactions." *Social Problems* 46: 440–59.
Eitzen, Stanley, and Maxine Baca Zinn. 2000. *Social Problems*. Boston: Allyn and Bacon.
Goldie, Terry. 2001. "Queer Nation?" In Terry Goldie (ed.), *In a Queer Country: Gay and Lesbian Studies in the Canadian Context*, pp. 7–26. Vancouver: Arsenal Pulp Press.
Gregg, Allan R. 2001/2002. "Scary New World." *Maclean's*, December 31–January 7: 22–25.
Hewlett, Sylvia Ann. 1992. *When the Bough Breaks: The Cost of Neglecting Our Children*. New York: Harper Perennial.
Hills, Stuart L. (ed.). 1987. *Corporate Violence: Injury and Death for Profit*. Lanham, MN: Rowman and Littlefield.
Jekielek, Susan M. 1998. "Parental Conflict, Marital Disruption and Children's Emotional Well-Being." *Social Forces* 76: 905–35.
May, Richard. 2000. "Human Development Report." *Journal of American Planning Association* 66: 219.
Merton, Robert K. 1968. *Social Theory and Social Structure*. New York: Free Press.
Mills, C. Wright. 1959. *The Sociological Imagination*. London: Oxford University Press.
Mouw, Ted, and Yu Xie. 1999. "Bilingualism and Academic Achievement of Asian Immigrants." *American Sociological Review* 64: 232–52.
Nader, Ralph, Nadia Milleron, and Duff Conacher. 1993. *Canada Firsts*. Toronto: McClelland and Stewart Inc.
Romer, D., R. Hornik, B. Stanton, M. Black, X. Li, I. Ricardo, and S. Feigelman. 1997. "'Talking Computers': A Reliable and Private Method to Conduct Interviews on Sensitive Topics with Children." *Journal of Sex Research* 34: 3–9.
Schwalbe, Michael. 1998. *The Sociologically Examined Life: Pieces of the Conversation*. Mountain View, CA: Mayfield Publishing Company.
Skeen, Dick. 1991. *Different Sexual Worlds: Contemporary Case Studies of Sexuality*. Lexington, MA: Lexington Books.
Thomas, W. I. [1931] 1966. "The Relation of Research to the Social Process." In Morris Janowitz (ed.), *W. I. Thomas on Social Organization and Social Personality*, pp. 289–305. Chicago: University of Chicago Press.
Wilson, John. 1983. *Social Theory*. Englewood Cliffs, NJ: Prentice-Hall.

Chapter 2

Adetunji, Jacob. 2000. "Trends in Under-5 Mortality Rates and the HIV/AIDS Epidemic." *Bulletin of the World Health Organization* 78(10): 1200–6.
American Psychiatric Association. 2000. *Diagnostic and Statistical Manual of Mental Disorders*, 4th ed., Text Revision DSM–TR. Washington, DC: American Psychiatric Association.
Antezana, Fernando S., Claire M. Chollat-Traquet, and Derik Yach. 1998. "Health for All in the 21st Century." *World Health Statistics Quarterly* 51: 3–6.
Armstrong, Pat, Hugh Armstrong, and Claudia Fegan. 1998. *Universal Health Care: What the United States Can Learn from the Canadian Experience*. New York: The New Press.
Arnold, Tom. 2001. "Drugs Account for 15.5% of Health Care Spending." *National Post*, March 15: A11.
Ash, Russell. 2001. *The Top 10 of Everything: Canadian Edition 2002*. Toronto: Dorling Kindersley Limited.

Barlow, Maude, and Elizabeth May. 2000. *Frederick Street: Life and Death on Canada's Love Canal*. Toronto: HarperCollins.

Bibby, Reginald W. 2001. *Canada's Teens: Today, Yesterday, and Tomorrow*. Toronto: Stoddart.

Bricker, Darrell, and Edward Greenspon. 2001. *Searching for Certainty: Inside the New Canadian Mindset*. Toronto: Doubleday Canada.

Brundtland, Gro Harlem. 2000. "Mental Health in the 21st Century." *Bulletin of the World Health Organization* 78(4): 411.

Canadian Aboriginal News. 2001. "Innu, Health Officials Settle Differences over Treatment for Gas Sniffers." http://www.canadianaboriginal.com/health/health26b.htm.

Canadian Centre on Substance Abuse. 1999. *Canadian Profile, 1999: Alcohol, Tobacco, and Other Drugs*. Ottawa: Canadian Centre on Substance Abuse and Centre for Addiction and Mental Health.

CMA (Canadian Medical Association). 1999. *Access to Health Care in Canada Report*. http://www.cma.ca/advocacy/access/index.asp.

———. 2001. "Canadians Give a B Grade to the Health Care System" (news release). August 13. http://www.cma.ca/cma/common/displayPage.do?pageID=/staticContent/HTML/N012/adovcacy/news/2001/08-13.htm.

Canadian Mental Health Association. 2002. "Depression and Manic Depression." http://www.cmha.ca/english/store/mh-pamphlets/mh.

Canadian Psychiatric Association. 2002. "Anxiety, Depression and Manic Depression." http://www.cpa-apc.org/MIAW/pamphlets/Anxiety.arp.

Cockerham, William C. 1998. *Medical Sociology*, 7th ed. Upper Saddle River, NJ: Prentice Hall.

Diamond, Catherine, and Susan Buskin. 2000. "Continued Risky Behavior in HIV-Infected Youth." *American Journal of Public Health* 90(1): 115–18.

Drivers.com. 2001. "Banning Phone Use While Driving a 'No-Brainer.'" May 29. http://www.drivers.com/cgs-bin/go.cgi?type=ART&id=000000387&static=1.

Everett, Sherry A., Rae L. Schnuth, and Joanne L. Tribble. 1998. "Tobacco and Alcohol Use in Top-Grossing American Films." *Journal of Community Health* 23: 317–24.

Family Care International. 1999. "Safe Motherhood." http://www.safemotherhood.org/init_facts.htm.

Feachum, Richard G. A. 2000. "Poverty and Inequality: A Proper Focus for the New Century." *The International Journal of Public Health* (Bulletin of the World Health Organization) 78: 1–2.

Garfinkel, P. E., and D. Goldbloom. 2000. "Mental Health—Getting Beyond Stigma and Categories." *Bulletin of the World Health Organization* 78(4): 503–5.

"Global Summary of the HIV/AIDS Epidemic, December 2000." 2001. "News." *Bulletin of the World Health Organization* 79(1): 78.

Goldstein, Michael S. 1999. "The Origins of the Health Movement." In Kathy Charmaz and Debora A. Paterniti (eds.), *Health, Illness, and Healing: Society, Social Context, and Self*, pp. 31–41. Los Angeles: Roxbury Publishing Co.

Gottlieb, Scott. 2000. "Oral AIDS Vaccine to Be Tested in the Republic of Uganda." *Bulletin of the World Health Organization* 78(7): 946–56.

Graham, Mel. 1999. "Budget 2000 and People with Disabilities." *Abilities: Canadian Lifestyle Magazine for People with Disabilities* 41 (Winter): 48.

Grant, Karen R. 1993. "Health and Health Care." In Peter S. Li and B. Singh Bolaria (eds.), *Contemporary Sociology: Critical Perspectives*, pp. 394–409. Toronto: Copp-Clark Pitman.

Health Canada. 1999a. *Toward a Healthy Future: Second Report on the Health of Canadians*. Prepared by the Federal, Provincial, and Territorial Advisory Committee on Population Health for the Meeting of Ministers of Health, Charlottetown, PEI, September.

———. 1999b. *Statistical Report on the Health of Canadians*. December 25. http://www.hc-sc.gc.ca/hppb/phdd/report/state/eng/over.html.

———. 2002a. "HIV and AIDS Among Women in Canada." *HIV/AIDS Epi Update*, April. http://www.hc-sc.gc.ca/pphb-dgspsp/publicat/epiu-aepi/hiv-vih/women_e.html.

———. 2002b. "HIV and AIDS Among Youth in Canada." *HIV/AIDS Epi Update*, April. http://www.hc-sc.gc.ca/pphb-dgspsp/publicat/epiu-aepi/hiv-vih/youth_e.html.

———. 2002c. "National HIV Prevalence and Incidence Estimates for 1999: No Evidence of a Decline in Overall Incidence." *HIV/AIDS Epi Update*, April. http://www.hc-sc.gc.ca/pphb-dgspsp/publicat/epiu-aepi/hiv-vih/estima_e.html.

Higgins, Michael. 2002. "Twelve in Manitoba being tested for West Nile." *National Post*, July 29: A1.

Inciardi, James A., and Lana D. Harrison. 1997. "HIV, AIDS, and Drug Abuse in the International Sector." *Journal of Drug Issues* 27: 1–8.

Johnson, Tracy L., and Elizabeth Fee. 1997. "Women's Health Research: An Introduction." In Florence P. Haseltine and Beverly Greenberg Jacobson (eds.), *Women's Health Research: A Medical and Policy Primer*, pp. 3–26. Washington, DC: Health Press International.

Joint United Nations Programme on HIV/AIDS. 2000a. "AIDS and Population." http://www.unaids.org.

———. 2000b. "AIDS: Men Make a Difference: World AIDS Campaign." http://www.unaids.org.

———. 2000c. "HIV/AIDS and Development." http://www.unaids.org.

———. 2000d. "Innovative Approaches to HIV Prevention." http://www.unaids.org.

———. 2000e. "Report on the Global HIV/AIDS Epidemic—June 2000." http://www.unaids.org/epidemic_update/report/Epi_report_chap_glo_estim.htm.

Kennedy, Mark. 1999. "Doctors Warn Ottawa to Heed Physician Shortages Right Away." *National Post*, August 3: A6.

———. 2001. "Health Costs Rocket Past $100B." *National Post*, December 19: A1, A6.

Kerzner, Lana, and David Baker. 1999. *A Canadians with Disability Act?* May 14. http://www.hc-sc.gc.ca.

Kessler, Ronald C., Katherine A. McGonagle, Shanyang Zhao, Christopher B. Nelson, Michael Hughes, Suzann Eshleman, Hans-Ulrich Wittchen, and Kenneth S. Kendler. 1994. "Lifetime and 12-Month Prevalence of DSM-III-R Psychiatric Disorders in the United States." *Archives of General Psychiatry* 51: 8–19.

Kitchener-Waterloo Record. 1999. "What's up with Viagra Decision?" November 25: A16.

Lantz, Paula M., James S. House, James M. Lepkowski, David R. Williams, Richard P. Mero, and Jieming Chen. 1998. "Socioeconomic Factors, Health Behaviors, and Mortality: Results from a Nationally Representative Prospective Study of U.S. Adults." *Journal of the American Medical Association* 279: 1703–8.

LaPorte, Ronald E. 1997. "Improving Public Health via the Information Superhighway." June 8, 1998. http://www.the-scientist.library. upenn.edu/yr1997/august/ opin_97018.html.

Lay, Carolyn. 2000. "Family Planning Access Is Seen as Key Determinant in Maternal Well Being." *Popline* 22: 3.

Lerer, Leonard B., Alan D. Lopez, Tord Kjellstrom, and Derek Yach. 1998. "Health for All: Analyzing Health Status and Determinants." *World Health Statistics Quarterly* 51: 7–20.

Marshall, Katherine. 2001. "Working with Computers." *Perspectives on Labour and Income* 13(2): 5–11.

Miller, K., and A. Rosenfield. 1996. "Population and Women's Reproductive Health: An International Perspective." *Annual Review of Public Health* 17: 359–82.

Milne, Celia. 2002. "Condition Critical." *Maclean's*, June 3: 40–41.

Mitchell, Alana. 1995. "Down's Transplant Bid Poses Dilemma." *The Globe and Mail*, April 28: A1, A10.

Morse, Minna. 1998. "The Killer Mosquitoes." *Utne Reader* (May–June): 14–15.

Murray, C., and A. Lopez (eds.). 1996. *The Global Burden of Disease*. Boston: Harvard University Press.

National Center for Health Statistics. 2000. *Health, United States, 2000 with Adolescent Health Chartbook*. Hyattsville, MD: U.S. Government Printing Office.

National Council of Welfare. 2001. "Welfare Rates." http://www.ncwc-nbes.net/htmdocument.htm.

Nelson, Adie, and Barrie W. Robinson. 2002. *Gender in Canada*, 2nd ed. Toronto: Pearson Education Canada Inc.

Ostrof, Paul. 1998. "Readers Write: My Chair." *The Sun* (August): 33–40.

Parsons, Talcott. 1951. *The Social System*. New York: The Free Press.

Pate, Russell R., Michael Pratt, Steven N. Blair, William L. Haskell, Caroline A. Macera, Claude Bouchard, David Buchner, Walter Ettiger, Gregory W. Health, Abby C. King, Andrea Kriska, Arthur L. Leon, Bess H. Marcus, Jeremy Morris, Ralph S. Paffenbarger, Kevin Patrick, Michael L. Pollock, James M. Rippe, James Sallis, and Jack H. Wilmore. 1995. "Physical Activity and Public Health: A Recommendation from the Centers for Disease Control and Prevention and the American College of Sports Medicine." *Journal of the American Medical Association* 273(5): 402–6.

"Poverty Threatens Crisis." 1998. *Popline* 20 (May–June): 3.

Rice, Amy L., Lisa Sacco, Adnan Hyder, and Robert E. Black. 2000. "Malnutrition as an Underlying Cause of Childhood Deaths Associated with Infectious Diseases in Developing Countries." *Bulletin of the World Health Organization* 78(10): 1207–21.

Royal Commission on Aboriginal Peoples. 1996. *Looking Forward, Looking Back: Report of the Royal Commission on Aboriginal Peoples*, Vol. 1. Ottawa: Supply and Services Canada.

Rustein, Shea O. 2000. "Factors Associated with Trends in Infant and Child Mortality in Developing Countries During the 1990s." *Bulletin of the World Health Organization* 78(10): 1256–70.

Safe Motherhood Initiative. 1998. "Fact and Figures." September 24. http://www.safemotherhood.org/ init_facts.htm.

Scott, K. 1997. "Indigenous Canadians." In D. McKenzie, R. William, and E. Single (eds.), *Canadian Profile, 1997: Alcohol, Tobacco and Other Drugs*. Ottawa: Canadian Centre on Substance Abuse.

Shkilnyk, Anastasia. 1985. *A Poison Stronger than Love*. New Haven, CT: Yale University Press.

Simmie, Scott, and Julie Nunes. 2001. *The Last Taboo: A Survival Guide to Mental Health Care in Canada*. Toronto: McCelland and Stewart Ltd.

Statistics Canada. 1998a. *Canada Yearbook 1999*. Ottawa: Ministry of Industry.

———. 1998b. *The Daily*, October 29. http://www.statcan.ca/Daily/ English/981029/d981029.htm.

———. 1998c. "Health Reports: Multiple-Risk Behaviour in Teenagers and Young Adults 1994/95." *The Daily*, October 29. http://www.statcan.ca/english/ads/ 82-003-X1B/10-98.htm.

———. 2002. "Deaths, 1999." *The Daily*, May 7. http://www.statcan.ca/Daily/ English/020507/d020507b.htm.

Stine, Gerald J. 1998. *Acquired Immune Deficiency Syndrome: Biological, Medical, Social, and Legal Issues*. Upper Saddle River, NJ: Prentice Hall.

Szasz, Thomas. [1961] 1970. *The Myth of Mental Illness: Foundations of a Theory of Personal Conduct*. New York: Harper and Row.

Turner, Linda A., Margaret Cyr, Robert A. Kinch, Robert Liston, Michael S. Kramer, Martha Fair, and Maureen Heaman. 2002. "Under-Reporting of Maternal Mortality in Canada: A Question of Definition." *Chronic Diseases in Canada*, 23(1). http://www.hc-sc. gc.ca/pphb-dgspsp/publicat/ cdic-mcc-23-1/d_e.html.

U.S. Department of Health and Human Services. 1999. *Mental Health: A Report of the Surgeon General: Executive Summary*. Rockville, MD: U.S. Government Printing Office.

UNICEF (United Nations Children's Fund). 2001. *The State of the World's Children, 2001*. New York: UNICEF. http://www.unicef.org/sowco1/pdf.

United Nations Population Fund. 2000. *The State of World Population Report 2000*.

http://www.unfpa.org/SWP/2000/english/index.

Verbrugge, Lois M. 1999. "Pathways of Health and Death." In Kathy Charmaz and Debora A. Paterniti (eds.), *Health, Illness, and Healing: Society, Social Context, and Self*, pp. 377–94. Los Angeles: Roxbury Publishing Co.

Visschedijk, Jan, and Silvere Simeant. 1998. "Targets for Health for All in the Twenty-First Century." *World Health Statistics Quarterly* 51: 56–67.

Ward, Darrell E. 1999. *The AmFAR AIDS Handbook*. New York: W.W. Norton & Company.

Weitz, Rose. 2001. *The Sociology of Health, Illness, and Health Care: A Critical Approach*, 2nd ed. Belmont, CA: Wadsworth Publishing Co.

Williams, David R., and Chiquita Collins. 1999. "U.S. Socioeconomic and Racial Differences in Health: Patterns, and Explanations." In Kathy Charmaz and Debora A. Paterniti (eds.), *Health, Illness, and Healing: Society, Social Context, and Self*, pp. 349–76. Los Angeles: Roxbury Publishing Co.

WHO (World Health Organization). 1946. "Constitution of the World Health Organization." New York: World Health Organization Interim Commission.

———. 1997. "Fact Sheet No. 178: Reducing Mortality from Major Childhood Killer Diseases." July 28, 1998. http://www.cdc.gov/ogh/frames.htm.

———. 1998. "Fifty Facts from the World Health Report 1998." August 8. http://www.who.int/whr/1998/factse/htm.

———. 2000. *The World Health Report 2000*. http://www.who.int.

———. 2001. *The World Health Report 2001*. http://www.who.int.

World Health Organization and United Nations Joint Programme on HIV/AIDS. 1998. "Report on the Global HIV/AIDS Epidemic— June 1998." August 8. http://www.who.int/emchiv/global_report/data/globrep_e/pdf.

WHO [World Health Organization] International Consortium on Psychiatric Epidemiology. 2000. "Cross-National Comparisons of the Prevalences and Correlates of Mental Disorders." *Bulletin of the World Health Organization* 78(4): 413–26. http://www.who.int/bulletin/tableofcontents/2000/vol.78no.4.html.

Chapter 3

Alcohol Alert. 2000. "Mechanisms of Addiction." *National Institute on Alcohol Abuse and Alcoholism* 46 (April): 2.

AP (Associated Press). 1999. "Alcoholism Touches Millions." December 30. http://abcnews.go.com.

Auditor General (of Canada). 2001. *2001 Report of the Auditor General of Canada*. http://www.oag-bvg.gc.ca/domino/reports.nsf/html/0111xe06.html.

AAP (Australian Associated Press). 1998. "Genetics of Alcoholism." *Institute of Alcohol Studies Update*. London: IAS Publications.

Becker, H. S. 1966. *Outsiders: Studies in the Sociology of Deviance*. New York: Free Press.

Bibby, Reginald W. 2001. *Canada's Teens: Today, Yesterday, and Tomorrow*. Toronto: Stoddart.

Bureau of Justice Statistics. 1992. "Drugs, Crime, and the Justice System: A National Report from the Bureau of Justice Statistics." U.S. Department of Justice, Office of Justice Programs. Washington, DC: U.S. Government Printing Office, Superintendent of Documents.

CCSA (Canadian Centre on Substance Abuse). 1999. *Canadian Profile, 1999: Alcohol, Tobacco, and Other Drugs*. Ottawa: Canadian Centre on Substance Abuse and Centre for Addiction and Mental Health.

Cloud, John. 2000. "The Lure of Ecstasy." *Time*, June 5: 63–72.

Cooper, M., R. Corrado, A. M. Karlberg, and L. P. Adams. 1992. "Aboriginal Suicide in British Columbia: An Overview." *Canada's Mental Health* (September): 19–23.

DEA (Drug Enforcement Administration). 2000. "An overview of Club Drugs." *Drug Intelligence Brief*, February. 1–10. Washington, DC: U.S. Department of Justice.

Dembo, Richard, Linda Williams, Jeffrey Fagan, and James Schmeidler. 1994. "Development and Assessment of a Classification of High Risk Youths." *Journal of Drug Issues* 24: 25–53.

Department of Finance Canada. 2002. "Government Announces Tobacco Tax Increases to Discourage Smoking." June 17. http://www.fin.gc.ca/news/02/02-052e.html.

Department of Justice. 1998. "How Do Canadian Crime Rates Compare to Those of Other Countries?" *Justice Research Notes* 5 (April): 17–8.

Duke, Steven, and Albert C. Gross. 1994. *America's Longest War: Rethinking Our Tragic Crusade against Drugs*. New York: G.P. Putnam and Sons.

Duster, Troy. 1995. "The New Crisis of Legitimacy in Controls, Prisons, and Legal Structures." *American Sociologist* 26: 20–29.

Easley, Margaret, and Norman Epstein. 1991. "Coping with Stress in a Family with an Alcoholic Parent." *Family Relations* 40: 218–24.

EMCDDA (European Monitoring Centre for Drugs and Drug Addiction). 2001. *Annual Report on the State of the Drugs Problem in the European Union Online: 2001*. http://annualreport.emcdda.org/index.html.

Feagin, Joe R., and C. B. Feagin. 1994. *Social Problems*. Englewood Cliffs, NJ: Prentice-Hall.

Fife, R. 1999. "Police Chiefs Get through to the Top." *National Post*, April 22.

Francis, Craig. 2000. "Europe Mellows Out over Cannabis." CNN.com, October 9. http://www.cnn.com/2000/world/europe/10/09/drugs.law.

Gentry, Cynthia. 1995. "Crime Control through Drug Control." In Joseph F. Sheley (ed.), *Criminology*, 2nd ed., pp. 477–93. Belmont, CA: Wadsworth.

Gfellner, B. M., and J. D. Hundelby. 1995. "Patterns of Drug Use Among Native and White Adolescents: 1990–1993." *Canadian Journal of Public Health* 86: 95–97.

Giffen, P. J., S. Endicott, and S. Lambert. 1991. *Panic and Indifference: The Politics of Canada's Drug Laws*. Ottawa: Canadian Centre on Substance Abuse.

Green, Melvyn. 1986. "The History of Canadian Narcotics Control: The Formative Years." In Neil Boyd (ed.), *The Social Dimensions of Law*, pp. 24–40. Scarborough, ON: Prentice Hall.

Gusfield, Joseph. 1963. *Contested Meanings: The Construction of Alcohol Problems*. Madison: University of Wisconsin Press.

Hackler, James C. 2000. *Canadian Criminology: Strategies and Perspectives*, 2nd ed. Scarborough, ON: Prentice Hall Allyn and Bacon Canada.

Health Canada. 1999. *Statistical Report on the Health of Canadians*. December 25. http://www.hc-sc.gc.ca/hppb/phdd/report/stat/eng/over.html.

———. 2001. "Research Results for First Half of 2001—February to June 2001." http://www.hc-sc.gc.ca/heces-sesc/tobacco/research/ctums/ctums_first_2001.html.

———. 2002a. "HIV/AIDS Among Aboriginal Persons in Canada: A Continuing Concern." *HIV/AIDS Epi Update*, April. http://www.hc-sc.gc.ca/pphb-dgspsp/publicat/epiu-aepi/hiv-vih/aborig_e.html.

———. 2002b. *The Scoop on Smoking—Health Canada for Youth*. http://www.hc-sc.gc.ca/hecs-sesc/tobacco/youth/scoop.html.

———. 2002c. "Smoking Rates Continue to Drop." June 26. http://www.hc-sc.gc.ca/english/media/releases/2002/2002_52.htm.

———. 2002d. "Research Tobacco Use Monitoring Survey (CTUMS) Annual Results, 2001." http://www.hc-sc.gc.ca/hecs-sesc/tobacco/research/ctums/2001/summary.html.

HHS (U.S. Department of Health and Human Services). 1998. "Tobacco Use Continues to Rise among High School Students in the U.S." *Substance Abuse and Mental Health Service Administration*. Press release, April 2. Washington, DC.

ISDD (Institute for Study of Drug Dependence—Drug Scope). 1999. "UK Trends and Updates." http://www.isdd.co.uk/trends/introduction1.html.

Jarvik, M. 1990. "The Drug Dilemma: Manipulating the Demand." *Science* 250: 387–92.

Johnson, Holly. 1996. *Dangerous Domains: Violence Against Women in Canada*. Scarborough, ON: Nelson.

Join Together. 1998. "Inhalant Abuse." *Hot Issues*, July 11. http://www.jointogether.org/sa/issues/hot_issues/inhalants/default.html.

Klutt, Edward C. 2000. "Pathology of Drug Abuse." http://www.medlib-utah.edu/WebPath.

Leinwand, Donna. 2000. "20% Say They Used Drugs with Their Mom or Dad..." *USA Today*, August 24: 1A.

Leonard, K. E., and H. T. Blane. 1992. "Alcohol and Marital Aggression in a National Sample of Young Men." *Journal of Interpersonal Violence* 7: 19–30.

Lipton, Douglas S. 1994. "The Correctional Opportunity: Pathways to Drug Treatment for Offenders." *Journal of Drug Issues* 24: 331–48.

MacCoun, Robert J., and Peter Reuter. 2001. "Does Europe Do It Better? Lessons from Holland, Britain and Switzerland." In D. Stanley Eitzen and Craig S. Leedham (eds.), *Solutions to Social Problems*, pp. 260–264. Boston: Allyn and Bacon.

Mayell, Hillary. 1999. "Tobacco on Course to Become World's Leading Cause of Death." *National Geographic News*. http://ngnews/news/1999/121499.

McCaffrey, Barry. 1998. "Remarks by Barry McCaffrey, Director, Office of National Drug Control Policy, to the United Nations General Assembly: Special Session on Drugs." Office of National Drug Control Policy. http://www.whitehousedrugpolicy.gov/news/speeches.

McLellan, A. Anne. 2002. "Medical Marijuana." *National Post*, August 29: A19.

Morgan, Patricia A. 1978. "The Legislation of Drug Law: Economic Crisis and Social Control." *Journal of Drug Issues* 8: 53–62.

Murphy, Judge Emily. 1922. *The Black Candle*. Toronto: Thomas Allen.

NIAAA (National Institute on Alcohol Abuse and Alcoholism). 2000. "Tenth Special Report on Alcohol and Health to the U.S. Congress." Washington, DC.

NIDA (National Institute on Drug Abuse). 1999. "Principles of Effective Treatment." NIDA. National Institute of Health. Publication No. 99-4180. Washington, DC.

———. 2000a. "Researcher Announces Latest study on Drug Dependence and Abuse." News Releases. http://www.nida.nih.gov.

———. 2000b."Club Drugs." Community Alert Bulletin. http://www.nida.nih.gov/ClubAlert/Clubdrugalert.html.

Nylander, Albert, Tuk-Ying Tung, and Xiaohe Xu. 1996. "The Effect of Religion on Adolescent Drug Use in America: An Assessment of Change." American Sociological Association Meetings, August. San Francisco, CA.

ONDCP (Office of National Drug Control Policy). 1998. "Trends in Drug Use: Part II: Cocaine." *Pulse Check* (Winter). http://www.health.org/pulse98/trend2.html.

———. 2000. "The Link between Drugs and Crime." Chapter II. *The National Drug Control Strategy 2000 Annual Report*. http://whitehousedrugpolicy.gov.

Remington, Robert. 2001. "Runner's Parents 'Living the Pain.'" *National Post*, December 6: A3.

Rorabaugh, W. J. 1979. *The Alcoholic Republic: An American Tradition*. New York: Oxford University Press.

Roth, J. A. 1994. *Psychoactive Substances and Violence*. Rockville: National Institute of Justice, U.S. Department of Justice.

Rychtarik, Robert G., Gerald J. Connors, Kurt H. Dermen, and Paul Stasiewicz. 2000. "Alcoholics Anonymous and the Use of Medications to Prevent Relapse." *Journal of Studies on Alcohol* 61: 134–41.

Sheldon, Tony. 2000. "Cannabis Use among Dutch Youth." *British Medical Journal* 321: 655.

Solomon, Robert. 1999. "Alcohol and Drug Law." In Canadian Centre on Substance Abuse, *Canadian Profile, 1999: Alcohol, Tobacco and Other Drugs*, pp. 295–315. Ottawa: Canadian Centre on Substance Abuse and Centre for Addiction and Mental Health.

Statistics Canada. 2001. "Impact of Smoking on Life Expectancy and Disability." *The Daily*, June 22. http://www.statcan.ca/Daily/English/010622/d010622a.htm.

———. 2002a. "Control and Sale of Alcoholic Beverages." *The Daily*,

July 12. http://www.statcan.ca/
Daily/English/020712/
d020712b.htm.

———. 2002b. "Crime Statistics,
2001." *The Daily*, July 17.
http://www.statcan.ca/Daily/
English/020717/d020717b.htm.

Sullivan, Thomas, and Kenrick S.
Thompson. 1994. *Social Problems*.
New York: Macmillan.

Tubman, J. 1993. "Family Risk Factors, Parental Alcohol Use, and
Problem Behaviors Among School-
Aged Children." *Family Relations*
42: 81–86.

Van Dyck, C., and R. Byck. 1982.
"Cocaine." *Scientific American* 246:
128–41.

Van Kammen, Welmoet B., and Rolf
Loeber. 1994. "Are Fluctuations in
Delinquent Activities Related to the
Onset and Offset in Juvenile Illegal
Drug Use and Drug Dealing?"
Journal of Drug Issues 24: 9–24.

Wechsler, Henry, George Dowdall,
Andrea Davenport, and William
Dejong. 1998. "Binge Drinking on
Campus: Results of a National
Study." Higher Education Center.
http://www.edc.org/hes/pubs/
binge.html.

White, Helene Raskin, and Erich W.
Labouvie. 1994. "Generality versus
Specificity of Problem Behavior:
Psychological and Functional Dif-
ferences." *Journal of Drug Issues* 24:
55–74.

Witters, Weldon, Peter Venturelli, and
Glen Hanson. 1992. *Drugs and
Society*, 3rd ed. Boston: Jones and
Bartlett.

World Drug Report. 1997. "Report
Highlights." United Nations Inter-
national Drug Control Program.
New York: United Nations.

Wysong, Earl, Richard Aniskiewicz,
and David Wright. 1994. "Truth
and Dare: Tracking Drug Education
to Graduation and as Symbolic Politics." *Social Problems* 41: 448–68.

Chapter 4

ABCNews. 2001. "U.S.–Russia Child
Porn Bust." http://www.abcnews.
go.com/sections/world/Daily/News/
childpornbust_010326.htm.

Anderson, Elijah. 1994. "The Code of
the Streets: Sociology of Urban
Violence." *Atlantic* 273(5): 80–91.

Ash, Russell. 2001. *The Top 10 of Everything: Canadian Edition 2002*. Toronto:
Dorling Kindersley Limited.

Becker, Howard S. 1963. *Outsiders:
Studies in the Sociology of Deviance*.
New York: Free Press.

Besserer, Sandra. 2002. "Criminal Victimization: An International Perspective: Results of the 2000
International Crime Victimization
Survey." *Juristat* 22(4), May. Catalogue no. 85-002-XPE.

Bibby, Reginald W. 1995. *The Bibby
Report: Social Trends Canadian Style*.
Toronto: Stoddart.

———. 2001. *Canada's Teens: Today,
Yesterday, and Tomorrow*. Toronto:
Stoddart.

Bourrie, Mark. 1999. "Compensating
the Innocent." *Canadian Lawyer*
(November/December): 29–32.

Brantingham, Paul J., Shihong Mu,
and Arvind Verma. 1995. "Patterns
in Canadian Crime." In Margaret
A. Jackson and Curt T. Griffiths
(eds.), *Canadian Criminology: Perspectives on Crime and Criminality*,
2nd ed., pp. 187–246. Toronto:
Harcourt Brace and Company,
Canada.

Bryant, Marian E. 1999. "Sentencing
Aboriginal Offenders." *Law Now*
(October/November): 20–21.

Business Network on Crime Prevention. 2001. "The Cost of Crime."
http://www.crime-prevention.org/
english/publications/economic/
invest/cost_e.html.

Campaign 2000. 2001. *Canada's Non-
Governmental Organization Report
Submitted for the United Nations
General Assembly Special Session*,
September 19–21.
http://www. campaign2000.ca.

CCJS (Canadian Centre for Justice
Statistics). 1999. "Overview of the
National Justice Statistics Initiative
and the Canadian Centre for Jus-
tice Statistics." In Canadian Centre
for Justice Statistics, *The Juristat
Reader: A Statistical Overview of the
Canadian Justice System*, pp. v–vi.
Toronto: Thompson Educational
Publishing, Inc.

Chesney-Lind, Meda, and Randall G.
Shelden. 1998. *Girls, Delinquency
and Juvenile Justice*. Belmont, CA:
Wadsworth.

Chua-Eoan, Howard, and Tim
Latimer. 1999. "Beware of the

PokéMania." *Time*, Canadian edition, November 22: 60–67.

Chwialkowska, Luiza. 2001. "Anti-
Terrorism Bill Becomes Law."
National Post, December 19: A6.

CATW (Coalition Against Trafficking
in Women). 1997. "Promoting Sex
Work in the Netherlands." *Coalition
Report* 4(1). http://www.uri.
edu/artsci/wms/hughes/catw.

Conklin, John E. 1998. *Criminology*,
6th ed. Boston: Allyn and Bacon.

COPS. 1998. "About the Office of
Community Oriented Policing
Services (COPS)."
http://communitypolicing.org/
copspage.html.

Department of Justice. 2002a. "Highlights of Anti-Terrorism Act."
http://www.canada.justice.gc.ca/
en/news/nr/2001/doc_27787.html.

———. 2002b. "Canada's Youth Criminal Justice Act: A New Law—
A New Approach."
http://www.canada.justice.gc.ca/
en/dept/pub/ycja/youth_html.

———. 2002c. "Organized Crime Legislation Comes into Force."
http://www.canada.justice.gc.ca/
en/news/nr/2002/doc_29525.html.

deSouza, Paul. 2002. "Youth Court
Statistics, 2000/01." *Juristat* 22(3),
March. Catalogue no. 85-002-
XPE.

DiIulio, John. 1999. "Federal Crime
Policy: Time for a Moratorium."
Brookings Review 17(1): 17.

Doyle, Roger. 2000. "The Roots of
Homicide." *Scientific American*
(October). http://www.sciam.com/
2000.

Economist, The. 2000. "Dead Man
Walking Out." June 10: 21–23.

Erikson, Kai T. 1966. *Wayward
Puritans*. New York: John Wiley
and Sons.

Evans, John, and Alexander Himelfarb. 2000. "Counting Crime." In
Rick Linden (ed.), *Criminology: A
Canadian Perspective*, 4th ed.,
pp. 60–93. Toronto: Harcourt Brace
and Company.

Fattah, Ezzat A. 1991. *Understanding
Criminal Victimization: An Introduction to Theoretical Victimology*. Scarborough, ON: Prentice Hall.

Fedorowycz, Orest. 1999. "Homicide
in Canada, 1998." *Juristat* 19(10),
October. Catalogue no. 85-002-
XIE.

Felson, Marcus. 1998. *Crime and Everyday Life*, 2nd ed. Thousand Oaks, CA: Pine Forge Press.

Fields, Gary. 2000. "Victims of Identity Theft Often Unaware They've Been Stung." *USA Today*, March 15: 6A.

Finckenauer, James O. 2000. "Meeting the Challenge of Transnational Crime. *National Institute of Justice Journal* (July): 2–7.

Gannon, Marie. 2001. "Crime Comparisons Between Canada and the United States." *Juristat* 21(11), December. Catalogue no. 85-002-XPE.

Garey, M. 1985. "The Cost of Taking a Life: Dollars and Sense of the Death Penalty." *U.C. Davis Law Review* 18: 1221–73.

Gest, Ted, and Dorian Friedman. 1994. "The New Crime Wave." *U.S. News and World Report*, August 29: 26–28.

Global Report on Crime and Justice. 1999. United Nations: Office of Drug Control and Crime Prevention. http://www.uncjin.org/special/overview.html.

Gorelick, David A. 1992. "Pathophysiological Effects of Cocaine in Humans: Review of Scientific Issues." *Journal of Addictive Diseases* 11(4): 97–110.

Hackler, James C. 2000. *Canadian Criminology: Strategies and Perspectives*, 2nd ed. Scarborough, ON: Prentice Hall Allyn and Bacon Canada.

Hagan, John. 2000. "White-Collar and Corporate Crime." In Rick Linden (ed.), *Criminology: A Canadian Perspective*, 4th ed., pp. 459–82. Toronto: Harcourt Brace and Company.

Hartnagel, Timothy F. 2000. "Correlates of Criminal Behaviour." In Rick Linden (ed.), *Criminology: A Canadian Perspective*, 4th ed., pp. 94–136. Toronto: Harcourt Brace and Company.

Hirschi, Travis. 1969. *Causes of Delinquency*. Berkeley: University of California Press.

Hochstetler, Andrew, and Neal Shover. 1997. "Street Crime, Labor Surplus, and Criminal Punishment, 1980–1990." *Social Problems* 44(3): 358–67.

Human Rights Watch. 2000. *Human Rights Watch World Report 2000*.

United States. http://www.hrw.org/wr2k/us.html.

INTERPOL. 1998. "INTERPOL Warning: Nigerian Crime Syndicate's Letter Scheme Fraud Takes on New Dimension." Press releases. http://www.kenpubs.co.uk/INTERPOL.COM/English/pres/nig.html.

Jacobs, David. 1988. "Corporate Economic Power and the State: A Longitudinal Assessment of Two Explanations." *American Journal of Sociology* 93: 852–81.

Janoff-Bulman, Ronnie, C. Timko, and L. Carli. 1985. "Cognitive Biases in Blaming the Victim." *Journal of Experimental Social Psychology* 23: 161–77.

John Howard Society. 1999. *Check & Balance: The Facts about Facts*. Toronto: The John Howard Society of Ontario.

Koenig, Daniel J. 2000. "Conventional or 'Street' Crime." In Rick Linden (ed.), *Criminology: A Canadian Perspective*, 4th ed., pp. 396–429. Toronto: Harcourt Brace and Company.

Kong, Deborah, and Jon Swartz. 2000. "Experts See Rash of Hack Attacks Coming..." *USA Today*, September 27: 1B.

Kong, Rebecca. 1999. "Canadian Crime Statistics, 1997." In Canadian Centre for Justice Statistics, *The Juristat Reader: A Statistical Overview of the Canadian Justice System*, pp. 117–37. Toronto: Thompson Educational Publishing, Inc.

Laub, John, Daniel S. Nagan, and Robert Sampson. 1998. "Trajectories of Change in Criminal Offending: Good Marriages and the Desistance Process." *American Sociological Review* 63 (April): 225–38.

Lehrur, Eli. 1999. "Communities and Cops Join Forces." *Insight on the News* 15(3), January 25: 16.

Liebman, James S., Jeffery Fagan, and Valerie West. 2000. "A Broken System: Error Rates in Capital Cases, 1973–1995." http://justice.policy.net/jpreport.

Lipsey, M. W. and D. B. Wilson. 1998. "Effective Intervention for Serious Juvenile Offenders: A Synthesis of Research." In R. Loeber and David Farrington (eds.), *Serious and Vio-*

lent Offenders. Thousand Oaks, CA: Sage Publications.

Logan, Ron. 2001. "Crime Statistics in Canada, 2000." *Juristat* 21(8), July. Catalogue No. 85-002-XPE.

Lonmo, Charlene. 2001. "Adult Correctional Services in Canada, 1999–2000." *Juristat* 21(5), July. Catalogue no. 85-002-XPE.

MacIntyre, John. 1999. "...and Counting." *Canadian Lawyer* (November/December): 6.

Madriz, Esther. 2000. "Nothing Bad Happens to Good Girls." In Frances Moulder (ed.), *Social Problems of the Modern World*, pp. 293–97. Belmont, CA: Wadsworth.

Merton, Robert. 1957. "Social Structure and Anomie." In *Social Theory and Social Structure*. Glencoe, IL: Free Press.

Miller, Melissa. 1999. "Identity Theft Is a Growing Problem and Legislatures Are Responding." *Missouri Digital News*. http://mdn.org/1999/stories/theft.html.

Moore, Elizabeth, and Michael Mills. 1990. "The Neglected Victims and Unexamined Costs of White Collar Crime." *Crime and Delinquency* 36: 408–18.

Murray, Mary E., Nancy Guerra, and Kirk Williams. 1997. "Violence Prevention for the Twenty-First Century." In Roger P. Weissberg, Thomas Gullota, Robert L. Hampton, Bruce Ryan, and Gerald Adams (eds.), *Enhancing Children's Awareness*, pp. 105–28. Thousand Oaks, CA: Sage Publications.

Myths and Facts about the Death Penalty. 1998. "Death Penalty: Focus on California." http://members.aol.com/Dpfocus/facts.htm.

National Research Council. 1994. *Violence in Urban America: Mobilizing a Response*. Washington, DC: National Academy Press.

OJP (Office of Justice Programs). 1998. "Gallery 37." http://www.ojp.usdoj.gov/nij/innvprog/gallery.htm.

Olmsted, A. D. 1988. "Morally Controversial Leisure." *Symbolic Interaction* 11: 277–87.

Pertossi, Mayra. 2000. "ANALYSIS— Argentine Crime Rate Soars." September 27. http://news.excite.com.

Roberts, Julian, and Thomas Gabor. 1990. "Race and Crime: A

Critique." *Canadian Journal of Criminology,* 92(2), April: 291–313.

Sanday, P. R. 1981. "The Sociocultural Context of Rape: A Cross-Cultural Study." *Journal of Social Issues* 37: 5–27.

Seagrave, J. 1997. *Introduction to Policing in Canada.* Scarborough, ON: Prentice Hall.

Shabalin, Victor, J. J. Albini, and R. E. Rogers. 1995. "The New Stage of the Fight against Organized Crime in Russia." *IASOC: Criminal Organization* 10(1): 19–21.

Sherrill, Robert. 2000. "A Year in Corporate Crime." In Frances Moulder (ed.), *Social Problems in the Modern World,* pp. 302–8. Belmont, CA: Wadsworth.

Siegel, Larry. 2000. *Criminology.* Belmont, CA: Wadsworth.

Solicitor General. 1999. "Organized Crime." http://www.sgc.gc.ca/EFact/eorgcrime.htm.

———. 2002. "Factsheets." http://www.sgc.ca/Efact/emyths.htm.

Stamler, Rodney T. 2000. "Organized Crime." In Rick Linden (ed.), *Criminology: A Canadian Perspective,* 4th ed., pp. 429–58. Toronto: Harcourt Brace and Company.

Statistics Canada. 1998. *Canada Yearbook 2000.* Ottawa: Ministry of Industry.

———. 2001. "Crime Statistics, 2000." *The Daily,* July 19. http://www.statcan.ca/Daily/English/010719/d010719b.htm.

———. 2002. "Crime Statistics, 2001." *The Daily,* July 17. http://www.statcan.ca/Daily/English/020717/d020717b.htm.

Steffensmeier, Darrell, and Emilie Allan. 1995. "Criminal Behavior: Gender and Age." In Joseph F. Sheley (ed.), *Criminology: A Contemporary Handbook,* 2nd ed., pp. 83–113. Belmont, CA: Wadsworth.

Sutherland, Edwin H. 1939. *Criminology.* Philadelphia: Lippincott.

Swartz, Joel. 1978. "Silent Killers at Work." In M. David Ermann and Richard Lundman (eds.), *Corporate and Governmental Deviance,* pp. 114–28. New York: Oxford University Press.

Thomas, Mikhail. 2002. "Adult Criminal Court Statistics, 2000/01."

Juristat 22(2), March. Catalogue no. 85-002-XPE.

Tufts, Jennifer. 2000. "Public Attitudes Toward the Criminal Justice System." *Juristat* 20(12), December. Catalogue no. 85-002-XPE.

United Nations. 1997. "Crime Goes Global." Document No. DPI/1518/SOC/CON/30M. New York: United Nations.

———. 2000. "UN Acts to Advance Restorative Justice." http://www.restorativejustice.org/conference/UN.RJ_UNbody.htm.

Warner, Barbara, and Pamela Wilcox Rountree. 1997. "Local Social Ties in a Community and Crime Model." *Social Problems* 4(4): 520–36.

White, Michael, 1999. "GM Ordered to Pay Accident Victims $49 B." *National Post,* July 10: A1.

Williams, Linda. 1984. "The Classic Rape: When Do Victims Report?" *Social Problems* 31: 459–67.

Worden, Amy. 2000. "More Whites than Blacks Evade Death Penalty." http://www.apbnews.com/newscenter/breakingnews/2000/07/24deathpleas0/24_01.html.

Chapter 5

Amato, Paul R. 2001. "The Consequences of Divorce for Adults and Children." In Robert M. Milardo (ed.), *Understanding Families Into the New Millennium: A Decade in Review,* pp. 488–506. Minneapolis: National Council on Family Relations.

Ambert, Anne-Marie. 1998. "Divorce: Facts, Figures and Consequences." Vanier Institute of the Family. http://www.vifamily.ca/cft/divorce/divorce.htm.

Anderson, Kristin L. 1997. "Gender, Status, and Domestic Violence: An Integration of Feminist and Family Violence Approaches." *Journal of Marriage and the Family* 59: 655–59.

Arnold, Tom. 2002. "Common-law Families on the Rise." *National Post,* October 23: A9.

Beitchman, J. H., K. J. Zuker, J. E. Hood, G. A. daCosta, D. Akman, and E. Cassavia. 1992. "A Review of the Long-Term Effects of Child Sexual Abuse." *Child Abuse and Neglect* 16: 101–19.

Berne, L. A., and B. K. Huberman. 1996. "Sexuality Education Works: Here's Proof." *Education Digest* (February): 25–29.

Bibby, Reginald W. 2001. *Canada's Teens: Today, Yesterday, and Tomorrow.* Toronto: Stoddart.

Browning, Christopher R., and Edward O. Laumann. 1997. "Sexual Contact between Children and Adults: A Life Course Perspective." *American Sociological Review* 62: 540–60.

Bunge, Valerie Pottie. 2000. "Spousal Violence." In Statistics Canada, *Family Violence in Canada: A Statistical Profile 2000,* pp. 11–21. Catalogue no. 85-224-XIE. Ottawa: Minister of Industry.

Clark, Charles. 1996. "Marriage and Divorce." *CQ Researcher* 6(18): 409–32.

Code, Ruth. 2001. "Children in Shelters for Abused Women." In Statistics Canada, *Family Violence in Canada: A Statistical Profile 2001.* July. Catalogue No. 85-224-XIE. Ottawa: Minister of Industry.

Cole, Charles L., Anna L. Cole, and Jessica G. Gandolfo. 2000. "Marriage Enrichment for Newlyweds: Models for Strengthening Marriages in the New Millennium." Poster presentation at the 62nd Annual Conference of the National Council on Family Relations, November 10–13. Minneapolis, MN.

Coontz, Stephanie. 2000. "Marriage: Then and Now." *Phi Kappa Phi Journal* 80: 10–15.

Crawford, Trish. 1997. "Sexual Health Programs Are at Risk." *Toronto Star,* August 23: M1.

Demo, David H. 1992. "Parent-Child Relations: Assessing Recent Changes." *Journal of Marriage and the Family* 54: 104–17.

Demo, David H., Mark A. Fine, and Lawrence H. Ganong. 2000. "Divorce as a Family Stressor." In P. C. McKenry and S. J. Price (eds.), *Families & Change: Coping with Stressful Events and Transitions,* 2nd ed., pp. 279–302. Thousand Oaks, CA: Sage Publications.

DiLillo, D., G. C. Tremblay, and L. Peterson. 2000. "Linking Childhood Sexual Abuse and Abusive Parenting: The Mediating Role of

Maternal Anger." *Child Abuse and Neglect* 24: 767–79.

"Domestic Violence and Homelessness." 1998. *NCH Fact Sheet No. 8*. National Coalition for the Homeless.

Dranoff, Linda Silver. 2001. *Everyone's Guide to the Law*. Toronto: HarperCollins Publishers Ltd.

Drummond, Tammerlin. 2000. "Mom on Her Own." *Time*, August 28: 54–55.

Edin, Kathryn. 2000. "What Do Low-Income Single Mothers Say about Marriage?" *Social Problems* 47(1): 112–33.

Edwards, Tamala M. 2000. "Flying Solo." *Time*, August 28: 49–53.

Elliott, D. M., and J. Briere. 1992. "The Sexually Abused Boy: Problems in Manhood." *Medical Aspects of Human Sexuality* 26: 68–71.

Eltahawy, Mona. 2000. "Giving Wives a Way Out." *U.S. News & World Report* 128(9), March 6: 35.

Emery, Robert E. 1999. "Postdivorce Family Life for Children: An Overview of Research and Some Implications for Policy." In R. A. Thompson and P. R. Amato (eds.), *The Postdivorce Family: Children, Parenting, and Society*, pp. 3–27. Thousand Oaks, CA: Sage Publications.

Family Court Reform Council of America. 2000. "Parental Alienation Syndrome." 31441 Santa Margarita Parkway, Suite A184. Rancho Santa Margarita, CA 92688.

Fedorowycz, Orest. 1999. "Homicide in Canada, 1998." *Juristat* 19(10), October. Catalogue no. 85-002-XIE.

Flory, Heather. 2000 (Spring). "I Promise to Love, Honor, Obey...and Not Divorce You: Covenant Marriage and the Backlash Against No-Fault Divorce." *Family Law Quarterly* 34(1): 133–48.

Gardner, Richard A. 1998. *The Parental Alienation Syndrome*, 2nd ed. Cresskill NJ: Creative Therapeutics, Inc.

Gelles, Richard J. 1993. "Family Violence." In Robert L. Hampton, Thomas P. Gullotta, Gerald R. Adams, Earl H. Potter III, and Roger P Weissberg (eds.). *Family Violence: Prevention and Treatment*,

pp. 1–24. Newbury Park, CA: Sage Publications.

———. 2000. "Violence, Abuse, and Neglect in Families." In P. C. McKenry and S. J. Price (eds.), *Families & Change: Coping with Stressful Events and Transitions*, 2nd ed., pp. 183–207. Thousand Oaks, CA: Sage Publications.

Gelles, Richard J., and Jon R. Conte. 1991. "Domestic Violence and Sexual Abuse of Children: A Review of Research in the Eighties." In Alan Booth (ed.), *Contemporary Families: Looking Forward, Looking Back*, pp. 327–40. Minneapolis: National Council on Family Relations.

Global Study of Family Values. 1998. The Gallup Organization. April 13. http://198.175.140.8/Special_Reports/family.htm.

Harrington, Donna, and Howard Dubowitz. 1993. "What Can Be Done to Prevent Child Maltreatment?" In Robert L. Hampton, Thomas P. Gullotta, Gerald R. Adams, Earl H. Potter III, and Roger P. Weissberg (eds.), *Family Violence: Prevention and Treatment*, pp. 258–80. Newbury Park, CA: Sage Publications.

Health Canada. 1999. *Statistical Report on the Health of Canadians*. December 25. http://www.hc-sc.gc.ca/hppb/phdd/report/ state/eng/over.html.

Henry, Ronald K. 1999. "Child Support at a Crossroads: When the Real World Intrudes Upon Academics and Advocates." *Family Law Quarterly* 33(1), Spring: 235–64.

Hewlett, Sylvia Ann, and Cornel West. 1998. *The War against Parents: What We Can Do for Beleaguered Moms and Dads*. Boston: Houghton Mifflin Company.

Hochschild, Arlie Russell. 1989 *The Second Shift: Working Parents and the Revolution at Home*. New York: Viking/Penguin.

———. 1997. *The Time Bind: When Work Becomes Home and Home Becomes Work*. New York: Henry Holt and Company.

Hogan, D. P., R. Sun, and G. T. Cornwell. 2000. "Sexual and Fertility Behaviors of American Females Aged 15–19 Years: 1985, 1990, and 1995. *American Journal of Public Health* 90: 1421–25.

Island, David and Patrick Letellier. 1991. *Men Who Beat the Men Who Love Them: Battered Gay Men and Domestic Violence*. New York: Haworth.

"In the News." 1998. Family Violence Prevention Fund. May 16. http:// www.igc.org/fund/materials/speakup/02_13_98.htm.

Jacobs, C. D., and E. M. Wolf. 1995. "School Sexuality Education and Adolescent Risk-Taking Behavior." *Journal of School Health* 65: 91–5.

Jasinski, J. L., L. M. Williams, and J. Siegel. 2000. "Childhood Physical and Sexual Abuse as Risk Factors for Heavy Drinking among African-American Women: A Prospective Study." *Child Abuse and Neglect* 24: 1061–71.

Jekielek, Susan M. 1998. "Parental Conflict, Marital Disruption and Children's Emotional Well-Being." *Social Forces* 76: 905–35.

Johnson, Holly and Tina Hotton. 2001. "Spousal Violence." In Statistics Canada, *Family Violence in Canada: A Statistical Profile 2001*, pp. 26–41. July. Catalogue no. 85-224-XIE. Ottawa: Minister of Industry.

Johnson, Michael P. and Kathleen Ferraro. 2001. "Research on Domestic Violence in the 1990s: Making Distinctions." In Robert M. Milardo (ed.), *Understanding Families Into the New Millennium: A Decade in Review*, pp. 167–182. Minneapolis: National Council on Family Relations.

Jorgensen, Stephen R. 2000. "Adolescent Pregnancy Prevention: Prospects for 2000 and Beyond." Presidential Address at the National Council on Family Relations 62nd Annual Conference, November 11. Minneapolis, MN.

Kaufman, Joan, and Edward Zigler. 1992. "The Prevention of Child Maltreatment: Programming, Research, and Policy." In Diane J. Willis, E. Wayne Holden, and Mindy Rosenberg (eds.), *Prevention of Child Maltreatment: Developmental and Ecological Perspectives*, pp. 269–95. New York: John Wiley & Sons.

Knox, David (with Kermit Leggett). 1998. *The Divorced Dad's Survival Book: How to Stay Connected with Your Kids*. New York: Insight Books.

Kong, R. 1997. "Criminal Harassment in Canada." *Canadian Social Trends* 45 (Autumn): 29–33.

Krug, Ronald S. 1989. "Adult Male Report of Childhood Sexual Abuse by Mothers: Case Description, Motivations, and Long-Term Consequences." *Child Abuse and Neglect* 13: 111–9.

Kurdek, Lawrence A. 1994. "Areas of Conflict for Gay, Lesbian and Heterosexual Couples: What Couples Argue About Influences Relationship Satisfaction." *Journal of Marriage and the Family*, 56(4): 923–34.

Lanz, Jean B. 1995. "Psychological, Behavioral, and Social Characteristics Associated with Early Forced Sexual Intercourse among Pregnant Adolescents." *Journal of Interpersonal Violence* 10: 188–200.

Le Bourdais, Celine, Neill Ghislaine, and Pierre Turcotte. 2001. "The Changing Face of Conjugal Relationships." *Canadian School Trends* (Spring): 14–17.

Leite, Randy W., and Patrick C. McKenry. 2000. "Aspects of Father Status and Post-Divorce Father Involvement with Children." Poster session at the National Council on Family Relations 62nd Annual Conference, November 10–13. Minneapolis, MN.

Lewin, Tamar. 2000. "Fears for Children's Well-Being Complicates a Debate Over Marriage." *The New York Times on the Web*, November 4. http://www.nytimes.com/2000/11/04/arts/04MARR.html.

Lloyd, Sally A. 2000. "Intimate Violence: Paradoxes of Romance, Conflict, and Control." *National Forum* 80(4): 19–22.

Lloyd, S. A., and B. C. Emery. 1993. "Abuse in the Family: An Ecological, Life-Cycle Perspective." In T. H. Brubaker (ed.), *Family Relations: Challenges for the Future*, pp. 129–52. Newbury Park, CA: Sage Publications.

———. 2000. *The Dark Side of Courtship: Physical and Sexual Aggression*. Thousand Oaks CA: Sage Publications.

Locke, Daisy, Sara Beattie, and Sean Miller. 2001. "Homicide of Children and Youth." In Statistics Canada, *Family Violence in Canada:*

A Statistical Profile 2001, pp. 15–18. July. Catalogue no. 85-224-XIE. Ottawa: Minister of Industry.

Lockhart, L. L., White, B. W., V. Causby, and A. Issac. 1994. "Letting Out the Secret: Violence in Lesbian Relationships." *Journal of Interpersonal Violence* 9(4): 469–92.

Luker, Kristin. 1996. *Dubious Conceptions: The Politics of Teenage Pregnancy*. Cambridge, MA: Harvard University Press.

Marlow, L., and S. R. Sauber. 1990. *The Handbook of Divorce Mediation*. New York: Plenum.

McKay, Alexander, Eleanor Maticka-Tyndale, and Michael Barrett. 2000. "Adolescent Sexual and Reproductive Health in Canada: A Review of National Data Sources and Their Limitations." *Canadian Journal of Human Sexuality* 9(1), March: 41–65.

Monson, C. M., G. R. Byrd, and J. Langhinrichsen-Rohling. 1996. "To Have and to Hold: Perceptions of Marital Rape." *Journal of Interpersonal Violence* 11: 410–24.

Morrison, N. 1987. "Separation and Divorce." In M. J. Dymond (ed.), *The Canadian Woman's Legal Guide*, pp. 125–43. Toronto: Doubleday.

Morton, M. 1990. "Controversies within Family Law." In M. Baker (ed.), *Families: Changing Trends in Canada*, pp. 211–40. Toronto: McGraw-Hill Ryerson.

National Center for Injury Prevention and Control. 2000. "Intimate Partner Violence Fact Sheet." National Center for Injury Prevention and Control. Mailstop K60, 4770 Buford Highway NE, Atlanta, GA 30341-3724.

National Coalition for the Homeless. 1999. NCH Fact Sheet #1. "Why Are People Homeless?" http:// www.nationalhomeless.org/causes.html.

National Council of Welfare. 1999. *Children First: A Pre-Budget Report by the National Council of Welfare*. Autumn. http://www.ncwcnbes.net.htmdocument/reportchildfirst.htm.

Nelson, B. S., and K. S. Wampler. 2000. "Systemic Effects of Trauma in Clinic Couples: An Exploratory Study of Secondary Trauma Resulting from Childhood Abuse."

Journal of Marriage and Family Counseling 26: 171–84.

Nielsen, L. 1999. "College Aged Students with Divorced Parents: Facts and Fiction." *College Student Journal* 33: 543–72.

Nock, Steven L. 1995. "Commitment and Dependency in Marriage." *Journal of Marriage and the Family* 57: 503–14.

Novac, S., J. Brown, and C. Bourbonnais. 1996. *No Room of Her Own: A Literature Review on Women and Homelessness*. Canadian Mortgage and Housing Corporation. May 1, 2000. http://www.cmhc-schl.gc.ca/cmhc.html.

Parker, Marcie, R. Edward Bergmark, Mark Attridge, and Jude Miller-Burke. 2000. "Domestic Violence and its Effect on Children." *National Council on Family Relations Report* 45(4): F6–F7.

Pasley, Kay, and Carmelle Minton. 2001. "Generative Fathering after Divorce and Remarriage: Beyond the 'Disappearing Dad.'" In T. F. Cohen (ed.), *Men and Masculinity: A Text Reader*, pp. 239–48. Belmont, CA: Wadsworth.

Peterson, Karen S. 1997. "States Flirt with Ways to Reduce Divorce Rate." *USA Today*, April 10: D1–2.

Peterson, Richard R. 1996. "A Reevaluation of the Economic Consequences of Divorce." *American Sociological Review* 61: 528–36.

Popenoe, David. 1993. "Point of View: Scholars Should Worry about the Disintegration of the American Family." *Chronicle of Higher Education*, April 14: A48.

———. 1996. *Life without Father*. New York: Free Press.

Renzetti, Claire M., and Charles H. Milley. 1996. *Violence in Gay and Lesbian Domestic Partnerships*. Newbury Park, CA: Sage Publications.

Resnick, Michael, Peter S. Bearman, Robert W. Blum, Karl E. Bauman, Kathleen M. Harris, Jo Jones, Joyce Tabor, Trish Beubring, Renee E. Sieving, Marcia Shew, Marjore Ireland, Linda H. Berringer, and J. Richard Udry. 1997. "Protecting Adolescents from Harm." *Journal of the American Medical Association* 278(10), September 10: 823–32.

Riedmann, Agnes, Mary Ann Lamanna, and Adie Nelson. 2003.

Marriages and Families: Making Choices in a Diverse Society, 1st Canadian ed. Toronto: Thomson Nelson.

Russell, D. E. 1990. *Rape in Marriage.* Bloomington: Indiana University Press.

Schacht, Thomas E. 2000. "Protection Strategies to Protect Professionals and families Involved in High-Conflict Divorce." *UALR Law Review* 22(3): 565–92.

Scott, K. L. and D. A. Wolfe. 2000. "Change Among Batterers: Examining Men's Success Stories." *Journal of Interpersonal Violence* 15: 827–42.

Shapiro, Joseph P., and Joannie M. Schrof. 1995. "Honor Thy Children." *U.S. News and World Report*, February 27: 39–49.

Singh, Susheela and Jacqueline E. Darroch. 2000. "Adolescent Pregnancy and Childbearing: Levels and Trends in Developed Countries." *Family Planning Perspectives* 32(1): 14–23.

Spiegel, D. 2000. "Suffer the Children: Long-Term Effects of Sexual Abuse." *Society* 37: 18–20.

Stanley, Scott M., Howard J. Markman, Michelle St. Peters, and B. Douglas Leber. 1995. "Strengthening Marriage and Preventing Divorce: New Directions in Prevention Research." *Family Relations* 44: 392–401.

Statistics Canada. 1998a. "1996 Census: Sources of Income, Earnings and Total Income, and Family Income." *The Daily*, May 12. http://www.statscan.ca:80/Daily/English/980512/d980512.htm.

———. 1998b. *Canada Yearbook 1999.* Ottawa: Minister of Industry.

———. 1998c. *The Daily*, March 28. http://www.statcan.ca/Daily/English/980328/d980328.htm.

———. 2000a. "Divorces, 1998." *The Daily*, September 28. http://www.statcan.ca/Daily/English/000928/d000928.htm.

———. 2000b. *Family Violence in Canada: A Statistical Profile 2000.* Catalogue no. 885-224-XIE. Ottawa: Minister of Industry.

———. 2000c. "Women in Canada 2000." *The Daily*, September 14. http://www.statcan.ca/Daily/English/000914/d000914c.htm.

———. 2001. *Family Violence in Canada: A Statistical Profile 2001.*

Catalogue No. 85-224-XIE. Ottawa: Ministry of Industry.

———. 2002. "Divorce." *The Daily*, December 2. http://www.statcan.ca/Daily/English/021202/d021202f.htm.

Stock, J. L., M. A. Bell, D. K. Boyer, and F. A. Connell. 1997. "Adolescent Pregnancy and Sexual Risk-Taking among Sexually Abused Girls." *Family Planning Perspectives* 29: 200–3.

Straus, Murray. 2000. "Corporal Punishment and Primary Prevention of Physical Abuse." *Child Abuse and Neglect* 24: 1109–14.

Thakkar, R. R., P. M. Gutierrez, C. L. Kuczen, and T. R. McCanne. 2000. "History of Physical and/or Sexual Abuse, and Current Suicidality in College Women." *Child Abuse and Neglect* 24: 1345–54.

Thompson, Ross A., and Paul R. Amato. 1999. "The Postdivorce Family: An Introduction to the Issues." In R. A. Thompson and P. R. Amato (eds.), *The Postdivorce Family: Children, Parenting, and Society*, pp. xi–xxiii. Thousand Oaks, CA: Sage Publications.

Thompson, Ross A., and Jennifer M. Wyatt. 1999. "Values, Policy, and Research on Divorce." In R. A. Thompson and P. R. Amato (eds.), *The Postdivorce Family: Children, Parenting, and Society*, pp. 191–232. Thousand Oaks, CA: Sage Publications.

Trocme, Nico and David Wolfe. 2001. "The Canadian Incidence Study of Reported Child Abuse and Neglect." In Statistics Canada, *Family Violence in Canada: A Statistical Profile 2001*, pp. 4–14. July. Catalogue no. 85-224-XIE. Ottawa: Minister of Industry.

United Nations Development Programme. 2000. *Human Development Report 2000.* Cary, NC: Oxford University Press.

Vanier Institute of the Family. 2000. *Profiling Canada's Families II.* Nepean, ON: Vanier Institute of the Family.

Ventura, Stephanie J., Sally C. Curtain, and T. J. Matthews. 2000. "Variations in Teenage Birth Rates, 1991–1998." National Vital Statistics Reports 48(6), April 24.

Viano, C. Emilio. 1992. "Violence Among Intimates: Major Issues

and Approaches." In C. E. Viano (ed.), *Intimate Violence: Interdisciplinary Perspectives*, pp. 3–12. Washington, DC: Hemisphere.

Waite, L., and M. Gallagher. 2000. *The Case for Marriage: Why Married People are Happier, Healthier and Better off Financially.* New York: Doubleday.

Walker, Alexis J. 2001. "Refracted Knowledge: Viewing Families Through the Prism of Social Science." In Robert M. Milardo (ed.), *Understanding Families into the New Millennium: A Decade in Review*, pp. 52–65. Minneapolis: National Council on Family Relations.

Wherry, Aaron. 2002. "Shelternet.ca aims to reach women across the country." *The Globe and Mail*, August 13: A18.

Whiffen, V. E., J. M. Thompson, and J. A. Aube. 2000. "Mediators of the Link between Childhood Sexual Abuse and Adult Depressive Symptoms." *Journal of Interpersonal Violence* 15: 1100–20.

Willis, Diane J., E. Wayne Holden, and Mindy Rosenberg. 1992. "Child Maltreatment Prevention: Introduction and Historical Overview." In Diane J. Willis, E. Wayne Holden, and Mindy Rosenberg (eds.), *Prevention of Child Maltreatment: Developmental and Ecological Perspectives*, pp. 1–14. New York: John Wiley and Sons.

Chapter 6

Adler, Jerry. 1994. "Kids Growing up Scared." *Newsweek*, January 10: 43–50.

AOA (Administration on Aging). 2000. "Demographic Changes." http://www.aoa.gov/stats/aging21/demography.html.

Anetzberger, Georgia J., Jill E. Korbin, and Craig Austin. 1994. "Alcoholism and Elder Abuse." *Journal of Interpersonal Violence* 9: 184–93.

Arluke, Arnold, and Jack Levin. 1990. "'Second Childhood': Old Age in Popular Culture." In W. Feigelman (ed.), *Readings on Social Problems*, pp. 261–65. Fort Worth, TX: Holt, Rinehart and Winston.

Arnold, Tom. 1999. "Older Heart-Attack Patients Less Likely to Get

Vital Drugs." *National Post,* November 30: A5.

Begley, Sharon. 2000. "The Stereotype Trap." *Newsweek,* November 6: 66–68.

Bibby, Reginald W. 2001. *Canada's Teens: Today, Yesterday, and Tomorrow.* Toronto: Stoddart.

Boudreau, François A. 1993. "Elder Abuse." In R. L. Hampton, T. P. Gullota, G. R. Adams, E. H. Potter III, and R. P. Weissberg (eds.), *Family Violence: Prevention and Treatment,* pp. 142–58. Newbury Park, CA: Sage Publications.

Brazzini, D. G., W. D. McIntosh, S. M. Smith, S. Cook, and C. Harris. 1997. "The Aging Woman in Popular Film: Underrepresented, Unattractive, Unfriendly, and Unintelligent." *Sex Roles* 36: 531–43.

Brooks-Gunn, Jeanne, and Greg Duncan. 1997. "The Effects of Poverty on Children." *Future of Children* 7(2): 55–70.

Campaign 2000. 2002. *Putting Promises into Action: A Report on a Decade of Child and Family Poverty in Canada.* May. http://www.campaign2000.ca.

CARP (Canadian Association of Retired Persons). 2002. http://www.fifty-plus.net.

Canadian Press. 1999. "Older Drivers More at Risk." *Kitchener-Waterloo Record,* November 17: B11.

Covell, Katherine. 2001. *Canada's Non-Governmental Organizations Report.* Submitted for the United Nations General Assembly Special Session September 19–21, 2001 (on behalf of the Canadian Coalition for the Rights of Children), February 2001.

Cowgill, Donald, and Lowell Holmes. 1972. *Aging and Modernization.* New York: Appleton-Century-Crofts.

Cummings, Elaine, and William Henry. 1961. *Growing Old: The Process of Disengagement.* New York: Basic Books.

DeAngelis, Tori. 1997. "Elderly May Be Less Depressed Than the Young." *APA Monitor* (October). http://www.apa.org/monitor/oct97/elderly.html.

DHHS (Department of Health and Human Services). 1998. "Statement of Jeanette Takamura." U.S. Department of Health and Human Services, Administration on Aging. June 8. http://www. aoa.dhhs.gov/pr/graying.html.

Dranoff, Linda Silver. 2001. *Everyone's Guide to the Law.* Toronto: Harper-Collins Publishers Ltd.

Dube, Francine. 2002. "25% of Households Have Only One Person." *National Post,* October 23: A9.

Duncan, Greg, W. Jean Yeung, Jeanne Brooks-Gunn, and Judith Smith. 1998. "How Much Does Childhood Poverty Affect the Life Chance of Children?" *American Sociological Review* 63: 402–23.

Fields, Jason, and Kristin Smith. 1998. "Poverty, Family Structure, and Child Well-Being." Population Division. Washington, DC: U.S. Bureau of Census.

Fine, Sean. 1999. "How Canada Broke Its Pledge to Poor Children." *The Globe and Mail,* November 24: A14.

GLARP (Gay and Lesbian Association of Retiring Persons). 2000. http://www.gaylesbianretiring.org/about.htm.

Goldberg, Beverly. 2000. *Age Works.* New York: Free Press.

Harris, Kathleen, and Jeremy Marmer. 1996. "Poverty, Paternal Involvement and Adolescent Well-Being." *Journal of Family Issues* 17(5): 614–40.

Health Canada. 1999. *Statistical Report on the Health of Canadians.* December 25. http://www.hc-sc.gc.ca/hppb/phdd/report/state/eng/over.html.

Ingrassia, Michelle. 1993. "Growing up Fast and Frightened." *Newsweek,* November 22: 52–53.

Kendall, Diana, Jane Lothian Murray, and Rick Linden. 2000. *Sociology in Our Times,* 2nd Canadian ed. Scarborough, ON: Nelson Thomson Learning.

Kinsella, K., and C. M. Taeuber. 1993. *An Aging World.* Washington, DC: U.S. Bureau of the Census.

Knoke, David, and Arne L. Kalleberg. 1994. "Job Training in U.S. Organizations." *American Sociological Review* 59: 537–46.

Krahn, H. K., and Lowe, G. S. 1993. *Work, Industry, and Canadian Society,* 2nd ed. Scarborough, ON: Nelson.

Lindsay, Colin. 2000. "Income." In *Women in Canada: A Gender-Based Statistical Report,* pp. 135–54. Catalogue No. 89-503-XPE. Ottawa: Statistics Canada.

Livni, Ephrat. 2000. "Exercise, the Anti-Drug." September 21. http://abcnews.go.com/sections/living/Daily/News/depression_elderly000921.htm.

Matras, Judah. 1990. *Dependency, Obligations, and Entitlements: A New Sociology of Aging, the Life Course, and the Elderly.* Englewood Cliffs, NJ: Prentice-Hall.

Miner, Sonia, John Logan, and Glenna Spitze. 1993. "Predicting Frequency of Senior Center Attendance." *Gerontologist* 33: 650–57.

National Council of Welfare. 1998. *Profiles of Welfare: Myths and Realities: A Report by the National Council of Welfare.* Spring. http://www.ncwcnbes.net/htmdocument/reportprowelfare.repprowelfare.htm.

Nelson, Adie, and Barrie W. Robinson. 2002. *Gender in Canada,* 2nd ed. Toronto: Prentice Hall.

NIH (National Institute of Health). 2000. "Nation's Children Gain Many Areas." NIH News release, July 13. http://www.nih.gov/news/pr/jul2000.

Nikiforuk, Andrew. 1999. "A Question of Style." *Time,* May 31: 58–59.

Novak, Mark. 1997. *Aging and Society: A Canadian Perspective,* 3rd ed. Scarborough, ON: Nelson.

Peterson, Peter. 2000. "Gray Dawn." In Frances Moulder (ed.), *Social Problems of the Modern World,* pp. 126–133. Belmont, CA: Wadsworth.

Picard, Andre. 2002. "Tagging Alzheimer's Patients." *The Globe and Mail,* October 18: A10.

Pillemer, Karl, and Beth Hudson. 1993. "A Model Abuse Prevention Program for Nursing Assistants." *Gerontologist* 33(1): 128–31.

Purvis, Andrew. 1999. "Tapestry." *Time,* May 31: 33–34.

Reidmann, Agnes, Mary Ann Lamanna, and Adie Nelson. 2003. *Marriages and Families.* Toronto: Thomson Nelson.

Riley, Matilda W., and John W. Riley. 1992. "The Lives of Older People and Changing Social Roles." In Hugh Lena, William Helmreich, and William McCord (eds.), *Issues in Society,* pp. 220–31. New York: McGraw-Hill.

Riley, Matilda White. 1987. "On the Significance of Age in Sociology." *American Sociological Review* 52 (February): 1–14.

Schieber, Sylvester. 2000. "The Global Aging Crisis." *Electric Perspectives* 25: 18–28.

Seeman, Teresa E., and Nancy Adler. 1998. "Older Americans: Who Will They Be?" *National Forum* (Spring): 22–5.

Simon-Rusinowitz, Lori, Constance Krach, Lori Marks, Diane Piktialis, and Laura Wilson. 1996. "Grand-parents in the Workplace: the Effects of Economic and Labor Trends." *Generations* 20(1): 41–44.

Statistics Canada. 1998. *Canada Year-book*. Ottawa: Ministry of Industry.

———. 2002. "2001 Census: Canada." http://www12.statcan.ca/english/census01/products/analytic/companion/age/canada.cfm.

Thurow, Lester C. 1996. "The Birth of a Revolutionary Class." *New York Times Magazine*, May 19: 46–47.

Townson, Monica. 1995. *Financial Futures: Mid-Life Prospects for a Secure Retirement*. Ottawa: Canadian Advisory Council on the Status of Women.

UNICEF (United Nations Children's Fund). 1998. "The First Nearly Universally Ratified Human Rights Treaty in History." *Status*. Washington, DC: UNICEF. http://www.unicef.org/crc/status.html.

———. 2000. "Convention on the Rights of the Child: FAQ." UNICEF. http://www.unicef.org/crc/html.

Vallis, Mary. 2002. "'Sadness, Shame' Over Sex Scandal." *National Post*, July 29, 2002: A1, A7.

Vanier Institute of the Family. 2000. *Profiling Canada's Families II*. Nepean, ON: Vanier Institute of the Family.

Weissberg, Roger P., and Carol Kuster. 1997. "Introduction and Overview: Let's Make Healthy Children 2010 a National Priority." In Roger Weissberg, Thomas Gullotta, Robert Hampton, Bruce Ryan, and Gerald Adams (eds.), *Enhancing Children's Well-Being*, pp. 1–16. Thousand Oaks, CA: Sage Publications.

Wittaker, Terri. 1996. "Violence, Gender and Elder Abuse." In Brid Featherstone (ed.), *Violence and Gender Relations: Theories and Inter-ventions*, pp. 147–60. Thousand Oaks, CA: Sage Publications Inc.

Yamaguchi, Mari. 2000. "Japan is Fastest Growing Graying Country." *The Washington Post*, May 30: A2.

Chapter 7

Adamson, N., L. Briskin, and M. McPhail. 1988. *Feminists Organizing for Change: The Contemporary Women's Movement in Canada*. Don Mills, ON: Oxford University Press.

Anderson, Margaret L. 1997. *Thinking about Women*, 4th ed. New York: Macmillan.

Anderson, John, and Molly Moore. 1998. "The Burden of Woman-hood." In Robert Jackson (ed.), *Global Issues 98/99*, pp. 170–75. Guilford, CT: Dushkin/McGraw-Hill.

Atcheson, E., M. Eberts, E. Symes, and J. Stoddart. 1984. *Women and Legal Action*. Ottawa: Canadian Advisory Council on the Status of Women.

Austin, Jonathan D. 2000. "U.N. Report: Women's Unequal Treat-ment Hurts Economies." CNN.com, September 20. http://www.cnn.com/2000/world/europe/09/20.un.population.report.

Bacchi, C. L. 1983. *Liberation Deferred? The Ideas of the English-Canadian Suf-fragists, 1877–1918*. Toronto: University of Toronto Press.

Baker, Robin, Gary Kriger, and Pamela Riley. 1996. "Time, Dirt and Money: The Effects of Gender, Gender Ideology, and Type of Earner Marriage on Time, House-hold Task, and Economic Satisfac-tion Among Couples with Children." *Journal of Social Behavior and Personality* 11: 161–77.

Bannon, Lisa. 2000. "Why Girls and Boys Get Different Toys." *The Wall Street Journal*, February 14: B1.

Basow, Susan A. 1992. *Gender: Stereo-types and Roles*, 3rd ed. Pacific Grove, CA: Brooks/Cole.

Begley, Sharon. 2000. "The Stereotype Trap." *Newsweek*, November 6: 66–68.

Bell, Stewart. 2002. "Pakistan Tribal Court Sentenced Teen To Be Gang-Raped for Her Brother's Indiscre-tion." *National Post*, July 4: A1, A12.

Beutel, Ann M., and Margaret Mooney Marini. 1995. "Gender and Values." *American Sociological Review* 60: 436–38.

Bianchi, Susanne M., Melissa A. Milkie, Liana C. Sayer, and John Robinson. 2000. "Is Anyone Doing the Housework? Trends in the Gender Division of Household Labor." *Social Forces* 79: 191–228.

Bittman, Michael and Judy Wajcman. 2000. "The Rush Hour: The Char-acter of Leisure Time and Gender Equity." *Social Forces* 79: 165–89.

Burger, Jerry M., and Cecilia H. Solano. 1994. "Changes in Desire for Control over Time: Gender Dif-ferences in a Ten-Year Longitudinal Study." *Sex Roles* 31: 465–72.

Burke, R.J. 1994. "Canadian Business Students' Attitudes Towards Women as Managers." *Psychological Reports* 75: 1123–29.

Cassidy, B., R. Lord, and N. Mandell. 1998. "Silenced and Forgotten Women: Race, Poverty, and Dis-ability." In N. Mandell (ed.), *Femi-nist Issues: Race, Class and Sexuality*, 2nd ed., pp. 26–54. Scarborough, ON: Prentice Hall Allyn and Bacon Canada.

CAUT (Canadian Association of Uni-versity Teachers) *Bulletin*. 2002. "Ivory Towers: Feminist Audits Years 2002 Figures." http://www.caut.ca/english/issues/women/Audit2002.asp.

Cejka, Mary Ann, and Alice Eagly. 1999. "Gender Stereotypic Images of Occupations Correspond to the Sex Segregation of Employment." *Personality and Social Psychology Bul-letin* 25: 413–23.

Chard, Jennifer. 2000. "Women in a Visible Minority." In *Women in Canada 2000: A Gender-Based Statis-tical Report*, pp. 219–27. Ottawa: Statistics Canada.

Cianni, Mary, and Beverly Romberger. 1997. "Life in the Corporation: A Multi-Method Study of the Experi-ences of Male and Female Asian, Black, Hispanic and White Employees." *Gender, Work and Orga-nization* 4: 116–29.

Cohen, Theodore. 2001. *Men and Mas-culinity*. Belmont, CA: Wadsworth.

Dranoff, Linda Silver. 2001. *Everyone's Guide to the Law*. Toronto: Harper-Collins Publishers Ltd.

Driedger, D. 1993. "Discovering Disabled Women's History." In L. Carty (ed.), *And Still We Rise*, pp. 173–88. Toronto: Women's Press.

Errington, J. 1993. "Pioneers and Suffragists." In S. Burt, L. Code, and L. Dorney (eds.), *Changing Patterns: Women in Canada*, 2nd ed., pp. 59–91. Toronto: McClelland and Stewart.

Evans, Lorraine, and Kimberly Davies. 2000. "No Sissy Boys Here." *Sex Roles* (February): 255–71.

Fitzgerald, Louise F., and Sandra L. Shullman. 1993. "Sexual Harassment: A Research Analysis and Agenda for the '90s." *Journal of Vocational Behavior* 40: 5–27.

Fitzpatrick, Catherine. 2000. "Modern Image of Masculinity Changes with Rise of New Celebrities." *Detroit News*, June 24. http://detnews.com/2000/religion/0006/24.

Frank, J. 1994. "Voting and Contributing: Political Participation in Canada." In *Canadian Social Trends: A Canadian Studies Reader* 2, pp. 333–57. Toronto: Thompson Educational Publishing.

Goldberg, Stephanie. 1997. "Making Room for Daddy." *American Bar Association Journal* 83: 48–52.

Henslin, J., and A. Nelson. 1997. *Essentials of Sociology*. Scarborough, ON: Allyn and Bacon.

Hochschild, Arlie. 1989. *The Second Shift: Working Patterns and the Revolution at Home*. New York: Viking Penguin.

Hunter, A., and M. Denton. 1984. "Do Female Candidates 'Lose' Votes?" *Canadian Review of Sociology and Anthropology* 2: 395–406.

IWRP (International Women's Right's Project). 2000. "The First CEDAW Impact Study." http://www. yorku.ca/iwrp/cedawReport.

Kalb, Claudia. 2000. "What Boys Really Want." *Newsweek*, July 2. http://www.msnbc.com/news/428301.asp.

Kenworthy, Lane, and Melissa Malami. 1999. "Gender Inequality in Political Representation: A Worldwide Comparative Analysis." *Social Forces* 78: 235–69.

Kilbourne, Barbara S., George Farkas, Kurt Beron, Dorothea Weir, and Paula England. 1994. "Returns to Skill, Compensating Differentials, and Gender Bias: Effects of Occupational Characteristics on the Wages of White Women and Men." *American Journal of Sociology* 100: 689–719.

Klein, Matthew. 1997. "Blue Jeans." *American Demographics* (August): 23.

———. 1998. "Women's Trip to the Top." *American Demographics* (February): 22.

Kopelman, Lotetta M. 1994. "Female Circumcision/Genital Mutilation and Ethical Relativism." *Second Opinion* 20: 55–71.

Leeman, Sue. 2000. "The More things Change..." September 20. http:// abcnews.go.com/sections/living/Daily/News/women_unreport00920.html.

Leo, John. 1997. "Fairness? Promises, Promises." *U.S. News and World Report* 123(4): 18.

Lindsay, Colin. 2000. "Income and Earnings." In *Women in Canada 2000: A Gender-Based Statistical Report*, pp. 135–218. Ottawa: Statistics Canada.

Long, J. Scott, Paul D. Allison, and Robert McGinnis. 1993. "Rank Advancement in Academic Careers: Sex Differences and the Effects of Productivity." *American Sociological Review* 58: 703–22.

Lorber, Judith. 1998. "Night to His Day." In Amanda Konradi and Martha Schmidt (eds.), *Reading Between the Lines*, pp. 213–20. Mountain View, CA: Mayfield Publishing.

Macklin, A. 1992. "*Symes v. M.N.R.*: Where Sex Meets Class." *Canadian Journal of Women and the Law* 5: 498.

Maclean's. 2002. "Death by stoning." September 2: 14.

Mandell, N. 1995. "Introduction." *Feminist Issues: Race, Class and Sexuality*, pp. vii–xxi. Scarborough, ON: Prentice Hall Allyn and Bacon Canada.

Marini, Margaret Mooney, and Pi-Ling Fan. 1997. "The Gender Gap in Earnings at Career Entry. *American Sociological Review* 62: 588–604.

Martin, Patricia Yancey. 1992. "Gender, Interaction, and Inequality in Organizations." In Cecilia Ridgeway (ed.), *Gender, Interaction, and Inequality*, pp. 208–31. New York: Springer-Verlag.

McCammon, Susan, David Knox, and Caroline Schacht. 1998. *Making Choices in Sexuality*. Pacific Grove, CA: Brooks/Cole Publishing Co.

Mensh, Barbara, and Cynthia Lloyd. 1997. "Gender Differences in the Schooling of Adolescents in Low-Income Countries: The Case of Kenya." *Policy Research Working Paper* no. 95. New York: Population Council.

Morin, Richard, and Megan Rosenfeld. 2000. "The Politics of Fatigue." In Kurt Finsterbusch (ed.), *Annual Editions: Social Problems*, pp. 152–54. Guilford, CT: Dushkin/McGraw-Hill.

Mossman, Mary Jane. 1997. *Readings on Law, Gender, Equality*. Materials prepared for the study use of students at Osgoode Hall School of Law of York University.

———. 1998. "The Paradox of Feminist Engagement with Law." In N. Mandell (ed.), *Feminist Issues: Race, Class, and Sexuality*, pp. 180–207. Scarborough, ON: Prentice Hall Allyn and Bacon Canada.

National Post. 1999. "Job Ad Seeking Only Women Draws Criticism." August 6: A4.

NCFM (National Coalition of Free Men). 1998. "Historical." Manhasset, NY: NCFM. http://ncfm.org.

Nelson, Adie, and Barrie W. Robinson. 2002. *Gender in Canada*, 2nd ed. Toronto: Pearson Education Canada Inc.

Nichols-Casebolt, Ann, and Judy Krysik. 1997. "The Economic Well-Being of Never and Ever-Married Mother Families." *Journal of Social Service Research* 23(1): 19–40.

Normand, Josee. 2000. "Education." In *Women in Canada 2000: A Gender-Based Statistical Report*, pp. 85–96. Ottawa: Statistics Canada.

Olson, Josephine E., Irene H. Frieze, and Ellen G. Detlefsen. 1990. "Having It All? Combining Work and Family in a Male and a Female Profession." *Sex Roles* 23: 515–34.

Pollock, William. 2000a. *Real Boys' Voices*. New York: Random House.

———. 2000b. "The Columbine Syndrome." *National Forum* 80: 39–42.

Population Reference Bureau. 1999. "World Population: More than Just Numbers." Washington, DC. http://www.prb.org.

Purcell, Piper, and Lara Stewart. 1990. "Dick and Jane in 1989." *Sex Roles* 22: 177–85.

Rabin, Sarah. 2000. "Feminists Take CEDAW Into Our Own Hands." National Organization for Women. http://63111.42.146/cgs/gs_article.asp?ArticleD=1863.

Reid, Pamela T., and Lillian Comas-Diaz. 1990. "Gender and Ethnicity: Perspectives on Dual Status." *Sex Roles* 22: 397–408.

Robinson, John P., and Suzanne Bianchi. 1997. "The Children's Hours." *American Demographics* (December): 1–6.

Rosenberg, Janet, Harry Perlstadt, and William Phillips. 1997. "Now that We Are Here: Discrimination, Disparagement, and Harassment at Work and the Experience of Women Lawyers." In Dana Dunn (ed.), *Workplace/Women's Place*, pp. 247–59. Los Angeles: Roxbury.

Rubenstein, Carin. 1990. "A Brave New World." *New Woman* 20(10): 158–64.

Sachs, Susan. 2000. "In Iran, More Women Leaving Nest for University." *The New York Times on the Web*, July 22. http://www10.nytimes.com/library/world/mideast.

Sadker, Myra, and David Sadker. 1990. "Confronting Sexism in the College Classroom." In S. L. Gabriel, and I. Smithson (eds.), *Gender in the Classroom: Power and Pedagogy*, pp. 176–87. Chicago: University of Illinois Press.

Sapiro, Virginia. 1994. *Women in American Society*. Mountain View, CA: Mayfield.

Schneider, Margaret, and Susan Phillips. 1997. "A Qualitative Study of Sexual Harassment of Female Doctors by Patients." *Social Science and Medicine* 45: 669–76.

Schroeder, K. A., L. L. Blood, and D. Maluso. 1993. "Gender Differences and Similarities between Male and Female Undergraduate Students Regarding Expectations for Career and Family Roles." *College Student Journal* 27: 237–49.

Schwalbe, Michael. 1996. *Unlocking the Iron Cage: The Men's Movement, Gender Politics, and American Culture*. New York: Oxford University Press.

Sheehan, Molly. 2000. "Women Slowly Gain Ground in Politics." In *Vital Signs: The Environmental Trends that Are Shaping Our Future*, ed. Linda Starke. pp. 152–53. New York: W.W. Norton Company.

Signorielli, Nancy. 1998. "Reflections of Girls in the Media: a Content Analysis across Six Media." Overview. http://childrennow.org/media/mc97/ReflectSummary.html.

Smolken, Rachael. 2000. "Girls SAT Scores Still Lag Boys." *Post Gazette*. http://www.post-gazette.com/headlines/20000830sat2.asp.

Sommers, Christina Hoff. 2000. *The War Against Boys: How Misguided Feminism Is Harming Young Men*. New York: Simon and Schuster.

Stark, R. 1992. *Sociology*, 4th ed. Belmont, CA: Wadsworth.

Statistics Canada. 1998. "1996 Census: Labour Force Activity, Occupation and Industry, Place of Work, Mode of Transportation to Work, Unpaid Work." *The Daily*, March 17. http://www.statcan.ca/Daily/English/980317/d980317.htm.

———. 1999. *The Daily*, April 14. http://www.statcan.ca/Daily/English/990417/d990417.htm.

———. 2000. *Women in Canada 2000: A Gender-Based Statistical Report*. Ottawa: Statistics Canada.

———. 2001. "Impact of Smoking on Life Expectancy and Disability." *The Daily*, June 22. http://www.statcan.ca/Daily/English/010622/d010622a.htm.

———. 2003a. "The Changing Profile of Canada's Labour Force." *2001 Census: Analysis Series*. Catalogue no. 96F0030XIE2001009 (released February 11, 2003), p. 36.

———. 2003b. "Earnings of Canadians: Making a Living in the New Economy." Catalogue 96F0030XIE2001013. http://www12.statcan.ca/english/census01/Products/Analytic/companion/earn/charts/menwom.cfm.

———. 2003c. "Education in Canada: Raising the Standard." Catalogue 96F0030XIE2001012, pp. 34, 36. http://www12.statcan.ca/english/census01/products/Analytic/companion/educ/contents.cfm.

Tam, Tony. 1997. "Sex Segregation and Occupational Gender Inequality in the United States: Devaluation or Specialized Training?" *American Journal of Sociology* 102(6): 1652–92.

Tannen, Deborah. 1990. *You Just Don't Understand: Women and Men in Conversation*. New York: Ballantine Books.

Tomaskovic-Devey, Donald. 1993. "The Gender and Race Composition of Jobs and the Male/Female, White/Black Pay Gap." *Social Forces* 72(1): 45–76.

United Nations. 2000a. "Convention on the Elimination of all Forms of Discrimination Against Women." http://un.org/womenwatch/daw/cedaw.

———. 2000b. "Strengthening Women's Economic Capacity." United Nations Development Fund for Women. http://www.unifem.undp.org/economic.htm.

———. 2000c. *The World's Women 2000: Trends and Statistics*. New York: United Nations Statistics Division.

United Nations Development Programme. 1997. *Human Development Report 1997*. New York: Oxford University Press.

——— 1999. *Human Development Report 1999*. New York: Oxford University Press.

——— *2001 Human Development Report 2001*. New York: Oxford University Press.

Van Willigen, Marieke, and Patricia Drentea. 1997. "Benefits of Equitable Relationships: The Impact of Sense of Failure, Household Division of Labor, and Decision-Making Power on Social Support." Presented at the Meeting of the American Sociological Association, Toronto, Ontario, August.

Whitla, W. 1995. "A Chronology of Women in Canada." In N. Mandell (ed.), *Feminist Issues: Race, Class and Sexuality*, pp. 315–53. Scarborough, ON: Prentice Hall Canada.

Wilkins, K. 1996. "Causes of Death: How the Sexes Differ." *Canadian Social Trends* 41: 11–7.

Williams, Christine L. 1995. *Still a Man's World: Men Who Do Women's Work*. Berkeley: University of California Press.

Williams, John E., and Deborah L. Best. 1990. *Measuring Sex Stereotypes: A Multination Study*. London: Sage Publications.

Wilmot, Alyssa. 1999. "First National Love Your Body Day a Big Success." Press release. *National Organization for Women Newsletter* (Winter). http://www.now.org.

Wine, J. D., and J. L. Ristock (eds.). 1991. "Introduction: Feminist Activism in Canada." In *Women and Social Change: Feminist Activism in Canada*, pp. 1–18. Toronto: James Lorimer.

Witt, S. D. 1996. "Traditional or Androgynous: An Analysis to Determine Gender Role Orientation of Basal Readers." *Child Study Journal* 26: 303–18.

WIN (Women's International Network) News. 2000. "Reports from around the World." (Autumn): 50–58.

World Bank. 2001. "Engendering Development." *World Bank Policy Research Report*. http://www.worldbank.org/gender/pur/newsummary.htm.

WHO (World Health Organization). 2001. "Prevalence Rates for FGM." http://www.who.int/frh-whd/FGM.

Yamaguchi, Mari. 2000. "Female Government Workers Face Harassment." http://news.excite.com/news/ap/001227/05/int.Japan.

Yumiko, Ehara. 2000. "Feminism's Growing Pains." *Japan Quarterly* 47: 41–48.

Zimmerman, Marc A., Laurel Copeland, Jean Shope, and T. E. Dielman. 1997. "A Longitudinal Study of Self-Esteem: Implications for Adolescent Development." *Journal of Youth and Adolescence* 26(2): 117–41.

Chapter 8

Abella, Irving. 1999. "Anti-Semitism." In James H. Marsh (ed.), *The Canadian Encyclopedia: Year 2000 Edition*, p. 90. Toronto: McClelland and Stewart, Inc.

Abella, Irving, and H. Troper. 1998. *None Is Too Many: Canada and the Jews of Europe, 1933–1948*. Toronto: Lester Publishing.

Beaudoin, Gerald A. 1999. "Keegstra Case." In James H. Marsh (ed.), *The Canadian Encyclopedia: Year 2000 Edition*, pp. 1237. Toronto: McClelland and Stewart, Inc.

Behiels, M.D. 1999. "Francophone-Anglophone Relations." In James H. Marsh (ed.), *The Canadian Encyclopedia: Year 2000 Edition*, pp. 909–13. Toronto: McClelland and Stewart, Inc.

Bibby, Reginald W. 2001. *Canada's Teens: Today, Yesterday, and Tomorrow*. Toronto: Stoddart.

Blackwell, Tom. 2002. "Racial Tension Peaked after Sept. 11 attacks." *National Post*, July 16: A7.

Boyd, Monica. 2000. "Canada's Refugees Flows: Gender Inequality." *Canadian Social Trends* 3: pp. 84–7. Toronto: Thompson Educational Publishing.

Breton, R. 1988. "French-English Relations." In J. E. Curtis and L. Tepperman (eds.), *Understanding Canadian Society*, pp. 557–85. Toronto: McGraw-Hill Ryerson Limited.

Bricker, Darrell, and Edward Greenspon. 2001. *Searching for Certainty: Inside the New Canadian Mindset*. Toronto: Doubleday Canada.

Burnet, Jean. 1999. "Multiculturalism." In James H. Marsh (ed.), *The Canadian Encyclopedia: Year 2000 Edition*, p. 1535. Toronto: McClelland and Stewart, Inc.

Children Now. 2000a. *Fall Colors I: How Diverse is the 1999–2000 Prime-Time Season?* http://www.childrennow.org.

———. 2000b. *Fall Colors II: Exploring the Quality of Diverse Portrayals on Prime-Time Television*. http://www.childrennow.org.

Claxton-Oldfield, Stephen, and Sheila M. Keefe. 1999. "Assessing Stereotypes about the Innu of Davis Inlet, Labrador." *Canadian Journal of Behavioural Sciences* 31(2): 86–91.

Cohen, Mark Nathan. 1998. "Culture, Not Race, Explains Human Diversity." *Chronicle of Higher Education* 44(32): B4–B5.

Columbo, J. R. 1986. *1001 Questions about Canada*. Toronto: Doubleday.

Conley, Dalton. 1999. *Being Black, Living in the Red: Race, Wealth, and Social Policy in America*. Berkeley: University of California Press.

Crauford-Lewis, M. 1999. "Nunavut." In James H. Marsh (ed.), *The Canadian Encyclopedia: Year 2000 Edition*, p. 1686. Toronto: McClelland and Stewart, Inc.

Deziel, Shanda, and Amy Cameron. 2001/2002. "Overbites." *Maclean's*, December 31–January 7: 11.

Doerr, A. 1999. "Royal Commission on Aboriginal Peoples." In James H. Marsh (ed.), *The Canadian Encyclopedia: Year 2000 Edition*, pp. 3–4. Toronto: McClelland and Stewart, Inc.

Donakowski, D. W., and V. M. Esses. 1996. "Native Canadians, First Nations, or Aboriginals: The Effects of Labels on Attitudes toward Native Peoples." *Canadian Journal of Behavioural Science* 28: 86–91.

Dreidger, L. 1999. "Prejudice and Discrimination." In James H. Marsh (ed.), *The Canadian Encyclopedia: Year 2000 Edition*, pp. 1888–92. Toronto: McClelland and Stewart, Inc.

Etzioni, Amitai. 1997. "New Issues: Rethinking Race." *Public Perspective* (June–July): 39–40. May 11, 1998. http://www.ropercenter.unconn.edu/pubper/pdf/!84b.htm.

Fitzhugh, T. V. 1991. *The Dictionary of Geneology*, 3rd ed. London: A. and C. Black.

Frideres, J. S. 1993. "Health Promotion and Indian Communities: Social Support or Social Disorganization." In B. Singh Bolaria and R. Bolaria (eds.), *Racial Minorities, Medicine and Health*, pp. 269–95. Halifax, NS: Fernwood.

Gaertner, Samuel L., and John F. Dovidio. 2000. *Reducing Intergroup Bias: The Common Ingroup Identity Model*. Philadelphia: Taylor & Francis Group.

Goldstein, Joseph. 1999. "Sunbeams." *The Sun* 277(January): 48.

Granastein, Ron. 2002. "Al-Qaida's Here." *Toronto Sun*, September 6: 4.

Guillebeau, Christopher. 1999. "Affirmative Action in a Global Perspective: The Cases of South Africa and Brazil." *Sociological Spectrum* 19(4): 443–65.

Guinier, Lani. 1998. Interview with Paula Zahn. *CBS Evening News*, July 18.

Gurin, Patricia. 1999. "New Research on the Benefits of Diversity in College and Beyond: An Empirical Analysis." *Diversity Digest* (Spring): 5–15. Washington, DC: Association of American Colleges and Universities.

"Hate on Campus." 2000. *Intelligence Report* 98 (Spring): 6–15.

Healey, Joseph F. 1997. *Race, Ethnicity, and Gender in the United States: Inequality, Group Conflict, and Power.* Thousand Oaks, CA: Pine Forge Press.

Health Canada. 1999. *Toward a Healthy Future: Second Report on the Health of Canadians.* Prepared by the Federal, Provincial, and Territorial Advisory Committee of Population Health for the Meeting of Ministers of Health, Charlottetown, PEI, September.

Henry, Frances, and Carol Tator. 1985. "Racism in Canada: Social Myths and Strategies for Change." In Rita M. Bienvenue and Jay E. Goldstein (eds.), *Ethnicity and Ethnic Relations in Canada,* 2nd ed., pp. 321–35. Toronto: Butterworths.

Henry, Frances, Carol Tator, Winston Mattis, and Tim Rees. 1995. *The Colour of Democracy.* Toronto: Harcourt Brace.

hooks, bell. 2000. *Where We Stand: Class Matters.* New York: Routledge.

Horwood, Harold. 1969. *Newfoundland.* Toronto: Macmillan.

Humphreys, Debra. 1999. "Diversity and the College Curriculum: How Colleges & Universities Are Preparing Students for a Changing World." *DiversityWeb.* http://www.inform.umd.edu/ EdRes/Topic/Di...Leadersguide/ CT/curriculum_briefing.html.

"Intelligence Briefs." 2000. *SPLC Report,* 30(3), September: 3.

Intelligence Report. 1998. *Teaching Tolerance* 89 (Winter). Montgomery, AL: Southern Poverty Law Center.

Janigan, Mary. 2002. "Immigrants." *Maclean's,* December 16: 10–25.

Jensen, Derrick. 2001. "Saving the Indigenous Soul: An Interview with Martin Prechtel." *The Sun* 304 (April): 4–15.

Keita, S. O. Y., and Rick A. Kittles. 1997. "The Persistence of Racial Thinking and the Myth of Racial Divergence." *American Anthropologist* 99(3): 534–44.

Kilgour, David. 1988. *Uneasy Patriots: Western Canadians in Confederation.* Edmonton: Lone Pine Press.

Kleg, Milton. 1993. *Hate, Prejudice, and Racism.* Albany: State University of New York Press.

Kunz, Jean Lock, Anne Milan, and Sylvain Schetagne. 2000. *Unequal Access: A Canadian Profile of Racial Differences in Education, Employment & Income.* Toronto: Canadian Race Relations Foundation. http://www.crr.ca.

KW Record. 2002. "Feeling the Backlash." September 3: C11.

Landau, Elaine. 1993. *The White Power Movement: America's Racist Hate Groups.* Brookfield, CT: Millbrook Press.

Leggon, Cheryl B. 1999. "Introduction: Race and Ethnicity—A Global Perspective." *Sociological Spectrum* 19(4): 381–85.

Levin, Jack, and Jack McDevitt. 1995. "Landmark Study Reveals Hate Crimes Vary Significantly by Offender Motivation." *Klanwatch Intelligence Report* August: 7–9.

Lieberman, Leonard. 1997. "Gender and the Deconstruction of the Race Concept." *American Anthropologist* 99(3): 545–58.

Liu, Marian. 2000. "Asian Americans Divided Over Web's 'Mr. Wong.' *San Francisco Chronicle,* August 16. http://www.sfgate.com/cgi-bin/ article.cgi?file=chronicle/archive/ 2000/08/16/DD35504.DTL.

Lofthus, Kai R. 1998. "Swedish Biz Decries Racist Music." *Billboard,* January 24: 71, 73.

Maclean's. 1999a. "Skinheads Sentenced." November 29: 33.

———. 1999b. "What Makes a Canadian?" December 20: 45–48.

———. 2001/2002. "Since Sept. 11: The Responses Show How Terrorism and War Have Left Their Mark." December 31–January 7: 38–39.

Marger, Martin N. 2000. *Race and Ethnic Relations: American and Global Perspectives,* 5th ed. Belmont, CA: Wadsworth.

Molnar, Stephen. 1983. *Human Variation: Races, Types, and Ethnic Groups,* 2nd ed. Englewood Cliffs, NJ: Prentice-Hall.

Mosher, Clayton J. 1998. *Discrimination and Denial: Systemic Racism in Ontario's Legal and Criminal Justice System, 1892–1961.* Toronto: University of Toronto Press.

Nash, Manning. 1962. "Race and the Ideology of Race." *Current Anthropology* 3: 258–88.

National Post. 1999a. "StatsCan Debates: How Canadian Are We?" November 30: A1.

———. 1999b. "Conditions Curtail Quebec's Right to Self-Determination." December 11: A11.

———. 1999c. "Clarity Act Fails to Arouse Separatist Sentiments." December 15: A7.

Niemonen, Jack. 1999. "Deconstructing Cultural Pluralism." *Sociological Spectrum* 19(4): 401–19.

Noh, S., and M. Belser. 1999. "Perceived Racial Discrimination, Depression, and Coping: A Study of Southeast Asian Refugees in Canada." *Journal of Health and Social Behavior* 40(3): 193–207.

Race Relations Reporter. 1999. Volume VII (8), October 15. New York: CH II Publishers, Inc. 200 West 57th St., New York, NY 10019.

Ray, Peter. 2002. "Arabs, Muslims Still Live in Fear of Attacks." *Toronto Star,* March 23: A20.

Roberts, J. 1995. "Disproportionate Harm: Hate Crime in Canada." http://ftp.nizkor.org/hweb/orgs/ Canadian/canada/justice/ disproportionate-harm.

Rowe, Frederick W. 1977. *Extinction: The Beothuks of Newfoundland.* Toronto: McGraw-Hill Ryerson.

Schaefer, Richard T. 1998. *Racial and Ethnic Groups,* 7th ed. New York: HarperCollins.

Sher, J. 1983. *White Hoods: Canada's Klu Klux Klan.* Vancouver: New Star Books.

Shipler, David K. 1998. "Subtle vs. Overt Racism." *Washington Spectator* 24(6), March 15: 1–3.

Statistics Canada. 1998. "1996 Census: Ethnic Origin, Visible Minorities." *The Daily,* February 17. http:// www.statcan.ca/Daily/ English/980217/d980217/ d980217.htm.

———. 2003a. "Canada's Ethnocultural Portrait: The Changing Mosaic." 2001 Census: Analysis Series. Catalogue no. 96F0030XIE2001008.

———. 2003b. "Census of a Population: Immigration, Birthplace, Birthplace of Parents, Citizenship, Ethnic Origin, Visible Minorities and Aboriginal Peoples." *The Daily,* January 21. http://www.statcan.ca/ Daily/English/030121/d030121.htm.

———. 2003c. "Education in Canada: Raising the Standard." Catalogue 96F0030XIE2001012. http://www12.statcan.ca/english/census01/products/Analytic/companion/educ/contents.cfm.

———. 2003d. "Earnings of Canadians: Making a Living in the New Economy." Catalogue 96F0030XIE2001013. http://www12.statcan.ca/english/census01/Products/Analytic/companion/earn/charts/menwom.cfm.

Stodolska, M., and E. L. Jackson. 1998. "Discrimination in Leisure and Work Experience by a White Ethnic Minority Group." *Journal of Leisure Research* 30(1): 23–41.

Such, P. 1978. *The Vanished People: The Beothuk People of Newfoundland.* Toronto: NC Press.

Weiner, Nan. 2001. "Employment barriers still block Aboriginals & Visible Minorities." *CAUT Bulletin*, April: A9, A10.

Wheeler, Michael L. 1994. *Diversity Training: A Research Report.* New York: The Conference Board.

Williams, Eddie N., and Milton D. Morris. 1993. "Racism and Our Future." In Herbert Hill and James E. Jones Jr. (eds.), *Race in America: The Struggle for Equality*, pp. 417–24. Madison: University of Wisconsin Press.

Winks, Robin W. 1999. "Slavery." In James H. Marsh (ed.), *The Canadian Encyclopedia Year 2000 Edition*, p. 2174. Toronto: McClelland and Stewart, Inc.

Zack, Naomi. 1998. *Thinking about Race.* Belmont, CA: Wadsworth Publishing Co.

Chapter 9

Alsdorf, Matt. 2001. "Portugal Grants Rights to Gay Couples." PlanetOut.com, March 16. http://www.planetout.com/news/article-print.html?2001/03/16/2.

Anderssen, Erin. 1999. "Gay-Bashing Preacher Calls Off Protest." *The Globe and Mail*, June 29. http://www.egale.ca/archives/press/9906299gm.htm.

Arnold, Tom. 2002. "Common-Law Families on the Rise." *National Post*, October 23: A9.

Arnup, Katherine (ed.). 1995. *Lesbian Parenting: Living with Pride and Prejudice.* Charlottetown, PEI: gynergy books.

Associated Press. 2001. "Vancouver Gay Man Beaten to Death: Police Suspect Hate Crime." http://www.planetqnews.com/0812/11.shtml.

Bailey, Martha. 2000. *Marriage and Marriage-Like Relationships.* http://www.lcc.gc/ca/cgi-bin/repee_en.c...y%2C+Martha&language=en&range=1&numdoc.

Baldwin, Tammy. "Never Doubt." Speech delivered at Millennium March, Washington, DC, April 2000.

Bayer, Ronald. 1987. *Homosexuality and American Psychiatry: The Politics of Diagnosis*, 2nd ed. Princeton, NJ: Princeton University Press.

Benkov, Laura. 1994. *Reinventing the Family: The Emerging Story of Gay and Lesbian Parents.* New York: Crown Publishers.

Besen, Wayne. 2000. "Introduction." In Human Rights Campaign, *Feeling Free: Personal Stories: How Love and Self-Acceptance Saved Us from "Ex-Gay" Ministries*, p. 7. Washington, DC: Human Rights Campaign Foundation.

Black, Dan, Gary Gates, Seth Sanders, and Lowell Taylor. 2000 (May). "Demographics of the Gay and Lesbian Population in the United States: Evidence from Available Systematic Data Sources." *Demography* 37(2): 139–54.

Brannock, J. C., and B. E. Chapman. 1990. "Negative Sexual Experiences with Men among Heterosexual Women and Lesbians." *Journal of Homosexuality* 19: 105–10.

"Brazilian Killers Sentenced." 2001. PlanetOut.com, February 15. http://www.planetout.com/news/article-print.html?2001/02/15/1.

Bricker, Darrell, and Edward Greenspon. 2001. *Searching for Certainty: Inside the New Canadian Mindset.* Toronto: Doubleday Canada.

Brown, Laura S. 2000. "Dangerousness, Impotence, Silence, and Invisibility: Heterosexism in the Construction of Women's Sexuality." In Cheryl Brown Travis and Jacquelyn W. White (eds.), *Sexuality, Society, and Feminism: Psy-*

chology of Women, pp. 273–97. Washington, DC: American Psychological Association.

Bullough, Vern L. 2000. "Transgenderism and the Concept of Gender." *International Journal of Transgenderism.* Special issue 4(3), July–September.

Bush, Irene R., and Anthony Sainz. 2001. "Competencies at the Intersection of Difference, Tolerance, and Prevention of Hate Crimes." In Mary E. Swigonski and Robin S. Mama (eds.), *From Hate Crimes To Human Rights: A Tribute to Matthew Shepard*, pp. 205–24. New York: Haworth Press.

Butler, Amy C. 2000. "Trends in Same-Gender Sexual Partnering, 1988–1998." *The Journal of Sex Research* 37(4): 333–43.

Button, James W., Barbara A. Rienzo, and Kenneth D. Wald. 1997. *Private Lives, Public Conflicts: Battles over Gay Rights in American Communities.* Washington, DC: CQ Press.

Chase, Bob. 2000. "NEA President Bob Chase's Historic Speech from 2000 GLSEN Conference." http://www.glsen.org/templates/resources/record.html?section=14&record=255.

"Constitutional Protection." 1999. GayLawNet, February 14. http://www.nexus.net.au/~dba/news.html#top.

Craig, Kellina M. 2002. "Examining Hate-Motivated Aggression: A Review of the Social Psychological Liteature on Hate Crimes as a Distinct Form of Aggression." *Aggression & Violent Behavior* 7(1), January–February: 85–101.

Dawson, Lorne. 1993. "Religion and Legitimacy." In Peter S. Li and B. Singh Bolaria (eds.), *Contemporary Sociology: Critical Perspectives*, pp. 311–27. Toronto: Copp Clark Pitman.

De Cecco, John P., and D. A. Parker. 1995. "The Biology of Homosexuality: Sexual Orientation or Sexual Preference?" *Journal of Homosexuality* 28: 1–28.

D'Emilio, John. 1990. "The Campus Environment for Gay and Lesbian Life." *Academe* 76(1): 16–9.

Deziel, Shanda. 2000. "Gaily Prime Time." *Maclean's*, October 30: 54.

Doell, R.G. 1995. "Sexuality in the Brain." *Journal of Homosexuality* 28: 345–56.

Dozetos, Barbara. 2001. "School Shooter Taunted as 'Gay.'" PlanetOut.com, March 7. http://www.planetout.com/news/article-print.html?2001/03/07/1.

Dranoff, Linda Silver. 2001. *Everyone's Guide to the Law.* Toronto: Harper-Collins Publishers Ltd.

Drinkwater, Gregg. 2001. "Netherlands to Celebrate First Gay Marriages." PlanetOut.com, March 30. http://www.planetout.com/news/article-print.html?2001/03/2.

Durkheim, Emile. 1993. "The Normal and the Pathological." Originally published in *The Rules of Sociological Method, 1938.* In Henry N. Pontell (ed.), *Social Deviance,* pp. 33–63. Englewood Cliffs, NJ: Prentice-Hall.

EGALE. 1999. "Press Release." June 7. http://www.egale.ca/politics.motion.htm.

———. 2001. "Svend Robinson Introduces Bill, EGALE Renews Call for Hate Crimes Protection In Wake of Murder of Gay Man in Vancouver." Press release, November 22. http://www.egale.ca/pressrel/011122.htm.

Esterberg, K. 1997. *Lesbian and Bisexual Identities: Constructing Communities, Constructing Selves.* Philadelphia: Temple University Press.

Faulkner, Anne H., and Kevin Cranston. 1998. "Correlates of Same-Sex Sexual Behavior in a Random Sample of Massachusetts High School Students." *Journal of Public Health* 88 (February): 262–66.

Firestein, B. A. 1996. "Bisexuality as Paradigm Shift: Transforming Our Disciplines." In B. A. Firestein (ed.), *Bisexuality: The Psychology and Politics of an Invisible Minority,* pp. 263–91. Thousand Oaks, CA: Sage.

Fisher, John. 1999. *A Report on Lesbian, Gay and Bisexual Youth Issues in Canada.* Ottawa: EGALE.

Flowers, Paul, and Katie Buston. 2001. "'I Was Terrified of Being Different': Exploring Gay Men's Accounts of Growing-Up in a Heterosexist Society." *Journal of Adolescence.* Special Issue: Gay, Lesbian, and Bisexual Youth. 24(1), February: 51–65.

Fone, Byrne. 2000. *Homophobia: A History.* New York: Henry Holt and Company.

Frank, Barney. 1997. Foreword. In J. W. Button, B. A. Rienzo, and K. D. Wald, *Private Lives, Public Conflicts: Battles over Gay Rights in American Communities.* Washington DC: CQ Press.

Frank, David John, and Elizabeth H. McEneaney. 1999. "The Individualization of Society and the Liberalization of State Policies on Same-Sex Relations, 1984–1995." *Social Forces* 77(3): 911–44.

Franklin, Sarah. 1993. "Essentialism, Which Essentialism? Some Implications of Reproductive and Genetic Techno-Science." *Journal of Homosexuality* 24: 27–39.

Freedman, Estelle B., and John D'Emilio. 1990. "Problems Encountered in Writing the History of Sexuality: Sources, Theory, and Interpretation." *Journal of Sex Research* 27: 481–95.

Fulford, Robert. 2002. "Man Bites Man." *Toronto Life* (September): 61–65.

Gallup Organization. 2000. "Gallup Poll Topics: A–Z." http://www.gallup.com/poll/indicators/indhomosexual.asp.

Garnets, L., G. M. Herek, and B. Levy. 1990. "Violence and Victimization of Lesbians and Gay Men: Mental Health Consequences." *Journal of Interpersonal Violence* 5: 366–83.

Gay and Lesbian International Lobby. 2000. "Recognition of Gay and Lesbian Partnerships in Europe." http://www.steff.suite.dk/partner.htm.

Gilbert, Michael. 2000. "The Transgendered Philosopher." *International Journal of Transgenderism.* Special issue 4(3), July–September.

Goldie, Terry. 2001. *In a Queer Country: Gay & Lesbian Studies in the Canadian Context.* Vancouver: Arsenal Pulp Press.

Goode, Erica E., and Betsy Wagner. 1993. "Intimate Friendships." *U.S. News and World Report,* July 5: 49–52.

Hamer, D., P. F. Copeland, S. Hu, V. L. Magnuson, N. Hu, and A. M. L. Pattatucci. 1993. "A Linkage Between DNA Markers on the X Chromosome and Male Sexual Orientation." *Science* 261: 321–27.

Herdt, Gilbert. 2001. "Social Change, Sexual Diversity, and Tolerance for Bisexuality in the United States." In Anthony R. D'Augelli and Charlotte J. Patterson (eds.), *Lesbian, Gay, and Bisexual Identities and Youth: Psychological Perspectives,* pp. 267–83. New York: Oxford University Press.

Herek, Gregory M. 1989. "Hate Crimes against Lesbians and Gay Men." *American Psychologist* 44: 948–55.

———. 1990. "The Context of Anti-Gay Violence: Notes on Cultural and Psychological Heterosexism." *Journal of Interpersonal Violence* 5: 316–33.

Homophobia 101: Teaching Respect for All. 2000. The Gay, Lesbian, and Straight Education Network. http://www.glsen.org.

Honore, Carl. 2000. "'Male Egg' Could Enable Two Men to Conceive a Child." *National Post,* September 26: A1, A12.

Human Rights Campaign. 2000a. *Feeling Free: Personal Stories: How Love and Self-Acceptance Saved Us from "Ex-Gay" Ministries.* Washington, DC: Human Rights Campaign.

———. 2000b. *The State of the Workplace for Lesbian, Gay, Bisexual and Transgendered Americans, 2000.* Washington, DC: Human Rights Campaign Foundation.

International Gay and Lesbian Human Rights Commission. 1999. "Antidiscrimination Legislation." http://www.iglhrc.org/news/factsheets/990604-antidis.html.

"Jail, Death Sentences in Africa." 2001. PlanetOut.com, February 21. http://www.planetout.com/news/articleprint.html?2001/02/21/2.

Kinsey, A. C., W. B. Pomeroy, C. E. Martin, and P. H. Gebhard. 1953. *Sexual Behavior in the Human Female.* Philadelphia: W. B. Saunders.

Kirkpatrick, R. C. 2000. "The Evolution of Human Sexual Behavior." *Current Anthropology* 41(3): 385.

Kite, M. E., and B. E. Whitley, Jr. 1996. "Sex Differences in Attitudes toward Homosexual Persons,

Behavior and Civil Rights: A Meta-analysis." *Personality and Social Psychology Bulletin* 22: 336–52.

Klassen, Albert D., Colin J. Williams, and Eugene E. Levitt. 1989. *Sex and Morality in the United States*. Middletown, CT: Wesleyan University Press.

Lambda Legal Defense and Education Fund. 2000. *Student Advocacy for University Anti-Bias Policies that Include Sexual Orientation*. Publications, July 6. http://www.lambdalegal.org.

LAWbriefs. 2000. "Recent Developments in Sexual Orientation and Gender Identity Law." *LAWbriefs* 3(3), Fall.

Lever, J. 1994. "The 1994 Advocate Survey of Sexuality and Relationships: The Men." *Advocate,* August 23: 16–24.

Louderback, L. A., and B. E. Whitley. 1997. "Perceived Erotic Value of Homosexuality and Sex-Role Attitudes as Mediators of Sex Differences in Heterosexual College Students' Attitudes toward Lesbians and Gay Men." *Journal of Sex Research* 34: 175–82.

Maclean's. 1996. "Untitled." November 4.

———. 2002. "Acceptable but not equal." June 3: 12.

Mathison, Carla. 1998. "The Invisible Minority: Preparing Teachers to Meet the Needs of Gay and Lesbian Youth." *Journal of Teacher Education* 49: 151–55.

Michael, Robert T., John H. Gagnon, Edward O. Laumann, and Gina Kolata. 1994. *Sex in America: A Definitive Survey*. Boston: Little, Brown.

Mohr, Richard D. 1995. "Anti-Gay Stereotypes." In P. S. Rothenberg (ed.), *Race, Class, and Gender in the United States*, 3rd ed., pp. 402–8. New York: St. Martin's Press.

Moore, David W. 1993. "Public Polarized on Gay Issue." *Gallup Poll Monthly* 331 (April): 30–34.

Moser, Charles. 1992. "Lust, Lack of Desire, and Paraphilias: Some Thoughts and Possible Connections." *Journal of Sex and Marital Therapy* 18: 65–69.

Murphy, Timothy F. 2001. "Commentary: Lesbian, Gay, Bisexual, and Transgender Medical Students and their Ethical Conflicts." *Journal of the Gay & Lesbian Medical Association.* Special issue 5(1), March: 31–35.

Nagle, Matt. 2001. "Gay Man Murdered in Vancouver's Stanley Park." *Seattle Gay News*, November 23. http://www.sgn.org/2001/11/23.

National Gay and Lesbian Task Force. 2001. "Specific Anti-Same-Sex Marriage Laws in the U.S.—January 2001." http://www.ngltf.org/downloads/marriagemap0201.pdf.

Nugent, Robert, and Jeannine Gramick. 1989. "Homosexuality: Protestant, Catholic, and Jewish Issues: A Fishbone Tale." *Journal of Homosexuality* 18: 7–46.

Patterson, Charlotte J. 2001. "Family Relationships of Lesbians and Gay Men." In Robert M. Milardo (ed.), *Understanding Families Into the New Millennium: A Decade in Review*, pp. 271–88. Minneapolis, MN: National Council on Family Relations.

Paul, J.P. 1996. "Bisexuality: Exploring/Exploding the Boundaries." In R. Savin-Williams and K. M. Cohen (eds.), *The Lives of Lesbians, Gays, and Bisexuals: Children to Adults*, pp. 436–61. Fort Worth, TX: Harcourt Brace.

Peele, S., and R. DeGrandpre. 1995. "My Genes Made Me Do It." *Psychology Today* 28(4), July/August: 50–53.

Pillard, Richard C., and J. Michael Bailey. 1998. "Human Sexuality Has a Heritable Component." *Human Biology* 70 (April): 347–65.

Platt, Leah. 2001. "Not Your Father's High School Club." *The American Prospect* 12(1): A37–A39.

Price, Jammie, and Michael G. Dalecki. 1998. "The Social Basis of Homophobia: An Empirical Illustration." *Sociological Spectrum* 18: 143–59.

Rice, G., C. Anderson, N. Risch, and G. Ebers. 1999. "Male Homosexuality: Absence of Linkage to Microsatellite Markers at Xq28." *Science* 284(5415), April 23: 665–67.

Rosin, Hanna, and Richard Morin. 1999. "In One Area, Americans Still Draw a Line on Acceptability." *Washington Post,* National Weekly Edition, 16(11), January 11: 8.

Sanday, Peggy R. 1995. "Pulling Train." In P. S. Rothenberg (ed.), *Race, Class, and Gender in the United States*, 3rd ed., pp. 396–402. New York: St. Martin's Press.

Schellenberg, E. Glenn, Jessie Hirt, and Alan Sears. 1999. "Attitudes Toward Homosexuals Among Students at a Canadian University." *Sex Roles* 40 (1/2): 139–52.

Simon, A. 1995. "Some Correlates of Individuals' Attitudes toward Lesbians." *Journal of Homosexuality* 29: 89–103.

"Sodomy Fact Sheet: A Global Overview." 2000. The International Gay and Lesbian Human Rights Commission. 1360 Mission Street, San Francisco, CA, 94103.

Stone, Sharon D. (ed.). 1990. "Lesbian Mothers: Organizing." In *Lesbians in Canada*, pp. 191–205. Toronto: Between the Lines.

Sullivan, A. 1997. "The Conservative Case." In A. Sullivan (ed.), *Same-Sex Marriage: Pro and Con*, pp. 146–54. New York: Vintage Books.

Thompson, Cooper. 1995. "A New Vision of Masculinity." In P. S. Rothenberg (ed.), *Race, Class, and Gender in the United States*, 3rd ed., pp. 475–81. New York: St. Martin's Press.

The United Methodist Church and Homosexuality. 1999. February 16. http://religioustolerance.org/hom_umc.htm.

Weston, Kath. 1991. *Families We Choose: Lesbians, Gays, Kinship*. New York: Columbia University Press.

Wetzel, Janice Wood. 2001. "Human Rights in the 20th Century: Weren't Gays and Lesbians Human?" In Mary E. Swigonski and Robin S. Mama (eds.), *From Hate Crimes to Human Rights: A Tribute to Matthew Shepard*, pp. 15–31. New York: Haworth Press.

Wilcox, Clyde, and Robin Wolpert. 2000. "Gay Rights in the Public Sphere: Public Opinion on Gay and Lesbian Equality." In Craig A. Rimmerman, Kenneth D. Wald, and Clyde Wilcox (eds.), *The Politics of Gay Rights*, pp. 409–32. Chicago: University of Chicago Press.

Yang, Alan. 1999. *From Wrongs to Rights 1973 to 1999: Public Opinion on Gay and Lesbian Americans Moves Toward Equality*. New York: The

Policy Institute of the National Gay and Lesbian Task Force.

Yogis, J. A., R. R. Duplak, and J. R. Trainor. 1996. *Sexual Orientation and Canadian Law: An Assessment of the Law Affecting Lesbian and Gay Persons.* Toronto: Emond Montgomery Publications Limited.

Chapter 10

Albelda, Randy, and Chris Tilly. 1997. *Glass Ceilings and Bottomless Pits: Women's Work, Women's Poverty.* Boston, MA: South End Press.

Alex-Assensoh, Yvette. 1995. "Myths about Race and the Underclass." *Urban Affairs Review* 31: 3–19.

Ash, Russell. 2001. *The Top 10 of Everything: Canadian Edition 2002.* Toronto: Dorling Kindersley Limited.

Barlow, Maude, and Bruce Campbell. 1995. *Straight through the Heart.* Toronto: HarperCollins Publishers Ltd.

Bricker, Darrell, and Edward Greenspon. 2001. *Searching for Certainty: Inside the New Canadian Mindset.* Toronto: Doubleday Canada.

Briggs, Vernon M. Jr. 1998. "American-Style Capitalism and Income Disparity: The Challenge of Social Anarchy." *Journal of Economic Issues* 32(2): 473–81.

Brown, Lester R. 2001. "Eradicating Hunger: A Growing Challenge." In Lester R. Brown, Christopher Flavin, and Hilary French (eds.), *State of the World 2001*, pp. 43–62. New York: W.W. Norton & Co.

Canada Customs and Revenue Agency. 2002. "About the Canada Child Tax Benefit (CCTB)." http://www.ccra-adrc.gc.ca/benefits/faq_about-e.html.

Canadian Centre for Policy Alternatives Monitor. 1999. September. http://www.policyalternatives.ca.

Canadian Council on Social Development. 2001. "Highlights: The Progress of Canada's Children 2001." March. http://www.ccsd.ca/pubs/2001/pcc2001/hl.htm.

Centre for Social Justice. 2001a. "Racial Background and Economic Inequality." http://www.socialjustice.org/issues/equity.html.

———. 2001b. "Wealth of the Top 20% of Families Surges 39% since

1984, while the Bottom Sinks." March 15. http://www.socialjustice.org/media/releas/wealthgap.html.

Chossudovsky, Michel. 1998. "Global Poverty in the Late Twentieth Century." *Journal of International Affairs* 52(1): 293–303.

Conley, Dalton. 2001. "Capital for College: Parental Assets and Post-secondary Schooling." *Sociology of Education* 74(January): 59–72.

Corak, Miles. 1998. "Getting Ahead in Life: Does Your Parents' Income Count?" *Canadian Social Trends* 49 (Summer): 6–15.

Coyne, Andrew. 1997. "Poverty Study Raises Questions." *Kitchener-Waterloo Record*, July 17: A7.

Cracker, David A., and Toby Linden, (eds.). 1998. *Ethics of Consumption: The Good Life, Justice, and Global Stewardship.* Lanhan, MD: Rowman & Littlefield.

Daub, Shannon, and Margaret Young. 1999. "Families Need More than Tax Fairness." http://www.policyalternatives.ca.

Davis, Kingsley, and Wilbert Moore. 1945. "Some Principles of Stratification." *American Sociological Review* 10: 242–49.

Deen, Thalif. 2000. "NGOs Call For UN Poverty Eradication Fund." Global Policy Forum. http://www.globalpolicy.org/msummit/millenni/millfor3.htm.

Dranoff, Linda Silver. 2001. *Everyone's Guide to the Law.* Toronto: HarperCollins Publishers Ltd.

Duncan, Greg J., and Jeanne Brooks-Gunn. 1997. "Income Effects across the Life Span: Integration and Interpretation." In Greg J. Duncan and Jeanne Brooks-Gunn (eds.), *Consequences of Growing Up Poor*, pp. 596–610. New York: Russell Sage Foundation.

Economic Policy Institute. 2000. "Issue Guide to the Minimum Wage." http://www.epinet.org/Issuesguides/minwage/minwagefaq.html.

Fawcett, 1999. "Disability in the Labour Market: Barriers and Solutions." *Perception* 23(3), December. Canadian Council on Social Development. http://www.ccsd.ca/perception/233/disab.htm.

Flavin, Christopher. 2001. "Rich Planet, Poor Planet." In Lester R. Brown, Christopher Flavin, and Hilary French (eds.), *State of the World 2001*. Worldwatch Institute. New York: W.W. Norton & Co.

Galabuzi, Grace Edward. 2001. *Canada's Creeping Economic Apartheid: The Economic Segregation and Social Marginalization of Racialised Groups*, 2nd ed. Toronto: CSJ Foundation for Research and Education.

Gans, Herbert J. 1972. "The Positive Functions of Poverty." *American Journal of Sociology* 78 (September): 275–388.

Global Poverty Report. 2000. G8 Okinawa Summit, July 2000.

Government of Canada. 1999. *National Child Benefit Progress Report 1999.* http://www.socialunion.gc.ca/NCB-99/html.

Guest, Dennis. 1999a. "Social Security." In James H. Marsh (ed.), *The Canadian Encyclopedia: Year 2000 Edition*, pp. 2200–4. Toronto: McClelland and Stewart, Inc.

———. 1999b. "Family Allowance." In James H. Marsh (ed.), *The Canadian Encyclopedia: Year 2000 Edition*, pp. 1815–16. Toronto: McClelland and Stewart, Inc.

Health Canada. 1999. *Toward a Healthy Future: Second Report on the Health of Canadians.* Prepared by the Federal, Provincial, and Territorial Advisory Committee on Population Health for the Meeting of Ministers of Health, Charlottetown, PEI, September 1999.

Hill, Lewis E. 1998. "The Institutional Economics of Poverty: An Inquiry into the Causes and Effects of Poverty." *Journal of Economic Issues* 32(2): 279–86.

Human Resources Development Canada. 2001. "What is the CESG?" http://www.hrdc-drhc.gc.ca/brib/learnlit/cesg/013/001_e.shtml.

Kennedy, Bruce P., Ichiro Kawachi, Roberta Glass, and Deborah Prothrow-Stith. 1998. "Income Distribution, Socioeconomic Status, and Self-Rated Health in the U.S.: Multilevel Analysis." *British Medical Journal* 317(7163): 917–22.

Knickerbocker, Brad. 2000. "Nongovernmental Organizations are Fighting and Winning Social, Political

Battles." Global Policy Forum. http://www.globalpolicy.org/ngos/00role.htm.

Krahn, Harvey. 1994. "Social Stratification." In Robert Brym (ed.), *New Society Brief Edition: Sociology for the Twenty-First Century*, pp. 2.1–2.31. Toronto: Harcourt Brace Jovanovich.

Larin, Kathryn. 1998. "Should We Be Worried about the Widening Gap between the Rich and the Poor?" *Insight on the News* 14(5): 24–28.

Lewis, Oscar. 1966. "The Culture of Poverty." *Scientific American* 2(5): 19–25.

———. 1998. "The Culture of Poverty: Resolving Common Social Problems." *Society* 35(2): 7–10.

Luker, Kristin. 1996. *Dubious Conceptions: The Politics of Teenage Pregnancy*. Cambridge, MA: Harvard University Press.

MacGregor, Karen. 2002. "It's Porridge for the Poor, and Oysters for the VIPs." *The Globe and Mail*, August 29: A13.

Maclean's. 1999. "What Makes a Canadian?" December 20: 44–8.

Mann, Judy. 2000 (May 15). "Demonstrators at the Barricades Aren't Very Subtle, but They Sometimes Win." *The Washington Spectator*, 26(10): 1–3.

Mayer, Susan E. 1997. *What Money Can't Buy: Family Income and Children's Life Chances*. Cambridge, MA: Harvard University Press.

Mead, L. 1992. *The New Politics of Poverty: The Non-Working Poor in America*. New York: Basic Books.

Mishel, Lawrence, Jared Bernstein, and John Schmitt. 2001. *The State of Working America 2000/2001*. Ithaca, NY: Cornell University Press.

Moscovitch, Allan. 1999. "Welfare State." In James H. Marsh (ed.), *The Canadian Encyclopedia: Year 2000 Edition*, pp. 2493–96. Toronto: McClelland and Stewart, Inc.

Narayan, Deepa. 2000. *Voices of the Poor: Can Anyone Hear Us?* New York: Oxford University Press.

National Council of Welfare. 1997. "Canada Welfare Incomes." http://csf.colorado.edu/lists/psn/dec97/0071.html.

———. 1998. *Profiles of Welfare: Myths and Realities: A Report by the National Council of Welfare*. Spring.

http://www.ncwcnbes.net/htmdocument/reportprowelfare.repprowelfare.htm.

———. 1999a. *Children First: A Pre-Budget Report by the National Council of Welfare*. Autumn. http://www.ncwcnbes.net/htmdocument/reportchildfirst/repchildfirst.htm.

———. 1999b. "No Such Thing as a 'Typical' Welfare Case, Says National Council of Welfare Report." http://www.ncwcnbes.net/htmdocument/reportprowelfare/PRESSPROWELFARE. htm.

———. 1999c. *Preschool Children: Promises to Keep*. Spring. http://www.ncwcnbes.net/htmdocument/reportpromise/firstpag.htm.

———. 2000. *Poverty Profile 1998*. Ottawa: Ministry of Public Works.

———. 2002a. "Fact Sheet: Welfare Recipients." http://www.ncwcnbes.net/htmdocument/principales/numberwelfare.htm.

———. 2002b. *Poverty Profile 1999*. http://www.ncwcnbes.net/htmdocument/reportpovertypro000/Introduction.html.

Orlikow, Lionel. 1999. "Students, Financial Aid." In James H. Marsh (ed.), *The Canadian Encyclopedia: Year 2000 Edition*, pp. 2264–65. Toronto: McClelland and Stewart, Inc.

Paul, James A. 2000. "NGOs and Global Policy-Making." Global Policy Forum. http://www.globalpolicy.org/ngos/analysis/anal00htm.

Ross, David P., and Clarence Lochhead. 1999. "Poverty." In James H. Marsh (ed.), *The Canadian Encyclopedia: Year 2000 Edition*, pp. 1880–82. Toronto: McClelland and Stewart, Inc.

Ross, David P., E. Richard Shillington, and Clarence Lochhead. 1994. *The Canadian Fact Book on Poverty*. Ottawa: Canadian Council on Social Development.

Sarlo, Christopher. 1992. *Poverty in Canada*. Vancouver: The Fraser Institute.

———. 1996. *Poverty in Canada*. Vancouver: The Fraser Institute.

Schenk, Christopher. 2001. *From Poverty Wages to a Living Wage*. Toronto: CJS Foundation for Research and Education.

Seccombe, Karen. 2001. "Families in Poverty in the 1990s: Trends, Causes, Consequences, and Lessons Learned." In Robert M. Milardo (ed.), *Understanding Families into the New Millennium: A Decade in Review*, pp. 313–32. Minneapolis, MN: National Council on Family Relations.

Speth, James Gustave. 1998. "Poverty: A Denial of Human Rights." *Journal of International Affairs* 52(1): 277–86.

Statistics Canada. 1998a. *Canada Yearbook 1999*. Ottawa: Minister of Industry.

———. 1998b. *The Daily,* May 12. http://www.statscan.ca:80/Daily/English/980512/d980512.htm.

———. 2000. "Family Income 1998." *The Daily*, June 12. http://www.statcan.ca/Daily/English/000612/d000612a.htm.

———. 2002. "Gender Pay Differentials: Impact of the Workplace." *The Daily*, June 19. http://www.statcan.ca/Daily/English/020619/d0201619b.htm.

Streeten, Paul. 1998. "Beyond the Six Veils: Conceptualizing and Measuring Poverty." *Journal of International Affairs* 52(1): 1–8.

United Nations. 1997. *Report on the World Social Situation, 1997*. New York: United Nations.

United Nations Development Programme. 1997. *Human Development Report 1997*. New York: Oxford University Press.

———. 2000. *Human Development Report 2000*. New York: Oxford University Press.

Van Kempen, Eva T. 1997. "Poverty Pockets and Life Chances: On the Role of Place in Shaping Social Inequality." *American Behavioural Scientist* 41(3): 430–50.

Vonnegut, Kurt Jr. 1968. *Welcome to the Monkey House: A Collection of Short Works*. New York: Delacorte Press/S. Lawrence.

Wilson, William J. 1987. *The Truly Disadvantaged: The Inner City, the Underclass, and Public Policy*. Chicago: University of Chicago Press.

Wilson, William J. 1996. *When Work Disappears: The World of the New Urban Poor*. New York: Knopf.

World Bank. 2001. *World Development Report: Attacking Poverty, 2000/2001*. Herndon, VA: World Bank and Oxford University Press.

Wren, Christopher S. 2001. "U.N. Report Maps Hunger 'Hot Spots.'" *The New York Times on the Web*, January 9. http://www.nytimes.com/2001/01/01/09/world/09HUNG.html.

Yalnizyan, A. 1998. *The Growing Gap.* Toronto: Centre for Social Justice.

Chapter 11

Ambrose, Soren. 1998. "The Case against the IMF." *Campaign for Human Rights Newsletter* 12, December 8. http://www.summersault.co…wsletter/news12.html.

Ash, Russell. 2001. *The Top 10 of Everything: Canadian Edition 2002.* Toronto: Dorling Kindersley Limited.

Aubin, Benoit, Julian Beltrame, Brian Bergman, John DeMont, Sharon Doyle Driedger, Sue Ferguson, Danylo Hawaleshka, John Intini, and Ken MacQueen. 2002. "*Maclean's* Leaders of Tomorrow." *Maclean's*, September 9: 20–30.

Bassi, Laurie J., and Jens Ludwig. 2000 (January). "School-to-Work Programs in the United States: A Multi-Firm Case Study of Training, Benefits, and Costs." *Industrial and Labor Relations Review* 53(2): 219.

Bavendam, James. 2000. "Managing Job Satisfaction." Special Reports, Volume 6: 1–2. Bavendam Research Incorporated. http://www.bavendam.com.

Bell, Daniel. 1973. *The Coming of Post-Industrial Society.* New York: Basic Books.

Bellan, Ruben C. 1999. "Foreign Investment." In James H. Marsh (ed.), *The Canadian Encyclopedia: Year 2000 Edition*, pp. 884–85. Toronto: McClelland and Stewart, Inc.

Benjamin, Medea. 1998. "What's Fair about Fair Labor Association (FLA)?" *Sweatshop Watch.* http://www.sweatshopwatch.org/swatch/headlines/1998/org/swatch/headlines/1998/gex_fla.html.

Bettelheim, Adriel. 1998. "Sleep Deprivation." *CQ Researcher* 8(24): 553–76.

Bracey, Gerald W. 1995. "The Fifth Bracey Report on the Condition of Public Education." *Phi Delta Kappan* (October): 149–62.

Bricker, Darrell, and Edward Greenspon. 2001. *Searching for Certainty: Inside the New Canadian Mindset.* Toronto: Doubleday Canada.

Canadian Council on Social Development. 2001. *The Progress of Canada's Children 2001—Highlights.* March. http://www.ccsd.ca/pubs/2001/pcc2001.hl.htm.

Canadian Global Almanac. 2002. Edited by Susan Girvan. Toronto: Macmillan Canada.

Caston, Richard J. 1998. *Life in a Business-Oriented Society: A Sociological Perspective.* Boston: Allyn and Bacon.

Coleman, James. 1994. *The Criminal Elite: The Sociology of White Collar Crime*, 3rd ed. New York: St. Martin's Press.

Conrad, Peter. 1999. "Wellness in the Work Place: Potentials and Pitfalls of Work-Site Health Promotion." In K. Charmaz and D. A. Paterniti (eds.), *Health, Illness, and Healing: Society, Social Context, and Self*, pp. 263–75. Los Angeles: Roxbury Publishing Company.

Danaher, Kevin. 1998. "Are Workers Waking Up?" Global Exchange: Education for Action. December 17. http://www.globalexchange.org/education/economy/laborday.html.

Doherty, Gillian. 2001. "Moving Towards Achieving Quality Child Care." In Gordon Cleveland and Michael Krashinsky (eds.), *Our Children's Future: Child Care Policy in Canada*, pp. 126–41. Toronto: University of Toronto Press.

Dorman, Peter. 2001. "Child Labour in the Developed Economies." Geneva: International Labour Office.

Durkheim, Emile. [1893] 1966. *On the Division of Labor in Society*, trans. G. Simpson. New York: Free Press.

Eitzen, Stanley, and Maxine Baca Zinn (eds.) 1990. *The Reshaping of America: Social Consequences of the Changing Economy.* Englewood Cliffs, NJ: Prentice-Hall.

Epstein, Gerald, Julie Graham, and Jessica Nembhard (eds.). 1993. "Third World Socialism and the Demise of COMECON." In *Creating a New World Economy: Forces of Change and Plans of Action*, pp. 405–20. Philadelphia: Temple University Press.

Feather, Norman T. 1990. *The Psychological Impact of Unemployment.* New York: Springer-Verlag.

Frederick, James and Nancy Lessin. 2000. "Blame the Worker: The Rise of Behavioral-Based Safety Programs." *Multinational Monitor* 21(11), November. http://www.essential.org/monitor/mm2000/00november/toc.html.

Galinsky, Ellen, and James T. Bond. 1998. *The 1998 Business Work-Life Study.* New York: Families and Work Institute.

Galinsky, Ellen, James E. Riesbeck, Fran S. Rodgers, and Faith A. Wohl. 1993. "Business Economics and the Work-Family Response." In *Work-Family Needs: Leading Corporations Respond*, pp. 51–54. New York: The Conference Board.

Ghalam, Nancy Zukewich. 2000. "Paid and Unpaid Work." In Statistics Canada, *Women in Canada 2000: A Gender-Based Statistical Report*, pp. 97–134. Ottawa: Statistics Canada.

"Global Labor Repression." 2000. Behind the Lines. *Multinational Monitor* 21(11), November. http://www.essential.org/monitor/mm2000/00november/toc.html.

Global March against Child Labor. 1998. "Global March against Child Labor." 1998. December 12. http://children.globalmarch-us.org.

Greenhouse, Steven. 2000. "Anti-Sweatshop Movement Is Achieving Gains Overseas." *The New York Times on the Web*, January 26. http://nytimes.com.

Hallsworth, Alan. 1993. "The External Trade of Canada." In *The U.S.A. and Canada*, pp. 432–39. London, U.K.: Europa Publications.

Hargis, Michael J. 2001. "Bangladesh: Garment Workers Burned to Death." Industrial Worker #1630, 98(1), January/February. http://parsons.ww.org/~iw/jan2001/stories/intl.html.

Health Canada. 1999. *Statistical Report on the Health of Canadians.* December 25. http://www.hc-sc.gc.ca/hppb/phdd/report/state/eng/over.html.

Hochschild, Arlie Russell. 1997. *The Time Bind: When Work Becomes Home and Home Becomes Work.* New York: Henry Holt and Company.

Human Rights Watch. 2000. "Unfair Advantage: Workers' Freedom of Association in the United States Under International Human Rights Standards." http://www.hrw.org/reports/2000/uslabor.

———. 2001. *World Report 2001.* http://www.hrw.org.

International Labour Organization. 2000. "Statistics: Revealing a Hidden Tragedy." http://www.ilo.org/public/...ish/standards/idec/simpoc/stats/4stt.htm.

———. 2001. *World Employment Report 2001: Life at Work in the Information Economy.* Geneva: International Labour Organization.

Kennedy, Joseph II. 1996. "Keynote Address." In *Forced Labor: The Prostitution of Children,* pp. 1–6. Washington, DC: U.S. Department of Labor, Bureau of International Labor Affairs.

Klein, Naomi. 2000. *No Logo: Taking Aim at the Brand Name Bullies.* Toronto: Vintage Canada.

Koch, Kathy. 1998. "High-Tech Labor Shortage." *CQ Researcher* 8(16): 361–84.

Krahn, Harvey and Graham Lowe. 1993. *Work, Industry and Canadian Society.* Scarborough, ON: Nelson Canada.

Lenski, Gerard, and J. Lenski. 1987. *Human Societies: An Introduction to Macrosociology,* 5th ed. New York: McGraw-Hill.

Leonard, Bill. 1996. "From School to Work: Partnerships Smooth the Transition." *HR Magazine (Society for Human Resource Management).* December 8, 1998. http://www.shrm.org/hrmag...articles/0796cov.htm.

Levitan, Sar A., Garth L. Mangum, and Stephen L. Mangum. 1998. *Programs in Aid of the Poor,* 7th ed. Baltimore: Johns Hopkins University Press.

Liem, Joan H., and G. Ramsey Liem. 1990. "Understanding the Individual and Family Effects of Unemployment." In J. Eckenrode and S. Gore (eds.), *Stress between Work and Family,* pp. 175–204. New York: Plenum Press.

Marshall, Katherine. 1999. "Employment after Childbirth." *Perspectives*

on Labour and Income, Autumn: 15–25. Catalogue No. 75-001-XPE.

Maule, C.J. 1999. "Multinational Corporation." In James H. Marsh (ed.), *The Canadian Encyclopedia: Year 2000 Edition,* pp. 1536. Toronto: McClelland and Stewart Inc.

Mishel, Lawrence, Jared Bernstein, and John Schmitt. 2001. *The State of Working America, 2000–2001.* Economic Policy Institute Series. Ithaca, NY: Cornell University Press.

Multinational Monitor. 2000. "Editorial: What is Society Willing to Spend on Human Beings?" *Multinational Monitor* 21(11), November. http://www.essential.org/monitor/mm2000/00november/.

National Council of Welfare. 1999a. *Children First: A Pre-Budget Report by the National Council of Welfare.* http://www.ncwcnbes.net/htmdocument/reportchildrenfirst.htm.

———. 1999b. *Preschool Children: Promises to Keep.* http://www.ncwcnbes.net/htmdocument/reportpromise/firstpag.html

National Safety Council. 1997. *Accident Facts 1997 Edition.* Itasca, IL: National Safety Council.

Parker, David L. (with Lee Engfer and Robert Conrow). 1998. *Stolen Dreams: Portraits of Working Children.* Minneapolis: Lerner Publications Company.

Reidmann, Agnes, Mary Ann Lamanna, and Adie Nelson. 2003. *Marriages and Families.* Toronto: Thomson Nelson.

Report on the World Social Situation. 1997. New York: United Nations.

Robie, Chet, Ann Marie Ryan, Robert A. Schmieder, Luis Fernando Parra, and Patricia C. Smith. 1998. "The Relation between Job Level and Job Satisfaction." *Group and Organizational Management* 23(4): 470–86.

Ross, Catherine E., and Marylyn P. Wright. 1998. "Women's Work, Men's Work, and the Sense of Control." *Work and Occupations* 25(3): 333–55.

Rotstein, Abraham. 1999. "Economic Nationalism." In James H. Marsh (ed.), *The Canadian Encyclopedia,*

Year 2000 Edition, pp. 716–17. Toronto: McClelland and Stewart, Inc.

Silvers, Jonathan. 1996. "Child Labor in Pakistan." *Atlantic Monthly* 277(2): 79–92.

Simone, Rose. 1999. "Couple Speak Out about Dangers of Toxic Substances in Workplace." *KW Record,* November 10: B7.

Statistics Canada. 1998a. *Canadian Profile 2000.* Ottawa: Ministry of Industry.

———. 1998b. *Canada Yearbook 1999.* Ottawa: Ministry of Industry.

———. 1999. "Labour Force Update: An Overview of the Labour Market." *The Daily,* January 27.

———. 2002. "Unionization." *The Daily,* August 24. http://www.statcan.ca/Daily/English/000824/d000824d.htm.

———. 2003. "Earnings of Canadians: Making a Living in the New Economy." *The Daily,* March 11. http://www12.statcan.ca/english/census01/Products/Analytic/companion/earn/contents.cfm.

Tremblay, Stephane, Nancy A. Ross, and Jean-Marie Berthelot. 2002. "Regional Socio-Economic Context and Health." *Supplement to Health Reports* 13. Catalogue no. 92-003. Ottawa: Statistics Canada.

U.S. Department of Labor. 1995. "By the Sweat and Toil of Children." *The Use of Child Labor in U.S. Agricultural Imports and Forced and Bonded Child Labor,* Vol. 2. Washington, DC: U.S. Department of Labor, Bureau of International Labor Affairs.

"Underage and Unprotected: Child Labor in Egypt's Cotton Fields." 2001. *Human Rights Watch* 13(1), January.

UNICEF (United Nations Children's Fund). 1997. *State of the World's Children, 1997.* New York: United Nations.

———. 2000. *The Progress of Nations 2000.* New York: United Nations.

Went, Robert. 2000. *Globalization: Neoliberal Challenge, Radical Responses.* Sterling, VA: Pluto Press.

Yanz, Lynda, and Bob Jeffcott. 1997. "Fighting Sweatshops/Building Solidarity: Exposing the Gap." *Canadian Dimensions* 31(4), October: 25–9.

Chapter 12

AAUW (American Association of University Women). 1998. "Report Finds Separating by Sex Not the Solution to Gender Inequity in School." Press release (2300). http://aauw.org.

Aberle-Grasse, Melissa. 2000. "The Washington Study Service-Learning Year of Eastern Mennonity University: Reflections on 23 Years of Service Learning." *American Behaviorial Scientist*, 43: 848–57.

Appleby, Timothy. 2000. "Weapons Turn Up More Often at Schools: Police." *The Globe and Mail*. February 18: A18.

Ascher, Carol, Norm Fruchter, and Robert Berne. 1997. *Hard Lessons: Public Schools and Privatization*. New York: Twentieth Century Fund.

Ash, Russell. 2001. *The Top 10 of Everything: Canadian Edition 2002*. Toronto: Dorling Kindersley Limited.

Associated Press. 1998. "Education Becomes Major Political Issue as Candidates Listen to Voters." *New York Times*, September 20: A5.

Bankston, Carl, and Stephen Caldas. 1997. "The American School Dilemma: Race and Scholastic Performance." *Sociological Quarterly* 38(3): 423–29.

Barlow, Maude, and Heather-Jane Robertson. 1994. *Class Warfare: The Assault on Canada's Schools*. Toronto: Key Porter Books.

Barton, Paul. 1992. *America's Smallest School: The Family*. Princeton, NJ: Educational Testing Service.

Bender, David, and Bruno Leone (eds.). 1994. *Culture Wars: Opposing Viewpoints*. San Diego, CA: Greenhaven Press Inc.

Bibby, Reginald W. 2001. *Canada's Teens: Today, Yesterday, and Tomorrow*. Toronto: Stoddart.

Bracey, Gerald W. 1998. "Are U.S. Students Behind?" *The American Prospect* 37 (March–April): 54–70. http://www.prospect.org/archives/37/37bracfs.html.

Bricker, Darrell, and Edward Greenspon. 2001. *Searching for Certainty: Inside the New Canadian Mindset*. Toronto: Doubleday Canada.

Brown, Roy J. 1999. "Special Education." In James H. Marsh (ed.), *The

Canadian Encyclopedia: Year 2000 Edition*, pp. 741–42. Toronto: McClelland and Stewart, Inc.

Bushweller, Kevin. 1995. "Turning Our Backs on Boys." *Education Digest* (January): 9–12.

Call, Kathleen, Lorie Grabowski, Jeylan Mortimer, Katherine Nash, and Chaimun Lee. 1997. "Impoverished Youth and the Attainment Process." Presented at the annual meeting of the American Sociological Association, Toronto, Canada, August.

Campaign 2000. 2001. "Child Poverty in Canada: Report Card 2000." Toronto Campaign 2000.

Canadian Council on Social Development. 1999. *Thinking Ahead: Trends Affecting Public Education in the Future*. Ottawa: Canadian Council on Social Development.

———. 2001. *The Progress of Canada's Children 2001—Highlights*. http://www.ccsd.ca/pubs/2-1/pcc2001.hl.htm.

Canadian Global Almanac. 2000. Edited by Susan Girvan. Toronto: Macmillan Canada.

Canadian Press. 2000. "School Violence: Read All about It." *The Globe and Mail*, May 6: A15.

Chard, Jennifer. 2000. "Women in a Visible Minority." In *Women in Canada 2000: A Gender-Based Statistical Report*, pp.219–44. Ottawa: Statistics Canada.

Chernos, Saul. 1998. "Alternative Route." *Education Today*, 10(1), Winter: 12–5.

Clark, Warren. 1999. "Paying off Student Loans." *Canadian Social Trends* 51 (Winter): 24–8.

Cohen, Warren. 1998. "Vouchers for Good and Ill." *U.S. News and World Report*, April 27: 46.

Conciatore, Jaqueline. 2000. "Study Shows that More than Half of American Colleges Now Have Diversity Requirements." *Black Issues in Higher Education* 17: 22.

Covell, Katherine. 2001. *Canada's Non-Governmental Organizations Report*. Submitted for the United Nations General Assembly Special Session September 19–21 (on behalf of the Canadian Coalition for the Rights of Children), February 2001.

Crane, Jennifer. 1999. "Help Troublemakers, Schools Told: Expelling

Kids Breeds Violence, Psychiatrist Says." *Toronto Star*, May 24: A2.

Curtis, James E., and Ronald D. Lambert. 1994. "Ideology and Social Change." In Lorne Tepperman, James E. Curtis, and R. Jack Richardson (eds.), *The Social World*, 3rd ed., pp. 710–58. Toronto: McGraw-Hill.

Digest of Educational Statistics. 2001. Chapters 1–6. National Center for Educational Statistics. http://nces.ed.gov/pubs2001/digest.

Doherty, G. 1997. *Zero to Six: The Basis for School Readiness*. Ottawa: Applied Research Branch, Human Resources Development Canada (#R-97-8E).

Evans, Lorraine, and Kimberly Davies. 2000. "No Sissy Boys Here." *Sex Roles* (February): 255–71.

Fact Sheet. 2000. "2000 Head Start Fact Sheet." Research and Statistics. Washington, DC: Department of Health and Human Services.

Fichten, Catherine S., Maria Barile, and Evelyn Reid. 1999. "Computer Technologies and Women with Disabilities: Is There Common Ground?" *1999 SWC Supplement*, pp. 5, 10. Ottawa: CAUT.

Fullan, Michael. [1982] 2001. *The New Meaning of Educational Change*, 3rd ed. New York: Teachers College Press.

George, Jane. 1998. "Kuujjuaq Daycare Thrives on Federal Head Start Program." *Nunatsiaq News*, October 29.

Ghalam, Nancy Z. 2000. "Paid and Unpaid Work." In *Women in Canada 2000: A Gender-Based Report*, pp. 97–134. Ottawa: Statistics Canada.

Gilbert, Sid, and Bruce Orok. 1993. "School Leavers." *Canadian Social Trends* (Winter): 2–7.

Goldberg, Carey. 1999. "After Girls Get Attention, Focus is on Boys' Woes." In *Themes of the Times: New York Times*, p. 6. Upper Saddle River, NJ: Prentice-Hall.

Government of Canada. 2001. "Early Intervention Programs." http://www.hrdc-drhc.gc.ca.

Hammonds, Bruce. 2002. "The Latest Ideas on School Reform by Michael Fullan." *Leading and Learning for the 21st Century*, June 29, pp. 1, 3. http://www.leading-learning.co.nz/newsletters/vol101-no03-2002.html.

Harrington, Rick. 1999. "Tragedy in Taber." *Time* (Canadian edition) 135(18), April 26: 22–23.

Health Canada. 1999. *Statistical Report on the Health of Canadians.* December 25. http://www.hc-sc.gc.ca/hppb/ phdd/report/state/eng/over.html.

Henry, Frances, Carol Tator, Winston Mattis, and Tim Rees. 2000. *The Colour of Democracy: Racism in Canadian Society*, 2nd ed. Toronto: Harcourt Brace Canada.

Jencks, Christopher, and Meredith Phillips. 1998. "America's Next Achievement Test: Closing the Black-White Test Score Gap." *The American Prospect* (September/ October): 44–53.

Johnson, Ann Dowsett. 1999. *Maclean's*, November 15: 31

———. 2001. "Survival of the Fittest." *Maclean's*, April 23. http://www.macleans.ca.

Kanter, Rosabeth Moss. 1972. "The Organization Child: Experience Management in a Nursery School." *Sociology of Education* 45: 186–211.

Kozol, Jonathan. 1991. *Savage Inequalities: Children in America's Schools.* New York: Crown Publishers.

Lam, Julia. 1997. "The Employment Activity of Chinese-American High-School Students and Its Relationship to Academic Achievement." Presented at the Annual Meeting of the American Sociological Association, Toronto, Ontario, August.

Lareau, Annette. 1989. *Home Advantage: Social Class and Parental Intervention in Elementary Education.* Philadelphia: Falmer Press.

Levin, Macolm. 1999. "Alternative Education." In James H. Marsh (ed.), *The Canadian Encyclopedia: Year 2000 Edition*, p. 732. Toronto: McClelland and Stewart, Inc.

Levinson, Arlene. 2000. "Study Evaluates Higher Education." Excite.News. http://www.excite.com/news/ ap/00130/08/grading.

Literacy. 2000. "Basic Literacy." Literacy Volunteers of America. http://www.literacyvolunteers.org/ about/basic.

Livingstone, D.N. 1999. "Educational Opportunity." In James H. Marsh (ed.), *The Canadian Encyclopedia: Year 2000 Edition*, pp. 743–44. Toronto: McClelland and Stewart, Inc.

Mackie, Marlene. 1991. *Gender Explorations in Canada: Further Explorations.* Toronto: Butterworths.

MacKinnon, Mark, Tu Thanh Ho, and Timothy Appleby. 2000. "Violence, Fear, Hit Canada's High Schools." *The Globe and Mail*, April 21: A1, A5.

Maclean's. 2002. "Ruling against Bullying." April 8: 14.

Mahoney, Jill. 2003. "New Edmonton Bylaw Aims to Fight Bullying." *The Globe and Mail*, March 12: A8.

Merton, Robert K. 1968. *Social Theory and Social Structure.* New York: Free Press.

Muller, Chandra, and Katherine Schiller. 2000. "Leveling the Playing Field?" *Sociology of Education* 73: 196–218.

Murnane, Richard J. 1994. "Education and the Well-Being of the Next Generation." In Sheldon H. Danziger, Gary D. Sandefur, and Daniel H. Weinberg (eds.), *Confronting Poverty: Prescriptions for Change*, pp. 289–307. New York: Russell Sage Foundation.

Natriello, Gary. 1995. "Dropouts: Definitions, Causes, Consequences, and Remedies." In Peter W. Cookson Jr. and Barbara Schneider (eds.), *Transforming Schools*, pp. 107–28. New York: Garland Publishing Co.

Noddings, Nel. 1995. "A Morally Defensible Mission for Schools in the Twenty-First Century." *Phi Delta Kappan* (January): 365–68.

Orlikow, Lionel, and Frank Peters. 1999. "Educational Organization." In James H. Marsh (ed.), *The Canadian Encyclopedia: Year 2000 Edition*, pp. 736–39. Toronto: McClelland and Stewart, Inc.

Osborne, Ken. 1988. *Educating Citizens: A Democratic Socialist Agenda for Canadian Education.* Toronto: Our Schools/Our Selves.

Population Reference Bureau. 1999. "World Population: More than Just Numbers." http://www.prb.org.

Ray, Carol A., and Roslyn A. Mickelson. 1993. "Restructuring Students for Restructured Work: The Economy, School Reform, and Non-College-Bound Youths." *Sociology of Education* 66: 1–20.

Rosenthal, Robert, and Lenore Jacobson. 1968. *Pygmalion in the Classroom: Teacher Expectations and Pupils' Intellectual Development.* New York: Holt, Rinehart and Winston.

Ross, David. 1998. "Rethinking Child Poverty." *Insight, Perception* 22(1): 9–11.

Schaefer, Richard T., Robert P. Lamm, Penny Biles, and Susannah J. Wilson. 1996. *Sociology: An Introduction.* Toronto: McGraw-Hill Ryerson.

Schmidt, Sarah. 2001. "U of T Law School Looks at Raising Tuition to $25,000." *National Post*, December 12: A1, A17.

Schofield, John. 1999. "Learning on the Front Lines." *Maclean's*, January 15: 90–94.

Schrag, Peter. 1997. "The New-Myth of Our Failing Schools." *The Atlantic Monthly* (October). http://www.theatlantic.com/issues/ 97oct/fail.htm.

Shanker, Albert. 1996. "Mythical Choice and Real Standards." In Michael Darby (ed.), *Reducing Poverty in America*, pp. 154–72. Thousand Oaks, CA: Sage.

Sokoloff, Heather. 2001a. "OECD Shows Alberta No. 1 in Reading Skills." *National Post*, December 5: A1, A17.

_____. 2001b. "Wealth Affects Test Scores." *National Post*, December 5: A17.

Sommers, Christina Hoff. 2000. *The War Against Boys: How Misguided Feminism Is Harming Young Men.* New York: Simon and Schuster.

Sowell, Thomas. 1994. "Multicultural Education Is Harmful." In David Bender and Bruno Leone (eds.), *Culture Wars: Opposing Viewpoints*, pp. 104–8. San Diego, CA: Greenhaven Press, Inc.

Statistics Canada. 1998. *Canada Yearbook 1999.* Ottawa: Minister of Industry.

———. 2003. "Education in Canada: Raising the Standard." Catalogue 96F0030XIE2001012. http://www12.statcan.ca/english/ census01/products/Analytic/ companion/educ/contents.cfm.

Summary Report. 2001. "Building Their Futures." http://www2.acf.dhhs.gov/programs/ hsb/EHS.

Sunter, S. 1993. "Juggling School and Work." *Perspectives on Labour and Income* (Spring): 15–21.

Toronto Board of Education. 1993. *The 1991 Every Secondary Student*

Survey, Part II: Detailed Profiles of Toronto's Secondary School Students. Toronto: Toronto Board of Education Research Services.

U.S. Newswire. 2000. "Fact Sheet: Building a Stronger Global Partnership." http://www.usnewswire.com/topnews/current_releases.

United Nations Population Fund. 1999. "Campaign Issues: Facing the Facts." Face to Face. http://www.facecampaign.org.

Vago, Steven, and Adie Nelson. 2003. *Law and Society.* Toronto: Pearson Educational Publishing.

Waldie, Paul. 1999. "Best Brains Likely to Leave Canada." *National Post,* August 28: A1, A2.

Waterman, Alan. S. (ed.). 1997. *Service-Learning: Applications from the Research.* Mahwah, NJ: Lawrence Erlbaum Associates Publishers.

Webb, Julie. 1989. "The Outcomes of Home-Based Education: Employment and Other Issues." *Educational Review* 41: 121–33.

Whitehead, Fred (ed.). 1994. *Culture Wars: Opposing Viewpoints.* San Diego, CA: Greenhaven Press, Inc.

Wilgoren, Jodi. 2001. "Calls for Change in the Scheduling of the School Day." *The New York Times on the Web,* January 10. http://www.nytimes.com/2001/01/10/nyregion/10scho.html.

Winters, Rebecca. 2000. "From Home to Harvard." *Time,* September 11. http://www.time.com/time/magazine/articles.

Zlotkowski, E. 1996. "Opportunity for all: linking service-learning and business education." *Journal of Business Ethics* 1: 5–19.

Chapter 13

AAUW (American Association of University Women). 2000. "Tech-Savvy: Educating Girls in the New Computer Age." http://www.aauw.org/2000/techsavvybd.

Abraham, Carolyn. 2002. "First peek at fetus is no longer a blur." *The Globe and Mail,* August 13: A1, A7.

Addison, John T., Douglas Fox, and Christopher Ruhm. 2000. "Technology, Trade Sensitivity, and Labor Displacement." *Southern Economic Journal* 66: 682–99.

Ash, Russell. 2001. *The Top 10 of Everything: Canadian Edition 2002.* Toronto: Dorling Kindersley Limited.

Bell, Daniel. 1973. *The Coming of Post-Industrial Society: A Venture in Social Forecasting.* New York: Basic Books.

Beniger, James R. 1993. "The Control Revolution." In Albert H. Teich (ed.), *Technology and the Future,* pp. 40–65. New York: St. Martin's Press.

Boles, Margaret, and Brenda Sunoo. 1998. "Do Your Employees Suffer from Technophobia?" *Workforce* 77(1): 21.

Brand, Bob. 2000. "DotComGuy." September 1. http://thebee.com/bweb.

Brin, David. 1998. *The Transparent Society: Will Technology Force Us to Choose between Privacy and Freedom?* Reading, MA: Addison Wesley.

Bush, Corlann G. 1993. "Women and the Assessment of Technology." In Albert H. Teich (ed.), *Technology and the Future,* pp. 192–214. New York: St. Martin's Press.

Carey, Patricia M. 1998. "Sticking It Out in the Sticks." *Home Office Computing* 16: 64–69.

Ceruzzi, Paul. 1993. "An Unforeseen Revolution: Computers and Expectations, 1935–1985." In Albert H. Teich (ed.), *Technology and the Future,* pp. 160–74. New York: St. Martin's Press.

Clarke, Adele E. 1990. "Controversy and the Development of Reproductive Sciences." *Social Problems* 37(1): 18–37.

Conrad, Peter. 1997. "Public Eyes and Private Genes: Historical Frames, New Constructions, and Social Problems." *Social Problems* 44: 139–54.

DotComGuy, Inc. 2001. http://dotcomguy.com.

Dranoff, Linda Silver. 2001. *Everyone's Guide to the Law.* Toronto: HarperCollins Publishers Ltd.

Durkheim, Emile. [1925] 1973. *Moral Education.* New York: Free Press.

Edwards, Steven. 2001. "Canada Eighth in Technology Race." *National Post,* July 10: A8.

Ehrenfeld, David. 1998. "A Techno-Pox upon the Land." *Harper's* (October): 13–17.

Eibert, Mark D. 1998. "Clone Wars." *Reason* 30(2): 52–54.

Fenna, Donald. 1999. "Internet." In James H. Marsh (ed.), *The Canadian Encyclopedia, Year 2000 Edition,* pp. 1181–82. Toronto: McClelland and Stewart, Inc.

Fix, Janet L. 1994. "Automation Makes Bank Branches a Liability." *USA Today,* November 28: B1.

Geddes, John. 1999. "Making Babies." *Maclean's,* December 6: 53–56.

GIP (Global Internet Project). 1998. "The Workplace." http://www.gip.org/gip2g.html.

Glendinning, Chellis. 1990. *When Technology Wounds: The Human Consequences of Progress.* New York: William Morrow.

Global Reach. 2000. "Global Internet Statistics." http://www.glreach.com/globstats/index.

Goodman, Paul. 1993. "Can Technology Be Humane?" In Albert H. Teich (ed.), *Technology and the Future,* pp. 239–55. New York: St. Martin's Press.

Hafner, Katie. 1999. "Horse and Blender, Car and Crockpot." In *Themes of the Times: N.Y. Times,* p. 1. Upper Saddle River, NJ: Prentice Hall.

Hayes, Frank. 1998. "Age Bias an IT Reality." *Computerworld* 32(46): 12.

Health Canada. 1999. *Statistical Report on the Health of Canadians.* http://www.hc-sc.gc.ca/hppb/phdd/report/stat/eng/over.html.

Hormats, Robert D. 2001. "Asian Connection." *Across the Board* 38: 47–50.

Hosmer, Ellen. 1986. "High Tech Hazards: Chipping Away at Workers' Health." *Multinational Monitor* 7 (January 31): 1–5.

IFR (International Federation of Robotics). 1997. "1997 Key Data for the World Robot Market." http://www.ifr.org.

Johnson, Jim. 1988. "Mixing Humans and Nonhumans Together: The Sociology of a Door-Closer." *Social Problems* 35: 298–310.

Kahn, A. 1997. "Clone Mammals… Clone Man." *Nature,* March 13: 119.

Kelly, Jason. 1997. "Technophobia." *Atlanta Business Chronicle,* August 18. http://www.amcity.com/atlanta/stories/1997/08/18/focus1.html.

Kuhn, Thomas. 1973. *The Structure of Scientific Revolutions.* Chicago: Chicago University Press.

Lemonick, Michael D. 1999. "Smart Genes?" *Time*, September 13: 40–44.

Lemonick, Michael, and Dick Thompson. 1999. "Racing to Map Our DNA." *Time Daily*, 153: 1–6. http://www.time.com.

Levy, Pierre. 1997. "Cyberculture in Question: A Critique of the Critique." *Revue-du-Mauss* 9: 111–26.

Levy, Steven. 1995. "TechnoMania." *Newsweek*, February 27: 25–29.

Lewin, Tamar. 1998. "Serious Gender Gap Remains in Technology." *N.Y. Times News Service*, October 18.

Macklin, Ruth. 1991. "Artificial Means of Reproduction and Our Understanding of the Family." *Hastings Center Report*, January/ February: 5–11.

Maclean's. 1999a. "Move Over." September 27: 20–23.

———. 1999b. "Sperm Bank Caution." July 19: 51.

Makris, Greg. 1996. "The Myth of a Technological Solution to Television Violence." *Journal of Communication Inquiry* 20: 72–91.

Markoff, John. 2000. "Report Questions a Number in Microsoft Trial." *The New York Times on the Web*, August 28. http://www.nytimes.com/ library/tech/00/08.

McCormick, S.J., and Richard A. 1994. "Blastomere Separation." *Hastings Center Report*, March/April: 14–16.

McDermott, John. 1993. "Technology: The Opiate of the Intellectuals." In Albert H. Teich (ed.), *Technology and the Future*, pp. 89–107. New York: St. Martin's Press.

Mehlman, Maxwell H., and Jeffery R. Botkin. 1998. *Access to the Genome: The Challenge to Equality*. Washington, DC: Georgetown University Press.

Merton, Robert K. 1973. "The Normative Structure of Science." In Robert K. Merton (ed.), *The Sociology of Science*. Chicago: University of Chicago Press.

Mesthene, Emmanuel G. 1993. "The Role of Technology in Society." In Albert H. Teich (ed.), *Technology and the Future*, pp. 73–88. New York: St. Martin's Press.

National Post. 1999. "French Schools to Hand out Morning-After Pills." November 30: A11.

Negroponte, Nicholas. 1995. "Nicholas Negroponte: The Multimedia Today Interview." *Multimedia Today*, July–September: 86–88.

Normand, Jessie. 2000. "Education." In *Women in Canada 2000: A Gender-Based Statistical Report*, pp. 85–96. Ottawa: Statistics Canada.

Ogburn, William F. 1957. "Cultural Lag as Theory." *Sociology and Social Research* 41: 167–74.

Papadakis, Maria. 2000. "Complex Picture of Computer Use in Home Emerges." National Science Foundation, March 31. NSF000-314.

Pascal, Zachary G. 1996. "The Outlook: High Tech Explains Widening Wage Gap." *Wall Street Journal*, April 22: A1.

Perrolle, Judith A. 1990. "Computers and Capitalism." In James M. Henslin (ed.), *Social Problems Today*, pp. 336–42. Englewood Cliffs, NJ: Prentice-Hall.

Pollack, Andrew. 2000. "Nations Agree on Safety Rules for Biotech Food." *The New York Times*, January 30. http://www.nytimes.com/ library/national/science.

Postman, Neil. 1992. *Technopoly: The Surrender of Culture to Technology*. New York: Alfred A. Knopf.

Potter, Ned. 2001. "First Reading: Scientists Detail Human Genetic Code." ABCNews.com, February 11. http://www.abcnews.go.com. sections/wnt/Daily/News/.

Powers, Richard. 1998. "Too Many Breakthroughs." Op-Ed. *New York Times*, November 19: 35.

Quick, Rebecca. 1998. "Technology: Pieces of the Puzzle—Not So Private Lives: Will We Have Any Secrets in the Future?" *Wall Street Journal*, November 13: R27.

Rabino, Isaac. 1998. "The Biotech Future." *American Scientist* 86(2): 110–12.

Regalado, Antonio. 2000. "The Great Gene Grab." *Technology Review* 103: 48–55.

Reuters. 2000. "U.S. Unlikely to Follow Britain's Human Clone Lead." August 17. http://www.nytimes.com/library/ national/science.

Richardson, W.G. 1999. "Technology." In James H. Marsh (ed.), *The Canadian Encyclopedia: Year 2000 Edition*, pp. 2297–301. Toronto: McClelland and Stewart, Inc.

Rifkin, Jeremy. 1996. *The End of Work: The Decline of the Global Labor Force and the Dawn of Post-Market Era*. Berkeley, CA: Putnam.

Rosenberg, Jim. 1998. "Troubles and Technologies." *Editor and Publisher* 131(6): 4.

Sampat, Payal. 2000. "Internet Use Accelerates." In Linda Starke (ed.), *Vital Signs: The Environmental Trends that Are Shaping Our Future*, p. 94. New York: W.W. Norton Company.

Schwartz, John. 2001. "Wassail Beats Lucres." *The New York Times*, January 8: C4.

Shand, Hope. 1998. "An Owner's Guide." *Mother Jones*, May/June: 46.

Statistics Canada. 1998. *Canada Yearbook 1999*. Ottawa: Minister of Industry.

———. 1999. *Science Statistics*. 23(6), November. Catalogue 88-001-XIB.

———. 2000. "Therapeutic Abortions 1998." *The Daily*, December 18. http://www.statcan.ca/Daily/ English/001218/d001218d.htm.

———. 2003a. Earnings of Canadians: Making a Living in the New Economy." http://www12.statcan.ca/english/ census01/Products/Analytic/ companion/earn/canada.cfm.

———. 2003b. "Education in Canada: Raising the Standard." Catalogue 96F0030XIE2001012. Ottawa: Statistics Canada.

———. 2003c. "Survey of Innovation." *The Daily*, January 13. http://www.statcan.ca/English/ Daily/030113/d030113e.htm.

Stenger, Richard. 2000. "Does Dot-ComGuy Live in e-utopia or a Publicity Hut?" January 25. http://www.cnn.com/2000/TECH/ computing/01/25/dotcomguy.

Toffler, Alvin. 1970. *Future Shock*. New York: Random House.

Wallace, Bruce. 1999. "Say It Ain't So." *Maclean's*, July 5: 14–19.

Weinberg, Alvin. 1966. "Can Technology Replace Social Engineering?" *University of Chicago Magazine* 59 (October): 6–10.

Welter, Cole H. 1997. "Technological Segregation: A Peek Through the Looking Glass at the Rich and Poor in an Information Age." *Arts Education Policy Review* 99(2): 1–6.

White, Lawrence. 2000. "Colleges Must Protect Privacy in the Digital Age." *The Chronicle of Higher Education*, June 30: B5–6.

Winner, Langdon. 1993. "Artifact/ Ideas as Political Culture." In Albert H. Teich (ed.), *Technology and the Future*, pp. 283–94. New York: St. Martin's Press.

Witt, Louise. 2000. "Why Would Anyone Listen to a Guy Named DotComGuy?" *Business Week Online*, August 4. http://www.businessweek.com.

World Employment Report. 2001. "Digital Divide is Wide and Getting Wider." Geneva: International Labor Organization. http://www.ilo.org/public/english/bureau/inf/pkits/wer2001.

Chapter 14

Agbese, Pita Ogaba. 1995. "Nigeria's Environment: Crises, Consequences, and Responses." In *Environmental Policies in the Third World: A Comparative Analysis,* edited by O. P. Dwivedi, and Dhirendra K. Vajpeyi, pp. 125–44. Westport, CT: Greenwood Press.

"A Prescription for Reducing the Damage Caused by Dams." 2001. *Environmental Defense* XXXII(2), March.

Associated Press. 2000. "Daimler-Chrysler Corporation Quits Global Climate Coalition." *Environmental News Network*, January 7. http://www.enn.com/news/.

Bergman, Lester V. 1998. "Cataract Development: It's Cumulative." *Environmental Health Perspectives* 106(12), December. February 1, 1999. http://ehpnet1.niehs.nih.gov/docs/1998/06-12/forum.html.

Black, Harvey Karl. 1999. "Complex Cleanup." *Environmental Health Perspectives* 107(2), February 1. http://ehpnet1.niehs.nih.gov/docs/1999/07-2/focus-abs.html.

Boland, Reed, Sudhakar Rao, and George Zeidenstein. 1994. "Honoring Human Rights in Population Policies: From Declaration to Action." In Gita Sen, Adrienne Germain, and Lincoln C. Chen (eds.), *Population Policies Reconsidered: Health, Empowerment, and Rights*, pp. 89–105. Boston: Harvard School of Public Health.

Bongaarts, John, and Susan Cotts Watkins. 1996. "Social Interactions and Contemporary Fertility Transitions." *Population and Development Review* 22(4): 639–82.

Brown, Lester R. 1995. "The State of the World's Natural Environment." In John J. Macionis, and Nijole V. Benokraitis (eds.), *Seeing Ourselves: Classic, Contemporary, and Cross-Cultural Readings in Sociology*, 3rd ed., pp. 411–16. Englewood Cliffs, NJ: Prentice-Hall.

———. 1998. "The Future of Growth." In Lester R. Brown, Christopher Flavin, and Hilary French (eds.), *State of the World 1998*. New York: W.W. Norton & Co.

Brown, Lester R., Christopher Flavin, and Hilary French. 1998. *State of the World 1998*. New York: W.W. Norton & Co.

Brown, Lester R., Gary Gardner, and Brian Halwell. 1998. *Beyond Malthus: Sixteen Dimensions of the Population Problem*. World Watch Paper 143. Washington, DC: World Watch Institute.

Bruce, Nigel, Rogelio Perez-Padilla, and Rachel Albalak. 2000. "Indoor Air Pollution in Developing Countries: A Major Environmental and Public Health Challenge." *Bulletin of the World Health Organization*, 78(9): 1078–92.

Buss, Dale. 2001. "Green Cars." *American Demographics* (January).

Canadian Global Almanac 2000. Edited by Susan Girvan. Toronto: Macmillan Canada.

Catley-Carlson, Margaret, and Judith A. M. Outlaw. 1998. "Poverty and Population Issues: Clarifying the Connections." *Journal of International Affairs* 52(1): 233–43.

CELA (Canadian Environmental Law Association). 1999. "Water Watch Summit a Huge Success." Media Release. September 19. http://www.web.net/~cela/mr990919.htm.

"China Phasing Out One-Child Policy." 2000. *Popline* 22 (May–June): 1.

Cincotta, Richard P., and Robert Engelman. 2000. *Human Population and the Future of Biological Diversity*. Washington, DC: Population Action International.

Cooper, Mary H. 1998. "Population and the Environment." *CQ Researcher* 8(26): 601–24.

"Corporate Spotlight." 2001. *Adbusters* 34 (March/April): 38.

Cray, Charlie. 2001. "Taking on Toxics 1: Stopping POPs." *Multinational Monitor* 22(1&2).

Denson, Bryan. 2000. "Shadowy Saboteurs." *The IRE Journal* (Investigative Reports and Editors, Inc.) 23 (May/June): 12–14.

DesJardins, Andrea. 1997. "Sweet Poison: What Your Nose Can't Tell You about the Dangers of Perfume." January 20, 1999. http://members.aol.com/enviroknow/perfume/sweet_poison.htm.

DaVanzo, Julie, David M. Adamson, Nancy Belden, and Sally Patterson. 2000. *How Americans View World Population Issues: A Survey of Public Opinion*. Santa Monica, CA: Rand Corporation.

Dionis, Joanna. 1999. "Handle with Care." *Mother Jones* (January–February): 25.

Engelman, Robert, Richard P. Cincotta, Bonnie Dye, Tom Gardner-Outlaw, and Jennifer Wisnewski. 2000. *People in the Balance: Population and Natural Resources at the Turn of the Millennium*. Washington, DC: Population Action International.

Fisher, Brandy E. 1998. "Scents and Sensitivity." *Environmental Health Perspectives* 106(12). February 1, 1999. http://ehpnet1.niehs.nih.gov/docs/1998/106-12/focus-abs.html.

———. 1999. "Focus: Most Unwanted." *Environmental Health Perspectives* 107(1). February 1, 1999. http://ehpnet1 niehs.nih.gov/docs/1999/107-1/focus-abs.html.

Flavin, Christopher. 2000. "Wind Power Booms." In Lester R. Brown, Michael Renner, and Brian Halwell (eds.), *Vital Signs 2000*, pp. 56–57. New York: W.W. Norton & Co.

French, Hilary. 2000. "Environmental Treaties Gain Ground." In Lester R. Brown, Michael Renner, and Brian Halwell (eds.), *Vital Signs 2000*, pp. 134–35. New York: W.W. Norton & Co.

Fridleifsson, Ingvar B. 2000. "Globeglance: Energy 2000." *United Nations Chronicle Online Edition* XXXVII(2):1–4.

Gardner, Gary. 1998. "Sanitation Access Lacking." In Lester R. Brown, Michael Renner, and Christopher Flavin (eds.), *Vital Signs 1998*, pp. 70–71. New York: W.W. Norton and Co.

"Global Corporations Join Us to Reduce Greenhouse Gas Emissions." 2000. *Environmental Defense* XXXI(4), November: 5.

Hager, Nicky and Bob Burton. 2000. *Secrets and Lies: The Anatomy of an Anti-Environmental PR Campaign*. Monroe, ME: Common Courage Press.

Halwell, Brian. 2000. "World Population Passes 6 Billion." In Lester R. Brown, Michael Renner, and Brian Halwell (eds.), *Vital Signs 2000*, pp. 98–99. New York: W.W. Norton & Co.

Hunter, Lori M. 2001. *The Environmental Implications of Population Dynamics*. Santa Monica, CA: Rand Corporation.

Intergovernmental Panel on Climate Change. 2001a. *Climate Change 2001: The Scientific Basis*. United Nations Environmental Programme and the World Meteorological Organization. http://www.ipcc.ch.

———. 2001b. *Climate Change 2001: Impacts, Adaptation, and Vulnerability*. United Nations Environmental Programme and the World Meteorological Organization. http://www.ipcc.ch.

Jan, George P. 1995. "Environmental Protection in China." In O. P. Dwivedi and Dhirendra K. Vajpeyi (eds.), *Environmental Policies in the Third World: A Comparative Analysis*, pp. 71–84. Westport, CT: Greenwood Press.

"Japanese Toy Firm Offers Employees Fertility Incentives." 2000. *Popline* 22 (May–June): 2.

Jensen, Derrick. 1999. "The War on Truth: The Secret Battle for the American Mind: An Interview with John Stauber." *Sun* 279 (March): 6–15.

———. 2001. "A Weakened World Cannot Forgive Us: An Interview with Kathleen Dean Moore." *The Sun* 303 (March): 13.

Kaplan, Sheila, and Jim Morris. 2000. "Kids at Risk." *U.S. News & World Report*, June 19: 47–53.

Karliner, Joshua. 1998. "Corporate Greenwashing." *Green Guide* 58 (August): 1–3.

Kemps, Dominic. 1998. "Deaths, Diseases Traced to Environment." *Popline* 20 (May–June): 3.

Koenig, Dieter. 1995. "Sustainable Development: Linking Global Environmental Change to Technology Cooperation." In O. P. Dwivedi and Dhirendra K. Vajpeyi (eds.), *Environmental Policies in the Third World: A Comparative Analysis*, pp. 1–21. Westport, CT: Greenwood Press.

Lenssen, Nicolas. 2000. "Nuclear Power Rises Slightly." In Lester R. Brown, Michael Renner, and Brian Halwell (eds.), *Vital Signs 2000*, pp. 54–55. New York: W.W. Norton & Co.

Lindauer, Wendy. 1999. "Fact Sheet: Sick Building Syndrome." *Environmental Health Center*. February 1. http://www.nsc.org/ehc/indoor/sbs.htm.

Lipke, David J. 2001. "Good for Whom?" *American Demographics*, January.

Livernash, Robert, and Eric Rodenburg. 1998. "Population Change, Resources, and the Environment." *Population Bulletin* 53(1): 1–36.

Mason, Karen Oppenheim. 1997. "Explaining Fertility Transition." *Demography* 34(4): 443–54.

McGinn, Anne Platt. 2000. "Endocrine Disrupters Raise Concerns." In Lester R. Brown, Michael Renner, and Brian Halwell (eds.), *Vital Signs 2000*, pp. 130–31. New York: W.W. Norton & Co.

McMichael, Anthony J., Kirk R. Smith, and Carlos F. Corvalan. 2000. "The Sustainability Transition: A New Challenge." *Bulletin of the World Health Organization* 78(9): 1067.

McVey, Wayne Jr., and Warren Kalbach. 1995. *Canadian Population*. Scarborough, ON: Nelson Canada.

Mead, Leila. 1998. "Radioactive Wastelands." *The Green Guide* 53 (April 14): 1–3.

Mitchell, Jennifer D. 1998. "Before the Next Doubling." *World Watch* 11(1): 21–29.

Mittelstaedt, Martin. 2002. "Nuclear Mishap's Toll to Be Measured." *The Globe and Mail*, July 17: A4.

Mokhiber, Russell, and Robert Weissman. 2000. "National Breast Cancer Industry Month." *Focus on the Corporation*, October 26. http://www.corporatepredators.org.

National Environmental Education and Training Foundation and Roper Starch Worldwide. 1999. *1999 NEETF/Roper Report Card*. Washington, DC: National Environmental Education and Training Foundation.

"Nukes Rebuked." 2000. *The Washington Spectator* 26(13), July 1: 4.

PBS. 2001. "Trade Secrets: A Moyers Report." http://www.pbs.org/tradesecrets/program/program.html.

Pimentel, David, Maria Tort, Linda D'Anna, Anne Krawic, Joshua Berger, Jessica Rossman, Fridah Mugo, Nancy Doon, Michael Shriberg, Erica Howard, Susan Lee, and Jonathan Talbot. 1998. "Ecology of Increasing Disease: Population Growth and Environmental Degradation." *BioScience* 48 (October): 817–27.

Population Institute. 1998. "1998 World Population Overview and Outlook 1999." January 29, 1999. http://www.populationinstitute.org/overview98.html.

———. 1999. *World Population Awareness Week: The Year of 6 Billion*. Washington, DC: The Population Institute.

———. 2000. *World Population Awareness Week 2000: Saving Women's Lives—A Guide to Action*. Washington, DC: The Population Institute.

Population Reference Bureau. 2000a. "2000 World Population Data Sheet." June. http://www.prb.org/prb/pubs/wpds2000/.

———. 2000b. "How Does Family Planning Influence Women's Lives?" *MEASURE Communication: Reports: Women 2000 Policy Briefs*. Washington, DC: Population Reference Bureau.

———. 2000c. "Is Education the Best Contraceptive?" *MEASURE Communication: Reports: Women 2000 Policy Briefs*. Washington, DC: Population Reference Bureau.

Reese, April. 2001. "Africa's Struggle with Desertification." *Population Reference Bureau*, February. http://www.prb.org/regions/africa/africa_desertification.html.

Renner, Michael. 1996. *Fighting for Survival: Environmental Decline, Social Conflict, and the New Age of Insecurity*. New York: W.W. Norton and Co.

Scholand, Michael. 2000. "Compact Fluorescents Light Up the Globe." In Lester R. Brown, Michael Renner and Brian Halwell (eds.), *Vital Signs 2000*, pp. 60–61. New York: W.W. Norton & Co.

Speirs, Rosemary. 2000. "For Boomers, Minivans Are Still a Big Gas." *Toronto Star*, March 11: A24.

Stanford, Jim. 2002. "Hot Air Over Kyoto." *THIS* magazine (July/August): 12–13.

Statistics Canada. 1998. *Canada Yearbook 2000*. Ottawa: Ministry of Industry.

———. 1999. *The Daily*, October 5. http://www.statcan.ca/Daily/English/991005/d991005.htm.

Stiefel, Chana. 2000. "Gaping Ozone Hole." *Science World* 57(6), November 27: 5.

Stover, Dawn. 1995. "The Nuclear Legacy." *Popular Science*, August: 52–83.

Suzuki, David, and Holly Dressel. 2002. *Good News For a Change: Hope For a Troubled Planet*. Toronto: Stoddart.

Switzer, Jacqueline Vaughn. 1997. *Green Backlash: The History and Politics of Environmental Opposition in the U.S.* Boulder, CO: Lynne Rienner Publishers.

"The Delicate Balance." 1994. *The National Center for Environmental Health Strategies* 5(3–4). 1100 Rural Avenue, Voorhees, NJ, 08043.

Tuxill, John. 1998. *Losing Strands in the Web of Life: Vertebrate Declines and the Conservation of Biological Diversity*. Worldwatch Paper 141. Washington, DC: Worldwatch Institute.

United Nations Development Programme. 2001. *Human Development Report 2001*. New York: Oxford.

United Nations Population Division. 2001. *World Population Prospects: The 2000 Revision*. New York: United Nations.

United Nations Population Fund. 1997. *1997 State of the World Population*. New York: United Nations.

———. 2000. *The State of the World Population 2000*. New York: United Nations.

Vajpeyi, Dhirendra K. 1995. "External Factors Influencing Environmental Policy-making: Role of Multilateral Development Aid Agencies." In O. P. Dwivedi and Dhirendra K. Vajpeyi (eds.), *Environmental Policies in the Third World: A Comparative Analysis*, pp. 24–45. Westport, CT: Greenwood Press.

"Water Wars Forecast if Solutions Not Found." 1999. *Environment News Service*, January 1. http://ens.lycos.com/ens/jan99/1999L-01-01-02.html.

Weiner, Tim. 2001. "Terrific News in Mexico City: Air is Sometimes Breathable." *The New York Times on the Web*, January 5. http://www.nytimes.com/2001/01/05/world/05MEXI.html.

Wood, Stanley, Kate Sebastian, and Sara J. Scherr. 2000. *Agroecosystems: Pilot Analysis of Global Ecosystems*. Washington, DC: International Food Policy Research Institute and World Resources Institute.

World Resources Institute. 1998. *Climate, Biodiversity, and Forests: Issues and Opportunities Emerging from the Kyoto Protocol*. Baltimore, MN: World Resource.

———. 2000. *People and Ecosystems: The Fraying Web of Life*. Washington, DC: World Resources Institute.

Zabin, L. S., and K. Kiragu. 1998. "The Health Consequences of Adolescent Sexual and Fertility Behavior in Sub-Saharan Africa." *Studies in Family Planning* 2, June 29: 210–32.

Zwingle, Erla. 1998. "Women and Population." *National Geographic*, October: 35–55.

Name Index

Subject Index